International Lactation Consultant Association

ILCA

# CORE CURRICULUM FOR LACTATION CONSULTANT PRACTICE

Edited by

## Marsha Walker

JONES AND BARTLETT PUBLISHERS

*Sudbury, Massachusetts*

BOSTON    TORONTO    LONDON    SINGAPORE

## World Headquarters

Jones and Bartlett Publishers
40 Tall Pine Drive
Sudbury, MA 01776
978-443-5000
info@jbpub.com
www.jbpub.com

Jones and Bartlett Publishers
Canada
2406 Nikanna Road
Mississauga, ON L5C 2W6
CANADA

Jones and Bartlett Publishers
International
Barb House, Barb Mews
London W6 7PA
UK

Library of Congress Cataloging-in-Publication Data

Core curriculum for lactation consultant practice / Marsha Walker [editor].
   p. cm.
  Includes bibliographical references and index.
  ISBN 0-7637-1038-5 (alk. paper)
   1. Breast feeding—Study guides. 2. Lactation—Study guides. 3. Breast feeding—Study and teaching. 4. Lactation—Study and teaching. I. Title: At head of title: International Lactation Consultant Association. II. Walker, Marsha. III. International Lactation Consultant Association.
RJ216.C657 2002
610.2'69'071—dc21

2001041706

### Production Credits

Acquisitions Editor: Penny M. Glynn
Associate Editor: Christine Tridente
Production Editor: Elizabeth Platt
Editorial Assistant: Thomas R. Prindle
Manufacturing Buyer: Amy Duddridge
Cover Design: Philip Regan
Design and Composition: D&G Limited, LLC
Printing and Binding: Malloy Lithographics

Printed in the United States of America.

05 04 03    10 9 8 7 6 5 4 3

# CONTENTS

# ACKNOWLEDGMENTS

The creation of this Core Curriculum has been the work of many. I especially wish to thank the contributors for a job well done. Their dedication to the lactation consultant profession is an example for all. I also wish to acknowledge the production staff from Jones and Bartlett whose patience and perseverance helped bring this resource to fruition.

Lastly, I wish to thank my long suffering husband, Hap, for the encouragement and support needed to accomplish this project; my son Justin and my daughter Shannon who served as my original lactation core curriculum and from whom I learned so much; and our son-in-law Tom, who along with Shannon has just blessed us with our granddaughter Haley, who makes it all worthwhile.

# Preface

Lactation consulting is an emerging allied health profession. While the term *lactation consultant* is a generic one, only those who have passed a criterion-referenced exam administered by the International Board of Lactation Consultant Examiners can use the credential International Board Certified Lactation Consultant (IBCLC) after their name. The IBCLC credential serves to both protect the public and define the areas where practitioners must develop competency. This book can be used for several purposes, the first of which is as a study guide for those who wish to sit for the IBCLC certification exam. This study guide is based on the exam blueprint, with each section corresponding to an area tested on the exam. Each individual practitioner should assess his or her own level of knowledge, experience, and expertise in order to develop an effective study plan. Second, this text will be useful in staff development, for orientation of new staff, and as a resource for aspiring and established lactation consultants. The content of this core curriculum is designed to reflect the scope of knowledge upon which lactation consulting is based.

This text is not designed to be the sole source of a practitioner's information, however. Within its pages reside hundreds of citations from a broad spectrum of disciplines that contribute to a holistic reservoir of supporting information. Charts and figures serve to enrich the learner's understanding and retention of the information. The authors who participated in the creation of this resource bring a wealth of knowledge and experience to a forum that is designed to ultimately benefit the mothers, babies, and families to whom we are responsible. I hope this text will be helpful to all of you who are using it, and I am honored to be its editor.

*Marsha Walker, RN, IBCLC*
Editor

# CONTRIBUTORS

Genevieve Becker, IBCLC, MSc, Reg Nutr, PGCertEd

Freelance breastfeeding education consultant/researcher, BEST Services, Galway, Ireland

Priscilla G. Bornmann, JD

Attorney/member, McKinley & Bornmann, P.L.C., Alexandria, Virginia

Karin Cadwell, RN, PhD, IBCLC

Healthy Children Project, Sandwich, Massachusetts

Marie Davis, RN, IBCLC

Perinatal educator and lactation consultant, Kaiser Permanente, Riverside, California; clinical instructor, UCLA Lactation Consultant Training Program

Elsa Regina Justo Giugliani, MD, PhD, IBCLC

Professor of pediatrics, Federal University of Rio Grande do Sul, Porto Alegre, Brazil

Karen Kerkhoff Gromada, MSN, RN, IBCLC

Director, Breastfeeding Answer Center

Thomas W. Hale, RPh, PhD

Associate professor of pediatrics, Texas Tech University School of Medicine, Amarillo, Texas

Joy Heads, RN, CM, Grad Certificate Bioethics, MHPEd, IBCLC

Clinical nurse consultant—lactation, Royal Hospital for Women, South Eastern Sydney Area Health Service, New South Wales, Australia

Kay Hoover, MEd, IBCLC

Lactation consultant, Philadelphia Department of Public Health, Division of Early Childhood, Youth and Women's Health, Philadelphia, Pennsylvania

Vergie I. Hughes, RN, MS, IBCLC

Director, Lactation Education Resources, Fairfax, Virginia

Heather Jackson, RGON, RM, AND, MA, IBCLC

Lactation consultant, midwife, BirthCare, Auckland, New Zealand

Judith Lauwers, BA, IBCLC

Executive director, BSC Center for Lactation Education, Chalfont, Pennsylvania

Chele Marmet, BS, MA, IBCLC

The Lactation Institute, Encino, California

Kristin Montgomery, PhD, RNC, IBCLC

Assistant Professor, School of Nursing, University of Texas at Austin, Austin, Texas

Sallie Page-Goertz, MN, CPNP, IBCLC

Assistant clinical professor, Kansas University School of Medicine; pediatric nurse practitioner and lactation consultant, Kansas University Children's Center, Kansas City, Kansas

Molly Pessl, BSN, IBCLC

Coordinator of Professional Education, Family Maternity Services, Evergreen Hospital Medical Center, Kirkland, Washington

Carol A. Ryan, RN, MSN(c), IBCLC

Manager, Perinatal Education, Parenting Services, Georgetown University Hospital, Washington, D.C.

JoAnne Scott, MA, IBCLC

Executive director, International Board of Lactation Consultant Examiners, Falls Church, Virginia; commissioner, National Commission of Certifying Agencies, Washington, D.C.

Ellen Shell, IBCLC

The Lactation Institute, Encino, California

Noreen Siebenaler, MSN, RN, IBCLC

Lactation consultant, Fairview Health Services, Fairview Southdale Hospital, Edina, Minnesota

Angela Smith, RN, CM, BA, IBCLC

Nursing unit manager KGV, Royal Prince Alfred Hospital; Partner, Australian Professional Lactation Education Services, Sydney, Australia

Linda J. Smith, BSE, FACCE, IBCLC

Owner, Bright Future Lactation Resource Centre, Dayton, Ohio

Amy Spangler, RN, MN, IBCLC

President, Daddy, Mommy, and Me, Atlanta, Georgia

Mary Rose Tully, MPH, IBCLC

Director, Lactation Services, UNC Women's and Children's Hospitals, Chapel Hill, North Carolina

Cynthia Turner-Maffei, MA, IBCLC

Lead faculty, Healthy Children 2000 Project, Inc., Sandwich, Massachusetts

Marsha Walker, RN, IBCLC

President, Lactation Associates; executive director, National Alliance for Breastfeeding Advocacy (Research, Education, and Legal Branch), Weston, Massachusetts

Barbara Wilson-Clay, BSEd, IBCLC

Private practice lactation consultant, Austin Lactation Associates, Austin, Texas

Ruth E. Worgan, RN, CM, C&FH, IBCLC

Midwife and lactation consultant, Centre for Family Health and Midwifery, University of Technology, Sydney, Australia

# MATERNAL BREASTFEEDING ANATOMY

*Marsha Walker, RN, IBCLC*

## OBJECTIVES

- Describe the process of breast development.
- Locate the major structures of the breast.
- Describe the function of the major structures of the breast.
- Discuss variations of breast anatomical structures.

## Introduction

The medical term for the breast is the mammary gland, which comes from the Latin word *mamma*, meaning "the breast." Gabrielle Palmer describes lactation as "such a spectacular survival strategy that we call ourselves after the mammary gland, mammals . . . animals that suckle their young." The mammary gland is the only organ that is <u>not fully developed</u> at birth. The gland undergoes three major phases of growth and development before pregnancy and lactation: in utero, during the first two years of life, and at puberty. The breast provides both <u>nutrition</u> and <u>nurturing.</u> The lactation consultant requires a basic understanding of the structures and functions of the breast in order to provide proper breastfeeding management guidelines and to troubleshoot problems should they arise.

## Breast Development: Mammogenesis

### Embryo

- Breast development begins during the fourth week of gestation when a primitive milk streak develops bilaterally from the axilla to the groin.
- This milk streak becomes the mammary milk ridge, or milk line, by the fifth week.
- The paired breasts develop from this line of glandular tissue.
- Thickening and inward growth into the chest wall continues during weeks seven through eight.

- Between weeks 12 and 16, specialized cells differentiate into the smooth muscle of the nipple and areola.
- Fifteen to 25 epithelial strips are formed that represent future secretory alveoli.
- Lactiferous ducts and their branches form and open into a shallow epithelial depression known as the mammary pit.
- The pit becomes elevated, forming the nipple and areola. An inverted nipple is the failure of the pit to elevate.
- A lumen (canal) is formed in each part of the branching system after 32 weeks of gestation.
- Near term, 15 to 25 mammary ducts form the fetal mammary gland.
- After birth, the neonate's mammary tissue—under the influence of maternal hormones—might secrete colostral-like fluid called witch's milk.
- Additional nipple or breast tissue can develop anywhere along the milk line, becoming especially prominent during pregnancy and lactation.
- This additional tissue is called accessory or supernumerary nipples.

## Puberty

- During childhood, the breasts simply keep pace with general physical growth.
- Ductal and lobular growth begins and continues through puberty, resulting in the growth of the breast parenchyma (functional parts: ducts, lobes, and alveoli) with its surrounding fat pad.
- At 10 to 12 years of age, primary and secondary ducts grow and divide, forming terminal end buds that later become the alveoli (small sacs where milk is secreted) in the mature female breast.
- During each menstrual cycle, proliferation and active growth of ductal tissue takes place.
- Complete development of mammary function occurs during pregnancy.
- Some illnesses, chemotherapy, therapeutic radiation to the chest, chest surgery, or injuries to the chest might affect development.
- Fat composition of the breast gives it its size and shape. Size is not related to functional capacity but might indicate milk storage potential.

## Structure of the Breast

- The breast is located in the superficial fascia (fibrous tissue beneath the skin) between the second rib and the sixth intercostal space.
- Mammary glandular tissue, known as the Tail of Spence (see Figure 1-1), projects somewhat into the axillary region.

**Figure 1-1** Quadrants of the left breast and axillary Tail of Spence

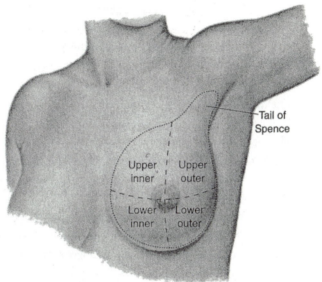

- The Tail of Spence is distinguished from supernumerary tissue because it connects to the normal duct system.
- The breast includes two major divisions: the parenchyma and the stroma.
- The parenchyma is composed of the alveolar gland with tree-like, ductular, branching alveoli that are in turn composed of secretory acinar units in which the ducts terminate.
- Each cluster of alveoli cells is surrounded by a contractile unit of myoepithelial cells that are responsible for ejecting milk into the ductules.
- Ductules from the 15 to 25 lobes converge into larger lactiferous ducts that widen under the areola into lactiferous sinuses.
- The stroma includes the connective tissue, fat tissue, blood vessels, nerves, and lymphatics.
- Suspensory ligaments called Cooper's ligaments run vertically through the breast and attach the deep layer of subcutaneous tissue to the dermis layer of the skin.
- The skin of the breast includes the nipple and areola.
- The nipple is a conical elevation located in the center of the areola.
- The nipple contains 15 to 25 milk ducts, smooth muscle fibers, sebaceous and apocrine sweat glands, and dense innervation of sensory nerve endings.
- The nipple is surrounded by the areola—a circular, darkly pigmented area.

- The areola usually darkens and enlarges during pregnancy and is elastic like the nipple.
- Montgomery's tubercles, containing ductular openings of sebaceous and lactiferous glands and sweat glands, are present in the areola.
- The areola does not contain fat but is constructed of smooth muscle and collagenous, elastic, connective tissue fibers in radial and circular arrangements.
- The Montgomery glands become enlarged during pregnancy, resembling small, raised pimples.
- They secrete a very small amount of milk as well as a substance that lubricates and protects the nipples (see Figures 1-2 and 1-3).
- Nipple erection is supported by fibroelastic tissue and local venostaisis that decrease the surface area of the areola and facilitate the draining of the lactiferous sinuses.
- The muscle arrangement of longitudinal inner muscles and outer circular and radial placed muscles make the nipple erect when contracted.
- When the nipple becomes erect, it changes shape to a smaller, firmer, and more prominent projection to aid the infant in latching on.
- The bulk of the nipple is composed of smooth muscle that functions as a closure mechanism to keep milk from continuously leaking.
- The breast is highly vascular, with 60 percent of the blood to the breast supplied by the internal mammary artery and 30 percent supplied by the lateral thoracic artery (see Figure 1-4).

**Figure 1-2**   Frontal view of lactating breast

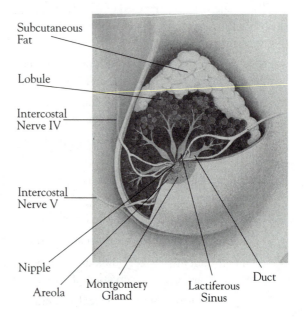

Subcutaneous Fat

Lobule

Intercostal Nerve IV

Intercostal Nerve V

Nipple

Areola

Montgomery Gland

Lactiferous Sinus

Duct

**Figure 1-3** Side view of lactating breast

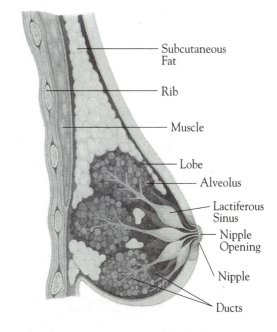

**Figure 1-4** Arterial blood supply to the breast

**Key**

1. subclavian artery
2. superior thoracic artery
3. internal thoracic artery
4. major pectoralis muscle
5. perforating branches of the internal mammary artery
6. arterial plexus around areola
7. intercostal arteries
8. pectoral branches of the lateral thoracic artery
9. circumflex scapular artery
10. minor pectoralis muscle
11. subscapular artery
12. lateral thoracic artery
13. pectoral branch of the thoracoacromial artery
14. axillary artery
15. deltoid branch of the thoracoacromial artery

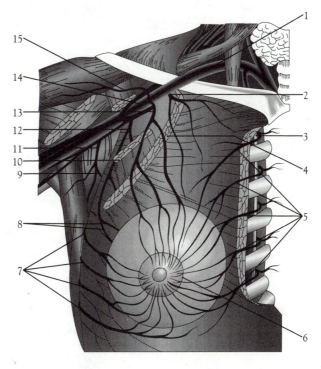

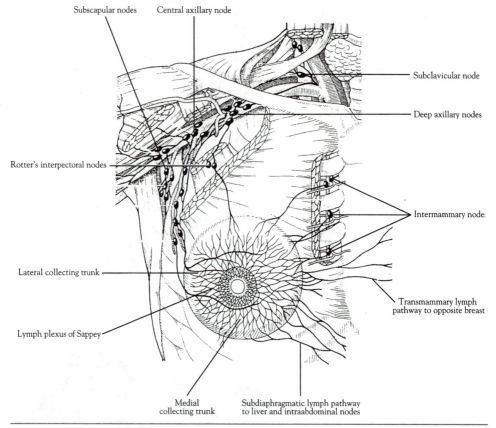

**Figure 1-5**   Lymph drainage of breast

- The lymphatic system of the breast collects excess fluids from tissue spaces, bacteria, and cast-off cell parts and drains these mainly to the axillary lymph nodes (see Figure 1-5).

- The nerves of the breast are mainly from branches of the fourth, fifth, and sixth intercostal nerves.

- The fourth intercostal nerve penetrates the posterior aspect of the breast at the four o'clock position on the left breast and at the eight o'clock position on the right, supplying the greatest amount of sensation to the areola (see Figure 1-6).

- The areola is the most sensitive part of the breast, followed by the general skin of the breast, and then the nipple which has the least sensitivity.

- The fourth intercostal nerve becomes more superficial as it reaches the areola, where it divides into five branches.

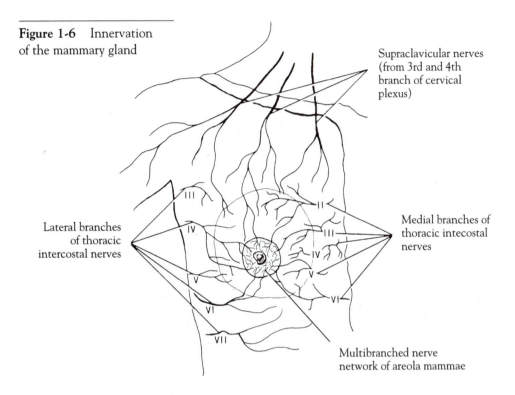

**Figure 1-6**   Innervation of the mammary gland

Supraclavicular nerves (from 3rd and 4th branch of cervical plexus)

Lateral branches of thoracic intercostal nerves

Medial branches of thoracic intecostal nerves

Multibranched nerve network of areola mammae

- The lowermost branch penetrates the areola at the five o'clock position on the left breast and at the seven o'clock position on the right breast.
- Trauma to this nerve might result in some loss of sensation in the breast.
- If the lowermost branch is severed, loss of sensation to the nipple and areola might result.
- Trauma or severing of this nerve could result from breast augmentation or reduction surgery.
- The nerve supply to the innermost areas of the breast is sparse.
- Aberrant sensory or autonomic nerve distributions in the nipple/areola complex could affect the let-down reflex and secretion of prolactin and oxytocin.

## Variations

- Breasts vary in size, shape, color, and placement on the chest wall (see Table 1-1 and Figure 1-7).

**Table 1-1**    Breast Types Classified by Physical Characteristics

| | |
|---|---|
| Type 1 | Round breasts, normal lower and medial and lateral quadrants |
| Type 2 | Hypoplasia of the lower medial quadrant |
| Type 3 | Hypoplasia of the lower medial and lateral quadrants |
| Type 4 | Severe constrictions, minimal breast base |

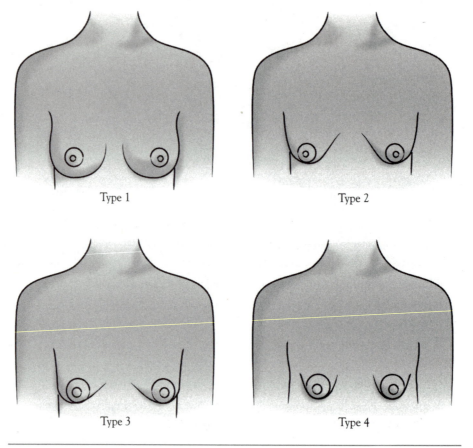

**Figure 1-7**    Breast classifications

- In a nonpregnant woman, the mature breast weighs about 200g.
- During pregnancy near term, the breast can weigh between 400 and 600g.

- During lactation, the breast can weigh 600 to 800g.
- Hypermastia—the presence of accessory mammary glands.
  - Hyperthelia—nipples without accompanying mammary tissue.
  - Accessory nipples and glandular tissue can be found along the milk line; these can lactate and undergo malignant changes.
- Hypertrophy—abnormally large breasts; hyperplasia refers to overdevelopment.
- Hypoplastia—underdevelopment of the breasts.
- Hypomastia—abnormally small breasts.
  - Hypoplastic breasts can be described as tubular or tuberous, sometimes with large areolas, and frequently asymmetric with the breasts being widely spaced from each other.
  - These breasts present an increased risk for insufficient milk.
  - Osborne classification.
    - Unilateral hypoplasia; contralateral breast normal
    - Bilateral hypoplasia with asymmetry
    - Unilateral hyperplasia; normal contralateral breast
    - Bilateral hyperplasia with asymmetry
    - Unilateral hypoplastic; contralateral breast is hypoplastic
    - Unilateral hypoplasia of the breast, thorax, and pectoral muscles (Poland's syndrome)
- Tied, retracted, or inverted nipple (see Figure 1-8).
  - Poor nipple protractility is not uncommon in primigravid women.
  - Protractility improves during the pregnancy.
  - True inversion is rare.
  - When the areola is compressed and the nipple retracts, it indicates a tied nipple caused by the persistence of fibers from the original invagination of the mammary dimple.
- Other nipple variations.
  - Bulbous—Might be difficult for a baby to grasp, especially a small baby.
  - Dimpled—Increases the risk for maceration as the nipple lies enveloped by the areola.
  - Bifurcated.
  - Double.
  - Skin tag—A skin tag can be removed during pregnancy if it is large or appears in a place where significant pain could occur.

**Figure 1-8**    Five basic types of nipples

| Type of Nipple | Before Stimulation | After Stimulation |
|---|---|---|
| **Common nipple**<br><br>The majority of mothers have what is referred to as a *common nipple*. It protrudes slightly when at rest and becomes erect and more graspable when stimulated. A baby has no trouble finding and grasping this nipple in order to pull in a large amount of breast tissue and stretch it to the roof of his mouth. | | |
| **Flat nipple**<br><br>The *flat nipple* has a very short shank that makes it less easy for the baby to find and grasp. In response to stimulation, this nipple remains essentially unchanged. Slight movement inward or outward may be present, but not enough to aid the baby in finding and initially grasping the breast on center. This nipple may benefit from the use of a syringe to increase protractility. | | |
| **Inverted-appearing nipple**<br><br>An *inverted-appearing nipple* may appear inverted but becomes erect after stimulation. This nipple needs no correction and presents no problems with graspability. | | |
| **Retracted nipple**<br><br>The *retracted nipple* is the most common type of inverted nipple. Initially, this nipple appears to be graspable. However, on stimulation, it retracts, making attachment difficult. This nipple responds well to techniques that increase nipple protrusion. | | |
| **Inverted nipple**<br><br>The truly *inverted nipple* is retracted both at rest and when stimulated. Such a nipple is very uncommon and more difficult for the baby to grasp. All techniques used to enhance protractility of breast tissue can be used to improve attachment. Even if the nipple remains retracted, the baby should be able to latch on if the mother helps form her breast into his mouth. | | |

# References

Auerbach KG, Riordan J. Clinical lactation: A visual guide. Sudbury, MA: Jones and Bartlett Publishers, 2000.

Huggins KE, Petok ES, Mireles O. Markers of lactation insufficiency: A study of 34 mothers. Current Issues in Clinical Lactation—2000. Sudbury, MA: Jones and Bartlett Publishers, 2000: 25–35.

Lauwers J, Shinskie D. Counseling the nursing mother. 3rd ed. Sudbury, MA: Jones and Bartlett Publishers, 2000: ch. 6, 87–106.

Lawrence RA, Lawrence RM. Breastfeeding: A guide for the medical profession. St. Louis, MO: Mosby, Inc., 1999: ch. 2, 35–57.

Osborne MP. Breast development and anatomy. In: Harris JR, Henderson IC, Hellman S, Kinney DW, eds. Breast disease. Philadelphia, PA: J. B. Lippincott, 1987: 1–15.

Palmer G. The politics of breastfeeding. London: Pandora Press, 1988:13.

Riordan J, Auerbach KG. Breastfeeding and human lactation, 2nd ed. Sudbury, MA: Jones and Bartlett Publishers, 1998: 93–98.

Wilson-Clay B, Hoover K. The breastfeeding atlas. Austin, TX: LactNews Press, 1999.

# Infant Anatomy for Feeding

*Chele Marmet, BS, MA, IBCLC and Ellen Shell, IBCLC*

## Objectives

- Locate and name the cranial and facial bones, sutures, fontanelles, joints, and processes on the infant skull.
- Name and describe the function of the 12 pairs of cranial nerves.
- Locate, name, and describe the function and innervation of the muscles of sucking and mastication.
- Locate, name, and describe the anatomical features of an infant's oral cavity.
- Identify the reference, atypical, and abnormal infant head and oral cavity.
- Describe the oral reflexes related to breastfeeding.

## Introduction

Familiarity with the anatomy of the infant's head is important as a basis for understanding the normal structure and function in infant feeding and as a reference for analyzing and correcting breastfeeding problems. The term "reference" is a nonjudgmental term that is used to describe the most common example or the greatest representation of a population, rather than the term "norm." It is necessary to distinguish between normal variations and abnormalities, both of which might cause breastfeeding problems. The lactation consultant requires an understanding of how infant anatomical structures and motions combine to enable the infant to take in nutrients and to determine his or her requisite milk supply. The newborn's oral anatomy is his or her primary way of relating to the world. Appropriate and accurate anatomical assessment aids the lactation consultant in assessing the normal and recognizing deviations that are amenable to intervention.

### Basic Concepts of Anatomic Terminology

1. reference—used to describe the most common example
2. body planes—used to facilitate uniformity in descriptions of the body

    a. midsagittal—the plane vertically dividing the body through the midline into right and left halves

    b. sagittal—any plane that is parallel to the midsagittal line, vertically dividing the body into right and left portions

    c. coronal (frontal)—any plane dividing the body into anterior (ventral) and posterior (dorsal) portions at right angles to the sagittal plane

    d. transverse (cross, horizontal)—plane dividing the body into superior and inferior portions

3. Directions and Positions

    a. cranial, superior, rostral—uppermost or above

    b. caudal, inferior—lowermost or below

    c. anterior, ventral—toward the front

    d. posterior, dorsal—toward the back

    e. medial—nearest the midline of the body

    f. lateral—toward the side

    g. proximal—nearest the point of attachment or origin

    h. distal—away from the point of attachment or origin

    i. superficial—on the surface

    j. deep—below the surface

    k. ipsilateral—pertaining to the same side

    l. contralateral—pertaining to the opposite side

4. Terms

    a. alveolus—a small cavity

    b. process—projections on a bone

    c. meatus—a passage or channel, especially the external opening of a canal

    d. foramen—a natural hole or passage, especially one into or through a bone

    e. lumen—the cavity or channel within a tube or tubular organ

    f. sinus—a recess, cavity, or hollow space

    g. protuberance—a projecting part, process, or swelling

    h. fontanel—junctions of cranial bones covered by a tough membrane

5. Body Positions

    a. prone—lying face down

    b. supine—lying on the back

6. Joints

    a. temporomandibular (TMJ)—opens and closes the jaw; lateral displacement of the mandible

    b. suture—a joint that does not move; the bones are united by a thin layer of fibrous tissue

7. Muscles

    a. involuntary—contraction not induced by will

    b. voluntary—subject to voluntary control

    c. visceral/smooth—found in digestive and respiratory tracts

    d. cardiac/striated—involuntary muscle possessing a striated appearance of voluntary muscles

    e. skeletal/striated—voluntary, striated; gross and fine motor movements

    f. origin—the more fixed attachment of a muscle that serves as a basis of action

    g. insertion—the moveable attachment where the effects of movement are produced

8. systems—groups of organs that form the general structural plan of the body

    a. skeletal—bones, cartilage, and membranous structures that protect and support the soft parts of the body and that supply levers for movement

    b. muscular—facilitates movement

    c. cardiovascular—pumps and distributes blood

    d. lymphatic—drains tissue spaces and carries absorbed fat in the blood

    e. nervous—controlling system of the body

    f. endocrine—chemical regulator of body functions

    g. integument—skin (hair, nails, sebaceous, and sweat glands); insulation, temperature, and water regulation

    h. respiratory—brings oxygen to and eliminates carbon dioxide from the blood

    i. digestive—converts food into substances that the body can absorb and utilize

    j. urinary—forms and eliminates urine and maintains homeostasis

    k. immune—protection from and reaction to disease and infection

    l. reproductive—perpetuation of the species

## Location of the Skeletal System of the Infant's Head, Face, and Neck

1. Bones

    a. occipital—forms the back and base of the cranium; contains the foramen magnum through which the spinal cord passes

    b. frontal—forms the forehead, roof of the nasal cavity, and orbits (bony sockets containing the eyes)

    c. parietal—sides and roof of the cranium

    d. temporal—sides and base of the cranium; houses the middle and inner ear structures

    e. ethmoid—between the nasal bones and sphenoid; forms part of the anterior cranial floor, medial walls of the orbits, and part of the nasal septum

    f. nasal—upper bridge of the nose

    g. vomer—posterior nasal cavity; forms a portion of the nasal septum

    h. lacrimal—anterior, medial wall of the orbit

    i. zygomatic arch—prominence of the cheeks and part of the lateral wall and floor of the orbits

    j. palatine—posterior nasal cavity between the maxillae and sphenoid

    k. maxilla—upper jaw

    l. mandible—lower jaw

    m. inferior nasal concha—lateral wall of the nasal cavity

    n. hyoid bone—horseshoe-shaped bone suspended from the styloid process of the temporal bone

2. sutures—found only in the skull

    a. coronal—line of articulation between the frontal bone and the two parietal bones

    b. sagittal—line of articulation between the two parietal bones in the midline

    c. lambdoidal—anterior articulation between the occipital and parietal bones

3. fontanels—the membranous intervals between the angles of the cranial bones in infants

    a. anterior fontanel—a diamond-shaped interval where the frontal angles of the parietal bones meet the two separate halves of the frontal

    b. posterior fontanel—a triangular interval at the union of the lambdoid and sagittal sutures

    c. sphenoidal fontanel—irregularly shaped interval on either side of the skull

    d. mastoid fontanel—interval on either side of the skull

## Innervation of the Mouth and Suckling Motion

1. cranial nerves

    a. CN I olfactory—smell

    b. CN II optic—sight

    c. CN III oculomotor—innervates external muscles for several movements of the eye

    d. CN IV trochlear—innervates muscles that move the eye up and down

    e. CN V trigeminal—three branches; muscles of mastication

    f. CN VI abducens—moves the eye up temporarily

    g. CN VII facial—muscles for facial expression

    h. CN VIII vestibulocochlear—hearing and equilibrium

    i. CN IX glossopharyngeal—taste

    j. CN X vagus—larynx, pharynx

    k. CN XI spinal accessory—muscles of the neck and shoulder

    l. CN XII hypoglossal—muscles of the tongue

2. Cranial Nerves Related to Suckling

| Structure | Cranial Nerve/Sensory | Cranial Nerve/Motor |
|---|---|---|
| Mouth | CN V (shape/texture) | CN VII |
| Tongue | CNVII, IX (taste) | CN XII |
| Jaw | CN V (position of TMJ) | CN |

Adapted from Wolf LS, Glass RP. Feeding and swallowing disorders in infancy: assessment and management. Tucson, AZ: Therapy Skill Builders, 1992.

3. Cranial nerves related to swallowing; 26 muscles and six cranial nerves must coordinate for swallowing

| Structure | Cranial Nerve/Sensory | Cranial Nerve/Motor |
|---|---|---|
| Palate | CN V, IX | CN V, VII, IX, X |
| Tongue | CN IX | CN V, VII, XII |
| Pharynx | CN V, X | CN IX, X |
| Larynx | CN X | CN IX, X |

Adapted from Wolf LS, Glass RP. Feeding and swallowing disorders in infancy: assessment and management. Tucson, AZ: Therapy Skill Builders, 1992.

   a. Cranial nerve palsies (partial paralysis) or damage might impair the suck, swallow, and breathe cycle (see Figure 2-1 and Figure 2-2).

## Muscles of Mastication and Suckling

   a. temporalis—raises the mandible; closes the mouth; draws the mandible backward

   b. masseter—closes the jaw

   c. medial pterygoid—raises the mandible; closes the mouth

   d. lateral pterygoid—brings the jaw forward

   e. buccinator—compresses the cheek and retracts the angle

   f. orbicularis oris—closes the lips

**Figure 2-1**  Muscles and nerves used in suckling and swallowing, sagittal section. (Reprinted with permission from M. Biancuzzo, *Breastfeeding the Newborn: Clinical Strategies for Nurses.* St. Louis: Mosby, Inc.)

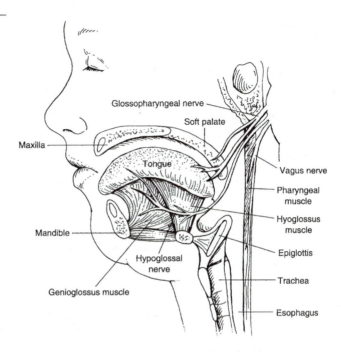

**Figure 2-2**  Lateral view (Reprinted with permission from M. Biancuzzo, *Breastfeeding the Newborn: Clinical Strategies for Nurses.* St. Louis: Mosby, Inc.)

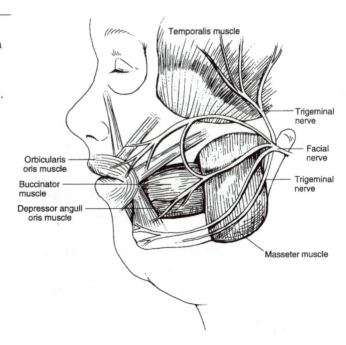

## Muscles Moving the Tongue

a. genioglossus—depresses and thrusts the tongue forward

b. styloglossus—draws the tongue upward and backward

c. stylohyoid—draws the hyoid and tongue upward

d. digastric—raises the hyoid or opens the mouth

e. mylohyoid—elevates the hyoid; supports the mouth floor

f. hyoglossus—depresses the tongue

g. geniohyoid—elevates and draws the hyoid forward

## Muscles Moving the Throat

a. sternohyoid—depresses the hyoid and larynx

b. omohyoid—depresses the hyoid

c. sternothyroid—depresses the thyroid cartilage

d. thyrohyoid—raises and changes the form of the larynx

## Anatomy of the Head, Mouth, and Pharynx of the Newborn as it Relates to Feeding

1. Oral Cavity (Mouth)
   a. Bounded by the roof, floor, lips, and cheeks (see Figure 2-3)
   b. Roof consists of the palatine process of the maxilla and the palatine bone (hard palate)
   a. Transitions posteriorly into the soft palate and uvula
   c. Floor consists of the mandible spanned by the mylohyoid, geniohyoid, and front of the digastric muscle
   d. The orbicularis oris surrounds the lips.
   e. Cheeks are defined by the buccinator and masseter muscles; sucking pads that consist of fatty tissue are encased in the cheek to provide stability for the sucking pattern; helps assure that the nipple/areola is in contact with the sides of the mouth
   f. Jaw is small and retracted
   g. The tongue fills the entire oral cavity and touches the roof and floor of the mouth as well as the lateral gum lines and cheeks
      i. lingual frenulum—a fold of mucous membrane extending from the floor of the mouth to the midline of the under surface of the tongue
      ii. labial frenum—the membrane that attaches the upper lip to the gum ridge

**Figure 2-3**   Mouth and pharynx of the newborn and adult
*(Pre-Feeding Skills—A Comprehensive Resource for Feeding Development.*
Copyright © 1987 by Therapy Skill Builders, a Harcourt Health Sciences Company. Reproduced by permission. All rights reserved.)

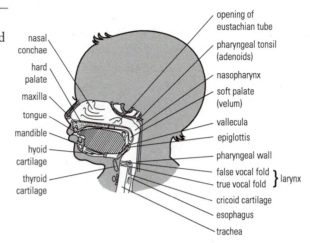

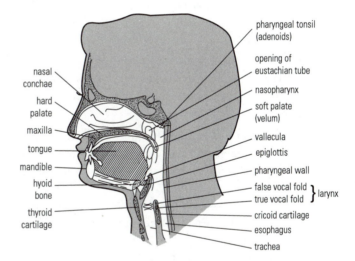

2. pharynx—a soft tube at the back of the throat

   a. oropharynx—composed of the area between the elevated soft palate and the epiglottis

   b. nasopharynx—section of the pharynx between the nasal choanae and the elevated soft palate; the eustachian tubes originate in the nasopharynx

   c. hypopharynx—extends from the base of the epiglottis to the cricopharyngeal sphincter

3. larynx—gateway to the trachea composed of cartilage suspended by muscles and ligaments to the hyoid bone and cervical vertebrae
   a. Contains the epiglottis, which closes during swallowing
   b. Contains the vocal cords, which also close during swallowing in order to protect the airway
4. trachea—a semirigid tube that branches into the primary bronchi leading to each lung; the posterior aspect is a membranous wall that abuts the soft tissue of the esophagus
5. esophagus—a thin, muscular tube that extends to the stomach and distends as food is propelled through it by peristaltic motion

## The Palate

1. Function
   a. The hard palate assists with positioning and stability of the nipple within the mouth.
   b. The hard palate works in conjunction with the tongue in order to compress the nipple.
   c. The soft palate works with the tongue to create the posterior seal of the oral cavity.
   d. The soft palate elevates during the swallow, closing off the nasal cavity and allowing the passage of the bolus.
2. Reference palate
   a. The hard palate should be intact and smoothly contoured.
      i. In utero and after birth, the shape of the hard palate is contoured by the continual pressure of the tongue as it rests against the palate with the mouth closed.
   b. Submucous clefts of the soft palate cannot be visualized.
      i. Might see a translucent zone in the middle of the soft palate.
      ii. Bifid uvula.
      iii. Absent or notched posterior nasal spine.
3. Variations and Abnormalities of the Palate
   a. high palate—the palate or a portion of the palate is very high, altering the shallow saucer shape
   b. wide palate or flat palate—reduced arch
   c. narrow palate—has a pinched shape
   d. short and long palates—shorter or longer than the typical one inch from the alveolar ridge to the point where the soft palate folds down
   e. channel palate—midline groove usually from the prolonged presence of orotracheal tubes

    f. V arch—a high palate, but at midline, the sides of the palate narrow

    g. bony prominences—uncommon; more common is an Epstein pearl (accumulation of epithelial cells or also called a retention cyst) located at the juncture of the hard and soft palates

    h. sloped palate—sudden declines in the normal curve

    i. bubble palate—concavities of the hard palate confined with a rim

    j. cleft—a complete opening in the hard or soft palate resulting from the failure of the palatal shelves to meet and fuse in the midline during the seventh to eighth week of gestation

## Mandible Placement

1. Reference
   a. Upper and lower jaw loosely opposed
   b. Both gun ridges in direct opposition

2. Deviations
   a. recessed jaw—the lower gum ridge is posterior to the upper gum ridge
   b. micrognathia—an excessively small or posteriorly positioned mandible; internally, the tongue is also posteriorly positioned in relation to the oral cavity

## Tongue

1. Reference
   a. Brings the nipple into the mouth, shaping it and stabilizing its position
   b. Provides a compression force to express milk from the nipple
   c. Forms a central groove to channel fluid toward the pharynx
   d. Assists in forming a bolus in preparation for the swallow
   e. The tongue is soft with a rounded tip
   f. Lies on the bottom of the mouth with a slight central groove

2. Variations
   a. tongue tip elevation—the tip of the tongue is in opposition to the upper gum ridge or the palate behind the alveolar ridge
   b. humped—in an anterior-posterior direction
   c. bunched—compressed in a lateral direction
   d. retracted—held posteriorly in the mouth well behind the alveolar ridges
   e. protruded—the tip rests forward, on the lips or over the lower gum ridge
   f. A short or tight lingual frenulum is referred to as tongue-tie or ankyloglossia

## Oral Reflexes

1. Adaptive
   a. rooting reflex—touching or stroking the baby's lips or cheek causes him or her to turn his or her head toward the stimulus and open the mouth
   b. sucking reflex—a light touch of the nipple or a finger to the lips or tongue initiates the complex movements of the suckle
   c. swallowing—elicited by a bolus of fluid impacting the sensory receptors of the soft palate and back of the mouth; has both reflexive and voluntary properties (see Figure 2-4 and Figure 2-5)
2. Protective
   a. gag reflex—protects the baby from ingesting items that are too large for the esophagus; is elicited in the newborn at the mid-tongue area
   b. cough reflex—mechanism that protects the airway from the aspiration of liquids; should be the primary consideration in decisions regarding the safety of infant feeding

**Figure 2-4**  Midsagittal section of cranial and oral anatomy of an adult while swallowing.

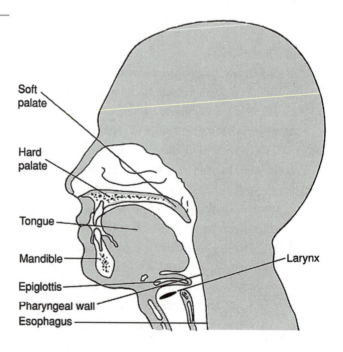

Soft palate

Hard palate

Tongue

Mandible

Epiglottis

Pharyngeal wall

Esophagus

Larynx

**Figure 2-5** Midsagittal section of cranial and oral anatomy of an infant while swallowing

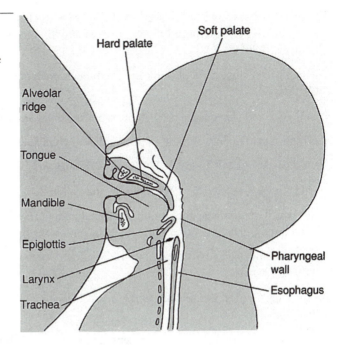

## References

Berg KL. Tongue-tie (ankyloglossia) and breastfeeding: a review. *J Hum Lact* 1990; 6:109–112.

Berg K. Two cases of tongue-tie and breastfeeding. *J Hum Lact* 1990; 6:124–126.

Bly L. The components of normal movement during the first year of life and abnormal motor development (monograph). Neuro-Developmental Treatment Association, Inc., Oak Park, IL: NDTA, 1983.

Bosma JF, ed. Oral sensation and perception: the mouth of the infant. Springfield, IL: Charles C. Thomas, 1972.

Brazelton TB. Neonatal behavioral assessment scale. Clinics in developmental medicine, No. 88. Philadelphia, PA: J. B. Lippincott Company.

Brown D. Tongue-tie. *Br Med J* 1959; 2:952.

Catlin FI. Tongue-tie. *Arch Otolaryng* 1971; 94:548–557.

Cullum IM. An old wives' tale. *Br Med J* 1959; 2:497–498.

Danner S, Wilson-Clay B. Breastfeeding the infant with cleft lip/palate. Lactation consultant series, Auerbach KG, ed. Schaumburg, IL: La Leche League International, Unit 10, 1986.

Diamond MD, Scheibel AB, Elson LM. The human brain coloring book. New York: Harper Collins, 1991.

Fleiss P, et al. Ankyloglossia: a cause of breastfeeding problems. *J Hum Lact* 1990; 6:128–129.

Good ME. Breastfeeding and the short frenulum. *J Hum Lact* 1987; 3:154–156.

Grant JCB. An atlas of anatomy. Baltimore: Williams and Wilkins, 1956.

Gray H. Gray's anatomy. New York: Barnes and Noble Books, 1995.

Hazelbaker A. Assessment tool for lingual frenulum function (ATLFF): Use in a lactation consultant private practice. Encino, CA: Lactation Institute, 1993.

Huggins K. Ankyloglossia—one lactation consultant's personal experience. *J Hum Lact* 1990; 6:123–124.

Ingram TTS. Clinical significance of the infantile feeding reflexes. *Physiol Behavior* 1962; 26:327–329.

Jain E. Tongue-tie (ankyloglossia). Presented at First Annual International Meeting, Academy of Breastfeeding Medicine: Physicians and Breastfeeding: A new alliance. Rochester, NY: October 1996.

Jain E. Tongue-tie: impact on breastfeeding. Complete management including frenotomy (video). Lakeview Breastfeeding Clinic, 6628 Crowchild Trail SW, Calgary, Alberta, Canada T3E 5R8, 1996.

Kapit W, Elson L. The anatomy coloring book. New York: Addison Wesley, 1993.

Marmet C, Shell E. Lactation forms: A guide to lactation consultant charting. Encino, CA: Lactation Institute Publications, 1993.

Marmet C, Shell E, Marmet R. Neonatal frenotomy may be necessary to correct breastfeeding problems. *J Hum Lact* 1990; 6:117–121.

Marmet C, Shell E. Training neonates to suck correctly. MCN 1984; 9:401–407.

Masaitis NS, Kaemps JW. Developing a frenotomy policy at one medical center: A case study approach. *J Hum Lact* 1996; 12:229–232.

Mathewson RJ, Siegel MJ, McCanna DL. Ankyloglossia: A review of the literature and a case report. *J Dent Child* 1966; 33:238–243.

McBride M, Danner S. Sucking disorders in neurologically impaired infants: Assessment and facilitation of breastfeeding. *Clin Perinatol* 1987; 14:109–130.

Messner AH, Lalakea ML, Aby J, et al. Ankyloglossia: Incidence and associated feeding difficulties. *Arch Otol Head Neck Surg* 2000; 126:36–39.

Milani-Comparetti A. The neurophysiologic and clinical implications of studies on fetal motor behavior. *Sem Perinatol* 1981; 5:183–189.

Miller JG, Miller JH. The controversial issue of breastfeeding for infants with cleft palate. Info Med Medical Research and Publishing #1, 5035-49 St Innisfail, Alberta, Canada, 1996.

Mohrbacher N. Nursing a baby with a cleft lip or palate. *Leaven* 1994; Mar/Apr:19–23.

Morris S, Klein M. Pre-feeding skills. Tucson, AZ: Therapy Skill Builders, 1987.

Mukai S, Mukai C, Asaoka K. Ankyloglossia with deviation of the epiglottis and larynx. *Ann Otol Rhinol Laryngol* 1991; 100:3–20.

Netter F. Atlas of human anatomy. East Hanover, NJ: Novartis, 1997.

Notestine GE. The importance of the identification of ankyloglossia (short lingual frenulum) as a cause of breastfeeding problems. *J Hum Lact* 1990; 6:113–115.

Oldfield MC. Tongue-tie. *Br Med J* 1959; 2:1181–1182.

Oldfield MC. Congenitally short frenula of the upper lip and tongue. *Lancet* 1955; 1:528–530.

Palmer B. The influence of breastfeeding on development of the oral cavity: A commentary. *J Hum Lact* 1998; 14:93–98.

Riordan J, Auerbach KG, eds. Breastfeeding and human lactation, 2nd ed. Sudbury, MA: Jones and Bartlett Publishers, 1998.

Sears W. Growing together. Schaumberg, IL: La Leche League International, 1987.

Smith W, et al. Physiology of sucking in the normal infant using real-time ultrasound. *Radiology* 1985; 156:379.

Smith W, Erenberg A, Nowak A. Imaging evaluation of the human nipple during breastfeeding. *Am J Dis Child* 1988; 142:76–78.

Smithells RW. Spontaneous rupture of tongue-tie. *Br Med J* 1959; 1:236.

Strauss RP, Davis JU. Prenatal detection and fetal surgery of clefts and craniofacial abnormalities in humans: Social and ethical issues. *Cleft Palate J* 1990; 27(2):176–183.

Snyder J. Variation in infant palatal structure and breastfeeding. Encino, CA: Lactation Institute, 1995.

Snyder JB. Bubble palate and failure to thrive: a case report. *J Hum Lact* 1997; 13:139–143.

Ward N. Ankyloglossia: A case study in which clipping was not necessary. *J Hum Lact* 1990; 6:126–127.

Weatherly-White RCA. Early repair and breastfeeding for infants with cleft lip. *Plast Reconst Surg* 1987; 79:879–887.

Weber F, et al. An untrasonographic study of the organization of sucking and swallowing by newborn infants. *Dev Med Child Neurol* 1986; 28:19–24.

Widstrom AM, Thingstrom-Paulsson J. The position of the tongue during rooting reflexes elicited in newborn infants before the first suckle. *Acta Paediatr* 1993; 83:281–283.

Widstrom AM, et al. Short-term effects of early suckling and touch of the nipple on maternal behavior. *Early Hum Dev* 1990; 21:153–163.

Wiessinger D, Miller M. Breastfeeding difficulties as a result of tight lingual and labial frena: A case report. *J Hum Lact* 1995; 11:313–316.

Wilson J. Oral-motor function and development in children. Proceedings of May 1977 symposium, Division of Physical Therapy, Department of Medical Allied Health Professions, School of Medicine, University of North Carolina, Chapel Hill, NC: 1977.

Wilton JM. Sore nipples and slow weight gain related to a short frenulum. *J Hum Lact* 1990; 6:122–123.

Wolf LS, Glass RP. Feeding and swallowing disorders in infancy. Tucson, AZ: Therapy Skill Builders, 1992.

Wong D. Essentials of pediatric nursing. St. Louis: Mosby, 1996.

Woolridge M. Anatomy of infant sucking. *Midwifery* 1986; 2:164–171.

# Physiology of the Breast during Pregnancy and Lactation

*Marsha Walker, RN, IBCLC*

## Objectives

- Discuss the hormonal control of mammary growth during pregnancy.
- Describe the processes of lactogenesis I, II, and III.
- List the hormones of lactation and their function.
- Describe the neuroendocrine control of milk ejection.
- Discuss the feedback inhibitor of lactation.
- Define autocrine (local) control of milk synthesis.
- Explain the process of milk synthesis.

## Introduction

The breast is a remarkable endocrine organ that experiences growth, differentiation, and lactation in response to a complex interplay of hormones and stimulation. Mammogenesis (the development of the mammary gland and related structures within the breast) occurs throughout fetal, adolescent, and adult life. The hormonal environment of pregnancy finishes preparing the breasts to assume the role of nourishing the infant following birth. After delivery, a profound change occurs in the hormonal milieu—enabling an elaborate system of neuroendocrine feedback to produce and deliver milk of a changing composition to meet the needs and stores of the infant as he or she grows and develops. The breasts are capable of full lactation from 16 weeks of pregnancy onward. Milk does not "come in" because it is already present before delivery in the form of colostrum. Abundant production is suppressed by inhibiting hormones until placental delivery, when the change in hormonal checks and balances and the stimulus of infant suckling signals the breasts to produce copious amounts of milk. The lactation consultant benefits from a familiarity with this cascade of events and its influence on normal and abnormal lactation.

## The Breasts during Pregnancy

1. Final preparation for lactation
   a. Early in the first trimester, mammary epithelial cells proliferate, ductal sprouting and branching are initiated, and lobular formation occurs.
   b. The ducts proliferate into the fatty pad, and the ductal end buds differentiate into alveoli.
   c. Increases occur in mammary blood flow, interstitial water, and electrolyte concentrations.
   d. Mammary blood vessels increase their luminal diameters and form new capillaries around the lobules.
   e. During the last trimester, secretory cells fill with fat droplets and the alveoli are distended with colostrum.
   f. Mammary epithelial proliferation declines and alveolar epithelium differentiates for secretory function.

2. Hormonal control of breast development during pregnancy
   a. Placental lactogen, prolactin, and chorionic gonadotrophin contribute to the accelerated growth.
   b. Ductular sprouting is attributed to estrogen, and lobular formation occurs in response to progesterone.
   c. Prolactin is necessary for complete growth of the gland and is secreted by the anterior pituitary gland.
   d. Prolactin exerts its effect through receptors for the initiation of milk secretion located on the alveolar cell surfaces.
   e. Prolactin levels rise during sleep and throughout pregnancy.
   f. In a non-nursing mother, prolactin levels drop to normal at two weeks postpartum.
   g. Estrogen and progesterone levels increase during pregnancy.
   h. 17beta-estradiol is required for mammary growth and epithelial proliferation during pregnancy.
   i. Progesterone stimulates lobuloalveolar growth while suppressing secretory activity.
   j. Prolactin is prevented from exerting its effect on milk excretion by the elevated levels of progesterone; prolactin-inhibiting factor is secreted by the hypothalamus in order to negatively control prolactin's effects.
   k. Progesterone sensitizes mammary cells to the effects of insulin and growth factors and might be involved in the final preparation of the gland for lactogenesis.
   l. Glucocorticoids enhance formation of the lobules during pregnancy.
   m. Thyroid hormones increase the responsiveness of mammary cells to prolactin and can improve lactational performance.

n. Three main hormones are necessary for lactation to begin: prolactin, insulin, and hydrocortisone.

o. Supportive metabolic hormones include insulin, cortisol, thyroid-parathyroid hormone, and growth hormone.

p. Lactogenesis I, occurring around 16 weeks prenatally, is when the breast is first capable of synthesizing unique milk components; placental lactogen is thought to be responsible.

q. The prepartum secretion, or colostrum, shows a gradually increasing presence of lactose, casein, and alpha-lactalbumin.

*I capable*
*II copious*
*III maintenance*

## Delivery and Lactogenesis II

1. Placental expulsion following delivery precipitates an abrupt decline in levels of placental lactogen, estrogens, and progesterone.

   a. A decline in progesterone levels is thought to be the initiating event for Lactogenesis II.

   b. This decline in progesterone acts in the presence of lactogenic hormones, such as prolactin and glucocorticoids for full lactogenic activity.

2. A sharp rise in citrate and alpha-lactalbumin occurs at the onset of Lactogenesis II.

   a. Lactogenesis II is the onset of copious milk secretion between 30 and 72 hours following delivery.

   b. Lactogenesis II might be delayed up to 24 hours in women who have type I diabetes mellitus; there might be a temporary imbalance in the amount of insulin required for glucose homeostasis and insulin required for the initiation of lactation.

3. Prolactin levels remain elevated for about three months postpartum with sharp spikes of prolactin released with suckling; after the third month, basal prolactin levels fall to normal.

   a. Prolactin increases the concentration of its own receptor; thus, the prepartum surge of prolactin probably is important for the onset of copious milk production.

   b. While prolactin is necessary for milk secretion, its levels are not directly related to the volume of milk produced; i.e., prolactin becomes permissive in its function.

   c. Prolactin release occurs only in response to direct stimulation of the nipple/areola.

## Lactogenesis III

1. Previously called galactopoiesis; is simply the maintenance of lactation.

2. Milk production refers to the volume of milk removed from the breast at a feeding/expression.

3. Milk synthesis refers to the accumulation of milk within the breast.
   a. The rate of milk synthesis refers to the rate at which newly synthesized milk is accumulating within the breast.
   b. Milk production is correlated to the needs of the baby.
4. Local or autocrine control regulates the short-term milk synthesis of the breasts.
   a. For mothers initiating lactation, the mothers who breastfeed more frequently produce more milk.
   b. If an infant's demand for milk increases, he or she might choose to feed at the same frequency but increase the amount of milk taken at each breastfeeding.
   c. An infant removes approximately 76 percent of the available milk at a feeding.
   d. Milk synthesis responds to the varying amount of residual milk remaining in the breast after a feeding.
   e. The storage capacity of breasts varies greatly among women.
      i. The measured storage capacity of a breast increases with breast size.
      ii. Storage capacity is related to how the infant's demand for milk is met by the mother.
      iii. Women who have small breasts are capable of secreting as much milk over a 24 hour period as women who have large breasts; however, they might need to feed their baby more frequently.
   f. The degree to which the breast is emptied signals the amount of milk to be made for the next feeding.
      i. The greater the degree of emptying at a feeding, the greater the rate of milk synthesis after that feed.
      ii. Milk production will not be limited by the frequency of breast emptying as long as the actual frequency of breast emptying is greater than the minimum frequency that is needed to prevent engorgement.
      iii. The total storage capacity of women's breasts varies widely, as does the infant's demand for milk.
   g. Milk synthesis is controlled independently in each breast to a considerable degree.
   h. Milk also contains a whey protein called the _Feedback Inhibitor of Lactation_ (FIL) that has strong effects on the mammary secretory cell.
   i. Its concentration increases with longer periods of milk accumulation, downregulating the production of milk.
5. Neuroendocrine involvement in milk ejection.
   a. Oxytocin is responsible for the milk ejection reflex, or let-down reflex.
   b. Milk ejection occurs when direct stimulation to sensory neurons in the areola results in the release of oxytocin from the posterior pituitary.

    c. Oxytocin causes a contraction of the myoepithelial cells surrounding the alveoli, forcing milk into the collecting ducts of the breast.

    d. Impulses from the cerebral cortex, ears, and eyes can also elicit the release of oxytocin through exteroceptive stimuli (such as hearing a baby cry).

    e. Suckling stimulates the pulsatile release of oxytocin at about one-minute intervals.

    f. Variable and intermittent bursts of oxytocin are also seen from pre-nursing stimuli and mechanical stimulation from a breast pump.

    g. Oxytocin causes shortening of the ducts without constricting them, thus increasing milk pressure.

    h. The milk ejection reflex serves to increase the intraductal mammary pressure and to maintain it at levels that are sufficient to overcome the resistance to the outflow of milk from the breast.

    i. A simultaneous and closed secretion of oxytocin occurs into brain regions of the mother where it has a calming affect, lowers maternal blood pressure and cortisol levels, decreases anxiety and aggressive behavior, and permeates the areas of the brain associated with mothering and bonding behaviors.

    j. Some women feel the milk ejection reflex as increased pressure or tingling within the breast or as shooting pains, whereas some women never feel the milk ejection reflex at all.

    k. Mothers, especially multiparous women, will also feel uterine cramping for the first few days after birth with each breastfeeding.

    l. Mothers might also report increased thirst, a warm or flushed feeling, increased heat from the breasts, or a feeling of sleepiness.

    m. Milk ejection signs can be seen when the baby begins gulping milk (when the rapid pattern of two sucks per second decreases to one suck or so per second with swallowing).

6. Milk synthesis

    a. The cells lining both the alveoli and the smaller ductules appear capable of secreting milk.

    b. They do so continuously at the rate of approximately 1.6g of milk per gram of tissue per 24 hours.

    c. The milk is stored in the alveoli and in small ducts adjacent to the cells that secrete it, compressing and flattening the cells.

    d. Five pathways are involved in milk synthesis.

        i. Pathway I: Protein Secretion

           (1) The most important proteins synthesized by the mammary cell are casein, lactoferrin, alpha-lactalbumin, and lysozyme.

      (2) Protein synthesis begins in the nucleus with the transcription of specific mRNAs that code for milk proteins and pass into the cytoplasm, where they serve as templates.

      (3) Proteins pass to the Golgi apparatus, where phosphate and sugar groups are added.

      (4) Calcium enters this compartment and aggregates the casein molecules into micelles containing large amounts of calcium and phosphate.

      (5) The secretory vesicles migrate to the apical membrane, fuse with it, and release their contents.

  ii. Pathway II: Lactose Secretion

      (1) Alpha-lactalbumin forms a complex with the enzyme galactosyl-transferase, catalyzing the synthesis of lactose from glucose and UDP-galactose.

      (2) Lactose concentration is 200mM, or about 7 percent by weight.

      (3) Another 30mM of sugar is added to the milk as glycosyl groups on milk proteins; these are oligosaccharides that vary according to the mother's ABO blood type and are involved in disease protection.

  iii. Pathway III: Milk Fat Synthesis

      (1) The substrate for milk fat synthesis comes from two sources: mammary alveolar cells synthesize the shorter chain fatty acids (10 to 16 carbons) from glucose, and fatty acids derived from plasma sources are synthesized in adipose tissue and are the longer chain fatty acids (16 to 20 carbons).

  iv. Pathway IV: Monovalent Ion Secretion into Milk

      (1) Low ion concentrations of sodium, potassium, and chloride are maintained by mechanisms in the apical membrane.

  v. Pathway V: Plasma Protein Secretion into Milk

      (1) A plasma membrane receptor binds immunoglobulin A (IgA) from the plasma to the mammary alveolar cell. IgA is released from the apical membrane into the milk.

      (2) Other hormones (such as prolactin, insulin, growth factors, and so on) have receptors on mammary cells and most likely find their way into milk through pathway V.

e. Mammary cells become competent to secrete milk proteins at midpregnancy but are kept in check by high circulating levels of steroids, particularly progesterone.

f. Most milk products secreted during pregnancy find their way back into the plasma via the leaky junctions (spaces between the mammary alveolar cells).

# References

Arthur PG, Jones TJ, Spruce J, Hartmann PE. Measuring short-term rates of milk synthesis in breast-feeding mothers. *Quarterly J Exp Physiol* 1989; 74:419–428.

Arthur PD, Smith M, Hartmann PE. Milk lactose, citrate, and glucose as markers of lactogenesis in normal and diabetic women. *J Pediatr Gastroenterol Nutr* 1989; 9:488–496.

Cox DB, Pwens RA, Hartmann PE. Blood and milk prolactin and the rate of milk synthesis in women. *Exp Physiol* 1996; 81:1007–1020.

Cregan MD, Hartmann PE. Computerized breast measurement from conception to weaning: Clinical implications. *J Hum Lact* 1999; 15:89–96.

Daly SEJ, Kent JC, Huynh DQ, et al. The determination of short-term breast volume changes and the rate of synthesis of human milk using computerized breast measurement. *Exp Physiol* 1992; 77:79–87.

Daly SEJ, Di Rosso A, Owens RA, Hartmann PE. Degree of breast emptying explains changes in the fat content, but not fatty acid composition, of human milk. *Exp Physiol* 1993; 78:741–755.

Daly SEJ, Owens RA, Hartmann PE. The short-term synthesis and infant-regulated removal of milk in lactating women. *Exp Physiol* 1993; 78:209–220.

Daly SEJ, Hartmann PE. Infant demand and milk supply. Part 1. Infant demand and milk production in lactating women. *J Hum Lact* 1995; 11:21–26.

Daly SEJ, Hartmann PE. Infant demand and milk supply. Part 2. The short-term control of milk synthesis in lactating women. *J Hum Lact* 1995; 11:27–37.

Daly SEJ, Kent JC, Owens RA, Hartmann PE. Frequency and degree of milk removal and the short-term control of human milk synthesis. *Exp Physiol* 1996; 81:861–875.

Kaplan CR, Schenken RS. Endocrinology of the breast. Chapter 3 in Mitchell GW, Bassett LW, eds. The female breast and its disorders. Baltimore: Williams & Wilkins, 1990: pp. 22–44.

Lawrence RA, Lawrence RM. Breastfeeding: a guide for the medical profession. Chapter 3. St. Louis: Mosby, Inc. 1999: pp. 59–94.

Neville MC. The physiological basis of milk secretion. Part 1. Basic physiology. *Ann NY Acad Sci* 1990; 586:1–11.

Peaker M, Wilde CJ. Milk secretion: autocrine control. *News in Physiol Sci* 1987; 2:124–126.

Peaker M, Wilde CJ. Feedback control of milk secretion from milk. *J Mammary Gland Biol Neoplasia* 1996; 1:307–315.

Prentice A, Addey CVP, Wilde CJ. Evidence for local feedback control of human milk secretion. *Biochem Soc Trans* 1989; 17:122.

Riordan J. Anatomy and physiology. Chapter 4 in Riordan J, Auerbach KG, eds. Breastfeeding and human lactation, 2nd ed. Sudbury, MA: Jones and Bartlett Publishers, 1998: 93–119.

Uvnas-Moberg K, Widstrom A-M, Werner S, et al. Oxytocin and prolactin levels in breast-feeding women. *Acta Obstet Gynecol Scand* 1990; 69:301–306.

Uvnas-Moberg K, Eriksson M. Breastfeeding: Physiological, endocrine and behavioral adaptations caused by oxytocin and local neurogenic activity in the nipple and mammary gland. *Acta Paediatr* 1996; 85:525–530.

Whitworth N. Lactation in humans. *Psychoneuroendocrinology* 1988; 13:171–188.

Wilde CJ, Addey CVP, Boddy LM, Peaker M. Autocrine regulation of milk secretion by a protein in milk. *Biochem J* 1995; 305:51–58.

Wilde CJ, Prentice A, Peaker M. Breastfeeding: matching supply with demand in human lactation. *Proc Nutr Soc* 1995; 54:401–406.

# Physiology of the Infant

*Amy Spangler, RN, MN, IBCLC*

## Objectives

- Define the terms *sucking* and *suckling*.
- Discuss the difference between nutritive and non-nutritive suckling.
- List factors that can influence or contribute to suckling abnormalities.
- Describe oral motor and feeding development.
- Discuss the complete suck cycle.
- Describe the parameters of newborn adaptation to extrauterine life.

## Introduction

Suckling is a complex and discrete, inborn behavioral response by which infants obtain their food. Infants are uniquely designed to remove milk from the breast over a range of variables for which they show remarkable skills for adaptation. Infants use two methods for removing milk from the breast: generation of negative or subatmospheric pressure within the oral cavity as the jaw drops and use of positive pressure when the jaw elevates in order to facilitate the peristaltic motion of the tongue along the teat. The human infant is born with advanced feeding skills but demonstrates immaturity in other areas that are affected by both breast milk and the act of breastfeeding. The lactation consultant benefits from a working knowledge of suckling mechanics and the needs and stores of the newborn.

### The Science of Suckling

I  All mammals are characterized by their ability to lactate.

II  Suckling patterns are unique to each mammal species.

III  The principal mechanism of milk removal that is common to all mammals is the contractile response of the mammary myoepithelium subsequent to the release of oxytocin from the posterior pituitary (Lawrence, 1999).

IV Effective provision of milk requires a storage system (alveoli), exit channels (ducts), a prehensile appendage (areola), an expulsion mechanism (the milk ejection reflex), and a retention mechanism (sympathetic activity).

V Central nervous system control of milk ejection ensures milk ejection only under circumstances that are conducive to effective milk removal.

## Sucking versus Suckling

I The terms suckling and sucking are often used interchangeably.

A. Historically, the baby sucked and the mother suckled.

B. Suckling: The removal of milk from the breast through compression of the milk sinuses by peristaltic movements of the tongue from front to back.

1. The rate is variable up to 1 suckle/second.

2. There is an inverse relationship between rate and flow; increased flow equals a decreased rate.

3. The suck volume ranges 0.14ml/suck to 0.10ml/suck from beginning to ending of the feed.

4. Suck volume in the first breast increases and stabilizes after approximately two minutes.

5. The suck volume in the second breast decreases from the peak until end of feed, supporting the theory that milk remains unconsumed in the breast (Pollitt, et al, 1981).

6. Control of milk intake comes under intrinsic control of the infant during the first month (Woolridge, et al, 1982).

7. As milk is depleted from the breast, several sucks per swallow can occur.

C. Sucking is known as the creation of a vacuum in the absence of liquid.

1. Short, rapid bursts of sucking can be observed at the beginning of a breastfeeding.

D. Nutritive suckling and non-nutritive sucking.

1. Nutritive suckling facilitates the transfer of milk from the breast.

2. Non-nutritive sucking facilitates little or no milk transfer.

a. Increases peristalsis

b. Enhances the secretion of digestive fluids

c. Decreases crying

d. An example of non-nutritive sucking is the spontaneous sucking that occurs during sleep when a finger or pacifier is placed in the infant's mouth

## Coordinated Suckling Sequence (Woolridge, 1986)

**I** A teat is formed as the nipple elongates two to three times its length and half its width (see Figure 4-1).

**II** Fat pads in the cheeks form a seal that facilitates the creation of a vacuum.

**III** Negative pressure in the mouth holds the nipple and breast in place.

**IV** Upward movement of the jaw traps milk in the milk sinuses and compresses the sinuses between the hard palate above and the tongue below.

**V** Positive pressure of the tongue against the teat and increased intraductal pressure result in milk ejection.

**Figure 4-1**    Complete suck cycle

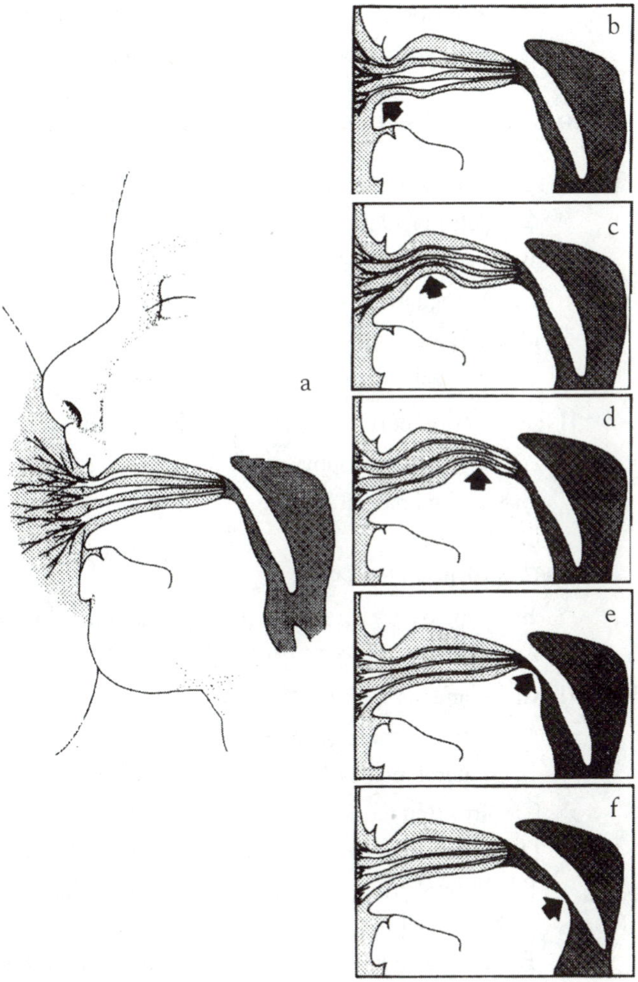

**VI** Anterior to posterior peristaltic movements of the tongue against the teat evacuate the milk.

Lateral margins of the tongue cup around the nipple, creating a central trough or groove that channels milk to the back of the throat.

The anterior portion of the tongue provides most of the compression while the posterior portion is initially elevated to form a seal and is then depressed in its central portion.

**VII** Accumulation of milk in the oral cavity triggers a swallow.

**VIII** A 1:1:1 suckle-swallow-breathe sequence occurs; two sucks to one breath.

    A. During an uncoordinated sequence, breathing is interrupted.

    B. Occlusion of nasal passages results in interruption of the sequence.

    C. Each cycle of jaw and tongue movement occurs every 1.5 seconds.

## Factors that Influence Suckling or Contribute to Suckling Abnormalities

  **I** Abnormalities of the face, mouth, or pharynx

    A. Cleft lip/palate

    B. Macroglossia—large tongue

    C. Micrognathia—small or receding jaw

    D. Ankyloglossia—tongue-tie

    E. High palatal arch

  **II** Dysfunction of the central or peripheral nervous or musculature system

    A. Muscular dystrophy

    B. Cerebral palsy

    C. Prematurity

    D. Down syndrome

    E. Central nervous system (CNS) infections (for example, toxoplasmosis, cytomegalovirus, or bacterial meningitis)

  **III** Miscellaneous

    A. Maternal analgesia/anesthesia

    B. Prenatal medications that cause sleepiness in the baby

    C. Birth trauma

    D. Premature separation of mother and infant

    E. Hospital policies/practices that limit the length and/or frequency of breastfeedings

    F. Early introduction of artificial nipples and/or breast milk substitutes

G. Crying prior to a feeding

H. An increased room temperature decreases sucking

## Oral Motor and Feeding Development

I Four weeks' gestation—tongue beginning to form

II Eight weeks' gestation—taste buds form; fetus exhibits an avoidance response to stimuli around his or her mouth

III Nine weeks' gestation—stimulation of the lips elicits mouth movement

IV 10 weeks' gestation—hard and soft palates form

V 12 weeks' gestation—the fetus swallows fluid

VI 14 weeks' gestation—the avoidance response to stimuli around the face and mouth increases; stimulation of the tongue elicits a tongue retraction

VII 18 weeks' gestation—the fetus approximates his or her hand and mouth

VIII 20 weeks' gestation—swallowing is present

IX 24 weeks' gestation—sucking is present; the fetus turns his or her head toward oral stimulation

X 26 weeks' gestation—the gag reflex is present; this reflex is strongest in the full-term infant and disappears by 6 months of age

XI 28 weeks' gestation—the phasic bite and transverse tongue reflexes are present; tongue protrusion is present at 40 weeks but disappears by 6 months of age

XII 32 weeks' gestation—the rooting reflex is present; peaks at 40 weeks and disappears by 3 months of age

XIII 32 weeks' gestation—the fetus is able to coordinate suck and swallow actions

XIV 36 weeks' gestation—the olfactory system begins to mylenate

XV 37 weeks' gestation—the fetus is able to coordinate suck, swallow, and breathe actions

XVI 40 weeks' gestation—the oral area is highly sensitive and active; tongue protrusion, gag reflex, flexion posture, and olfactory preferences exist

## Oral Anatomy

I 0 to 6 months of age

A. Oral cavity short from top to bottom

B. Hard palate short, wide, and slightly arched with corrugated surface (rugae)

C. Soft palate and epiglottis approximated

D. Tongue fills oral cavity

E. Frenulum anchors tongue to floor of mouth

F. Fat pads in cheeks

G. Jaw is recesssed with the lower gum line slightly behind the upper gum line

II  6 months to 1 year of age

A. Oral cavity elongates vertically and becomes more spacious

B. Soft palate and epiglottis are no longer in close proximity

C. Tongue elevates and acquires a front-back movement

D. Frenulum stretches to facilitate tongue movement

## Newborn Adaptation to Extrauterine Life (Biancuzzo, 1999)

I  Gastrointestinal function

A. Normal infants require <u>90–120 kcal</u>/kg/24 hours to support metabolic needs (Committee on Nutrition, 1993). Underfeeding can result in slow weight gain or failure to thrive.

B. When given the opportunity, normal newborns exhibit the following suckling behavior during the immediate postpartum period (Righard et al, 1990):

  ✱ 1. 15 minutes—infant roots and sucks

  2. 34 minutes—infant exhibits hand-to-mouth movements

  3. 55 minutes—infant exhibits spontaneous attachment and suckling

C. Gastrointestinal tract facilitates ingestion, digestion, motility, secretion of digestive juices, absorption, and elimination.

  1. Ingestion—Human milk provides 67 kcal/100 ml, or 20 kcal/oz. Normal infants who are fewer than 4 months of age require 90–120 kcal/kg/24 hr, or 2.5 oz/lb/day.

    a. Gastric capacity 5–15 cc; colostrum production 30–100ml/24 hr

    b. Daily milk yield increases rapidly during the first one to five days to 500ml and more slowly during the next three to five months to 750–800ml

  2. Digestion—Human milk is easily digested, limiting the need for mechanical or chemical means of digestion and the subsequent production of colicky symptoms.

    a. The mean gastric half emptying time is <u>47 minutes</u> (range 16–86 minutes) in breastfed babies.

    b. The mean gastric half emptying time is <u>65 minutes</u> (range 27–98 minutes) in formula-fed babies.

    c. Breastfeeding causes the release of several gastrointestinal hormones, such as gastrin and cholecystokinin (CCK), which take part in not only digestion, but also metabolism of ingested food; they promote the glucose-induced insulin release.

     d. Gastrin is released in response to protein intake.

     e. CCK is released mainly in response to fat intake.

     f. CCK also induces satiety as well as post-feeding sedation and sleep; it is also released in response to sucking; might partly explain why breastfed infants frequently fall asleep at the breast whether or not milk is actually flowing.

3. Motility—Colostrum acts as a laxative on the lower bowel, facilitating the excretion of bilirubin and reducing the risk of hyperbilirubinemia.

4. Secretion—Digestive enzymes are scarce in the newborn; therefore, the enzymes in human milk compensate (specifically, amylase and bile salts).

5. Absorption—Human milk enhances the absorption of needed nutrients (iron specifically).

6. Elimination—Breastfed infants have a distinct stool pattern:

| | |
|---|---|
| • Meconium | 0–24 hours |
| • Transitional stools | By 2–3 days after birth |
| • Milk stools | By 4–7 days after birth |

7. Stooling and voiding patterns—Normal newborns should have at least one wet diaper and one bowel movement on day one, two wet diapers and two bowel movements on day 2 (and so on), until day six and beyond, when diaper counts are typically eight or more wet diapers and three or more bowel movements each 24 hours.

     a. This pattern differs from the frequency of voiding, which is approximately 2–6 times per day for the first 48 hours and 5–25 times per day, subsequently.

     b. The quantity of urine is approximately 15–60ml/24 hours for the full-term newborn on days 1 and 2; 50–300ml on days 3–10; 11 days until the 2 months output is approximately 250–400 ml/24 hours; and from 3–12 months about 400–500ml/24 hours.

     c. Voiding size is approximately 19.3ml ± 4.1ml from birth to 30 days and 27.1ml ± 5.5ml from 31–60 days.

8. Liver function

     a. Glucuronyl transferase activity is 1 percent that of the adult at birth.

     b. The infant reaches the adult level at 6 to 12 weeks.

     c. The infant is dependent on glucose and oxygen to form uridine diphosphate (UDP-GT).

     d. Hypoglycemia can impair this process.

     e. Predisposes the infant to elevated bilirubin levels.

D. Microbial environment of the neonatal gut.

   1. The gastrointestinal (GI) tract of a normal fetus is sterile.

2. The neonatal GI tract undergoes rapid growth and maturational change following birth; infants have a functionally immature and immunonaive gut at birth.

3. Tight junctions of the GI mucosa take many weeks to mature and close the gut to whole proteins and pathogens.

✱ 4. Secretory IgA from colostrum and breast milk coats the gut, passively providing immunity during the time of reduced neonatal gut immune function.

5. During and after the birth process, microbes from the mother and the surrounding environment colonize the GI tract of the infant; babies born by cesarean section show altered development of gut flora because the first microbes the baby is exposed to are from equipment, air, and other infants (with the medical and nursing staff serving as vectors for transfer).

6. Gut flora of breastfed babies is characterized by bifidobacteria and reduced numbers of pathogenic bacteria; once dietary supplementation begins, the bacterial profile of the breastfed infant resembles that of formula-fed babies.

7. Relatively small amounts of formula supplementation of a breastfed baby will result in shifts from a breastfed to a formula-fed microbial environment; the flora becomes indistinguishable from adult flora within 24 hours; when breast milk is again given exclusively, it can take two to four weeks for the intestinal environment to return again to a state favoring gram-positive bacteria (thus the risk in giving "just one bottle").

8. Babies born by cesarean section, preterm infants, and full-term infants requiring intensive care are at an increased risk of acquiring hospital-derived microbes that can also carry antibiotic resistance.

9. Infants requiring intensive care acquire intestinal organisms slowly, and the establishment of bifidobacteria is retarded; a delayed bacterial colonization of the gut with a limited number of bacterial species tends to be virulent.

10. Fresh breast milk minimizes the ecological disturbance of the gut from these conditions.

E. Cardiopulmonary function.

1. A newborn must make the transition from fetal to postnatal circulation with immediate closure of the foramen ovale, closure within three to four days of the ductus arteriosus, and closure later of the ductus venosus.

2. The newborn must exhibit the ability to coordinate suckling, swallowing, and breathing.

F. Thermoregulation.

1. "Brown fat" is deposited during the 28th week of gestation and makes up 2 to 6 percent of the total body weight of the infant; it is highly vascular and designed for heat production.

2. The newborn has an immature thermoregulatory system and is therefore at risk for hypothermia (especially premature infants); <u>cold stress can lead</u> to metabolic acidosis, a decrease in arterial blood oxygen level, and hypoglycemia.

3. Infants who are in skin-to-skin contact with the mother maintain their body temperature better than when separated and placed in a bassinet (cot).

4. Axillary temperature of the newborn ranges from 36.5°C to 37°C (97.6°F–98.6°F); a neutral thermal environment for infants is 32°C–34°C (89.6°F–93.2°F).

G. Fluid balance.

1. Normal infants require about 80–100ml of water per kilogram of body weight per 24 hours. Human milk is 87 percent water and satisfies all of the fluid needs of an exclusively breastfed infant.

2. Normal infants are born with extra body fluid and might experience fluid loss after birth and subsequent weight loss; however, weight loss should be carefully monitored.

3. Babies of mothers who have had epidural labor medication might lose more weight in the first days than babies from mothers who have not had an epidural (8 oz. or 226g versus 5 oz. or 142g in the first 24 hours).

H. Sleep-wakefulness states include deep sleep, light sleep, drowsiness, quiet alert, active alert, and crying.

1. Birth–2 hours—Quiet alert (the best time to initiate breastfeeding).

2. 2–20 hours—Light and deep sleep (the infant will not breastfeed).

3. After 20 hours—Continuum of states.

4. Infants who are in active alert or crying states will need to be calmed before they can breastfeed effectively.

5. Optimize feeding opportunities by alerting to early feeding cues, including rooting, sucking sounds, rapid eye movements, or hand-to-mouth movements.

6. Infants whose mothers have received labor medications, both regional and IV, might demonstrate deficiencies in both state and motor control.

7. The sleep organization of breastfed infants is different than formula-fed babies; breastfed infants show a longer sleep latency, lower body temperature and heart rate, increased non-REM sleep, more night wakenings, and an accelerated central nervous system development.

I. Sensory needs.

1. Vision—limited but can see objects up to about 8 inches away

2. Hearing—similar to that of an adult; can identify familiar sounds

3. Smell—more developed than that of an adult; guides the newborn to the breast

4. Taste—fully developed; can distinguish sweet, sour, and bitter tastes

5. Touch—perceives touch in all parts of the body (especially the perioral area)

# References

Ardran GM, Kemp PH, Lind J. A cineradiographic study of bottle feeding. *Br J Radiology* 1958; 31:11–22.

Ardran GM, Kemp PH, Ling J. A cineradiographic study of breastfeeding. *Br J Radiology* 1958; 31:156–162.

Biancuzzo M. Breastfeeding the newborn clinical strategies for nurses. St. Louis: C.V. Mosby Company, 1999.

Bowen-Jones A, Thompson C, Drewett RF. Milk flow and sucking rates during breastfeeding. *Dev Med Child Neurol* 1982; 24:626–633.

Butte NF, Jensen CL, Moon JK, et al. Sleep organization and energy expenditure of breastfed and formula-fed infants. *Pediatr Res* 1992; 32:514–519.

Chetwynd AG, Diggle PJ, Drewett RF, Young B. A mixture model for sucking patterns of breastfed infants. *Statistics in Medicine* 1998; 17:395–405.

Christensson K, Siles C, Moreno L, et al. Temperature, metabolic adaptation and crying in healthy full-term newborns cared for skin-to-skin or in a cot. *Acta Paediatr* 1992; 81:488–493.

Cloherty JP, Stark AR, eds. Manual of neonatal care. Boston, MA: Little Brown and Company, 1991.

Committee on Nutrition, American Academy of Pediatrics. Pediatric nutrition handbook. Elk Grove Village, IL: American Academy of Pediatrics, 1993.

Dai D, Walker WA. Protective nutrients and bacterial colonization in the immature human gut. *Adv Pediatr* 1999; 46:353–382.

Drewett R, Woolridge M. Sucking patterns of human babies on the breast. *Early Hum Dev* 1979; 3:315–320.

Eregie CO. Observations on urinary frequency in exclusively breastfed neonates. *E Afr Med J* 1998; 75:576–578.

Goellner MH, Ziegler EE, Fomon SJ. Urination during the first three years of life. *Nephron* 1981; 28:174–178.

Gronlund MM, Lehtonen OP, Eerola E, Kero P. Fecal microflora in healthy infants born by different methods of delivery: permanent changes in intestinal flora after cesarean delivery. *J Pediatr Gastroenterol Nutr* 1999; 28:19–25.

Host A, Husby S, Osterballe O. A prospective study of cow's milk allergy in exclusively breastfed infants. *Acta Paediatr Scan* 1988; 77:663–670.

Kron RE, Litt M. Fluid mechanics of nutritive sucking behaviour: the suckling infant's oral apparatus analysed as a hydraulic pump. *Med & Biol Engng* 1971; 9:45–60.

Lawrence RA. Breastfeeding: A guide for the medical profession, 5th ed. St. Louis: C.V. Mosby Company, 1999.

Mackie R, Sghir A, Gaskins HR. Developmental microbial ecology of the neotanal gastrointestinal tract. *Am J Clin Nutr* 1999; 69(Suppl):1035S–1045S.

Merry H, Montgomery A. Do breastfed babies whose mothers have had labor epidurals lose more weight in the first 24 hours of life? *ABM News and Views* 2000; 6(3):21.

Pollitt E, et al. Changes in nutritive sucking during a feed in two-day and thirty-day-old infants. *Early Human Dev* 1981; 5:201.

Prieto CR, Cardenas H, Salvatierra AM, et al. Sucking pressure and its relationship to milk transfer during breastfeeding in humans. *J Reproduction and Fertility* 1996; 108:69–74.

Righard L, et al. Effect of delivery room routine on success of first breastfeed. *Lancet* 1990; 336:1105.

Rubaltelli FF, Biadaioli R, Pecile P, Nicoletti P. Intestinal flora in breast- and bottle-fed infants. *J Perinat Med* 1998; 26:186–191.

Saarinen KM, Juntunen-Backman K, Jarvenpaa AL, et al. Supplementary feeding in maternity hospitals and the risk of cow's milk allergy: A prospective study of 6209 infants. *J Allergy Clin Immunol* 1999; 104:457–461.

Scammon RE, Doyle LO. Observations on the capacity of the stomach in the first ten days of life. *Am J Dis Child* 1920; 20:516–538.

Smith WL, Erenberg A, Nowak A, Franken EA. Physiology of sucking in the normal term infant using real-time US. *Radiology* 1985; 156:379–381.

Uvnas-Moberg K, Widstrom AM, Matchini G, Winberg J. Release of GI hormones in mother and infant by sensory stimulation. *Acta Paediatr Scand* 1987; 76:851–860.

Van den Driessche M, Peeters K, Marien P, et al. Gastric emptying in formula-fed and breastfed infants measured with the 13-C-Octanoic acid breath test. *J Pediatr Gastroenterol Nutr* 1999; 29:46–51.

Voloschin LM, Althabe O, Olive H, Diena V, Repezza B. A new tool for measuring the suckling stimulus during breastfeeding in humans: the orokinetogram and the Fourier series. *J Reproduction and Fertility* 1998; 114:219–224.

Weber F, Woolridge M, Baum J. An ultrasonographic study of the organization of sucking and swallowing by newborn infants. *Dev Med Child Neurol* 1986; 28:19–24.

Woolridge MW, et al. The continuous measurement of milk intake at a feed in breast-fed babies. *Early Human Dev* 1982; 6:365.

Woolridge MW. The "anatomy" of infant sucking. *Midwifery* 1986; 2:164–171.

Woolridge M, Drewett R. Sucking rates of human babies on the breast: A study using direct observation and intraoral pressure measurements. *J Repro Infant Psychology* 1986; 4:69–75.

Zetterstrom R, Bennet R, Nord KE. Early infant feeding and micro-ecology of the gut. *Acta Paediatr Jpn* 1994; 36:562–571.

# The Biochemistry of Human Milk

*Linda J. Smith, BSE, FACCE, IBCLC*

## Objectives

- Discuss the differences between colostrum, transitional, and mature milk.
- Describe human milk components and their functions.
- Discuss the influence of the mother's diet on breast milk composition.

## Introduction

Human milk is a unique food designed specifically for the needs of a human infant. Nutritional and anti-infective components are woven into a tapestry of growth-promoting elements, enzymes to aid in the digestion and absorption of nutrients, and a fatty acid profile that optimizes brain growth and development. The ingredients of breast milk are not interchangeable with manufactured milks or nutrients from other species. The protein and fat content of human milk reflects the identity of a species that requires close contact and frequent feedings. Human milk is not a means of supplying added benefits to an infant's diet; rather, it is the reference food and nature's plan for nourishing young humans. The lactation consultant will benefit from a knowledge of human milk composition to educate parents in the importance of supplying breast milk for their baby.

   I Human milk is species-specific.

      A. "The unique feature of human milk is that virtually every component examined plays some extranutritional role. The elegance of the system is remarkable—the more so the more we learn about it."—Judy Hopkinson, PhD

         1. Mother's milk matches much more than 50 percent of the baby's genetic material. Milk from other species and plant-based fluids are genetically different from the infant.

         2. The unique balance of nutrients and other components most closely matches milks of species that require a high maternal investment and frequent feedings.

3. Human milk composition is not static or uniform like artificial baby milks.

   a. Colostrum one to five days post birth evolves to:

   b. Transitional milk 6–13 days post birth

   c. Mature milk 14 days and beyond

4. High bioavailability

   a. Little residue

   b. Low solute load

5. Human milk has 200-plus identified constituents, and many more are unexamined.

6. Contains the aromas and flavors of the mother's diet, which the baby smelled and tasted in utero.

7. Milk from other animals contains deficiencies and excesses of one or more components, only some of which can be modified for infant consumption.

B. Colostrum: the "first milk" secreted by the mammary gland from 12–16 weeks of pregnancy into the early postpartum days; undergoes a gradual change in composition toward "mature" milk.

   1. High density; thick, almost gel-like; generally yellow-colored fluid

      a. Low volume: range 10–100ml/day, average 30ml

      b. Ideal for the infant's tiny stomach, with 2–20ml per feeding during the first three days

      c. Immature kidneys cannot tolerate a large fluid volume.

      d. The baby's physiologic stomach capacity is 4–7ml at birth

      e. 67kcal/dl (18.76kcal/oz)

      f. Yellow color due to the presence of beta-carotene

      g. 2 percent fat content in colostrum

   2. Its primary function is protective—sealing the gut lining to prevent the adherence of pathogens.

      a. Secretory Immunoglobulin A (sIgA) is especially high.

      b. White cells, especially polymorphonucleocytes (90 percent of cells in colostrum).

      c. Other immune factors: lactoferrin, lysozyme; epidermal growth factor, interleukin 10, and many others.

      d. Its laxative effect clears meconium with its reservoir of bilirubin.

      e. Growth factors stimulate the infant's system.

      f. Contains at least two separate antioxidants.

      g. Contributes to the establishment of the bifidus flora (non-pathogenic) in the digestive tract.

   3. Different in composition from mature milk
      a. Lower in lactose, fat, and water-soluble vitamins
      b. Higher in Vitamin A, Vitamin E, and carotenoids
      c. Higher in protein, sodium, zinc, chloride, and potassium
      d. Compositional changes begin around 30–40 hours postbirth with an increase in lactose and a resultant increase in fluid volume

C. Water
   1. Water makes up the majority (87.5 percent) of human milk.
   2. All other components are dissolved, dispersed, or suspended in water.
   3. Human milk provides all the water a baby needs, even in hot and arid climates.

D. Proteins and nonprotein nitrogen compounds in mature milk
   1. Whey to casein ratio
      a. Earlier studies suggested 80:20.
      b. New research suggests a variation during the course of lactation, from 90:10 in early lactation; 60:40 in mature milk; and 50:50 in late lactation (Kunz 1992).
      c. Whey predominates in human milk. Casein predominates in cow (bovine) milk.
   2. Total protein in mature milk is 0.8–1.0 percent (the lowest of all mammals).
   3. 19 amino acids essential to human development
      a. Taurine—develops the brain and retina, membrane stabilization, and inhibitory neurotransmitter; not found in bovine milk
      b. Tyrosine
      c. Phenylalanine—much higher levels in cow's milk
   4. Casein proteins
      a. Phosphoproteins—binds calcium and results in a cloudy/opaque/white color
      b. Forms soft, flocculent curds that are easily digested
   5. Whey proteins—available for digestion and perform specific functions
      a. Alpha-lactalbumin
         i. No counterpart in bovine milk and plant-based (soy) "milks"
         ii. Bovine milk is high in beta-lactoglobulin, which is not found in human milk
         iii. Regulates milk synthesis
         iv. Mucins bind pathogens; kill cancer cells in vitro

b. Lactoferrin

   i. Iron transport and absorption

   ii. Competes with bacteria to bind iron

   iii. Antibacterial

   iv. Essential growth factor for B- and T-cell lymphocytes

   v. Promotes the growth of lactobacilli

   vi. Produced in mammary epithelial cells, milk ducts, and other regions of the body; speculated to have local as well as systemic protective properties

c. sIgA

   i. Other immunoglobulins: IgG, IgM, and IgE

   ii. sIgA is the most important immunoglobulin

     (1) Coats mucosal surfaces to prevent adherance and penetration by pathogens

     (2) Aids in apoptosis (programmed cell death)

d. Lysozyme

   i. Serum albumin

e. Enzymes (more than 40 identified to date)

   i. Aid in the digestion of the nutrients in milk

   ii. Compensatory digestive enzymes

   iii. Stimulate neonatal development

     (1) No active enzymes in processed cow milk or infant formulas

   iv. Lipase—digests fats; breaks down fatty acid chains

   v. Bile salt-stimulated lipase—anti-protozoan; acts on *Giardia* and other organisms that cause diarrhea

   vi. Lysozyme—attacks cell walls of pathogens

   vii. Amylase—digests polysaccharides/starch

   viii. Alkaline phosphatase

     (1) Peroxidases—act like hydrogen peroxide; oxidize bacteria

     (2) Xanthine oxidase

     (3) Sulfhydryl oxidase

     (4) Glutathione peroxidase

f. Hormones and hormone-like substances

   i. Prolactin (different from mother's serum prolactin)

   ii. Prostaglandins—anti-inflammatory properties

   iii. Oxytocin

   iv. Adrenal and ovarian steroids

        v. Relaxin

       vi. Insulin

     vii. Thyroid hormones: TRH, TSH, and Thyroxine (T4)

  g. Growth factors

     i. Epidermal growth factors—aid gut and other tissue maturity

     ii. Nerve growth factor

    iii. Insulin-like growth factor

6. Nonprotein nitrogen compounds

  a. Urea

  b. Creatine

  c. Creatinine

  d. Uric acid

  e. Glucosamine

  f. Alpha-amino nitrogen

  g. Nucleic acids

  h. Nucleotides

  i. Polyamines

E. Carbohydrates

1. Principal carbohydrate in human milk is lactose; disaccharide (galactose plus glucose) is found only in milk.

  a. Supplies 40 percent of the baby's energy needs.

  b. Synthesis begins at lactogenesis II, approximately 30–40 hours postbirth.

     i. The rise in lactose secreted in the cell draws water into secretion by osmosis.

     ii. Directly influences milk volume.

    iii. Colostrum is 4 percent lactose on day one; rapidly increases while fluid is still considered colostrum.

  c. Of all mammals, human milk is highest in lactose.

     i. Largest brain of all animals at birth.

     ii. 7.2g/100ml—sweetest of all milks.

    iii. Component of galactolipids needed for *central nervous system* (CNS) development

  d. Lactose is the primary carbohydrate in milk and the least variable (most consistent).

     i. Humans produce lactase (the enzyme to digest the lactose) until age 2 1/2 to 7 years or older.

        ii. Lactase is a brush border intestinal enzyme that is present by 24 weeks of fetal life.

       iii. Its concentration at term is two to four times that seen at 2–11 months of age.

       iv. Genetically determined; decreases with age.

       v. Lactose assists in the absorption of calcium and iron.

       vi. Primary lactose intolerance is extremely rare.

2. Oligosaccharides

  a. Stimulate lactobacillus bifidus

  b. Block pathogens from attaching to gut

  c. Protect against enterotoxins in the gut; bind to bacteria

3. Bifidus factor—a combination of several different oligosaccharides

  a. With lactose, promotes the growth of lactobacillus bifidus in the infant's gut

  b. Suppresses pathogens

  c. Thought to contribute to the unique aroma of exclusively breastmilk stools

4. Other carbohydrates

  a. Glycopeptides

  a. Fructose

  c. Galactose

F. Fats (lipids)

1. Provide up to 50 percent of the calories in milk.

2. The fat content of mature milk ranges from 3.5 percent to 4.5 percent.

3. The ratio of saturated to unsaturated fat is relatively stable at 42 percent saturated, 57 percent unsaturated.

4. Smoking decreases the fat content of milk.

5. Lipases (enzymes) are released simultaneously.

  a. Break down long-chain fatty acids; aid in digestion.

  b. Free fatty acids kill bacteria (including *Giardia*).

6. 98 percent of lipids are encased in globules; the membrane coating prevents clumping.

7. Fats in milk vary and are difficult to measure.

  a. In colostrum, fat is in higher proportion (concentration) than in mature milk.

  b. In mature milk, fat is in higher total volume but lower in concentration than in colostrum.

  c. Total fat is only somewhat related to the mother's diet; the profile of fatty acid chain-length varies with diet (refer to the following information).

    d. Fat levels increase within each feed (foremilk to hindmilk).

    e. Fat levels increase as the breast "empties"; 70 percent of fat variation is related to relative "fullness" or emptiness of the breast (Hartmann).

    f. The concentration of fat is inversely related to milk volume (Hachey, Butte, and Dewey).

8. Triglycerides predominate.

    a. Lipases break down triglycerides into free fatty acids.

9. Cholesterol in human milk.

    a. Unique metabolic effects.

    b. Essential part of all membranes.

    c. Cholesterol is an important constituent of brain tissue and is necessary for the laying down of the myelin sheath, which is involved in nerve conduction in the brain, along with DHA (docosohexaenoic acid) and AA (arachidonic acid).

    d. Breastfed babies have higher cholesterol levels than formula-fed infants.

    e. There is little to no cholesterol in infant formula.

10. Fatty acids

    a. Long-chain polyunsaturated fatty acids specific to infant needs.

        i. Central role in cognitive development, vision, and nerve myelinization.

        ii. Might be conditionally essential to newborns (Koletzko).

        iii. DHA and AA are especially important to brain maturation.

    b. Can be synthesized from precursors (linolenic and linoleic acids).

    c. Preformed dietary DHA is better synthesized into nervous tissue than that synthesized from linolenic acid.

11. Phospholipids

12. Sterols—a component of lipid membranes

13. Fat-soluble vitamins

    a. Vitamin A and carotene.

    b. Vitamin D is a group of related fat-soluble compounds with antirachitic (rickets) activity.

    c. Also found in milk in an aqueous form.

        i. Exclusive breastfeeding results in normal infant bone mineral content when the maternal vitamin D status is adequate and the infant is regularly exposed to sunlight; breastfed infants require about 30 minutes of sunlight exposure per week if wearing only a diaper or two hours per week if fully clothed without a hat; darkly pigmented infants require a greater exposure to sunlight; only if the infant or mother is not regularly exposed to sunlight or if the mother's intake of vitamin D is low would supplements for the infant be indicated.

d. Vitamin E—functions as an antioxidant.

e. Vitamin K—highest in colostrum; later manufactured in infant gut; localized in the milk fat globule with hindmilk containing a two-fold higher vitamin K concentration than milk from a full pumping.

G. Water-soluble vitamins; show variations due to stage of lactation, maternal intake, and if delivery takes place before term; the breast does not synthesize these water-soluble vitamins, so their origin is maternal plasma derived from the maternal diet.

1. Thiamin

2. Riboflavin

3. Niacin

4. Panthothenic acid

5. Biotin

6. Folate

7. Vitamin B6

8. Vitamin B12—needed by the baby's developing nervous system; vitamin B occurs exclusively in animal tissue, is bound to protein, and is minimal to absent in plant protein; a vegetarian mother who consumes no animal products could have milk deficient in vitamin B12 and need an acceptable source of intake

9. Vitamin C (higher in milk than in maternal plasma)

10. Inositol

11. Choline

H. Cells

1. Macrophages

a. Contain IgA

b. 90 percent of cells in mature milk

c. Phagocytosis

d. Make/facilitate lactoferrin, complement

2. Leukocytes

3. Lymphocytes—10 percent of cells; T-cells and B-cells; humoral immunity

4. Epithelial cells

5. Neutrophil granulocytes

6. Chemical mediators released by cells and injured/inflamed tissue cause more white cells to move into the area in order to facilitate healing.

I. Minerals

1. Macronutrient elements; numerous factors affect the levels of minerals in human milk; during pregnancy, involution, and mastitis, the junctions between the alveolar cells are open, enabling sodium and chloride to enter the milk space drawing water with them; under these conditions, milk has much higher concentrations of sodium and potassium and decreased concentrations of lactose and potassium; the presence of high sodium concentrations in human milk can be diagnostic of either mastitis or low milk volume secretion

   a. Calcium
   b. Phosphate
   c. Magnesium
   d. Potassium
   e. Sodium
   f. Chloride
   g. Sulfate
   h. Citrate

2. Trace elements

   a. Copper
   b. Chromium
   c. Cobalt
   d. Iron—full-term infants are born with large physiologic stores of iron in the liver and hemoglobin, which—along with the iron in breast milk—is sufficient to meet the requirements for iron for about the first six months if babies are exclusively breastfed; approximately 50 percent of iron is absorbed from breast milk compared with 7 percent from fortified infant formulas and 4 percent from fortified infant cereals; iron concentrations in breast milk are not influenced by the maternal iron status or intake; lactose, which promotes iron absorption, is higher in breast milk especially compared to some commercial formulas (some of which contain no lactose at all)
   e. Iodine
   f. Fluoride
   g. Zinc
   h. Manganese
   i. Selenium

J. Constituents have more than nutritive functions
1. Alpha-lactalbumin
    a. Nutrient synthesis
    b. Carries metals
    c. Prevents infection
2. Lactoferrin
    a. Transports iron
    b. Prevents infection
    c. Prevents inflammation, including necrotizing enterocolitis (NEC)
    d. Promotes tissue growth and the growth of lactobacilli in the gut
3. sIgA: most important immunoglobulin
    a. The infant receives 0.5g/day in the first month
    b. Prevents inflammation
    c. Active against enveloped viruses, rotaviruses, polioviruses, RSV, enteric and respiratory bacteria, and intestinal parasites
    d. Stimulates infant production of sIgA
    e. General and specific protection against pathogens
4. Epidermal growth factor
    a. Prevents inflammation
    b. Promotes growth
    c. Catalyzing reactions
5. Lipids: break down products (free fatty acids) active against enveloped viruses and intestinal parasites
6. Oligosaccharides: Active against enteric and respiratory bacteria
7. Beta-carotene: an antioxidant and nutrient
8. Anti-inflammatory and pharmacologically active components
    a. Prostaglandins
    b. Ovarian steroids
    c. Gonadotropins
    d. Somatostatin
    e. Prolactin
    f. Insulin
K. Antiinfectious agents: found in many components of milk
1. Lipids
2. Proteins

  a. Lactoferrin, sIgA, lysozymes

  b. Enzymes—bile salt-stimulated lipase active against protozoa

3. Nonspecific factors

  a. Complement

  b. Interferon

  c. Bifidus factor

  d. Antiviral factors

4. Cells

  a. T- and B-lymphocytes

  b. Macrophages

  c. Neutrophils

L. Variations in human milk composition

1. Changes within a feed (for example, fat increases during each feed)

2. Differences between breasts; changes over the 24-hour day

  a. Fat levels increase as the breast "empties."

  b. They still maintain the foremilk-to-hindmilk differential.

3. Changes over the short and long term of a lactation cycle (days to months to years)

  a. Zinc decreases slightly.

  b. The whey-to-casein ratio changes—casein increases proportionally to whey.

  c. Calcium decreases.

  d. DHA levels change.

4. Preterm milk

  a. Higher protein, sodium, and chloride than mature milk

  b. Lower lactose level than mature milk

  c. Fatty acids parallel intrauterine levels and profiles

5. Colored milk

  a. Might be caused by something in the maternal diet or medication

  b. No known harmful effect on the infant

  c. If bright red, investigate the cause while continuing to breastfeed/provide milk to the baby

6. Odor and flavor influenced by mother's diet

M. Influence of mother's diet

| Milk Component | Affected by Mother's Diet? |
|---|---|
| Total milk volume | No, except possibly in maternal starvation conditions |
| Carbohydrates | No |
| Proteins | No |
| Lipids | Fatty acid profile only (total fats unaffected) |
| Cellular components | No |
| Immune factors | No |
| Fat-soluble vitamins | Slight variance related to fat levels in milk |
| Water-soluble vitamins | Yes |
| Minerals | No: macronutrient elements; iron, chromium, and cobalt. Slight/possible: iodine, fluoride, zinc, manganese, selenium, and lead |

N. Influence of heat treatments on milk components

| Component | Effect of Pasteurization (in Degrees Celsius) | Effect of Boiling | Effect of Freezing |
|---|---|---|---|
| Cellular components | Destroyed at 62.5°C/30 min. | | Destroyed |
| Lipids | | Stable | Increased breakdown into free fatty acids after freezing and thawing |
| Minerals | Stable | | Stable |
| Lactoferrin | 2/3 loss at 62.5°C/30 min. | | |
| Secretory IgA | Stable at 56°C/30 min. | Destroyed | |
| Lysozyme | Stable at 62.5°C/30 min. | Mostly destroyed/ 15–30 min. | |
| Other immunoglobulins | Stable at 56°C/30 min. | | |
| Bifidus factor | | Stable | |
| Gangliosides | | Stable | |

O. Recommendations for milk storage for healthy term infants (Hamosh, 1996)—assumes that milk is collected in a clean environment with sanitary collection procedures

| | |
|---|---|
| Air temperature 100°F/38°C | Not recommended |
| Air temperature 77°F/25°C | Up to four hours |
| Air temperature 59°F/15°C | 24 hours in Styrofoam chest with blue ice "freezer pack" |
| Refrigerator | 3–5 days |
| Freezer | Two weeks to 12 months or more, depending on the type of freezer (self-defrosting freezers warm the milk, thereby shortening the storage time) |
| Preferred containers | Glass with secure tops/lids |
| Acceptable containers | Rigid plastic containers, clear or cloudy, with secure tops |

# References

Akre J, ed. Infant feeding, the physiological basis. *Bull WHO*, Supplement to Vol. 67 (1989). Geneva: World Health Organization, 1991.

Allen JC, Keller RP, Archer P, Neville MC. Studies in human lactation: milk composition and daily secretion rates of macronutrients in the first year of lactation. *Am J Clin Nutr* 1991; 54:69–80.

Black R. Lactation specialist self-study modules #1–4. Sudbury, MA: Jones and Bartlett Publishers, 1998.

Guidelines for the establishment and operation of a donor human milk bank. Sandwich, MA: Human Milk Banking Association of North America, 1994.

Hamosh M, Ellis LA, Pollock DR, Henderson TR, Hamosh P. Breastfeeding and the working mother: effect of time and temperature of short-term storage on proteolysis, lipolysis, and bacteria growth in milk. *Pediatrics* 1996;97(4):492–498.

Institute of Medicine (Subcommittee on Nutrition during Lactation, Food and Nutrition Board). Nutrition during lactation. Washington, D.C.: National Academy of Sciences, 1991.

Jensen R. Handbook of milk composition. London: Academic Press, 1995.

Jocson MA, Mason EO, Schanler RJ. The effects of nutrient fortification and varying storage conditions on host defense properties of human milk. *Pediatrics* 1997; 100:240–243.

Kleinman RE, ed. Pediatric nutrition handbook, 4th ed. Elk Grove Village, IL: American Academy of Pediatrics, 1998.

Kunz C, Lonnerdal B. Re-evaluation of the whey protein/casein ratio of human milk. *Acta Paediatr* 1992 Feb; 81(2):107–112.

Lawrence RA. Breastfeeding, a guide for the medical profession, 4th ed. St. Louis, MO: Mosby, 1994.

Lawrence R. A review of the medical benefits and contraindications to breastfeeding in the United States (Maternal and Child Health Technical Information Bulletin). Arlington, VA: National Center for Education in Maternal and Child Health, October 1997.

Lonnerdal B, Forsum E. Casein content of human milk. *Am J Clin Nutr* 1985 Jan; 41(1):113–120.

Neville MC, Neifert M. Lactation: Physiology, nutrition and breastfeeding. New York, NY: Plenum Press, 1983.

Neville MC, Allen JC, Archer PC, et al. Studies in human lactation: milk volume and nutrient composition during weaning and lactogenesis. *Am J Clin Nutr* 1991; 54:81–92.

Raiha NC. Nutritional proteins in milk and the protein requirement of normal infants. *Pediatrics* 1985; 1:136–141.

Recommendations for collection, storage and handling of mother's milk for her own infant in the hospital setting. Sandwich, MA: Human Milk Banking Association of North America, 1993.

Riordan J, Auerbach K. Breastfeeding and human lactation, 2nd ed. Sudbury, MA: Jones and Bartlett Publishers, 1998.

Sanchez-Hildago VM, Flores-Huerta S, Matute G, et al. Whey protein/casein ratio and nonprotein nitrogen in preterm human milk during the first 10 days postpartum. *J Pediatr Gastroenterol Nutr* 1998 Jan; 26(1):64–69.

The womanly art of breastfeeding, 6th ed. Schaumburg, IL: La Leche League International, 1997.

Worthington-Roberts B, Williams SR. Nutrition in pregnancy and lactation, 5th ed. St. Louis, MO: Mosby, 1993.

# Nutrition for Lactating Women

*Genevieve Becker, IBCLC, MSc, Reg Nutr, PGCertEd*

## Objectives

- Discuss the nutritional recommendations for pregnant women and breastfeeding women.
- Explain weight patterns during pregnancy and lactation.
- Describe the effects of the maternal diet on breast milk composition.
- Suggest suitable food choices, taking into account cultural practices and individual preferences.
- Evaluate the need for referral to a nutrition specialist or to another health care specialist.

## Introduction

A woman's nutrition can affect her health and the health of her child. Women might be particularly motivated to make nutritional changes during pregnancy and breastfeeding. Misconceptions abound regarding the amounts and types of foods to consume or avoid, however. The woman sitting in front of the *lactation consultant* (LC) brings with her a nutritional history/status, eating patterns, and food beliefs. The LC needs to provide information and suggestions that are compatible with the woman's lifestyle and beliefs and that are within the woman's ability. This chapter covers the basic information that the LC might need when assisting the mother. The goals are to provide appropriate nutrition information and recommendations, to identify women at nutritional risk, and to refer if necessary.

### Assessment and Referral

The following risk factors that occur pre-conception, during pregnancy, or while breastfeeding require referral for detailed assessment and advice from a nutritionist/dietitian:

- A *Body Mass Index* (BMI) of less than 19.8 (very underweight); refer to Figure 6-1[1]
- A BMI of greater than 26 (overweight or obese)

[1] BMI is calculated by weight (kg)/height (m). Charts with the calculations already done are widely available.

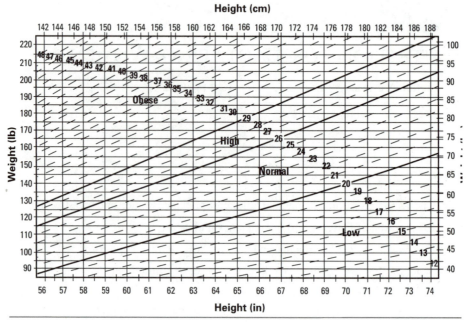

**Figure 6-1**   Chart for estimating BMI category and BMI

- Teenagers who are within less than four years of menarche (the adolescent diet is typically low in iron and vitamin A)
- Conditions such as *insulin-dependent diabetes mellitus* (IDDM), gastrointestinal malabsorption conditions, metabolic disease such as phenylketonuria (PKU), or eating disorders
  - Insulin requirements in a diabetic mother will change following delivery and during lactation.
  - IDDM can delay lactogenesis for up to two to three days.
  - Diabetic mothers might need an increase in calories, carbohydrates, and protein.
  - If the blood sugar is elevated high enough, acetone is released and can be transmitted to the baby through the breast milk.
  - Several days of acetone exposure can enlarge the baby's liver.
  - Mother's will increase their carbohydrate intake and/or their insulin dosage.
  - Blood sugar that is too low could lead to diabetic shock, releasing epinephrine into the mother's system and potentially inhibiting the let-down reflex and milk production.
- Self-diagnosed allergy or other special diets that exclude a major food group
- Higher-order multiples

- Excessive recent weight gain or weight loss
- Closely spaced pregnancies (including miscarriages)
- Poor nutrition might be a marker for other problems
- Poverty, cultural beliefs, physical disability, limited intellectual ability, or psychological problems might restrict food choices
- Refer to the appropriate services as needed

# General Nutritional Recommendations

## Pre-Conception

The LC might see a few women before their first pregnancy; however, the time after the birth of one child might be the pre-conception period before the next pregnancy.

Recommendations to the woman at this time include the following:

- Establish a healthy eating pattern that includes a variety of foods based on the food pyramid (refer to Figure 6-2).
- Aim for the recommended weight range.
- Either severe underweight or overweight conditions can affect the ability to conceive.
- Low pre-pregnancy maternal weight is linked with low infant birth weight.
- Reduce weight in advance of conception to lessen the risk of nutritional inadequacy.

**Figure 6-2**  The food guide pyramid

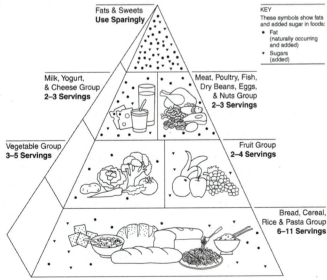

- Assure that height and weight are accurately recorded so that measurements during pregnancy are correct.

- Assure that iron levels in the blood are assessed and corrected if needed by dietary advice and/or supplementation.

- Haemoglobin below 12.0g/dl or serum ferritin below 20μg/l are indications of iron deficiency in the non-pregnant woman.

- Assure that a folic acid supplement to reduce the risk of neural tube defects has been recommended.

- Remind mothers to reduce the risks of food-borne illnesses, such as *Listeria* and *Salmonella*, by following general food hygiene practices.

## Pregnancy

- Nutrients provide growth for the fetus as well as stores for use during lactation.

- Pregnancy enhances fat deposition.

- Fetal growth retardation, congenital defects, and maternal anaemia are linked to low nutritional status during pregnancy.

- Low maternal weight gain during pregnancy has also been associated with diminished milk production and lower fat concentration in breast milk (refer to Figure 6-3).

- Obesity is linked with maternal hypertension and impaired glucose tolerance.

- Excessive energy restriction during pregnancy might restrict other nutrient intakes and also lead to ketosis, which can compromise fetal mental development.

- Most women store 2–4kg (4.8–9.6lb) of fat during pregnancy in anticipation of lactation.

Recommendations at this time include the following:

- Eat a healthy, varied diet and pay particular attention to iron, calcium, and vitamin D (plus, if vegetarian, vitamin B12).

- Watch weight gain.

- Take nutritional supplements if prescribed.

- Avoid non-prescribed supplements, particularly vitamin A.

- Assure that a source of folic acid is provided.

- Reduce the intake of caffeine and food additives if high.

- Avoid smoking and smoky areas, alcohol, and non-prescribed medicines or street drugs.

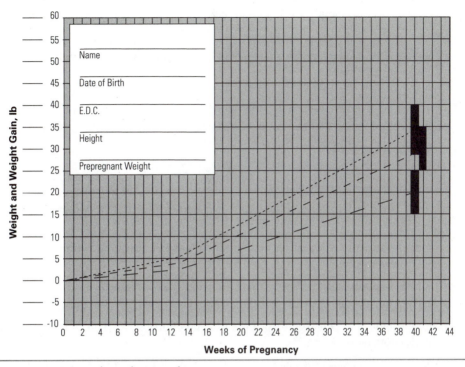

**Figure 6-3**   Prenatal weight gain chart

## Labor, Birth, and the Hospital Stay

- Routine fasting during labor has not been shown by controlled trials to reduce the risk of Mendelson's syndrome and might have negative effects on the mother and baby (NCT, 1996).
- Hospital diets are designed for ill patients, not hard-laboring healthy women.
- Menus might not facilitate cultural food beliefs.
- Access to food might be limited, with long gaps between meals.
- Mothers should not have to choose between eating their own meal and feeding their infant; flexibility in meal service is needed (facility to keep food hot/cold or to reheat meals).

## Lactation

- Lactation is a normal physiological process in a woman who is generally healthy.
- Special diets or foods are not needed.

- Mothering is hard work, and all mothers who are caring for young children need to eat well.
- Lactation increases the body's efficiency in its use of energy and the uptake of nutrients.

Recommendations at this time include the following:

- Eat a healthy, varied diet and pay particular attention to iron, calcium, and vitamin D (plus, if vegetarian, vitamin B12).
- Drink to thirst.
- Weight loss should be gradual—not more than 1lb (0.5kg) per week.
- Breastfeeding, healthy food choices, and gentle exercise can assist with gradual weight loss.
- Women who eat to habit rather than hunger might gain weight at weaning when their energy needs decline.
- Women do not need to eat special foods or avoid specific foods.
- A lactating mother's diet typically provides 50–55 percent of calories from carbohydrates, 12–15 percent of calories from protein, and less than 30 percent of calories from fat.
- Mothers should reduce the amount of trans fatty acids (solid fats) consumed through fats.

## Energy

- The caloric cost of producing one litre of milk is approximately 940kcal.
- The caloric intake for lactating women based on mathematical calculations is as high as 2700 calories per day.
- Many women do not consume this many calories and remain healthy and active with an abundant milk supply (refer to Figure 6-4).

## Protein

- The recommended intake is 65g/day during the first six months and 62g/day during the second six months.
- Protein from animal sources contains all eight *essential amino acids* (EAAs).
- Protein from vegetable sources might be low in one or more EAA.
- Food choices can be combined in the vegetarian diet to provide complementary proteins.

**1989 Recommended Dietary Alllowances (RDA)**

| AGE (YR) | (kcal) ENERGY | (g) PROTEIN | (µg RE) VITAMIN A | (mg α-TE) VITAMIN E | (µg) VITAMIN K | (mg) VITAMIN C | (mg) THIAMIN | (mg) RIBOFLAVIN | (mg NE) NIACIN | (mg) VITAMIN B6 | (µg) FOLATE | (µg) VITAMIN B12 | (mg) IRON | (mg) ZINC | (µg) IODINE | (µg) SELENIUM |
|---|---|---|---|---|---|---|---|---|---|---|---|---|---|---|---|---|
| **Infants** | | | | | | | | | | | | | | | | |
| 0.0—0.5 | 650 | 13 | 375 | 3 | 5 | 30 | 0.3 | 0.4 | 5 | 0.3 | 25 | 0.3 | 6 | 5 | 40 | 10 |
| 0.5—1.0 | 850 | 14 | 375 | 4 | 10 | 35 | 0.4 | 0.5 | 6 | 0.6 | 35 | 0.5 | 10 | 5 | 50 | 15 |
| **Children** | | | | | | | | | | | | | | | | |
| 1–3 | 1300 | 16 | 400 | 6 | 15 | 40 | 0.7 | 0.8 | 9 | 1.0 | 50 | 0.7 | 10 | 10 | 70 | 20 |
| 4–6 | 1800 | 24 | 500 | 7 | 20 | 45 | 0.9 | 1.1 | 12 | 1.1 | 75 | 1.0 | 10 | 10 | 90 | 20 |
| 7–10 | 2000 | 28 | 700 | 7 | 30 | 45 | 1.0 | 1.2 | 13 | 1.4 | 100 | 1.4 | 10 | 10 | 120 | 30 |
| **Males** | | | | | | | | | | | | | | | | |
| 11–14 | 2500 | 45 | 1000 | 10 | 45 | 50 | 1.3 | 1.5 | 17 | 1.7 | 150 | 2.0 | 12 | 15 | 150 | 40 |
| 15–18 | 3000 | 59 | 1000 | 10 | 65 | 60 | 1.5 | 1.8 | 20 | 2.0 | 200 | 2.0 | 12 | 15 | 150 | 50 |
| 19–24 | 2900 | 58 | 1000 | 10 | 70 | 60 | 1.5 | 1.7 | 19 | 2.0 | 200 | 2.0 | 10 | 15 | 150 | 70 |
| 25–50 | 2900 | 63 | 1000 | 10 | 80 | 60 | 1.5 | 1.7 | 19 | 2.0 | 200 | 2.0 | 10 | 15 | 150 | 70 |
| 51+ | 2300 | 63 | 1000 | 10 | 80 | 60 | 1.2 | 1.4 | 15 | 2.0 | 200 | 2.0 | 10 | 15 | 150 | 70 |
| **Females** | | | | | | | | | | | | | | | | |
| 11–14 | 2200 | 46 | 800 | 8 | 45 | 50 | 1.1 | 1.3 | 15 | 1.4 | 150 | 2.0 | 15 | 12 | 150 | 45 |
| 15–18 | 2200 | 44 | 800 | 8 | 55 | 60 | 1.1 | 1.3 | 15 | 1.5 | 180 | 2.0 | 15 | 12 | 150 | 50 |
| 19–24 | 2200 | 46 | 800 | 8 | 60 | 60 | 1.1 | 1.3 | 15 | 1.6 | 180 | 2.0 | 15 | 12 | 150 | 55 |
| 25–50 | 2200 | 50 | 800 | 8 | 65 | 60 | 1.1 | 1.3 | 15 | 1.6 | 180 | 2.0 | 15 | 12 | 150 | 55 |
| 51+ | 1900 | 50 | 800 | 8 | 65 | 60 | 1.0 | 1.2 | 13 | 1.6 | 180 | 2.0 | 10 | 12 | 150 | 55 |
| **Pregnant** | +300 | 60 | 800 | 10 | 65 | 70 | 1.5 | 1.6 | 17 | 2.2 | 400 | 2.2 | 30 | 15 | 175 | 65 |
| **Lactating** | | | | | | | | | | | | | | | | |
| 1st 6 mo. | +500 | 65 | 1300 | 12 | 65 | 95 | 1.6 | 1.8 | 20 | 2.1 | 280 | 2.6 | 15 | 19 | 200 | 75 |
| 2nd 6 mo. | +500 | 62 | 1200 | 11 | 65 | 90 | 1.6 | 1.7 | 20 | 2.1 | 260 | 2.6 | 15 | 16 | 200 | 75 |

**1997 Dietary Reference Intakes (DRI)**

| AGE (YR) | (µg) VITAMIN D | (mg) CALCIUM | (mg) PHOSPHORUS | (mg) MAGNESIUM | (mg) FLUORIDE |
|---|---|---|---|---|---|
| **Infants** | | | | | |
| 0.0—0.5 | 5 | 210 | 100 | 30 | 0.01 |
| 0.5—1.0 | 5 | 270 | 275 | 75 | 0.5 |
| **Children** | | | | | |
| 1–3 | 5 | 500 | 460 | 80 | 0.7 |
| 4–8 | 5 | 800 | 500 | 130 | 1.1 |
| **Males** | | | | | |
| 9–13 | 5 | 1300 | 1250 | 240 | 2.0 |
| 14–18 | 5 | 1300 | 1250 | 410 | 3.2 |
| 19–30 | 5 | 1000 | 700 | 400 | 3.8 |
| 31–50 | 5 | 1000 | 700 | 420 | 3.8 |
| 51–70 | 10 | 1200 | 700 | 420 | 3.8 |
| 71+ | 10 | 1200 | 700 | 420 | 3.8 |
| **Females** | | | | | |
| 9–13 | 5 | 1300 | 1250 | 240 | 2.0 |
| 14–18 | 5 | 1300 | 1250 | 360 | 2.9 |
| 19–30 | 5 | 1000 | 700 | 310 | 3.1 |
| 31–50 | 5 | 1000 | 700 | 320 | 3.1 |
| 51–70 | 10 | 1200 | 700 | 320 | 3.1 |
| 71+ | 10 | 1200 | 700 | 320 | 3.1 |
| **Pregnant** | | * +40 | | | |
| **Lactating** | * | * | * | * | |

*Values are the same as for other women of comparable age.*

*Note:* Appendix G presents additional RDA tables showing recommended energy intakes and estimated safe and adequate daily dietary intakes and estimated minimum requirements for selected vitamins and minerals. Appendix 1 presents the Recommended Nutrient Intakes (RNI) For Canadians.
*Source:* RDA reprinted with permission from *Recommended Dietary Allowances,* 10th edition ©1989 by the National Academy of Sciences. Courtesy of the National Academy Press, Washington, D.C.: Committee on Dietary Reference Intakes, *Dietary Reference Intakes for Calcium, Phosphorus, Magnesium, Vitamin D, and Fluoride* (Washington, D.C.: National Academy Press, 1997).

**Figure 6-4**    Recommended Dietary Intakes

## Vitamins and Minerals

### Iron

- Ideally, anemia should be corrected pre-conception.
- Supplements should be used selectively because they have side effects, including constipation and nausea.

- Absorption increases during pregnancy, and there is no loss through menstruation, so women who start their pregnancy with good iron levels and who eat iron-rich foods should not need routine iron supplements.

- Hemodilution (increased blood volume) during pregnancy is normal and affects hemoglobin measurements; serum ferritin is a better indicator at this time.

- Iron levels in breast milk are independent of maternal blood levels.

- Vitamin C enhances iron absorption.

## Vitamin D

- Aids calcium absorption.

- Food sources—whole and fortified milk, eggs, cheese, margarine, and oily fish

- Sunlight is a good source.

- If sunlight is restricted (due to climate, clothing, lifestyle, or beliefs), a supplement for the mother and/or the baby might be needed during the last trimester of pregnancy and during breastfeeding.

- Light-skinned babies need approximately 30 minutes per week of sun exposure in a diaper or two hours per week if fully clothed and wearing a hat.

- Dark-skinned babies who receive this minimum exposure or less might require a 5–7.5 μg/day vitamin D supplement.

- Low maternal stores of vitamin D during pregnancy will result in low levels in the infant.

- Breast milk concentrations reflect maternal levels.

- Over-supplementation can be potentially toxic.

## Calcium

- Calcium absorption is reduced by phytates in high fiber foods.

- Maternal intake has little effect on breast milk levels of calcium.

- Calcium absorption, metabolism, and excretion can change in response to intake and requirements (Prentice, 1994).

- Calcium requirements have been extensively studied with mixed conclusions.

- Women who avoid or are allergic or intolerant of dairy products might need other food choices that are high in calcium, or if this situation is not possible, a 600mg/day elemental calcium supplement might be necessary.

- Bone loss occurs during lactation; however, remineralization occurs following the return of menstrual cycles.

- This loss and recovery are independent of dietary intake.

- Studies suggest that this turnover process results in greater bone mass in women who have breastfed than in women who did not breastfeed, thus decreasing the risk of osteoporosis.

### Fluid

- Increasing fluid intake does not increase milk supply unless the mother is severely dehydrated.
- Decreasing fluid intake does not reduce engorgement or suppress a high milk volume.
- Forcing fluids beyond what the body requires can decrease milk production.
- If maternal urine is scant or dark colored, suggest an increase in fluid intake.
- Sugary or salty fluids will increase thirst.
- Remind mothers that it is not necessary to drink milk to make milk.
- Mothers should simply drink to thirst.

## Recommended Intake Tables

A diet containing less than the recommended intake is not necessarily deficient in a particular nutrient; however, it indicates a need for further assessment (refer to Table 6-1 and Table 6-2).

**Table 6-1**   Foods Containing Nutrients Needed during Lactation

| Nutrient Needed | Foods Rich in This Nutrient |
| --- | --- |
| Calcium | Milk, cheese, yogurt, fish with edible bones, tofu processed with calcium sulfate, bok choy, broccoli, kale, collard, mustard, and turnip greens, breads made with milk |
| Zinc | Meat, poultry, seafood, eggs, seeds, legumes, yogurt, whole grains (bioavailability from this source is variable) |
| Magnesium | Nuts, seeds, legumes, whole grains, green vegetables, scallops, oysters (in general, this mineral is widely distributed in food rather than concentrated in a small number of foods) |
| Vitamin B6 | Bananas, poultry, meat, fish, potatoes, sweet potatoes, spinach, prunes, watermelon, some legumes, fortified cereals, and nuts |
| Thiamine | Pork, fish, whole grains, organ meats, legumes, corn, peas, seeds, nuts, fortified cereal grain (widely distributed in foods) |
| Folate | Leafy vegetables, fruit, liver, green beans, fortified cereals, legumes, and whole-grain cereals |

Source: Institute of Medicine. *Nutrition during lactation.* Washington, DC: National Academy Press; 1991: 231.

**Table 6-2**  Menu Suggestions That Implement the Recommendations in the Food Pyramid

| Food Group | Minimum Recommended Number of Servings Daily (with Sample Food Servings) | Nonpregnant (1900 Calories) | Pregnant or Lactating (2200 Calories) |
|---|---|---|---|
| Milk or milk products | 1 cup low fat milk or yogurt<br>1 1/2 oz. cheddar cheese<br>1 cup pudding<br>1 1/4 cups low fat ice cream<br>2 cups cottage cheese<br>1 cup tofu (soybean curd) | 2 | 3 |
| Meats and meat substitutes | Cooked lean meat, fish, or poultry<br>Cheddar cheese<br>1/2 cup cottage cheese<br>1 cup dried beans or peas<br>4 tbsp. peanut butter | 5–7 ounces | 7 ounces |
| Eggs | | 1 | 1–2 |
| Fruits | (Include Vitamin C-rich choice)<br>1/2 cup cooked or juice<br>1 cup raw<br>1 medium-sized fruit | 2–4 | 3–4 |
| Vegetables | (Choose from dark leafy and starch vegetables. Variety is recommended.)<br>1/2 cup cooked<br>1 cup raw | 3–5 | 4–5 |
| Grains | (Whole grain, fortified, or enriched)<br>1 slice breat<br>1 cup ready-to-eat cereal<br>1/2 cup cooked cereal, pasta, or grits | 6–11 | 9–11 |

## Nutrient and Vitamin Chart

| Key Nutrient | RDI for Ages 23–50 | Important Sources | Important Functions |
|---|---|---|---|
| Water and liquids | N 4 C; P 6–8 C; L 8+ C | Water, juice, milk. | Carries nutrients to and waste products away from cells. Provides fluid for increased blood and amniotic fluid volume. Helps regulate body temperature and aids digestion. Comments: Often neglected. Is an important nutrient. |
| Protein amino acids | N 50g; P 60g; L 64g | Animal: Meat, fish, eggs, milk, cheese, yogurt. Plant: Dried beans and peas, peanut butter, nuts, whole grains and cereals, soy milk, meat substitutes. | Constitutes part of the structure of every tissue cell, such as muscle, blood, and bone. Supports growth and maintains healthy body cells. Constitutes part of enzymes, some hormones and body fluids. Helps form antibodies that increase resistance to infection. Builds and repairs tissues, helps build blood and amniotic fluid. Supplies energy. Comments: Fetal requirements increase by about 1/3 in late pregnancy as the baby grows. |
| *Minerals* | | | |
| Calcium | N 800–1200mg; P 1200mg; L 1200mg | Animal: Milk, cheese, yogurt, egg yolk, whole canned fish, ice cream. Plant: Whole grains, almonds, filberts, green leafy vegetables. | Combines with other minerals within a protein framework to give structure and strength to bones and teeth. Assists in blood clotting. Functions in normal muscle contraction and relaxation, and normal nerve transmission. Helps regulate the use of other minerals in the body. Comments: Fetal requirements increase by about 2/3 in late pregnancy. |
| Phosphorus | N 1000mg; P 1200mg; L 1200mg | Animal: Milk, cheese, lean meats. | Helps build bones and teeth. Comments: Calcium and phosphorus exist in a constant ratio in the blood. An excess of either limits utilization of calcium. |

*(continues)*

**Table 6-2** (*Continued*)

| Key Nutrient | RDI for Ages 23–50 | Important Sources | Important Functions |
|---|---|---|---|
| | | *Minerals* | |
| Iron | N 18mg; P 30–60mg; L 18+ mg | Animal: Liver, red meats, egg yolk. Plant: Whole grains, leafy vegetables, nuts, legumes, dried fruits, prune and apple juice. | Aids in utilization of energy. Combines with protein to form hemoglobin, the red substance in blood that carries oxygen to and carbon dioxide from the cells. Prevents nutritional anemia and its accompanying fatigue. Increases resistance to infection. Functions as part of enzymes involved in tissue respiration. Provides iron for fetal storage. Comments: Fetal requirements increase tenfold in final 6 weeks of pregnancy. Supplement of 30–60 mg of iron daily recommended by National Research Council. Continued supplementation for 2–3 months postpartum is recommended to replenish iron. |
| Zinc | N 15mg; P 20mg; L 25mg | Animal: Meat, liver, eggs, and seafood, especially oysters. | A component of insulin. Important in growth of skeleton and nervous system. Comments: Deficiency can cause fetal malformation of skeleton and nervous system. |
| Iodine | N 150μcg; P 175μcg; L 200μcg | Animal: Seafood. Plant: Iodized salt. | Helps control the rate of body's energy use, important in Thyroxine production. Comments: Deficiency may produce goiter in infant. |
| Magnesium | N 400mg; P 450mg; L 450mg | Plant: Nuts, cocoa, green vegetables, whole grains, dried beans, peas. | Co-enzyme in energy and protein metabolism, enzyme activator, tissue growth, cell metabolism, muscle action. Comments: Most is stored in bones. Deficiency may produce neuromuscular dysfunctions. |

| Key Nutrient | RDI for Ages 23–50 | Important Sources | Important Functions |
|---|---|---|---|
| *Fat-Soluble Vitamins* | | | |
| Vitamin A | N 800 RE; P 1000 RE; L 1200 RE | Animal: Butter, whole milk, cheese, fortified lowfat milk, liver. Plant: Fortified margarine, green and leafy vegetables, orange vegetables, fruits. | Assists formation and maintenance of skin and mucous membranes that line body cavities and tracts, such as nasal passages and intestinal tract, thus increasing resistance to infection. Essential in development of enamel-forming cells in gum tissue. Helps bone and tissue growth and cell development. Functions in visual processes, thus promoting healthy eye tissues and eye adaptation in dim light. Comments: Is toxic to the fetus in very large amounts. Can be lost with exposure to light. |
| Vitamin D | N 5μcg; P 800μcg; L 10μcg | Animal: Fortified milk, fish liver oils. Plant: Fortified margarine, sun on skin. | Promotes the absorption of calcium from the digestive tract and the deposition of calcium in the structure of bones and teeth. Comments: Toxic to fetus in excessive amounts. Is a stable vitamin. |
| Vitamin E | N 8mg; P 10mg; L 13mg | Vegetable oils, leafy vegetables, cereals, meat, eggs, milk. | Tissue growth, cell wall integrity, red blood cell integrity. Comments: Enhances absorption of Vitamin A. |
| *Water-Soluble Vitamins* | | | |
| B; Vitamins and folic acid | N 400μcg; P 800μcg; L 600μcg | Liver, green leafy vegetables, yeast. | Hemoglobin synthesis, involved in DNA and RNA synthesis, co-enzyme in synthesis of amino acids. Comments: Water-soluble vitamins are interdependent on each other. Deficiency leads to anemia. Can be destroyed in cooking and storage. Supplement of 200–400 μ cg/day is recommended by the National Research Council. Oral contraception use many reduce serum level of folic acid. |
| Niacin | N 13mg; P 15mg; L 18mg | Pork, organ meats, peanuts, beans, peas, enriched grains. | Coenzyme in energy and protein metabolism. Comments: Stable; only small amounts lost in food preparation. |

*(continues)*

Table 6-2  (*Continued*)

| Key Nutrient | RDI for Ages 23-50 | Important Sources | Important Functions |
|---|---|---|---|
| | | *Water-Soluble Vitamins* | |
| Riboflavin | N 1.2mg; P 1.5mg; L 1.7–1.9mg | Animal: Milk products, liver, red meat. Plant: Enriched grains. | Aids in utilization of energy. Functions as part of a co-enzyme in the production of energy within body cells. Promotes healthy skin, eyes, and clear vision. Protein metabolism. Comments: Severe deficiencies lead to reduced growth and congenital malformations. Oral contraceptive use may reduce serum concentrations. |
| B1-Thiamin | N 1.0mg; P 1.4mg; L 1.5mg | Pork, beef, liver, whole grains, legumes. | Co-enzyme in energy and protein metabolism. Comments: Its availability limits the rate at which energy from glucose is produced. |
| B6 Pyrodoxine | N 1.6mg; P 2.2mg; L 2.1mg | Unprocessed cereals, grains, wheat germ, bran, nuts, seeds, legumes, corn. | Important in amino acid metabolism and protein synthesis. Fetus requires more for growth. Comments: Excessive amounts may reduce milk production in lactating women. |
| B12 | N 2.0μcg; P 2.2μcg; L 2.6μcg | Animal: Milk, cheese, eggs, meat, liver, fish. Plant: Fortified soy milk, cereals, meat substitutes. | Assists in the maintenance of nerve tissue. Coenzyme in protein metabolism, important in the formation of red blood cells. Comments: Deficiency leads to anemia and central nervous system damage. Is manufactured by microorganisms in intestinal tract. Oral contraceptive use may reduce serum concentrations. |
| Vitamin C | N 60mg; P 80mg; L 100mg | Citrus fruits, berries, melons, tomatoes, chili peppers, green vegetables, potatoes. | Tissue formation and integrity, "cement" substance in connective and vascular substances, increases iron absorption. Comments: Large doses in pregnancy may create a larger than normal need in infant. Benefits of large doses in preventing colds have not been confirmed. |

Data from The Food Pyramid: How to make it work for you. *Consumer Reports on Health*, September, 1996; Charbonneau, K. "Nutrition Continuum." *International Journal of Childbirth Education* 8:16–18, 1993.

L, lactating; N, nonpregnant; P, pregnant; RDI, reference daily intake.

From Worthington-Roberts B and Williams SR. *Nutrition in pregnancy and lactation*, St. Louis, MO, Times Mirror/Mosby College Publishing; 1989 and *www.nal.usda.gov*.

> "Women living under a wide variety of circumstances in the United States and elsewhere are capable of fully nourishing their infants by breastfeeding them."
>
> "Mothers are able to produce milk of sufficient quantity and quality to support growth and promote the health of infants—even when the mother's supply of nutrients and energy is limited." (Nutrition during Lactation, Institute of Medicine, 1991)

## Weight Patterns

- In the past, mothers were advised to consume high levels of nutrients; however, it is now known that a lactating woman's body is very efficient at producing milk (Frigerio et al, 1991).
- Body stores provide about 200 calories per day.
- An increase of 300–500 calories per day (over non-pregnant requirements) is recommended and can be met by nutritious snacks or additions to meals; however, many women consume less than this amount and their babies grow well.
- Weight is linked to culture. A thin nursing mother might be viewed as ideal or as indicating that her family did not care for her well, depending on the culture.
- Return to pre-pregnancy weight is influenced by the following:
  - Previous weight
  - Weight gain during pregnancy
  - Parity
  - Lifestyle and beliefs
  - Maternal age
  - Level of physical activity
  - Caloric intake
- Breastfeeding mothers tend to lose more weight than non-breastfeeding women, primarily due to differences in weight loss after three months.
- Weight loss greater than 6.5lb (3kg) in the early weeks might indicate that sufficient food is not being consumed.
- Mothers can safely lose 0.5–1 pound (0.45kg) per week.
- Caloric intake should not drop below 1800 kcal.
- Lactating mothers typically consume between 1800–2200 kcal per day with no adverse effects on the baby.
- Mothers should avoid fad or crash diets and diet medications.

- Energy intakes of approximately 15 percent less than those currently recommended are compatible with full lactation, full activity, and gradual weight loss; the 2700 kcal per day recommendation might be in excess of what many mothers actually need to consume.

## Groups That Have Special Nutritional Needs

### Young Mothers

- Young mothers are still growing and thus have higher nutrient requirements.
- Counseling might be needed to discuss food choices.

### Malnourished Women

- Improve the maternal intake to benefit both the mother and the baby.
- Feeding the breastfeeding mother is more cost effective than providing breast milk substitutes for the infant.
- Inadequate nutrition is linked to socio-economic issues, and purely nutritional interventions are unlikely to succeed if these issues are not also addressed.
- Severely malnourished mothers might have reduced breast milk levels of water-soluble vitamins, lactose, and fat concentration; however, infants who are allowed to self-regulate their intake will usually take sufficient lower fat milk to meet their needs.

### Eating Disorders

- A woman who has anorexia or bulimia needs to be under the care of suitable health professionals.
- Anorexia: Breast milk composition might be affected as described under the Malnourished Women section.
- Concern for her infant's well being might motivate an anorexic mother to address her disorder.
- Bulimia: Wide variations in intake might affect the nutritional status.
- Little information is available on the effect of bulimia on milk composition.

### Multiples

- During pregnancy, the mother might need to eat very small, frequent meals due to her womb pushing upwards.
- During breastfeeding, nutrient needs are increased above the needs of a mother who is breastfeeding a single infant.
- The mother might need to discuss ways of finding time to eat.

**Breastfeeding and Pregnancy**

- Nutrient needs are generally increased.
- The mother might need suggestions on coping with morning sickness and finding time to eat while also caring for a toddler.

**Vegetarian**

- Vegetarians who are knowledgeable about their diet can have very healthy diets.
- There are a number of vegetarian diets that are classified as follows:
  - Vegan—no animal proteins, including egg and milk
  - Semi-vegetarian—vegetables, milk products, seafood, and poultry (avoids red meat)
  - Lacto-vegetarians consume milk and milk products, such as cheese and ice cream, in addition to plant foods
  - Ovo-vegetarians consume plant foods and eggs
  - Lacto-ovo-vegetarians consume plant foods, dairy products, and eggs (no meat, seafood, or poultry)
  - Fruitarians consume fruits, nuts, olive oil, and honey
  - Macrobiotic—the advanced form is usually nutritionally inadequate for lactating women
- Vegetarian mothers who do not regularly receive some exposure to the sun might need a vitamin D supplement (mothers who reside in northern latitudes, work indoors, wear cultural clothing that covers their skin, and so on).
- Pregnant vegetarians should be encouraged to eat foods or supplements that are rich in vitamin B12 in order to enhance lactation.
- Alternative sources for vitamin B12 include the following:
  - Red Star brand yeast T6635+ contains active vitamin B12; a rounded teaspoon of yeast powder, or 2 teaspoons of mini-flake yeast, or 2.5 tablespoons of large-flake yeast provides 2.2 μg of vitamin B12
  - Fortified cereal, such as Nutri-Grain; mothers can be encouraged to check the labels of cereals to assure that vitamin B12 is present
  - Fortified soy milk
  - Fortified meat analogues (food made from wheat gluten or soybeans to resemble meat, fish, or poultry)
  - A vitamin supplement that does not contain animal products

**Exercise**

- The mother who exercises strenuously will have increased energy needs.
- Moderate exercise has no adverse effect on breast milk, and elevated levels of lactic acid are not seen with moderate exercise.
- The possibility of breast refusal by the baby following extremely heavy exercise by the mother has been suggested to be caused by elevated levels of lactic acid.
- Mothers can feed the baby before exercising if this concern is present.
- Breastfeeding and exercising are compatible, and both should be encouraged.

## Effects on Food Choices

**Education**

- Formal education on healthy eating choices might be limited.
- A decrease in contact with older family members reduces "passed-down" information.
- Much of the mother's information might come from product advertisements.
- An opinion of what a healthy diet consists of might vary; ask what is eaten regularly rather than, "Do you eat well?"
- Imposing healthy eating rules that must be followed can make breastfeeding seem too difficult for some women; a more supportive approach is to present options and suggestions.
- Check that the information leaflets that you hand out do not imply that a special (expensive) diet must be followed or that the mother needs to keep charts of foods eaten.

## Cultural and Religious Beliefs

- Upbringing, habits, and beliefs affect food practices.
- Find out any common food practices of the cultural groups with which you work; be aware that every mother within that cultural group might not follow those practices.
- Your food choices might be very different from those of your client; yours are not necessarily better for her, nor are the practices of your culture—the norm by which you judge hers.
- Cultural practices that are beneficial, such as giving the mother particularly nourishing foods, should be encouraged; as long as the belief is not harmful, you should not interfere with the belief.
- Galactogogues are common in many cultures.
- Food preferences of other family members might decide what is eaten in the home.

- Some cultures might not recognize the high nutritional needs of a pregnant or nursing woman, and both the mother and other family members might resist changes.

## Economic

- A lack of money might limit the food that is available as well as the facilities to store and prepare the food.
- Distance from stores and lack of transportation might limit the purchase of foods, particularly those that are heavy to carry or that perish quickly.
- Establish what financial aid and food subsidy programs are available in your area, what they provide, and how to refer a woman to them.

## Time

- Time is needed to shop for food, prepare the food, and eat the food; a mother has many demands on her time, and snacking on convenience foods might be how she manages her time.
- Suggest foods that are easy and quick to prepare and that fit with the other demands on her time.
- Explore the availability of in-home help for women who are at a particular nutritional risk.

## Effects of Maternal Food Intake on the Breastfeeding Infant

### Milk Volume/Composition

- Increasing maternal energy intake and fluid does not increase milk volume unless the mother is very severely malnourished or dehydrated.
- Major nutrients and minerals, such as iron and calcium, are provided at a stable level in breast milk at the expense of maternal stores.
- In the chronically malnourished woman, vitamin A and B group stores are likely to be low; thus, breast milk levels of these vitamins might be low; supplement the mother.
- The volume of milk might also be somewhat diminished.
- Consuming fewer than 1500 kcal/day has been shown to decrease milk volumes.
- The kinds of fatty acids in milk but not the overall fat content are influenced by the maternal diet.
- Carbohydrate levels of breast milk are not affected by maternal intake; maternal diabetes does not affect breast milk carbohydrate levels.
- Factors other than nutrition, particularly nursing behavior and stress, have a greater effect on milk supply.

## Immunological Effects

- An adaptive mechanism keeps the iron level in milk at an optimum level to preserve the bacteriostatic role of lactoferrin (Zapata, 1994).
- Severely malnourished women might have slightly reduced levels of immunoglobulin levels in their milk, although studies are not conclusive.

## Colic and Allergy

- There is little evidence to support the belief that gassy or spicy foods, when eaten in moderation by the mother, cause problems in most breastfeeding infants.
- If a food is suspected of causing a problem, it can be eliminated for two weeks; if symptoms reappear when the food is reintroduced, it might be wiser to avoid it.
- Mothers who avoid a major food (such as wheat or dairy products) must give consideration to replacing those nutrients; referral to a dietitian might be needed.
- A mother who has a strong family history of milk protein intolerance might pass more beta-lactoglobulin through her milk, which could cause colic-type symptoms in her baby (Jakobsson, 1991).
- In high-risk allergic families, mothers might be advised to avoid peanuts and other potent allergens during pregnancy and breastfeeding (Anaphylaxis Campaign).
- Red pepper (with capsaicin) has been reported to cause dermatitis in the breastfed infant; infants of mothers who consume hot red pepper have been reported to develop a perianal rash.

## Caffeine

- Caffeine ingested by the mother in moderate amounts (up to five cups/day) does not cause a problem for most babies.
- The amount of caffeine available to the baby is 0.06–1.5 percent of the maternal dose.
- Preterm or ill infants might not metabolize it well, leading to accumulation and wakefulness.
- Caffeine is found in some medications, soft drinks (common in energy or sports drinks), coffee, and tea; theobromine is found in chocolate and in excessive amounts can have similar effects to caffeine.
- Herbal teas can contain active ingredients that are secreted into milk; cathartics such as buckhorn bark and senna might result in cramps and diarrhea in a baby; chamomile has been reported to possibly sensitize a susceptible baby to ragweed and cause an allergic reaction.

## Alcohol

- High intakes might impair the let-down reflex.
- The taste of milk might result in less milk consumed.
- A number of factors influence maternal blood alcohol concentrations, including body weight, amount of adipose tissue, stomach contents, how fast the alcohol is consumed, the amount of alcohol consumed, and the concentration of alcohol in the beverage being consumed (proof).
- Alcohol passes freely into milk and in large amounts might cause drowsiness, slow growth, and neurodevelopmental delays in the infant; alcohol achieves the same level in milk as in blood.
- Infants detoxify alcohol in the first four weeks of life at a rate approximately one-half that of an adult.
- Doses of more than 2g/kg completely block the milk ejection reflex.
- A high alcohol intake impairs the mother's ability to safely care for a child.
- Support to breastfeed might assist the motivation of a woman who wishes to reduce her alcohol intake.
- Peak alcohol levels in milk occur in 30–60 minutes on an empty stomach and in 60–90 minutes when consumed with food.
- It takes approximately 1 1/2–2 hours per ounce to metabolize alcohol in the adult.
- The alcohol content of milk falls as the blood levels fall due to back diffusion of alcohol from the milk to the blood stream.
- Pumping milk does not increase the speed of elimination of alcohol from the milk or from the body.

## Taste

- Breast milk flavor changes depending on the foods and spices that the mother consumes.
- Babies whose mothers eat a variety of foods, including highly flavored foods, are more accepting of a variety of solids when introduced (Sullivan and Birch, 1994).
- Babies suckled for 50 percent longer when milk was garlic flavored (Mennella, 1995).
- Babies suckled even longer when exposed to vanilla-flavored milk.
- Some babies will suck more when a novel flavor is introduced.

## Food Additives

- Artificial sweeteners
  - Aspartame metabolizes into phenylalanine and aspartic acid

- Would pose a risk to those who have phenylketonuria
- Milk levels of phenylalanine are only slightly elevated after ingesting aspartame
- Aspartame in moderation during lactation is presumed safe

## A Consultation

As an LC who is carrying out a consult with a nutritional focus, it is helpful to have the following:

- Basic nutrition knowledge in order to assess the mother's intake
- Awareness of the diversity of cultural practices
- Counselling skills to gather information and discuss choices
- Simple charting to record information that is gathered
- Education strategies to provide information to the mother
- Knowledge of other services that are available and how to refer to them

# References

Anderson PO. Alcohol and breastfeeding. *J Hum Lact* 1995; 11:321–323.

Bertelsen C, Auerbach KG. Nutrition and breastfeeding: the cultural connection. Lactation Consultant Series, Unit 11, LLLI and Avery Publishing, NY, 1987.

Butte NF, Garza C, Stuff JE, et al. Effect of maternal diet and body composition on lactational performance. *Am J Clin Nutr* 1984; 39:296.

Dusdieker LB, Booth BM, Stumbo PJ, et al. Effect of supplemental fluids on human milk production. *J Pediatr* 1985; 106:207.

Food and Nutrition Information Center, National Agricultural Library, U.S. Department of Agriculture, Agricultural Research Service maintains an extensive resource list on dietary supplements at: http://www.nal.usda.gov/fnic/pubs/bibs/gen/dietsupp.html.

Frigerio C, Schutz Y, Prentice A, et al. Is human lactation a particularly efficient process? *Euro J Clin Nutr* 1991; 45(9):459–462.

Hammer RL, Hinterman C. Exercise and dietary programming to promote maternal health fitness and weight management during lactation. *J Perinat Educ* 1998; 7:13–26.

Hattevig G, Sigurs N, Kjellman B. Effects of dietary avoidance during lactation on allergy in children at 10 years of age. *Acta Paediatr* 1999; 88(1):7–12.

Illingworth RS, Kilpatrick B. Lactation and fluid intake. *Lancet* 1953; 2:1175.

Illingworth PJ, Jung RT, Howie PW, et al. Diminution in energy expenditure during lactation. *Br Med J* 1986; 292:437.

Institute of Medicine: Nutrition during pregnancy. Washington, D.C.: National Academy Press, 1990.

Institute of Medicine: Nutrition during lactation. Washington, DC: National Academy Press, 1991

Jakobsson I. Food antigens in human milk. *Euro J Clin Nutr* (Suppl 1) 1991; 29–33.

Lauwers J, Shinskie D. Maternal health and nutrition. Chapter 7 in Counseling the nursing mother. Sudbury, MA: Jones and Bartlett Publishers, 2000: pp. 107–128.

Mangels R. The vegan diet during pregnancy and lactation. The Vegetarian Resource Group. http://www.vrg.org/nutrition/veganpregnancy.htm; accessed 1/6/01.

Mennella JA. Mother's milk: a medium for early flavour experiences. *J Hum Lact* 1995; 11(1):39–45.

Michaelsen K, et al. The Copenhagen Cohort Study on infant nutrition and growth: breast milk intake, human milk macronutrient content, and influencing factors. *Am J Clin Nutr* 1994; 59:600–611.

Ngai Fen Cheung. Diet therapy in the postnatal period—from a Chinese perspective. *Midwives*, 109(1302) 1996; 149: 190–193.

Olsen A. Nursing under conditions of thirst or excessive ingestion of fluids. *Acta Obstet Gynaecol Scand* 1940; 20:313.

Pengelley L, Gyte G. Eating and drinking in labour, a summary of the medical research to facilitate informed choice. United Kingdom: National Childbirth Trust, 1996.

Prentice AM, Prentice A. Energy costs of lactation. *Annual Rev Nutr* 1988; 8:63.

Prentice A. Maternal calcium requirements during pregnancy and lactation. *Am J Clin Nutr* 59(Suppl 2) 1994; 477S–483S.

Schulte P. Minimizing alcohol exposure of the breastfeeding infant. *J Hum Lact* 1995; 11:317–319.

Sullivan SA, Birch LL. Infant dietary experience and acceptance of solid foods. *Pediatrics* 1994; 93(2):271–277.

The Anaphylaxis Campaign, P.O. Box 149, Fleet, Hampshire GU13 9XU, England.

United States Department of Agriculture and United States Department of Health and Human Services. FNS-250. 1986 Cross-cultural counseling—a guide for nutrition and health counselors. Institute of Medicine: Nutrition during lactation. National Academy Press, Washington, D.C.: 1991.

## Multilingual Resources

Nutrition Education for New Americans Project Materials are available in 37 languages and include culturally appropriate food guide pyramids as well as hand-outs on healthy eating for adults, mothers and babies, elderly adults, and children. All are bilingual and copyright free. They can be downloaded from http://monarch.gsu.edu/nutrition/download.htm.

Chapter 7

# GUIDELINES FOR INFANT BREASTFEEDING

*Marie Davis, RN, IBCLC*

## Objectives

- Identify two things that will aid the baby in his or her transition to extrauterine life.
- Give at least two examples of physiological and psychological benefits to the mother and baby related to early first contact.
- Identify at least two routine hospital procedures that disrupt the normal first attachment needs of both mother and baby.
- List at least three things parents should be made aware of in the prenatal setting that can enhance first contact and that should be incorporated into the birth plan.
- State the significance of *amnionic fluid* (AF) transfer in relation to first contact.
- State one rationale for *skin-to-skin* (STS) contact between the mother and the neonate.

## Introduction

The establishment of lactation begins with the separation of the placenta. Birth interventions that disrupt the natural interaction between the mother and the infant in the immediate postpartum period can impact long-term breastfeeding success. For the past several decades, hospitals have used "an intensive care approach" during the transition period to extrauterine life, treating all newborns as "recovering patients until they have demonstrated evidence of smooth transition" (Thureen, Deacon, and O'Niell, 1999, p. 91). The medicalization of birth and postpartum processes drove women to breastfeeding failure through management (Lawrence and Lawrence, 1999). UNICEF's 10 Steps to Successful Breastfeeding, the Baby Friendly Hospital Initiative, and the breastfeeding statement from the American Academy of Pediatrics are directing maternity care away from an antiquated treatment model that applies to fewer than 10 percent of all newborns. A mother's breastfeeding experience can be "profoundly affected by what happens during the first hours after birth"

(Newman and Pitman, 2000, p. 43). The lactation consultant might not be present for the first mother-infant breastfeeding contact. She can, however, educate parents and medical providers about how critical this first step is toward successful breastfeeding and how to handle it safely and effectively.

## Teaching Points

- Encourage parents to have a written birth plan and feeding plan (Riordan and Auerbach, 1998) before hospital admission.

- Encourage hospitals and birth centers to limit nonessential routine interventions in labor and birth (Lauwers and Shinskie, 2000).

- More natural birth processes enhance the instinctual and reflexive aspects of breastfeeding.

- Mothers who initiate breastfeeding within an hour of birth breastfeed longer than those who have delayed contact.

- Labor medications and interventions dull breastfeeding and bonding processes (Powers and Slusser, 1997).

- Encourage parents and health care providers to recognize and facilitate the baby's reflexes for self attachment.

- Human imprinting is not discussed in pediatric texts.

- Comfort sucking and the formation of a nipple preference are genetically determined behaviors for imprinting on the mother's nipple (Lawrence and Lawrence, 1999).

- The baby recognizes his or her mother by oral, tactile, and olfactory modes.

- The baby learns the smell of amniotic fluid in utero and shows a preference for objects that are coated with amniotic fluid.

- This preference changes to a preference for the smell of the mother's milk four or five days after birth.
  - Babies who are exposed to the amniotic fluid smell cried less than those who were exposed to no odor or to the odor of the mother's breast (Varendi, Christensson, Porter, and Winberg; 1998).
  - Odors play an important role in the mediation of an infant's early behavior (Varendi, Christensson, Porter, and Winberg; 1998).

- Most babies from unmedicated births will self attach and suckle correctly in fewer than 50 minutes.

- If left undisturbed with the mother, the baby responds with an unlearned pattern of attachment; the process is innate.

- When a baby self attaches, he or she will attach correctly to the areola and not to the nipple alone.

- If separated from the mother for newborn procedures, the baby's initial suckling attempts are disturbed.
- Delayed gratification of the early sucking reflex might make it more difficult for the infant to suckle later on (Riordan and Auerbach, 1998).
- The infant might be too drowsy or stressed to latch on following routine newborn procedures.
- Organized breastfeeding behavior develops in a predictable way during the first hours of life; the pre-feeding sequence of behaviors include the following:
  - Licking movements precede and follow the rooting reflex in alert infants.
  - The tongue is placed on the floor of the mouth during this distinct rooting.
  - "Mouth and lip smacking movements begin, and the infant begins to drool. The baby then begins to move forward slowly, starts to turn the head from side to side, and open the mouth widely upon nearing the nipple. After several attempts, the lips latch on to the areola and not the nipple" (Kennell and Klaus, 1998, p. 6).
- A healthy infant should be given the opportunity to show hunger and optimal reflexes and attach to the areola by himself or herself (Lawrence and Lawrence, 1999).
- Forcing the infant to the breast is counterproductive; forcing the infant to the breast might disturb the rooting reflex and alter the tongue position as the infant reflexively raises his or her tongue to protect the airway.
- Birth plans and hospital protocols should include the following:
  - Provide labor support.
  - Support in labor has been shown to have positive effects on birth, bonding, and breastfeeding success (Langer et al., 1998; Kennell et al., 1991).
  - Family/primary support person, usually the baby's father.
- Doula.
  - Powerful force intrapartum; mother receives one-to-one support from the doula throughout labor.
  - Medical care cost reduction: a reduced need for medical interventions including pitocin, epidural anesthesia, and cesarean sections (Gordon et al., 1999; Klaus, Kennell, and Klaus, 1993; and Perez, 1998).
  - Shortened labors (averaging slightly less than six hours for the first-time mother).
  - The level of support has the greatest influence on successful labor and breastfeeding outcomes (Klaus, Kennell, and Klaus, 1993).
  - Postpartum doulas facilitate breastfeeding.
- Limit the use of labor interventions.
  - Artificial Rupture of Membranes (AROM).
  - Induction and augmentation (pitocin/prostaglandins).

- Analgesics; mothers who have been medicated during labor are more likely to leave the hospital without having established breastfeeding.
  - Narcotics, barbiturates can sedate the baby
  - Epidural analgesia; epidurals increase the risk of intrapartum maternal fever, leading to separation, septic workup for the baby, and the use of antibiotics; epidural babies have an increased risk of seizures; epidural mothers spend less time with their baby during the hospital stay; medications can depress the effectiveness of early suckling and interfere with state and motor control
  - Numerous analgesics might disturb and delay important newborn behaviors such as breast-seeking, latch-on, and suckling. Analgesics can depress developing breastfeeding behaviors such as stimulation of the mother's breast
- Excessive IV fluids; large amounts of IV fluids (especially with the addition of pitocin) increase the risk of maternal fluid retention, an edematous areola, and an inflated infant birth weight; diuresis of the excess fluid by the infant might be misconstrued as abnormal weight loss.
- Routine episiotomy; can be extremely painful for 7–10 days or more, making it difficult to become comfortable.
- Limit the use of instrument-assisted delivery by facilitating more natural birthing positions.
  - Vacuum extraction; increases the risk for intracranial hemorrhage and subgaleal hematoma, which are serious and can be fatal
  - Forceps
- Delay, minimize, or eliminate postpartum procedures that interfere with first contact; stress on the neonate from procedures can result in sensory overload and cause the baby to temporarily shut down in order to reorganize his or her nervous system.
- Keep the mother and infant together after birth; separation of the mother and the infant after birth has been shown to interfere with breastfeeding and bonding.
- The baby should be allowed to self attach.
- Provide for STS contact (Kangaroo Care) with the mother immediately after birth and for the first few hours after birth.
  - Skin-to-skin contact has been shown to help the infant regulate his body temperature, breathing, and heart rate faster than radiant warmers and incubators.
  - Babies might be genetically encoded against separation from their mothers (Christensson, 1995).
  - Babies who are separated from their mothers display "Separation Distress Calls" (Michelsson, 1996).
  - Crying occurs in pulses with separation from the mother and stops upon reunion.
  - "The most appropiate position for the healthy full-term newborn is in close body contact with the mother" (Christensson, 1995).

- If contact with the mother is not possible because of cesarean delivery or maternal condition, then STS contact with the father should be provided.
- STS has also been shown to assist pre-term infants (34–36 weeks gestation) with recovering from birth-related fatigue (Ludington-Hoe, 1999).

- Minimize suctioning.
  - Bulb and DeLee mucus suctioning of the mouth and/or nares might cause physical injury and/or cause nasal edema and stuffiness, making latch on and breathing difficult.
  - Routine suctioning of gastric contents.
    - Can result in electrolyte imbalances
    - Can result in injury to the oropharynx
    - Can cause retching
    - Can cause physiological changes, such as increased blood pressure and changes in heart rate
    - Disrupts prefeeding behavior, or cueing (Widstrom)
    - In the situations where intubation, visualization, and deep suctioning of the trachea and bronchial tree below the vocal cords are required due to possible meconium aspiration, suctioning should be done as gently as possible
    - Might affect the baby's desire to latch on for several days due to pain/injury to the oropharynx; might demonstrate oral defensiveness

- Bathing should be delayed until after the initial bonding period.
  - The vernix should be allowed to soak into the skin to lubricate and protect it.
  - Dry the infant except for the hands and forearms; leave some amniotic fluids on the hands and forearms; transferred amniotic fluid to the breast when the baby is placed skin to skin on the mother's chest might be beneficial for latching on.
  - Delay bathing to prevent the loss of amniotic fluid odors and thermal losses.

- Delay giving eye treatments, which can cause blepharospasm (will prevent the infant from opening the eyes); the mother has a high emotional need for eye-to-eye contact with the infant immediately after birth.

- Delay vitamin K injection until after first contact.

- Delay painful procedures such as circumcision until the baby has had several good feedings.

## Clinical Practice Implications

- First contact should occur as soon as possible after birth, usually within the first hour (American Academy of Pediatrics (AAP)).

- Mother and baby are in a heightened state of readiness (Riordan and Auerbach, p. 283).

- Quiet alert state might last up to two hours after birth; following this quiet alert period, the baby might be sleepy and not willing to nurse for as long as 24 hours (Riordan and Auerbach, 1998).

- First contact can last as long as 120 minutes.

- The baby might only lick or nuzzle the breast.

- The mother might need reassurance if she is concerned because the infant does not nurse as vigorously as expected.

- First contact has physiological effects:
  - Mother
    - Hormonal.
    - Maternal estrogen, progesterone, oxytocin, and prolactin are believed to be responsible for many mothering behaviors.
    - "Sensitive periods in biologic phenomena are times when events can alter later behaviors" (Lawrence and Lawrence, 1999, p. 201). For the human female, the first few hours after delivery is the sensitive period for bonding.
    - Oxytocin.
      - Induces uterine contractions.
      - Helps expel placenta.
      - Prevents excessive bleeding.
      - Oxytocin levels are significantly elevated at 15, 30, and 45 minutes post birth.
      - Oxytocin, known as the "cuddle hormone" (Lauwers and Shinskie, 2000, p. 4), has been associated with maternal bonding; thus, it is appropriate to optimize mother-infant interaction at this highest point of oxytocin by facilitating infant suckling (Lawrence and Lawrence, 1999, p. 249; Kennell and Klaus, 1991, p. 8).
      - Helps mold maternal behavior; oxytocin not only participates in a reflex arc to the target myoepithelial cells in the breast but also disperses into a closed system within the brain, bathing the area that is responsible for social preferences and affiliative behavior.
      - Oxytocin deficiency has been reported with epidural block.
      - Opiates can inhibit the sucking-induced oxytocin release.
      - Morphine administration can significantly reduce the oxytocin response to suckling.
      - Stimulates the release of gastrointestinal (GI) hormones such as insulin, cholecystokinin, somatostatin, and gastrin.
      - Causes the mother to feel relaxed or sedated and calmer.

- Increases skin temperature (flushing).
- Thirst.

✿ Prolactin.
  - The amount is proportional to the amount of nipple stimulation; prolactin is released in pulses directly related to nipple stimulation.
  - Often called "the milk-making hormone."
  - Often called the "mothering hormone," it stimulates a feeling of yearning for her baby (Lauwers and Shinskie, 2000) and a calming, relaxing, even euphoric effect (Riordan and Auerbach, 1998) during the feeding.

  ✿ Release can be inhibited by ergot preparations that are commonly used to control postpartum bleeding.

- Other hormones: gastrointestinal (19 hormones released by vagal signals alter gut hormones in mother and infant, coordinating their metabolisms)(Kennell and Klaus, 1998).

– Baby
  - Oxytocin contained in the mother's milk is destroyed in the baby's stomach.
  - Oxytocin found in neonatal serum is produced by the baby; whether oxytocin has a physiological effect on the neonatal gut or other systems is unknown (Lawrence and Lawrence, 1999).
  - Prolactin.
    - Present in milk; might be soothing/calming to the baby.
    - Biologically potent and absorbed by the infant; effects intestinal fluid and electrolyte absorption; sodium potassium and calcium in the newborn. (Riordan and Auerbach, 1998, and Lawrence and Lawrence, 1999)

– Early mother and infant contact helps the baby adapt to a new unsterile environment by colonizing skin, respiratory, and gastrointestinal tracts with the mother's microorganisms and immunities, such as sIgA.

– The mother's normal body flora, which tends to be nonpathogenic, will colonize her baby's body—but only if she is the first person to hold him, rather than a nurse, physician, or others (Lauwers and Shinskie, 2000).

– Swallowing causes digestive peristalsis and early passing of the bilirubin-laden meconium stool, reducing neonatal jaundice.

– Meconium is the first medium for lactobacillus bifidus, which is introduced through colostrum.

– Early mother-infant contact has emotional effects:
  - Mother: boosts mothering confidence
  - Baby: calms, relaxes, and stops crying

## Planning and Implementation

- For the first feeding immediately after birth, an atmosphere of tranquility must exist in the room.
- The role of the LC and medical providers is one of observant noninterference.
- Assist the mother into a comfortable position.
- Dry the infant except for his or her hands and forearms; the infant only needs to be clothed in a diaper.
- Place the baby near the breast or between the breasts on the mother's bare chest and cover both with a light blanket.
- Maternal and neonatal vital signs can be monitored with minimal interruption.
- Physiological concerns immediately postpartum:
  - Mother
    - Comfort: pain
    - Medications (narcotics/sedatives)
    - Epidurals
    - IV lines
    - Bleeding
    - Shaking/chills: Cover the mother and baby with a warm blanket, and place the radiant warmer over the mother and baby
    - Fatigue
  - Infant
    - Breathing
    - Circulation
    - Temperature regulation
    - Best accomplished by STS contact with the mother
    - Prevent thermal stress on the infant by turning off any air conditioning
    - Chilling an infant sets off a cascade of events, from hypothermia to hypoglycemia to tachypnea to mild acidosis to the extent of requiring a septic workup
  - Hypothermia is therefore more easily prevented than treated
- Recognize the emotional needs of the family unit; provide time for the mother and father to be alone for getting acquainted with their newborn.
  - Hidden cameras in research studies have revealed that some intimate attachment behaviors only occur in complete privacy, including kissing, licking, and tasting the infant.
  - Keep in mind that bonding comprises the attachment of both the mother and the father to their infant.

- Fathers find touching and talking to their newborn babies pleasing and necessary for forming close emotional ties.
- Allow the baby to take the lead in first contact; it is unnecessary to force the baby to the breast.
- Mother and infant can remain in skin-to-skin contact until they are both ready to nurse.
- When the baby begins to show an interest in latching on:
  - The baby will assume whatever position is natural to him or her.
  - Provide for the infant's safety.
  - Provide positional stability as needed.
  - The mother should be encouraged to use the most natural and comfortable position for her.
  - Give instructions/demonstrations of hand placement and/or positioning only when requested.
  - Use positive reinforcement and praise the mother's mothering abilities.
  - Avoid "take over" behaviors.

# References

Akre J, ed. Infant feeding: The physiological basis. World Health Organization, Geneva: 1989.

American Academy of Pediatrics. Breastfeeding and the use of human milk. Policy Statement RE9729 *Pediatrics* (1997) 100[6]:1035–1039. Reprint retrieved 5/1/98 from http://www.aap.org/policy/re9729.html.

Christensson K, Cabrera T, Christensson E, Uvnas-Moberg K, Winburg J. Separation distress call in the human neonate in the absence of maternal body contact. *Acta Paediatr* 1995; 84(5): 468–473.

Crowell M, Hill P, Humenick S. Relationship between obstetrical analgesia and time to effective breastfeeding. *J Nurs Midwifery* 1994; 30:150–155.

DiGirolamo AM, Grummer-Strawn LM, Fein S. Maternity care practices: implications for breastfeeding. Birth 2001; 28:94–100.

FDA Public Health Warning: Need for caution when using vacuum assisted delivery devices. May 21, 1998.

Gordon NP, Walton D, McAdam E, Derman J, Gallitero G, Garrett L. Effects of providing hospital-based doulas in health maintenance organization hospitals. *Obestetr Gynecol* 1999; 93(3):422–6.

Kennell J, Klaus M, McGrath S, Robertson S. Continuous emotional support during labor in a U.S. hospital. A randomized controlled trial. *JAMA* 1991; 256(17):2197–201.

Kennell JH, Klaus MH. Bonding: recent observations that alter perinatal care. *Pediatrics in Review* 1998; 19(1):4–12.

Klaus M, Kennell J, Klaus P. Mothering the mother. New York: Addison-Wesley, 1993.

Langer A, Compero L, Garcia C, Reynoso S. Effects of psychosocial support during labor and childbirth on breastfeeding, medical interventions, and mothers' well-being in a Mexican public hospital: A randomized clinical trial. *Br J Obstet Gynaecol* 1998; 105(10): 1056–63.

Lauwers J, Shinskie D. Counseling the nursing mother: A lactation consultant's guide, 3rd ed. Sudbury, MA: Jones and Bartlett Publishers, 2000.

Lawrence RA, Lawrence RM. Breastfeeding: A guide for the medical profession, 5th ed. New York: C.V. Mosby, 1999.

Lieberman E, Eichenwald E, Mathur G, et al. Intrapartum fever and unexplained seizures in term infants. *Pediatrics* 2000; 106:983–988.

Lieberman E, Lang JM, Frigoletto Jr F, et al. Epidural analgesia, intrapartum fever, and neonatal sepsis evaluation. *Pediatrics* 1997; 99:415–419.

Lindow SW, Hendricks MS, Nugent FA, et al. Morphine suppresses the oxytocin response in breastfeeding women. *Gynecol Obstet Invest* 1999; 48:33–37.

Ludington-Hoe SM, Anderson GC, Simpson S, et al. Birth-related fatigue in 34-36 week preterm neonates: rapid recovery with very early Kangaroo (Skin-to-Skin) Care. *J Obstet Gynecol Neonatal Nurs* 1999; 28(1): 94–103.

Matthews MK. The relationship between maternal labor analgesia and delay in the initiation of breastfeeding in healthy neonates in the early neonatal period. Midwifery 1989; 5:3–10.

Michelsson K, Christensesson K, Rothganger H, Winberg J. Crying in separated and nonseparated newborns: sound spectrographic analysis. *Acta Paediatr* 1996; 85(4): 471–475.

Nelson E, Panksepp J. Brain substrates of infant-mother attachment: contributions of opoids, oxytocin, and norepinephrine. *Neurosci Biobehav Rev* 1998; 22:437–452.

Newman J, Pitman T. Dr. Jack Newman's Guide to Breastfeeding. Toronto: Harper Collins, 2000.

Nissen E, Lilja G, Widstrom A-M, Uvnas-Moberg K. Elevation of oxytocin levels early postpartum in women. *Acta Obstet Gynecol Scand* 1995; 74:530–533.

Perez PG. Labor support to promote vaginal delivery. Baby Care Forum. Spring 1998: 1, 3.

Powers G, Slusser W. Breastfeeding update 2: Clinical lactation management. *Pediatrics in Review* 1997; 18(5): 147–161.

Ransjo-Arvidson A–B, Matthiesen A–S, Lilja G, et al. Maternal analgesia during labor disturbs newborn behavior: effects on breastfeeding, temperature and crying. Birth 2001; 28:5–12.

Righard L, Alade MO. Effect of delivery room routines on success of first breastfeed. *Lancet* 1990; 336(8723):1105–1107.

Righard L, et al. Breastfeeding patterns: comparing the effects on infant behavior and maternal satisfaction of using one or two breasts. *Birth* 1993; 20:182–185.

Righard L. How do newborns find their mother's breast? *Birth* 1995; 22:174–175.

Riordan J, Auerbach KG, eds. Breastfeeding and Human Lactation, 2nd ed. Sudbury, MA: Jones and Bartlett Publishers, 1998.

Riordan J, Riordan S. The effect of labor epidurals on breastfeeding. *Lactation Consultant Series* Two, Unit 4. Schaumburg, IL: La Leche League International, 2000.

Sepkowski C, Lester BM, Ostheimer GW, Brazelton TB. Neonatal effects of maternal epidurals. *Dev Med Child Neurol* 1994; 36:375–376.

Stainton MC, Edwards S, Jones B, Switonski C. The nature of maternal postnatal pain. *J Perinatal Educ* 1999; 8:1–10.

Steinbach MT. Traumatic birth injury-intracranial hemorrhage. *Mother Baby J* 1999; 4:5–14.

Thureen P, Deacon J, O'Niell P, Hernandez J, eds. Assessment and care of the well newborn. Philadelphia: W. B. Saunders, 1999.

Varendi H, Christensson K, Winberg J, Porter RH. Soothing effect of amniotic fluid smell in newborn infants. *Early Human Development* 1998; 51(1):47–55.

Walker M. Do labor medications affect breastfeeding? *J Hum Lact* 1997; 13:131–137.

Widstrom AM, Ransjo-Arvidson AB, Christensson K, et al. Gastric suction in healthy newborn infants. Effects on circulation and developing feeding behaviour. *Acta Paediatr Scand* 1987: 76(4): 566–572.

# Artificial Baby Milks (Infant Formula)

*Marsha Walker, RN, IBCLC*

## Objectives:

- Compare the components of breast milk and *artificial baby milk* (ABM).
- Describe the differences in growth and development between breastfed and artificially fed infants.
- Identify the effect of artificial feeding on the brain, immune system, and acute and chronic diseases in an ABM-fed baby.
- Explain some of the hazards of ABM.
- Evaluate the criteria for the complementary feeding of infants.

## Introduction

Many health care providers as well as the general public believe that the feeding of artificial baby milk (ABM) by bottle is equivalent to breastfeeding. Human milk is species-specific and has evolved throughout the millennia to facilitate the optimal growth and development of human infants. Breast milk is extremely complex, and its composition is most likely programmed by chemical communication between the mother and the infant, both pre- and postnatally. Formula does not duplicate the complexity, cannot provide the multiple tiers of disease protection, and cannot operate in the dynamic manner of human milk. Artificial baby milk simply fulfills the role of maintaining growth and development within normal limits.

## Components of Artificial Baby Milk

### General Concepts

1. Human milk is used as a general guide for nutrient content in ABM.
2. While ABM contains similar categories of nutrients as in breast milk, such as protein, fat, carbohydrates, vitamins, and minerals, it does not duplicate them.

3. ABM is an inert medium that has no bioactive components.

   a. ABM does not alter its composition to meet the changing needs of a growing infant.

   b. Unlike breast milk, ABM does not contain growth factors, hormones, live cells, immunologic agents, or enzymes.

4. The fatty acid profile of ABM does not resemble breast milk.

5. In general, the concentrations of nutrients in ABM are higher than those in human milk to compensate for their reduced bioavailability.

6. Commercial ABMs have many similarities to each other but can differ significantly from each other in the quality and quantity of nutrients.

7. There are a number of bodies worldwide that either oversee or make recommendations for the nutrient content of ABM.

   a. The *American Academy of Pediatrics, Committee on Nutrition* (AAP-CON)

   b. The *European Society of Paediatric Gastroenterology and Nutrition* (ESPGAN)

   c. The *Food and Agriculture Organization* (FAO), a part of the *United Nations* (UN)

   d. Codex Alimentarius

   e. *European Communities* (EC)

   f. The United States *Food and Drug Administration* (FDA)

8. There are numerous types of artificial baby milks:

   a. standard cow's milk based

   b. cow's milk based without lactose

   c. soy

   d. follow-on

   e. protein hydrolysate-based (hypoallergenic)

   f. preterm

   g. special formulations for metabolic problems

   h. amino acid based

   i. with added soy fiber (for diarrhea)

   j. with added rice solids (for reflux)

   k. follow-on preterm

9. ABM is available in three forms: ready-to-feed, concentrated liquid, and powder.

   a. The composition of ABM within each of these forms can differ, even among those from the same manufacturer.

   b. The composition of ABM differs between manufacturers and varies from country to country, depending on the legal requirements for content.

10. ABM products frequently change composition, receive new labels, change scoop sizes in the powdered variety, are discontinued, or experience changes in their recommended usage.

11. ABM has an expiration date after which it should be discarded.

12. ABM labels state the minimum amount of ingredients that are supposed to be present at any one time.

13. Overages (additional amounts) of some components are added to compensate for their degredation over the shelf life of the product.

14. ABM is frequently recalled or withdrawn from the market due to health and safety issues (see Table 8-1).

**Table 8-1**   Recalls of Infant Feeding Products

| Recall Class | Date | Product | Problem |
|---|---|---|---|
| III<br>Firm-initiated recall | 2000 | *Repackaged infant formula:* Isomil powder and concentrate, Similac with iron, low iron powder and concentrate, Neosure powder, Enfamil low iron and with iron powder, Enfamil Lacto-free powder, Prosobee soy powder, Nutramigen powder 2000–3000 cases | The infant formulas were repackaged in cardboard trays/boxes, which were misbranded. All lots of cardboard cases and trays were repackaged, labeled, and distributed by Unity Wholesale Grocery since April 25, 2000. |
| III | 2000 | Carnation Good Start, Alsoy, and Follow-up in 13-oz concentrate cans (2.5 million cans) (Nestle) | Processing may not have reached high enough temperatures to ensure sterility. |
| II | 1999 | Isomil ready-to-feed soy formula in 32-oz metal cans, 17,821 cases (106,926 cans) (Ross Laboratories) | Product was held in cans with a low level of can lid defects allowing for post-processing contamination. |

*(continues)*

**Table 8-1**    Recalls of Infant Feeding Products (continued)

| Recall Class | Date | Product | Problem |
|---|---|---|---|
| Manufacturer's voluntary recall | 1999 | ProSobee soy formula; 8-oz, ready-to-use cans sold in 4-pack cartons, 7000 cases (Mead Johnson) | Cans in batch mislabeled ProSobee when they actually contained vanilla Sustacal, an adult nutrition supplement. |
| | | | Consuming Sustacal has the potential to cause severe medical problems in infants, especially if they are ill, highly sensitive to milk proteins, or have galactosemia. Because it has a higher caloric density and renal solute load as compared to ProSobee, Sustacal also has the potential to cause dehydration in healthy infants. |
| I | 1999 | Heinz 3 Broccoli, Carrots and Cheese Junior Baby Food, 6-oz glass jars, 5,269 cases (24 jars/case) (Heinz USA) | Product contaminated with pieces of hard plastic. |
| III | 1999 | Carnation Follow-Up formula, 32-oz cans, 12,651 cases (6 cans/case) (Nestle USA) | Product has a lumpy, curdled appearance. |
| II | 1998 | Beginner strained carrots 25,760 cases of 2.5-oz jars (Heinz) | Product contains elevated levels of lead. |
| Manufacturer's voluntary recall | 1998 | Beginner strained carrots, Vegetable chicken dinner, 300,000 jars (Heinz) | 20-22µg/oz of lead/4 oz jar (usual intake is 4.1µg of lead/day from food). |
| II | 1997 | Gerber carrots for babies: 1st, 2nd, 3rd foods, 2,141,880 jars (Gerber) | Product contains high levels of arsenic. |
| III | 1997 | Isomil Soy Formula, 104 cases, 6 cans per case (Ross) | Did not contain the labeled amount of inositol. Product was originally formulated for distribution in the UK which did not require the addition of inositol. |

| Recall Class | Date | Product | Problem |
|---|---|---|---|
| II | 1997 | Carnation Follow-Up formula, 32-oz cans, 11,317 cases (6 cans/case) (Nestle) | Adulterated-produced under unsanitary conditions; linked with mild gastrointestinal illness; product is separated. |
| II | 1996 | Heinz Apple-Prune juice for infants, 4-oz bottles | Product contains lead in excess of 80 ppb. |
| Market Withdrawal | 1996 | Carnation Alsoy Concentrate liquid, 13-oz cans Carnation Nutritionals (Nestle) | Can top says "Do not add water." Mislabeling could lead to infants consuming undiluted, concentrated formula (side label states to add water). |
| III | 1996 | Balsam Springs Baby Water with fluoride in gallon containers (Veryfine Products) | Unfit for food due to seal microleakage and contamination with extraneous material. |
| III | 1996 | Gerber Graduates apple juice for toddlers, 46-oz clear, plastic bottles (Gerber) | Unfit for food due to vinegary and sour taste. |
| III | 1995 | Oral water nursette, 3-oz glass bottles (Bristol-Meyers Squibb) | Product is contaminated with chlorine. |
| II | 1994 | Carnation Good Start, concentrated liquid, 13-oz cans, 16,878 cases Carnation Nutritionals (Nestle) | Some cans contained non-pathogenic spoilage organisms indicating product could be contaminated with other microorganisms. |
| III | 1993 | Infant's Choice Water, calcium and fluoride added, sodium-free, in one gallon plastic jugs, 24,000 gallons, Magnetic Springs Water Co., Columbus, Ohio | Product is mislabeled. |
| I | 1993 | Soylac Powder infant formula, 14-oz cans, distributed in US and Canada (Nutricia, Inc) | Product is contaminated with *Salmonella*. |
| I | 1993 | Promil, supplemental food for infants and children, distributed in Thailand, spray dried at Maple Island, Inc.'s facility (Wyeth-Ayerst) | Manufactured under conditions in which it may have become contaminated with *Salmonella*. |

*(continues)*

**Table 8-1**   Recalls of Infant Feeding Products (continued)

| Recall Class | Date | Product | Problem |
|---|---|---|---|
| I | 1993 | Formance, fortified nutritional powder for use by pregnant and lactating women, 850g cans, spray dried at Maple Island, Inc.'s facility, distributed in Hong Kong (Ross Labs) | Manufactured under conditions under which it may have become contaminated with *Salmonella*. |
| II | 1993 | Nutramigen, 20 cal/oz, 3-oz glass nursettes, 102,048 bottles (Mead Johnson Nutritionals) | Product contaminated with glass particles. |
| II | 1993 | Gerber 2nd Foods brand oatmeal with applesauce and bananas, 4-oz jars, 25,590 cases (Gerber products) | Product contained glass particles. |
| III | 1993 | Isomil Soy Formula with iron, concentrated liquid, 13-oz cans (Ross Labs) | Product is in cans with peeling can liners. |
| II | 1993 | Nursoy Soy Protein, iron fortified concentrate, 13-oz cans, 10,250 cases (Wyeth-Ayerst) | Some contaminated with *Klebsiella pneumoniae* and *Pseudomonas aeruginosa*: hazard to infant health in form of gastrointestinal stress to infants and newborns. |
| I | 1990 | I-Soyalac Concentrated Infant Formula, 13-oz cans (Loma Linda Foods) | Product contaminated with heat-sensitive and heat-resistant bacteria. |
| III | 1989 | Similac PM 60/40 powder, 16-oz metal cans, low iron infant formula (Ross Labs) | Product deficient in vitamin D, below label claims for vitamin K. |
| III | 1989 | Carnation Good Nature Infant Formula, 32-oz containers, for babies over six months of age | Unfit for food because of physical appearance and will not pass through an ordinary bottle nipple. |
| III | 1989 | Nutramigen Iron Fortified Protein Hydrolysate Formula, 4- & 8-oz bottles (Mead Johnson) | Deficient in vitamin D. |
| III | 1986 | Soyalac Powder, 1.2-oz foil pouches as physician samples | Progressive vitamin A degredation. |

| Recall Class | Date | Product | Problem |
|---|---|---|---|
| II | 1986 | SMA Ready to Feed 32-oz cans (Wyeth Labs) | Curdling, discoloration, off odor. |
| II | 1985 | Gerber Meat Base Formula with iron, 15-oz cans of concentrated formula | Superpotent levels of vitamin A and subpotent levels of vitamin D. |
| I | 1985 | Kama-Mil Powder, 14- & 16-oz cans (Kama Nutritional Products) | Marked in violation of Infant Formula Act, deficient in folacin, vitamin D, and zinc. |
| I | 1985 | Nutra-Milk Powder infant formula, 8-, 10-, & 16-oz bottles | -as above- |
| I | 1985 | Kama-Mil Powder infant formula in 14-oz fiberboard cans, 14- & 16-oz | -as above- |
| I | | Pamphlet labeled in part "Edensoy" promotional material for Edensoy Soy Drinks (Eden Foods, Inc.) | Pamphlet erroneously suggests that Edensoy may be used as a substitute for mother's milk or for infant formula. |
| II | 1985 | Cow & Gate Improved Modified Infant Formula, 450g & 1kg cans, US Virgin Islands | Deficient in copper & linoleic acid, not in compliance with section 412 of Food, Drug and Cosmetic Act. |
| III | 1985 | Lactogen Brand Infant Milk Formula in powder form with iron, 450g, 227g, & 1135g cans (Cow & Gate) | -as above- |
| II | 1985 | 5% glucose water in 4-oz bottles (Ross Labs) | Glass particles in product due to bottle necks chipping. |
| III | 1984 | Similac with iron concentrate, 13-oz cans (Ross Labs) | Overprocessed, resulting in its becoming lumpy, brown, and unfit for food consumption. |
| II | 1983 | Soyalac Powder Milk-Free fortified soy formula, 16-oz cans (Loma Linda Foods) | Deficient in vitamin A. |

*(continues)*

**Table 8-1**    Recalls of Infant Feeding Products (continued)

| Recall Class | Date | Product | Problem |
|---|---|---|---|
| II | 1983 | Naturlac Infant Formula Powder, 22; 3/4-oz cans and trial size 32g packets (Fillmore Foods) | Copper levels below minimum required by Infant Formula Act, thiamine and vitamin B6 below label declaration. |
| I | 1982 | Nursoy Concentrated Liquid 13-oz cans, Nursoy Ready to Feed 32-oz cans (Wyeth Labs) | Deficient in vitamin B6. |
| I | 1982 | SMA Iron Fortified Concentrated Liquid 13-oz cans, SMA Iron Fortified Ready to Feed 32-oz cans, SMA Powder 16-oz cans, SMA E-Z Nurser Ready to Feed Nursettes (Wyeth Labs) | Deficient in vitamin B6; it contains less than stated on the label |

Source: FDA Enforcement Report, HFI-20, 5600 Fishers Lane, Rockville, MD 20857

Class I Recall: A product whose use will cause serious health consequences or death

Class II Recall: A product whose use may cause medically reversible health consequences

Class III Recall: A product whose use is not likely to cause adverse health consequences

© 2000 Marsha Walker, RN, IBCLC

## Selected Differences in Macronutrients

### Protein

1. ABM can have up to 50 percent more protein than human milk.

2. The whey-to-casein ratio of human milk changes over time from 90:10 in the early milk to 60:40 in mature milk and 50:50 in late lactation.

3. In ABM, cow's milk protein remains static—and depending on the brand, the levels could be 18:82, 60:40, or 100 percent whey.

4. Bovine casein is less-easily digested and forms a tough, rubbery curd in the infant's stomach, partially accounting for the slower gastric emptying time in ABM-fed babies.

5. There are compositional and functional differences between the casein and whey proteins in human milk and ABM. In ABM:

    a. Bovine alpha-lactalbumin is not well digested.

    b. There is no lactoferrin (an iron-binding protein).

    c. There are no immunoglobulins, such as secretory IgA (defense agents).

       i. ABM-fed babies can show lower or absent antibody levels to their immunizations (Zoppi, et al., 1983).

    d. There are no enzymes (digestive or defensive).

    e. There are few of the nonprotein nitrogen components found in breast milk.

       i. Random additions of a few nonhuman nucleotides have not been shown to decrease morbidity in ABM-fed infants.

6. Cow's-milk ABM uses processing procedures that exclude colostrum, milk fat globule membranes, and fractions that contain DNA from the final product—components that provide disease protection that is species-specific to the calf.

## Lipids (Fat)

1. Lipids provide 40 to 50 percent of the energy in cow's milk ABM.

2. During processing, cow's milk fat (butterfat) is removed and replaced with vegetable oils or a mixture of vegetable and animal fats for better digestibility and absorption.

3. These fats include coconut oil, palm oil, soy oil, corn oil, safflower oil, palm olein, high oleic safflower oil, high oleic sunflower oil, oleo (destearinated beef fat), and *medium-chain triglycerides* (MCT) oil.

4. The fatty acid profile differs significantly among various brands of ABM as well as between ABM and human milk.

5. ABM fats do not contain *docosahexaenoic* (DHA) and *arachidonic* (AA) acids, the *long-chain polyunsaturated fatty acids* (LCPUFA) found in human milk that are thought to be necessary for normal brain growth and development.

    a. Additions of these LCPUFA to some ABM brands does not replicate the complex human milk fatty acid pattern.

    b. Sources of these additives include fish heads, tuna eyeballs, egg yolks, evening primrose oil, micro algae, and fungal sources and must be provided in the correct ratio to avoid growth problems.

    c. Some infants who are fed ABM enriched with various combinations of these LCPUFA do not grow as well as with standard ABM or breast milk (Carlson, et al., 1991).

6. The brain composition of ABM-fed babies is measurably and chemically different than the brain of a breastfed baby, with DHA levels in ABM-fed term babies remaining static, decreasing in preterm infants, and increasing in breastfed babies (Cunnane, et al., 2000).

7. ABM contains little to no cholesterol. Cholesterol is present in human milk and increases during the course of lactation. Cholesterol is an essential part of all membranes and is involved with the laying down of the myelin sheath, which facilitates nerve conduction in the brain.

## Carbohydrates

1. Lactose is the principle sugar in human milk and in most other mammals' milk.

2. Human milk lactose:
   a. Favors the colonization of the infant's intestine with microflora that compete with and exclude pathogens
   b. Insures a supply of galactocerebrosides that are major components of brain growth
   c. Enhances calcium absorption

3. The use of cow's milk-based ABM with the lactose removed, all soy preparations, and some of the hydrolyzed ABM brands that have no lactose has an unknown effect on both brain development and disease outcomes in ABM-fed babies.

4. There are approximately 130 oligosaccharides (nonlactose carbohydrates) in human milk—10 times the amount found in cow's milk.

5. Human oligosaccharides inhibit pathogens from binding to their receptor sites in the gut and on mucous membranes.

6. Human oligosaccharides contain human blood group antigens, with women from different blood groups having distinct patterns contributing to the tailor-made disease protection within each mother-baby unit.

7. Oligosaccharides in the milk of other species confer protection to the young of that species. Random additions of a few nonhuman oligosaccharides into some brands of ABM would not be expected to generate a tier of disease protection, however, because oligosaccharides in breast milk are unique to human milk and have not been replicated synthetically.

## Vitamins and Minerals

1. ABM is fortified with water- and fat-soluble vitamins.

2. There are upper and lower limits for most of these.

3. Most brands of ABM contain far higher amounts of vitamins than human milk in order to offset their reduced absorption.

4. Excesses, deficiencies, and omissions of ingredients can and do occur in the manufacturing process.

5. Approximately 50 percent of the iron in human milk is absorbed compared to 7 percent from iron-fortified ABM and 4 percent from iron-fortified cereals.

## Defense Agents

1. ABM contains no defense agents for human babies to protect them from acute and chronic disease.

2. Some brands of ABM contain added nonhuman nucleotides or oligosaccharides, enabling the claim of enhanced immune response. The clinical significance of this addition has not been demonstrated.

## Growth Outcomes of Breastfed and ABM-Fed Infants

1. Breastfed and ABM-fed babies grow differently (Dewey, 1998).

2. Until recently, most practitioners in the United States used growth charts based on reference data compiled in 1977 by the United States National Center for Health Statistics (NCHS), which was adopted for international use by the World Health Organization (WHO).

3. For children younger than 24 months of age, the NCHS charts were based on data collected from a single community between 1929 and 1977 as part of the Fels Longitudinal Study.

4. The limitations of this data include the following:
   a. A small sample limited to Caucasian infants from middle-class families
   b. Measurements taken every three months instead of monthly
   c. Most infants were bottle-fed with few breastfed for more than three months

5. When the growth of a breastfed baby is compared to the 1977 NCHS growth chart, the typical pattern is a relatively rapid weight gain in the first two to three months, followed by a downward trend in percentile ranking thereafter.

6. This pattern can cause a perception of growth faltering, even if the infant is healthy and thriving.

7. A misdiagnosis of inadequate weight gain can lead to inappropriate supplementation.

8. Breastfed infants are lower in weight-for-length by 12 months than would be expected when using the NCHS reference charts.

9. Breastfed infants are leaner than ABM-fed babies, with the difference in fatness most evident at 9–12 months.

10. The DARLING study demonstrated that after three months of age, growth velocity in breastfed infants changes.

11. This difference reflects the biological norm, with the difference in weight gain representing excessive gain by ABM-fed babies rather than a slow gain by breastfed infants.

12. By two years of age, breastfed babies' growth is similar to the 1977 NCHS reference.

13. The greater fatness of ABM-fed infants might persist well into childhood and beyond.

14. Revised growth charts have been issued by the Centers for Disease Control and Prevention (CDC)/the National Center for Health Statistics based on more representative U.S. national data.

15. These charts represent a mixed feeding population (breastfed and formula-fed, not an exclusively breastfed one).

16. The new charts will more frequently classify an infant as underweight.

17. WHO is creating a new international growth chart for the first two years of life based on data from breastfed infants from healthy populations as the biological norm.

18. Preliminary charts from WHO might be useful as references in situations of suspected growth faltering (WHO, 1994).

## Effects of Artificial Feeding on the Brain and Immune System

1. ABM-fed infants and children demonstrate less-advanced cognitive development compared with breastfed children (Anderson, et al., 1999).

2. Lower mental development and IQ scores are seen at all ages through adolescence in ABM-fed children.

3. Infants who are fed formula have significantly lower DHA in the gray and white matter of the cerebellum, the area of the brain that coordinates movement and balance.

4. A deficiency of 8 to 10 IQ points in ABM-fed subjects is reported in most studies.

5. Central to this discrepancy are particular fatty acids, DHA and AA, which are found in human milk but are absent in ABM.

6. DHA and AA are found in abundance as structural lipids in the brain, retina, and central nervous system of infants.

7. ABM contains precursors of DHA and AA, linolenic and linoleic acid, from which an infant's immature liver is supposed to synthesize enough of these LCPUFA to meet the needs of the rapidly developing brain.

8. IQ studies are remarkably consistent in their demonstration of higher IQs that are dose dependant relative to the number of months that a child has been exclusively breastfed.

9. Neural maturation of ABM-fed preterm infants shows a deficit compared to those who are fed human milk.

10. Delayed maturation in visual acuity can occur in both term and preterm ABM-fed infants (Birch, et al., 1993).

11. Delayed maturation in visual acuity might affect other mental and physical functions later in development that are linked to the quality of early visual processing.

12. An IQ increase of as little as three points (1/5 of a standard deviation) from 100 to 103 would move a person from the 50th to the 58th percentile of the population and would potentially be associated with higher educational achievement, occupational achievement, and social adjustment.

13. Defense agents are poorly represented in cow's milk (Jensen, 1995).

14. Bovine colostrum and its antimicrobial agents are specific for the cow and are removed from milk during processing.

15. Human milk not only provides passive protection, but also directly modulates the immunologic development of the recipient infant (Goldman, 1998).

16. ABM-fed infants and children have increased risks and rates of:
    a. Allergic disease (Chandra, 1997)
    b. Asthma (Oddy, et al., 1999)
    c. Crohn's disease
    d. Ulcerative colitis
    e. *Insulin-dependent diabetes mellitus* (IDDM); see Vaarala, et al., 1999
    f. Some lymphomas (Davis, 1998)
    g. *Necrotizing enterocolitis* (NEC)
    h. Diarrheal disease (Scariati, et al., www.pediatrics.org/cgi/content/full/99/6/e5)
    i. Otitis media (Scariati, et al.)
    j. Lower respiratory tract illness (bronchiolitis, croup, bronchitis, and pneumonia)
    k. Obesity (Von Kries, et al., 1999)
    l. *Sudden Infant Death Syndrome* (SIDS)
    m. Sepsis
    n. Urinary tract infections (Pisacane, et al., 1992)
    o. Acute leukemia (Shu, et al., 1999)

17. Humoral and cellular immune responses to specific antigens (such as vaccines) given during the first year of life appear to develop differently in breastfed and ABM-fed babies.

18. Infants who are fed cow's milk-based ABM frequently demonstrate lower antibody titres to their immunizations than breastfed babies.

19. Infants who are fed soy ABM have even lower antibody titres, with some showing no response at all to some of their vaccines.

20. Qualitative and quantitative immunologic differences between human milk and cow's milk are striking.

21. Goldman, Chheda, and Garafolo (1998, 155–162) compare the relative expression of certain major antimicrobial proteins in human and bovine milk:

|  | Human | Bovine |
| --- | --- | --- |
| Secretory IgA | ++++ | + |
| IgG | + | ++++ |
| Lactoferrin | ++++ | + |
| Lactoperoxidase | ± | ++++ |
| Lysozyme | ++++ | ± |
| Complement | + | ++++ |

# Hazards of Artificial Baby Milk

## Genetically Modified Ingredients

1. Genetically engineered corn and soy have been found in numerous brands of ABM.
2. Transgenic ingredients pose the risk of introducing novel toxins, new allergens, and increased antibiotic resistance in infants.
3. Labeling of genetically modified ingredients is not required, so parents are unaware of whether they are feeding their baby transgenic foods.
4. The long-term effects of these ingredients on ABM-fed infants is unknown.

## Soy-Based ABM

1. Twenty-five percent of all ABM sold in the United States is soy.
2. Soy ABM is used much less extensively outside the United States.
3. Soy ABM might be allergenic in infants who are allergic to cow's milk protein.
4. Many soy preparations contain sucrose, which is a contributor to dental caries in babies who are fed soy ABM by bottle.
5. Soy is not recommended for preterm infants who have birth weights lower than 1800g, for the prevention of colic or allergy, or with infants who have cow's milk protein-induced enterocolitis or enteropathy.

6. Infants who are fed soy ABM can have circulating phytoestrogen concentrations that are 13,000–22,000 times higher than normal levels in early life (Setchell, K. D. et al., 1997).

7. This dose represents a 6- to 11-fold higher level of intake of isoflavones than that found to cause significant modifications to the hormonal regulation of the menstrual cycle in western women.

8. The consumption of soy ABM was associated with an increased occurance of premature thelarche (breast development in girls younger than eight years of age) in Puerto Rico and specifically in many girls before they were 18 months of age (Fremi-Titulaer, et al., 1986).

9. It is unknown what other effects these bioactive compounds might produce by creating steroid hormone imbalances by competition with enzymes that metabolize steroids and drugs or by influencing gonadal function.

10. ABM, especially soy and some hydrolyzed ABM, contains 35–1,500 times the amount of aluminum as in breast milk.

11. Aluminum can accumulate in bones and in the brain, and the effect of large amounts in infancy is unknown.

12. A positive association has been found between feeding infants soy ABM and the development of autoimmune thyroid disease.

13. Soy ABM components can act against the thyroid by inhibition of thyroid peroxidase and can have the potential to disrupt thyroid function even in the presence of added iodine.

## Follow-on ABM

1. Follow-on ABM is marketed for infants who are four months of age and older who are also receiving cereal and other solid foods.

2. The most significant difference in this category of products is that they are lower in fat than both breast milk and standard starter ABM.

3. Regular ABM and breast milk contribute 45–50 percent of the energy from fat.

4. Follow-on ABM can contribute as little as 37 percent energy from fat.

5. Current pediatric nutrition recommendations advise against lowering the fat intake of infants and children under the age of two years (Kleinman, 1998).

6. There are few additional sources of fat in the first year of life, and this period includes rapid growth and development with high energy requirements.

## Neurotoxins and Altered Behavior Patterns

1. Toxic pollutants can affect the brain in different ways.

2. The manganese (Mn) concentration in breast milk is very low (4–8µg/L). Cow's milk ABM is 10 times higher in Mn concentration (30–60µg/L than breast milk, while soy ABM has about a 50–75 times higher concentration than breast milk).

3. Mn lowers the levels of serotonin and dopamine—brain neurotransmitters that are associated with planning and impulse control.

4. Low levels of brain serotonin are known to cause mood disturbances, poor impulse control, and increased aggressive behavior.

5. There is little regulation of Mn uptake at young ages, and ABM-fed infants—especially those who are fed soy ABM—will have a much larger body burden of Mn.

6. Children who are raised from birth on ABM will absorb five times as much Mn as breastfed infants.

7. Altered brain chemistry combined with social stresses increases the risk of violent behavior.

8. Ingredients that contain processed free glutamic acid (monosodium glutamate, or MSG) and free aspartic acid (known neurotoxins) are used in ABM.

9. These are found in high levels in some hypoallergenic ABM brands and are cause for concern due to the underdeveloped blood-brain barrier that enables neurotoxins to be more accessible to the brain.

10. Schizophrenic patients are less likely to have been breastfed.

11. Some infants who were fed a chloride-deficient brand of ABM in 1978–1979 showed cognitive delays, language disorders, visual motor and fine motor difficulties, and attention deficit disorders at ages 8–9 years (Kaleita, et al., 1991).

# Contaminants in ABM and Water Used for Reconstitution

1. Silicon contamination can be seen in ABM with levels ranging from 746–13,811ng/ml. Breast milk of women who do not have silicone implants contains approximately 51.05ng/ml of silicon, while those who have implants show 55.45ng/ml (Semple, et al., 1998).

2. Lead intoxication can occur when hot tap water or lead-containing water is boiled and is used to reconstitute concentrated or powdered ABM (Shannon, et al., 1992).

3. Boiling concentrates lead, arsenic, cadmium, and other contaminants in water.

4. Infants who are fed ABM that has been reconstituted with nitrate-contaminated water are at risk for potentially fatal methemoglobinemia. The baby's system converts nitrates to nitrites, resulting in hemoglobin being converted to methemoglobin that cannot bind molecular oxygen (Dusdieker, et al., 1994).

5. This risk increases if babies are younger than six months of age and are also fed baby food that has high concentrations of nitrates, such as green beans and bananas.

6. Atrazine is a weed killer found in the water supplies in agricultural areas. Atrazine is a carcinogen at high levels. ABM-fed infants can obtain a lifetime dose by age five. Most ready-to-feed ABM contains water that has atrazine filtered out of it before it is used for processing (Houlihan, et al., www.ewg.org).

## Container Hazards

1. Phthalates are used as plasticizers and are testicular toxins and estradiol imitators. All 15 brands of ABM tested in the United Kingdom contained phthalates.

2. Bisphenol-A is used in the production of polycarbonate plastics and has been found in plastic baby bottles. This chemical can leach from the container and has been known to be estrogenic since 1938 (Larkin, 1995).

3. Bisphenol-A resins are used as lacquers to coat metal products such as food cans. This chemical can leach into the contents of cans during autoclaving. Some of the tested cans were concentrated milk-based ABM.

4. Bottle-fed babies are at risk for scald and burn injuries from bottles heated on the stove or in a microwave oven.

5. Babies who are fed by bottle have increased rates of malocclusion (Labbok, 1990). Muscles involved with breastfeeding are either immobilized (masseter and obicularis oris), overactive (chin muscle), or malpositioned (the tongue is pushed backwards) during artificial feeding (Inoue, et al., 1995), contributing to abnormal dentofacial development in the child (Palmer, 1998).

6. Bottle feeding is positively correlated with finger sucking, which can deform the maxillary arch and palate.

7. ABM is acidogenic and might play a significant role in the development of early dental caries in infants (Sheikh, et al., 1996).

8. Baby bottles that are decorated with name-brand soft drink logos, noncarbonated beverage logos, and juice logos encourage parents to give infants the respective beverage from the bottle.

# Errors in ABM Preparation and Inappropriate Foods

1. Babies who are fed powdered ABM are at risk for hyperosmolar (overconcentrated) feedings. Reports have been noted of mothers losing the measuring scoop, using graduated markings on a bottle that was brought home from the hospital, adding extra ABM to help a small baby grow faster, and so on.

2. Babies are also at risk for underconcentrated feedings if mothers use less powdered ABM per bottle to make the supply last longer.

3. Oral water intoxication can result not only from overly dilute ABM, but also from supplemental feedings of solute-free tap water, juice, tea, soda, and bottled drinking water marketed for infants (Keating, et al., 1991).

4. Rapid ingestion of water over a short period of time can cause hyponatremic seizures and brain swelling.

5. Infants who ingest 260ml–540ml (9–19 oz) of solute-free water can become symptomatic over a relatively short period of time (90 minutes to 48 hours).

# Cardiorespiratory Disturbances

1. Both preterm and full-term infants who are fed by bottle are at an increased risk of cardiopulmonary disturbances, including prolonged airway closure and obstructed respiratory breaths due to repeated rapid swallowing.

2. Preterm infants have shown decreased oxygen saturations accompanied by apnea (an absent airflow for more than 20 seconds), bradycardia (a heart rate of fewer than 100 beats per minute), and cyanosis (blue coloring) during bottle feeding due to frequent swallowing and limited breathing time with high-flow nipples.

# Costs

1. The direct cost of ABM to families for one year in the United States ranges from $500–$1,200 or more. In Canada, this amount can be $150 greater per month or more. In some developing countries, the cost of ABM can exceed 100 percent of the yearly family income.

2. The U.S. government is the single largest purchaser of ABM in the world for the *Women, Infants, and Children* (WIC) supplemental food program.

# Exclusive versus Partial Breastfeeding

1. The absence of standard definitions for breastfeeding prevents precision and comparability in research, causing inaccuracies and confusion at both policy-making and clinical levels.

2. A schema for defining breastfeeding has been devised. By using and describing the terms *full*, *partial*, and *token*, the authors further subdivide these terms based on patterns of feedings (Labbock, et al., 1990).

3. These breastfeeding patterns might occur at any stage of the child's life and are not associated with age.

4. Precise definitions of breastfeeding in well-controlled research show that the protective effects of breast milk are afforded in a dose-response manner.

5. The less breast milk a baby receives, the higher the risk for disease and adverse cognitive development.

6. Even partial breastfeeding confers some measure of disease protection.

7. Exclusive breastfeeding is becoming an endangered practice.

8. Exclusive breastfeeding rates for infants who are younger than 4 months old range from 19 percent in Africa to 49 percent in Southeast Asia. In the United States, 46.2 percent of babies are breastfeeding exclusively in hospitals and 13.8 percent are breastfeeding at 6 months of age.

9. Healthy, full-term, normal breastfeeding infants do not need supplements of water, glucose water, ABM, and so on unless a medical indication exists.

10. Supplements displace breast milk intake and can lead to increased morbidity, early cessation of breastfeeding, and interference with the bioavailability of certain key nutrients and disease-protective factors in breast milk.

11. Some babies will receive culturally valued supplements or ritual foods, such as tea, vitamin drops, honey, butter, and so on (but in very small amounts). While these supplements and foods are not necessary, most pose no problem to breastfeeding. Honey can carry the possibility of infecting the infant with botulism, however, and should not be given to infants who are younger than one year of age.

## Complementary Feeding: Starting Solids

1. For several decades, the World Health Organization has issued recommendations regarding the appropriate age to begin complementary feeding (WHO, 1998).

2. These recommendations have varied and have sparked debate about whether recommendations should be the age range of 4 to 6 months or if the phrase "at about 6 months" expresses the desired flexibility and protection of infant health.

3. Studies show that in affluent populations, introducing solid foods before 6 months of age has little impact on the total energy intake or growth.

4. Studies show that there is no growth advantage in the complementary feeding of breastfed infants in developing countries prior to 6 months of age. The results of a WHO systematic review supports the recommendation of exclusive breastfeeding for about 6 months.

5. The American Academy of Pediatrics states that exclusive breastfeeding is ideal nutrition and is sufficient to support optimal growth and development for approximately the first six months after birth (American Academy of Pediatrics, 1997).

6. At about 6 months of age, the normal infant begins using his or her iron stores.

7. Iron, energy, zinc, vitamin A, and calcium might be limiting nutrients with breast milk consumption alone sometime after 6 months of age.

8. The neuromuscular and gastrointestinal systems are beginning to mature around 6 months of age.

9. While infants at this age can physically manage food, the efficiency of consumption of different types of foods varies considerably with age.

10. It is practically impossible to supply enough iron from unmodified complementary foods to meet the calculated needs of an infant who is between 6–11 months of age without unrealistically high intakes of animal products.

11. Therefore, iron-fortified cereals or other iron-fortified foods are usually introduced as the first solids where available.

12. Iron deficiency can result when using iron-fortified cereal and whole cow's milk during the second six months of life, however. This condition results from a combination of poor bioavailability of electrolytic iron in some cereals and the composition of cow's milk, which makes iron less available to the infant.

13. Giving infants coffee or tea can have a strong inhibitory effect on iron absorption from foods that are consumed in the same meal or from iron supplements.

14. Once complementary foods are introduced at about 6 months of age, special transitional foods (for example, with semi-solid consistency and adequate energy and nutrient densities) are recommended.

15. Breastfed infants from 6–8 months of age can receive (in addition to breast milk) two to three meals per day depending on the population's nutritional status and the energy density of the complementary foods.

16. Children who are older than 8 months can receive at least three meals per day.

## Inappropriate Foods

1. The definition of "inappropriate" foods will vary with the population that is being discussed.

2. Generally, cow's milk or the fluid milk of other species is not recommended during infancy due to its displacement of breast milk, possible microbial contamination, an inappropriate blend of nutrients, and gastrointestinal blood loss when fresh milk is consumed.

3. Local foods that have a low nutrient density might need to be fortified.

4. Solid foods, such as cereals, should not be given to young babies to make them sleep through the night.

5. Solid foods should not be diluted and put in bottles for young babies to consume.

6. Acceptance of semi-solid food is not an indication of maturity.

7. Parents might need help in resisting the pressure from health care providers, baby food manufacturers, and grandmothers to introduce solids before six months.

8. Water and fruit juices are unnecessary for exclusively breastfed babies during their first six months.

9. If commercial baby foods are used, parents should be counseled to avoid those that contain modified food starch or added sugar or salt, or those that have multiple ingredients.

10. Soy milk that is used in addition to or in place of ABM is inappropriate.

11. Coffee creamers, flour and water mixtures, adult beverages, and carbonated or alcoholic drinks are inappropriate.

12. Baby bottles decorated with name-brand logos of juices and carbonated and non-carbonated beverages encourage parents to give infants the respective beverage from the bottle. Kool-Aid, soft drinks, sports drinks, soda, and so on are typically put in these bottles.

# References

American Academy of Pediatrics, Work Group on Breastfeeding. Breastfeeding and the use of human milk. *Pediatr* 1997; 100:1035–1039.

Anderson JW, Johnstone BM, Remley DT. Breastfeeding and cognitive development: A meta-analysis. *Am J Clin Nutr* 1999; 70:525–535.

Birch E, Birch D, Hoffman D, Hale L, et al. Breastfeeding and optimal visual development. *J Pediatr Ophthalmol Strabismus* 1993; 30:30–38.

Carlson SE, Cooke RJ, Rhodes PG, Peeples JM, Werkman SH, Tolley EA. Long-term feeding of formulas high in linolenic acid and marine oil to very low birth weight infants: Phospholipid fatty acids. *Pediatr Res* 1991; 30:404–412.

Chandra RK. Five-year follow-up of high-risk infants with family history of allergy who were exclusively breastfed or fed partial whey hydrolysate, soy, and conventional cow's milk formulas. *J Pediatr Gastroenterol Nutr* 1997; 24:380–388.

Cunnane SC, Francescutti V, Brenna JT, Crawford MA. Breastfed infants achieve a higher rate of brain and whole body docosahexaenoate accumulation than formula-fed infants not consuming dietary docosahexaenoate. *Lipids* 2000; 35:105–111.

Davis MK. Review of the evidence for an association between infant feeding and childhood cancer. *Intl J Cancer Suppl* 1998; 11:29–33.

Dewey KG. Growth patterns of breastfed infants and the current status of growth charts for infants. *J Hum Lact* 1998; 14:89–92.

Dusdieker LB, Getchell JP, Liarakos TM, et al. Nitrate in baby foods: Adding to the nitrate mosaic. *Arch Pediatr Adolesc Med* 1994; 148:490–494.

Expert consultation on the optimal duration of exclusive breastfeeding. Conclusions and recommendations. Geneva, WHO, March 28–30, 2001, http://www.who.int/inf-pr-2001/en/note2001-07.html.

Fremi-Titulaer LW, Cordero JF, Haddock L, et al. Premature thelarche in Puerto Rico. A search for environmental factors. *Am J Dis Child* 1986; 140:1263–1267.

Goldman AS, Chheda S, Garofalo R. Evolution of immunologic functions of the mammary gland and the postnatal development of immunity. *Pediatr Res* 1998; 43:155–162.

Houlihan J, Wiles R. Into the mouths of babes: bottle-fed infants at risk from atrazine in tap water. Washington, DC: Environmental Working Group, 1999. http://www.ewg.org.

Inoue N, Sakashita R, Kamegai T. Reduction of masseter muscle activity in bottle fed babies. *Early Hum Dev* 1995; 42:185–193.

Jensen RG, ed. Handbook of milk composition. San Diego, CA: Academic Press, Inc., 1995.

Kaleita TA, Kinsbourne M, Menkes JH. A neurobehavioral syndrome after failure to thrive on chloride-deficient formula. *Dev Med Child Neurol* 1991; 33:626–635.

Keating J, Schears GJ, Dodge PR. Oral water intoxication in infants: an American epidemic. *Am J Dis Child* 1991; 145:985–990.

Kleinman RE, ed. Pediatric nutrition handbook, 4th edition. Elk Grove Village, IL: Committee on Nutrition, American Academy of Pediatrics, 1998.

Kuczmarski RJ, Ogden CL, Grummer-Strawn L, et al. CDC growth charts: United States. Advance data from vital and health statistics; no. 314. Hyattsville, MD: National Center for Health Statistics, 2000. http://www.cdc.gov/growthcharts.

Labbok MH, Hendershot G. Does breastfeeding protect against malocclusion? An analysis of the 1981 Child Health Supplement to the National Health Interview Survey. *Am J Prev Med* 1987; 3:227–232.

Labbok M, Krasovec K. Toward consistency in breastfeeding definitions. *Stud Fam Plan* 1990; 21:226–230.

Larkin, M. Estrogen: Friend or foe? *FDA Consumer* 1995; April:25–29.

Oddy WH, Holt PG, Sly PD, et al. Association between breastfeeding and asthma in 6-year-old children: Findings of a prospective birth cohort study. *BMJ* 1999; 319:815–819.

Palmer B. The influence of breastfeeding on the development of the oral cavity: a commentary. *J Hum Lact* 1998; 14:93–98.

Pisacane A, Graziano L, Mazzarella G, et al. Breastfeeding and urinary tract infections. *J Pediatr* 1992; 120:87–89.

Scariati PD, Grummer-Strawn LM, and Fein SB. A longitudinal analysis of infant morbidity and the extent of breastfeeding in the United States. *Pediatrics* 1997; 99:e5, http://www.pediatrics.org/cgi/content/full/99/6/e5.

Semple JL, Lugowski SJ, Baines CJ, et al. Breast milk contamination and silicone implants: preliminary results using silicon as a proxy measurement for silicone. *Plast Reconstruct Surg* 1998; 102:528–533.

Setchell KDR, Zimmer-Nechemias L, Cai J, Heubi JE. Exposure of infants to phyto-estrogens from soy-based infant formula. *Lancet* 1997; 350:23–27.

Shannon MW, et al. Lead intoxication in infancy. *Pediatrics* 1992; 89:87–90.

Sheikh C, Erickson PR. Evaluation of plaque pH changes following oral rinse with eight infant formulas. *Pediatr Dent* 1996; 18:200–204.

Shu XO, Linet MS, Steinbuch M, et al. Breastfeeding and the risk of childhood acute leukemia. *J Natl Cancer Inst* 1999; 91:1765–1772.

Vaarala O, Knip M, Paronen J, et al. Cow's milk formula feeding induces primary immunization to insulin in infants at genetic risk for Type I diabetes. *Diabetes* 1999; 48:1389–1394.

Von Kries R, Koletzko B, Sauerwald T, et al. Breastfeeding and obesity: Cross sectional study. *BMJ* 1999; 319:147–150.

World Health Organization (WHO). Complementary feeding of young children in developing countries: a review of current scientific knowledge. WHO/NUT/98.1; Geneva, Switzerland, WHO, 1998.

World Health Organization Working Group on Infant Growth, Nutrition Unit. An evaluation of infant growth: A summary of analyses performed in preparation for the WHO Expert Committee on "Physical Status: The use and interpretation of anthropometry." Doc WHO/NUT/94.8, Geneva: Switzerland, WHO, 1994.

Zoppi G, Gasparini R, Mantovanelli F, et al. Diet and antibody response to vaccinations in healthy infants. *Lancet* 1983; 2:11–14.

# Allergenic Protection and Defense Agents and Systems in Human Milk

*Linda J. Smith, BSE, FACCE, IBCLC*

## Objectives

- Describe the general classes of components in human milk that contribute to disease protection.
- Discuss the action of the disease-protective factors.
- Discuss the role of breastfeeding in long-term protection against chronic diseases.
- Identify maternal infectious diseases that are compatible with breastfeeding.
- Describe contraindications to breastfeeding.

## Introduction

The mother serves as the baby's immune system. There are multiple mechanisms whereby milk components protect the nursling: an active attack of pathogens, binding nutrients that are needed by pathogens, and enhancing the growth and maturation of the infant's own immune system. The mother's secretory immune system provides targeted protection against pathogens to which she (or the baby) has been exposed. Sensitized B-lymphocytes begin manufacturing targeted sIgA. The lymphocytes and the targeted sIgA migrate to the breast and pass into the milk, where they are ingested by the baby and provide additional protection in the infant's gut. Milk contains soluble components with immunological properties and living cells that are immunologically specific.

Breastfeeding is rarely contraindicated in maternal infection. Breastfeeding is strongly protective against allergy, delaying the onset and lessening the symptoms in the child. Dietary prophylaxis during pregnancy and exclusive breastfeeding for six months has a strongly protective effect. Breastfeeding avoids infant exposure to dietary allergens and slows or prevents the absorption of allergens through the gut. Epidemiological evidence of short-term and long-term benefits of breastfeeding to the infant and mother continues to accumulate. Lactation affects the woman's reproductive system, mediates her responses to stress, and reduces the risk of several cancers. Breastfeeding protects the baby from numerous infections, improves cognitive and neurological development, and reduces the risk of many long-term and chronic diseases and conditions.

I The mother serves as the baby's immune system.

A. Prebirth and early postbirth

1. The placenta passes maternal antibodies to the baby that persist for several weeks to months. The fetus also breathes and ingests/digests amniotic fluid, which provides significant amounts of protein.

2. Colostrum is exceedingly concentrated with anti-infective properties. Evolutional evidence suggests that the earliest function of colostrum was to protect the young, with nutrition being a secondary purpose.

3. Human babies have a proportionally longer duration of colostrum feedings than other mammals.

B. Actions/features of milk components that protect the infant and the lactating breast

1. Actively bind to pathogens, which prevents their passage through the permeable infant gut mucosa. Components are highly targeted to foreign pathogens and ignore the infant's healthy gut flora.

2. Bind and reduce the availability of nutrients, vitamins, and/or minerals that pathogens need.

3. Cellular components directly attack pathogens through phagocytosis.

4. They trigger and enhance the development and maturation of infant's own immune system, including increased effectiveness of immunizations.

5. Support optimal growth and maturation of the infant gut, respiratory, and urogenital tracts.

6. Prevent or reduce inflammation in infant organs and tissues, which protects them from infection.

7. Stimulate the infant's immune system; macrophages and T-lymphocytes provide immunologic maturation stimulus through cytokine production.

C. The role of breastfeeding in long-term protection against chronic diseases is well documented, although the specific mechanisms are not fully understood.

D. The secretory immune system (entero-mammary and broncho-mammary pathways) provides protection against specific organisms to which the mother or infant has been exposed.

1. The mother is exposed to a pathogen by ingestion, inhalation, or other contact, including pathogens that her baby has picked up. The pathogen comes in contact with the mucous membranes in her gut and bronchial tree, triggering an "alarm" in the mother's immune system.

2. T-lymphocytes located in the mother's gut (in the Peyer's patches, or GALT: gut associated lymphoid tissue) and bronchial tree (BALT: bronchus associated lymphoid tissue) notice the new pathogen and pass on the specific message of "alarm" to nearby B-lymphocytes, which immediately begin production of sIgA that is targeted to that organism.

3. Sensitized B-lymphocytes migrate to the mother's secretory organs or mucosal surfaces. There, they secrete targeted sIgA into her blood, which is transported across the mammary secretory cells and is released into the milk. (In addition, more sIgA appears to be synthesized in the mammary glandular cells.)

4. Targeted sIgA appears in milk shortly after maternal exposure to the original pathogen. Some sensitized B-lymphocytes also pass into milk and are ingested by the baby and carry on their production of specific sIgA antibodies in the baby's gut.

5. The nursling ingests these targeted antibodies and sensitized, live lymphocytes in the next breastfeed. The child might not get sick at all, or the illness will be reduced in severity—even if the mother becomes ill. See Figure 9.1.

II Some specific protective components of milk:

   A. Cellular components directly attack pathogens, mobilize other defenses, and activate soluble components (Table 9-1). Although most live cells in the milk survive and continue to function in the infant's gastrointestinal (GI) tract, they are usually destroyed by freezing, boiling, and other heat treatments.

     1. Immunologically specific: T-lymphocytes; B-lymphocytes

     2. Accessory cells: neutrophils, macrophages, and epithelial cells

**Table 9-1**    Immune Benefits of Breast Milk at a Glance

*White Blood Cells in Breast Milk*

| Component | Action |
| --- | --- |
| B-Lymphocytes | Give rise to antibodies targeted against specific microbes. |
| Macrophages | Kill microbes outright in the baby's gut, produce lysozyme, and activate other components of the immune system. |
| Neutrophils | May act as phagocytes, injecting bacteria in baby's digestive system. |
| T-lymphocytes | Kill infected cells directly or send out chemical messages to mobilize other defenses. They proliferate in the presence of organisms that cause serious illness in infants. They also manufacture compounds that can strengthen a child's own immune response. |

**Figure 9-1**   Disease protection for the nursling is choreographed by the mother's own immune system. (Reproduced with permission from Dana Burns-Pizer.)

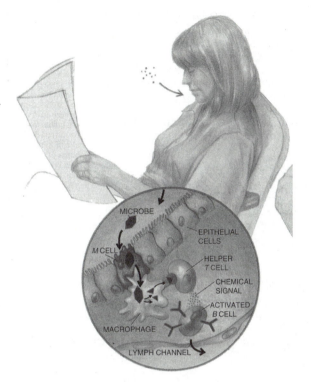

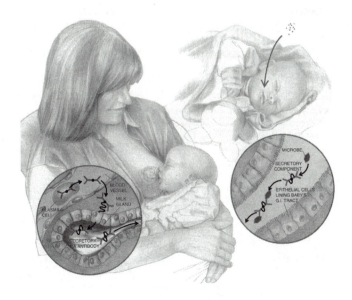

B. Soluble components have multiple protective functions, including binding pathogens, secreting chemical markers, and binding nutrients needed by pathogens. See Table 9-2.

   1. Immunoglobulins: sIgA, IgE, IgM, IgG, and IgE
   2. Nonspecific factors: complement, interferon, bifidus factor, and antiviral factors
   3. Carrier proteins: lactoferrin and transferrin
   4. Enzymes: lysozyme, lipoprotein lipase, and leukocyte enzymes

**Table 9-2**    Molecules in Breast Milk

| Component | Action |
| --- | --- |
| Antibodies of secretory IgA class | Bind to microbes in baby's digestive tract and thereby prevent them from passing through walls of the gut into body's tissues. |
| B12 binding protein | Reduces amount of vitamin B-2, which bacteria need in order to grow. |
| Bifidus factor | Promotes growth of *Lactobacillus bifidus*, harmless bacterium, in baby's gut. Growth of such nonpathogenic bacteria helps to crowd out dangerous varieties. |
| Fatty acids | Disrupt membranes surrounding certain viruses and destroy them. |
| Fibronecting | Increases antimicrobial activity of macrophages; helps to repair tissues that have been damaged by immune reactions in baby's gut. |
| Gamma-interferon | Enhances antimicrobial activity of immune cells. |
| Hormones and growth factors | Stimulate baby's digestive tract to mature more quickly. Once the initially "leaky" membranes lining the gut mature, infants become less vulnerable to microorganisms. |
| Lactoferrin | Binds to iron, a mineral many bacteria need to survive. By reducing the available amount of iron, lactoferrin thwarts growth of pathogenic bacteria. |
| Lysozyme | Kills bacteria by disrupting their cell walls. |
| Mucins | Adhere to bacteria and viruses, thus keeping such microorganisms from attaching to mucosal surfaces. |
| Oligosaccharides | Bind to microorgansims and bar them from attaching to mucosal surfaces. |

     5. Cytokines including interferon and interleukins

     6. Hormones and hormone-like substances

       a. Epidermal growth factor

       b. Prostaglandins

       c. Relaxin

       d. Somatostatin

       e. Gonadotropins and ovarian steroids

       f. Prolactin

       g. Insulin

C. Anti-inflammatory properties

     1. Human milk lacks the initiators of inflammation.

     2. Contains specific anti-inflammatory agents, such as:

       a. Lactoferrin

       b. Secretory IgA

       c. Lysozymes

       d. Prostaglandins

       e. Oligosaccarides

       f. Epidermal growth factor

D. Interaction of anti-inflammatory and anti-infective factors is more than the sum of the parts, thus protecting both the mammary gland and the infant from a vast array of pathogens. See Table 9-3.

**Table 9-3**   Antibacterial Factors Found in Human Milk

| Factor | Shown *in vitro* to be active against |
| --- | --- |
| Secretory IgA | E. coli (also pili, capsular antigens, CFA1) including enteropathogenic strains, C. tetani, C. diptheriae, K. pneumoniae, S. pyogenes, S. mutans, S. sanguins, S. mitis, S. agalactiae (group B streptococci), S. salvarius, S. pneumoniae, C. burnetti, H. influenzae, H. pylori, S. flexneri, S. boydii, S. sonnei, C. jejuni, N. meningitidis, B. pertussis, S. dysenteriae, C. trachomatis, Salmonella (6 groups), S. minnesota, P. aeruginosa, Campylobacter flagelin, S. flexneri virulence plasmid antigen, C. diphtheriae toxin, E. coli enterotoxin, V. cholerae enterotoxin, C. difficile toxins, H. influenzae capsule, S. aureus enterotoxin F, Candida albicans* |

*(continues)*

**Table 9-3**    *(Continued)*

| Factor | Shown *in vitro* to be active against |
| --- | --- |
| IgG | *E. coli, B. pertussis, H. influenzae* type b, *S. pneumoniae, S. agalactiae, N. mengingitidis,* 14 pneumoccoccal capsular polysaccharides, *V. cholerae* lipopolysaccharide, *S. flexneri* invasion plasmid-coded antigens, major opsonin for *S. aureus* |
| IgM | *V. cholerae* lipopolysaccharide, *E. coli, S. flexneri* |
| IgD | *E. coli* |
| Free secretory component** | *E. coli* colonization factor antigen I (CFA1), *C. difficile* toxin A |
| Bifidobacterium bifidum growth factors (oligosaccharides, glycopeptides); other Bifidobacteria growth factors (alpha-lactoglobulin, lactoferrin, sialyllactose) | Enteric bacteria |
| Factor finding proteins (zinc, vitamin B12, folate) | Dependent *E. coli* |
| Complement C1-C0 (mainly C3 and C4) | Killing of *S. aureus* in macrophages, *E. coli* (serum-sensitive) |
| Lactoferrin** | *E. coli, E. coli*/CFA1 or *S. fimbriae, Candida albicans*, Candida krusei*, Rhodotorula rubra*, H. influenzae, S. flexneri* |
| Lactoperoxidase | *Streptococcus, Pseudomonas, E. coli, S. typhimurium* |
| Lysozyme | *E. coli, Salmonella, M. lysodeikticus, S. aureus, P. fragi,* growing *Candida albicans** and *Aspergillus fumigatus** |
| Unidentified factors | *S. aureus, B. pertussis, C. jejuni, E. coli, S. typhimurium, S. flexneri, S. sonnei, V. cholerae, L. pomona, L. hyos, L. icterohaemorrhagiae, C. difficile* toxin B, *H. pylori, C. trachomatis* |
| Nonimmunoglobulin; (milk fat, proteins) | *C. trachomatis, Y. enterocolitica* |
| Carbohydrate | *E. coli* enterotoxin, *E. coli, C. difficile* toxin A |
| Lipids | *S. aureus, E. coli, S. epidermis, H. influenzae, S. agalactiae, L. monocytogenes, N. gonorrhoeae, C. trachomatis, B. parapertusis* heat-labile toxin, binds *Shigella*-like toxin-1 |

| Factor | Shown *in vitro* to be active against |
| --- | --- |
| Ganglioside GM1 | *E. coli* enterotoxin, *V. cholerae* toxin, *C. jejuni* enterotoxin, *E. coli* |
| Ganglioside GM3 | *E. coli* |
| Phosphatidylethanolamine | *H. pylori* |
| Sialyllactose | *V. cholerae* toxin, *H. pylori* |
| Mucin (muc-1; milk fat globulin membrane) | *E. coli* (S-fimbrinated) |
| Sialyloligosaccharides on sIgA(Fc) | *E. coli* (S-fimbrinated) adhesion |
| Glycoproteins (receptor-like) + oligosaccharides | *V. cholerae* |
| Clycoproteins (N-acetylneuramic-containing or terminal galactose) | *E. coli* (S-fimbrinated) |
| Glycoproteins (mannosylated) | *E. coli, E. coli* CFA11, fimbrae |
| kappa-Casein** | *H. pylori, S. pneumoniae, H. influenzae* |
| (Tri to penta) phosphorylated beta-casein | *H. influenzae* |
| Casein | *H. influenzae* |
| Xanthine oxidase (with added hypoxanthine) | *E. coli, S. enteridis* |
| alpha-Lactalbumin (variant) | *S. pneumoniae* |
| Glycolipid Gb3 | *S. dysenterae* toxin, shigatoxin of *Shigella* and *E. coli* |
| Sulphatide (sulpphogalactosylceramide) | *S. typhimurium* |
| Fucosylated oligosaccharides | *E. coli* heat stable enterotoxin, *C. jejuni, E. coli* |
| Analogues of epithelial cell receptors (oligosaccharides and sialylated oligosaccharides***) | *S. pneumonieae, H. influenczae* |
| Lewis antigens | *S. aureus, C. perfringens* |
| Soluble bacterial pattern recognition receptor CD14 | Bacteria (or LPS) activate this to induce immune response molecules from intestinal cells |

*(continues)*

**Table 9-3** *(Continued)*

| Factor | Shown *in vitro* to be active against |
| --- | --- |
| Milk cells (80% macrophages, 15% neutrophils, 0.3% B and 4% T lymphocytes) | By phagocytosis and killing: *E. coli*, *S. aureus*, *S. enteritidis*; by sensitized lymphocytes: *E. coli*; by phagocytosis: *Candida albicans\**, *E. coli*; lymphocyte stimulation: *E. coli* K antigen tuberculin; spontaneous monokines: simulated bylipopolysaccaride; induced cytokines: PHA, PMA + ionomycin; fibronectin helps in uptake by phagocytic cells. |

| Factors found at low level in human milk | Shown *in vitro* to be active against |
| --- | --- |
| Secretory leukocyte protease inhibitor (antileukocyte protease) | *E. coli*, *S. aureus*, growing *C. albicans\**, and *A. fumigatus\** |

*Fungi

**Contain fucosylated oligosaccharides

***One sialylated pentasaccharide (3'-sialyllactose-N-neotetraose; NE-1530) had no beneficial effect on otitis media in phase-2 clinical trials.

* Human milk contains nearly a thousand different oligosaccharides (determined by MALDI-mass spectrometry). Many have the potential to act as receptors for bacteria not listed in the table.

* Concentration of milk components in *Breastfeeding: unravelling the mysteries of mother's milk* (requires completion of free registration to Mecdscape)

From Proceedings of Breast Milk and Special Care Nurseries: Problems and Opportunities Conference. August 1995. Melbourne. Copyright J.T. May and Australian Lactation Consultants Association (ACLA) Victorian Branch, 1995.

**III** Selected maternal diseases and breastfeeding

    A. "Breastfeeding is rarely contraindicated in maternal infection . . . Documenting transmission of infection from mother to infant by breastfeeding requires not only the exclusion of other possible mechanisms of transmission but also the demonstration of the infectious agent in the breast milk and a subsequent clinically significant infection in the infant caused by a plausible infectious process." Robert Lawrence, MD, in Breastfeeding, a Guide for the Medical Profession, 5th ed., p. 563. See Table 9-4.

**Table 9-4** Antiparasite Factors Found in Human Milk

| Factor | Shown *in vitro* to be active against |
| --- | --- |
| Secretory IgA | *Giardia lamblia* (protozoa); *Entamoeba histolytica* (protozoa); *Schisteosoma mansoni* (blood fluke); *Cryptosporidium* (protozoa); *Toxoplasma gondii*; *Plasmodium falciparum* (malaria) |
| IgG | *Plasmodium falciparum* |

| Factor | Shown *in vitro* to be active against |
|---|---|
| Lipid (free fatty acids and monoglycerides) | *Giardia lamblia; Entamoeba histolytica; Trichomonas vaginalis* (protozoa); *Giardia intestinalis; Eimeria tenella* (animal coccidiosis) |
| Lactoferring (or pepsin-generated lactoferricin) | *Giardi lamblia, Plasmodium falciparum* |
| Unidentified | *Trypanosoma brucei rhodesiense* |
| Macrophages | *Entamoeba histolytica* |

From Proceedings of Breast Milk and Special Care Nurseries: Problems and Opportunities Conference. August 1995. Melbourne. Copyright J.T. May and Australian Lactation Consultants Association (ACLA) Victorian Branch, 1995. Updated October, 1998.

B. Viral diseases

1. Viral fragments for many diseases appear in mother's milk. These are not whole virus particles and do not appear to actually transmit disease. These fragments might act as a "vaccination" against the specific disease (for example, cytomegalovirus). See Table 9-5.

**Table 9-5**   Microbial Contaminants of Nucleic Acid Detected in Human Milk

| Contaminant | Number of Infections |
|---|---|
| *Viruses* **** | |
| Cytomegalovirus (or virus DNA) | About two thirds of infants consuming cytomegalovirus containing milk excrete virus after 3 weeks. Up to a half of CMV positive mothers have varying levels of infectious virus in their milk for up to 3 months. Present in preterm and mature milk, but low in colostrum. One death in an infant with an immunodeficiency syndrome. Symptoms may be seen in some preterm infants. |
| Human T-lymphotropic virus type 1 (or provirus DNA; p24 antigen) [causes adult T-cell leukaemia] | Transmitted to a quarter of infants almost exclusively through milk (cells) after 6 months of breast-feeding, in restricted geographical areas; seroconversion of infants occurs after 12—24 months. |
| Rubella virus | A quarter of infants seroconvert 4 weeks after consuming rubella (normal or vaccine strains) containing milk. Two thirds of vaccinated mothers can excrete virus in milk for up to 3 weeks. |

(*continues*)

**Table 9-5** *(Continued)*

| Contaminant | Number of Infections |
|---|---|
| Human immunodeficiency virus type 1 (and 2) (or provirus DNA or virus RNA; p24 antigen) | At least one third of transmissions to breast-fed infants is through milk. Most occur by 5—6 months of breast feeding. HIV RNA can be present in half of infected mothers' milk. |
| Herpes simplex virus type 1 (or DNA) [cold sores] | One infected by 6 days. Infects also from nipple lesions, but infants may also infect mothers. HSV-1 and HSV-2 DNA has been detected in milk cells. |
| Sin nombre (no name) hantavirus RNA [pulmonary syndrome] | Nil |
| Human herpesvirus 7 DNA (febrile illness) | No increased seroconversion (infection) in breast fed infants. |
| Hepatitis E | Milk is not a major source, transmitted during pregnancy. |
| Hepatitis B surface antigen (or virus DNA) | No increased seroconversion (infection) in breast fed infants. |
| B-type (retrovirus-like particles) | Nil |
| Hepatitis C RNA | Three infants had symptoms after breastfeeding for 3 months, from symptomatic mothers with high levels of virus. Others have found no infection from chronic infected mothers. Infants with hepC RNA may spontaneously clear the virus and not seroconvert. Present in nil to 20% of infected mothers' milk.* |
| Transfusion-transmission virus (TTV) DNA [no associated disease] | Can be present in the milk of half to three quarters of women who have TTV DNA in their serum and may be transmitted to infants, before breastfeeding begins or by later close contact. * |
| Human T-lymphotropic virus type II provirus DNA | Transmission occurs through milk |
| Varicella-zoster virus DNA | One? |
| Epstein-Barr virus DNA (glandular fever) | No increased seroconversion (infection) in breast-fed infants. |

| Contaminant | Number of Infections |
| --- | --- |
| *Bacteria* | |
| *Streptococcus agalactieae* (Group B streptococci) | Rare, one death; grows in milk ducts |
| Staphylococci | Rare |
| *Leptospira australis* | Rare |
| *Salmonella senftenberg* | One death; rare growth in milk ducts |
| *Salmonella typhimurium* | One |
| *Salmonella kottbus* | One; may grow in milk ducts. |
| *Listeria monocytogenes* | One? |
| *Brucella melitensis* | Rare |
| *Mycobacterium tuberculosis* (TB) | Nil? |
| *Mycobacterium paratuberculosis* | ? |
| *Coxiella burnetti* (Q fever) | ? |
| *Serratia marcescens* | ?; detected during infection in maternity wards |
| *Citrobacter freundii* | ?; detected during infection in maternity ward |
| *Candida albicans* *** | ?; can be found with nipple pain in mother |
| *Borrelia burgdorferi* DNA (Lyme disease) | ? |
| *Staphylococcus aureus* enterotoxin F | mother had toxic shock syndrome |
| *Parasites* | |
| *Trypanosoma cruzi** (Changas' disease) | ? |
| *Trichinella spiralis* (tissue worm) | ? |
| *Strongyloides fulleborni* (threadworm) | ? |
| *Necator americanus* (new world hookworm) | ? |
| *Toxoplasma gondii* | One? |
| *Schistosoma mansoni* antigens (blood fluke) | Hypersensitive allergy |
| *Onchocerca volvulus* antigens (skin worm) | Immune suppression |

*(continues)*

**Table 9-5**    *(Continued)*

| Contaminant | Number of Infections |
|---|---|
| | *Other* |
| Mycotoxins (aflatoxins, ochratoxin) | ?; fungal toxins from food mother has eaten |
| Creutzfeld-Jacob transmittable agent ** | - |

*Not detected in all studies

**Never confirmed (*N Engl J Med* 327: 649; 1992)

***Fungi

****Detection of virus nucleic acid (RNA or DNA) does not mean the virus is still intact and infectious

- Syphilis may come from breast lesions
- HIV-1 was possibly transferred in pooled unpasteurized milk that was fed to a young child for a 4 week period (up to 15% of donors could have been HIV positive). Estimates of the time before HIV infection starts to occur through milk vary widely, from 4 months to less than 1 month (most after 4–6 weeks).
- Infants daily intake through milk may be $10^5$ infected cells (HIV-1 or HTLV-1) or $10^4$ infectious virus (CMV or rubella), but each can be up to 100-fold higher.
- Virus infections of infants take at least 3 weeks of feeding. There is no evidence indicating that one feed of infected milk would cause a virus infection. Bacterial infections which are rarer can occur more quickly from untreated expressed milk, but usually take about 3 weeks of feeding; and can also be treated using antibiotics.
- Group B Streptococci > $10^5$ cfu/ml has been found in an asymptomatic mother.
- *No* human herpesvirus 6 DNA or hepatitis G / GB virustype C RNA has been detected in human milk.

From Proceedings of Breast Milk and Special Care Nurseries: Problems and Opportunities Conferences. August 1995. Melbourne. Copyright J.T. May and Australian Lactation Consultants Association (ACLA) -Victorian Branch, 1995.

2. Human milk contains specific components that are active against many viruses, including poliovirus, respiratory syncytial virus, rotavirus, and influenza virus. See Table 9-6.

**Table 9-6**    Antiviral Factors Found in Human Milk

| Factor | Shown *in vitro* to be active against |
|---|---|
| Secretory IgA | Polio types, 1, 2, 3*. Coxsackie types A9, B3, B5, echo types 6, 9, Semliki Forest virus, Ross River virus, rotavirus*, cytomegalovirus, reovirus type 3, rubella varicella-zoster virus, rhinovirus, herpes simplex virus, mumps virus, influenza, respiratory syncytial virus, human immunodeficiency virus, hepatitis C virus, hepatitis B virus, measles, sin nombre hantavirus. |
| IOgG | Rubella, cytomegalovirus, respiratory syncytial virus, rotavirus, human immunodeficiency virus, Epstein-Barr virus, sin nombre hantavirus. |

| Factor | Shown *in vitro* to be active against |
| --- | --- |
| IgM | Rubella, cytomegalovirus, respiratory syncytial virus, human immoundeficiency virus, sin nombre hantavirus. |
| Lipid (unsaturated fatty acids and monoglycerides) | Herpes simplex virus, Semliki Forest virus, influenza, dengue, Ross River virus, Japanese B encephalitis virus, sindbis, West Nile, Sendai, Newcstle disease virus, human immunodeficiency virus, respiratory syncytial virus, vesticular stomatitis virus, cytomegalovirus, mumps, measles, parainfluenza viruuses 1–4, coronavirus, bovine enterovirus (C12), poliovirus (C18). |
| Non-immunoglobulin macromolecultes | Herpes simplex virus, vesicular stomatitis virus, Coxsackie B4, Semliki Forest virus, reovirus 3, poliotype 2, cytomegalovirus, respiratory syncytial virus, rotavirus*. |
| alpha2-macroglobulin (like) | Influenza hemagglutinin, parainfluenza hemagglutinin. |
| Ribonuclease | Murine leukemia, human immunodeficiency virus |
| Haemagglutinin inhibitors | Influenza, mumps. |
| Lactadherin (mucin-associated glycoprotein) | Rotavirus* |
| Chondroitin sulphate (-like) | Human immunodeficiency virus |
| Sulphatide (sulphogalactosylceramide) | Human immunodeficiency virus |
| Secretory leukocyte protease inhibitor (colostrum levels) | Human immunodeficiency virus |
| *Bifidobacterium bifidum*** | Rotavirus (by increasing mucin) |
| sIgA + trypsin inhibitor | Rotavirus |
| Lactoferrin | Cytomegalovirus, human immunodeficiency virus, respiratory syncytial virus, herpes simplex virus type 1, hepatitis C, poliovirus type 1, and Friend retrovirus. Also binds to the virus receptors, low density lipoprotein receptor, and heparin sulphate proteoglycans. Hepatitis G***, rotavirus*** and Seoul hantavirus*** |
| Vitamin A | Herpes simplex virus 2, simian virus 40, cytomegalovirus |
| Lysozyme | Human immunodeficiency virus, ectromelia |

*(continues)*

**Table 9-6**   *(Continued)*

| Factor | Shown *in vitro* to be active against |
|---|---|
| Soluble intracellular adhesion; molecule 1 | Rhinoviruses (major-group) 3, 14, 54; Coxsackie A13 |
| Milk cells | Induced gamma-interferon: virus, PHA, or PMA and ionomycin; Induced cytokine: herpes simplex virus, respiratory syncytial virus; Lymphocyte stimulation: rubella, cytomegalovirus, herpes, measles, mumps, respiratory syncytial virus. |

| Factors found at very low levels in human milk | Shown *in vitro* to be active against |
|---|---|
| Prostaglandins E2, F2 alpha | Parainfluenza 3, measles |
| Prostaglandins E1 | Poliovirus, encephalomyocarditis virus, measles |
| Gangliosides GM1–3 | Rotavirus, respiratory syncytial virus |
| Heparin | Cytomegalovirus, respiratory syncytial virus, dengue |
| Glycolipid Gb4 | Human B19 parvovirus |

* Cytomegalovirus growth *in vitro* can be enhanced by the milk factors prostaglandins E1 or E2 or F2-alpha, sialyllactose or interleukin-8
* Rotavirus growth can be activated *in vitro* by fatty acids (C10, C16)
* HIV growth *in vitro* can be enhanced by prostaglandin E2 or (pro)cathepsin D.
*In vivo* protection also
**Used with *Streptococcus thermophilus*
***Only bovine so far, but human is normally identical

From Proceedings of Breast Milk and Special Care Nurseries: Problems and Opportunities Conference. August 1995. Melbourne. Copyright J.T. May and Australian Lactation Consultants Association (ACLA) - Victoria Branch, 1995.

3. Guidelines for breastfeeding or breast-milk feeding when the mother is actively infected with a viral illness *at the time the baby is born* are published periodically.

   a. See Lawrence, Breastfeeding, a Guide for the Medical Profession, 5th ed. or similar references for treatment protocols for specific illnesses. In most (but not all) cases, breastfeeding can proceed normally.

   b. Precautions are necessary when the mother is actively contagious with certain diseases *at the time of the baby's birth*. For example, a mother who has an active tuberculosis or chickenpox infection must be isolated from her newborn until she has been treated or is not contagious.

    c.  Even if the mother who has chickenpox or active tuberculosis is isolated, she can and should provide her milk for her infant because these diseases are not transmitted via breast milk.

    d.  Maternal Group B Streptococcal (GBS) infections are treated prenatally when identified or during the intrapartum period.

    e.  Acquisition of GBS through breast milk or breastfeeding is rare.

    f.  If a breastfed baby develops late-onset GBS, milk is cultured, the mother is treated, and breastfeeding or breast-milk administration continues.

C.  HIV/AIDS (and women who are infected with the HTLV virus)

    1.  At this writing, mother-to-child transmission of HIV/AIDS appears to occur mainly through direct blood contact at the time of birth or transplacentally in utero. Estimated rates of mother-to-child transmission range from 13–60 percent depending on the geographic area studied.

    2.  Some babies face the additional risk of becoming infected through breastfeeding, although the data are not conclusive in this respect. At this writing, the incremental *additional* risk of transmission via breastfeeding ranges from 3 percent to 29 percent (AAP, November 1995), depending on a multitude of contributing factors.

    3.  Individual countries and medical associations have published specific policies based on local economic, health, and other conditions.

    4.  HIV-1 transmission through breast milk might be more dependent on the pattern of breastfeeding rather than on the total amount or duration of all breastfeeding.

    5.  Exclusive breastfeeding for approximately three months might carry half the risk of mother-to-child transmission of HIV-1 than mixed feeding (never breastfed = 18.8 percent; mixed-fed = 24.1 percent; exclusively breastfed for three months = 14.6 percent). Infants exclusively breastfed for three months or more had no excess risk of HIV infection over six months than those never breastfed. Once exclusive breastfeeding ends, if mixed breastfeeding continues, new mixed feeding-associated infections can occur (Coutsoudis et al., 2001).

    6.  WHO, UNICEF, and UNAIDS issued a joint policy statement in June 1998 containing these policy issues:

        a.  The human rights perspective

        b.  Preventing HIV infection in women

        c.  Health of mothers and children

        d.  Elements of establishing a policy concerning HIV and infant feeding

            i.  Supporting breastfeeding

            ii.  Access to voluntary, individual, and confidential counseling and testing

            iii.  Ensuring informed choice

            iv.  Preventing commercial pressures for artificial feeding

D.  Breastfeeding should continue to be promoted, protected, and supported in all populations worldwide. Health authorities consider the mother who is HIV positive to be an extraordinary circumstance. All women should have voluntary and confidential HIV testing and individualized counseling in order to make an informed decision regarding feeding their babies.

1.  Mothers who are HIV positive and decide not to breastfeed have several options:

a.  Mother's own modified milk (heat treatment inactivates the virus). See Table 9-7.

**Table 9-7**    Effect of Heat Treatment or Storgage on Antimicrobial Factors in Human Milk

| | Percentage of Activity Remaining* | | | |
|---|---|---|---|---|
| | Heat Treatment (15 seconds) | Heat Treatment (30 minutes) | Refrigeration (7 days) | Freezing (3 months) |
| | 72°C** Flash Pasteurization | 62.5°C "Holding method" Pasteurization | 56°C | 4°C | −15°C |
| Secretory IgA | 85 | 70 | 85 | 100 | 100 |
| IgM | | 0 | | | Decreased |
| IgG | | 70 | | 95 | Decreased |
| Lactoferrin (Iron-binding capacity) | 100 | 40 | 75 | | 100 |
| Complement C3 | | 0 | 0 | | 90 |
| Milk cells | 0 | 0 | 0 | | 10 |
| Lysozyme | 100 | 75 | 100 | | 90 |
| Vitamin A | | 100 | 100 | | 100 *** |
| Lipases (generator of antimicrobial lipids) | 3 | 0 | | 75 | 50 |
| Other factors **** (oligosaccharide, etc.) | 100 | 100 | 100 | 100 | 100 |
| Bacteriostatic activity (on added E. coli) | | Some decrease | Some decrease | No decrease | Decreases at 1 month |

*Percentage of Activity Remaining\**

| | Heat Treatment (15 seconds) | Heat Treatment (30 minutes) | | Refrigeration (7 days) | Freezing (3 months) |
|---|---|---|---|---|---|
| | 72°C** Flash Pasteurization | 62.5°C "Holding method" Pasteurization | 56°C | 4°C | −15°C |
| Cytomegalovirus | Nil | Nil | Can be some | Gone in a quarter of samples in 24 hours, all gone by 7 days | Gone in most samples after 24 hours, others decreased by 99% in 3 days |
| Skin bacteria | 99% gone | Nil | Nil | Same | Decreased |

*Values indicated are maximum values

**Special equipment needed for this high temperature treatment

***Minimum of 3 weeks

****These survive over 80°C for >30 minutes, while other listed factors are totally destroyed

- HIV is destroyed by milk pasteurization. HIV-1 is reduced ten-fold at 56°C for 121 seconds and at 62.5°C for 10 seconds in liquid; hepatitis B is killed and hepatitis C almost eliminated in serum at 60° C for 10 hours; parvovirus B19 (similar to TTV) is removed at 60°C for 3 hours or 30 minutes at 70°C in liquid.

- HTLV-1 (all cell-associated) is destroyed within 20 minutes at 56°C (or 10 minutes at 90°C), or by freezing at -20°C for 12 hours. Cell associated HIV provirus DNA is destroyed by bringing milk to a boil. Boiling milk destroys the immunoglubulins, lactoferrin, lysozyme and the milk's bacteriostaic activity.

- Mature milk stored at room temperature for up to 6 hours (27–32°C) does not normally have any increase in bacterial counts. However, S. epidermidis may have proliferated in a warm environment during collection and transport.

- Normally milk is not stored at 4°C for more than 48 hours and heat treated milk is stored frozen.

Based on a table in the Proceedings of Breast Feeding: The Natural Advantage Conference. October, 1997. Sydney. (c) J.T. May and Nursing Mothers' Association of Australia. November, 1997.

    i. Institutional pasteurization

    ii. Home pasteurization

2. Heating 450ml of water to the boiling point can cause heat transfer to a smaller jar of breast milk that is placed into the water.

3. A solar-powered breast milk pasteurizer device that will hold milk at 60°C for 30 minutes

         a. Banked donor human milk (all banked milk is donated by screened donors and is then pasteurized)

         b. Commercial infant formula

         c. Homemade formula

    4. The lactation consultant's role is to collect and compile current research, resources, and recommendations and share these with the mother and her primary care provider(s). She might also assist with weaning or other breastfeeding-related issues. The lactation consultant (LC) does not have a decision-making role in caring for families who have this disease.

    5. Careful attention to universal precautions is required of all health care providers.

         a. "Contact with breast milk does not constitute occupational exposure as defined by OSHA standards" (AAP, 1995).

         b. "Gloves are not recommended for the routine handling of expressed human milk; but should be worn by health care workers in situations where exposure to breast milk might be frequent or prolonged, for example, in milk banking" (WHO, CDC).

  E. Cross infection

    1. The baby's mouth and mother's breast are in intimate physical contact many times a day during breastfeeding.

    2. Any communicable disease/infection on either the nipple surfaces or the infant's mouth is quickly transmitted to the other.

    3. The dyad needs to be treated simultaneously until both (or all) sites are healthy. Examples include oral thrush and nipple candida, and a child who has strep throat infects the mother's nipple.

    4. Breastfeeding should continue during treatments.

# Summary of Maternal Infectious Diseases and Compatibility with Breastfeeding

Caution: Consult current medical references as new information becomes available. The primary care provider(s) must consider each situation individually. Contraindications to breastfeeding are rare.

| Disease | OK to Breastfeed in the United States?* | Conditions |
|---------|------------------------------------------|------------|
| Acute infectious disease | Yes | Respiratory, reproductive, GI infections |
| Active tuberculosis | Yes | If mother is actively infected at birth, separate until after mother has received two or more weeks of treatment; milk is still OK |
| Hepatitis A | Yes | |
| Hepatitis B | Yes | After infant receives HBIG, first dose before discharge |
| Hepatitis C | Yes | If no co-infections (such as HIV) |
| Herpes simplex | Yes | Except if lesion is on breast where the baby would contact |
| Herpes/Cytomegalovirus | Yes | |
| Herpes/Epstein-Barr | Yes | |
| Herpes/Varicella-zoster (chicken pox) | Yes | If mother is actively infected at birth, separate until mother becomes non-infectious; baby can still receive her milk |
| Lyme disease | Yes | As soon as mother begins treatment |
| Mastitis (infectious) | Yes | Milk stasis will exacerbate the illness. |
| Toxoplasmosis | Yes | |
| Venereal warts | Yes | |
| HIV or HTLV-1 | No | *HIV positive—see WHO/UNICEF guidelines |

*Adapted from Table 7 in Lawrence, R. *A Review of the Medical Benefits and Contraindications to Breastfeeding In the United States* (Maternal and Child Health Technical Information Bulletin). Arlington, VA: National Center for Education in Maternal and Child Health, October 1997.

IV Immunizing the nursing mother

    A. Lactating women can be immunized as recommended for other adults in order to protect against measles, mumps, rubella, tetanus, diphtheria, influenza, *Streptococcus pneumoniae*, Hepatitis A virus, Hepatitis B virus, varicella, and Rh immune globulin

    B. Inactivated polio virus if traveling to a highly endemic area

    C. Not smallpox (rarely indicated)

V   Protective effect of breastfeeding against allergy

   A.   Milk is species specific; a baby is never allergic to its own mother's milk. The baby and the mother share 50 percent of the same genetic material. No antibody response to the mother's milk has ever been documented.

   B.   SIgA in milk binds with and prevents the transport of dietary allergens until the infant gut is less permeable. This function is most important in the early months until the baby begins producing its own sIgA.

   C.   Breastmilk has a double effect:

      1.   Prevents/avoids the infant's exposure to non-human proteins

      2.   Slows or prevents the absorption of antigens through the infant gut

   D.   Prophylactic management of children who have a family history of atopic (allergic) disease.

   E.   Allergic disease has a strong hereditary basis.

   F.   47 percent incidence if both parents are allergic.

   G.   29 percent incidence if one parent is allergic.

   H.   13 percent incidence even if neither parent has a family history of allergy.

      1.   The only effective treatment is to reduce the allergenic load.

      2.   Dietary prophylaxis is clearly effective, especially in families who have a strong history.

         a.   Mothers have been advised to avoid common allergens during pregnancy (especially dairy products, fish, eggs, and peanuts), yielding mixed results in terms of allergy prevention in the child.

         b.   Exclusive breastfeeding for about six months.

         c.   Longer exclusive breastfeeding might be advantageous to the infant who has a family history of allergy.

   I.   Allergic disease is responsible for one-third of pediatric office visits, one-third of chronic conditions of children younger than age 17, and one-third of lost school days due to asthma. Allergic diseases are strongly linked to artificial feeding:

      1.   Eczema

      2.   Asthma

      3.   Hay fever

      4.   Gut and respiratory infection

      5.   Sudden death

      6.   Ulcerative colitis

   J.   All non-human milks currently available, including hydrolyzed or "hypoallergenic" products, have been shown to cause anaphylactic reactions in sensitive babies.

K.  Severe reactions have occurred, even at the "first" exposure. Researchers discovered that the infants who reacted so strongly had received feeds of cow's milk formula in a hospital nursery without the mother's knowledge or permission and without appropriate documentation on the infant's chart.

L.  Hypoallergenic formulas are not completely non-allergenic; they have the capacity to provoke anaphylactic shock in susceptible infants; hypoallergenic means that 90 percent of affected individuals will not be allergic to the product.

M.  Up to 60 percent of children who are allergic to cow's milk protein can also be sensitive to soy. The American Academy of Pediatrics does not recommend the use of soy formula when a documented allergy to cow's milk formula exists, because soy formula has not been demonstrated to reduce the development of atopy in infancy and childhood.

N.  The prevalence of cow's milk allergy ranges from .5 percent to 7.5 percent.

O.  Food allergy occurs in approximately 4–6 percent of children.

P.  Solid foods that are introduced before 15 weeks are associated with an increased probability of wheezing, respiratory illness, and eczema.

Q.  Partial breastfeeding or full formula feeding increases the risk for respiratory diseases.

R.  Exclusive breastfeeding for at least four months is protective against asthma by avoiding other milks.

S.  The age at which other milks are introduced rather than total breastfeeding length is more closely associated with atopy at six years of age.

T.  Cow's milk proteins are usually the first foreign antigens encountered by newborn infants in their diet.

U.  Intestinal absorption of macromolecules is greatest during the first two months of life, which is the critical time period for induction of a specific immune response to dietary antigens.

V.  An incomplete mucosal barrier and increased gut permeability are seen in altered immunologic responses.

W.  In infants who are prone to developing cow's milk allergy, short exposure to cow's milk-based formula in the hospital or exclusive breastfeeding combined with an infrequent intake of small amounts of cow's milk stimulates specific IgE antibody production.

X.  Frequent feeding of large volumes of cow's milk-based formula induces the development of non-IgE, mediated, delayed-type hypersensitivity to cow's milk.

Y.  Arbitrary, inadvertent, or unnecessary cow's milk-based formula supplementation given to susceptible breastfed babies during the first three days of life can sensitize these babies and provoke allergic reactions to cow's milk protein later in the first year of life.

Z.  Minute quantities of cow's milk proteins (beta-lactoglobulin) have been documented in the milk of some mothers, which could theoretically sensitize predisposed babies to cow's milk.

AA.  Regular exposure to large allergen doses induces tolerance, whereas small allergen doses might be sensitizing in allergy-prone people.

BB.  The prevalence of eczema and food allergy is highest between 1–3 years of age, and respiratory allergy has its highest prevalence between 5–17 years.

CC.  Breastfeeding also confers long-term protection against allergic sensitization.

1.  Breastfeeding for longer than one month with no other milk supplements offers significant prophylaxis against food allergy at three years and respiratory allergy at 17 years.

2.  Six months of breastfeeding significantly reduces eczema during the first three years and at adolescence.

3.  Allergic manifestations include recurrent wheezing, elevated IgE levels, eczema, atopic dermatitis, GI symptoms of diarrhea, vomiting, and blood in the stool.

DD.  Babies who demonstrate an allergic reaction to hydrolyzed formula might need to be fed with elemental or amino acid-derived formulas.

VI  Breastfed infants have different health, growth, and developmental outcomes than formula-fed babies.

A.  Breastfed babies have fewer sick baby visits to health care providers.

B.  A dose-response relationship exists between the amount of breast milk as the percentage of the infant's feed, with babies receiving exclusive breast milk for longer periods of time showing the least amount of disease and allergy.

C.  The more breast milk an infant receives during the first six months of life, the less likely he or she is to develop illness or allergy.

D.  Formula-fed babies have an increased risk and incidence of:

1.  Gastrointestinal disease

a.  Diarrhea—bacterial, viral, and parasitic

b.  NEC (necrotizing enterocolitis)

2.  Respiratory disease

a.  Otitis media

b.  Upper and lower respiratory infections

c.  Wheezing

d.  Asthma

e.  Allergies

3.  Urinary tract infections

4.  Deficient response to childhood immunizations

E. Formula-fed babies have a different brain composition than breastfed babies. Artificially fed babies acquire half the DHA as in the brain of a breastfed infant and can experience the following:

1. Discrepancy in visual acuity
2. Lower IQ
3. Poorer school performance
4. Increased risk for neurological dysfunction
5. Increased risk for specific language impairment
6. Lower DHA in the gray and white matter of the cerebellum, which coordinates movement and balance
7. Increased risk for multiple sclerosis

F. Long-term and chronic diseases are more common in artificially fed children, such as:

1. Obesity
2. Sudden Infant Death Syndrome (SIDS)
3. Juvenile rheumatoid arthritis
4. Childhood cancers, especially lymphomas and leukemia
5. Diabetes: insulin-dependent and non-insulin-dependent
6. GI disorders: Crohn's disease, ulcerative colitis
7. Autoimmune thyroid disease
8. Dental caries and dental fluorosis
9. Structural changes
   a. Inguinal hernia
   b. Bone mineralization
   c. Gastro-esophageal reflux
   d. Pyloric stenosis
10. Differences because of the act of breastfeeding:
   a. Orthodontic changes affecting bite and alignment; malocclusion; a deformed maxillary arch
   b. Oral muscle changes affecting speech and articulation

# References

Acheson L. Family violence and breastfeeding. *Arch Fam Med* 1995; 4:550–562.

Altemus M, Deuster PA, et al. Suppression of hypothalmic-pituitary-adrenal axis responses to stress in lactating women. *J Clin Endocrinol Metab* 1995; 80:2954–59.

American Academy of Pediatrics, Committee on Pediatric AIDS. Human milk, breastfeeding, and transmission of human immunodeficiency virus in the United States. *Pediatrics* 1995; 96:977–979.

American Academy of Pediatrics. Human Milk, Breastfeeding, and Transmission of Human Immunodeficiency Virus in the United States (RE9542). *Pediatrics* 1995; 96(5):977–979.

Aniansson G, Alm B, Andersson B, et al. A prospective cohort study on breast-feeding and otitis media in Swedish infants. *Pediatr Infect Dis J* 1994; 13:183–188.

Arnold L. HIV and breastmilk: What it means for milk banks. *J Hum Lact* 1993; 9(1):47–48.

Arnon SS. Breast feeding and toxigenic intestinal infections: Missing links in crib death? *Rev Infect Dis* 1984; 6:S193–S201.

Bahna SL. Milk allergy in infancy. *Ann Allergy* 1987; 59:131–136.

Bauer G, Ewald LS, Hoffman J, Dubanoski R. Breastfeeding and cognitive development of three-year-old children. *Psychological Reports* 1991; 68:1218.

Beaudry M, Dufour R, Marcoux S. Relation between infant feeding and infections during the first six months of life. *J Pediatr* 1995; 126:191–197.

Bergstrom E, Hernell O, Persson LA, Vessby B. Serum lipid values in adolescents are related to family history, infant feeding, and physical growth. *Atherosclerosis* 1995; 117:1–13.

Birch E, Birch D, Hoffman D, et al. Breastfeeding and optimal visual development. *J Pediatr Opthamol Strabismus* 1993; 30:33–38.

Bishop NJ, Dahlenburg SL, Fewtrell MS, et al. Early diet of preterm infants and bone mineralization at five years. *Acta Paediatrica* 1996; 85:230–236.

Braveman P, Egerter S, Pearl M, et al. Problems associated with early discharge of newborn infants. *Pediatrics* 1995; 96:716–726.

Buescher ES. Host defense mechanisms of human milk and their relations to enteric infections and necrotizing enterocolitis. *Clin Perinatol* 1994; 21(2):247–262.

Burr M, et al. Infant feeding, wheezing, and allergy: A prospective study. *Arch Dis Child* 1993; 68:724–728.

Butte N, et al. Heart rates of breastfed and formula-fed infants. *J Ped Gastro Nutr* 1991; 13:391–396.

Cavataio F, Iacono G, Montalto G, et al. Clinical and pH-metric characteristics of gastro-esophageal reflux secondary to cow's milk protein allergy. *Arch Dis Child* 1996; 75:51–56.

Centers for Disease Control and Prevention. Recommendations for assisting in the prevention of perinatal transmission of human T-lymphotropic virus type III/lymphadenopathy-associated virus and acquired immunodeficiency syndrome. *MMWR* 1985; 34:721–732.

Chandra RK. Five year follow-up of high-risk infants with family history of allergy who were exclusively breastfed or fed partial whey hydrolysate, soy, and conventional cow's milk formulas. *J Pediatr Gastroenterol Nutr* 1997; 24:380–388.

Chen Y. Synergistic effect of passive smoking and artificial feeding on hospitalization for respiratory illness in early childhood. *Chest* 1989; 95:1004–1007.

Chernishov VP, et al. Mucosal immunity of the mammary gland and immunology of mother/newborn interrelation. *Arch Immunol Ther Exp (Warsz)* 1990; 38(1-2):145–164.

Chua S, Arulkumaran S, Lim I, et al. Influence of breastfeeding and nipple stimulation on postpartum uterine activity. *Br J Obstet Gynaecol* 1994; 101:804–805.

Cochi SL, Fleming DW, Hightower AW, et al. Primary invasive Haemophilus influenzae type b disease: A population-based assessment of risk factors. *J Pediatr* 1986; 108:887–896.

Combs VL, Marino BL. A comparison of growth patterns in breast and bottlefed infants with congenital heart disease. *Pediatr Nurs* 1993; 19:175–179.

Coutsoudis A, Pillay K, Spooner E, et al. Influence of infant feeding patterns on early mother-to-child transmission of HIV-1 in Durban, South Africa: A prospective cohort study. *Lancet* 1999; 354:471–476.

Coutsoudis A, Pillay K, Kuhn L, et al. Method of feeding and transmission of HIV-1 from mothers to children by 15 months of age: Prospective cohort study from Durban, South Africa. *AIDS* 2001; 15:379–387.

Covert RF, Barman N, Domanico RS, et al. Prior enteral nutrition with human milk protects against intestinal perforation in infants who develop necrotizing enterocolitis. *Pediatr Res* 1995; 37:305A.

Crawford M. The role of essential fatty acids in neural development: Implications for perinatal nutrition. *Am J Clin Nutr* 1993; 57(suppl):703S–710S.

Crook W. Are you allergic? Jackson, TN: Professional Books, 1978.

Crook W. Tracking down hidden food allergy. Jackson, TN: Professional Books, 1980.

Crook W. You and allergy. Jackson, TN: Professional Books, 1980.

Cumming RG, Klineberg RJ. Breastfeeding and other reproductive factors and the risk of hip fractures in elderly women. *Int J Epidemiol* 1993; 22:684–691.

Cummings RD, et al. Epidemiology of osteoporosis and osteoporotic fractures. *Epidemiol Rev* 1985; 7:178–203.

Cunningham AS, Jelliffe DB, Jelliffe EFP. Breastfeeding and health in the 1980's: A global epidemiologic review. *J Pediatrics* 1991; 118(5):659–666.

Cunningham AS. Morbidity in breastfed and artificially fed babies. *J Pediatrics* 1979; 95:685–689.

Dallman PR. Progress in the prevention of iron deficiency in infants. *Acta Paediatr Scand* 1990; 365 Suppl.:28–37.

Davis D, et al. Infant feeding practices and occlusal outcomes: A longitudinal study. *J Can Dent Assoc* 1991; 57(7):593–594.

Davis MK, Savitz DA, Graubard BI. Infant feeding and childhood cancer. *Lancet* 1988; 2:365–368.

Dewey KG, Heinig J, Nommsen-Rivers L. Differences in morbidity between breastfed and formula-fed infants. *J Pediatr* 1995; 126:696–702.

Dewey KG, Heinig MJ, Nommsen LA. Maternal weight-loss patterns during prolonged lactation. *Am J Clin Nutr* 1993; 58:162–166.

Dewey KG, Heinig MJ, Nommsen LA, Peerson JM, Lonnerdal B. Breastfed infants are leaner than formula-fed infants at 1 y of age: The DARLING study. *Am J Clin Nutr* 1993; 57: 140–5.

Dewey KG, Heinig MJ, Nommsen LA, Peerson JM, Lonnerdal B. Growth of breastfed and formula-fed infants from 0 to 18 months: The DARLING study. *Pediatrics* 1992; 89:1035–1041.

Di Pietro J, et al. Behavioral and heart rate pattern differences between breastfed and bottle-fed neonates. *Develop Psych* 1988; 23(4):467–474.

Duncan B, Ey J, Holberg CJ, et al. Exclusive breastfeeding for at least 4 months protects against otitis media. *Pediatrics* 1993; 91:867–872.

Ellis MH, Short JA, Heiner DC. Anaphylaxis after ingestion of a recently introduced hydrolyzed whey protein formula. *J Pediatr* 1991; 118:74–77.

Falth-Magnusson K. Breast milk antibodies to foods in relation to maternal diet, maternal atopy and the development of atopic disease in the baby. *Int Arch Allergy Appl Immunol* 1989; 90(3):297–300.

Fishaut M, et al. Bronchomammary axis in the immune response to respiratory syncytial virus. *J Pediatr* 1981; 99(2):186–191.

Ford RPK, Taylor BJ, Mitchell EA, et al. Breastfeeding and the risk of sudden infant death syndrome. *Int J Epidemiol* 1993; 22:885–890.

Frank AL, Taber LH, Glezen WP, et al. Breastfeeding and respiratory virus infection. *Pediatrics* 1982; 70:239–245.

Frank JW, Newman J. Breastfeeding in a polluted world: Uncertain risks, clear benefits. *Can Med Assoc J* 1993; 149:33–37.

Freudenheim JL, Marshall JR, Graham S, et al. Exposure to breastmilk in infancy and the risk of breast cancer. *Epidemiology* 1994; 5:324–331.

Garofalo R, et al. Interleukin-10 in human milk. *Pediatr Res* 1995; 37(4 Pt 1):444–449.

Garofalo RP, et al. Cytokines, chemokines, and colony-stimulating factors in human milk: The 1997 update. *Biol Neonate* 1998; 74(2):134–142.

Gerstein HC. Cow's milk exposure and type I diabetes mellitus: A critical overview of the clinical literature. *Diabetes Care* 1994; 17(1):13–18.

Goldman AS, et al. Evolution of immunologic functions of the mammary gland and the postnatal development of immunity. *Pediatr Res* 1998; 43(2):155–162.

Goldman AS, et al. Host defenses: Development and maternal contributions. *Adv Pediatr* 1985; 32:71–100.

Goldman AS, et al. Immunologic factors in human milk during the first year of lactation. *J Pediatr* 1982; 100(4):563–567.

Goldman AS, et al. Transfer of maternal leukocytes to the infant by human milk. *Curr Top Microbiol Immunol* 1997; 222:205–213.

Goldman AS. Immunologic system in human milk. *J Pediatr Gastroenterol Nutr* 1986; 5(3):343–345.

Goldman AS. The immune system of human milk: Antimicrobial, antiinflammatory and immunomodulating properties. *Pediatr Infect Dis J* 1993; 12(8):664–671.

Gray RH, Campbell OM, Apelo R, et al. Risk of ovulation during lactation. *Lancet* 1990; 335:25–29.

Greco L, Auricchio S, Mayer M, et al. Case control study on nutritional risk factors in celiac disease. *J Pediatr Gastroenterol Nutr* 1988; 7:395–399.

Gwinn, ML et al. Pregnancy, breastfeeding, and oral contraceptives and the risk of epithelial ovarian cancer. *J Clin Epidemiol* 1990; 43(6):559–568.

Habbick BF, et al. Infantile hypertonic pyloric stenosis: A study of feeding practices and other possible causes. *CMAJ*, 1989; 140:401–404.

Hahn-Zoric M, et al. Antibody responses to parenteral and oral vaccines are impaired by conventional and low protein formulas as compared to breastfeeding. *Acta Paediatr Scand* 1990; 79:1137–1142.

Halken S, Host A, Hansen LG, et al. Effect of an allergy prevention programme on incidence of atopic symptoms in infancy. *Ann Allergy* 1992; 47:545–553.

Hanson LA, et al. Protective factors in milk and the development of the immune system. *Pediatrics* 1985; 75(1 Pt 2):172–176.

Hanson LA, et al. The immune response of the mammary gland and its significance for the neonate. *Ann Allergy* 1984; 53(6 Pt 2):576–582.

Harper R, et al. Developmental patterns of heart rate and heart rate variability during sleep and waking in normal infants and infants at risk for the Sudden Infant Death Syndrome. *Sleep* 1982; 5:28–38.

Harper RM, Hoffman HD, Eds: Sudden Infant Death Syndrome: Risk factors and basic mechanisms. New York: PMA Publishing, 1988; pp. 187–201.

Hasselbalch H, Jeppesen DL, Engelmann MDM, Michaelsen KF, Nielsen MB. Decreased thymus size in formula-fed infants compared with breastfed infants. *Acta Paediatrica* 1996; 85:1029–1032.

Heck H, de Castro JM. The caloric demand of lactation does not alter spontaneous meal patterns, nutrient intakes, or moods of women. *Physiol Behav* 1993; 54:641–648.

Heinig MH, Nommsen LA, Peerson MH, Lonnerdal B, Dewey KG. Energy and protein intakes of breastfed and formula-fed infants during the first year of life and their association with growth velocity: The DARLING study. *Am J Clin Nutr* 1993; 58:152–161.

Host, A. Importance of the first meal on the development of cow's milk allergy and intolerance. *Allergy Proc* 1991; 10:227–232.

Host A, Husby S, Osterballe O. A prospective study of cow's milk allergy in exclusively breastfed infants. *Acta Paediatr Scand* 1988; 77:663.

Howie PW, Forsyth JS, Ogston SA, Clark A, Florey C. Protective effect of breastfeeding against infection. *Br Med J* 1990; 300:11–16.

Hreschyshyn MN, et al. Associations of parity, breastfeeding, and birth control pills with lumbar spine and femoral neck bone densities. *Am J Obstet Gynecol* 1988; 159:318–322.

Iacono G, Carroccio A, Vatataio F, et al. Gastroesophageal reflux and cow's milk allergy in infants: A prospective study. *J Allergy Clin Immunol* 1996; 97:822–827.

Infante-Rivard C. Childhood asthma and indoor environmental risk factors. *American Journal of Epidemiology* 1993; 137:834–844.

Inoue N, Sakashita R, Kamegai T. Reduction of masseter muscle activity in bottle-fed babies. *Early Human Development* 1995; 42:185–193.

Institute of Medicine (Subcommittee on Nutrition during Lactation, Food and Nutrition Board). Nutrition during lactation. Washington DC: National Academy of Sciences, 1991.

Istre GR, Conner JS, Broome CV, et al. Risk factors for primary invasive Haemophilus influenzae disease: Increased risk from day care attendance and school-aged household members. *J Pediatr* 1985; 106:190–195.

Jeffery BS, Mercer KG. Pretoria pasteurization: A potential method for the reduction of postnatal mother-to-child transmission of the human immunodeficiency virus. *J Trop Pediatr* 2000; 46:219–223.

Jelliffe DB. Active anti-infective properties of human milk. *Lancet* 1971 Jul 17; 2(7716):167–168.

Johnstone JKAB, Kyle DJ. Meta-Analysis of the effect of breastfeeding on neurodevelopmental scores. Abstract presented at PUFA *in Infant Nutrition: Consensus and Controversies*. Barcelona, Spain: November 1996.

Jones EG, Matheney RJ. Relationship between infant feeding and exclusion from child care because of illness. *J Am Diet Assoc* 1993–7; 93(7):809–811.

Jorgensen MH, Hernell O, Lund P, Holmer G, Michaelsen KF. Visual acuity and erythrocyte docosahexaenoic acid status in breast-fed and formula-fed term infants during the first four months of life. *Lipids* 1996; 31:99–105.

Kajosaari M, et al. Prophylaxis of atopic disease by six months' total solid food elimination. Evaluation of 135 exclusively breast-fed infants of atopic families. *Acta Paediatr Scand* 1983.

Kalkwarf HJ, Specker BL, Heubi JE, et al. Intestinal absorption of women during lactation and after weaning. *Am J Clinl Nutr* 1996; 63:526–531.

Kennedy KI, Visness CM. Contraceptive efficacy of lactational amenorrhoea. *Lancet* 1992; 339:227–230.

Kjos SL, Henry O, Lee RM, Buchanan TA, Mishell DR. The effect of lactation on glucose and lipid metabolism in women with recent gestational diabetes. *Obstet Gynecol* 1993; 82:451–455.

Klaus MH. The frequency of suckling—neglected but essential ingredient of breastfeeding. *Obstet Gynecol Clin North Am* 1987; 14:623–633.

Koletzko S, Sherman P, Corey M, Griffiths A, Smith C. Role of infant feeding practices in development of Crohn's disease in childhood. *Br Med J* 1989; 298:1617–1618.

Kostraba JH, Cruickshanks KJ, et al. Early exposure to cow's milk and solid foods in infancy, genetic predisposition, and risk of IDDM. *Diabetes* 1993; 42:288–295.

Kovar MG, Serdula MK, Marks JS, et al. Review of the epidemiologic evidence for an association between infant feeding and infant health. *Pediatrics* 1984; 74:S615–S638.

Kramer F, et al. Breastfeeding reduces maternal lower-body fat. *J Am Diet Assoc* 1993; 93(4):429–433.

Labbock MH, Colie C. Puerperium and breastfeeding. *Curr Opin Obstet Gynecol* 1992; 4:818–825.

Labbok MH, Hendershot GE. Does breastfeeding protect against malocclusion? An analysis of the 1981 child health supplement to the National Health Interview Survey. *Am J Prev Med* 1987; 3(4):227–232.

Lanting CE, Fidler V, Huisman M, Touwan BD, Boersma ER. Neurological differences between 9-year-old children fed breastmilk or formula-milk as babies. *Lancet* 1994; 344(8933):1319–1322.

Lawrence R. A review of the medical benefits and contraindications to breastfeeding in the United States (Maternal and Child Health Technical Information Bulletin). Arlington, VA: National Center for Education in Maternal and Child Health, October 1997.

Lawrence RA, Lawrence RM. Breastfeeding: A guide for the medical profession, 5th ed. St. Louis: Mosby, 1999.

Lemons P, Stuart M, Lemons JA. Breastfeeding the premature infant. *Clin Perinatol* 1986; 13:111–122.

Lerman Y, Slepon R, Cohen D. Epidemiology of acute diarrheal diseases in children in a high standard of living rural settlement in Israel. *Pediatr Infect Dis C* 1994; 13:116–122.

Lucas A, Brooke OG, Morley R, et al. Early diet of preterm infants and development of allergic or atopic disease: Randomised prospective study. *Br Med J* 1990; 300:837–840.

Lucas A, Cole TJ. Breast milk and neonatal necrotising enterocolitis. *Lancet* 1990; 336:1519–1523.

Lucas A, Morley R, Cole TJ, Lister G, Lesson-Payne C. Breastmilk and subsequent intelligence quotient in children born preterm. *Lancet* 1992; 339:261–264.

Lucas A, Morley R, Cole TJ, Gore SM. A randomized multicentre study of human milk versus formula and later development in preterm infants. *Arch Dis Child* 1994; 70(2 Spec no); F141–146.

Machida HM, Catto Smith AG, Gall DG, Travenen C, Scott RB. Allergic colitis in infancy: Clinical and pathologic aspects. *J Pediatr Gastroenterol Nutr* 1994; 19:22–26.

Madsen BF. Solar-powered device decontaminates HIV-infected breast milk. Reuters Medical News. http://medscape.com/reuters/prof/2000/09/09.07/20000907drgd004.htm Accessed 9-10-2000.

Makrides M, Simmer K, Goggin M, et al. Erythrocyte docosahexaenoic acid correlates with the visual response of healthy, term infants. *Pediatr Res* 33 1993; (4 Pt 1) 425–427.

Mason T, Rabinovich CE, Fredrickson DD, et al. Breastfeeding and the development of juvenile rheumatoid arthritis. *J Rheumatol* 1995; 22:1166–1170.

Mayer EJ, Hamman RF, Gay EC, Lezotte DC, Savitz DA, Klingensmith GJ. Reduced risk of insulin-dependent diabetes mellitus (IDDM) among breastfed children. *Diabetes* 1988; 37:1625–1632.

Meier, P. Bottle and breastfeeding: Effects on transcutaneous oxygen pressure in preterm infants. *Nursing Research* 1988; 37:36–41.

Melton LJ, Bryant SC, Wahner HW, et al. Influence of breastfeeding and other reproductive factors on bone mass later in life. *Osteoporos Int* 1993; 3:76–83.

Merrett TG, Burr ML, Butland BK, et al. Infant feeding and allergy: Twelve-month prospective study of 500 babies in allergic families. *Ann Allergy* 1988; 61(6 pt 2):13–20.

Mestecky J, ed. Immunology of Milk and the Neonate. New York: Plenum Press, 1991.

Methemoglobinemia in an infant—Wisconsin 1992. *MMWR*, April 2, 1993; 42(12).

Meyers A, Hertzberg J. Bottle-feeding and malocclusion: Is there an association? *Am J Orthod Dentofac Orthop* 1988–92; 93(2):149–152.

Minchin M. Food for Thought. Sydney, Australia: Unwin Paperbacks, 1987.

Mitchell EA, Stewart MW, Becroft DM, et al. Results from the first year of the New Zealand cot death study. *NZ Med J* 1991; 104:71–76.

Mitchell EA, Taylor BJ, Ford RPK, et al. Four modifiable and other major risk factors for cot death: The New Zealand study. *J Paediatr Child Health* 1992; 28:S3–S8.

Monte WD, Johnston CS, Roll LE. Bovine serum albumin detected in infant formula is a possible trigger for insulin-dependent diabetes mellitus. *J Am Diet Assoc* 1994; 94:314–316.

Morrow-Tlucak M, Haude RH, Ernhart CB. Breastfeeding and cognitive development in the first 2 years of life. *Soc Sci Med* 1988; 26:635–639.

Neville MC, Neifert MR. Lactation: Physiology, nutrition and breastfeeding. New York: Plenum Press, 1983.

Newcomb PA, Storer BE, Longnecker MP, Mittendorf R, et al. Lactation and a reduced risk of premenopausal breast cancer. *N Engl J Med* 1994; 330:81–87.

Newman J. How breast milk protects newborns. *Sci Am* 1995 Dec; pp. 76–79.

Niemala M, Uhari M, Mottonen M. A pacifier increases the risk of recurrent otitis media in children in day care centers. *Pediatrics* 1995; 96:884–888.

Oddy WH, Holt PG, Sly PD, et al. Association between breastfeeding and asthma in six year old children: Findings of a prospective birth cohort study. *Br Med J* 1999; 319:815–819.

Odze RD, Wershil BK, Leichtner AM, Antonioli, DA. Allergic colitis in infants. *J Pediatr* 1995; 126:163–170.

Owen MJ, Baldwin CD, Swank PR, et al. Relation of infant feeding practices, cigarette smoke exposure, and group child care to the onset and duration of otitis media with effusion in the first two years of life. *J Pediatr* 1993; 123:702–711.

Paine R, Cable RD. Breastfeeding and infant health in a rural US community. *Am J Dis Child* 1982; 136:36–38.

Paradise JL, Elster BA, Tan L. Evidence in infants with cleft palate that breast milk protects against otitis media. *Pediatrics* 1994; 94:853–860.

Pettitt DJ, Forman MR, Hanson RL, Knowler WC, Bennett PH. Breastfeeding and incidence of non-insulin-dependent diabetes mellitus in Pima Indians. *Lancet* 1997; 350:166–168.

Pickering LK, Ed. 2000 Red book: Report of the committee on infectious diseases, 25th ed. Elk Grove Village, IL: American Academy of Pediatrics; 2000.

Pisacane A, De Visia B, Valiante A, et al. Iron status in breastfed infants. *J Pediatr* 1995; 127:429–431.

Pisacane A, DeLuca U, Vaccaro F, Valiante A, Impagliazzo N, Caracciolo G. Breastfeeding and inguinal hernia. *J Pediatr* 1995; 127:109–111.

Pisacane A, Graziano L, Mazzarella G, Scarpellino B, Zona G. Breastfeeding and urinary tract infection. *J Pediatr* 1992; 120:87–89.

Pisacane A, Graziano L, Zona G, et al. Breastfeeding and acute lower respiratory infection. *Acta Paediatr* 1994; 83:714–718.

Pisacane A, Impagliazzo N, DeCaprio C, Criscuolo L, Inglese A, da Silva MCMP. Breast feeding and tonsillectomy. *Br Med J* 1996; 312:746–747.

Pisacane A, Impagliazzo N, Russo M, Valiani R, Mandarina A, Florio C, Vivo P. Breastfeeding and multiple sclerosis. *Br Med J* 1994; 308:1411–1412.

Pisacane A, DeLuca U, Impagliazzo, et al. Breastfeeding and acute appendicitis. *Br Med J* 1995; 310:836–837.

Pooro E, et al. Early wheezing and breastfeeding. *J Asthma* 1993; 30(1):23–28.

Popkin BM, Adair L, Akin JS, et al. Breastfeeding and diarrheal morbidity. *Pediatrics* 1990; 86:874–882.

Powers NG, Naylor AJ, Wester RA. Hospital policies: Crucial to breastfeeding success. *Semin Perinatol* 1994; 18:517–524.

Procianoy RS, Fernandes-Filho PH, Lazaro L, et al. The influence of rooming-in on breastfeeding. *J Trop Pediatr* 1983; 29:112–114.

Radford A. The ecological impact of bottle feeding. *Breastfeeding Review* 1992–5 II(5):204–208.

Raisler J, Alexander C, O'Campo P. Breastfeeding and infant illness: A dose-response relationship? *Am J Pub Health* 1999; 89:25–30.

Rapp, D. Is this your child? Discovering and treating unrecognized allergies in children and adults. New York: Quill William Morrow, 1991.

Rapp D. Is this your child's world? New York: Bantam Books, 1996.

Reves R, et al. Child day care increases the risk of clinic visits for acute diarrhea and diarrhea due to rotovirus. *Am J Epidemiol* 1993; 137(1):97–107.

Rigas A, Rigas B, Glassman M, et al. Breastfeeding and maternal smoking in the etiology of Crohn's disease and ulcerative colitis in childhood. *Ann Epidemiol* 1993; 3:387–392.

Riordan J, Auerbach KG. Breastfeeding and human lactation, 2nd ed. Sudbury, MA: Jones and Bartlett Publishers, 1999.

Riva E, Agostoni C, Biasucci G, et al. Early breastfeeding is linked to higher intelligence quotient scores in dietary-treated phenlyketonuric children. *Acta Paediatr* 1996; 85:56–58.

Rogan WJ, Gladen BC. Breastfeeding and cognitive development. *Early Human Dev* 1993; 31:181–193.

Rosenblatt KA, Thomas DB, the WHO Collaborative Study of Neoplasia and Steroid Contraceptives. Prolonged lactation and endometrial cancer. *International Journal of Epidemiology* 1995; 24:499–503.

Rosenthal E, Schlesinger Y, Birnbaum Y, et al. Intolerance to casein hydrolysate formula. *Acta Paediatr Scand* 1991; 80:958–960.

Saarinen UM, Savilahti E. Infant feeding patterns affect the subsequent immunological features in cow's milk allergy. Clin Exp Allergy 2000; 30:400–406.

Saarinen UM, Kajosaari M. Breastfeeding as prophylaxis against atopic disease: Prospective follow-up study until 17 years old. *Lancet* 1995; 346:1,065–1,069.

Saarinen UM. Prolonged breastfeeding as prophylaxis for recurrent otitis media. *Acta Paediatr Scand* 1982; 71:567–571.

Saarinen UM. Need for iron supplementation in infants on prolonged breastfeeding. *J Pediatr* 1978; 93:177–180.

Sampson HA, James JM, Bernhisel-Broadbent J. Safety of an amino acid derived infant formula in children allergic to cow milk. *Pediatr* 1992; 463–465.

Sampson HA, Bernhisel-Broadbent J, Yang E, Scanlon SM. Safety of casein hydrolysate formula in children with cow milk allergy. *J Pediatr* 1991; 118:520–525.

Samuelsson U, Johansson C, Ludvigsson J. Breastfeeding seems to play a marginal role in the prevention of insulin-dependent diabetes mellitus. *Diabetes Res Clin Pract* 1993; 19:203–10.

Saylor JD, Bahna SL. Anaphylaxis to casein hydrolysate formula. *J Pediatr* 1991; 118:71–73.

Scariati PD, Grummer-Strawn LM, Fein SB. A longitudinal analysis of infant morbidity and the extent of breastfeeding in the US. *Pediatrics* 1997; 99(6):e5.

Schwartz RH, Amonette MS. Cow milk protein hydrolysate infant formulas not always "hypoallergenic." *J Pediatr* 1991; 118:839.

Scragg LK, Mitchell EA, Tonkin SL, et al. Evaluation of the cot death prevention programme in South Auckland. *N Z Med J* 1993; 106:8–10.

Setchell KDR, Zimmer-Nechemias L, Cai J, Heubi JE. Exposure of infants to phyto-estrogens from soy-based infant formula. *Lancet* 1997; 350:23–27.

Shu X-O, Clemens J, Zheng W, Ying DM, Ji BT, Jin F. Infant breastfeeding and the risk of childhood lymphoma and leukaemia. *Int J Epidemio* 1995; 24:27–32.

Sigman-Grant M, Peterson S, Moll M. Confirmation of breastfeeding as a protective factor from *Salmonellosis* in Pennsylvania infants. *FASEB J* Abstracts: Part 1:Vol 9(7), 1995; p. A183.

Silver LB, et al. Learning disabilities as a probable consequence of using chloride-deficient formula. *J Pediatr* 1989; 115:97–99.

Simopoulos A. Omega-3 fatty acids in health and disease and in growth and development. *Am J Clin Nutr* 1991; 54:438–463.

Singh H, Kaur L, Kataria FP. Enuresis: Analysis of 100 cases. *Indian Pediatrics* 1991; 28(4):375–380.

Slade HB, Schwartz SA. Mucosal immunity: The immunology of breast milk. *J Allergy Clin Immunol* 1987; 80(3):348–356.

Snyder JD, et al. Pyloric stenosis and eosinophilic gastroenteritis in infants. *J Ped Gastro Nutr* 1987; 6:543–47.

Sosa R, Kennell JH, Klaus M, et al. The effect of early mother-infant contact on breast feeding, infection and growth. In: Lloyd JK, ed. Breastfeeding and the mother. Amsterdam: Elsevier; 1976; 179–193.

Steinman HA. "Hidden" allergens in foods. *J Allergy Clin Immunol* 1996 Aug; 98(2):241–250.

Strimac JN, Chi DS. Significance of IgE level in amniotic fluid and cord blood for the prediction of allergy. *Ann Allergy* 1986, 61:133–136.

Strobel S. Dietary manipulation and induction of tolerance. *J Pediatr* 1992 Nov; 121(5 Pt 2):S74–9.

Sveger T. Breastfeeding, a 1-antitrypsin deficiency, and liver disease? *JAMA* 1985; 254:3036. Letter.

Takala AK, Eskola J, Palmgren J, et al. Risk factors of invasive Haemophilus influenzae type b disease among children in Finland. *J Pediatr* 1989; 115:694–701.

Tanoue Y, Oda S. Weaning time of children with infantile autism. *J Autism Developmental Disord* 1989; 19(3):425–434.

Teele DW, Klein JO, Rosner B. Beneficial effects of breastfeeding on duration of middle ear effusion after first episode of acute otitis media. *Pediatr Res* 1980; 14: 494 (Abstract 10).

Toms GL, et al. Secretion of respiratory syncytial virus inhibitors and antibody in human milk throughout lactation. *J Med Virol* 1980; 5(4):351–360.

Uauy R, et al. Effect of dietary Omega-3 fatty acids on retinal function of very-low-birthweight neonates. *Pediatr Res* 1990; 28(5):485–492.

Uauy R, et al. Visual and brain function measurements in studies of Omega-3 fatty acid requirements of infants. *J Pediatr* 1992; 120:S168–180.

Uauy R. Are Omega-3 fatty acids required for normal eye and brain development in the human? *J Ped Gastro Nutr* 1990; 11(3):296–302.

Udall JN, Dixon M, Newman AP, et al. Liver disease in a 1-antitrypsin deficiency: retrospective analysis of the influence of early breast vs. bottle feeding. *JAMA* 1985; 253:2679–2682.

Uhari M, Mantysaari K, Niemala M. A Meta-analytic review of the risk factors for acute otitis media. *Clinical Infectious Diseases* 1996; 22:1079–1083.

Uvnas-Moberg K, Eriksson M. Breastfeeding: physiological, endocrine and behavioural adaptations caused by oxytocin and local neurogenic activity in the nipple and mammary gland. *Acta Pediatr* 1996; 85:525–530.

Van Den Bosch CA, Bullough CHW. Effect of early suckling on term neonates' core body temperature. *Ann Trop Paediatr* 1990; 10:347–353.

Virtanen SM, Rasanen L, Aro A, et al. Infant feeding in Finnish children <7 yr of age with newly diagnosed IDDM. *Diabetes Care* 1991; 14:415–417.

Walterspiel JN, Morrow AL, Guerrero L, Ruiz-Palacios GM, Pickering LK. Secretory Anti-*Giardia lamblia* antibodies in human milk: Protective effect against diarrhea. *Pediatrics* 1994; 93:28–31.

Wang YS, Wu SY. The effect of exclusive breastfeeding on development and incidence of infection in infants. *J Hum Lact* 1996; 12(1):27–30.

Whorell PJ, Hodstack G, et al. Bottlefeeding, early gastroenteritis, and inflammatory bowel disease. *Br Med J* 1979; 1: 382.

Wiessinger D. Watch your language! *J Hum Lact* 1996; 12(1): 1–4.

Wilson AC, Forsyth JS, Greene SA, et al. Relation of infant diet to childhood health: 7 year follow-up of cohort of children in Dundee infant feeding study. *Br Med J* 1998; 316:21–25.

World Health Organization. Consensus statement from the consultation on HIV transmission and breastfeeding. *J Hum Lactation* 1992; 8:173–174.

World Health Organization, UNICEF, UNAIDS. HIV and infant feeding: Infant feeding options. Geneva: World Health Organization, 1998.

World Health Organization, UNICEF, UNAIDS. HIV and infant feeding: Guidelines for decision-makers. Geneva: World Health Organization, 1998.

Wright AL, Bauer M, Naylor A, et al. Increasing breastfeeding rates to reduce infant illness at the community level. *Pediatrics* 1998; 101:837–844.

Wright AL, Holberg CJ, Martinez FR, Morgan WJ, Taussig LM. Breastfeeding and lower respiratory tract illness in the first year of life. *Br Med J* 1989; 299:946–949.

Wright AL, Holberg CJ, Taussig LM, Martinez FD. Relationship of infant feeding to recurrent wheezing at age 6 years. *Arch Pediatr Adolescent Med* 1995; 149:758–763.

Yap PL, et al. The development of mammary secretory immunity in the human newborn. *Acta Paediatr Scand* 1981 Jul; 70(4):459–65.

Yoon PW, Black RE, Moulton LH, Becker S. Effect of not breastfeeding on the risk of diarrheal and respiratory mortality under 2 years of age in Metro Cebu, the Philippines. *Am J Epidemiol* 1996; 143:1142–1148.

Zeiger RS. Dietary aspects of food allergy prevention in infants and children. *J Pediatr Gastroenterol Nutr* 2000; 30:S77–S86.

Zeskind PS, et al. Rhythmic organization of heart rate in breastfed and bottle-fed newborn infants. *Early Dev and Parenting* 1992; (2):79–87.

Zimmer JP, et al. Relationship between serum prolactin, lactation and changes in maternal blood B-cell (CD19+) percents during the first 8 months post-partum. *J Reprod Immunol* 1996; 30(2-3):81–95.

Zoppi G, et al. Diet and antibody response to vaccinations in healthy infants. *Lancet* 1983; 2:11–14.

# Protection Against Chronic Disease

*Carol A. Ryan, RN, MSN(c), IBCLC*

## Objectives

- List selected chronic diseases that are affected by breastfeeding.
- Discuss long-term outcomes of the receipt of breast milk.
- Provide evidence-based support for the continued recommendation to breastfeed exclusively for about six months and to continue providing breast milk as long as possible as a preventive measure in reducing the incidence of chronic disease.

## Introduction

Medical research and clinical practice have long acknowledged the immediate benefits of human milk for the human infant. Continued research has explored and studied breastfed infants into their adulthoods. Researchers' findings have brought to light facts to the medical and general public's attention that support the long-term benefits of human milk for the world's community of children. Some of the most notable and life-sustaining outcomes have been seen in studies examining Crohn's disease, ulcerative colitis, *insulin-dependent diabetes mellitus* (IDDM), obesity, and certain childhood cancers (lymphomas and leukemia). Because these diseases and conditions can exact a devastating toll on the health of affected individuals and a crushing burden on the health care system's scarce dollars, the lactation consultant's knowledge of these issues will be important in health planning and in working both prenatally and postpartum with new families. Breastfeeding reduces the incidence of all of these diseases:

I  Crohn's disease—an inflammatory bowel disease

    A. Crohn's disease has increased in incidence since its recognition only several decades ago

    B. Noted in Western populations with Northern European and Anglo-Saxon cultures

    C. Noted also in developing countries, African-American, and Hispanic populations

    D. Occurs equally in both sexes

    E. More common in the Jewish population

    F.  Has a familial tendency and can overlap with ulcerative colitis

    G.  Peak incidences occur at ages 14 and 24 years

    H.  Appears as patchy inflammatory ulcerations on the mucosa of the intestinal wall with a combination of longitudinal and transverse ulcers and intervening mucosal edema

    I.  Causes inflammation of the small intestine, often in the ileum, but can affect the digestive system from the mouth to the anus

    J.  The inflammation extends into the deeper layers of the intestinal wall

    K.  The most common signs and symptoms include diarrhea with abdominal pain, fever, anorexia, weight loss, bleeding, and a right lower quadrant mass or fullness

    L.  Children who have Crohn's disease might suffer delayed development and stunted growth

    M.  Breast milk is essential for the development of normal immunological competence of the intestinal mucosa

    N.  People who have Crohn's disease are overrepresented in groups that have little to no breastfeeding history as infants

II  Ulcerative colitis—an inflammatory bowel disease

    A.  A chronic, nonspecific inflammatory and ulcerative disease arising in the colonic mucosa

    B.  Characterized most often as periods of bloody diarrhea with mucous, abdominal cramps varying in intensity and duration, and with intermittent exacerbations and remissions

    C.  Complications can be life threatening

    D.  Etiology is similar to Crohn's disease

    E.  Has a nonspecific microbial etiology

    F.  Familial tendency is less evident than in Crohn's disease

    G.  The major peak incidence is seen at 15–30 years of age, with a smaller peak at ages 50–70 years

    H.  The disease usually beings in the rectosigmoid area, extending proximally and eventually involving the whole colon (or perhaps including most of the large bowel at once); involves ulceration and inflammation of the inner lining of the colon and rectum

    I.  Human milk protects against many of these *gastrointestinal* (GI) diseases because it causes development of the normal immunologic competence of the intestinal mucosa and protects it from adhesion and penetration from bacteria, viruses, and foreign proteins that can compromise its integrity and provoke an inflammatory response

    J.  Human milk is also therapeutic to the damaged gut

**III** Insulin-dependent diabetes mellitus (IDDM)

  A. IDDM represents 10–15 percent of all incidences of diabetes mellitus.

  B. IDDM is clinically characterized by hyperglycemia (high blood sugar) and an inclination toward diabetic ketoacidosis (coma).

  C. Once diagnosed, IDDM requires insulin for life.

  D. IDDM occurs most often in childhood or adolescence.

  E. IDDM is the most predominant form of diabetes mellitus diagnosed before age 30.

  F. IDDM results from a genetically conditioned, immune-mediated, selective destruction of more than 90 percent of the insulin-secreting B cells in the pancreas.

  G. IDDM individuals have an increased risk for retinopathy, nephropathy, neuropathy, and atherosclerotic coronary and peripheral vascular disease and are very susceptible to infections.

  H. Children who have IDDM are approximately 30 percent less likely to have ever been breastfed.

    1. A significantly decreased risk for IDDM exists as infants are breastfed for lengths approaching 12 months.

    2. 2–26 percent of IDDM can be attributable to little or no breastfeeding and could be reduced by exclusive breastfeeding through at least three months of age.

  I. The biologic mechanisms that could lead to a protective effect by breastfeeding are not well understood.

    1. Diet might be a permissive factor in the development of IDDM.

    2. Newly diagnosed children have increased IgA and IgG antibodies to bovine beta-lactoglobulin.

    3. Cow's milk has been reported to be diabetogenic in two susceptible animal models.

    4. The destruction of the pancreatic beta cells that occurs in IDDM is autoimmune in nature.

    5. Several recessive genes map the risk of diabetes, but one or more environmental factors triggers the disease.

    6. Cow's milk is one of a number of environmental triggers.

    7. Exclusive breastfeeding with delayed exposure to cow's milk-based formula reduces the risk of diabetes.

    8. Whey protein *bovine serum albumin* (BSA) might be a trigger.

    9. Its antibodies can cross-react with a pancreatic beta cell surface protein, destroying it in an immune reaction attack.

    10. A possible sequence might include a specific immune memory established at the time of the dietary exposure to cow's milk.

11. The timing of gut closure, the presence of digestive enzymes such as trypsin, GI infections, and oral tolerance mechanisms might all collaborate to enable the initiation of the autoimmune response.

12. Clinical disease develops in about five to six per 1,000 hosts with the relevant genetic predisposition.

13. Prevention of exposure to cow's milk early in life eliminates a dietary trigger that is thought to initiate the autoimmune response.

14. Exposures to cow's milk and solid foods before three months of age might be particularly important in terms of diabetic risk.

    a. The age of introduction of alternative infant milks and solid foods is etiologically important.

    b. Sensitization to cow's milk could occur when very early exposure occurs before gut cellular tight junction closure or exposure during an infection-caused GI alteration when the intestinal barrier is compromised, enabling antigens to cross and initiate an immune reaction.

15. Children who have IDDM have a history of more frequent feedings with soy-based formula, showing twice as high anti-thyroid antibodies as breastfed children.

16. A high weight gain during the first 30 months of life (as seen in many non-breastfed babies) is associated with an increased risk of IDDM.

    a. Overfeeding with formula causes an increased demand for insulin, which might result in an increased beta-cell antigen presentation—helping explain the tendency to develop IDDM during periods of increased insulin demand.

**IV** Childhood cancer

  A. Lymphoma—a heterogeneous group of neoplasms arising in the reticuloendothelial and lymphatic systems

    1. Lymphoma is a cancer that is strongly associated with artificial feeding.

    2. Altered immunoregulation (disturbed immune competence) might contribute to an increased risk of lymphoproliferative disease because children with immune deficiencies have an increased risk for lymphoma.

    3. Immunoregulation might be altered in some children who were not breastfed during early exposure to viral infections.

  B. Hodgkin's disease—has features of a complex cellular immune disorder and of chronic infection

    1. A chronic disease with lymphoreticular proliferation of an unknown cause that might present itself in a localized or disseminated fashion.

    2. First peaks around 15–34 years of age and again around 60 years of age.

3. Presents with a wide variety of signs and symptoms, not necessarily occurring at the same time—some of which include (depending upon its stage) intense pruritis, fever, night sweats, weight loss, lymph node compression, and obstruction of internal organs.

4. Manifestations appear as the disease spreads from one site to another.

5. The rate of progression varies from relatively slow to aggressive.

6. Children who were never breastfed or who were breastfed only short term have a higher risk than those who were breastfed for greater than or equal to six months of developing Hodgkin's disease but not non-Hodgkin's lymphoma.

C. Leukemia

1. Leukemia is the most common childhood malignancy in Western countries and accounts for one-third of all cancers occurring in children younger than age 15.

2. Even short-term breastfeeding has been associated with a 21 percent reduction in risk of childhood acute leukemias.

3. Specific or nonspecific anti-infectious effects and early immune-stimulating effects of breast milk might work either independently or synergistically to protect children against acute leukemia.

V. Obesity

A. In industrialized countries, *overweight* and *obesity* represent the most common nutritional disorders in children and adolescents.

B. Overweight and obesity in children is increasing in prevalence.

C. This situation presents the concomitant risk from the associated health complications, such as diabetes, hypertension, and coronary artery disease.

D. Once established, it is highly likely that childhood obesity might become chronic and resistant to treatment.

E. Researchers have found a clear dose-dependent effect of the duration of breastfeeding on the prevalence of being overweight or obese at the time of school entry.

**Amount of Risk Reduction for Being Overweight and Obesity from Breastfeeding**

| Exclusive Breastfeeding for: | Overweight | Obesity |
| --- | --- | --- |
| less than or greater than months | 11% | 10% |
| 3–5 months | 13% | 35% |
| 6–12 months | 33% | 43% |
| greater than 12 months | 57% | 72% |

F. The protective effect might have a programming effect in preventing overweight conditions and obesity in later life.

G. Formula-fed infants have higher plasma concentrations of insulin, which could stimulate fat deposition and the early development of adipocytes (fat cells).

H. Breastfed babies do not consume as much energy and protein as formula-fed babies, which could contribute to a decreased *body mass index* (BMI) of children and adolescents who were breastfed.

I. Breastfed babies are leaner than formula-fed babies at one year of age.

# References

Akre J. Ed. Infant feeding: The physiologic basis. Geneva, Switzerland: World Health Organization, 1989.

American Academy of Pediatrics, Work Group on Cow's Milk Protein and Diabetes Mellitus. Infant feeding practices and their possible relationship to the etiology of diabetes mellitus. *Pediatrics* 1994; 94:752–755.

Bergstrand O, Hellers G. Breastfeeding during infancy and later development of Crohn's disease. *Scand J Gastroenterol* 1983; 18:903.

Borch-Johnson K, et al. Relation between breastfeeding and incidence rates of insulin dependent diabetes mellitus. *Lancet* 1984; 2:1083–1086.

Calkins BM, Mendeloff AI. Epidemiology of inflammatory bowel disease. *Epidemiol Rev* 1986; 8:60–91.

Chen Y, Yu S, Li W. Artificial feeding and hospitalization in the first 18 months of life. *Pediatrics* 1988; 81:58–62.

Clavano NR. Mode of feeding and its effect on infant mortality and morbidity. *J Trop Pediatr* 1982; 28:287–293.

Cunningham AS, Jelliffe DB, Jelliffe EFP. Breastfeeding and health in the 1980's: A global epidemiologic review. *J Pediatr* 1991; 118:659–666.

Davis MK, Savitz DA, Graubard. Infant feeding and childhood cancer. *Lancet* 1988; 2(8607):365–368.

Davis MK. Review of the evidence for an association between infant feeding and childhood cancer. *Int J Cancer Suppl* 1998; 11:29–33.

Dewey KG, et al. Breastfed infants are leaner than formula-fed infants at one year of age: The DARLING study. *Am J Clin Nutr* 1993; 57:140–145.

Dewey KG, Heinig J, Nommensen-Rivers LA. Differences in morbidity between breastfed and formula-fed infants. *J Pediatr* 1995; 126:697–702.

Dewey KG, et al. Growth of breastfed infants deviates from current reference data: A pooled analysis of US, Canadian, and European data sets. *Pediatrics* 1995; 96:495–503.

Fallot ME, Boyd JL, Oski FA. Breastfeeding reduces incidence of hospital admissions for infections in infants. *Pediatrics* 1980; 65:1,121–1,124.

Fomon SJ, Filer LJ, Thomas LN, et al. Indices of fatness and serum cholesterol at age eight years in relation to feeding and growth during early infancy. *Pediatr Res* 1984; 18:1233.

Fort P, Lanes R, Dahlem S, et al. Breastfeeding and insulin dependent diabetes mellitus in children. *J Am Coll Nutr* 1986; 5:439.

Gerstein HC. Cow's milk exposure and type I diabetes mellitus: A critical overview of the clinical literature. *Diabetes Care* 1994; 17:13–18.

Glatthaar D, Whitall DE, Welborn TA, et al. Diabetes in western Australian children: Descriptive epidemiology. *Med J Aust* 1988; 148:117.

Gulick EE. The effect of breastfeeding on toddler health. *Pediatr Nurs* 1986; 12:51–54.

Hamosh M. Does infant nutrition affect adiposity and cholesterol levels in adulthood? *J Pediatr Gastroenterol Nutr* 1988; 7:10.

Howie PW, Forsyth JS, Ogston SA, et al. Protective effect of breastfeeding against infection. *Br Med J* 1990; 300:11–16.

Jarrett RJ. Breastfeeding and diabetes. *Lancet* 1984; 2:1283.

Jason JM, Nieburg P, Marks JS. Mortality and disease associated with infant feeding practices in developing countries. *Pediatrics* 1984; 74:702–727.

Jelliffe DB, Jelliffe EFP. Human milk in the modern world. Oxford: Oxford University Press, 1978.

Johansson C, Samuelsson U, Ludvigsson J. A high weight gain early in life is associated with an increased risk of Type I (insulin dependent) diabetes mellitus. *Diabetologia* 1994; 37:91–94.

Karjalainen J, Martin J, Knip M, et al. A bovine albumin peptide as a possible trigger of insulin dependent diabetes mellitus. *N Engl J Med* 1992; 327:302–307.

Khin-Maung-U, Nyant Nyant W, Khin M, et al. Effect on clinical outcome of breastfeeding during acute diarrhea. *Br Med J* 1985; 290:587.

Koletzko S, Sherman P, Corey M, et al. Role of infant feeding practices in development of Crohn's disease in childhood. *Br Med J* 1989; 298:1617–1618.

Koopman JS, et al. Infant formulas and gastrointestinal illness. *Am J Pub Health* 1985; 75:477–480.

Kostraba JH, and Cruickshanks KJ, et al. Early exposure to cow's milk and solid foods in infancy, genetic predisposition, and risk of IDDM. *Diabetes* 1993; 42:288–295.

Kovar MG, et al. Review of the epidemiologic evidence for an association between infant feeding and infant health. *Pediatrics* 1984; 74:615–638.

Kramer MS, Barr RG, Leduc DG, et al. Determinants of weight and adiposity in the first year of life. *J Pediatr* 1985; 106:10.

Lawrence RA, Lawrence R. Breastfeeding: A guide for the medical profession. St. Louis, MO: Mosby, Inc., 1999.

Lebenthal E, Leung Y-K. The impact of development of the gut on infant nutrition. *Pediatr Ann* 1987; 16:211.

Lewis DS, Bertrand HA, McHahan CA, et al. Preweaning food intake influences the adiposity of young adult baboons. *J Clin Invest* 1986; 78:899.

Marmot MG, Page CM, Atkins E, et al. Effect of breastfeeding on plasma cholesterol and weight in young adults. *J Epidemiol* 1980; 34:164.

Mathur GP, et al. Breastfeeding and childhood cancer. *Ind Pediatr* 1993; 30:651–657.

Mayer EJ, Hamman RF, Gay EC, et al. Reduced risk of IDDM among breastfed children: The Colorado IDDM Registry. *Diabetes* 1988; 37:1625.

McKinney PA, Parslow R, Gurney KA, et al. Perinatal and neonatal determinants of childhood Type I diabetes. A case-control study in Yorkshire, UK. *Diabetes Care* 1999; 22(6):928–932.

Merck manual of diagnosis and therapy. 16th ed. Rathway, NJ: Merck Research Laboratories, 1992.

Miller RW, Fraumeni JF. Does breastfeeding increase the child's risk of breast cancer? *Pediatrics* 1996; 49:645.

Minchin M. Infant formula: A mass uncontrolled trial in perinatal care. *Birth* 1987; 14:25–35.

Mitra AK, Rabbani F. The importance of breastfeeding in minimizing mortality and morbidity from diarrhoeal diseases: The Bangladesh perspective. *J Diarrhoeal Dis Res* 1995; 13:1–7.

Monte WD, Johnston CS, Roll LE. Bovine serum albumin detected in infant formula is a possible trigger for insulin dependent diabetes mellitus. *J Am Diet Assoc* 1994; 94:314–316.

Motil KJ, et al. Human milk protein does not limit growth of breastfed infants. *J Pediatr Gastroenterol Nutr* 1997; 24:10–17.

Pettitt DJ, Forman MR, Hanson RL, et al. Breastfeeding and incidence of non-insulin dependent diabetes mellitus in Pima Indians. *Lancet* 1997; 350 (9072):166–168.

Pettitt DJ, Knowler WC. Long-term effects of the intrauterine environment, birth weight, and breastfeeding in Pima Indians. *Diabetes Care* 1998; Suppl 2:B138–B141.

Popkin BM, et al. Breastfeeding and diarrheal morbidity. *Pediatrics* 1990; 86:874–882.

Read L, et al. Changes in growth promoting activity of human milk during lactation. *Pediatr Res* 1984; 18:133–138.

Rennie J. Formula for diabetes? *Sci Am* 1992; 267:24.

Rigas A, et al. Breastfeeding and maternal smoking in the etiology of Crohn's disease and ulcerative colitis in childhood. *Ann Epidemiol* 1993; 3:387–392.

Riordan J. The cost of not breastfeeding. *J Hum Lact* 1997; 13:93–97.

Riordan J, Auerbach KG. Eds. Breastfeeding and human lactation, 2nd ed. Sudbury, MA: Jones and Bartlett Publishers, 1999.

Samuelson U, Johansson C, Ludvigsson, J. Breastfeeding seems to play a marginal role in the prevention of insulin dependent diabetes mellitus (IDDM) among breastfed children. *Diabetes* 1988; 37:1625–1632.

Sandiford P, et al. Why do child mortality rates fall? An analysis of the Nicaraguan experience. *Am J Public Health* 1991; 81:30–37.

Savilahti E, Saukkonen TT, Virtala ET, et al. Increased levels of cow's milk and beta-lactoglobulin antibodies in young children with newly diagnosed IDDM. *Diabetes Care* 1993; 16:984–989.

Scott FW. Cow milk and insulin dependent diabetes mellitus: Is there a relationship? *Am J Clin Nutr* 1990; 51:489–491.

Shing YW, Klagsburn M. Human and bovine milk contain different sets of growth factors. *Endocrinol* 1984; 115:273.

Shu XO, et al. Infant breastfeeding and the risk of childhood lymphoma and leukaemia. *Int J Epidemiol* 1995; 24:27–34.

Shu XO, Linet M, Steinbuch M, et al. Breastfeeding and risk of childhood acute leukemia. *J Natl Cancer Inst* 1999; 91:1765–1772.

Strabk V, Skulteyova M, Randuskova A, et al. Late effects of breastfeeding and early weaning: Seven year prospective study in children. *Endocr Regul* 1991; 25:53.

Tulldahl J, Pettersson K, Andersson SW, Hulthen L. Mode of infant feeding and achieved growth in adolescence: Early feeding patterns in relation to growth and body composition in adolescence. *Obesity Res* 1999; 7:431–437.

Vaarala O, et al. Cow's milk formula feeding induces primary immunization to insulin in infants at genetic risk for Type I diabetes. *Diabetes* 1999; 48:1389–1394.

Von Kries R, Koletzko B, Sauerwald T, et al. Breastfeeding and obesity: Cross sectional study. *Br Med J* 1999; 313:147–150.

Von Kries R, Koletzko B, Sauerwald T, et al. Does breastfeeding protect against childhood obesity? *Adv Exp Med Biol* 2000; 478:29–39.

Wade N. Bottle-feeding: Adverse effects of a Western technology. *Science* 1974; 184:45–48.

Walker M. A fresh look at the risks of artificial infant feeding. *J Hum Lact* 1993; 9:97–107.

Whitehead RG, Paul AA. Infant growth and human milk requirement: A fresh approach. *Lancet* 1978; 2:161–163.

Whorwell PJ, Hodstack G, et al. Bottle-feeding, early gastroenteritis, and inflammatory bowel disease. *Br J Med* 1979; 1:382.

Wilson JV, Self TW, Hamburger R. Severe cow's milk induced colitis in an exclusively breastfed neonate. *Clin Pediatr* 1990; 29:77–80.

Wood CS, et al. Exclusively breastfed infants: Growth and caloric intake. *Pediatr Nurs* 1988; 14:117–124.

World Health Organization Working Group on Infant Growth and Nutrition Unit. An evaluation of infant growth. Geneva: World Health Organization, 1994.

Yoneyama K, Nagata H, Asano H. Growth of Japanese breastfed and bottle-fed infants from birth to 20 months. *Annu Hum Biol* 1994; 21:597–608.

# PREGNANCY, LABOR, AND BIRTH COMPLICATIONS

*Marsha Walker, RN, IBCLC*

## OBJECTIVES

- Describe several maternal problems that can occur in the perinatal period.
- Plan for how breastfeeding can continue under adverse situations.
- Ascertain whether any of these conditions are present when working with a breastfeeding problem.
- Discuss how these situations can impact the baby and breastfeeding.

## Introduction

While pregnancy, labor, and birth are normal and natural processes, occasional problems arise that might have an impact on breastfeeding. These complications can change a mother's birth plan and might affect access to her infant after delivery. The lactation consultant will benefit from knowledge of the more common alterations in maternal health and strategies in order to circumvent any impediment to breastfeeding that might be present.

   I  Hypertensive disorders of pregnancy

     A. Preeclampsia is determined by increased blood pressure after 20 weeks of gestation (pregnancy-induced hypertension, or PIH) accompanied by proteinuria, edema, or both.

     B. Severe preeclampsia is a progression to higher blood pressure, more protein in the urine, oliguria (decreased urine output), cerebral or visual changes, severe headaches, epigastric pain, pulmonary edema, or cyanosis.

     C. Eclampsia (toxemia) denotes the occurrence of convulsions not caused by neurologic disease and usually occurs after 32 weeks gestation.

     D. Delivery is the only definitive treatment for PIH.

E. Preeclampsia occurs in 5–6 percent of otherwise normal pregnancies and more frequently in women who have chronic renal or vascular diseases such as diabetes, collagen vascular disease, or chronic hypertension.

F. Morbidity to the infant can include growth retardation, asphyxia in the fetus, or premature delivery in order to improve the mother's condition.

G. Some women who have preeclampsia develop an unusual manifestation of their disease that is called the HELLP syndrome:

   1. H = intravascular hemolysis

   2. EL = elevated aspartate aminotransferase (AST) and alanine aminotransferase (ALT) liver enzymes

   3. LP = low platelets

   4. HELLP most often occurs early in the third trimester and is thought to result from a circulating immunologic component

   5. Women who develop HELLP might also experience disseminated intravascular coagulation (DIC) and require intensive medical care

      a. DIC is caused by a process that consumes the plasma-clotting factors and platelets so that hemorrhage occurs

H. Women who have severe preeclampsia and eclampsia are usually hospitalized and placed on seizure precautions

I. Medications might continue after the baby is born.

J. The mother might be sedated and given antihypertensive medications and anti-convulsive medications, such as magnesium sulfate.

   1. Magnesium sulfate is compatible with breastfeeding.

K. Breastfeeding will depend on the condition of the mother and the baby.

L. Because it is important to reduce stress and other noxious stimuli that could provoke a seizure, breastfeeding might actually be therapeutic due to the calming and sedating effects of prolactin and oxytocin.

M. If the baby cannot go to the breast, arrangements need to be made for pumping breast milk.

II Cesarean delivery

A. Cesarean delivery is the most frequently performed surgery in the United States.

B. Cesarean delivery is compatible with breastfeeding and should not preclude the mother from nursing her infant as soon as she feels ready, including in the recovery room.

   1. Most incisions are a low segment transverse, enabling the mother to more comfortably position the baby for breastfeeding across her lap.

   2. Vertical incisions are usually done for a problem or in emergency childbirth.

C. Breastfeeding should not be delayed unless the mother and/or baby are unable to do so.

D. Occasionally, a mother might receive general anesthesia—in which case she can breastfeed as soon as she is awake and able to respond.

E. An unexpected cesarean delivery might be a significant disappointment to the mother, will increase the amount of pain experienced, and will limit her mobility temporarily.

F. Mothers might experience anger, resentment, remorse, grief, or relief at this point.

G. Mothers who are receiving pain medication intrathecally might be quite comfortable and ready to breastfeed soon after surgery.

H. Full-term, healthy babies and mothers can and should recover together.

I. Mothers will receive pain medication during their hospital stay, which can be as short as three days.

J. Pain medication is usually required for 72 hours and can be given immediately after a breastfeeding in order to permit the level to peak before the next feeding.

K. Some babies might be lethargic at first, especially if the labor was protracted and involved long exposure to analgesia or anesthesia.

L. Suctioning of the mouth and throat might temporarily cause oral defensiveness.

M. Finding a comfortable position in which to breastfeed can be worrisome to mothers; fathers and other helpers should be encouraged to lift and change the baby and help position the baby at the breast.

N. Mothers should breastfeed the baby 8–12 times each 24 hours and refrain from sending the baby to the nursery for long periods of time, where he or she is likely to receive bottles.

O. While cesarean mothers need their rest, visitors can be limited to allow for napping and breastfeeding during the day; mothers should breastfeed the baby during the night when the infant demonstrates readiness to feed.

P. Low-grade maternal fever can occur and should not interrupt breastfeeding.

Q. If the baby was born preterm or will be unable to breastfeed for some time, the mother should use a hospital-grade breast pump with a double collection kit to stimulate milk production.

R. If the baby is temporarily unable to latch on to the breast, the mother can hand-express colostrum into a spoon and spoon feed it to the baby.

S. Mothers might be given antibiotics, placing them at a higher risk for candida overgrowth.

T. Antibiotics also place the baby at an increased risk for altered gut flora.

**III** Retained placenta

    A. Subinvolution of the uterus due to retained placental fragments is typically diagnosed after the mother has been discharged from the hospital.

    B. It might present itself as bleeding that is uncharacteristic for the length of time post-delivery.

    C. Placenta retention can inhibit the lactation process by keeping inhibitory hormones at levels that are representative of pregnancy.

    D. Mothers might experience little to no breast fullness by days 3–5 and might still be producing colostrum when transitional milk should be seen.

    E. Failure to see breast engorgement might occur prior to excessive bleeding or hemorrhage.

    F. Curettage might be required, after which spontaneous milk flow should commence.

    G. Retained placenta can be suspected if the mother complains of little to no breast engorgement by day five, a colostrum stage of milk that persists beyond day four, an infant who is not satisfied at the breast, who has less than the normal amount of wet and soiled diapers per day, and who might be showing visible signs of jaundice, continued bright-red vaginal bleeding that continues to be heavy, and a uterus that might be painful to palpation and larger than expected.

**IV** Venous thrombosis

    A. Thrombosis is the formation of a blood clot inside a blood vessel.

    B. A reduction in this complication has been seen due to early ambulation following delivery, fewer operative deliveries using general anesthesia, and better health of pregnant women.

    C. Deep vein thrombosis is taken very seriously, because pulmonary embolism can result if thrombi formed in the legs migrate to the lungs.

    D. A pulmonary embolism can be fatal.

    E. Procedures to establish a diagnosis and systemic medications involved in treatment are considerations during lactation.

    F. Hormonal contraception is contraindicated.

    G. Scans using radioactive contrast media might be necessary to confirm a diagnosis.

    H. Radioactive materials vary in their half lives, with some requiring little disruption to breastfeeding and others requiring pumping and discarding milk for up to two weeks; the lactation consultant should ascertain the contrast medium being used, its half life, and when breastfeeding can recommence.

I. Anticoagulant treatment is used with medications such as heparin or newer, low-molecular anti-coagulants.

J. If long-term anticoagulant therapy is initiated, prothrombin time in the infant is usually monitored monthly and the infant might be given vitamin K if necessary.

K. Some mothers can experience a lengthy hospital stay or readmission and possible separation from their baby; plans must be made for continued breastfeeding and/or for the expressing of breast milk.

L. Some hospital units enable babies to room with their mothers if a caretaker is available to be responsible for the infant; because the mother might be on bed rest and pain medication, a helper is usually needed for baby care and infant access to the mother.

V Sheehan's syndrome

A. Sheehan's syndrome is caused by a postpartum hemorrhage and hypotension that is severe enough to decrease the blood flow to the pituitary gland, leading to an infarction and necrosis or other vascular injury to the pituitary gland.

B. It is the only commonly recognized endocrine disorder associated with lactation failure.

C. The pituitary is very sensitive to decreased blood flow at the end of pregnancy because of its vascularity and increased size.

D. With prolactin not being secreted, the breasts can involute and lactation might be suppressed.

E. Prolactin-stimulating drugs have been used to treat this condition.

F. Nasal oxytocin spray prior to each feeding might also be helpful.

G. Mild cases of pituitary disruption can occur with a delay in copious milk production and a slow start to breastfeeding.

VI Episiotomy

A. Episiotomy is the surgical incision of the perineum made to facilitate birth as the fetal head distends the perineum.

B. This procedure is often done in the United States as a routine procedure that is not supported by current research.

1. Midline episiotomy is an incision straight down towards the rectum.

2. Mediolateral episiotomy is angled down and off to one side.

C. It might be done therapeutically for shoulder dystocia to allow more room for manual maneuvers to free the impacted shoulders of the infant.

D. It is also used with forceps to provide more room for their application.

1. Forceps use has declined in the United States and can cause trauma to the baby, such as bruising to the face where the blades were applied, facial nerve paralysis, caput seccedaneum (localized soft-tissue swelling that crosses suture lines), cephalhematoma (hemorrhage into the subperiosteum that can also be associated with intracranial bleeding or skull fracture; seen more frequently with vacuum extraction).

2. Vacuum extraction does not need more room in the vagina than forceps do for application; some babies who have undergone this procedure have large blood losses, increased bilirubin levels, and feed poorly.

E. Research does not support the old rationale for this procedure being done to avoid ragged tears that supposedly did not heal as well as a surgical incision.

F. Naturally occurring lacerations involve less tissue and muscle impairment than do episiotomies.

G. Short-term pelvic muscle function is not improved by an episiotomy.

H. Apgar scores are not improved by episiotomies.

I. Complications of episiotomies include excessive blood loss, infection of the incision, necrotizing fasciitis, extension of the midline episiotomy into the rectal sphincter (which is a third-degree tear), and further extension into the anterior rectal wall (which is a fourth-degree perineal laceration).

J. Episiotomies can be extremely painful, with pain lasting up to two weeks or longer (necessitating pain medications); cold packs are usually applied immediately following delivery, and topical preparations and sitz baths are also used for pain and to hasten healing.

K. Mothers who have episiotomies often find it very hard to assume a comfortable position, especially when sitting upright.

L. This situation makes it even more difficult to position the baby properly for breastfeeding.

M. The sometimes extreme pain could interfere with the let-down reflex, impeding milk flow to the baby.

N. Mothers might find the side-lying position more comfortable if an episiotomy is especially painful.

O. Mothers can be counseled during the prenatal period to request that an episiotomy not be done unless absolutely necessary.

VII Postpartum infection

A. Postpartum infection processes might remain localized in the reproductive or genital area, urinary tract, or breasts or it might progress, resulting in metritis, endometritis, peritonitis, or parametritis.

B. Prenatal risk factors associated with postpartum infections include preexisting infections, chronic diseases, anemia, diabetes, obesity, and poor nutritional status.

C. Intrapartum risk factors include prolonged rupture of the membranes, frequent vaginal examinations, intrauterine fetal monitoring, intrauterine manipulation, lacerations in the reproductive tract, operative delivery, retained placental fragments, manual removal of the placenta, hematomas, postpartum hemorrhage, and improper aseptic technique.

D. Portals for bacterial entry include the placental site, the perineum, the episiotomy, cesarean incision, the vagina, the urinary tract, the breasts, and the lymphatic system along the uterine veins.

E. Perineal and vaginal infections are usually easily treated with antibiotics that are compatible with breastfeeding; these infections, however, are a source of significant discomfort for the mother (making positioning for breastfeeding cumbersome).

F. Endometritis is the infection of the lining of the uterus, which is the most frequent cause of postpartum infection.
   1. Early endometritis occurs within 48 hours of the delivery.
   2. Mothers might experience elevated temperatures or severe considerable pain and malaise.
   3. Early temperature rises are also seen with epidural anesthesia/analgesia.
   4. The most important risk factor is nonelective cesarean section after the onset of labor or rupture of the membranes.
   5. Treatment is usually with broad-spectrum antibiotics that are compatible with breastfeeding.
   6. The mother's condition will determine how breastfeeding proceeds.

G. Parametritis, or pelvic cellulites, is an extension of the infectious process beyond the endometrium into the broad ligaments.
   1. Typically occurs during the second week postpartum.
   2. Mothers might experience a persistent high fever, malaise, chills, lethargy, and marked pain over the affected area.
   3. The lactation consultant will need to remember to ask whether pain is present in areas other than the breasts, because some of these infections present with symptoms similar to mastitis.
   4. Intravenous antibiotics are used, and surgery might be required to drain an abscess.

5. Separation and interrupted breastfeeding might occur; arrangements for access to the baby and/or a breast pump might need to be arranged.

H. Urinary tract infections (UTIs) caused by urine retention after childbirth are not uncommon.

   1. Causes include trauma to the base of the bladder, use of regional anesthesia, increased capacity and decreased sensitivity of the puerperal bladder, and the use of oxytocin infusion after birth, which induces potent antidiuretic effects until the oxytocin is stopped and rapid diuresis follows.

   2. Catheterization is a frequent cause of UTIs because the insertion of the catheter introduces residual urine and bacteria into the bladder.

   3. Mothers can experience fever and considerable pain.

   4. Treatment includes antibiotic therapy that is compatible with breastfeeding, increased fluid intakes, and proper nutrition.

I. Cesarean incision infections occur in about 2 percent of mothers, even with the use of prophylactic antibiotics.

   1. The most common symptom is fever occurring on about the fourth day.

   2. Treatment is with antibiotics and less-frequent surgical drainage.

VIII Maternal side effects of labor medications that can affect breastfeeding

A. Some mothers feel drugged or "hung over" during the early postpartum period.

B. Many side effects of labor medications occur during labor and subside following delivery.

C. Oxytocin administration can cause potent antidiuretic effects on the mother; coupled with large amounts of IV fluids this might result in fluid retention, an edematous areola, and a possible delay in copious milk production due to interference with or blocking of oxytocin release from the pituitary.

   1. Morphine is known to block oxytocin release from the pituitary.

D. Epidural analgesia has been associated with the use of episiotomy, bladder catheterization, high spinal or intravasular injection of drugs with possible convulsions, respiratory paralysis, cardiac arrest, allergic shock, maternal nerve injury (through placement, catheter migration, or breakage), spinal headache from puncturing the dura, epidural patch to fix the spinal headache, increased core temperature leading to separation and septic workup of the baby, urinary incontinence or retention, long-term backache, headaches, abnormal motor and decreased sensation, and less time spent with the baby in the hospital.

# References

Goer H. Obstetric myths versus research realities: a guide to the medical literature. Westport, CT: Bergin & Garvey, 1995.

Lauwers J, Shinskie D. Counseling the nursing mother: A lactation consultant's guide, 3rd ed. Sudbury, MA: Jones and Bartlett Publishers, 2000.

Lawrence RA, Lawrence RM. Breastfeeding: A guide for the medical profession. St. Louis, MO: Mosby, Inc., 1999.

Nichols FH, Zwelling E. Maternal-newborn nursing: Theory and practice. Philadelphia, PA: W.B. Saunders Company, 1997.

Riordan J, Auerbach KG. Breastfeeding and human lactation, 2nd ed. Sudbury, MA: Jones and Bartlett Publishers, 1998.

Walker M. Do labor medications affect breastfeeding? *J Hum Lact* 1997;13:131-137.

# Breast Pathology

*Angela Smith, RN, CM, BA, IBCLC and Joy Heads, RN, CM, Grad Certificate Bioethics, MHPEd, IBCLC*

## Objectives

- Describe preventive and prophylactic measures for common breastfeeding problems related to the lactating breast.
- Differentiate between common presenting signs and symptoms.
- Identify appropriate interventions by the lactation consultant.
- Identify relevant educational issues associated with the mother with a breastfeeding problem.

## Introduction

There are a number of common problems related to the lactating breast. While most can either be prevented or improved, early recognition, prompt treatment and/or referral, and close follow-up might be required in order to preserve the breastfeeding experience. Some of these problems can be painful and extend over a period of time, which can be disappointing and frustrating to the new mother. Many have a number of therapeutic interventions that are based on long years of clinical experience, rather than on randomized, controlled trials. Most have a number of treatment options that clinicians have come to prefer but might vary from region to region and country to country. Some are seen in daily practice, and some are seen more rarely. All solutions to problems depend on careful assessment and management plans developed in conjunction with the mother.

## Normal Fullness

Engorgement is generally a preventable postpartum complication. Many women experience normal fullness when the "milk comes in." The increase in blood flow to the breast, triggered by the prolactin surge, is accompanied by an increase in milk volume and will result in normal fullness in most women. Restrictive feeding practices, poor attachment, and inefficient sucking will lead to incomplete removal of the milk, which will lead to the pathological problem of engorgement. Normal fullness can be differentiated from problematic engorgement of the breast.

1. The normally full breast will be larger, warmer, and uncomfortable; milk flow will be normal.
2. The engorged breast will look tight and shiny and milk flow may be compromised.

I Engorgement

A. Engorgement is a well-known but poorly researched aspect of lactation.

 1. The medical dictionary defines engorgement as congestion or distension with fluid.

B. Lactation literature refers to engorgement as the physiologic condition characterized by the painful swelling of the breasts associated with the sudden increase in milk volume, lymphatic and vascular congestion, and interstitial edema during the first two weeks following birth.

C. Engorgement is a normal physiologic process with a progression of events, not trauma or injury to the tissues. Breast fullness, the normal physiologic process, may progress to problematic engorgement if milk removal is compromised.

D. When milk production increases rapidly, the volume of milk in the breast can exceed the capacity of the alveoli to store it.

E. If the milk is not removed, over-distention of the alveoli can cause the milk-secreting cells to become flattened and drawn out and even to rupture.

F. The distention can partly or completely occlude the capillary blood circulation surrounding the alveolar cells, further decreasing cellular activity. This distention can partly or completely occlude the oxytocin-rich capillary blood reaching the myoepithelial complex.

G. Congested blood vessels leak fluid into the surrounding tissue space, contributing to interstitial edema, which further compresses and impedes the milk flow. A cycle of congestion/edema/poor flow/congestion can easily occur.

H. Pressure and congestion obstruct the lymphatic drainage of the breasts, stagnating the system that rids the breasts of toxins, bacteria, and cast-off cell parts—thereby predisposing the breast to mastitis (both inflammation and infection).

I. In addition, a protein called the *feedback inhibitor of lactation* (FIL) accumulates in the mammary gland during milk stasis, further reducing milk production.

J. Accumulation of milk and the resulting engorgement are a major trigger of apoptosis, or programmed cell death, that causes involution of the milk secreting gland, milk resorption, collapse of the alveolar structures, and the cessation of milk production.

K. Engorgement has also been classified as involving only the areola, only the body of the breast, or both.

 1. Areolar engorgement involves clinical observations of a swollen areola with tight, shiny skin, probably involving over-full lactiferous sinuses.

 2. A puffy areola is thought to be tissue edema caused by large amounts of intravenous fluids or pitocin received by some mothers during labor.

L. Minimal or no engorgement in the first week postpartum has been associated with insufficient milk, early supplementation, and a higher percentage of breastfeeding decline in the early weeks.

M. Rates of engorgement between 20 percent and 85 percent have been reported in the literature encompassing numerous definitions and are usually limited to the first few days postpartum.

N. Such reports described engorgement as peaking between days three and four declining thereafter; however, data from two unpublished masters theses suggested that mothers actually experience more than one peak of engorgement and that engorgement can continue for as long as 10 days or more (Csar, 1999, and Riedel, 1991).

O. Four patterns of engorgement have been described:

1. One experience of firm, tender breasts followed by a resolution of symptoms

2. Multiple peaks of engorgement followed by resolution

3. Intense and painful engorgement lasting up to 14 days

4. Minimal breast changes, demonstrating that the experience of engorgement is not the same for all mothers

P. Predicting an individual mother's risk for and the course of engorgement might not be possible, but some general principles can be of help in anticipating situations that predispose to a higher risk, including the following:

1. Failure to prevent or resolve milk stasis resulting from infrequent or inadequate drainage of the breasts; the higher the cumulative number of minutes of sucking during the early days postpartum, the less pain from engorgement that mothers describe.

2. Mothers who have small breasts (other than hypoplastic and tubular); while small breast size does not limit milk production, it can influence storage capacity and feeding patterns; mothers with small breast capacity might need to experience a greater number of breastfeedings over 24 hours than women with a larger milk storage capacity; Robson (1990) described a similar observation in engorged women who wore a significantly smaller bra cup size (34 percent) than women who did not become engorged (12.5 percent).

3. Previous breastfeeding experience, not parity, influences engorgement; second-time breastfeeding mothers experience greater levels of engorgement sooner with faster resolution than first-time breastfeeding mothers; breast engorgement for multiparous mothers who are breastfeeding for the first time is similar to primiparous breastfeeding mothers; Robson (1990) found that mothers in a non-engorged group were more likely to have never experienced engorgement following previous births than mothers in the engorged group; McLachlan et al. (1991) found that 70 percent of multiparous mothers experiencing engorgement in a current lactation had also experienced engorgement with previous babies.

4. Mothers with high rates of milk synthesis (hyperlactation) or large amounts of milk might see milk stasis magnified if infants consume less milk, if less milk is pumped, or whenever milk volume significantly exceeds milk removal.

5. Limited mother/infant contact in the early days by not rooming in or baby separated for medical reasons such as prematurity; Shiau (1997) demonstrated significantly less engorgement on day three in mothers who participated in skin-to-skin care of their full-term babies rather than standard nursery care.

Q. Numerous preventive strategies have been seen over the years, including restricting fluids, prenatal expression of colostrum, prenatal breast massage, postnatal breast massage, binding the breasts, or wearing a tight bra.

1. Mothers experience less-severe forms of engorgement with early frequent feedings, self-demand feedings, unlimited sucking times, and with babies who demonstrate correct suckling techniques. This remains the only proven preventive measure.

2. A more effective technique called alternate breast massage has been shown to significantly reduce the incidence and severity of engorgement while simultaneously increasing milk intake, increasing the fat content of the milk, and increasing the infant's weight gain.

   a. Alternate massage is a simple technique of massaging and compressing the breast during the baby's pause between sucking bursts; the technique alternates with the baby's sucking and is continued throughout the feeding on both breasts.

3. A plethora of treatment modalities have been put forward, both anecdotally and in literature, such as hot compresses, hot showers, soaking the breasts in a bowl of hot water, cold compresses after feedings, cold packs before feedings, ice packs, frozen bags of vegetables, both hot and cold therapy, oxytocin, proteolytic enzymes, stilbestrol, binding the breasts, manual expression, mechanical expression, no expression, lymphatic breast massage, ultrasound, frequent feedings, alternate massage, chilled cabbage leaves, room-temperature cabbage leaves, and the application of cabbage leaf extract.

   a. *Heat application*—in the form of hot compresses, hot showers or hot soaks are poorly researched and have usually been more of a comfort measure to activate the milk ejection reflex, rather than a treatment for edema; some mothers complain that heat exacerbates the engorgement and causes throbbing and an increased feeling of fullness

   b. *Warmth application*—where a milk ejection reflex is thought to be compromised or slow, warmth has been shown to improve oxytocin uptake

   c. *Soften areola prior to attachment*—a small amount of milk may need to be expressed to enable the baby to latch correctly. If areola edema is apparent, gentle massage and shaping of the areola may also be required

d. *Cold therapy*—cold applications in the form of ice packs, gel packs, frozen bags of vegetables, frozen wet towels, and so on have been studied under various application conditions; cold application triggers a cycle of vasoconstriction during the first 9–16 minutes where blood flow is reduced, local edema decreases, and lymphatic drainage is enhanced; this condition is followed by a deep tissue vasodilation phase lasting 4–6 minutes that prevents thermal injury; Robson (1990) discusses that the application of cold for 20 minutes would have a minimal vasoconstriction effect in the deeper breast tissue and that venous and lymphatic drainage would be enhanced in the deeper tissues due to the accelerated circulation to and from the superficial tissues; Sandberg (1998) reports on the application of cold packs for 20 minutes *before* each feeding on a small sample of women; mothers reported increased comfort compared to heat, decreased chest circumference, and no adverse affect on milk ejection or milk transfer

e. *Ultrasound*—thermal (continuous) ultrasound treatments of engorged breasts has not been shown to improve pain or edema

f. *Lymphatic breast drainage therapy*—a gentle massage of the lymphatic drainage channels in the breast; lymphatic drainage is thought to improve the movement of the stagnated fluid, reduce edema, and improve cellular function; Wilson-Clay (1999) reports the relief of discomfort and better subsequent milk yields during the pumping of three women who had unrelieved severe engorgement following manual lymphatic drainage therapy; this type of therapy should be only administered by professionals qualified to do so

g. *Chilled cabbage leaves*—Rosier (1988) anecdotally describes the use of chilled cabbage leaves that are applied to engorged breasts and are changed every two hours in a small sample of women as having a rapid effect on reducing edema and increasing milk flow; Nikodem et al. showed a non-significant trend in reduced engorgement in mothers who were using cabbage leaves; Roberts (1995) compared chilled cabbage leaves and gel packs, showing similar significant reduction in pain with both methods with two-thirds of the mothers preferring the cabbage due to a stronger, more immediate effect; Roberts et al. (1998) tudied the use of cabbage extract cream applied to the breasts, which had no more effect than the placebo cream

h. *Expressing milk*—refraining from expressing milk because the mother will "just make more milk" cannot be justified; hand expressing or pumping to comfort reduces the buildup of FIL, decreases the mechanical stress on the alveoli (preventing the cell death process), prevents blood circulation changes, alleviates the impedence to lymph and fluid drainage, decreases the risk of mastitis and compromised milk production, and feels good to the mother

R. It is not known what degree of engorgement or duration of milk stasis poses an unrecoverable situation.

S. The milk production in the alveoli that are not experiencing engorgement continues normally.

T. The breast is capable of compensating to a point.

II Plugged ducts

A. Besides engorgement, other conditions can contribute to milk stasis

B. Poor milk drainage from the breast due to physical obstruction of a milk duct is a common occurrence during lactation; this blockage is anecdotally thought to occur from pressures outside the breast, like a tight fitting bra or from straps on a baby carrier, mother's fingers, or a baby's fist.

C. This condition can often be traced back to ineffective drainage of the breast by factors such as a weak suck, an inefficiently feeding baby, poor attachment, disorganized or dysfunctional sucking, skipped or irregular feedings, or an oversupply.

D. The section of the breast behind this blockage might experience a focal area of engorgement; an older name for this was "caked breast."

E. Niebyl, Spence, and Parmley (1978) distinguished between an infection and focal breast engorgement; they explained that when milk secretions became inspissated (thickened by the absorption of fluid) or a duct became blocked, a segment of the breast could become swollen, firm, and tender as the ducts filled and then became distended with milk.

F. The mother might complain of tenderness, heat, or possibly redness over a palpable, pea-sized lump; the lump has well-defined margins and no fever is present.

G. Management is by hot compresses and massage of the affected area before and during breastfeeding; changing the baby's position at the breast so that the chin is adjacent to the lump will help (the area adjacent to the lower jaw will always be the most effectively emptied part of the breast).

H. A blocked nipple pore is another potential cause of milk stasis.

I. This condition is frequently described as a white dot or a whitehead on the tip of the nipple; this object is a solitary bleb occluding the opening of a duct, usually shiny, smooth, and less than a millimeter in diameter.

1. The bleb blocks the terminal opening for drainage of one of the lobes of the breast and as such could contribute to milk stasis in a larger area of the breast.

2. This condition causes pinpoint pain and might not disappear with warm soaks or proper latch and sucking.

3. This condition might require a health professional to open it with a sterile needle; it often reforms and requires repeated opening. Lawrence (1999) states that "the bleb probably represents a small pressure cyst formed at the end of the duct from milk seeping into this very elastic tissue."

J. Corpora amylacia have been described as white crystals caused by the aggregation and fusion of casein micelles in the alveoli to which further materials are added, which hardens them.

K. Other descriptions of milk expressed from blocked areas of the breast include reports of strings that look like spaghetti or lengths of fatty-looking material.

1. This type of blockage might account for the ropy texture of an obstructed area and the thought that thickened milk could be responsible for the blockage.

2. Lawrence (1999) describes improvement in this condition when the mother's diet contains only polyunsaturated fats and a lecithin supplement is added to meals.

## III  Mastitis

Mastitis is a preventable but common lactation complication. The onset is usually in the first three weeks postpartum or with abrupt weaning or sudden changes in breast usage. Mastitis is an inflammatory process, which may or may not progress on to a breast infection. The initial cause of mastitis is an unresolved increase in the intraductal pressure, first causing a flattening of the secretory cells; a paracellular pathway then may occur between the cells which allows the passage of some of the components in breast milk to leak into the interstitial tissue, resulting in an inflammatory response. This inflammatory response and resultant tissue damage can be a precursor to infective mastitis.

A. Mastitis is an inflammation of the breast and is usually associated with lactation, can be acute or chronic, and often occurs as a result of poor breastfeeding techniques.

B. This condition can progress to an infection and provoke serious sequelae, such as an abscess, if it is treated inappropriately.

C. The incidence of mastitis varies among studies; it is estimated to occur in 1–33 percent of lactating women.

D. Mastitis has a variety of definitions that usually describe different aspects of the problem and are often based on the symptoms or ultimate treatment approach; Lawrence (1999) differentiates two types of mastitis:

1. Acute puerperal mammary cellulitis, a non-epidemic mastitis involving interlobular connective tissue; this is the most common form of mastitis

2. Acute puerperal mammary adenitis, which was epidemic with an outbreak of skin infections in infants (a rare occurrence)

E. Niebyl, Spence, and Parmley (1978) describe mastitis by using the following symptoms:
  1. A fever greater than 38.5°C (100.4°F)
  2. Chills
  3. Aching
  4. Systemic illness
  5. A pink, tender, hot, swollen, and wedge-shaped area of the breast

F. Freed, Landers, and Schanler (1991) define mastitis as follows:
  1. Cellulitis of the interlobular connective tissue of the breast
  2. Symptoms include breast pain, swelling, erythema, and fever
  3. Infection is usually due to *Staphylococcus aureus* and occasionally a *Streptococcus* species
  4. Can occur at any time during lactation
  5. A plugged duct is a frequent precursor of infection

G. Thomsen, Espersen, and Maigaard (1984) looked microscopically at the milk itself to differentiate between milk stasis, inflammation, and infection; all of the mothers in their study complained of tender, red, hot, and swollen breasts.
  1. The diagnosis of a breast infection was made by counting (not culturing) leukocytes and bacteria in milk samples taken from the affected breast and studied under a microscope. They identified three clinical states:
     a. Milk stasis               $< 10^6$ leukocytes and $< 10^3$ bacteria/ml of milk
     b. Non-infectious inflammation     $> 10^6$ leukocytes and $< 10^3$ bacteria/ml of milk
     c. Infectious mastitis          $> 10^6$ leukocytes and $> 10^3$ bacteria/ml of milk
  2. They recommended that antibiotic use be prescribed for the last classification only; this type of laboratory analysis might or might not be practical depending on the clinical setting.

H. Confusion arises in defining mastitis because the words *mastitis* and *infection* are often used interchangeably by clinicians; the inflammation is frequently treated as if it were the infection.

I. Mastitis is an inflammatory condition of the breast that might or might not eventually or concurrently involve an infection.
  1. Most clinicians simply use a cluster of signs and symptoms to diagnose mastitis (the infection):
     - Fever > 38°C (100.4°F)
     - Flu-like aching
     - Red, tender, hot area
     - Chills
     - Pain/swelling at the site
     - Increased sodium levels in the milk (the baby might reject the breast due to the salty taste of the milk)
     - Red streaks extending toward the axilla side
     - Increased pulse

J. The highest occurrence is generally at two to three weeks postpartum.

K. Evans and Heads (1995) also found that the prevalence of mastitis fluctuated by season; the winter months, July and August in the southern hemisphere (January and February in the northern hemisphere), had the highest rates of any months. However, as the trend was not correlated with birth rates fluctuations, the findings are inconclusive.

L. The upper, outer quadrant of the breast was the most frequent site for infection to occur.

M. There seems to be a fairly equal distribution of cases between the right and left breasts. Bilateral mastitis occurs much less frequently.

N. Breast milk is not sterile, nor are the breast skin and lactiferous sinuses.

O. Matheson et al. (1988) noted that the bacterial counts of both pathogenic and non-pathogenic bacteria were indistinguishable between the mastitic and non-mastitic breasts in women who had unilateral mastitis; thus, the presence of bacteria was not necessarily a precursor for the development of an infection; generally, some other condition needs to be present in order to facilitate the development of an inflammatory or infective outcome.

P. Contributing factors include the following:

1. Milk stasis (engorgement)

   a. The condition commonly thought to contribute most towards increasing the risk of both inflammation and infection is milk stasis.

   b. If the pressure rises high enough, as with severe, unrelieved, and prolonged engorgement, small amounts of milk components will be forced out the tight junctions between the epithelial cells that line the ductal system into the surrounding breast tissue.

   c. This situation can cause a localized inflammatory response, which involves pain, local swelling, redness, and heat over the affected area and/or a general response of a rise in body temperature and pulse rate.

   d. Once the integrity of these tight junctions has been disrupted, it might be easier for it to happen again when similar circumstances increase the pressure in the breast; this situation might help explain why women who have had mastitis in a previous lactation have a greater chance of a recurrence of mastitis in the same or next lactation compared to women who have never had mastitis.

   e. The disruption of the tight junction integrity can also provide a partial explanation for why women develop recurrent mastitis within a particular lactation.

   f. If milk components also leak into the vascular channels, capillaries, and blood stream, it can account for the systemic response of fever, aches, fatigue, and general malaise that accompany mastitis (the infection).

g. The body's response to both the inflammatory agents in the milk (interleukin-1) and the antigenic response to the milk proteins (which are recognized as foreign) are thought to contribute to the flu-like symptoms above.

h. If milk stasis is allowed to persist, it might be the condition that provides the medium that is needed for bacterial overgrowth and that provokes an infection.

2. Inefficient milk removal

a. Inefficient milk removal, which leaves areas of the breast undrained for long periods of time, facilitates milk stasis, e.g., poor attachment.

b. The following list of conditions and situations can all contribute to residual milk backup:

- Scheduled, interrupted, or erratic feeding patterns
- A sudden change in the number of feeds
- Baby sleeping longer at night
- Sucking at breast displaced by pacifiers or bottles
- Breastfeeding technique (switching too soon from the first breast to the second before the baby has adequately drained the first side)
- short frenulum (tongue tie)
- baby with neurologic impairment
- mother or baby illness
- overabundant milk supply (hyperlactation)
- separation of mother and baby
- abrupt weaning
- baby's oral anatomy that leads to inefficient emptying of the breast, e.g., short frenulum, cleft palate, Pierre Robin syndrome

c. Overdistension of the breasts from any of these factors represents an increased risk for milk stasis.

d. Livingstone (1996) describes a maternal hyperlactation syndrome consisting of a mother with a high rate of milk synthesis and an abundant milk supply.

e. She lists several factors contributing to the development of mastitis in mothers who produce large quantities of milk:

i. A high rate of milk synthesis (greater than 60ml/hour)

ii. An abundant milk supply

iii. Weaning process

iv. Skipped feedings

v. Irregular breast drainage

vi. Switching to the second breast before the first is drained

vii. Poor positioning and latch on, leading to inefficient milk drainage

viii. Consistent failure to drain a segment of the breast

4. Cracked or damaged nipples

   a. Cracked or damaged nipples are often thought to contribute to mastitis.

   b. This disruption in skin integrity is surmised to provide the portal of entry for pathogenic organisms.

   c. Livingstone, Willis, and Berkowitz (1996) found that a break in the nipple integument associated with cracks, fissures, ulcers, or pus resulted in a 35 percent chance of *S. aureus* colonization; this chance was five times greater than when the skin was intact; mothers who had infants younger than one month who complained of moderate to severe nipple pain *and* who had cracks and fissures had a 64 percent chance of having positive skin cultures and a 54 percent chance of having *S. aureus* colonization.

5. Maternal stress and/or fatigue; Riordan and Nichols (1990) state that the most common factor that the women in their study associated with mastitis was fatigue; this retrospective recall helps identify a facilitating condition rather than a cause.

6. Use of nipple creams.

   a. Jonsson and Pulkkinen (1994) found that the use of a nipple cream several times a day was associated with an increased incidence of mastitis.

   b. Minchin (1985) also notes that the use of nipple creams or lotions could either damage the skin or alter the skin's natural defenses against infection.

   c. It has been hypothesized that the use of creams and lotions alters the pH of the nipple and areolar epithelium or blocks the glands of Montgomery or alters their secretions, reducing the natural protective factors of the areola.

   d. The use of nipple creams could also indicate the presence of sore or damaged nipples and could appear as one of a cluster of situations or conditions simply associated with mastitis.

7. The vast majority of confirmed cases of mastitis show *S. aureus* as the causative organism.

   a. Although lactating women might have potentially pathogenic bacteria on their skin or in their milk, most do not go on to develop mastitis (the infection).

   b. Conversely, in many women who actually develop an infection, pathogenic bacteria cannot be cultured in their milk.

8. Recurrent mastitis is usually caused by delayed or inadequate treatment of the initial mastitis.

   a. This condition most frequently recurs when the bacteria is resistant or not sensitive to the prescribed antibiotic, when antibiotics are not continued long enough, when the mother stopped nursing on the affected side, or when the initial cause of the mastitis was not addressed (such as milk stasis).

b. Clinicians can recommend that the mother continues to feed (or pump) on the affected side, that she take a full 10–14 day course of antibiotics, and that the cause or precipitating factors be identified and remedied.

c. At the first recurrence, Lawrence (1999) recommends milk cultures as well as cultures of the infant's nasopharynx and oropharynx.

d. Other family members can be cultured as necessary to identify the source of the bacteria to keep it from reinfecting the mother.

e. Culture and sensitivity testing is important to determine that the proper antibiotic is given.

f. Lawrence also states that if the infection is chronic, low-dose antibiotics can be instituted for the duration of the lactation (erythromycin 500mg/day).

g. Mothers with a history of mastitis in previous lactations need to be especially vigilant in preventing milk stasis and in assuring proper positioning and latch-on of the baby.

Q. Ultrasound examination of the breast is used when either a cyst or an abscess is suspected. If the breast shows a fluid-filled cavity, an abscess is likely to be present.

R. Prevention of mastitis begins with accurate breastfeeding guidelines that discourage situations that can result in milk stasis. Such basics would include the following:

1. Early, frequent, unrestricted access to the breast and correct breastfeeding techniques, which include the following:

   a. Proper positioning of the baby at the breast

   b. Correct latch on with minimal to no discomfort

   c. No pain during a breastfeeding

   d. Finishing the first breast before switching to the second

   e. Alternate massage to help a sleepy baby sustain sucking, which aids in better breast drainage

2. 24-hour rooming-in at the hospital, which promotes the prompt recognition of infant feeding cues, reduces skipped feedings (especially at night), and leads to more frequent breast drainage during the early days.

3. Avoiding early bottle use, which leaves the unsuckled breasts undrained for prolonged periods of time.

4. Avoiding the use of pacifiers, which displaces sucking from the breast; this situation causes the breasts to remain full of milk as the time between nursings increases.

5. Prompt attention to and correction of early warning signs to stop the progression of milk stasis, inflammation, infection, and possible abscess;

sore or cracked nipples require immediate attention not only to reduce bacterial overgrowth opportunities but also to prevent decreased frequency or length of feedings due to pain.

6. Plugged milk ducts can be massaged while the baby is sucking in order to encourage the removal of the blockage that is inhibiting milk flow from the affected area of the breast.

7. A sleepy baby or any baby who feeds inefficiently at the breast might need to be observed while feeding to improve the baby's ability to remove milk; if a baby remains an inefficient feeder for whatever reason, the mother might need to pump following feeds to ensure adequate milk drainage and to provide additional milk for the baby.

8. Adequate rest, help around the house and with other children, good nutrition, and proper hand washing before manual expression are common guidelines that can contribute to better overall health of the mother.

9. Limited milk expression might be needed if the baby abruptly starts sleeping for longer periods at night or if there is a substantial decrease in the number of breastfeedings for any reason.

10. Mothers who have a history of mastitis in previous lactations need to be especially vigilant in preventing milk stasis and in assuring proper positioning and latch-on of the baby.

11. Inflammation in the breast needs to be identified early (red patches on the breast and so on) and followed by appropriate interventions, such as increased number of feedings and alternate massage.

12. Engorgement can be managed with frequent feedings and alternate massage; if the baby cannot drain the breasts adequately, they should be pumped; the baby's milk needs and feeding skills will catch up to the milk supply.

13. Unrelieved engorgement contributes not only to an increased risk of milk stasis but also to the condition of insufficient milk at six to eight weeks.

S. While antibiotics treat the infection, they do not treat the underlying cause of mastitis; if a mother develops mastitis (the infection), then symptomatic treatments and antibiotic therapy must be joined by the third part of the intervention plan (which is identification and treatment of the underlying cause); failure to do so can lead to recurrent mastitis.

1. Treating the underlying cause

   a. Because milk stasis is the primary contributor to both inflammation and infection in the lactating breast, a feeding history and observation are important in determining the underlying cause.

   b. The clinician can troubleshoot by asking the following questions:

      i. Have there been any skipped or hurried feedings?

    ii. Is the mother limiting feeding time on the first side so that the baby will take the second breast?

    iii. Is an older baby starting to sleep longer at night?

    iv. Is there a plugged milk duct?

    v. Is there a blocked nipple pore?

    vi. Is the mother painfully engorged?

    vii. Are the nipples sore or cracked with decreased feeding times due to pain?

    viii. Has any type of surgery ever been performed on the breast(s)?

    ix. Has the baby been given bottles or pacifiers, which either decreased breast stimulation or changed the baby's suck?

    x. Has a young baby been given solid food to make him or her sleep longer?

    xi. Does the mother use nipple shields?

    xii. Is the baby sleepy or a slow feeder?

    xiii. Is the baby gaining weight?

    xiv. Has the mother been attending or hosting holiday functions?

    xv. Has the mother begun employment outside the house?

    xvi. Has the mother been ill, unduly stressed, or so fatigued that it is affecting her ability to function?

c. Observe a feeding at the breast:

    i. Is the baby positioned and latched correctly?

    ii. Can you verify milk transfer by observing the baby swallowing milk throughout the majority of the feeding?

    iii. Have all areas of the breast been drained following the feeding, or can milk stasis be felt upon palpation?

    iv. Does the mother obstruct milk flow by pressing down on the areola under the baby's nose?

    v. Is there nipple pain during a feeding?

    vi. Is the nipple creased, compressed, distorted, or white (in spasm) when the baby comes off the breast?

    vii. Does the baby suck or feed in an inefficient, weak, or uncoordinated manner, which leaves large amounts of residual milk in the breasts?

d. Identification of the cause and using the appropriate intervention can halt the inflammatory process and eliminate the progression to an infection.

       i. If the mother has a low-grade fever, aching, and a painful area in the breast, it is important that she seek help to identify and begin treatment for any of the underlying causes.

      ii. If pain caused by inflammation is treated with a non-steroidal anti-inflammatory (NSAID) drug, such as ibuprofen, reduction of inflammatory symptoms might be even more rapid.

     iii. If there is no improvement within 8–24 hours, if the mother continues to run a fever, if she has obvious signs of a bacterial infection (such as a discharge of pus from the nipple), or if she suddenly spikes a high fever, then she needs to contact her physician immediately.

T. Because mothers' milk is seldom examined under a microscope for bacterial and white cell counts, antibiotics are generally started based on symptoms, which include the following:

1. Fever of greater than 38.4°C (101°F)
2. A reddened, painful, swollen area of the breast
3. Aches, chills, or general malaise

U. Breast milk is seldom obtained for routine culture and sensitivity testing for proper antibiotic choice; however, culture and sensitivity testing should be undertaken if the following situations occur:

1. There is no response to antibiotics within two days.
2. If the mastitis recurs
3. If it is hospital-acquired mastitis
4. In severe or unusual cases

V. Because S. *aureus* is most commonly associated with breast infections, choices of antibiotics are generally penicillinase-resistant penicillins or cephalosporins, which are effective against S. *aureus*.

1. Other antibiotics that are used for mastitis include erythromycin, nafcillin, and clindamycin. In streptococcal infections, penicillin might be preferable.

W. A management plan includes the following:

1. Bed rest
2. Increased fluids for the mother
3. Pain medication (acetaminophen); ibuprofen could also be used as both a pain reliever and as an anti-inflammatory
4. Antibiotics for 10–14 days
5. Hot compresses prior to feedings to promote milk drainage
6. Continued nursing on *both* breasts; start the baby on the unaffected side to achieve milk ejection, then thoroughly drain the affected side

X. When the mastitis (the infection) is not treated properly, up to 10 percent can progress to an abscess.

Y. Mothers who are treated with antibiotics for mastitis might subsequently develop candida (a fungal infection).

Z. Empirical interventions to accompany antibiotic treatment of mastitic infections include the following:

　1. Immersing the affected breast in warm water before feeding

　2. Lying in a tub of hot water with the affected breast lower down and floating

　3. Feeding in a hands-and-knees position

　4. Vitamin C supplements

　5. There is no research-based support for these interventions during mastitis other than for simple treatment of the symptoms to help the mother feel better; these are frequently thought to relieve some of the underlying causes of mastitis

AA. Cantile (1988) reported on the concept of stripping pus from the milk ducts as a method of treating mastitis (adenitis or infected milk ducts) and of preventing abscesses.

　1. Stripping the breast involves compressing the breast tissue between the thumb and rib cage, moving down the affected area of the breast to the areola, and squeezing with the thumb and forefinger the entire length of the nipple.

　2. This procedure is thought to reestablish free milk flow by removing the pus that is blocking adequate breast drainage and to enable antibiotics in the milk to reach the infected areas.

　3. The process is very painful, and about 2 percent of mothers required demerol IM to handle the pain.

IV  Breast abscess

A. A breast abscess can be a complication of mastitis, which is usually the result of untreated mastitis, delayed treatment of mastitis, and/or inadequate or incorrect treatment of mastitis.

B. An abscess is a localized collection of pus that the body walls off; once encapsulated, it must be surgically drained/aspirated.

C. Risk factors for breast abscess include the following:

　1. Prior mastitis

　2. A delay in therapy

　3. Refusal to take antibiotics or an incomplete course taken

　4. Poor choice of antibiotics

　5. Antibiotic resistance

　6. Failure to drain the affected breast

7. Avoiding breastfeeding on the affected side

8. Acute weaning

D. Benson and Goodman (1970) classified abscesses as follows:

1. Subareolar (superficial and near the nipple)

2. Intramammary unilocular (a single area of pus deep in the breast and away from the nipple)

3. Submammary multilocular (having multiple sites of pus within the abscess)

E. They state that 23 percent are subareolar, 12 percent are intramammary unilocular, and the remaining 65 percent are intramammary and multilocular.

F. The most common offending organism is *S. aureus*, although other organisms are occasionally cultured from an abscess.

G. Prevention of an abscess resides on a continuum of:

1. Efficient milk transfer from breast to baby

2. Avoidance and/or intervention for milk stasis

3. Quick relief of breast inflammation

4. The prompt treatment of breast infection, which includes continued and frequent nursing or pumping on the affected side

5. Delay in seeking treatment for a breast infection is consistently associated with poorer lactation outcomes

6. Maternal education regarding gradual rather than abrupt weaning

H. It is not always possible to confirm or exclude the presence of an abscess by clinical examination alone.

I. Mammography might not reveal an abscess due to extreme tenderness of the breast and very dense tissue.

1. The mammographic features of an abscess are not specific.

J. The use of ultrasound can confirm the existence of the abscess and indicate a suitable site for the incision/aspiration, thus keeping the number and length of incisions to a minimum.

1. Ultrasound has the added benefit of excluding the presence of an abscess and thereby avoiding unnecessary surgery.

K. Surgical drainage of a breast abscess, even a large abscess, can be replaced by repeated aspiration.

1. Mothers can breastfeed throughout the course of the treatment and possibly avoid surgery, admission to the hospital, and separation from their baby and families.

L. Weaning or inhibiting lactation might hinder the rapid resolution of the abscess by producing increasingly viscid fluid that tends to promote rather than reduce breast engorgement.

1. The baby is not affected with continued breastfeeding.

2. Some babies, however, might refuse to feed from the affected side due to a change in the taste of the milk.

3. Following the onset of mastitis, changes in protein, carbohydrate, and electrolyte concentrations of milk from the affected breast have been observed; in particular, there is a decreased level of lactose and a marked rise in the concentrations of sodium and chloride; this situation has the temporary effect of causing the milk to taste salty.

V  Galactocele—a cyst in the ducts of the breast that contains a milky fluid; often called a milk retention cyst

A. The contents of the cyst at first are pure milk but change to a thickened cheesy or oily consistency.

B. The cyst is smooth and rounded and might cause milk to ooze from the nipple when it is pressed.

C. They are thought to be caused by the blockage of a milk duct.

D. The cyst can be aspirated but usually refills with milk.

E. If deemed necessary, it can be surgically removed under local anesthesia without interfering or interrupting breastfeeding; some spontaneously resolve.

F. Diagnosis can be made with ultrasound.

VI  Duct ectasia (also known as comedomastitis, varicocele tumor, or granulomatous mastitis)

A. Most common cause of a multicolored, sticky nipple discharge.

B. It starts as dilatation of the terminal ducts and can occur in pregnancy, although it is most commonly seen between the ages of 35 and 40.

C. An irritating lipid forms in the ducts, producing an inflammatory reaction and nipple discharge.

D. Women complain of burning, itching, pain, and swelling of the nipple and areola, which must be differentiated from symptoms of candida.

E. A palpable, wormlike mass might develop as the condition progresses that mimics cancer, with chronic inflammation leading to fibrosis.

F. Surgery is not indicated unless the condition becomes severe and bleeding commences from the nipple.

G. Lactation can aggravate this condition but is not contraindicated.

VII  Fibrocystic disease (also known as benign breast disease, cystic mastitis, mammary dysplasia, fibrocystic mastopathy, and chronic cystic mastopathy)

A. This condition is benign; palpable irregularities in breast tissue can be felt in varying degrees in response to the normal menstrual cycle.

B. These occur as proliferations of the alveolar system under hormonal influence.

C. Women might experience pain, tenderness, palpable thickenings, and nodules of varying sizes.

D. This condition might regress during pregnancy and does not contraindicate breastfeeding.

E. Some women describe varying degrees of relief from the condition when they eliminate caffeine from their diet and take vitamin E supplements.

**VIII** Other lumps, cysts, and discharges

A. Intraductal papilloma is a benign tumor or wartlike growth on the lining of a duct that bleeds as it erodes.

1. The discharge is usually spontaneous from a single duct, and a non-tender lump might be felt under the areola.

2. After serious disease has been ruled out, breastfeeding can continue; mothers are usually advised to pump the affected breast until the milk is clear of blood and continue breastfeeding on the other side; if the baby tolerates the milk, many can simply continue breastfeeding; the baby's stools might contain black flecks or become discolored and tarry temporarily.

3. If the discharge does not stop, the affected duct can be surgically removed.

4. Sometimes the first sign of this condition is when the baby spits up blood or when a mother who is pumping sees blood or pink tinged milk.

5. This condition is extremely upsetting to the mother; infant disease can be ruled out by checking the spit-up blood for fetal or adult hemoglobin (Apt test) to determine from whom the blood came.

B. Breast cancer—approximately 1–3 percent of masses diagnosed during pregnancy and lactation are malignant.

1. Prominent masses need prompt evaluation; mammography might be difficult to interpret; fine needle biopsy can be performed with minimal problems during lactation; ultrasound or magnetic resonance imagery (MRI) can be used to confirm a solid mass.

2. Treatment might include surgery, chemotherapy, and radiation therapy.

3. Infants are usually weaned from the breast if chemotherapy is necessary.

4. Young women who are treated with breast-conserving therapy and radiation for early stage cancer might experience subsequent full-term pregnancies and successful breastfeeding on the untreated breast, as well as in some women on the treated breast.

5. The milk volume of the treated breast might be diminished.

6. Sometimes a baby will refuse to nurse from a cancerous breast, which is the first clue that a problem exists.

7. Inflammatory breast cancer must be differentiated from mastitis and plugged ducts; lumps that do not disappear in a couple of days, that are fixed with no clearly defined margins, and a pink slightly swollen breast that does not resolve with frequent breastfeeding or anti-inflammatory/antibiotic medications should be evaluated by a physician.

8. Long-term breastfeeding (longer than 24 months per child) has shown an approximate 50 percent reduction in breast cancer risk.

9. A lifetime duration of lactation that totals 73–108 months has also demonstrated an approximately 50 percent reduction in risk.

10. Totals greater than 109 months show an approximate 66 percent reduction in the risk of breast cancer.

IX Augmentation mammoplasty

A. Implants for breast augmentation are done for a variety of reasons, such as asymmetric breasts, hypoplastic breasts, breast reconstruction from surgery, or more commonly to simply have bigger breasts.

B. Breasts undergoing augmentation might lack functional breast tissue, so the reason for the augmentation will impact breastfeeding management.

C. Some augmentation procedures are done on adolescents.

D. Lactation success will depend on the surgical technique used and if the breasts have sufficient functional breast tissue.

1. Infrasubmammary procedure, where the incision is made under the breast.

2. Periareolar, where the incision goes around the areola.

3. An axillary incision near the armpit.

4. Women who have a periareolar incision are at the highest risk for milk insufficiency.

5. All women who have had augmentation surgery face the possibility of this problem, however—not only from the site of the incision but also from nerve disruption and pressure from the implant on breast structures.

6. Mothers need close follow-up and strong encouragement to breastfeed early and often, paying close attention to engorgement and infant weight gain, especially in mothers who have sufficient glandular tissue.

E. Women who received silicone implants are usually concerned about the leakage of silicone into breast milk.

1. For the most part, silicone implants seem to pose little hazard to the breastfed baby.

2. Silicon measurements of infant formula shows vastly higher amounts in artificial baby milks than in breast milk from women who have implants.

F. Most implants used currently are saline filled.

**X** Reduction mammoplasty

   A. Women have breast-reduction surgery of breasts that are so large that they cause shoulder and back pain and interfere with normal activities and relationships.

   B. Full breastfeeding might not always be possible after reduction surgery, depending on the amount of tissue removed and the surgical technique used.

   C. Mothers have the best chance of lactation with the least amount of tissue removed, if the fourth intercostal nerve that branches to the breast and areola is left intact, and if the pedicle technique is used during surgery.

   D. Two techniques are commonly used for breast-reduction surgery:

     1. The pedicle technique leaves the nipple and areola attached to the breast gland on a stalk of tissue; a wedge is removed from the undersides of the breast; because for the most part, the breast tissue, blood supply, and some nerves remain intact, breastfeeding might have varying degrees of success.

     2. The free nipple technique (autotransplantation of the nipple) involves removing the nipple/areola entirely so that larger amounts of breast tissue can be removed; the blood supply to the nipple/areola is severed and nerve damage occurs; this situation might result in diminished sensations in the nipple/areola.

     3. Full breastfeeding is a possibility with the pedicle technique but not with the free nipple technique.

   E. Mothers who have breast-reduction surgery should be encouraged to breastfeed and provide as much breast milk as possible.

     1. Babies might need to be supplemented.

     2. Supplementation can often be done at the breast with a tube feeding device so that the mother and baby can enjoy each other and the breastfeeding experience.

**XI** Dermatitis involving the breast, nipple, and areola

Dermatitis may affect any area of skin on the body including the breasts. Dermatitis may be caused by contact with an allergen, viral dermatitis may be caused by herpes simplex infection, and bacterial dermatitis may occur with impetigo or staphylococcus infection. There is also a case report of a mother developing dermatitis on the nipple and areola after having developed an allergy to her infant's saliva.

   A. Paget's disease of the nipple (PDN) is a superficial manifestation of an underlying breast malignancy and is about 1–3 percent of all breast cancers.

     1. It appears as a unilateral, well-demarcated, red, scaly plaque involving the nipple or areola.

2. The mother might also complain of a serous or blood-tinged discharge, pain, crusting, itching, burning, skin thickening, redness, ulceration, or nipple retraction.

3. There is an underlying breast mass about 60 percent of the time.

4. The lesion tends to appear on the nipple first, then spreads to the areola.

5. Follow-up closely if the mother describes a broken blister on the nipple with discharge, persistent soreness that is not relieved with proper positioning, pain and itching of the whole nipple/areolar complex, and especially if the lesion is unilateral and confined to just the nipple area.

6. Biopsy establishes the diagnosis of Paget's disease.

B. Nipple eczema tends to present with redness, crusting, oozing, scales, fissures, blisters, excoriations (slits), or lichenification; mothers might complain of burning and itching, and the eczema can extend onto and beyond the areola.

1. This condition is usually treated with topical steroids and can occur on both nipples.

2. Allergic contact dermatitis can present in a similar manner and arise from the use of lanolin, emollients, or ointments containing beeswax or chamomile; the lactation consultant should ask what is being put on the nipples that might be causing this problem.

C. Psoriasis can affect any area of the breast and can present as a pink plaque that appears moist with minimal or no scale.

D. Seborrheic dermatitis can occur on the breast, most commonly in the mammary folds; it exhibits a greasy white or yellow scale on a reddened base and is treated topically with ketaconazole, zinc, or selenium sulfide preparations.

E. Herpes simplex with active oozing lesions on the nipple or areola requires a culture of the lesions and immediate treatment.

1. Breastfeeding on that side is interrupted until the lesions heal.

F. Mammary candidiasis (thrush)

Candidiasis is also known as thrush or Monilia. The offending organism *Candida albicans* is a commensal organism, i.e., we live in harmony with this organism until a change disrupts the balance between the fungus and its host, the human body. The best example of this is the use of antibiotics and the often resultant vaginal thrush. It can affect the breastfeeding dyad in many ways.

1. The organism C. *albicans*, found frequently in the vagina and gastrointestinal tract, is the most frequent cause of thrush in the oral cavity of a baby and for the superficial and ductal infection of the breast.

2. Diagnosis is frequently based on a cluster of symptoms rather than on laboratory evidence or a standard technique.

3. Intact dry skin is protective against C. *albicans*, while the warm moist nipple possibly damaged or eroded from poor position or improper sucking is a perfect host for colonization and infection.

4. C. *albicans* can exist in a number of forms from the spherical cells on the surface of the nipple to the invasive form that is capable of penetrating cell walls.

5. Infant symptoms of oral thrush range from no visible symptoms to a white plaque coating of the tongue to cottage-cheese like fungal colonies on the tongue, buccal mucosa, soft palate, gums, or tonsils.

6. These plaques, if wiped, might reveal a reddened or bleeding base.

7. A fiery-red diaper/nappy rash with glistening red patches, clear margins, and pustules that enlarge, appear outside the rash, and rupture, resulting in scaly and peeling skin, might be present on the baby.

8. An infected nipple might appear red, shiny, and have sloughing skin or be merely pink; the areola might have irregular shiny confluences.

9. Mothers complain of burning, itching, and stinging pain in the nipples that persists between feedings for many days and that is unresponsive to position changes, sucking corrections, or standard nipple creams.

10. Some mothers also complain of burning and shooting pain in the breasts, which needs to be differentiated from a bacterial infection that causes the same symptoms.

11. Proper identification of the infectious agent is seldom carried out.

12. Skin swabs of the nipple/areola can be examined under a microscope in a potassium hydroxide wet mount for the presence of superficial candidosis.

13. This examination enables the proper use of antifungals, because their excessive use has produced resistant strains; culturing can confirm the *Candida* species; milk cultures are difficult as milk components can inhibit fungal growth.

14. Both mother and baby should be treated simultaneously, even if the baby shows no signs in his or her mouth.

15. More than 40 percent of *Candida* strains are resistant to topical Nystatin (usually the first medication prescribed); other topical treatments can follow, including clotrimazole and miconazole; a 0.5 percent solution of gentian violet can be painted onto the nipple/areola and inside the baby's mouth once a day for 3–4 days; also recommended is the concomitant use of a combination nipple ointment composed of mupirocin 2 percent ointment (15g), Nystatin ointment 100,000units/ml (15g), Clotrimazole 10 percent (15g), and Betamethasone 0.1 percent ointment (15g (Newman).

16. Pacifiers are a continuous source of reinfection; all items coming into contact with the baby's mouth need to be boiled, bleached, or washed daily.

17. Iatrogenic factors increase the risk of *Candida*, including the use of antibiotics, oral contraceptives, and steroids.

18. If all topical medications fail to bring relief, systemic oral fluconazole can be prescribed for 14–28 days.

**XII** Abnormal nipple tenderness (sore) and damage

A. In late pregnancy and early breastfeeding, there is normal tenderness as nipple sensitivity is heightened. This peaks on Day 3–6 postpartum and is relieved as the volume of milk increases.

B. Women feel nipple discomfort as the collagen fibers are stretched with early sucking. This decreases as nipple flexibility increases.

C. Increased vascularity of the nipple and normal epithelial denudement can occur with perfect latch but will increase initial tenderness.

D. Transient latch-on pain may occur from lack of established keratin layer on the nipple epithelium.

E. Prior to milk-ejection, unrelieved negative pressure will increase nipple tenderness. This is relieved with milk ejection.

F. Protracted tenderness that lasts longer than a week and is felt throughout a feed is not normal and requires intervention.

G. Skin color, hair color, prenatal preparation, or limiting sucking time at the breast are not related to the discomfort experienced.

H. Pain during a feed is most commonly a result of incorrect latch.

I. Nipple pain/areola protactibility and baby's oral anatomy and functional suck will require assessment, review and/or correct positioning.

J. Eliminate impetigo, eczema, *C. albicans* overgrowth.

K. Observance of nipple shape as the baby detaches is diagnostic.

L. Nipple shape post-feed may present in a number of ways:
   1. Horizontal or vertical red or white stripes
   2. Asymmetrical stretching
   3. Blisters
   4. Fissures, cracks, or bleeding
   5. Sharp pain experienced in one or both nipples post-feed
   6. Blanching (vasospasm)

M. Nipple pain will be aggravated by engorgement and the level of nipple damage.

N. The individual response of the mother will mediate nipple pain.

O. Vasospasm of the nipple, Raynaud-like condition of the nipple.
   1. Described as extreme pain, stinging and burning of the nipple.

2. Shape of the nipple post-feed can indicate proper latch but pain evident.

3. Nipple appears blanched post-feed then the classic triphasic color change of white to blue to red is apparent.

4. Babies who bite at the breast, clench their jaw, or chew on the nipple can cause nipple spasms (spasms of the blood vessels within the nipple).

5. Some babies will clench their jaws in order to hang on and not lose the nipple; these babies actually need more support at the breast and benefit from sublingual pressure (gentle support under the chin where the tongue attaches) or the full jaw support of the Dancer hand position.

6. Symptomatic management of warm compresses, avoiding cold air and reduction of smoking may help.

7. Systematic management by Nifedipine may be considered.

P. Contributing factors include the following:

1. Transient latch-on pain might occur from a lack of an established keratin layer on the nipple epithelium.

2. Pain during a feeding can be attributed to:

   a. The nipple/areola not in the baby's mouth symmetrically or not in far enough

   b. Unrelieved negative pressure, which is present until the milk ejection reflex occurs and is relieved by the periodic swallowing of the baby

   c. The baby's lower and/or upper lip curled under rather than flared out

   d. Manipulation of the nipple/areola, such as squeezing it, tilting it up, pointing it down, or pushing it into the baby's mouth

   e. The baby's tongue behind the lower gum and pinching or biting the nipple

   f. The baby having tongue-tie (ankyloglossia)

   g. The mother leaning down over the baby to "insert" the breast into the baby's mouth

   h. The breast pushed sideways to the baby, rather than the baby's mouth centered over where the nipple points naturally

   i. Nipple preference (the mouth configured for feeding on an artificial nipple)

   j. A disorganized or dysfunctional sucking pattern

   k. Flat or retracted nipples

   l. The baby's mouth is not opened wide enough.

   m. Impetigo, eczema, or C. albicans overgrowth

# Management

- Suggest that the mother initiate the milk ejection reflex or express drops of colostrum before putting the baby to her breast.
- Review and/or correct positioning:
  - If in the cradle hold, the baby completely faces the mother and is held close with his or her legs wrapped around the mother's waist.
  - Four fingers are under the breast, and the thumb is on top with all fingers off the areola.
  - The baby is brought to the breast with his or her mouth centered below where the nipple points.
  - The baby's lips should touch the nipple; when his or her mouth opens to its most wide open point, the baby is drawn the rest of the way onto the breast.
  - If the baby does not open wide enough or if the nipple feels pinched, the mother can use the side of her index finger under her breast to gently pull down on the chin; this action also rolls out the lower lip.
  - Some babies who do not open wide enough might benefit from sucking on an adult's finger before feeds.
- The mother can massage and compress the breast to initiate milk flow if the baby does not begin sucking.
- If the baby pauses for long periods of time between sucking bursts, the mother can add the technique of alternate massage (squeezing the breast when the baby pauses, alternates with the sucking bursts).
- Avoid extension in the baby's back or neck; align the head and trunk; the mother can use the football (clutch) hold or prone infant positioning for a high-tone baby.
- The mother should avoid depressing the top of the breast or areola under the baby's nose to create an airway.
- A properly positioned baby should have the tip of the nose touching the breast and can breathe without assistance.
- The mother should also avoid the scissors hold on the areola if by doing so she compresses it and flattens an inverted nipple.
- The baby should be fed on cue 8–12 times each 24 hours; avoid trying to lengthen time intervals between feeds or feeding the baby a bottle in the nursery at night.
- Breast milk can be applied to the nipples following each feeding. Avoid creams, lotions, oils, and ointments unless medically indicated. Warm water compresses might provide relief as well as the use of hydrogel dressings.

- Avoid pacifiers (especially the flavored or scented ones as well as the orthodontic ones), artificial nipples on bottles, and nipple shields. Use alternative devices for supplemental feeds if needed (cup, syringe, dropper, feeding tube devices, and so on).

- Avoid squeezing the areola and pushing it into the baby's mouth. The baby's head should not be pushed into the breast.

- Flat nipples can be encouraged to protrude by using a modified syringe prior to each feeding in order to increase protractility.

# References

ALCA News. White spots (Corpora amylocea) 1992; 3:8–9.

Amir LH. Candida and the lactating breast: Predisposing factors. *J Hum Lact* 1991; 7:177–181.

Amir L, Hoover K, Mulford C. Candidiasis and breastfeeding. *Lactation Consultant Series* Unit 18. Schaumburg, IL: La Leche League International, 1995.

Amir LH, Garland SM, Dennerstein L, Fariah SJ. *Candida albicans:* Is it associated with nipple pain in lactating women? *Gynecol Obstet Invest* 1996; 41:30–34.

Barnes L. Cryotherapy: Putting injury on ice. *The Physician and Sports Medicine* 1979; 7:130–136.

Benson EA, Goodman MA. Incision with primary suture in the treatment of acute puerperal breast abscess. *Br J Surg* 1970; 57:55–58.

Benson EA. Management of breast abscesses. *World J Surg* 1989; 13:753–756.

Bertrand H, Rosenblood LK. Stripping out pus in lactational mastitis: A means of preventing breast abscess. *Canadian Med Assoc J* 1991; 145:299–306.

Bowles BC, Stutte PC, Hensley JH. New benefits from an old technique: Alternate massage in breastfeeding. *Genesis* 1987/1988; 9:5–9,17.

Brodribb W, ed. Breastfeeding management in Australia, 2nd ed. Merrily Merrily Enterprises, Australia, 1997.

Bucho BL, Pugh LC, Bishop BA, et al. Comfort measures in breastfeeding primiparous women. *JOGNN* 1993; 23:46–52.

Cantile HB. Treatment of acute puerperal mastitis and breast abscess. *Can Fam Physician* 1988; 34:2221–2227.

Carroll L, et al. Bacteriologic criteria for feeding raw breastmilk to babies on neonatal units. *Lancet* 1979; ii:732–733.

Centouri MD, Burmaz T, Rofani L, et al. Nipple care, sore nipples, and breastfeeding: A randomized trial. *J Hum Lact* 1999; 15: 127–132.

Chikly B. Lymph drainage therapy: Treatment for engorgement. International Lactation Consultant Association conference, August 2, 1999; Scottsdale, AZ. Audio tape: Repeat Performance 219.465.1234.

Connor AE. Elevated levels of sodium and chloride in milk from mastitic breasts. *Pediatrics* 1979; 63:910–911.

Coomes F, McIntyre E. Fibrocystic breast disease, Topics in Breastfeeding Set VI. Melbourne, Australia: Lactation Resource Centre, 1994.

Cowie AT, Forsyth IA, Hart IC. Hormonal control of lactation. Berlin: Springer Verlag, 1980.

Csar N. Breast engorgement: What is the incidence and pattern? Unpublished Masters thesis. University of Illinois, Chicago, IL: 1991.

Daly SEJ, Hartmann PE. Infant demand and milk supply. Part 2: The short-term control of milk synthesis in lactating women. *J Hum Lact* 1995; 11:27–37.

Dawson EK. Histological study of normal mamma in relation to tumour growth; mature gland in lactation and pregnancy. *Edinburgh Med J* 1935; 42:569.

Dever J. Mastitis: positive interventions. *Midwifery Today* 1992; 22:22–25.

Devereux WP. Acute puerperal mastitis: evaluation of its management. *Am J Obstet Gynecol* 1970; 108:78–81.

Dixon JM. Repeated aspiration of breast abscesses in lactating women. *Br Med J* 1988; 297:1517–1518.

Dixon JM, Mansel RE. ABC of breast disease. Symptoms, assessment and guidelines for referral. *Br Med J* 1994; 309(6956):722–726.

Dixon JM, Ravisekar O, Chetty U, Anderson TJ. Periductal mastitis and duct ectasia: Different conditions with different aetiologies. *Br J Surg* 1996; 83:820–822.

Drewett R, Kahn H, Parkhurst S, Whiteley S. Pain during breastfeeding: The first three months postpartum. *J Reprod Inf Psychol* 1987; 5: 183–186.

Eschenbach DA. Acute postpartum infections. *Emerg Med Clin North Am* 1985; 3:87–115.

Evans K, Evans R, Simmer K. Effect of method of breastfeeding on breast engorgement, mastitis and infant colic. *Acta Paediatr* 1995; 84:849–852.

Evans M, Heads J. Mastitis: Incidence, prevalence and cost. *Breastfeeding Rev* 1995; 3:65–72.

Ferris AM, Dalidowitz CK, Ingardia CM, et al. Lactation outcome in insulin dependent diabetic women. *J Am Diet Assoc* 1988; 88:317–322.

Ferris CD. Instrumentation system for breast engorgement evaluation. *Biomed Sci Instrum* 1990; 90:227–229.

Ferris CD. Hand-held instrument for evaluation of breast engorgement. *Biomed Sci Instrum* 1996; 96:299–304.

Fetherston C. Characteristics of lactation mastitis in a Western Australian cohort. *Breastfeeding Review* 1997; 5:5–11.

Fetherston C. Management of lactation mastitis in a Western Australian cohort. *Breastfeeding Review* 1997; 5:13–19.

Fetherston C. Risk factors for lactation mastitis. *J Hum Lact* 1998 14:2, 101–109.

Fetherston C. Mastitis in lactating women: Physiology or pathology? *Breastfeeding Rev* 2001; 9:1, 5–12.

Fildes V. Breasts, bottles and babies. Edinburgh: Edinburgh University Press, 1986; 85–86.

Foxman B, Schwartz K, Looman SJ. Breastfeeding practices and lactation mastitis. *Soc Sci Med* 1994; 38:755–761.

Freed GL, Landers S, Schanler RJ. A practical guide to successful breastfeeding management. *Am J Dis Child* 1991; 145:917–921.

Fulton AA. Incidence of puerperal and lactational mastitis in an industrial town of some 43,000 inhabitants. *Br Med J* 1945; May 19:693–696.

Geissler N. An instrument used to measure breast engorgement. *Nurs Res* 1967; 16:130–136.

Gibberd GF. Sporadic and epidemic puerperal breast infections: A contrast in morbid anatomy and clinical signs. *Am J Obstet Gynecol* 1953; 65:1038–1041.

Glover R. The engorgement enigma. *Breastfeeding Rev* 1998; 6:31–34.

Gupta R, Gupta S, Duggal N. Tubercular mastitis. *Int Surg* 1982; 67:422.

Hale T. Clinical therapy in breastfeeding patients. Amarillo, TX: Pharmasoft Publishing, 1999.

Harris LMD, Stevens FM, Frieberg A. Is breastfeeding possible after reduction mammoplasty? *J Plast Reconstr Surg* 1992; 89: 836–839.

Hayes R, Michell M, Nunnerley HB. Acute inflammation of the breast—the role of breast ultrasound in diagnosis and management. *Clin Radiol* 1991; 44:253–256.

Heads J, Higgins L. Perceptions and correlates of nipple pain. *Breastfeeding Rev* 1995; 3:2, 59–64.

Heinig MJ, Francis J, Pappagianis D. Mammary candidosis in lactating women. *J Hum Lact* 1999; 15:281–288.

Hesseltine HC, Freundlich CG, Hite KE. Acute puerperal mastitis: Clinical and bacteriological studies in relation to penicillin therapy. *Am J Obstet Gynecol* 1948; 55:778–788.

Hill PD, Humenick SS. The occurrence of breast engorgement. *J Hum Lact* 1994; 10:79–86.

Hocutt JE, Jaffe R, Rylander CR, Beebe JK. Cryotherapy in ankle sprains. *Am J Sports Med* 1982; 10:317–319.

Huggins KE, Petok ES, Mireles O. Markers of lactation insufficiency: A study of 34 mothers. Current Issues in Clinical Lactation 2000. Boston: Jones and Bartlett Publishers, 25–35.

Humenick SS, Hill PD, Anderson MA. Breast engorgement: Patterns and selected outcomes. *J Hum Lact* 1994; 10:87–93.

Iffrig MC. Nursing care and success in breastfeeding. *Nurs Clin N Amer* 1968; 3:345–354.

Illingworth RS, Stone DG. Self demand feeding in a maternity unit. *Lancet* 1952; I:683–687.

Inch S, Fisher C. Mastitis: Infection or inflammation. *The Practitioner* 1995; 239:472–476.

Inch S. Mastitis: A literature review. WHO, Division of Child Health & Development. Geneva, Switzerland: 1997.

Isbister C. Acute mastitis: A study of 28 cases. *Med J Aust* 1952; Dec 6:801–808, 1952.

Jeffrey JS. Treatment of acute puerperal mastitis. *Edinburgh Med J* 1947; 54:442–446.

Jonsson S, Pulkkinen MO. Mastitis today: Incidence, prevention and treatment. *Ann Chir Gynaecol Suppl* 1994; 208:84–87.

Kalstone C. Methicillin-resistant staphylococcal mastitis. *Am J Obstet Gynecol* 1989; 161:120.

Karstrup S, Khattar S, et al. Acute puerperal breast abscess: US-guided drainage. *Radiology* 1993; 188:807–809.

Kaufmann R, Foxman B. Mastitis among lactating women: Occurrence and risk factors. *Soc Sci Med* 1991; 33:701–705.

Kenny JF. Recurrent group B streptococcal disease in an infant associated with the ingestion of infected mother's milk. *J Pediatr* 1977; 91:158.

Kesaree N, Banapurmath CR, Banapurmath S, et al. Treatment of inverted nipples using a disposable syringe. *J Hum Lact* 1993; 9:27–29.

Kirkman W. Breast dermatitis. Le Leche League News, Great Britain. 1997; 97:6–7.

Lawlor-Smith LS, Lawlor-Smith CL. Raynaud's phenomenon of the nipple: A preventable cause of breastfeeding failure. *Med J Aust* 1996; 166:448.

Lawlor-Smith LS, Lawlor-Smith CL. Vasospasm of the nipple: A manifestation of Raynaud's phenomenon; case reports. *Br Med J* 1997; 314:644.

Lawrence RA. Breastfeeding: A guide for the medical profession, 5th ed. St. Louis: Mosby-Year Book, Inc., 1999.

Leary WG, Jr. Acute puerperal mastitis: A review. *Calif Med* 1948; 68:147–151.

Livingstone V. Too much of a good thing: Maternal and infant hyperlactation syndromes. *Can Fam Physician* 1996; 42:89–99.

Livingstone VH, Willis CE, Berkowitz J. *Staphylococcus aureus* and sore nipples. *Can Fam Physician* 1996; 42:654–659.

Livingstone V, Stringer IJ. The treatment of staphyloccocus aureus infected sore nipples: A randomised comparative study. *J Hum Lact* 1999; 15(3):241–246.

Marshall BR, Hepper JK, Zirbel CC. Sporadic puerperal mastitis: An infection that need not interrupt lactation. *JAMA* 1975; 233:1377–1379.

Marshall DR, Callam PP, Nicholson W. Breastfeeding after reduction mammoplasty. *Br J Plast Surg* 1994; 47:167–169.

Marti A, Feng Z, Altermatt HJ, Jaggi R. Milk accumulation triggers apoptosis of mammary epithelial cells. *Eur J Cell Biol* 1997; 73:158–165.

Matheson I, Aursnes I, Horgen M, Aabo O, Melby K. Bacteriological findings and clinical symptoms in relation to clinical outcome in puerperal mastitis. *Acta Obstet Gynecol Scand* 1988; 67:723–726.

McLachlan Z, Milne J, Lumley J, Walker B. Ultrasound treatment for breast engorgement: A randomised double blind trial. *Austr J Physiother* 1991; 37:23–29.

Menczer J, Eskin B. Evaluation of postpartum breast engorgement by thermography. *Obstet Gynecol* 1969; 33:260–263.

Minchin M. Breastfeeding matters: What we need to know about infant feeding. Victoria, Australia: Alma Publications and George Allen & Unwin Australia Pty Ltd, 1985.

Mohrbacher N, Stock J. The breastfeeding answer book. Schaumburg, IL: La Leche League International, 1997, p. 423.

Moon AA, Gilbert B. A study of acute mastitis of the puerperim. *J Obstet Gynecol Br Commonwealth* 1935; 42:268–282.

Moon JL, Humenick SS. Breast engorgement: Contributing variables and variables amenable to nursing intervention. *JOGNN* 1989; 18:309–315.

Neifert M, DeMarzo S, Seacat J, et al. The influence of breast surgery, breast appearance, and pregnancy-induced breast changes on lactation sufficiency as measured by infant weight gain. *Birth* 1990; 17:31–38.

Neubauer SH, Ferris AM, Hinckley L. The effect of mastitis on breast milk composition in insulin dependent diabetic and non-diabetic women. *FASEB J* 1990; 4:A915.

Neville MC, Neifert MR, eds. Lactation: Physiology, nutrition and breastfeeding. New York: Plenum Press, 1983.

Newman J, Pitman T. Dr. Jack Newman's guide to breastfeeding. Toronto, Ontario: HarperCollins Publishers Ltd., 2000.

Newton EN. Mastitis: cause, diagnosis, treatment. La Leche League International Individual Study Module #3, April 1997, from a talk at the La Leche League International 24th Annual Physician's Seminar, July 19, 1996, San Diego, CA.

Newton M, Newton N. Breast abscess: A result of lactation failure. *Surg Gynecol Obstet* 1950; 91:651–655.

Newton M, Newton N. Postpartum engorgement of the breast. *Am J Obstet Gynecol* 1951; 61:664–667.

Nicholson W, Yuen HP. A study of breastfeeding rates at a large Australian obstetric hospital. *Aust NZJ Obstet Gynaecol* 1995; 35:393–397.

Niebyl JR, Spence MR, Parmley TH. Sporadic (non-epidemic) puerperal mastitis. *J Repro Med* 1978; 20:97–100.

Nikodem VC, Danziger D, Gebka N, et al. Do cabbage leaves prevent breast engorgement? A randomized, controlled study. *Birth* 1993; 20:61–64.

Norwood S. Fibrocystic breast disease: An update and review. *JOGNN,* 1990; 129:116–121.

O'Hara RJ, Dexter SPL, Fox JN: Conservative management of infective mastitis and breast abscess after ultrasonographic assessment. *Br J Surg* 1996; 83:1413–1414.

Ogle KS, Davis S. Mastitis in lactating women. *J Fam Pract* 1988; 26:138–144.

Olsen G, Gorden R. Breast disorders in nursing mothers. *Am Fam Physician* 1990; 45:1509–1516.

Opri F. Mammary mycoses. *Chemotherapy* 1982; 28 (suppl1):61–65.

Peaker M, Wilde CJ. Feedback control of milk secretion from milk. *J Mamm Gland Biol Neoplasia* 1996; 1:307–314.

Pittard WB, et al. Bacteriostatic qualities of human milk. *J Pediatr* 1985; 107:240–243.

Prentice A, Prentice AM, Lamb WH. Mastitis in rural Gambian mothers and the protection of the breast by milk antimicrobial factors. *Trans R Soc Trop Med Hyg* 1985; 79:90–95.

Prentice A, Addey CVP, Wilde CJ. Evidence for local feedback control of human milk secretion. *Biochem Soc Trans* 1989; 15:122.

Prosser CG, Hartmann PE. Comparison of mammary gland function during the ovulatory menstrual cycle and acute breast inflammation in women. *Aust J Exp Bio Med Sci* 1983; 61:277–286.

Rench MA, Baker CJ. Group B streptococcal breast abscess in a mother and mastitis in her infant. *Obstet Gynecol* 1989; 73:875–877.

Riedel LJ. Breast engorgement: Subjective and objective measurements and patterns of occurrence in primiparous mothers. Masters thesis, Department of Nursing, University of Wyoming, Laramie, Wyoming: 118 pages, 1991.

Righard L, Alade MO. Sucking technique and its effect on success of breastfeeding. *Birth* 1992; 19:185–189.

Riordan J. A practical guide to breastfeeding. St. Louis: CV Mosby, 1983, pp. 149–156.

Riordan JM, Nichols FH. A descriptive study of lactation mastitis in long-term breastfeeding women. *J Human Lact* 1990; 6:53–58.

Riordan J, Auerbach KG. Breastfeeding and human lactation, 2nd ed. Sudbury, MA: Jones and Bartlett Publishers, 1998.

Roberts KL. A comparison of chilled cabbage leaves and chilled gelpaks in reducing breast engorgement. *J Hum Lact* 1995; 11:17–20.

Roberts KL, Reiter M, Schuster D. Effects of cabbage leaf extract on breast engorgement. *J Hum Lact* 1998; 14:231–236.

Robson BA. Breast engorgement in breastfeeding mothers. Doctoral dissertation, Case Western Reserve University, Cleveland, Ohio, 1990. UMI order #PUZ9023094.

Rosier W. Cool cabbage compresses. *Breastfeeding Rev* 1988; 12:28–31.

Sandberg CA. Cold therapy for breast engorgement in new mothers who are breastfeeding. Masters thesis, College of St. Catherine, St. Paul, MN, 1998.

Schreiner RL, Coates T. Possible breast milk transmission of group B streptococcal infection. *J Pediatr* 1977; 91:159.

Semmler D. The use of ultrasound therapy in the treatment of breast engorgement. *Austr Physiotherapy Association Natl Obstet and Gynecolo J* 1982; 2:18.

Shellshear M. Therapeutic ultrasound in postpartum breast engorgement. *Austr J Physiother* 1981; 27:15–16.

Shiau S-HH. Randomized controlled trial of Kangaroo Care with full term infants: Effects on maternal anxiety, breast milk maturation, breast engorgement, and breastfeeding status. Doctoral dissertation, Case Western Reserve University, Cleveland, Ohio: 1997.

Slaven S, Harvey D. Unlimited sucking time improves breast feeding. *Lancet* 1981; 1(8216):392–393.

Snowden HM, Renfrew MJ, Woolridge MW. Treatments to relieve breast engorgement during lactation (Protocol for a Chochrane Review). In: The Cochrane Library, Issue 2 2000. Oxford: update software.

Stevens K, Burrell HC, Evans AJ, Sibbering DM. The ultrasound appearance of galactocoeles. *Br J Radiol* 1997; 70:239–241.

Stutte PC, Bowles BC, Morman GY. The effects of breast massage on volume and fat content of human milk. *Genesis* 1988; 10:22–25.

Taylor MD, Way S. Penicillin treatment of acute puerperal mastitis. *Br Med J* 1946; Nov 16:731–732.

Thomsen AC, Housen KB, Moller BR. Leukocyte counts and microbiologic cultivation in the diagnosis of puerperal mastitis. *Am J Obstet Gynecol* 1983; 146:938–941.

Thomsen AC, Espersen T, Maigaard S. Course and treatment of milk stasis, noninfectious inflammation of the breast, and infectious mastitis in nursing women. *Am J Obstet Gynecol* 1984; 149:492–495.

Thorley V. Impetigo on the areola and nipple. *Breastfeeding Rev* 2000; 8:25–26.

Uvnas-Moberg K. Oxytocin may mediate the benefits of positive social interaction and emotions. *Psychoneuroendocrinology* 1998; 23:8 819–835.

Walia HS, Abraham TK, Shaikh H. Fungal mastitis: Case report. *Arch Chir Scand* 1987; 153:133–135.

Walker M. Mastitis. Lactation Consultant Series 2. La Leche League International, USA, 1999.

Waller H. The early failure of breastfeeding. *Arch Dis Child* 1946; 21:1–12.

Walsh A. Acute mastitis. *Lancet* 1949; 2:635–639.

Weichert CE. Prolactin cycling and the management of breastfeeding failure. *Adv Pediatr* 1980; 27:391–407.

West J, Rutsch M, Stocker S. *Streptococcus pneumoniae* as an agent of mastitis. *Eur J Clin Microbiol Infect Dis* 1995; 14:156–157.

Whitaker-Worth DL, Carlone V, Susser WS, et al. Dermatologic diseases of the breast and nipple. *J Am Acad Dermatol* 2000; 43:733–754.

Wilson-Clay B, Hoover K. The breastfeeding atlas. Austin, TX: LactNews Press, 1999.

Woolridge MW. Aetiology of sore nipples. *Midwifery* 1986; 2:172–176.

Woolridge MW. The 'anatomy' of infant sucking. *Midwifery* 1986; 2:164–171.

World Health Organisation: Mastitis: Causes and management. Geneva: WHO, 2000.

Zheng T, Duan L, Liu Y, et al. Lactation reduces breast cancer risk in Shandong Province, China. *Am J Epidemiol* 2000; 152:1129–1135.

# MATERNAL ACUTE AND CHRONIC ILLNESS

*Marsha Walker, RN, IBCLC*

## OBJECTIVES

- Describe the influence of acute and chronic maternal illness on breastfeeding and lactation.
- Identify breastfeeding management strategies to preserve breastfeeding under adverse situations.
- Discuss contraindications to breastfeeding.

## Introduction

Not only has there been an increase in the number of women choosing to breastfeed, but more women now than ever have been able to conceive and carry a pregnancy to term or near term under a variety of acute and chronic health conditions. Almost all of these mothers can breastfeed partially or totally even if they are taking medications or are experiencing viral or bacterial infections. The lactation consultant should gain familiarity with a number of the more common health challenges in order to better provide lactation care and services when met with maternal health problems.

I Pituitary disorders

A. Sheehan's syndrome (panhypopituitarism) caused by severe postpartum hemorrhage and hypotension can lead to the failure of the pituitary gland to produce gonadotropins.

1. Symptoms of severe Sheehan's syndrome include weight gain then loss postpartum, loss of pubic and axillary hair, intolerance to cold, low blood pressure, and vaginal and breast tissue atrophy.

2. Milder cases might see a delay in milk synthesis; frequent breastfeeding or pumping would be required in order to stimulate the number and sensitivity of breast prolactin receptors and to take advantage of what little prolactin might be available.

3. The role of the pituitary gland might be permissive rather than completely responsible for the success of lactation; women who have varying levels of prolactin have been shown to produce adequate amounts of milk for their infants.

4. The breast and body have compensatory mechanisms that make lactation a robust activity; autocrine control of milk production can fill in for a less-than-optimal hormonal environment.

B. Prolactinomas—prolactin-secreting adenomas.

1. Prolactin-secreting tumors that can produce amenorrhea and galactorrhea do not show a correlation with milk production.

2. Women can breastfeed with this condition.

3. Chronic, high levels of prolactin can also be caused by certain medication, excessive breast manipulation, hypothyroid states, hyperthyroid disease, chronic renal failure, and several less-frequently seen syndromes.

II  Insulin-dependent diabetes mellitus (IDDM)

A. Diabetes is a chronic disease of impaired carbohydrate metabolism.

1. Type 1 diabetes, or insulin-dependent diabetes mellitus (insufficient insulin).

2. Type 2 or late-onset diabetes that is usually not insulin dependent (inefficient use of insulin).

3. Gestational diabetes is a glucose intolerance that is seen in about 10–12 percent of pregnancies.

   a. Women who have gestational diabetes are more likely to develop IDDM if they do not lactate following the pregnancy.

B. The breast has insulin-sensitive tissue and requires insulin to initiate milk production.

1. There can be a 24-hour delay in lactogenesis II as the mother's body competes with the breasts for the available insulin.

C. Lactation has an insulin-sparing effect on the mother, which can cause lower insulin requirements during lactation; the constant conversion of glucose to galactose and lactose during milk synthesis lowers the insulin requirement.

1. The diabetic mother also needs extra calories while lactating.

D. Diabetic mothers should be encouraged to breastfeed.

1. Their infants might be large and are prone to hypoglycemia; therefore, very frequent feedings of colostrum are necessary; if mother and baby are separated, pumping should be instituted as soon as possible.

2. Some babies of diabetic mothers are observed in a nursery for a number of hours following birth; this separation increases the chances for supplemental bottles of formula and a long delay in putting the baby to the breast; hand-expressed colostrum is very valuable to these babies at this point for both

disease protection and to stabilize blood sugar levels; colostrum or breast-milk substitutes can be offered to the baby by cup, spoon, dropper, or tube feeding device.

   3. Insulin is a large molecule that does not pass into the milk of a mother on insulin replacement therapy.

E. Mothers who have diabetes might be more prone to infection, mastitis, and overgrowth of *Candida albicans*.

   1. Hypoglycemia in the mother might increase the release of epinephrine, reducing milk production and interfering with the milk ejection reflex.

   2. The presence of acetone signals the need for more calories and carbohydrates; acetone can be transferred to the milk and stress the newborn's liver.

III  Thyroid disease

A. The thyroid gland controls the body's metabolism and is involved with the hormones of pregnancy and lactation.

B. Because untreated hypothyroidism has a low probability for the maintenance of a pregnancy, most mothers who have this condition are already receiving thyroid replacement therapy (which is compatible with breastfeeding).

C. Low thyroid levels have been associated with low milk production and insufficient weight gain in some babies and should be examined in these situations.

D. Hypothyroidism has also been identified in postpartum mothers who have prolonged "baby blues," a new onset of depression, or extended fatigue.

E. Hyperthyroidism is an excess amount of thyroid hormone that can result in rapid weight loss, increased appetite, nervousness, heart palpitations, and a rapid pulse at rest.

   1. The ability to lactate is not compromised by this condition.

   2. Hyperthyroidism with bulging eyes is called Graves' disease.

   3. Laboratory examination of a blood sample can usually diagnose this condition; sometimes radioiodine studies are recommended and care must be taken to use a medium that is considered safe for lactation.

   4. Treatment is usually an antithyroid drug that is safe for the infant.

   5. Sometimes the baby's thyroid function is measured periodically.

IV  Cystic fibrosis (CF)

A. Cystic fibrosis is characterized by the dysfunction of the exocrine glands and includes chronic pulmonary disease, obstruction of the pancreatic ducts, and pancreatic enzyme deficiency.

B. Formerly, life expectancy was short with few women reaching adulthood.

C. In early stages, more sophisticated treatments are now enabling women to live into adulthood, reproduce, and breastfeed.

D. Concerns center around the mother maintaining her own weight and her health status, rather than quality or quantity of her breast milk.

1. Mothers who have CF usually need plenty of extra calories and supplements to their own diet in order to maintain their weight.

E. Individuals who have CF are chronic carriers of pathological bacteria such as *Staphylococcus aureus* and *Pseudomonas*.

1. Breast milk lymphocytes are sensitized to these pathogens carried by the mother and are passed to the baby in breast milk, protecting him or her from infections by these agents.

V   Phenylketonuria (PKU)

A. PKU is an inborn error of metabolism whereby the body lacks the enzyme to break down the amino acid phenylalanine, which can result in lowered intelligence.

B. Because of widespread newborn screening for this situation and early treatment, many women are reaching their childbearing years with normal intelligence.

C. Diet restrictions should not be discontinued at any age, especially in women.

1. Blood phenylalanine levels should be 4mg or lower in women.

2. Breastfeeding is compatible with the condition.

3. The milk of mothers who have PKU is of normal composition.

VI   Systemic Lupus Erythematosus (SLE)

A. SLE is an autoimmune disease of the connective tissue primarily affecting women of childbearing age.

B. Symptoms are diverse, exacerbated by pregnancy, and include the following: fatigue, fibromyalgia, joint redness and swelling, and a butterfly rash on the cheeks and nose.

C. Women who have SLE experience higher rates of miscarriage and delivery of preterm infants.

D. Raynaud's phenomenon is present in about 30 percent of cases.

E. Insufficient milk supply is the most frequent complaint during lactation; infant weight gain must be carefully watched, and babies might need supplementation.

F. Non-steroidal-antiinflammatory medications (NSAIDs) and corticosteroids are frequent medications that are given to handle symptoms.

G. Breastfeeding is especially beneficial to mothers who have SLE because it enables them to rest while feeding the baby and helps space out pregnancies.

VII   Osteoporosis

A. Osteoporosis is a condition of bone thinning that is generally associated with older, postmenopausal women.

B. A rare syndrome of osteoporosis has been identified during pregnancy and lactation that generally responds to increased calcium in the diet.

C. Normal lactation-associated bone mineral mobilization takes place and does not require drug therapy or nutritional supplements.

D. Bone loss can be measurable during lactation but returns to normal baseline following weaning.

E. Because a lactating woman's body is more efficient in energy use and nutrient uptake, lumbar bone density actually increases the longer a woman breastfeeds and the more infants she nurses.

F. Age, diet, body frame size, and weight-bearing exercise all contribute to good (or poor) bone health.

VIII Seizure disorders (epilepsy)

A. Mothers who have epilepsy can successfully breastfeed and should be encouraged to do so.

B. The major concern is the sedating effects on the baby of the maternal medications.

C. Antiepileptic drugs tend to make a baby sleepy and depress his or her sucking in the early days following birth until he or she is better able to handle drug clearance; it is important that mothers pump milk following feedings or if the baby feeds poorly in order to provide breast stimulation in the absence of adequate sucking from the baby during the early days.

D. Some mothers have been advised not to breastfeed because they might drop the baby if they have a seizure while breastfeeding; having this situation happen is no more likely to occur during breastfeeding than during bottle feeding and is a poor excuse not to breastfeed.

IX Migraine headaches

A. These severe episodic headaches tend to be worse during the first trimester of pregnancy and are sensitive to hormones and other triggers.

B. Many remedies, both pharmacologic and of a biofeedback nature, are used to help this condition.

C. It does not preclude breastfeeding.

D. When a mother experiences this type of headache and if it is severe enough, she might not feel well enough to breastfeed (although pumping is not much of a relief).

E. Mothers might want some extra milk in the freezer in case others need to feed the baby.

X Raynaud's phenomenon of the nipple

A. Raynaud's phenomenon is an intermittent ischemia (narrowing of the blood vessels) usually affecting the fingers and toes, especially when exposed to cold and more commonly seen in women.

B. This condition has been likened to descriptions by some women of blanching of the nipple either before, during, or after breastfeedings.

C. These nipple spasms have also been seen clinically as a result of babies biting at the breast, jaw clenching, and in the presence of severe nipple damage; such sucking variations need to be corrected to help eliminate the trigger to the spasms.

D. The mother feels extreme pain during this nipple spasm, which might continue to spasm and relax for up to 30 minutes after a feeding.

E. Exposure to cold can exacerbate this problem.

F. Some maternal medications, such as fluconazole and oral contraceptives, might be associated with vasospasm.

G. Mothers usually feel relief from warm compresses to the breasts or a heating pad.

H. Other anecdotal remedies for this condition that have not been thoroughly studied include the following:

   1. Ibuprofen
   2. Nifedipine (5mg three times per day for one week)
   3. Supplemental calcium (2000mg/day)
   4. Supplemental magnesium (1000mg/day)

**XI** Surgery

A. Breastfeeding can continue through almost all situations that require surgery.

B. Concern is over anesthetic and pain medications, the mother's ability to hold and feed the baby, access to the baby, access to a breast pump, and the ability to pump on a regular basis.

C. Babies might be able to room with the mother during her hospital stay as long as an assistant is present to care for the baby; otherwise, the baby can be brought to the hospital for feedings; if this situation is not possible, the mother should have access to a hospital-grade electric breast pump with a double collection kit; if she is physically unable to pump, then the nurse or caretaker can pump the breasts for her.

D. With elective surgery, the mother has time to arrange for access to the baby, a private room, and perhaps pump extra milk and freeze it for use any time she is unavailable to feed.

**XII** Viral infections

A. Breastfeeding is rarely contraindicated in maternal infection.

B. Exceptions relate to specific infectious agents with strong evidence of transmission and to the association of increased morbidity and mortality in the infant.

C. Cytomegalovirus (CMV)—one of the human herpes viruses.

   1. Congenital infections are usually asymptomatic but can result in later hearing loss or learning disability.

2. Infections acquired at birth from maternal cervical secretions or breast milk are usually not associated with symptoms.

3. Infants who have congenital or acquired CMV do better if they are breastfed because of the antibody protection delivered through breast milk.

4. Nonbreastfed infants can be infected through other secretions, including saliva, and receive no protective antibodies or other host resistance factors that are present in breast milk; they can have significant health effects from the disease, including microcephaly and mental retardation; high rates of transmission occur in child-care centers.

5. Term infants can be fed breast milk when the mother is shedding virus in her milk because of the passively transferred maternal antibodies.

6. Preterm infants can develop the disease, even from breast milk; recommendations include freezing the breast milk for 3–7 days at –20°C, which destroys the virus.

D. Herpes simplex virus.

1. Infection in the early neonatal period is serious and can be fatal.

2. The infection is most frequently transmitted to the baby through the birth canal.

3. Only lesions on the breast would require a temporary interruption of breastfeeding until the lesions have completely cleared.

4. Active lesions elsewhere on the body should be covered, and the mother should be instructed to wash her hands before handling the infant; breastfeeding is not affected.

5. A mother who has cold sores on her lips should refrain from kissing and nuzzling the baby until the lesions have crusted and dried.

E. Herpes varicella-zoster (chicken pox).

1. If maternal chicken pox occurs within six days of delivery and no lesions are present in the mother or the baby, mother and baby should be isolated from each other.

2. When the mother becomes noninfectious (6–10 days), she can be with her baby.

3. The mother will need to pump breast milk, which can and should be given to the baby (as long as there are no active lesions on the breast).

F. Respiratory syncytial virus (RSV).

1. RSV is a common cause of respiratory illness in children.

2. Mortality can be high in neonates, especially preterm babies or ill full-term babies.

3. There is no reason to stop breastfeeding during maternal RSV infection (breast milk might be protective against severe RSV).

4. Infants who have RSV should breastfeed.

G. Human immunodeficiency virus 1 (HIV-1).

1. HIV-1 can be transmitted through breast milk, but the relative risk is not well quantified.

2. HIV-1 antibodies also occur in the breast milk of infected women; breast milk in vitro is capable of neutralizing the HIV virus.

3. A major dilemma in estimating the risk from breastfeeding is in the difficulty in determining when the HIV infection actually occurs in the infant.

4. Current standards of the United States *Occupational Safety and Health Administration* (OSHA) do not require gloves for the routine handling of expressed human milk; health workers should wear gloves in situations where exposure to expressed breast milk would be frequent or prolonged, such as in milk banking.

5. Expressed breast milk from HIV-positive mothers can be made safe for infant consumption and should be carefully considered for use, especially in areas of the world where breast-milk substitute use would pose a grave threat to the life of the infant.

6. Refer to Chapter 9, "Immunology, Infectious Disease, and Allergy Prophylaxis."

H. Hepatitis.

1. The varying types of hepatitis carry different risks of contagion, pathways of exposure, treatments, and preventive measures.

2. Hepatitis A is an acute illness and is usually transmitted through food-borne and water-borne routes as well as commonly in child-care settings through fecal contamination.

   a. A newborn can be infected by vertical transmission from an infected mother during delivery.

   b. The baby should be isolated from other babies in the nursery (such as rooming-in).

   c. Gamma globulin is given to the baby if the mother developed the disease within two weeks of the delivery.

   d. The mother will also receive gamma globulin.

   e. Breastfeeding should proceed as usual.

3. Hepatitis B can cause a wide variety of infections, from asymptomatic conversion to fulminant fatal hepatitis.

   a. Mandatory prenatal testing reveals the mother's status prior to delivery.

   b. Infants who are born to mothers who have the active disease or who are active carriers receive hepatitis B specific immunoglobulin (HBIG) at birth or soon after, followed by an immunization program.

   c. As soon as HBIG is given, breastfeeding should begin.

4. Hepatitis C infection has an insidious onset, with many people not aware that they are affected.

   a. The risk of infection via breast milk is very low.

   b. Concern arises if a mother has a co-infection, such as HIV.

   c. Because the virus might be inactivated in the infant's gastrointestinal tract or neutralized in colostrum, mothers who have hepatitis C can and should breastfeed.

5. Hepatitis D, E, and G

   a. Not much is known about transmission of the forms of hepatitis through breastfeeding.

   b. Hepatitis D is usually a co-infection or superimposed on a hepatitis B infection.

   c. Once immunoglobin has been given and the vaccine has begun, breastfeeding should proceed as usual.

   d. Hepatitis E is self-limited and is not a chronic disease (usually associated with water contamination).

   e. Breastfeeding has not been shown to transmit this disease and should proceed as usual.

   f. Hepatitis G seems associated with blood transfusions but has not been shown to be transmitted through breast milk.

   g. Reports of infected mothers breastfeeding infants are few, but no clinical infections have been reported.

XIII. Tuberculosis

  A. Breastfeeding is not contraindicated in women who have previously positive skin tests and no evidence of disease.

    1. A mother who has had a recent conversion to a positive skin test should be evaluated for the disease, and if there is no sign of disease, breastfeeding should begin or continue.

    2. If a mother has suspicious symptoms, she might need to pump milk and have it fed to the baby until a diagnosis is made.

    3. In developed countries where there is easy access to an electric breast pump, mothers might need to pump milk during the time they are being evaluated.

    4. If there is confirmation of the disease, the mother needs to be treated and breastfeeding can begin or resume after two weeks of maternal therapy.

    5. In developing countries where nonbreastfed infants have a high mortality rate, breastfeeding is not interrupted.

    6. If it is safe for the mother to be in contact with her baby, then it is safe to breastfeed.

# References

De Coopman J. Breastfeeding after pituitary resection: support for a theory of autocrine control of milk supply? *J Hum Lact* 1993; 9:35–40.

Lawrence RA. A review of the medical benefits and contraindications to breastfeeding in the United States (Maternal and Child Health Technical Information Bulletin). Arlington, VA: National Center for Education in Maternal and Child Health, 1997.

Lawrence RA, Lawrence RM. Breastfeeding: A guide for the medical profession, 5th ed. St. Louis, MO: Mosby, Inc., 1999.

Mohrbacher N, Stock J. The breastfeeding answer book. Revised edition. Schaumburg, IL: La Leche League International, 1997.

Pickering LK, ed. 2000 Red Book: Report of the commission on infectious diseases, 25th ed. Elk Grove Village, IL: American Academy of Pediatrics, 2000.

Riordan J, Auerbach KG. Breastfeeding and human lactation, 2nd ed. Sudbury, MA: Jones and Bartlett Publishers, 1998.

# INSUFFICIENT MILK SUPPLY

*Kay Hoover, MEd, IBCLC*

## OBJECTIVES

- Delineate between a real and perceived insufficient milk supply.
- Discuss the etiology of insufficient milk.
- Describe potential indicators of insufficient milk.
- List options for improvement of an insufficient milk supply.

## Introduction

An insufficient supply of breast milk continues to be the major reason given by mothers worldwide for the discontinuation of breastfeeding during the first 6–8 weeks postpartum. This reason is also commonly given around four months of age. Whether the problem is real or perceived is addressed by a careful history and breastfeeding assessment. True low milk supply can be caused by a number of factors (overlapping etiologies) and is often a combination of these factors. Perceived low milk supply is an interpretation by the mother of an infant's behavior of being unsettled after being breastfed or asking for frequent feedings and experiencing slow weight gain. Many of the mothers reporting infant fussiness after breastfeeding will give the baby a bottle of formula to "satisfy" the infant. Topping off the baby usually begins a downward spiral of insufficient milk unless interrupted. The percentage of mothers reporting insufficient milk in the literature varies, with many reports not differentiating between real and perceived insufficiency. Probably no more than 1–2 percent of women actually cannot lactate.

  **I** Physiologic basis for insufficient milk (Woolridge, 1995)

    A. Milk production at five days is highly variable, with mothers producing between 200–900g/24 hours.

    B. Over the following 3–5 weeks, milk output is progressively calibrated to the baby's needs, increasing in most cases but sometimes decreasing.

C. Interference with the calibration of the breasts during this time can cause the breasts to calibrate at an inappropriate level. Such interferences include the following:

1. Supplemental feeds of water or formula that cause the breasts to make less milk or calibrate at an inappropriately low level

2. A baby who does not efficiently remove milk from the breast

3. Unrelieved engorgement

4. A mother of a preterm infant who does not express her milk to her peak yield, just to the transient limited needs of the small baby at the time

5. A limited number of feedings

6. Feedings that are not long enough

D. Following initiation of milk production, milk output rises to about 700g/24 hours by 4–6 weeks of age.

1. The rate of increase is about 175g/week; after about six weeks, the rate of milk increase slows to about 4g/week.

2. 750g/24 hours meets the needs of the average singleton infant, even beyond the six week period.

3. While the infant continues to grow normally after six weeks, his or her energy requirements per kilogram of body weight decreases.

4. Milk output is not constrained at 750g/24 hours because mothers of twins are quite capable of outputs of 1500g/24 hours.

E. If breast milk production is to be sustained, milk must be consistently and effectively removed.

1. Unremoved milk exerts an inhibitory effect on milk production, down-regulating the amount produced through chemical (feedback inhibitor of lactation) and physical (pressure atrophy of milk secreting cells) means.

II Descriptions of insufficient milk

A. Mothers can present with an infant who shows slow or static weight gain or weight loss.

B. Mothers often describe an unsettled baby who fusses after feedings; a baby who feeds for long periods at the breast; and a baby who feeds constantly at the breast and fusses when put down.

C. Perceptions by the mother that her supply is low due to softer breasts, breasts feeling less full, and cessation of leakage.

D. Mothers simply doubt their ability to make sufficient milk.

III Classification of apparent milk insufficiency (Woolridge, 1995)

A. Class I: Unsubstantiated low milk supply

1. The vast majority of "insufficient milk supply"

2. Based on a history and breastfeeding assessment, management can include the following:

a. Technical improvements in position, latch-on, and sucking; use of alternate massage (massage and compress the breast during pauses between sucking bursts) to sustain sucking, increase volume and fat content per feed, and adequately drain breasts; and teaching the indicators of swallowing

b. Teaching feed management

i. Number of times each 24 hours = 8–12 in the early weeks.

ii. Clustered or bunched feedings in the late afternoon and early evening are normal.

iii. Frequency days can occur anytime, and the baby should be need-fed.

iv. The baby should drain the first breast before being placed at the second.

v. No time limitations at the breast, such as five minutes on the first side so that the baby will take both sides.

vi. The baby should feed at night; breastfeeding should not be skipped at night.

vii. Avoid the use of sleep-through-the-night baby training programs that do not enable night feeds.

viii. Avoid parenting programs that attempt to control how frequently a baby can be breastfed.

ix. Assure that the cause of sore nipples is addressed (positioning or inefficient sucking patterns).

x. Advise mothers not to decrease the number of breastfeedings to "let the breasts fill."

c. Support and encouragement

i. Might be beneficial to educate significant others, including the father and grandmothers of the baby, regarding breastfeeding norms in order to eliminate the pressure to give bottles or to not breastfeed as much.

ii. Mothers might need pain relief from episiotomy, cesarean incision, and back pain from labor or the epidural.

B. Class IIa: Physiological low milk supply where mothers make 150–350g/24 hours

1. Does not respond to normal routine advice and support.

2. Might require pumping breast milk after feedings to increase the degree of drainage of the breasts.

C. Class IIb: Iatrogenic low milk supply with milk output of less than 450g/24 hours

1. Might have seen evidence of higher milk output at an earlier stage, but output has dropped due to poor management.

2. Mothers might have been engorged and told not to pump milk because they would just make more milk (low milk production is a result of this advice).

3. Preterm mothers might have been told that they did not need to pump more milk than what the baby required at the time, causing a low calibration of milk yield.

4. Mothers might have been encouraged not to feed the baby at night.

5. The baby might have been supplemented with formula, preventing a higher calibration of the milk production.

6. Breastfeeding might have been interrupted or delayed for a variety of reasons, such as hyperbilirubinemia, hypoglycemia, maternal medication use (oral, injectable, implanted, or transdermal contraceptives), maternal illness, mastitis, and infant illness without concomitant pumping of the breasts.

7. Maternal smoking, recreational drugs such as alcohol, and herbal preparations or seasonings (such as sage or mint).

8. Insufficient weight gain during pregnancy; an eating disorder.

9. After six weeks, this condition might be more difficult to reverse.

D. Class IIc: behaviorally induced low milk supply with a milk output of less than 450g/24 hours

1. Factors here include the baby's behaviors

2. An adverse reaction to the breast from being pushed onto the breast by pressure on the back of the head; oral defensiveness from suctioning or intubation

3. Sleepy babies from maternal labor medications; breathing problems; sucking on artificial nipples or pacifiers; a behavioral lack of persistence; an overactive let-down reflex; conditions where the control a baby normally exerts over the feeding process has been overridden

E. Class III: pathophysiological lactation failure with milk output of less than 150g/24 hours

1. Intrinsic problem of maternal origin

   a. Mammary hypoplasia (breasts do not undergo normal growth and development during pregnancy)

   b. Breasts can be asymmetric, tubular, and lacking in sufficient glandular tissue

   c. Retained placental products (which is reversible)

   d. Necrosis of the anterior pituitary due to hypotensive episode; postpartum hemorrhage (Sheehan's syndrome)

   e. Endocrine deficiency (a lack of sufficient progesterone, which is responsible for the proliferation of alveolar tissue; could see this condition in a luteal phase defect, where the mother is estrogen dominant with an adequate ductal network but with deficient alveolar tissue)

    f. Low thyroid hormone

    g. Anemia

    h. History of chest tubes

    i. Breast surgery, such as augmentation or reduction mammoplasty; breast milk insufficiency has been particularly noted when periareolar incisions are used

    j. Polycystic ovary syndrome (can present with a number of hormonal aberrations, such as low progesterone levels, insulin resistance, elevated estrogen levels, and high levels of testosterone and adrostenedione (with their possible effect of down regulating estrogen and prolactin receptors)

**IV** Management of milk insufficiency

  A. Recognizing who is at risk, anticipating insufficient milk, and preventing iatrogenic factors reduces the chances of low milk production.

    1. Potential indicators of those who are at risk for insufficient milk include the following:

      a. Mothers who are less informed about breastfeeding

      b. Making the decision to breastfeed later in pregnancy

      c. Intending to breastfeed for a short or limited period of time

      d. Being less confident about their ability to breastfeed; mothers who are tentative and say that they are going to "try" to breastfeed

      e. Being sensitive to a lack of privacy

      f. Receiving less encouragement from male partners and mothers-in-law

      g. Having a poorer health status and more problems with illness while breastfeeding

      h. Infants of mothers who have insufficient milk also tend to weigh less at birth, be fussier, and be poorer feeders

        i. A chronically fussy baby can disrupt a mother's fragile confidence in her ability to breastfeed.

        ii. These babies are more frequently complimented with formula after breastfeeding because of the perception that the fussiness is caused by not getting enough milk.

        iii. Complementing or supplementing with formula can, in some cases, be an initial marker rather than a cause of milk insufficiency.

      i. Poor feeding by the baby can relate to maternal labor medications, birth injuries from forceps or vacuum extraction, and chronic maternal medications

  B. Therapeutic interventions depend on the cause of the problem.

1. Mothers should be taught how to position their baby at the breast, what constitutes an effective latch-on, and how to know when the baby is swallowing milk.

2. Nipple pain during a feeding can indicate that the baby is not positioned correctly or is not suckling correctly; each increases the likelihood of poor milk transfer, less milk removed from the breast, and less milk synthesized to replace it.

3. Mothers should be taught infant behavioral feeding cues, be encouraged to eliminate watching the clock, and to feed the baby when he or she demonstrates feeding readiness.

   a. Feeding cues include rapid eye movements under the eyelids, sucking movements of the mouth and tongue, hand-to-mouth movements, body movements, and small sounds; these indicate a light sleep state moving to alertness when the baby is more likely to feed efficiently; babies who are in a deep sleep state do not breastfeed; feeding at proscribed intervals might catch the baby repeatedly at times when he or she is not "available" to feed.

   b. Babies should be fed 8–12 times each 24 hours; feedings should not be skipped, complemented, or supplemented unless medically indicated; mothers should manually express or pump milk if the baby cannot go to the breast.

   c. Mothers should demonstrate an awareness of cluster or bunched feedings that typically occur in the late afternoon or early evening.

   d. Alternate massage can be used to initiate and sustain suckling at the breast; some babies require the presence of milk flow to regulate their sucking.

   e. Mothers should know how to gauge whether their baby is getting enough milk; diaper counts and weight gain are typical indicators.

   f. Sudden weight loss during the early days in a baby whose mother had pitocin and/or large amounts of IV fluids during labor should not be confused with insufficient milk intake.

4. Diabetic mothers can have a 24-hour delay in lactogenesis II and should breastfeed their baby very frequently.

5. Mothers who have had any type of breast surgery should feed their baby very frequently, and a weight check should be done no later than 48 hours following discharge.

   a. Some of these mothers might be able to synthesize a partial supply of breast milk that is adequate during the early weeks but that does not reach a sufficient amount to fully meet the needs of the growing baby; some mothers might need to supplement; the supplement can be delivered through a tube feeding device if the mother desires to feed the baby at the breast.

6. If pumping is recommended, the breasts can be expressed following each breastfeeding to more thoroughly drain the breasts; the degree of drainage and the frequency of drainage influences milk production.

   a. Mothers who are pumping for preterm infants should be encouraged to start pumping as soon as possible in the hospital; milk quantity should exceed by 50 percent the infant's requirement at hospital discharge; the ideal quantity is 750–1000ml/day by day 10; this quantity is predictive of milk output at five weeks.

V Pharmacologic interventions

A. Galactogogues have been used for millennia to support and increase a mother's milk supply.

B. Every culture has its favored herbs, concoctions, and remedies for this condition.

C. There are also prescription medications that are used to improve milk production, most of which were never intended for use as a galactogogue; they typically increase the amount of prolactin secreted by the mother by inhibiting the secretion of dopamine by the mother's hypothalamus; dopamine inhibits the release of prolactin.

   1. Major tranquilizers such as chlorpromazine (Largactil and Thorazine) and haloperidol (Haldol) typically increase milk production as a side effect; however, significant side effects of sedation, fatigue, and neurological aberrations preclude their use for insufficient milk supply; sulpiride is used as an antipsychotic in some countries and also increases milk production, but its side effects are similar to tranquilizers, and it is used only in emergency or disaster situations.

   2. Metoclopramide (Reglan and Maxeran) is used quite successfully to increase a faltering milk supply, especially in the preterm mother; some mothers experience depression as a side effect; mothers who have a history of depression might not be good candidates for use of this medication; other mothers find significant benefits from its use.

   3. Domperidone (Motilium; not available in the United States) is used for the treatment of certain gastrointestinal disorders; it is quite effective at increasing milk production without the side effects of metoclopramide.

   4. Thyrotropin-releasing hormone (TRH) has been used successfully to increase prolactin levels and milk production; side effects can include hyperthyroidism in larger doses.

   5. Human growth hormone (HGH) has been shown to significantly increase milk production in both term and preterm mothers; adverse effects have not been reported in either mothers or babies.

   6. Oxytocin nasal spray used prior to each breast pumping during the first week postpartum in preterm mothers showed a dramatic increase in milk output with no side effects.

D. Herbs are used throughout the world to increase milk production; herbs that have pharmacologic properties act as drugs; little quality control exists over herbal preparations; concentrations of ingredients as well as ingredients themselves vary from one manufacturer to another and are not standardized; dosage is anecdotal and some herbs have side effects; herbal preparations are not regulated and can be adulterated; herbs by themselves do not fix problems caused by infrequent nursing or ineffective suckling; herbal therapy is usually used in conjunction with a plan to remedy what is causing the low milk supply.

1. Some herbs should be avoided by breastfeeding mothers, such as those that decrease milk production; herbal antihistamines such as mahuang (*Ephedra*) and osha root (*Ligusticum porteri*) as well as herbs containing steroid-like ingredients such as licorice (*Glycerrhiza glabra*), ginseng (*Panex quinquefolium*), sage (*Saliva officinalis*), black walnut (*Juglandis regia*), and yarrow (*Achillea milleolium*).

2. A few of the many herbal galactogogues include red clover blossoms (*Trifolium pratense*), nettles (*Urtica dioica*), blessed thistle (*Cnici benedicti herba*), alfalfa, borage (*Borago officinalis*), fennel seeds, milk thistle, and fenugreek (*Trigonella foenum-graecum*) capsules.

3. Fenugreek seems to work best as 2–3 capsules taken three times per day rather than prepared as a tea.

VI  Alternative therapy

A. Acupuncture has been used in China for low milk production since 256 A.D.

1. Reports indicate that acupuncture is most effective if started with 20 days post delivery; little to no results will be obtained if started after six months.

2. Milk production can start to increase as soon as 2–4 hours following treatment or as late as 72 hours; the faster the response, the better the outcome.

3. Acupuncture might be a good choice for preterm mothers.

4. There seem to be few (if any) side effects.

# References

Ball DE, Morrison P. Oestrogen transdermal patches for postpartum depression in lactating mothers—a case report. *Cent Afr J Med* 1999; 45:68–70.

Bodley V, Powers D. Patient with insufficient glandular tissue experiences milk supply increase attributed to progesterone treatment for luteal phase defect. *J Hum Lact* 1999; 15:339–343.

Breier BH, Milsom SR, Blum WF, et al. Insulin-like growth factors and their binding proteins in plasma and milk after growth hormone-stimulated galactopoiesis in normally lactating women. *Acta Endocrinol* 1993; 129:427–435.

Clavey S. The use of acupuncture for the treatment of insufficient lactation (Que Ru). *Am J Acupuncture* 1996; 24:35–46.

Desmarais L, Browne S. Inadequate weight gain in breastfeeding infants: Assessments and resolutions. Lactation consultant series Unit 8. New York: Avery Publishing Group, 1990.

Greiner T, van Esterik P, Latham MC. The insufficient milk syndrome: An alternative explanation. *Med Anthropol* 1981; 5:233–260.

Gunn AJ, Gunn TR, Rabone DL, et al. Growth hormone increases breast milk volumes in mothers of preterm infants. *Pediatrics* 1996; 98:279–282.

Gussler JD, Briesemeister LH. The insufficient milk syndrone: A biocultural explanation. *Med Anthropol* 1980; 4:145–174.

Harris L, Morris SF, Freiberg A. Is breastfeeding possible after reduction mammoplasty? *Plast Reconstruct Surg* 1992; 89:836–839.

Henly SJ, Anderson CM, Avery MD, et al. Anemia and insufficient milk in first-time mothers. *Birth* 1995; 22:87–92.

Hill PD. Insufficient milk supply syndrome. *NAACOG's Clin Issues Perinat Women's Health Nursing* 1992; 3:605–612.

Hill PD. The enigma of insufficient milk supply. MCN 1991; 16:313–316.

Hill PD, Aldag J. Potential indicators of insufficient milk supply syndrome. *Res Nurs Health* 1991; 14:11–19.

Hill PD, Humenick SS. Insufficient milk supply. Image: *J of Nurs Scholar* 1989; 21:145–148.

Hillervik-Lindquist C. Studies on perceived breast milk insufficiency: a prospective study in a group of Swedish women. *Acta Paediatr Scand* 1991; 80(Suppl 376):6–27.

Hillervik-Lindquist C, Hofvander Y, Sjolin S. Studies on perceived breast milk insufficiency. III. Consequences for breast milk consumption and growth. *Acta Paediatr Scand* 1991; 80:297–303.

Hopkinson J, Schanler R, Fraley J, et al. Milk production by mothers of premature infants: Influence of cigarette smoking. *Pediatr* 1992; 90:934–938.

Huggins KE. Fenugreek: One remedy for low milk production. *Medela Rental Roundup* 1998; 15:16–17.

Huggins KE, Petok ES, Mireles O. Markers of lactation insufficiency: A study of 34 mothers. In: Auerbach K, ed. Current issues in clinical lactation 2000. Sudbury, MA: Jones and Bartlett Publishers, 2000; 25–35.

Hughes V, Owen J. Is breastfeeding possible after breast surgery? MCN 1993; 18:213–217.

Hurst NM. Lactation after augmentation mammoplasty. Obstet Gynecol 1996; 87:30–34.

Kennedy KI, Short RV, Tully MR. Premature introduction of progestin-only contraceptive methods during lactation. Contracept 1997; 55:347–350.

Kopec K. Herbal medications and breastfeeding. J Hum Lact 1999; 15:157–161.

Marasco L, Marmet C, Shell E. Polycystic ovary syndrome: A connection to insufficient milk supply? J Hum Lact 2000; 16:143–148.

Miczak M. Herbs and healthy lactation. Mothering Magazine 1996; Spring:60–63.

Milsom SR, Breier BH, Gallaher BW, et al. Growth hormone stimulates galactopoiesis in healthy lactating women. Acta Endocrinol 1992; 127:337–343.

Milsom SR, Rabone DL, Gunn AJ, Gluckman PD. Potential role for growth hormone in human lactation insufficiency. Horm Res 1998; 50:147–150.

Morton JA. Ineffective suckling: A possible consequence of obstructive positioning. J Hum Lact 1992; 8:83–85.

Neifert M. Breastfeeding after breast surgical procedure or breast cancer. NAACOG's Clin Iss Perinat Women's Health Nurs: Breastfeeding 1992; 3:673–682.

Neifert M, DeMarzo S, Seacat J, et al. The influence of breast surgery, breast appearance, and pregnancy-induced breast changes on lactation sufficiency as measured by infant weight gain. Birth 1990; 17:31–38.

Neifert MR, McDonough SL, Neville MC. Failure of lactogenesis associated with placental retention. Am J Obstet Gynecol 1981; 140:477–478.

Neifert M, Seacat J. Lactation insufficiency: A rational approach. Birth 1987; 14:182–190.

Neifert M, Seacat J, Jobe WE. Lactation failure due to insufficient glandular development of the breast. Pediatr 1985; 76:823–828.

Neubauer S, Ferris S, Chase C, et al. Delayed lactogenesis in women with insulin-dependent diabetes mellitus. Am J Clin Nutr 1993; 58:54–60.

Nice F, Coghlan RJ, Birmingham BT. Herbals and breastfeeding; http://www.uspharmacist.com/NewLook/Display/Article.cfm?item_num=581. Accessed 10/6/2000.

Ostrom K, Ferris A. Prolactin concentrations in serum and milk of mothers with and without insulin-dependent diabetes. Am J Clin Nutr 1993; 58:49–53

Renfrew MJ, Lang S, Woolridge M. Oxytocin for promoting successful lactation. Cochrane Database Syst Rev 2000; (2):CD000156.

Ruis H, Rolland R, Doesburg W, et al. Oxytocin enhances onset of lactation among mothers delivering prematurely. *Br Med J* (Clin Res Ed) 1981; 283(6287):340–342.

Salariya E, Easton P, Cater J. Breast feeding and milk supply failure. *J Mat Child Health* 1980; 5:38–42.

Sheehan HL, Murdoch R. Post-partum necrosis of the anterior pituitary: Pathological and clinical aspects. *J Obstet Gynecol Br Empire* 1938;45:456–489

Tully J, Dewey KG. Private fears, global loss: A cross-cultural study of the insufficient milk syndrome. *Medical Anthropol* 1985; Summer: 225–243.

Tyson JE, Perez A, Zanartu J. Human lactational response to oral thyrotropin releasing hormone. *J Clin Endocrinol Metab* 1976; 43:760–768.

Verronen P. Breast feeding: Reasons for giving up and transient lactational crises. *Acta Paediatr Scand* 1982; 71:447–450.

Walker M. Functional assessment of infant breastfeeding patterns. *Birth* 1989; 16:140–147.

Walker M. Management of selected early breastfeeding problems seen in clinical practice. *Birth* 1989; 16:148–158.

Willis C, Livingstone V. Infant insufficient milk syndrome associated with maternal postpartum hemorrhage. *J Hum Lact* 1995; 11:123–126.

Woolridge M. Breast feeding: Physiology into practice. Ch 2. Davies DP, ed. Nutrition in child health. London: Royal College of Physicians of London Press, 1995, pp. 13–31.

# Induced Lactation and Relactation

*Ruth E. Worgan, RN, CM, C&FH, IBCLC*

## Objectives

- Describe the differences between induced lactation and relactation.
- Discuss the historical basis and indications of induced lactation and relactation.
- List the necessary breast development required for lactation.
- List indications for inducing lactation and relactation.
- List and discuss the action of medications prescribed to induce lactation and relactation.
- Describe physical actions that can assist in inducing lactation and relactation.
- Describe different options of management for inducing lactation and relactation.

## Introduction

Induced lactation and relactation have occurred and still occur in varying incidences in breast-feeding societies. The physiology is not well understood, nor has it been well researched. The nutritional, immunological, and hormonal components of induced and relactated breast milk is also lacking within research, with only minimal number of papers being published. This situation, however, has not diminished the incidence in some societies—with it becoming more common with the increase in breastfeeding rates in western countries.

Breast development and maturation during pregnancy is a precursor to lactation; however, history and literature has shown that a woman can induce lactation and breastfeed without the preparatory effect of pregnancy and birth. When breast stimulation has commenced, many women experience breast fullness and tenderness.

## Definitions of Induced Lactation and Relactation

Induced lactation—stimulation of the breast to lactate in order for an infant to be breastfed where pregnancy has been absent

Relactation—restimulation of lactation following the cessation of lactation following birth or untimely weaning at any age

## Clinical Indications

Induced lactation and relactation have been practiced in most cultures and for a variety of reasons.

Induced lactation has been practiced when:

1. A mother adopts a baby and desires to breastfeed (sometimes referred to as adoptive breastfeeding).

2. A relative/friend wet nurses an infant if the biological mother is unable (for example, in the cases of maternal HIV, maternal death, the maternal inability to breastfeed because of a physical abnormality, or a maternal absence).

3. Emergency or disaster situations exist.

Relactation has been practiced when:

1. The mother weans and wishes to recommence breastfeeding.

2. The infant recommences breastfeeding following weaning.

3. The infant becomes sick upon weaning and the mother wishes to recommence breastfeeding.

4. The inability to initiate breastfeeding at birth exists due to maternal/infant illness and/or separation.

5. The inability to initiate breastfeeding at birth exists due to conditions such as prematurity, infant illness, oral-facial anomalies, or hospitalization.

6. The inability to breastfeed exists due to maternal physical anomalies (such as inverted nipples).

7. The infant is intolerant or allergic to breast-milk substitutes.

8. Emergency or disaster situations exist.

## Induced Lactation—Clinical Practice Assessment

I History

  A. Previous pregnancies

    1. Has the woman had previous pregnancies/children?

      a. If so, how many?

      b. Duration of pregnancies

      c. How long ago?

      d. Reason for adoption

    e. History of infertility (for example, hormonal)

    f. Other hormonal abnormalities, such as thyroid or pituitary disorders

  B. Previous breastfeeding experience

    1. Has the mother breastfed previous children, and if so, for how long?

    2. Did she have any breastfeeding problems? If so, what?

    3. When and reason(s) for weaning

    4. Previous breastfeeding education (classes, reading, and videos)

  C. Cultural influences

    1. Assess the mother's concerns regarding modesty.

    2. What are her expectations about her ability to make breast milk?

    3. What are her expectations about her ability to breastfeed?

    4. Assess her support system.

    5. What are her religious beliefs regarding breast milk and breastfeeding affecting the mother-infant relationship?

  D. Reasons for wishing to breastfeed an adopted baby

    1. Many mothers wish to breastfeed in order to normalize the arrival of a child and to simulate the experience of biological motherhood.

    2. They might wish to enhance the mother-infant relationship and increase the opportunity for close attachment.

    3. They might feel that it would be healthier for the baby and that they would not want the baby to miss out on the experience.

**II** Prior to receiving the infant

  A. How long will it be until she receives the child to be breastfed?

  B. How old will the child be when he or she commences breastfeeding?

    1. What type of milk is the child being fed at present?

    2. How is the child being currently fed (for example, wet nursed, via bottle, by a cup)?

    3. Babies who are older than six months might not be willing to breastfeed.

      a. Babies at 2–3 months of age might be as likely to accept the breast as to reject it.

      b. After the first week of trying to breastfeed, the older the baby is when introduced to the breast, the less willing the baby might be to suckle.

**III** Breasts and nipples

  A. The size and shape of the breasts

    1. Scars, anomalies noted, history of any surgical procedures

    2. Breast size and shape (for example, tubular, asymmetrical, or pendulous)

B. The size and shape of the nipples and areola
1. Normal, inverted, flat, and retracted
2. Nipple anomalies and supernumerary nipples
3. Areola anomalies
4. The direction the nipple points will influence the position of baby's mouth.

## Planning and Implementation

I Expected outcome
A. Counseling
1. Emphasize the breastfeeding relationship.
a. Might never achieve full lactation
b. Realisitic levels of achievement
c. Center upon the baby being content to nurse at the breast
2. First milk drops expected from one to six weeks
3. If the baby is suckling, breastmilk can be observed as early as one to two weeks
C. Support from family and friends
1. Support from family and friends is necessary.
2. Support, encouragement, and appropriate information from the care giver is required.

II Establishing lactation
A. Expressing
1. Assess the mother's comfort with expressing.
2. Teach and assess the ability to hand express breast milk.
3. Assess the availability and type of hand and electric breast pumps.
4. Assess the mother's ability to pump/express.
5. Assess the mother's ability to achieve expression frequency (at least six times in 24 hours/15 minutes each expression).
B. Stimulation to induced breast milk production
1. Stimulation of parenchymal breast tissue for development and maturation prior to breastfeeding
a. Some women have induced lactation by expressing and nursing the baby.
b. Nipple stimulation has been reported to include the following:
i. Nipple exercises for four weeks prior to acquiring the baby, every three to four hours
ii. Breast massage
iii. The baby nursing at the breast

        iv. Often using a tube feeding device that delivers milk while simultaneously suckling at the breast

2. Some mothers might not have breast secretions prior to putting the baby to the breast.

    a. Mothers who have previously breastfed are more likely to have milk prior to putting the adopted baby to the breast.

    b. Tandem nursing does not guarantee a full milk supply for the newly adopted baby.

3. Lactogogues/galactogogues

    a. Estrogen and progesterone (Ano, et al., 1979 and Auerbach and Avery, 1979); caution as a high risk of deep vein thrombosis

4. Stimulation of prolactin during expression/breastfeeding (Auerbach and Avery, 1979)

    a. Metoclopramide (Auerbach and Avery, 1980; Banapurmath, et al., 1993; Bose, et al., 1981; and Brown, 1973)

    b. Domperidone (Brown, 1978 and Budd, et al., 1993)

    c. Sulpiride (Cheales-Siebenaler, 1999; Clavey, 1996; and Cohen, 1971)

    d. Thyrotropin-releasing hormone (Creel, et al., 1991 and Emery, 1996)

    e. Chlorpromazine (Auerbach and Avery, 1979; Ehrenkranz, et al., 1986; Fleiss, 1988; and Hale, 2000)

    f. Human growth hormone (Hofmeyr, et al., 1985)

    g. Theophylline (Hofmeyr, et al., 1985)

5. Stimulation of oxytocin for the milk-ejection reflex

    a. Syntocinon (Hormann, 1977)

6. Non-drug/natural galactagogues

7. Most information is anecdotal and should be used with caution or has been found to be detrimental to lactation; many mothers think that dietary supplements or increasing fluid intake will stimulate milk production; most of these have never been shown to affect milk synthesis.

8. Fleiss (Jelliffe, et al., 1972) in 1988 considered more than 30 herbs to be galactagogues; other suggestions include the following:

    a. Brewer's yeast

    b. Beer (Kauppila, et al., 1983) as an inhibitory factor

    c. Herbs/herbal teas (Kesaree, et al., 1993)

    d. Garlic (Kleinman, et al., 1980)

    e. Chicken soup

    f. Anise (Kramer, 1995)

    g. Fennel

h. Fenugreek (Kulski, et al., 1981)

i. Acupuncture

j. Hypnosis

C. The most common problems adoptive mothers might encounter:

  a. Getting the baby to nurse

  b. Worry about the baby getting enough milk

  c. Fatigue

  d. Lack of sufficient preparation time

  e. Issues over decreasing supplements

  f. Expressing/feeding equipment difficulties

D. Discomforts and/or physiological responses to induced lactation

  a. Nipple pain

  b. Breast pain

  c. Nipple and breast changes

  d. Signs of milk ejection

  e. Menstrual irregularities

  f. Appetite changes

  g. Weight changes

E. Infant suckling

  1. Skin-to-skin (STS) contact.

    a. Begin skin contact when the baby is not hungry and is contented.

  2. Establish breastfeeding.

    a. Facilitate good positioning.

      i. Begin to nurse the infant on the side on which he or she is used to being fed (for example, bottle fed on the left side, startbreastfeeding on the left breast).

    b. Facilitate good attachment.

    c. Facilitate short, frequent breastfeeds (8–12 each 24 hours).

    d. Do not force the infant to the breast or to breastfeed.

    e. Do not allow the infant to cry at the breast; the breastfeeding experience needs to be pleasurable.

      i. Partial feeding via a bottle, cup, finger feeding with a feeding tube, or syringe prior to breastfeeds.

      ii. Breastfeed the baby when he or she is drowsy.

      iii. Breastfeed in a darkened, quiet room.

    f. If complementary feeds are given via a bottle, bottle feed on both the left and right side or cup-feed the baby in an upright position.

    g. Gradually decrease other milks and foods as appropriate.

        i. Do not dilute formula.

        ii. Do not restrict the amounts of supplements.

        iii. Do not keep the baby hungry in an attempt to encourage him or her to feed at the breast.

        iv. Avoid lengthy milk expression sessions.

        v. Avoid lengthy breastfeeding attempts.

    h. Decrease/eliminate the use of bottles, teats, and pacifiers.

    i. A supplemental feeding tube device can assist if the baby is unwilling to suckle at a nonproductive breast.

    j. Continue expressing and galactogogues for maximum stimulation.

    k. Once lactation is established, wean slowly off expressing and/or galactogogues.

    l. Some babies will require supplementation as long as the mother nurses.

# Evaluation

  **I** Mother-infant relationship

    A. Developing a harmonious mother-infant bond/relationship

    B. Facilitated by skin-to-skin contact

      1. Mother-infant dyad happy and contented

  **II** Infant breastfeeding

    A. Infant suckling at the mother's breast

      1. The infant is contented to suckle at the breast for increasing periods

      2. Document swallowing actions

  **III** Mother producing breastmilk

    A. Mother producing breastmilk in increasing quantities

      1. Milk secretion commencing; observed at expression

  **IV** Infant receiving some nutrition from breast

    A. Milk/food intake from other sources diminishing

      1. Reduction of the infant's need to use formula/supplementary foods

      2. Changes in stools, which might vary through the day

      3. Diaper counts (urinary output) remain normal

      4. Pre- and post-feed weights can assess amounts of milk obtained directly from the breasts if necessary

       5. Weight checks every 3–5 days and then weekly to assure adequate weight gain

V  Infant taking all nutrition from breast

    A. Infant receiving only breast milk from breastfeeding

       1. Cessation of supplementary formulas/foods

       2. Cessation of requiring bottles, cups, and so on

    B. Expressing for stimulation gradually decreasing

       1. Maintain milk production by infant breastfeeding

       2. Gradual reduction of expression

    C. Galactogogues gradually decreasing

       1. Maintain milk production by infant breastfeeding

       2. Gradual reduction of the use of galactogogues

## Relactation—Clinical Practice

Many aspects of relactation are similar to induced lactation.

## Assessment

I  History

    A. Previous pregnancies

       1. Has the woman had previous pregnancies/children?

          a. If so, how many?

          b. Duration of pregnancies

          c. How long ago?

    B. Previous breastfeeding experience

       1. Has the mother breastfed previous children? If so, for how long?

       2. Did she have any breastfeeding problems?

       3. When and reason for weaning

       4. Previous breastfeeding education (classes, reading, videos, and so on)

          a. What is the mother's experience/knowledge of breastfeeding?

    C. Current infant breastfeeding experience

       1. Did she breastfeed this infant? If so, for how long?

       2. What were her reasons for not breastfeeding/weaning?

       3. Did she have any difficulties breastfeeding this infant?

          a. Infant-related?

          b. Mother-related?

       4. How and what is the infant currently being fed?

    D. Infant's current health status

    1. Age of infant

       a. Babies who are fewer than three months old might be more willing to accept the breast.

       b. Babies who are older than 12 months and who have a long history of breastfeeding might return to the breast with fewer problems, having not lost the ability to breastfeed.

    2. Birth details (for example, normal, forceps, vacuum extraction, cesarian, or birth asphyxia)

    3. Health history of the infant to date

    4. Is the infant thriving and well?

    5. Physical growth and development check

    6. Have factors related to feeding difficulties been addressed (such as tongue tie, developmental lag, or hypertonic bite)?

  C. Cultural influences

    1. Assess the mother's concerns regarding modesty.

    2. What are her expectations about her ability to breastfeed?

    3. What are her expectations about her infant's ability to suckle?

    4. Assess the mother's support system (family/friends might require information).

    5. Is the mother seeing anyone else for breastfeeding assistance?

II Breasts and nipples assessment

  A. Size and shape of breasts

    1. Scars, anomalies noted

    2. Breast size and shape (tubular, asymmetric)

  B. Size and shape of nipples and areola

    1. Inverted, flat, retracted

    2. Nipple anomalies, supernumerary nipples

    3. Areola anomalies

    4. The direction the nipple points will influence the position of the baby's mouth.

  C. Breast milk production

    1. Is the mother producing any breast milk at present?

    2. How long has it been since the last breastfeed/expressed breast milk?

## Planning and Implementation

I Expected outcome—encourage a focus on the breastfeeding relationship

  A. Counseling

    1. Emphasize the breastfeeding relationship.

    2. Might never achieve full lactation.

3. Realistic levels of achievement.

4. Center upon having the baby content to nurse at the breast.

5. Achievement depends on the baby's feeding history and his or her ability to learn and to remember how to breastfeed effectively.

6. If the baby is suckling, breast milk can be observed as early as one to two weeks.

B. Support from family and friends

1. Support from family and friends is necessary.

2. Support, encouragement, and appropriate information from the caregiver is required.

II Re-establishing lactation

A. Infant suckling at the breast

1. Establish breastfeeding.

a. Establish regular skin-to-skin contact.

b. Facilitate good positioning and attachment.

c. Facilitate frequent breastfeeding.

d. Do not force the baby to breastfeed.

e. Ensure a pleasurable breastfeeding experience.

i. Do not allow the baby to cry at the breast.

ii. Soothe the baby away from the breast before resuming breastfeeding.

f. Gradually decrease other milks and foods as appropriate.

g. Decrease/eliminate the use of bottles, teats, and pacifiers.

h. A supplemental feeding device can assist.

i. Expressing and galactogogues, if used, for maximum stimulation.

j. Once lactation is established, wean slowly off expressing and/or galactogogues.

B. Stimulation to induced breast milk production

1. The stimulation of parenchymal breast tissue to recommence breast milk production

a. Many women have achieved relactation by expressing and nursing the baby alone.

C. Expressing

1. Assess the mother's comfort with expressing.

2. Teach and assess the ability to hand express.

3. Assess the availability and type of hand and/or electric breast pumps.

4. Assess the ability to pump express.

5. Assess the mother's ability to achieve expression frequency (minimum six times in 24 hours/15 minutes each expression).

D. Lactogogues/galactogogues

1. Stimulation of prolactin during expression/breastfeeding (Auerbach and Avery, 1981)

   a. Metoclopramide (Auerbach and Avery, 1980; Banapurmath, et al., 1993; Bose, et al., 1981; and Brown, 1973)

   b. Domperidone (Brown, 1978, and Budd, et al., 1993)

   c. Sulpiride (Cheales-Siebenaler, 1999; Clavey, 1996; and Cohen, 1971)

   d. Thyrotropin-releasing hormone (Creel, et al., 1991 and Emery, 1996)

   e. Chlorpromazine (Auerbach and Avery, 1979; Ehrenkranz, et al., 1986; Fleiss, 1988; and Hale, 2000)

   f. Human growth hormone (Hofmeyr, G. et al., 1985)

   g. Theophylline (Hofmeyr, et al., 1985)

2. Stimulation of oxytocin for the milk ejection reflex

   a. Skin-to-skin contact

   b. Syntocinon (Hormann, and Savage, 1998)

3. Non-drug/natural galactogogues

   Most information is anecdotal and should be used with caution.

   Fleiss (in Jelliffe, et al., 1972) considers more than 30 herbs to be galactagogues.

   a. Brewer's yeast

   b. Beer (Kauppila, et al., 1983) has an inhibitory effect

   c. Herbs/herbal teas (Kesaree, et al., 1993)

   d. Garlic (Kleinman, et al., 1980)

   e. Chicken soup

   f. Anise (Kramer, 1995)

   g. Fennel/fenugreek (Kulski, et al., 1981)

   h. Acupuncture

# Evaluation

I Mother-infant relationship

A. Developing a harmonious mother-infant bond/relationship

1. The mother-infant dyad is happy and contented.

II Infant breastfeeding

A. Infant suckling at the mother's breast

1. Infant contented to suckle at the breast for increasing periods.

2. Document swallowing actions.

**III** Mother producing breast milk

    A. Mother producing breast milk in increasing quantities

        1. Milk secretion commencing; observed at expression

**IV** The infant is receiving some nutrition from the breast.

    A. Milk/food intake from other sources diminishing

        1. Reducing the need of the infant to use formula/supplementary foods

        2. Stool changes, which can vary through the day

        3. Weight checks every 3–5 days to assure adequate intake

**V** Infant taking all nutrition from the breast

    A. Infant receiving only breast milk from breastfeeding

        1. Cessation of supplementary formulas/foods

        2. Cessation of the infant requiring bottles, cups, and so on

    B. Expressing for stimulation gradually decreasing

        1. Maintain milk production by infant breastfeeding

        2. Gradual reduction of expression

    C. Galactogogues gradually decreasing

        1. Maintain milk production by infant breastfeeding

        2. Gradual reduction of the use of galactogogues

**VI** Problems

        1. Relactation is not always easy, nor is it necessarily easier than induced lactation.

        2. Baby not taking the breast

        3. Baby not getting enough to eat

        4. Fatigue

        5. Unreliable milk ejection reflex

# Milk Composition of Induced Breast Milk and Relactation

- Induced lactational milk is shown in other species (for example, bovine and rat) to be similar to normal pregnancy-induced lactation.

- Only a small number of papers have been published, however, to evaluate the constituents of induced lactational breast milk.

- Relactation breast milk is not well described or researched in literature; following literature searches, no reported studies have been found on the constituents of relactated breast milk.

Vorherr in 1978 (Hofmeyr, et al., 1985), Kleinman, et al. (Lawrence, et al., 1999), and Kulski, et al., (McNeilly, et al., 1974) have reported the constituents of induced lactational breast milk (Table 15-1).

**Table 15-1**    Composition of Induced Lactaton Breast Milk

| Components | Normal Breast Milk | Induced Lactation Breast Milk |
|---|---|---|
| Fat (g/dl) | 3.7 | |
| Lactose (g/dl) | 7.0 | 5.4 |
| Total protein (g/dl) | 1.2 | 1.6 |
| Sodium (mg/dl) | 15 | 22 |
| Potassium (mg/dl) | 50 | 19.8 |
| Calcium (mg/dl) | 35 | |
| Chlorine (mg/dl) | 45 | 18.4 |
| Phosphorous (mg/dl) | 15 | |
| Ash (mg/dl) | 20 | |

Vorherr, H. Human lactation and breastfeeding. In Larson B. Lactation. New York, Academic Press, 1978.

Kleinman, R.; Jacobson, L.; Hormann, E.; and Walker, W. Protein values of milk samples from mothers without biologic pregnancies. *J Pediatr* 1980; 97: 612.

Kulski, J.; Hartmann, P.; Saint, W.; Giles, P.; and Gutteridge, D. Changes in milk composition of nonpuerperal women. *Am Obstet Gynecol* 1981;139:597.

- The research on induced lactational breast milk is still very limited and contradictory.
- Kulski, et al. (McNeilly, et al., 1974) noted that at the commencement of milk production, colostrum was produced for approximately one week, and by one month it resembled mature milk.
- Kleinman, et al. (Lawrence, et al., 1999), however, found that protein levels differed in five mothers whom they studied.
- Early colostral milk (zero to five days) had protein levels of 3.6g/dl, reducing to 1.6g/dl day 6 to 15 and 0.8g/dl by day 16 and longer.
- By comparison, induced-lactation breast milk had protein levels of 1.6g/dl in the first five days.
- This situation indicates that a colostral phase did not occur.
- Similar results were obtained when they also looked at albumin, sIgA, and alpha-lactalbumin levels.

# References

Ano T, Shioji T, et al. Augmentation of puerperal lactation by oral administration of sulpiride. *J Clin Endo Metabol* 1979; 48(3):478–482.

Auerbach K, Avery J. Induced lactation: A study of adoptive nursing in 240 women. *Am J Dis Children* 1981; 135:340–334.

Auerbach K, Avery J. Relactation: A study of 366 cases. *Pediatrics* 1980; 65:236.

Auerbach KG, Avery JL. Nursing the adopted infant: Report from a survey. Denver, CO: Resources in Human Nurturing International, 1979. Monograph Number Five.

Auerbach KG, Avery JL. Relactation after an untimely weaning: Report from a survey. Denver, CO: Resources in Human Nurturing International, 1979. Monograph Number Two.

Auerbach KG, Avery JL. Relactation after a hospital-induced separation: Report from a survey. Denver, CO: Resources in Human Nurturing International, 1979. Monograph Number Four.

Banapurmath CR, Banapurmath SC, Kesaree N. Initiation of relactation. *Indian Pediatr* 1993; 30:1329–1332.

Bose C, Dercole J, Lester A, et al. Relactation by mothers of sick and premature infants. *Pediatrics* 1981; 67:565–569.

Brown R. Breastfeeding in modern times. *Am J Clin Nutr* 1973; 26:556.

Brown R. Relactation: An overview. *Pediatrics* 1977; 60:116–120.

Brown RE. Relactation with reference to application in developing countries. *Clin Pediatr* 1978; 17:333–337.

Budd S, Erdman S, Long D, et al. Improved lactation with metoclopramide. *Clin Pediatr* 1993; 32:53–57.

Cheales-Siebenaler NJ. Induced Lactation in an Adoptive Mother. *J Hum Lact* 1999; 15(1):41–43.

Clavey S. The use of acupuncture for the treatment of insufficient lactation (Que Ru). *Am J Acupuncture* 1996; 24:35–46.

Cohen R. Breastfeeding without pregnancy. *Pediatrics* 1971; 48:996–997.

Creel S, Monfort S, Wildt D, et al. Spontaneous lactation is an adaptive result of pseudopregnancy. *Nature* 1991; 351:660.

Ehrenkranz R, Ackerman B. Metoclopramide effect on faltering milk production by mothers of premature infants. *Pediatrics* 1986; 78:614–62.

Emery MM. Galactogogues: Drugs to induce lactation. *J Hum Lact* 1996; 12(1):55–57.

Fleiss P. Herbal Remedies for the breastfeeding mother. *Mothering* 1988; 48: 68–70.

Hale T. Medications and mothers' milk, 9th ed. Amarillo, TX: Pharmasoft Medical Publishing, 2000.

Hofmeyr G, Van Iddekinge B. Domperidone and lactation. *Lancet* 1983; I: 647.

Hofmeyr G, et al. Domperidone: Secretion in breastmilk and effect on puerperal prolactin levels. *B J Obstet Gynaecol* 1985; 92:141–144.

Hormann E, and Savage F. Relactation: Review of Experience and Recommendations for Practice. WHO/CHS/CAH98.14, 1998.

Hormann E. Breastfeeding the adopted baby. *Birth Fam J* 1977; 4:165–172.

Jelliffe DB, Jelliffe EFP. Non-puerperal induced lactation. *Pediatrics* 1972; 50:170–171.

Kauppila A, Kivinen S, Ylikorkala O. Metoclopramide and breastfeeding: Transfer into milk and the newborn. *Eur J Clin Pharmacol* 1983; 25:819–823.

Kauppila A, Kivinen S, Ylikorkala O. A dose response relation between improved lactation and metoclopramide. *Lancet* 1981; 1:1175–1177.

Kesaree N, Banapurmath C, Shamanur K. Treatment of inverted nipples using a disposable syringe. *J Hum Lact* 1993; 9(1):27–29.

Kleinman R, Jacobson L, Hormann E, Walker W. Protein values of milk samples from mothers without biologic pregnancies. *J Pediatr* 1980; 97:612.

Kramer P. Breastfeeding of adopted infants. *Br Med J* (letter) 1995; 310:188.

Kulski J, Hartmann P, Saint W, et al. Changes in milk composition of nonpuerperal women. *Am Obstet Gynecol* 1981; 139:597.

Lawrence RA, Lawrence RM. Breastfeeding: A guide for the medical professional. 5th ed. St. Louis: Mosby, Inc., 1999.

McNeilly A, Thorner M, Volans G, et al. Metoclopramide and prolactin. *Br Med J* 1974; 2:729.

Menella J, Beauchamp G. The transfer of alcohol to human milk. *N Engl J Med* 1993; 325: 981–985.

Menella J, Beauchamp G. Beer, breastfeeding and folklore. *Devel Psychobiol* 1993; 26(8): 459–466.

Menella J, Beauchamp G. The effects of repeated exposure to garlic-flavored milk on the nursling's behavior. *Pediatr Res* 1994; 34:805–808.

Miczak M. Herbs and healthy lactation. *Mothering* 1996; 78:60–63.

Milsom S, Breier B, Gallaher B, et al. Growth hormone stimulates galactopoesis in healthy lactating women. *Acta Endocrinol* 1992; 127:337–343.

Nemba K. Induced lactation: A study of 37 non-puerperal mothers. *J Trop Paediatr* 1994; 40:240–242.

Peters F. Lactation and breastfeeding: Physiology, clinical aspects and pathophysiology of breast glandular function—Milk production and breastfeeding under special conditions. *Br J Obstet Gynecol* 1987; 26:8: p. 74.

Peters F, Schulaze-Tollert J, and Schuth W. Thyrotrophin-releasing hormone: A lactation promoting agent? *Br J Obstet Gynecol* 1991; 98:880–985.

Phillips V. Non-puerperal lactation among Australian Aboriginal women. Part I. Nursing Mothers' Association of Australia News 1969; 5(4). Repr as NMAA Res Bull No. 1.

Phillips V. Relactation in mothers of children over 12 months. *J Trop Pediatr* 1993; 39:45–47.

Riordan J, Auerbach K. Breastfeeding and human lactation, 2nd ed. Sudbury, MA: Jones and Bartlett Publishers, 1998.

Rogers IS. Relactation. *Early Hum Dev* 1997; 49 Suppl:S75–S81.

Ruis H, Rollan R, Doseburg W, Broeders G, Corbey R. Oxytocin enhances onset of lactation among mothers delivering prematurely. *Br Med J* 1981; 283(6287):340–342.

Slome C. Non-puerperal lactation in grandmothers. *J Pediatr* 1956; 49:550.

Sousa PLR, Barros FC, Pinheiro GNM, Gazalle RV. Re-establishment of lactation with metoclopramide. *J Trop Pediatr* 1975; 21:214.

Sutherland A, Auerbach KG. Relactation and induced lactation. Lactation Consultant Series, Unit 1 1985; La Leche League International.

Takeda S, Kuwabara Y, Mizuno M. Concentrations and origin of oxytocin in breastmilk. *Endocrinol Japon* 1986; 33(6):821–826.

Thompson NM. Relactation in a newborn intensive care setting. *J Hum Lact* 1996; 12(3):233–235.

Thorley V. Relactation and induced lactation: Bibliography and resources. Brisbane Lactation Education Services and Support, Brisbane, Australia, 2000.

Vargas L. Traditional breastfeeding methods in Mexico. In Raphael D, ed. Breastfeeding and food policy in a hungry world. New York: Academic, 1979.

Vorherr H. Human lactation and breastfeeding. In Larson B, ed. Lactation. New York: Academic Press, 1978.

Waletzky L, Herman E. Relactation. *Am Fam Pract* 1976; 14:69–74.

Wiles D, Orr M, Kolakowska T. Chlorpromazine levels in plasma and milk of nursing mothers. *Br J Clin Pharmacol* 1978; 5:272–273.

Ylikorkala O, Kauppila A, Kivinen S, et al. Treatment of inadequate lactation with oral sulpiride and bucal oxytocin. *Obstet Gynecol* 1984; 63:57–60.

Ylikorkala O, Kauppila A, Kivinen S, et al. Sulpiride improves inadequate lactation. *Br Med J* 1982; 285:249–251.

Zimmerman MA. Breastfeeding the adopted newborn. *Pediatr Nurs* 1981; January-February: 9–12.

# MATERNAL PHYSICAL IMPAIRMENTS

*Noreen Siebenaler, MSN, RN, IBCLC*

## OBJECTIVES

- List five maternal impairments that might create barriers to successful breastfeeding.

- State four different types of breastfeeding assistance that are most appropriate to offer breastfeeding mothers who have physical, visual, or hearing impairments.

- Describe four psychological benefits that physically impaired, visually impaired, or hearing-impaired mothers might experience when they choose to breastfeed.

- List three community services that are available to physically impaired, visually impaired, or hearing-impaired mothers who choose to breastfeed.

## Introduction

An increasing number of women who have physical impairments are choosing to conceive and breastfeed their infants. Many of these mothers find that breastfeeding is more convenient than bottle-feeding because there are none of the inconveniences related to bottle-feeding, such as mixing, pouring, and measuring. Despite the protests that often arise from their well-meaning families, who feel that these mothers should not breastfeed due to limited energy and ability, many mothers continue to choose to breastfeed.

Breastfeeding is one infant caretaking activity that the physically impaired mother is often able to accomplish without assistance. For mothers who need assistance with their activities of daily living, breastfeeding remains possibly the only thing they are exclusively able to do for their infants. Both of these situations might be empowering for a physically impaired woman by demonstrating that her body is capable of nourishing her baby without assistance. Breastfeeding makes parenting with a disability functionally easier.

Women who have been physically impaired for a long time are usually more knowledgeable than anyone else about their abilities and limitations. Creativity and referral to appropriate resources and identification of individuals who are genuinely supportive of the mother's breastfeeding goals are keys to assisting these mothers in accomplishing their definition of successful breastfeeding.

I  Carpal Tunnel Syndrome

  A. Physiology:

    1. A painful disorder of the wrist and hand that causes parasthesia (numbness and tingling) of the hand.

    2. More common in women, especially during pregnancy and menopause.

    3. Caused by compression on the median nerve between the inelastic carpel ligament and other structures within the carpel tunnel (a pathway for the median nerve that innervates the palm and radial side of the hand).

    4. Compression of the median nerve causes weakness, pain with opposition of the thumb, burning, tingling, or aching sometimes radiating to the forearm and shoulder joint. Pain is intermittent or constant and is often most intense at night.

    5. Diagnosis by electromyography (EM).

  B. Treatment

    Symptomatic:

    1. Splinting of the hand and forearm

    2. Elevation of the arm to relieve the swelling of soft tissue

    3. Oral analgesics

    4. Range of motion exercises for wrist and fingers in order to prevent atrophy

    5. Corticcosteroid injections often bring dramatic relief of pain

    6. Surgical intervention involving division of the volar carpal ligament to relieve nerve pressure is occasionally needed to relieve symptoms

  C. Possible effect on breastfeeding

    1. Difficulties with positioning baby at the breast using one hand

    2. Cannot easily pick up the baby or move the baby between breasts

    3. Limited ability to use two hands to assist the baby with latch on

    4. Reduced finger dexterity to open and close bra

  D. Methods of assisting

    1. A firm breastfeeding pillow that goes around the mother's waist and attaches on the side

    2. Football (clutch) position using pillows to hold the baby in position

    3. Breastfeed one breast per feeding

    4. Practice latch on by using one hand

    5. Velcro bra attachments for opening and closing bra

II  Multiple Sclerosis

  A. Physiology

    1. Multiple sclerosis is a progressive autoimmune disease that attacks the central nervous system, causing widespread removal of the nerve coverings (myelin) of the brain and spinal cord.

a. Symptoms usually appear between the ages of 20 and 40 and can impact a number of physiological functions, including vision, gait, memory, strength and can contribute to extreme fatigue.

b. Its cause is unknown but is thought to have an immunogenetic-viral link.

c. Some pregnant women with MS may experience fewer symptoms of the disease during pregnancy.

2. First symptoms are usually abnormal sensations in the extremities or on one side of the face.

3. These sensations include numbness and tingling, muscle weakness, vertigo, and visual disturbances such as nystagmus, diplopia, double vision, and partial blindness.

4. Urinary tract disorders and difficulty walking are also common as multiple sclerosis continues throughout life, with periods of exacerbation and remission.

5. As the disease progresses, the intervals between exacerbations grow shorter and disability becomes greater.

6. A greater-than-normal amount of protein in cerebrospinal fluid is characteristic of multiple sclerosis; however, the diagnosis is difficult to make because many other conditions affect the nervous system and produce similar symptoms.

B. Treatment

1. Corticosteroids and other medications are used to treat symptoms of MS, such as bladder and bowel problems and visual disturbances.

2. Physical therapy helps to postpone or prevent specific disabilities.

C. Possible effect on breastfeeding

1. All medications should be evaluated for their passage into breast milk and for any effect they might have on the baby.

2. The possible risks of the medication need to be weighed carefully against the benefits of breastfeeding.

3. Fatigue associated with multiple sclerosis is increased due to the addition of the fatigue experienced by most women who are caring for a newborn.

4. Symptoms of multiple sclerosis are more likely to increase during the postpartum period for both breastfeeding and bottle-feeding women due to decreases in serum hormonal levels (Riordan and Auerbach, 1999).

5. The mother might experience increased weakness and have difficulty picking up or holding her baby.

6. Families and friends who provide care and support for mothers who have multiple sclerosis might believe that breastfeeding causes additional stress and fatigue for the mother. They might "take over" most infant care and feeding activities, advising the mother to limit or discontinue breastfeeding.

D. Methods of assisting

1. Encourage and assist the mother with learning to breastfeed comfortably while lying down so that she can rest while feeding her baby.

2. Suggest that the mother try using multiple pillows as supports for her arms while breastfeeding if she has muscular weakness (Figure 16-1).

3. A baby sling might make breastfeeding easier if the mother experiences limited coordination and muscular weakness (Figure 16-2).

4. Educate the mother and the family and friends who assist her by providing information regarding the evidence that breastfeeding six months or longer might provide the baby with protection from multiple sclerosis later in life (Pisacane et al., 1994).

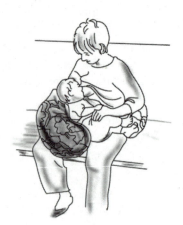

**Figure 16-1**    Supportive positioning for mothers with MS

**Figure 16-2**    A support suggestion for muscular weakness

Cholesterol and the long chain fatty acids in breast milk are necessary components of the myelin sheath that surround nerve fibers. Since it is believed that a virus in adults attacks this nerve covering causing MS, mothers and their family should understand the important contribution human milk makes in protecting the baby from developing the disease as an adult.

5. Discuss with the mother and her family and friends who assist her the special advantages that breastfeeding offers to mothers who have physical impairments:

   a. Breastfeeding saves energy because it is not necessary to prepare or buy formula.

   b. A breastfed baby is statistically healthier, saving trips to the doctor's office with ear infections, digestive problems, and allergies.

   c. Unlike bottle-feeding, a breastfeeding mother can breastfeed lying down, enabling her to rest while she feeds her baby.

   d. Breastfeeding helps build a close emotional bond between mother and baby that might be more difficult to develop if others take over the baby's care (*The Breastfeeding Answer Book*, 1997).

   e. Provide family members and friends with many choices related to ways to assist the mother that exclude feeding the baby.

Women with MS often undergo a number of drug therapies and may find that breastfeeding could be interrupted depending on the medications needed. Mothers can be advised to pump and freeze milk during remission times to have it available if necessary during exacerbations of the disease.

III Spinal cord injury

A. Physiology

   1. The extent and level of injury determines whether a woman who has a spinal cord injury will be able to breastfeed (Halbert, 1998).

   2. The extent of injury is described as complete or incomplete.

      a. Complete is the loss of all motor and sensory function at the level of the injury and below.

      b. Incomplete enables either some sensory or motor function at the level of the injury and below.

   3. The level of the injury determines the level of function lost.

      a. The higher the injury, the more severe the loss of function.

      b. Injury to the cervical area can result in the inability of the mother to breathe by herself (C 1-3) to having good upper-extremity use (C 6-8).

      c. Injuries further down the spinal cord enable more independence in function.

      d. T1-level injuries result in paraplegia with complete upper-extremity function.

    4. A decrease in milk production can be seen after six weeks postpartum in a breastfeeding mother who has an injury at the T6 level and higher.

        a. This decrease is caused by the lack of sympathetic nervous system feedback at and above the T6 level.

        b. In high-level injuries, neurological impulses are not able to reach the pituitary gland.

        c. Due the lack of sympathetic feedback, myoepithelial cells in the breast do not contract.

        d. For nipple stimulation to effectively stimulate milk production, the spinal cord injury must be at or below the point of origin for the fourth, fifth, and sixth intercostal nerves (Halbert, 1998).

B. Possible effect on breastfeeding

    1. In a woman who has a spinal cord injury below the T6 level, breastfeeding is possible as long as she has adequate nipple stimulation to release prolactin from the pituitary.

    2. Limited ability to hold or lift the baby.

    3. Increased susceptibility to sore nipples due to the mother's inability to support her infant and her breasts correctly during feedings.

    4. Family and friends might discourage breastfeeding by bottle-feeding the baby or by suggesting that the mother becomes (or will become) too tired feeding every few hours and needs more rest.

C. Methods of assisting

    1. Advise the use of breastfeeding pillows that support the baby.

    2. Demonstrate and provide one-to-one help when the mother is learning how to use positioning aids.

    3. Recommend a baby carrier that fits "in front."

    4. Assist the mother until she expresses confidence in her ability to utilize this device.

    5. Discuss with the mother and her helpers any adjustments that are necessary to adapt her environment to facilitate breastfeeding, such as wheelchair access to the baby's crib (Figure 16-3).

D. Prevent sore nipples

    1. Teach the mother how to air-dry expressed breast milk onto her nipples after breastfeeding.

    2. Observe breastfeeding and show the mother how to attach the baby correctly.

    3. If mild nipple soreness is present, suggest air exposure.

E. Discuss with family members and friends ways to assist and support the mother with breastfeeding.

**Figure 16-3**
Pillows help
maintain baby
for positioning
in a wheelchair

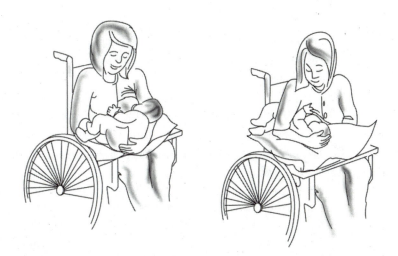

1. Provide opportunities for and encourage frequent rest periods.

2. Take care of grocery shopping, meal preparation, and housekeeping.

3. Obtain and offer the mother frequent nutritious snacks and drinks.

4. Assist with positioning the baby for breastfeeding, burping, changing diapers, and other infant care activities.

5. Verbally support the mother's breastfeeding choice, realizing the significant influence of the advice of friends and family members on the mother due to the increased vulnerability of the immediate postpartum period.

IV  Visual impairment/hearing impairment

A. Physiology

1. Loss of sight or hearing results in increased dependence upon, and development of, the remaining senses of touch, smell, and taste.

2. Mothers who cannot see or hear their infants care for and bond with them through their sense of touch and smell, which are often very sensitive, and through intuitive sensitivity (Martin, 1992).

3. These senses become highly developed due to their loss of sight and hearing.

4. There is no physiologic reason why mothers who are visually or hearing impaired should not breastfeed.

B. Possible effect on breastfeeding

1. Breastfeeding is usually much easier and economical for visually impaired or hearing-impaired mothers becuase there are no bottles to prepare and clean.

2. Understanding and responding to their baby's feeding cues before crying begins is important for both hearing-impaired and visually impaired mothers.

3. When mothers begin breastfeeding before the baby cries, the feedings are easier and mothers breastfeed longer with fewer problems (Marasco and Barger, 2000).

4. Breastfeeding enhances maternal/infant bonding for visually impaired and hearing-impaired mothers through the sense of touch.

C. Methods of assisting

1. Methods of assisting are the same as for sighted mothers.

2. Use appropriate voice tone and touch.

3. Concentrate on what information needs to be communicated because mother cannot see what you are doing.

4. Sign language as a communication method to accompany one-to-one breastfeeding assistance for hearing-impaired mothers might be available within the mother's clinic, hospital, or community.

5. Telephone systems specifically designed for hearing-impaired individuals are easily available for home use.

6. Mothers use these systems to call lactation consultants when questions or problems arise.

7. Resources for visually impaired/hearing-impaired mothers: Braille communications and audio tapes for visually impaired mothers are available from La Leche League International.

V  Arthritis

A. Physiology

1. Defined as any inflammatory condition of the joints characterized by pain and swelling (Anderson et al., 1994)

2. Types are osteoarthritis and rheumatoid arthritis

a. Osteoarthritis

i. The most common form of arthritis, resulting in the degeneration of joints within the body.

ii. Begins with pain after exercise or use of the joints.

iii. Inflammation of the synovial membrane of the joint is common late in the disease.

iv. The cause of osteoarthritis is unknown but is thought to be related to chemical, mechanical, genetic, metabolic, and endocrine factors.

v. Emotional stress aggravates the condition.

vi. Involvement of the hip, knee, or spine usually causes more disability than other areas that might be affected.

(1) Treatment includes rest and the use of anti-inflammatory drugs.

(2) With severe pain, intra-articular injections of corticosteriods might give relief.

b. Rheumatoid arthritis

  i. A chronic, destructive, sometimes deforming, collagen disease that has an autoimmune component.

  ii. Results in a symmetric inflammation of the synovium (fluid surrounding the joints) and swelling of the joints.

  iii. Usually first appears in early middle age and most often in women.

  iv. Characterized by exacerbations and remissions.

  v. Stress aggravates rheumatoid arthritis.

  vi. Advice includes the avoidance of situations known to cause anxiety, worry, fatigue, and other stressors.

  vii. Treatment includes sufficient rest, exercise in order to maintain joint function, medications for the relief of pain and to reduce inflammation, orthopedic intervention to prevent deformities, and excellent nutrition with weight loss if needed.

  viii. Symptoms usually go into remission during pregnancy and then relapse postpartum.

  ix. Exacerbations postpartum are often more of a problem for breastfeeding women due to the pro-inflammatory affects of prolactin on this condition (Brennan and Silman, 1994; Brennan et al., 1996).

B. Possible effect on breastfeeding relationship

  1. Breastfeeding might be simpler than artificial feeding for a mother who has arthritis if her hands and arms are stiff or if movement is difficult because breastfeeding requires less-complex movements.

  2. Mothers will need additional rest due to the sometimes overwhelming fatigue, stiffness, and pain that occur postpartum (Figure 16-4).

  3. The worsening of symptoms often happens when the baby needs care or feeding during the early morning, late evening, and during the night.

  4. Medications that are used to decrease pain and inflammation are usually compatible with breastfeeding.

---

**Figure 16-4** This jacket for arthritis sufferers has a Velcro™ closure for easy access, and the jacket helps keep the mother's stiff shoulders warm.

Velcro

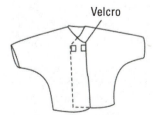

5. Methotrexate therapy, used for severe cases, has been found to be compatible with breastfeeding in low doses (Hale, 1999).

6. Breastfed babies can be less likely to develop juvenile arthritis and other autoimmune disorders.

7. Breastfeeding can provide a protective effective (Brun and Nilssen, 1995), decreasing maternal mortality from rheumatoid arthritis.

C. Methods of assisting

1. Encourage the mother to breastfeed lying down in order to promote periods of rest.

2. Involve the physiotherapist if possible to assist with designing an exercise maintenance program that will maintain joint range of motion, mobility, and minimize stiffness and pain.

3. Removable braces or splints support joints and can reduce fatigue.

4. Place the baby high enough in front or on the side of the mother to directly face her when feeding so there is no downward pull on the mother's arms.

5. The baby might need to be placed on top of two pillows for height or on a wrap-around feeding pillow.

6. A sling keeps the baby well supported, enables the mother's arms to be free during feeding, and makes it easier to move from place to place carrying the baby.

7. Family members and friends who are advocates of breastfeeding and who will provide assistance in the form of housekeeping, grocery shopping, and meal preparation support this mother's dedication to her infant and to her new role.

VI Myasthenia gravis

A. Physiology

1. Myasthenia gravis (MG) comes from the Greek and Latin words meaning grave muscular weakness.

2. Prevalence in the United States is 14/100,000 population.

3. The most common form of MG is a chronic autoimmune neuromuscular involvement of voluntary muscle groups.

4. Involuntary heart muscle, smooth muscle of the gut, blood vessels, and uterine muscle are not affected.

5. Muscles most frequently involved are ones that control eye movements, eyelids, chewing, swallowing, coughing, and facial expressions.

6. Muscles that control breathing and movements of the arms and legs might also be affected.

7. There is usually no pain experienced with this form of autoimmune disease.

8. If neck muscles are involved and are in spasm, pain in the back of the neck and head might be present.

9. Weakness and fatigue of specific muscle groups are the most common symptoms of MG.

10. Remission of symptoms is common and can last for long periods of time.

B. Possible effect on breastfeeding

1. Weakness and fatigue of arm and neck muscles can result in difficulty with positioning and attachment.

2. Fatigue associated with specific muscle groups increases the need for rest periods.

3. If impaired mobility is present, the mother's home environment will need to be adjusted so that she can function independently while caring for her infant.

4. Successful breastfeeding builds the mother's confidence and self esteem.

5. Adequate and appropriate support from family, friends, health care professionals, and the community positively influence the success of the breastfeeding relationship that these mothers have chosen.

C. Methods of assisting

1. Positioning aids in the form of wrap-around pillows.

2. Assist the mother with learning to breastfeed while lying down.

3. Discuss the mother's need for assistance and rest with family and friends and encourage appropriate interventions.

4. Medications used to treat MG (anticholinesterase agents, corticosteroids, and immunosuppressive agents) are generally compatible with breastfeeding.

VII   Internet resources for physically impaired mothers

A. "Through The Looking Glass" (TLG). A community nonprofit organization formed in 1982. A resource center for families in which one or more members has a disability. TLG's mission is to create, demonstrate, and encourage resources and model early intervention services that are nonpathological and empowering. TLG consults with parents and professionals nationally and internationally. The Internet address is www.lookingglass.org/links.htm.

B. National Association of the Deaf (NAD): www.nad.org/

C. Deaf Counseling, Advocacy, and Referral Agency: www.dcara.org

D. American Council of the Blind: www.acb.org

E. American Foundation for the Blind: www.igc.apc.org/afb/

F. La Leche League International; audiotapes and Braille: www.lalecheleague.org

G. Arthritis Foundation: www.arthritis.org

H. Rheumatoid arthritis: www.helioshealth.com

I. Rheumatoid arthritis: www.webmd.lycos.com/conditioncenter?doi-rha

J. Myasthenia Gravis Foundation of America: www.myasthenia.org

K. National Disability Organization and Agencies: www.pacer.org/natl/yellowna.htm

L. National Multiple Sclerosis Society: www.nmss.org

International Multiple Sclerosis Support Foundation: www.msnews.org

Multiple Sclerosis Association of America: www.msaa.com

Multiple Sclerosis Foundation: www.msfacts.org

National Institute of Neurological Disorders and Stroke: www.ninds.nih.gov

# References

Anderson K, Anderson L, Glanze W. Mosby's medical, nursing, and allied health dictionary, 4th ed. St. Louis: Mosby Yearbook, 1994: 124–125.

Barrett JH, Brennan P, Fiddler M, Silman A. Breast-feeding and postpartum relapse in women with rheumatoid and inflammatory arthritis. *Arthritis Rheum* 2000; 43:1010–1015.

Bowles BC. Breastfeeding consultation in sign language. *J Hum Lact* 1991; 7:21.

Brennan P, Ollier B, Worthington J, et al. Are both genetic and reproductive associations with rheumatoid arthritis linked to prolactin? *Lancet* 1996; 348:106–109.

Brennan P, Silman A. Breastfeeding and the onset of rheumatoid arthritis. *Arthr Rheum* 1994; 37:808–813.

Brun JF, et al. Breastfeeding, other reproductive factors and rheumatoid arthritis: A prospective study. *Br J Rheumatol* 1995; 34:542–546.

Carty E, Conine TA, Hall L. Comprehensive health promotion for the pregnant woman who is disabled. *J Nurse Midwif* 1990; 35:133–142.

Eggum M. Breastfeeding with multiple sclerosis. AWHONN Lifelines 2001; Feb/March: 37–40.

Halbert L. Breastfeeding in the woman with a compromised nervous system. *J Hum Lact* 1998; 14:327–331.

Hale T. Clinical therapy in breastfeeding patients. Amarillo, TX: Pharmasoft Publishing, 1999.

Hale T. Medications and mothers milk, 9th ed. Amarillo, TX: Pharmasoft Publishing, 2000.

Jorgensen C, Picot MC, Bologna C, Sany J. Oral contraception, parity, breast feeding, and severity of rheumatoid arthritis. *Ann Rheum Dis* 1996; 55:94–98.

Lawrence RA, Lawrence RM. Medical complications of the mother, Chapter 15. Breastfeeding a guide for the medical profession, 5th ed. St. Louis: Mosby, Inc., 1999: 558–562.

Marasco L, Barger J. Examining the evidence for cue feeding of breastfed infants. Retrieved June 9, 2000 from www.fix.net/~rprewett/evidence.html

Martin Cookson D. La Leche League and the mother who is blind. *Leaven* 1992; 5:67–68.

Mohrbacher N, Stock J. The breastfeeding answer book. Shaumburg, IL: La Leche League International, 1997: 471–480.

Nelson LM, et al. Risk of multiple sclerosis exacerbation during pregnancy and breastfeeding. *JAMA* 1988; 259:441–443.

Pisacane A, Impagliazzo N, Russo M, et al. Breastfeeding and multiple sclerosis. *Br Med J* 1994; 308:1411–1412.

Riordan J, Auerbach KG. Breastfeeding and human lactation, 2nd ed. Sudbury, MA: Jones and Bartlett Publishers, 1998: 558–562.

Thomson VM. Breastfeeding and mothering one-handed. *J Hum Lact* 1995; 11:211–215.

Wade M, Foster N, Cullen L, et al. Breast and bottle-feeding for mothers with arthritis and other physical disabilities. *Prof Care Mother Child* 1999; 9:35–38.

# PRETERM INFANTS

*Ruth Worgan, RN, CM, C&FH, IBCLC and Heather Jackson, RGON, RM, AND, MA, IBCLC*

## OBJECTIVES

- Discuss the nutritional needs of a preterm infant and indications when breast milk alone might not be meet all nutritional requirements.
- Describe the influence of maturation on the ability to breastfeed.
- Discuss the establishment of breast milk supply and maintenance for a mother who has a preterm baby.
- List the scientific evidence for early feeding.
- List and discuss the three phases to establishing full breastfeeding when an infant is preterm.
- Describe the need for well-planned discharge for the breastfeeding preterm baby.
- Describe the advantages and disadvantages of alternative methods of receiving breast milk for a preterm baby who is unable to sustain full feeding at the breast.

## Introduction

Establishing breastfeeding for a preterm infant can be a challenge. Problems involve how to provide adequate nutrients in a form that the infant can absorb and utilize and in amounts that promote optimum growth and development without causing unnecessary stress to the immature infant. Mother's own breast milk is the most appropriate milk to provide not only adequate nutrition, but also protection from disease and infections and promote the growth and maturation of the neonate. Infants not fed mother's own breast milk have an increased morbidity and mortality rate in all areas of the world.

Support and appropriate management in establishing breast milk and maintaining the supply when the baby is unable to initiate the lactation process is critical to the successful outcome. The lactation consultant must take into consideration the special needs of the preterm baby and incorporate these considerations into her knowledge of the physiological process of breastfeeding the normal, healthy, term baby. The preterm infant is not just a smaller version of a full-term baby, but instead demonstrates distinct differences in the physiology of almost all body systems. The age of viability has edged toward smaller and smaller babies surviving birth as early as 23–24 weeks. This situation presents a unique set of hurdles in achieving optimal short-term nutrition and long-term goals of physical and cognitive development. Mothers of preterm infants experience challenges that are unique to the preterm condition in addition to the uncertainty and stress that is involved in a life event that has an uncertain outcome.

# Preterm Infant Needs

## Definition

- A preterm baby is defined as birth prior to the 37th week of gestation.
- Infants weighing less than 2,500g are referred to as low birth weight.
- Infants weighing less than 1,500g are referred to as very low birth weight.
- Infants weighing under 1,250g are often referred to as extremely low birth weight.

    Gestational age and weight need to be assessed together as in infants who are intrauterine growth retarded (IUGR) or small for dates (SFD)

- All preterm infants are not the same.
- Feedings for a 2,000g preterm infant usually vary only in volume and frequency from the full-term infant.
- The metabolizable energy requirement is approximately 109 kcal/kg/day.

## Issues

I The preterm infant has special needs in order to facilitate normal growth and development:

   A. Needs to maintain blood sugars above 2.5mM/L

   B. Needs to support and maintain temperature control

   C. Nutritional requirements that are unique to each infant

   D. Mechanical obstacles to feeding

   E. Skin-to-skin contact

II The lactation consultant needs to be familiar with common problems of these infants and their effects on feeding, such as the following:

   A. Respiratory distress syndrome

    B. Necrotizing enterocolitis—a potentially fatal inflammation with cell death in the lining of the intestines; preterm infants who are fed formula demonstrate a 6–10 times greater incidence of NEC compared to preterm babies who are fed breast milk

    C. Hyperbilirubinemia

    D. Intracranial hemorrhage

    E. Hyperglycemias

    F. Bronchopulmonary dysplasia (BPD)

**III** Close contact with the mother and family members is beneficial for not only bonding, but also for maturation, growth, and development of the infant.

    A. Emotional development should be encouraged and maintained as much as possible.

    B. Skin contact and verbal interaction should be facilitated and supported.

    C. Mothers and fathers should be part of the health care team and part of the decision-making process regarding the care of their infant.

    D. In many countries, the breastfeeding rates for this population are lower than for the population of full-term deliveries.

    E. In some countries, the breastfeeding duration is often shorter than for full-term infants.

    F. Rates of breastfeeding initiation and duration can be improved when mothers are provided with consistent, current, and evidence-based expressing and breastfeeding guidelines.

**IV** Needs of mother and father who have a preterm baby

    A. Support and education of parenting a preterm infant.

    B. Facilitating parental infant care in the nursery.

    C. Establishment and maintenance of lactation by expression.

    D. Maintaining equipment and safe storage of milk.

    E. Open visiting/accommodations for parents with their baby.

    F. It is not unusual for the mother of the preterm baby to be ill as a result of complications of the pregnancy or labor.

    G. Consideration of how to best support her in her goal to breastfeed needs special consideration and skilled, knowledgeable health professionals.

    H. Milk expression and breastfeeding can be highly significant for the mother.

    I. These two actions are contributions to the infant's care that only the mother can make.

    J. It represents a normalization of an abnormal event.

K. It is a caregiving behavior that does not have to be forfeited because of the preterm birth.

L. Mothers have identified five positive outcomes or rewards from their preterm breastfeeding experience and have concluded that the rewards outweigh the efforts:

1. The health benefits of breast milk

2. Knowing that they gave their infants the best possible start in life

3. Enjoyment of the physical closeness and the perception that their baby preferred breastfeeding to bottles

4. Making a unique contribution to the infant's care

5. Breastfeeding was more convenient

M. Mothers should be provided with information to make an informed decision regarding breastfeeding.

N. Withholding information in attempts to avoid making mothers feel guilty if they do not breastfeed robs women of the right to make these decisions based on factual information.

## Nutritional Considerations

- The optimal growth of preterm infants is typically compared to the growth curve that they would have followed had they remained in utero.

- While this target can be achieved more easily in babies who have higher gestational ages, the extremely low birth weight baby has a high energy requirement but limited volume tolerance.

- Preterm breast milk offers a unique set of advantages to the preterm infant, but the extremely low birth weight baby might have gaps in certain nutrients due to the high needs coupled with the inability to consume the volume of breast milk required.

## Components of Preterm Breastmilk

I Review the components of preterm breastmilk.

A. Gross et al. in 1980 reported the differences and changes in preterm breast milk compared to full-term breast milk, with preterm breast milk having higher concentrations of calories, lipids, protein, sodium, chloride, potassium, iron, and magnesium.

B. The addition of extra nutrients, vitamins, and minerals need only arise when inadequate growth and serum metabolites is becoming evident in the preterm infant or with the extremely low birth weight baby.

C. Calcium and phosphorus are the most commonly limiting macrominerals.

D. Preterm breast milk is optimally suited to the maturation of systems and the growth and immunological requirements of the preterm infant.

E. Preterm breast milk is essential to the preterm baby due to his limited renal concentration and diluting capacities, a large surface area in relation to weight, and insensible water loss.

F. The breast milk of mothers of preterm infants matures to the levels of term milk at about four to six weeks.

G. After the first month, preterm milk might not meet all the nutritional needs of the growing preterm infant, and caloric intake might be inadequate for growth (particularly in preterm infants who are born under 30 weeks' gestation and/or are born at less than 2.5kg).

H. Risks associated with adding fortification to breastmilk are the following:
   1. Significantly slower gastric emptying times and, therefore, implications for feed intolerance
   2. The neutralizing effect on some of the anti-infective properties of human milk
   3. Increasing the risk of infection
   4. The incomplete absorption of additives such as MCT oil (medium chain triglyceride)
   5. Increased osmolarity of fortified milks increasing the morbidity from gastrointestinal disease
      a. Fortification might influence short-term outcomes, such as weight gain and bone mineralization, but long-term growth and developmental outcomes have not been shown to be enhanced by fortification.
      b. Bone mineral content at 8–12 years of age in children who are born preterm and are fed breast milk is as high or higher than children who are born at term.

I. Human milk can be fortified with commercial fortifiers that include cow's milk-based protein, electrolytes, and a number of vitamins and minerals.

J. Human milk can be fortified with specific nutrients, such as calcium and phosphorus.

K. Fortification is usually begun after full enteral feeding is established and is discontinued before discharge from the neonatal intensive care unit (NICU).

L. Hindmilk supplementation is a process using the hindmilk portion of expressed milk (lactoengineering) as a concentrated source of lipids, providing a high-calorie, low-volume, low osmolaric, readily absorbable supplement.

M. Hindmilk and commercial fortifiers are used for different purposes; commercial fortifiers are used to supplement essential nutrients; hindmilk provides a concentrated source of lipids and calories.

N. "Lactoengineering" can further refine and tailor the milk to a specific baby's needs.

    1. The lipid and caloric content of breast milk can be estimated with the creamatocrit.

    2. The creamatocrit is derived from centrifuging a small milk specimen in a capillary tube, separating the lipid portion, and then measuring the content as a percentage of total milk volume.

O. Some nutrient loss can occur through enteral feeding tubes; lipids can adhere to the lumen of a feeding tube and not reach the infant; this is more common when giving continuous enteral feeds.

P. The greatest lipid losses occur with continuous slow infusions, therefore causing a recommendation for bolus feedings (intermittent gavage) when possible.

Q. If infusion pumps are used, the syringe should be tilted upward at a 25–45-degree angle so that the lipids rise to the leur of the syringe and are infused first.

R. Early enteral feedings of breast milk (0.5 to 1ml) before the baby is actually ready to be fed by mouth are sometimes used to prime the gut; these are variously referred to as trickle feeds, trophic feeds, or gastrointestinal (GI) priming feeds and are based on the concept that gastrointestinal hormones are absent in the gut of infants who have never been fed; trophic feeds facilitate protective gut flora, improve bowel emptying of meconium, and decrease morbidity and mortality from NEC; more mature motor patterns in the gut are seen with these small feeds.

S. There are many guidelines for the progression of premature infant feeding throughout the world. Practices depend on the level and availability of technology within each country and within each individual nursery. Many nurseries are now trialing Kangaroo Care, which reduces or changes the need for extensive policies for initiating and maintaining breastfeeding in the preterm infant.

Some published examples of preterm infant feeding regimes are as follows:

I Steichen JJ, Krug-Wispe SK, Tsang RC. Breastfeeding the low birth weight preterm infant. *Clin Perinatol* 1987; 14:131–161.

  For use with the preterm infant weighing less than 1,500g:

A. Use refrigerated milk from the preterm infant's mother when it is available and has been collected within 48 hours of feeding.

B. When fresh milk is not available, use frozen human milk from the infant's mother. This milk should be provided in the sequence that it was collected to provide the greatest nutritional benefit.

C. When the preterm infant is tolerating human milk at greater than 100ml/kg/day, supplementation with a human milk fortifier is started.

D. If the mother's milk supply is inadequate to meet her infant's feeding needs, pooled human milk supplemented with a human milk fortifier or an infant formula designed for preterm feeding is used.

E. Fortification of human milk is recommended until the infant is taking all feedings from the breast directly or when he or she weighs 1,800g to 2,000g, depending on the nursery policy regarding infant discharge weight. During the transition from feeding human milk by gavage or bottle and nipple to feeding at the breast, only these feedings given by gavage or bottle require fortification.

F. Multivitamin supplementation is started once feeding tolerance has been established. This supplementation varies depending on the composition of the human milk fortifier.

G. Iron supplementation providing 2mg/kg/day is started by the time the infant has doubled his or her birth weight.

II  Valentine CJ, Hurst NM. A six-step feeding strategy for preterm infants. *J Hum Lact* 1995; 11:7–8.

A. Infants begin 10–20 cc/kg/day of expressed breast milk (oral-gastric, bolus, or continuous drip by using an automated syringe pump) and are progressed daily at the same rate (if tolerated) to the goal of 150cc/kg/day of expressed breast milk. During this time period, infants are transitioning off parenteral nutrition.

B. Once the baby is receiving 150cc/kg/day, a powdered human milk fortifier is added at two packets per 100cc of mother's milk; after 24 hours of tolerance, this amount is increased to four packets per 100cc of mother's milk.

C. If infant growth falters (less than 15g/kg/day), then the volume of fortified human milk is increased to 160–180cc/kg/day. Other clinical factors associated with slow growth are first ruled out (for example, acidosis or anemia).

D. If growth remains (less than 15g/kg/day), we use fortified hindmilk at 180cc/kg/day and fortify as above.

E. If growth falters, the infants are supplemented with corn oil 0.5cc every three hours given as a bolus rather than mixed with the milk.

F. If growth falters, four feedings are replaced with premature formula, and four fortified breast milk feeds are continued.

III Stine MJ, Breastfeeding the premature newborn: a protocol without bottles. *J Hum Lact* 1990; 6:167–170.

A. Gavage feeding until the infant is in stable condition and can tolerate short periods outside the isolette.

B. Practice sessions at the breast followed by gavage feeding.

C. When the infant consistently latches on during maternal visits, feeds with swallowing for five minutes, and demonstrates steady weight gain, the amount of supplement should be based on observations of feeding at the breast.

D. Supplemental milk is given by a nasogastric tube as needed. None is given if the infant breastfed well for five minutes with swallowing.

E. Half the usual volume is given if the infant breastfed for less than five minutes.

F. The full amount of supplement is given if the infant did not breastfeed.

IV Hopkinson J, Texas Children's Hospital

A. Start with practice sessions/non-nutritive feeding at the breast.

B. Practice latch-on on a drained breast.

C. Skin-to-skin contact for a half-hour before feeding at the breast.

D. One unsupplemented feeding at the breast (replace one tube feeding with feeding at the breast).

E. Do not measure pre- and post-feed weight.

F. Take the baby's weight the next morning.

G. If the weight is acceptable, continue one unsupplemented breastfeeding per day until the weight has been good for three days.

H. Add another unsupplemented feeding at the breast.

I. When the weight has been good for three days on two unsupplemented feeds at the breast, add a third (and so on).

V Kliethermes PA, Cross ML, Lanese MG, Johnson KM, Simon SD. Transitioning preterm infants with nasogastric tube supplementation: Increased likelihood of breastfeeding. *JOGNN* 1999; 28:264–273.

A. Supplementation provided through an indwelling number 3.5 French nasogastric tube when the mother was not available to breastfeed or if additional supplemental feedings were required

B. Daily weights, with supplements reduced gradually as the infant consistently meets or surpasses the expected weight gain of 20–30g/day

C. Nasogastric tube removed 24–48 hours prior to discharge with supplements given if needed by cup

D. Stine's protocol with the following definitions:

E. Breastfeeds well:

1. Good latch-on with a wide-open mouth and lips flanged

2. Areola drawn in with sucking

3. Tongue is down and cupped; infant retains a vacuum when the forehead is gently pushed away from the breast

4. No dimpling of infant's cheeks

5. Long draws with rhythmical sucking and audible swallowing

6. Mother requires minimal help with positioning and latch-on

7. Breastfeeding is greater than or equal to 5–8 minutes.

F. Breastfeeds fairly:

1. Occasional latch-on
2. Short sucks, fewer long draws, infrequent audible swallowing, mother requires help with positioning
3. Time of active suckling is less than five minutes

G. Breastfeeds poorly (non-nutritive or introductory phase):

1. Some rooting or licking movements
2. No latch-on
3. Mother requires assistance with positioning

# Advantages of Preterm Breast Milk

I   Mother's own breast milk is the optimal milk for the preterm infant. Donor breast milk is the next optimal choice with preterm formula, and then full-term formula being the last choice. Mobidity and mortality rates increase significantly when the infant is not fed breast milk. Preterm infants who are fed human milk accrue a number of beneficial outcomes and advantages over being fed preterm infant formula:

A. The achievement of greater enteral feeding tolerance and more rapid advancement to full enteral feeds; physiologic amino acids and fatty acid profiles enhance the digestion and absorption of these nutrients; low real solute load

B. Gastric half emptying time in a formula-fed preterm infant can be up to twice the time as in a breast milk-fed baby (25 minutes versus 51 minutes)

C. The presence of active enzymes that supplement those that are lacking in the underdeveloped gut; trophic factors that hasten the maturation of the preterm gut

D. Reduced risk and severity of necrotizing enterocolitis, sepsis, and nosocomial infections (both acute and long term)

E. Reduced risk of allergy in atopic families

F. Weight gain of not just fat and water, but also bone and other tissue

G. Optimal development of visual acuity and retinal health; retinopathy of prematurity has been reported to be 2.3 times higher in formula-fed preterm infants

H. Cognitive and neurodevelopmental outcomes are enhanced, with preterm infants who have been fed breast milk showing higher IQs; the long-chain polyunsaturated fatty acids DHA and AA that are present in breast milk but not in many formulas are considered to be closely linked with this outcome

I. Helps to protect the baby from environmental pathogens; particularly important in a special care nursery with many staff handling the baby and with invasive treatments

# Maturation and Influences on Sucking, Swallowing, and Breathing Coordination

I The ability of an infant to breastfeed depends on the suck, swallow, and breathing coordination of the innate reflexes.

  A. Esophageal peristalsis and swallowing have been seen in the fetus as early as 11 weeks of gestation.

  B. Sucking has been described between 18–24 weeks.

  C. Lactase, a brush border intestinal enzyme that digests lactose, is present at 24 weeks.

  D. Lingual and gastric lipases are detectable at 26 weeks.

  E. The gag reflex is seen in preterm babies of 26–27 weeks.

  F. Rooting is seen around 32 weeks.

  G. The coordination of suck, swallow, and breathe actions is seen at 32–35 weeks.

  H. Some babies as young as 28 weeks are able to lick expressed milk from the mother's nipple.

  I. At 28–30 weeks, some oral feeding might be possible at the breast or by cup.

  J. From 32–34 weeks, some babies might be able to take a complete breastfeed once or twice a day.

  K. From 35 weeks onward, efficient breastfeeding that maintains adequate growth is possible.

  L. Preterm infants are characterized by a weak suck, a lack of coordination between sucking, swallowing, and breathing, a baby who tires easily, and a baby who has low muscle tone.

  M. Immature suck pattern.

    1. Three to five sucks per burst

    2. A pause of equal duration, often detaching from the breast

  N. Transitional suck pattern.

    1. 6 to 10 sucks per burst

    2. Burst = pause duration with occasional detaching

    3. An apneic episode can follow longer suck bursts

  O. Mature suck pattern.

    1. 10–30 sucks per burst

    2. Brief pauses

    3. Suck/swallow = 1:1 ratio

  P. Disorganized sucking is a lack of rhythm of the total sucking activity.

Q. Dysfunctional sucking is the interruption of the feeding process by abnormal movements of the tongue and jaw.

II Non-nutritive sucking (sucking without taking milk).

  A. Has a number of advantages, including increasing the infant's weight gain, linking a full stomach with the act of sucking, and a soothing experience.

  B. Non-nutritive sucking opportunities are sometimes provided by a pacifier or an artificial nipple during gavage feedings.

  C. When possible, it is more advantageous for non-nutritive sucking to occur at the mother's emptied breast during gavage feeding.

    1. Non-nutritive sucking defines sucking without obtaining breast milk.

      a. Can be observed from 18 weeks' gestation

      b. Rate of two sucks per second

      c. Weak, uncoordinated flutter sucking

      d. Full-term babies also perform non-nutritive sucking

      e. Absence of swallow

## Scientific Basis for Breastfeeding a Preterm Infant

I No scientific evidence links growth/weight milestones, the ability to suck bottles, or the inability to measure accurate intake as reasons for delaying offering a preterm baby the opportunity to attempt breastfeeding.

  A. Until recently, it was widely assumed that breastfeeding was more tiring and that bottle-feeding was less work; consequently, preterm infants were required to demonstrate the ability to consume an entire bottle-feed before being introduced to breastfeeding.

  B. Prolonged bottle-feeding in the absence of breastfeeding frequently leads to feeding patterns that do not transfer well to the breast.

  C. Bottle-feeding when a mother is wishing to breastfeed, undermines her efforts of expressing and supplying her breast milk for her infant.

  D. Early breastfeeding has been shown to be less stressful to a preterm infant than bottle-feeding.

  E. Bottle-feeding has been shown to produce adverse and undesirable physiologic and biochemical changes in small babies, including hypoxia, apnea, bradycardia, oxygen desaturation, hypercarbia, and reduced minute and tidal volume hypothermia, and irregular breathing frequency.

II When the infant's condition is stable enough to be held by the parents, it is deemed appropriate to be put to the breast for skin-to-skin contact (Kangaroo Care).

A. Breast/chest cuddles by the parents usually stabilize the baby.

B. Babies can be placed in skin-to-skin care when they are very young and mechanically ventilated.

C. Skin-to-skin contact provides warmth, love, and comfort; there is no reason to restrict the length of skin-to-skin care unless the baby becomes unstable.

D. Mothers who provide Kangaroo Care report that their infants make rooting and mouthing movements toward the nipple, note feelings of milk ejection and leaking, and often express larger amounts of milk especially immediately following a Kangaroo Care session. Kangaroo Care or skin-to-skin is a special type of holding where the baby is dressed only in a diaper and placed inside the mother's shirt or top, snuggled between her breasts. Fathers can provide this type of holding also.

E. Babies in Kangaroo Care demonstrate more stable respirations, heart rates, and temperatures; they spend less time crying and more time in a quiet alert state and deep sleep; most studies show that these babies enjoy a greater weight gain and earlier discharge home.

F. Early breastfeeding practice can be a component of skin-to-skin care as a gradual transition to the breast.

III Readiness to breastfeed depends on the individual baby's cues.

A. There are no universally agreed-upon criteria for when to initiate feedings at the breast.

B. Traditionally, babies needed to be of a certain weight or gestational age before attempts were made at the breast; these criteria did not have a scientific basis.

C. The literature supports the observations that the infants vary considerably in their ability to consume measurable amounts of milk at the breast and require an individualized approach to initial feeding readiness.

D. The transition to the breast can be gradual, with daily non-nutritive sessions at the breast advancing to limited periods of sucking on a partially drained breast.

E. There are numerous protocols used to transition the baby to the breast; while some use bottles in the absence of the mother, many protocols currently use gavage feeding or cup feeding in the mother's absence.

IV Positions for breastfeeding the preterm infant.

A. The preterm infant usually feeds in positions that provide extra support for the head and torso.

B. The baby's entire head can be encircled by the mother's hand, or she can use the Dancer hand position for jaw stability; the preterm infant's head is heavy in relation to the weak neck musculature that is supposed to support it.

C. Failure to provide suitable head and jaw stability can result in a baby not latching on to the breast effectively, in a baby that tires quickly, or in biting the nipple in order to hang on.

D. Typical positions include the underarm/clutch or football hold or the transitional (across the lap) position.

E. The preterm baby might have difficulty opening his or her mouth wide enough.

F. Sucking pressures are lower in preterm babies, increasing the difficulty in actually drawing the nipple and areola into the mouth.

V Intake of milk while breastfeeding.

A. If doing Kangaroo Care breastfeeding, intake can be assessed as daily weights or weights every two days.

B. Intake can be estimated by the use of pre- and post-feed weights if accuracy is paramount early on; pre- and post-feed weights are helpful in situations where decisions must be made regarding the amounts of supplement, determination of milk transfer problems, or simple reassurance to the mother or staff.

C. Staff and parent observation of the breastfeed can also estimate an adequate or inadequate feed.

D. Mother's milk supply also plays a part in assessing infant intake.

E. Daily weights or weights every second day are used as the baby begins taking more milk at the breast and decreasing the supplement used.

F. Preterm infants often do not demonstrate a predictable, cue-based feeding pattern until close to their corrected term age.

G. Intake-related problems can also be helped by the use of a tube feeding device at the breast that delivers additional milk as the baby suckles the breast.

H. Indications for this device can include the following:

1. A baby who latches on to the breast but exerts low sucking pressures
2. Lack of sucking rhythm
3. Wish to supplement at breast
4. Mother who has a limited milk supply
5. Slow milk ejection reflex

I. When limited intake is a result of the baby's inability to draw in enough of the nipple/areola (or if the areola is puffy or the nipple is very large in relation to the baby's mouth), a thin nipple shield has been successfully used on a temporary basis until the baby is capable of forming a teat by himself or herself.

J. One of the major concerns of preterm mothers relates to whether the infant is consuming adequate volumes of milk by breastfeeding.

1. Mothers might perceive that their infant is not taking the majority of the milk available.

2. Babies might slip off the breast, fall asleep at the breast, or simply stop feeding.

3. These immature feeding patterns are gradually replaced with more mature ones as the baby nears his or her term-corrected age.

4. Milk transfer is dependent on milk supply, milk ejection, and infant sucking.

   a. If sucking is immature, then interventions can be targeted toward optimizing milk production and milk ejection in order to compensate for weak or immature sucking patterns.

   b. Mothers usually need to continue using the breast pump after the baby has been discharged; this device might be needed after each feeding or only a couple of times each day.

   c. Experts recommend that the mother produce about 50 percent more milk than the infant needs at discharge; the increased volume helps the milk flow freely in the presence of a weaker suck.

   d. The baby should finish the first breast before being placed on the other side.

## Establishing Full Breastfeeding

I  Phase One: Initiate lactation by the expression and collection of breast milk.

   A. Lactation should be initiated with a breast pump as early as possible following delivery, preferably with one to two hours.

   B. Some units utilize hand expression rather than mechanical expression.

   C. Mothers should plan to pump 8–12 times each 24 hours for the first 7–10 days for optimal milk yield; this plan might change to fewer pumping sessions if that maintains this level of production.

   D. This plan should yield 800–1000ml of milk daily.

   E. An abundant milk supply at this point greatly reduces the risk of insufficient milk later.

   F. It also supports a 50 percent oversupply that is intended to provide a cushion; if the milk production drops with a setback in the baby, it can be fractioned in order to provide hindmilk supplements and aids the infant in extracting milk from a full breast with freely flowing milk.

   G. Mothers might find that massaging and compressing each breast during expression contributes to increased milk yields, a more thorough draining of the breast, and a higher fat content of the expressed milk.

   H. Mothers should plan to use a hospital-grade electric breast pump with double collection kits.

   I. Simultaneous milk pumping can increase prolactin levels, increase milk yield, and reduce the time spent pumping.

    J. Mother's milk should be fed to preterm infants immediately after it is pumped. Fresh breast milk is preferable for preterm infants.

    K. Frozen colostrum can be given first before fresh breast milk if the baby cannot be fed enterally for the first few days. This is also good for priming the infant's gut.

    L. Fresh breast milk can be refrigerated 24–48 hours before use.

    M. Breast milk can be frozen for later use, it should be used in the order it was expressed; frozen milk can be used up to 24 hours after thawing.

    N. Low milk volume is a common problem, especially if the baby cannot come to the breast for several weeks or if the baby was born extremely early; a number of possible interventions have proven helpful.

    O. Encourage the baby to suckle at the emptied breast; pump during or right after skin-to-skin contact.

    P. Pump at the baby's bedside.

    Q. Medications such as metoclopramide or domperidone.

    R. Oxytocin to enhance milk ejection and a more thorough draining of the breasts.

    S. Acupuncture.

    T. Human growth hormone.

**II** Phase Two: Early introduction of the infant to the breast (Kangaroo Care)

    A. May require continuous/hourly gavage feedings of expressed breast milk in the beginning until full milk feeds are tolerated

    B. Use of breast milk for mouth care

    C. Maintenance of milk supply by expression

**III** Phase Three: Optimizing early feedings

    A. Optimal positioning and attachment of the infant

    B. Football (clutch) hold, transitional hold, and use of the Dancer hand position

    C. Feeding regime transitional

    D. Scheduled feeds might be useful until the baby is mature enough to begin cue-based feeding

    E. The feeding frequency might move from two to three hourly gradually over time

    F. Combination of breastfeeds and alternative methods until mature enough to sustain all feeding at the breast

    G. Might require small, frequent breastfeeds when fully breastfeeding at the beginning

**IV** Phase Four: Transition to cue-based, full breastfeeding

    A. Will occur over time with most babies able to achieve cue-based feeding by the time they are term equivalent

    B. Assess the readiness to breastfeed

        1. Show signs of demand sucking

        2. Awake and alert at feed times

        3. Sucking on gavage tubing or fist

        4. Mouthing

    C. Able to sustain a full breastfeed

    D. Able to sustain full breastfeeding on demand and gain adequate weight

## Discharge Planning

- Parents require a detailed plan of caring/parenting their preterm baby after discharge with support and encouragement for ongoing care; information should include the following:
  - Signs that the baby is getting enough breast milk; weight checks; pre- and post-feed weights if necessary; diaper counts of wet diapers and bowel movements
  - Expected feeding patterns; eight feeds at least per 24 hours with one prolonged sleep period of up to five hours; cues that indicate the baby is available to feed
  - Continued use of a breast pump until the baby is vigorous and fully established at the breast
  - Proper use of breastfeeding aids, such as a nursing supplement (tube feeding device), supervision of the use of a nipple shield if started; close follow-up should be provided to move toward full breastfeeding
  - Where to get support and assistance; mothers should be referred to a lactation consultant or other health professional who has expertise in preterm infants

## References

Affonso D, Bosque E, Wahlberg V, Brady JP. Reconciliation and healing for mothers through skin-to-skin contact provided in an American tertiary-level intensive care nursery. Neonatal Network 1993; 12:25–32.

Als H, Gilkerson L. Developmentally supportive care in the neonatal intensive care unit. *Zero to Three* 1995; 15:2–10.

Anderson GC. Current knowledge about skin-to-skin (Kangaroo) care for preterm infants. *J Perinatology* 1991; 11:216–226.

Arenson J. Discharge teaching in the NICU: The changing needs of NICU graduates and their families. *Neonatal Network* 1988; 7:29–30, 47–52.

Armstrong HC. Breastfeeding low birthweight babies: advances in Kenya. *J Hum Lact* 1987; 3:34–37.

Arnold LDW, Larson E. Immunologic benefits of breast milk in relation to human milk banking. *Am J Infection Control* 1993; 21:235–242.

Auer C, Gromada KK. A case report of breastfeeding quadruplets: Factors perceived as affecting breastfeeding. *J Hum Lact* 1998; 14:135–141.

Auerbach KG, Walker M. When the mother of a premature infant uses a breast pump: What every NICU nurse needs to know. *Neonatal Network* 1994; 13:23–29.

Baker BJ, Rasmussen TW. Organizing and documenting lactation support of NICU families. *JOGNN* 1997; 26:515–521.

Barnes LP. Lactation consultation in the neonatal intensive care unit. *MCN* 1991; 16:167.

Becker PT, Grunwald PC, Moorman J, Stuhr S. Effects of developmental care on behavioral organization in very-low-birth-weight infants. *Nursing Research* 1993; 42:214–220.

Bell RP, McGrath JM. Implementing a research-based kangaroo care program in the NICU. *Nursing Clinics of North America* 1996; 31:387–403.

Bell EH, Geyer J, Jones L. A structured intervention improves breastfeeding success for ill or preterm infants. *MCN* 1995; 20:309–314.

Bier JB, Ferguson A, Anderson L, et al. Breast-feeding of very low birth weight infants. *J Pediatr* 1993; 123:773–779.

Bier JB, Ferguson A, Cho C, et al. The oral motor development of low-birth-weight infants who underwent orotracheal intubation during the neonatal period. *AJDC* 1993; 147:858–862.

Bier JB, Ferguson AE, Morales Y, et al. Comparison of skin-to-skin contact with standard contact in low birth weight infants who are breastfed. *Arch Pediatr Adolesc Med* 1996; 150:1265–1269.

Bishop NJ, Dahlenburg SL, Fewtrell MS, et al. Early diet of preterm infants and bone mineralization at age five years. *Acta Paediatr* 1996; 85:230–236.

Bosque EM, Brady JP, Affonso DD, Wahlberg V. Physiologic measures of kangaroo versus incubator care in a tertiary-level nursery. *JOGNN* 1995; 24: 219–226.

Bowles BC, Stutte PC, Hensley JH. Alternate massage in breastfeeding. *Genesis* 1988; 9:5–9, 17.

Brooten D, Kumar S, Brown LP, et al. A randomized clinical trial of early hospital discharge and home follow-up of very-low-birth-weight infants. *N Engl J Med* 1986; 315:934–939.

Charpak N, Ruiz-Pelaez JG, Charpak Y. Rey-Martinez Kangaroo mother program: An alternative way of caring for low birth weight infants? One year mortality in a two cohort study. *Pediatrics* 1994; 94:804–810.

Chen C-H, Wang T-M, Chang H-M, Chi C-S. The effect of breast- and bottle-feeding on oxygen saturation and body temperature in preterm infants. *J Hum Lact* 2000; 16:21–27.

Clavey S. The use of acupuncture for the treatment of insufficient lactation. *Am J of Acupuncture* 1996; 24:35–46.

Costello A, Chapman J. Mothers' perceptions of the care-by-parent program prior to hospital discharge of their preterm infants. *Neonatal Network* 1998; 17:37–42.

D'Appolito K. What is an organized infant? *Neonatal Network* 1991; 10:23–29.

Dowling D, Danner SC, Coffey PM. Breastfeeding the infant with special needs. March of Dimes Nursing Module, 1997.

Drosten-Brooks F. Kangaroo care: Skin-to-skin contact in the NICU. *MCN* 1993; 18:250–253.

Durand R, Hodges S, LaRock S, et al. The effect of skin-to-skin breastfeeding in the immediate recovery period on newborn thermoregulation and blood glucose values. *Neonatal Intensive Care* 1997; March/April: 23–27.

Ehrenkranz RA, Ackerman BA. Metoclopramide effect on faltering milk production by mothers of premature infants. *Pediatrics* 1986; 78:614–620.

Elizondo AP. Nursing case management in the neonatal intensive care unit, part 2: Developing critical pathways. *Neonatal Network* 1995; 14:11–19.

Elliott S, Reimer C. Postdischarge telephone follow-up program for breastfeeding preterm infants discharged from a special care nursery. *Neonatal Network* 1998; 17:41–45.

El-Mohandes, et al. Bacterial contaminants of collected and frozen human milk used in an intensive care nursery. *Am J Infection Control* 1993; 21:226–230.

Erenberg A, Nowak AJ. Palatal groove formation in neonates and infants with orotracheal tubes. *Am J Dis Child* 1984; 138:974–975.

Evanochko CM. Bacterial growth in expressed breast milk in continuous feeding setups in the NICU. *Neonatal Network* 1995; 14:52.

Ewer AK, Yu VYH. Gastric emptying in preterm infants: The effect of breast milk fortifier. *Acta Paediatr* 1996; 85:1112–1115.

Farquharson J, Jamieson EC, Logan RW, et al. Age- and dietary-related distributions of hepatic arachidonic and docosahexaenoic acid in early infancy. *Pediatr Res* 1995; 38:361–365.

Feher SDK, Berger LR, Johnson JD, Wilde JB. Increasing breast milk production for premature infants with a relaxation/imagery audiotape. *Pediatrics* 1989; 83:57–60.

Fewtrell MS, Prentice A, Jones SC, et al. Bone mineralization and turnover in preterm infants at 8–12 years of age: The effect of early diet. *J Bone Miner Res* 1999; 14:810–820.

Forsyth TJ, Maney LA, Ramirez A, et al. Nursing case management in the NICU: Enhanced coordination for discharge planning. *Neonatal Network* 1998; 17:23–34.

Forte A, Mayberry LJ, Ferketich S. Breast milk collection and storage practices among mothers of hospitalized neonates. *J Perinatology* 1987; 7:35–39.

Gale G, Franck L, Lund C. Skin-to-skin (Kangaroo) holding of the intubated premature infant. *Neonatal Network* 1993; 12:49–57.

Gennaro S, Brooten D, Bakewell-Sachs S. Postdischarge services for low-birth-weight infants. *JOGNN* 1991; 20:29–36.

Glass RP, Wolf LS. A global perspective on feeding assessment in the neonatal intensive care unit. *Am J Occupational Therapy* 1994; 48:514–526.

Goldman AS, Chheda S, Keeney SE, et al. Immunologic protection of the premature newborn by human milk. *Sem Perinatol* 1994; 18:495–501.

Griffin TL, Meier PP, Bradford LP, et al. Mother's performing creamatocrit measures in the NICU: Accuracy, reactions, and cost. *JOGNN* 2000; 29:249–257.

Groh-Wargo S, Toth A, Mahoney K, et al. The utility of a bilateral breast pumping system for mothers of premature infants. *Neonatal Network* 1995; 14:31–36.

Gross SJ, David RJ, Bauman L, et al. Nutritional composition of milk from mothers delivering preterm and at term. *J Pediatrics* 1980; 96:641–644.

Gunn AJ, Gunn TR, Rabone DL, et al. Growth hormone increases breast milk volumes in mothers of preterm infants. *Pediatrics* 1996; 98:279–282.

Gupta A, Khanna K, Chattree S. Cup feeding: An alternative to bottle feeding in a neonatal intensive care unit. *J Trop Pediatr* 1999; 45:108–110.

Hamosh M. Digestion in the premature infant: The effects of human milk. *Sem Perinatol* 1994; 18:485–494.

Hamosh M, et al. Breastfeeding and the working mother: Effect of time and temperature of short-term storage on proteolysis, lipolysis, and bacterial growth in milk. *Pediatrics* 1996; 97:492–498.

Harrison H. The principles for family-centered neonatal care. *Pediatrics* 1993; 92:643–650.

Hill AS, Rath L. The care and feeding of the low-birth-weight infant. *J Perinat Neonatal Nurs* 1993; 6:56–68.

Hill PD, Hanson KS, Mefford AL. Mothers of low birthweight infants: Breastfeeding patterns and problems. *J Hum Lact* 1994; 10:169–176.

Hill PD, Andersen JL, Ledbetter RJ. Delayed initiation of breast-feeding the preterm infant. *J Perinat Neonatal Nurs* 1995; 9:10–20.

Hill PD, Brown LP, Harker TL. Initiation and frequency of breast expression in breastfeeding mothers of LBW and VLBW infants. *Nurs Research* 1995; 44:352–355.

Hill PD, Aldag JC, Chatterton RT. The effect of sequential and simultaneous breast pumping on milk volume and prolactin levels: A pilot study. *J Hum Lact* 1996; 12:193–199.

Hill PD, Ledbetter RJ, Kavanaugh KL. Breastfeeding patterns of low birth weight infants after hospital discharge. *JOGNN* 1997; 26:189–197.

Hill PD, Aldag JC, Chatterton, Jr. RT. Breastfeeding experience and milk weight in lactating mothers pumping for preterm infants. *Birth* 1999; 26:233–238.

Hill PD, Aldag JC, Chatterton RT. Effects of pumping style on milk production in mothers of non-nursing preterm infants. *J Hum Lact* 1999; 15:209–216.

Hopkinson JM, Schanler RJ, Garza C. Milk production by mothers of premature infants. *Pediatrics* 1988; 81:815–820.

Hopkinson JM, Schanler RJ, Fraley JK, Garza C. Milk production by mothers of premature infants: Influence of cigarette smoking. *Pediatrics* 1992; 90:934–938.

Hurst NM, Valentine CJ, Renfro L, et al. Skin-to-skin holding in the neonatal intensive care unit influences maternal milk volume. *J Perinatol* 1997; 17:213–217.

Hurst NM, Myatt A, Schanler RJ. Growth and development of a hospital-based lactation program and mother's own milk bank. *JOGNN* 1998; 27:503–510.

Inoue N, Sakashita R, Kamegai T. Reduction of masseter muscle activity in bottle-fed babies. *Early Human Development* 1995; 42:185–193.

Jocson ML, Mason EO, Schanler RJ. The effects of nutrient fortification and varying storage conditions on host defense properties of human milk. *Pediatrics* 1997; 100:240–243.

Jones E. Breastfeeding in the preterm infant. *Modern Midwife* 1994; 4:22–26.

Kavanaugh K, Mead L, Meier P, Mangurten HH. Getting enough: Mothers' concerns about breastfeeding a preterm infant after discharge. *JOGNN* 1995; 24:23–32.

Kavanaugh K, Meier P, Zimmerman B, Mead L. The rewards outweigh the efforts: Breastfeeding outcomes for mothers of preterm infants. *J Hum Lact* 1997; 13:15–21.

Kirsten D, Bradford L. Hindmilk feedings. *Neonatal Network* 1999; 18:68–70.

Kliethermes P, Cross MD, Lanese MG, et al. Transitioning preterm infants with nasogastric tube supplementation: Increased likelihood of breastfeeding. *JOGNN* 1999; 28:264–273.

Koenig JS, Davies AM, Thach BT. Coordination of breathing, sucking, and swallowing during bottle feedings in human infants. *J Appl Physiol* 1990; 69:1623–1629.

Lang S, Lawrence CJ, Orme RL. Cup feeding: An alternative method of infant feeding. *Arch Dis Child* 1994; 71:365–369.

Lang S. Breastfeeding special care babies. Philadelphia: W.B. Saunders, 1997.

Lawhon G, Melzar A. Developmental care of the very low birth weight infant. *J Perinatal Neonatal Nursing* 1988; 2:56–65.

Lucas A, Morley R, Cole TJ, et al. Breast milk and subsequent intelligence quotient in children born preterm. *Lancet* 1992; 339:261–264.

Lucas A, Fewtrell MS, Morley R, et al. Randomized outcome trial of human milk fortification and developmental outcome in preterm infants. *Am J Clin Nutr* 1996; 64:142–151.

Lucas A, Cole TJ. Breast milk and necrotising enterocolitis. *Lancet* 1990; 336:1519–1523.

Ludington-Hoe SM, Thompson C, Swinth J, et al. Kangaroo care: Research results, and practice implications and guidelines. *Neonatal Network* 1994; 13:19–27.

Ludington-Hoe SM, Swinth JY. Developmental aspects of kangaroo care. *JOGNN* 1996; 25:691–703.

Ludington S. Kangaroo care: The best you can do for your preterm infant. New York: Bantam Books, 1993.

Luukkainen P, Salo MK, Nikkari T. The fatty acid composition of banked human milk and infant formulas: The choices of milk for feeding preterm infants. *Eur J Pediatr* 1995; 154:316–319.

Makrides M, Neumann MA, Gibson RA. Effect of maternal docosahexaenoic acid (DHA) supplementation on breast milk composition. *Eur J Clin Nutr* 1996; 50:352–357.

Malhotra N, Vishwambaran L, Sundaram KR, Narayanan I. A controlled trial of alternative methods of oral feeding in neonates. *Early Hum Dev* 1999; 54:29–38.

Martell M, Martinez G, Gonzalez M, et al. Suction patterns in preterm infants. *J Perinatal Medicine* 1993; 21:363–369.

Matthew OP. Respiratory control during nipple feeding in preterm infants. *Pediatric Pulmonology* 1988; 5:220–224.

Matthew OP. Science of bottle feeding. *J Pediatr* 1991; 119:511–519.

Matthew OP. Breathing patterns of preterm infants during bottle feeding: Role of milk flow. *J Pediatr* 1991; 119:960–965.

McCoy R, Kadowaki C, Wilks S, Engstrom J, Meier P. Nursing management of breast feeding for preterm infants. *J Perinatal Neonatal Nursing* 1988; 2:42–55.

Medoff-Cooper B, Verklan T, Carlson S. The development of sucking patterns and physiologic correlates in very-low-birth-weight infants. *Nursing Research* 1993; 42:100–105.

Meier P, Pugh EJ. Breast-feeding behavior of small preterm infants. MCN 1985; 10:396–401.

Meier P, Anderson GC. Responses of small preterm infants to bottle- and breast-feeding. MCN 1987; 12:97–105.

Meier P, Wilks S. The bacteria in expressed mothers' milk. MCN 1987; 12:420–423.

Meier P. Bottle- and breast-feeding: Effects on transcutaneous oxygen pressure and temperature in preterm infants. *Nursing Research* 1988; 37:36–41.

Meier PP, Engstrom JL, Mangurten HH, et al. Breastfeeding support services in the neonatal intensive-care unit. JOGNN 1993; 22:338–347.

Meier PP, Engstrom JL, Crichton CL, et al. A new scale for in-home test-weighing for mothers of preterm and high risk infants. *J Hum Lact* 1994; 10:163–168.

Meier PP, Engstrom JL, Fleming BA, et al. Estimating intake of hospitalized preterm infants who breastfeed. *J Hum Lact* 1996; 12:21–26.

Meier PP, Brown LP. State of the science: Breastfeeding for mothers and low birth weight infants. *Nursing Clinics of North America* 1996; 31:351–365.

Meier PP, Brown LP. Breastfeeding a preterm infant after NICU discharge: Reflections on Ryan's story. *Breastfeeding Abstracts* 1997; 17:3–4.

Meier PP, Brown LP, Hurst NM, et al. Nipple shields for preterm infants: Effect on milk transfer and duration of breastfeeding. *J Hum Lact* 2000; 16:106–114.

Mennella JA, Beauchamp GK. The human infants' response to vanilla flavors in mother's milk and formula. *Infant Behavior and Development* 1996; 19:13–19.

Milsom SR, Breier BH, Gallaher BW, et al. Growth hormone stimulates galactopoiesis in healthy lactating women. *Acta Endocrinologica* 1992; 127:337–343.

Moran M, Radzyminski SG, Higgins K, et al. Maternal Kangaroo (skin-to-skin) care in the NICU beginning 4 hours postbirth. MCN 1999; 24:74–79.

Moro GE, Minoli I, Ostrom M, et al. Fortification of human milk: Evaluation of a novel fortification scheme and of a new fortifier. *J Pediatr Gastroenterol Nutr* 1995; 20:162–172.

Narayanan I. Human milk for low birthweight infants: Immunology, nutrition and newer practical technologies. *Acta Paediatr Jpn* 1989; 31:455–461.

Newell SJ, Chapman S, Booth IW. Ultrasonic assessment of gastric emptying time in the preterm infant. *Arch Dis Child* 1993; 69:32–36.

Nyqvist KH, Sjoden PO, Ewald U. Mothers' advice about facilitating breastfeeding in a neonatal intensive care unit. *J Hum Lact* 1994; 10:237–243.

Nyqvist KH, Rubertsson C, Ewald U, et al. Development of the preterm infant breastfeeding behavior scale (PIBBS): A study of nurse-mother agreement. *J Hum Lact* 1996; 12:207–219.

Nyqvist KH, Ewald U, Sjoden PO. Supporting a preterm infant's behavior during breastfeeding: A case report. *J Hum Lact* 1996; 12:221–228.

Nyqvist KH, Sjoden P-O, Ewald U. The development of preterm infants' breastfeeding behavior. *Early Human Development* 1999; 55:247–264.

Orlando S. The immunologic significance of breast milk. *JOGNN* 1995; 24:678–683.

Palmer MM. Identification and management of the transitional suck pattern in premature infants. *J Perinat Neonatal Nurs* 1993; 7:66–75.

Pardou A, et al. Human milk banking: Influence of storage processes and of bacterial contamination on some milk constituents. *Biology of the Neonate* 1994; 65:302–309.

Polberger S, Lonnerdal B. Simple and rapid macronutrient analysis of human milk for individualized fortification: Basis for improved nutritional management of very-low-birth-weight infants? *J Pediatr Gastroenterol Nutr* 1993; 17:283–290.

Quan R, Yang C, Rubinstein S, et al. The effect of nutritional additives on anti-infective factors in human milk. *Clinical Pediatrics* 1994; June:326–329.

Ruis H, Rolland R, Doesburg W, et al. Oxytocin enhances onset of lactation among mothers delivering prematurely. *Br Med J* 1981; 283:340–342.

Saunders RB, Friedman CB, Stramoski PR. Feeding preterm infants: Schedule or demand? *JOGNN* 1991; 20:212–218.

Schanler RJ, Hurst NM. Human milk for the hospitalized preterm infant. *Seminars in Perinatology* 1994; 18:476–484.

Schanler RJ. Human milk fortification for premature infants. *Am J Clin Nutr* 1996; 64:249–250.

Schanler RJ, Shulman RJ, Lau C, et al. Feeding strategies for premature infants: Randomized trial of gastrointestinal priming and tube feeding method. *Pediatrics* 1999; 103:434–439.

Schanler RJ, Shulman RJ, Lau C. Feeding strategies for premature infants: Beneficial outcomes of feeding fortified human milk versus preterm formula. *Pediatrics* 1999; 103:1150–1157.

Schanler RJ, Hurst NM, Lau C. The use of human milk and breastfeeding in premature infants. *Clinics in Perinatology* 1999; 26:379–398.

Shivpuri CR, Martin RJ, Carlo WA, Fanaroff AA. Decreased ventilation in preterm infants during oral feeding. *J Pediatr* 1983; 103:285–289.

Siddell EP, Froman RD. A national survey of neonatal intensive care units: Criteria used to determine readiness for oral feedings. *JOGNN* 1994; 23:783–789.

Stine MJ. Breastfeeding the premature newborn: A protocol without bottles. *J Hum Lact* 1990; 6:167–170.

Stutte PC, Bowles BC, Morman GY. The effects of breast massage on volume and fat content of human milk. *Genesis* 1988; 10:22–25.

Thompson DG. Critical pathways in the intensive care and intermediate care nurseries. *MCN* 1994; 19:29–32.

Usowicz AG, Dab SB, Emery JR, et al. Does gastric acid protect the preterm infant from bacteria in unheated human milk? *Early Human Development* 1988; 16:27–33.

Valentine CJ, Hurst NM, Schanler RJ. Hindmilk improves weight gain in low-birth-weight infants fed human milk. *J Pediatr Gastroenterol Nutr* 1994; 18:474–477.

Van den Driessche M, Peeters K, Marien P, et al. Gastric emptying in formula-fed and breast-fed infants measured with the 13C-octanoic acid breath test. *J Pediatr Gastroenterol Nutr* 1999; 29:46–51.

Walker M. Breastfeeding premature babies. Lactation Consultant Series Unit 14, New York: Avery Publishing Group, Inc., 1990.

Walker M. Management guidelines for breastfeeding mothers with LBW infants. *J Perinat Educ* 1992; 1:25–30.

Walker M. Breastfeeding the premature infant. Chute G: NAACOG's *Clin Iss Perinat Women's Health Nurs* 1992; 3(4):620–633.

Walker M. Breastfeeding your premature or special care baby: A practical guide for nursing the tiny baby. Weston, MA: Lactation Associates, 1998.

Wang CD, Chu PS, Mellen BG, Shenai JP. Creamatocrit and the nutrient composition of human milk. *J Perinatology* 1999; 19:343–346.

Williamson MT, Murti PK. Effects of storage, time, temperature, and composition of containers on biologic components of human milk. *J Hum Lact* 1996; 12:231–235.

Wolf LS, Glass RP. Feeding and swallowing disorders in infancy: Assessment and management. Tucson, AZ: Therapy Skill Builders, 1992.

# HYPERBILIRUBINEMIA AND HYPOGLYCEMIA

*Sallie Page-Goertz, MN, CPNP, IBCLC*

## OBJECTIVES

- Define the characteristics of physiologic jaundice versus breastfeeding-associated jaundice versus breast-milk jaundice.
- Describe the breastfeeding management of an infant who is experiencing breastfeeding-associated jaundice, breast-milk jaundice, and pathologic jaundice.
- List strategies for the prevention of breastfeeding-associated jaundice.
- List the criteria for referral for medical evaluation.
- List the risk factors for the development of hypoglycemia.
- Describe breastfeeding management of an infant who has hypoglycemia.
- List measures for preventing hypoglycemia in a newborn infant.

## Introduction

During the newborn period, two problems that impact and are impacted by breastfeeding management are hyperbilirubinemia and hypoglycemia. Appropriate breastfeeding routines, awareness of the risk factors, and the continuous assessment of a newborn are critical elements in preventing or reducing morbidity from these two concerns. There are increasing reports in the literature of infants who are experiencing complications from hyperbilirubinemia and concurrent dehydration. Such cases are preventable when the mother-infant dyad receives a high standard of care.

## Hyperbilirubinemia

Hyperbilirubinemia is the presence of elevated bilirubin. Extremely high levels of bilirubin can cause kernicterus, which is damage to the brain caused by the accumulation of bilirubin in brain tissue. Often, the lactation consultant is asked to evaluate and manage the breast-feeding of an infant who has hyperbilirubinemia during the first few days of life. Jaundiced infants might present to the consultant's practice with family members who are unaware of the significance of the jaundice. In certain situations, a jaundiced infant might also have excessive weight loss and other underlying health problems contributing to his or her problems. There might even be life-threatening situations related to associated dehydration. These children must be seen in conjunction with a primary health care provider.

I  Bilirubin physiology of the normal newborn
   A. Red blood cells (RBCs) break down after birth with the transition to a higher-oxygen environment.
   B. Bilirubin is one of the break-down products of these RBCs that is released into the bloodstream.
   C. Bilirubin is bound to albumin in the bloodstream and carried to the liver, where it is conjugated with gulcuronide.
   D. Bilirubin is then excreted via the bile duct into the intestine.
   E. Bilirubin is excreted by defecation through the stool.
   F. Many factors can lead to:
      1. An increased amount of circulating bilirubin beyond the liver's capability to metabolize it
         a. Birth trauma
         b. Polycythemia (placenta-to-infant or twin-to twin transfusion)
         c. Ineffective feeding (breastfeeding-associated jaundice)/delayed defecation with a recirculation of bilirubin
      2. Interference with the liver's capability to metabolize bilirubin
         a. In-born errors of metabolism
         b. Hypothyroidism
         c. Possibly breast-milk jaundice
      3. Interference with the body's ability to excrete bilirubin
         a. Ineffective feeding (breastfeeding-associated jaundice) and delayed defecation
         b. Intestinal obstruction
         c. Other congenital gastrointestinal disorders

II Risk factors for hyperbilirubinemia
   A. Maternal factors
      1. Diabetes
      2. Anatomic breast abnormality
      3. Breast surgery, especially breast reduction
      4. A retained placenta
      5. Endocrine dysfunction

      6. Hypertension/Eclampsia

      7. Family history of RBC disorders (such as spherocytosis or G6PD)

  B. Labor and delivery factors

      1. Epidural analgesia

      2. Birth trauma

      3. Mother-infant separation

      4. Delayed first feeding

  C. Infant risk factors

      1. Sleepy infant/infrequent feedings

      2. Ineffective breastfeeding

      3. Congenital oral facial anomalies (for example, cleft palate, ankyloglossia, or Pierre Robin syndrome)

      4. Congenital heart disease/neurologic impairment (for example, Trisomy 21)

      5. Oral motor difficulties

      6. Small for gestational age/prematurity

**III** Approach to the jaundiced infant

  A. Quick appraisal to determine the immediate need for a medical evaluation

      1. Lethargic, unable to arouse

      2. Refusal to feed

      3. Excessive weight loss (greater than or equal to 10 percent)

      4. Vomiting

      5. Inadequate urine or stool output for the infant's age

  B. History

      1. Infant history

         a. Assess for the presence of the risk factors previously listed

         b. Assess the color of urine—should be yellow, not orange

         c. Presence of uric acid crystals in the urine (brick dust appearance in the diaper); an indicator of dehydration, but is also common in the first few days of life

         d. Assess the infant's behavior over the past 24–48 hours: Waking to feed? Content after feedings? Fussy and not satisfied with feedings?

      2. Maternal history

         a. Health history—underlying risk factors (see previously listed factors)

         b. Breast health history—underlying risk factors (see previously listed factors)

         c. Breast/nipple pain or discomfort

         d. Evidence of a let-down

3. Feeding history
   a. Frequency of feeds
   b. Length of active feeding
   c. Swallows present
   d. Number of voids and stools per 24 hours
   e. Mother's perception of galactogenesis

C. Physical assessment
   1. Infant
      a. General appearance of the infant
      b. Level of vigor—alert/active versus difficult to arouse/lethargic
      c. Evidence of dehydration? Skin turgor, mucus membranes
      d. Presence of any congenital oral facial anomalies or other syndromes
      e. Current weight and the percent below birth weight
      f. Estimation of the bilirubin level based on the extent of the jaundice color on the infant's body
   2. Feeding assessment
      a. Latch-on technique
      b. Presence/frequency and length of the bursts of swallows
      c. Impact of change of feeding positions on the quality of feeding
   3. Maternal breast assessment
      a. Evidence of scars/marked asymmetry
      b. Evidence of nipple trauma

D. See Table 18-1 for a summary and comparison of the findings related to different causes of jaundice in newborn infants.

E. Medical management of hyperbilirubinemia
   1. Establishment of a definitive cause
   2. Treatment based on the definitive cause
   3. Interventions to decrease bilirubin levels if they are at potentially dangerous or high levels (see Table 18-2)
      a. Phototherapy—under the influence of phototherapy lights, photo-isomers of bilirubin are formed that are more easily excreted by the liver
         i. Phototherapy lights or fiberoptic blankets are used
      b. Exchange transfusion—rarely needed in the case of extremely high bilirubin levels; not responsive to intensive phototherapy
      c. Tin—mesoporphyrin (Sn-MP), a new medication being discussed in the literature—a metal that inhibits bilirubin formation. One or two injections are administered to the infant, usually resulting in a rapid fall in bilirubin

**Table 18-1** Comparison of Common Causes of Indirect Hyperbilirubinemia in the Term Newborn Infant[*]

| | Physiologic Jaundice | Breastfeeding-Associated Jaundice | Breast-Milk Jaundice |
|---|---|---|---|
| Onset of clinical jaundice | 48–72 hours | 48–72 hourse | 5–10 days of age |
| Peak | Day 3–5 | Day 3–5+ | Day 15 |
| Rate of rise | 2mg/dL/day | 5mg/dL/day | 1–2mg/dL/day |
| Cause | RBC breakdown | Starvation/delayed defecaton | Unknown |
| Condition of infant | Thriving; normal weight loss; normal output; clinically jaundiced | Lethargic/fussy; excessive weight loss; ineffective feeding; scant urine/stool output; signs of dehydration | Thriving; clinically jaundiced |
| Breastfeeding management | Monitor in order to ensure effective breastfeeding and initiation of normal weight gain | Increase caloric intake; intervene to establish effective breastfeeding; assist with supplementation; stimulate milk supply | No intervention needed |
| Medical management | Monitor; return visit at 72 hours of age; phototherapy per guidelines (seldom needed) | Phototherapy per guidelines; supplementation if indicated | Monitor bilirubin until stable; consider brief interruption of mother's milk feedings (preferable to avoid this strategy) |

[*]Adapted from Page-Goertz S and McCamman S. Hyperbilirubinemia in the Breastfed Infant, Lectures to Go. Overland Park, Kansas: Best Beginnings Productions, 1996. With permission from Best Beginnings Productions.

        levels without the need for phototherapy. This medication is not commonly used at this time

   F.  Danger signs that indicate an *immediate* need for referral to the primary care health provider:

      1.  Excessive weight loss of greater than or equal to 10 percent below birth weight

      2.  History of brick dust urine or inadequate urine output for the age of the infant

**Table 18-2**   Management of Hyperbilirubinemia in the Healthy Term Newborn[*]

| Age in Hours | Total Serum Bilirubin Level, mg/dL (µmol/L) | | | |
|---|---|---|---|---|
| | Consider phototherapy | Phototherapy | Exchange transfusion if intense phototherapy fails | Exchange transfusion and intense phototherapy |
| ≤ 24 | An infant demonstrating jaundice at this age does not meet the criteria of a healthy infant and needs further evaluation. | | | |
| 25–48 | ≥ 12(205) | ≥ 15(260) | ≥ 20(340) | ≥ 25(430) |
| 49–72 | ≥ 15(260) | ≥ 18(310) | ≥ 25(430) | ≥ 30(510) |
| 72 | ≥ 17(290) | ≥ 20(340) | ≥ 25(430) | ≥ 30(510) |

[*]Adapted with permission of the American Academy of Pediatrics from: Provisional Committee for Quality Improvement and Subcommittee on Hyperbilirubinemia. Practice parameter: management of hyperbilirubinemia in the healthy term newborn. *Pediatrics* 94(4): 560, 1994.

   3. Vomiting

   4. Refusing to feed

   5. Excessive sleeping or continued fretfulness

   6. Jaundiced color below the umbilicus

II. Pathologic causes of indirect hyperbilirubinemia

   These children must be under the care of a primary health care provider in addition to receiving assistance from a lactation consultant.

   A. Introduction

      1. When to suspect pathologic causes

         a. Infant who has an onset of jaundice within the first 24 hours of life

         b. Newborn infant who has rapidly rising levels of bilirubin

         c. Infant who has persistent jaundice and is not thriving

      2. Breastfeeding implications

         a. Breastfeeding does not need to be interrupted

         b. Ineffective breastfeeding can increase the bilirubin levels due to the resultant decreased defecation (causing the delayed passage of bilirubin in the stool; breastfeeding-associated jaundice)

B. Pathologic causes of indirect hyperbilirubinemia

1. Excessive hemolysis:

a. G6PD, hereditary spherocytosis, ABO/Rh incompatibility; bruising—cephalohematoma, or other bruising related to birth trauma (often observed as related to vacuum extraction or forceps delivery)

2. Infection—usually includes increased, direct bilirubin

3. Metabolic/endocrine abnormalities

a. Inborn errors of metabolism, such as galactosemia or hypothyroidism

4. Delayed defecation

a. Intestinal obstruction—meconium ileus; other congenital intestinal anomalies

b. Inadequate intake—breastfeeding-associated jaundice (see following discussion)

C. Feeding management of an infant who has pathologic hyperbilirubinemia

1. Effective breastfeeding

2. Supplement at the breast if the infant has increased caloric needs

3. The only reason to discontinue breastfeeding is galactosemia

**III** Breastfeeding-associated jaundice

These infants are jaundiced due to poor feeds, inadequate caloric intake, and delayed defecation. They might be significantly dehydrated as well, occasionally presenting to the practitioner in a life-threatening condition. Quick appraisal and timely referral to the primary care health provider is a critical component of the lactation consultant's responsibilities.

A. Introduction

1. Physiology

a. An infant who is not feeding effectively experiences jaundice related to the delay in the passage of meconium

b. Meconium contains conjugated bilirubin

c. If the meconium is not passed in a timely manner, the bilirubin can become reabsorbed from the intestine into the bloodstream where it must be conjugated by the liver again to attempt to excrete it

2. Health implications for the infant

a. Ineffective feeding is also associated with inadequate fluid intake and resultant dehydration

b. Severe hyponatremic dehydration can result from the lack of fluid intake; is potentially a life threatening situation

     c. Insufficient caloric and fluid intake results in excessive weight loss that is typically greater than 8 percent below birth weight

     d. Kernicterus can result if the bilirubin levels remain greater than 25–30mg/dL in the term infant

B. Typical infant with breastfeeding-associated jaundice

  1. History

     a. Onset of jaundiced appearance at 48–72 hours of age

     b. Delayed or scant meconium output

     c. Scant urine output

     d. Either infrequent, ineffective feeds or frequent, ineffective feedings

     e. Either lethargic with few requests for feedings or very fussy and not content after feedings

  2. Physical assessment

     a. Thin, jaundiced infant

     b. Lethargic, difficult to arouse or fussy, and difficult to console

  3. Feeding assessment

     a. Problems with latch-on

     b. Scant swallows noted during the feeding

     c. Maternal engorgement might be noted

C. Management (see also Chapter 21, "Slow Weight Gain/Failure to Thrive")

  1. Establish effective breastfeeding techniques and routines

  2. Supplement at the breast as indicated with expressed mother's milk or a human milk substitute

  3. Initiate additional stimulation of the milk supply

  4. Monitoring of bilirubin per primary care provider's instruction

  5. Weight check within 24 hours

  6. If supplement is used, reduce the amount based on the infant's feeding capabilities, weight gain, and hydration status

  7. The child's primary health care provider will make a decision regarding the need for phototherapy or other intervention (refer to Table 18-2)

  8. Although medical therapy might be effective in reducing the bilirubin levels, the infant still needs a careful feeding evaluation and assessment in order to assure adequate hydration and weight gain

D. Prevention

  1. Early initiation of breastfeeding

  2. Frequent breastfeeding

  3. Effective breastfeeding

4. Early follow-up with the primary care provider (within 48–72 hours of birth) for an assessment of the weight, hydration, and breastfeeding effectiveness

E. Education and counseling

1. Explain to the family the reason for the jaundiced color and the implications related to breastfeeding.

2. Teach the family how to determine whether the infant is feeding effectively.

3. Provide the family with written information regarding the clinical indicators of sufficient intake and infant danger signals.

4. Assist the mother with techniques for the stimulation of milk supply:

   a. Frequent, effective feeding; hand or mechanical expression as an adjunct if a supplement has been recommended.

5. If phototherapy is required, advocate the avoidance of mother-infant separation.

6. If a supplement is required, teach the family how to obtain the additional mother's milk.

7. Work with the primary care provider to develop a feeding plan that is individualized to the infant-mother dyad's particular needs.

8. Provide families with a feeding diary to record feelings, supplement amounts, and the infant's output.

F. Evaluation

1. The infant's weight will stabilize, with 15–30g weight gain/day at Day 5–6 of life.

2. Bilirubin levels will decrease with the onset of effective feeding and resultant defecation; normally, there will be a rapid fall in the bilirubin level if effective feeding is established within 12–24 hours, which often eliminates the need for medical therapy.

3. Maternal milk supply will increase as evidenced by infant weight/hydration/defecation patterns and the ability to withdraw the supplement.

4. The breastfeeding relationship will be maintained and strengthened based on the previous parameters.

5. Failure of the infant to improve within 12–24 hours can indicate other underlying problems and a need for reappraisal by the primary care health provider.

III Breast-milk jaundice

Infants who have breast-milk jaundice are healthy breastfed infants who have no pathologic cause of indirect hyperbilirubinemia. They are breastfeeding effectively, have good weight gain, and have no signs or symptoms of illness. The diagnosis of breast-milk jaundice is made by exclusion; that is, other causes of delayed onset hyperbilirubinemia need to be ruled out either by history or laboratory testing.

A. Introduction
    1. Physiology—not well understood
    2. Tends to recur in subsequent infants
    3. No other health implications/risks for the infant

B. History
    1. Onset of jaundice between 5–10 days of age
    2. Other siblings might have experienced this condition
    3. Infant is vigorous, feeding well, and gaining weight

C. Physical assessment
    1. Level of jaundice
    2. Alertness
    3. Assess the weight status

D. Breastfeeding assessment
    1. Expect effective breastfeeding

E. Management
    1. Assure continued, effective breastfeeding
    2. The health provider will decide on the frequency of bilirubin monitoring.
        a. Typically, bilirubin may be monitored until the levels stop rising
        b. An infant who has additional risk factors, such as prematurity or ethnicity, might experience levels requiring phototherapy
        c. Some health providers will interrupt breastfeeding for 12–24 hours
            1. Bilirubin levels will drop precipitously
            2. This situation firmly establishes the diagnosis of breast-milk jaundice
            3. It is not thought to be necessary by most experts
            4. Interruption of breastfeeding might also permanently alter the breastfeeding relationship between the mother and her infant
            5. If phototherapy is required, advocate for the avoidance of mother-infant separation

F. Education and counseling
    1. Reassure the family that the infant is not ill
    2. Work with the primary care provider to develop a breastfeeding plan
    3. If breastfeeding is interrupted, teach the mother how to maintain her milk supply

G. Evaluation
1. Maintenance of the breastfeeding relationship
2. Continued, normal weight gain
3. A gradual decrease in jaundice appearance over 3–12 weeks

# Hypoglycemia

Hypoglycemia in newborn infants is of concern due to the potential detrimental effect that sustained hypoglycemia has on the infant's neurologic outcome. Certain infants have a higher risk for experiencing hypoglycemia. Effective breastfeeding provides the newborn infant with sufficient calories to prevent hypoglycemia in a normal infant. If risk factors are present, the infant's effective breastfeeding and intake of normal amounts of colostrum might not be sufficient to support the newborn's unusual metabolic demands. In these cases, a supplement might be required. The baby's primary health care provider will determine whether calories are best supplied as an oral supplement or by using intravenous glucose infusion.

I Introduction
  A. Physiology
    1. The fetus receives energy continuously via the placenta.
    2. Glycogen reserves that are available for conversion to glucose during the immediate neonatal period are laid down during the later part of the third trimester.
    3. Newborns have a greater demand for glucose than children and adults due to their large brain-to-body weight.
    4. Premature infants have an even greater demand for glucose and have limited to absent glycogen reserves.
    5. Glucose is the primary nutrient for brain metabolism and the maternally derived supply terminates at delivery.
    6. At birth, there is a transition period as glucose homeostasis is established by the infant.
       a. There is a change in glucoregulatory hormones as follows:
          i. Increased epinephrine
          ii. Increased norepinephrine
          iii. Increased glucagon
       b. The net effect is mobilization of glycogen and fatty acids.
       c. The collective activities that maintain glucose homeostasis is called counterregulation, which consists of the following:
          i. Glycogenolysis—the mobilization and release of glycogen from body stores to form glucose

        ii. Gluconeogenesis—the production of glucose by the liver and kidneys from non-carbohydrate substrates such as fatty acids and amino acids

    d. The rate of glucose production is 4-6mg/kg/minute.

        i. 3.7mg/kg/minute is needed to meet the requirements of the brain.

        ii. About 70% is provided by glucose oxidation with the rest being provided from alternative fuels.

        iii. Alternative brain fuels are also produced, such as ketone bodies.

    e. After 12 hours, the baby is dependent on glucose made from milk components (20–50%) and gluconeogenesis to maintain blood glucose (galactose, amino acids, glucerol, lactate) as well as free fatty acids from fat stores and milk.

        i. Breast milk is more ketogenic than formula, enabling the breastfed baby to create high levels of alternative fuels until the milk supply increases enough to draw upon milk components for glucose synthesis.

        ii. High levels of ketone bodies enable breastfed babies to demonstrate lower measured blood glucose levels, but still maintain the optimum production of brain fuels.

  7. Glycogen stores are converted to glucose (glycogenolysis), rapidly depleting glycogen stores over the first hours of life; liver glycogen stores are 90% depleted by three hours and gone by 12 hours.

  8. Fat metabolism provides a glucose substrate beginning at 2–3 days of age.

  9. Hypoglycemia is most likely to occur after the first 2–3 hours of birth, before fat metabolism has begun, and particularly if any other risk factors are present (see below).

  10. Infants who are born prior to 38 completed weeks have limited glycogen reserves.

  11. Infants who have intrauterine growth retardation or who are small for gestational-age infants have limited fat reserves.

  12. Infants of diabetic mothers (who have been producing large amounts of insulin in response to maternal hyperglycemia in utero) quickly deplete their glycogen stores after birth due to hyperinsulinism.

B. Definition of hypoglycemia

  1. No consensus on the definition of hypoglycemia in a full-term infant; hypoglycemia is a continuum of falling blood glucose levels, not an arbitrary number.

  2. The range of recommended level is serum glucose is 25–40mg/dL.

C. Testing for hypoglycemia

  1. AAP recommendations for glucose screening.

    a. Universal screening is not recommended.

    b. Screen infants who are at risk.

2. Which infants should be screened?
   a. Any infant who is symptomatic
      i. Weak cry, apnea, cyanosis, hypothermia, irritability, lethargy, feeding problems, and tremors or seizures
   b. Infants meeting high-risk criteria—large or small for gestational age, infant of a diabetic mother, babies who have been axphyxiated, those with sepsis, cold stress, Rh disease, or with congestive heart failure
3. Which screening method?
   a. Reagent strips/photometry screening methods
      i. Accuracy depends on exactly following the directions
      ii. Significant variability of the results depends on the individual who is performing the test
      iii. The results are affected by hemoglobin values
   b. Confirm abnormal screening results with a serum glucose level sent to a laboratory
   c. Do not delay treatment while waiting for the serum glucose results
D. Health implications for a breastfed infant
   1. Hypoglycemia is linked to later developmental difficulties
   2. Delay in first feeding and ineffective breastfeeding can contribute to the development of hypoglycemia, even in low-risk infants

II Risk factors for hypoglycemia in a full-term newborn
A. Maternal history
   1. Gestational diabetes
   2. Diabetes
   3. Anatomic or physiologic disorders affecting lactogenesis
   4. Hypertension—pregnancy induced or essential
B. Labor and delivery management factors
   1. Maternal intravenous fluids using dextrose and water solutions
   2. Cool room temperature
   3. Separation from mother
   4. Delayed feeding
   5. Crying that is not responded to
C. Infant
   1. Large for gestational age—more than 4,000g
   2. Small for gestational age—under 2,500g
   3. Intrauterine growth retardation
   4. Prematurity (= 37 completed weeks of gestation)

**III** Prevention of hypoglycemia in a newborn infant

    A. Labor and delivery management

        1. If intravenous fluids are used, choose balanced electrolyte solutions rather than dextrose and water for the laboring woman

        2. Have a neutral thermal environment

        3. Avoid cold stress in the infant

            a. Towel dry

            b. Keep skin-to-skin contact with the mother, and cover the dyad

        4. Avoid allowing the baby to cry because crying rapidly depletes glycogen stores

    B. Feeding routine

        1. Early first feeding

        2. Frequent feeding

        3. Assure effective feedings

        4. Avoid a dextrose water complement or supplement

            i. After the first few hours, the major determinant of blood glucose concentration is the interval between feeds

            ii. Babies separated from their mother have lower body temperatures, cry more, and have lower blood glucose levels

    C. Post-discharge follow-up

        1. Perform an early follow-up at 48 hours of age to assure the well being and establishment of effective breastfeeding

        2. Teach families the early symptoms of hypoglycemia

**IV** Implementation and planning

    A. Monitor the infant closely to assess for signs of hypoglycemia

    B. Notify the primary health care provider if the infant is symptomatic

    C. Assure effective breastfeeding

    D. If feeding is ineffective or the infant's glucose levels are low, initiate supplementation according to the health provider's recommendation (expressed mother's milk or human milk substitute is preferred to glucose water for the prevention of rebound hypoglycemia)

    E. Supplement at the breast if the infant is able to feed properly

    F. If the infant unable to sustain suckling at the breast, feed away from the breast by using a method that is best suited to the infant's capabilities and the parents' and provider's preference

        1. The mother can hand express colostrum into a spoon and spoon feed it frequently to her baby

2. The protein and fat in colostrum provide substrates for gluconeogenesis, enhance ketogenesis, and increases gut motility and gastric emptying time which causes a rapid absorption of nutrients

G. The health care provider might prefer to use intravenous glucose if the initial feedings are not sufficient enough to increase the infant's serum glucose level

H. All infants require close monitoring after discharge by either home or office visits with a health care provider at 48–72 hours of age in order to assess well-being

   1. Recent case reports describe breastfed infants who had no other risk factors yet became symptomatic on day three, presenting with seizures at home (Moore and Perlman, 1999). Each of these infants was found to have experienced feeding difficulties

   2. Hume *et al.* (1999) reported on pre-term infants (a gestation of less than or equal to 37 weeks) who were at risk for hypoglycemia at the time of discharge. Their findings stressed the importance of timely feedings to avoid hypoglycemia at home

**V** Education and counseling

A. Explain to the family the short-term feeding implications for an infant who has low blood sugar

B. If supplementation is needed, assist the mother with initiating milk expression

C. Assist the mother in administering oral supplementation if ordered

D. Assure that the family understands the importance of a timely return visit to the health care provider

E. Teach the family the indicators of effective breastfeeding

F. Teach the family the symptoms of hypoglycemia

**VI** Evaluation

A. The infant will be able to maintain blood glucose without the need for supplementation

B. Breastfeeding will be established prior to dismissal from the birthing site

# References—Jaundice and Breastfeeding

Auerbach K, Gertner LM. Breastfeeding and human milk: Their association with jaundice in the neonate. *Clinics in Perinatology* 1987; 14(1):89–107.

Cooper WO, Atherton HD, Kahana M, Kotagal UR. Increased incidence of severe breastfeeding malnutrition and hypernatremia in a metropolitan area. *Pediatrics* 1995; 96(5):957–960.

DeCarvalho M, Hall M, Havey D. Effects of water supplementation on physiological jaundice in breastfed babies. *Arch Dis Child* 1981; 56:568–569.

DeCarvalho M, Kalus MH, Merkatz RB. Frequency of breastfeeding and serum bilirubin concentration. *Am J Dis Child* 1982; 136:737–738.

Elander G, Lindberg T. Hospital routines in infants with hyperbilirubinmeia influence the duration of breastfeeding. *Acta Paed Scand* 1986; 75:798–812.

Gartner LM. On the question of the relationship between breastfeeding and jaundice in the first 5 days of life. *Semin Perinatol* 1994; 18(6):502–509.

Gourley GR, Kreamer K, Cohnen M, Kosorok MR. Neonatal Jaundice and diet. *Archives Pediatr Adolescent Med* 1999; 153:184–188.

Grunebaum E, Amir J, Merlob P, Mimouni M, Varsano I. Breast milk jaundice: Natural history, familial incidence and late neurodevelopmental outcome of the infant. *Eur J Pediatr* 1991; 150:267–270.

James JM, Williams SD, Osborn LM. Discontinuation of breast-feeding infrequence among jaundiced neonates tested at home. *Pediatrics* 1993; 153–155.

Johnson JD, Angelus P, Aldrich M, Skipper BJ. Exaggerated jaundice in Navajo neonates. *Am J Dis Child* 1986; 140:889–890.

Kemper KJ, Forsyth BW, McCarthy P. Jaundice, terminating breastfeeding and the vulnerable child. *Pediatrics* 1989; 84(5):773–775.

Kemper KJ, Forsyth BW, McCarthy P. Persistent perceptions of vulnerability following neonatal jaundice. *Am J Dis Child* 1990; 144:238–241.

Maisels, MJ, Gifford K. Normal serum bilirubin levels in the newborn and the affect of breastfeeding. *Pediatrics* 1986; 78(5):837–843.

Martinez JC, Garcia HO, Otheguy LE, Drummond GS, Kappas A. Control of severe hyperbilirubinemia in full-term newborns with the inhibitor of bilirubin production Sn-mesoporphyrin. *Pediatrics* 1999; 103(1):1–5.

Martinez JC, Maisels MJ, Otheguy L, Garcia H, Savorani M, Mogni B, Martinez JC Jr. Hyperbilirubinemia in the breast-fed newborn: A controlled trial of four interventions. *Pediatrics* 1993; 91:470–473.

Newman TB, Klebanoff MA. Hyperbilirubinemia and long-term outcome. *Pediatrics* 1993; 92(5):651–657.

Newman TB, Maisels MJ. Evaluation and treatment of jaundice in the term newborn: A kinder, gentler approach. *Pediatrics* 1992; 89:809–818.

Provisional Committee for Quality Improvement and Subcommittee on Hyperbilirubinemia. Practice parameter: Management of hyperbilirubinemia in the healthy term newborn. *Pediatrics* 1994; 94(4):558–565.

Seidman DS, Stevenson DK, Ergaz Z, Gale R. Hospital readmission due to neonatal hyperbilirubinemia. *Pediatrics* 1995; 96(4):727–729.

Sward-Comunelli S, Welhoelter J, Harris K, Hall RT. Bilirubin levels and weight change in infants with early hospital discharge versus prolonged hospital stay. *J Perinatol* 1996; 16(1):211–214.

Ymauchi Y, Yamanouchi I. Breastfeeding frequency during the first 24 hours after birth in full-term neonates. *Pediatrics* 1990; 86(2):171–175.

## References—Hypoglycemia

Academy of Breastfeeding Medicine. Guidelines for glucose monitoring and treatment in term breastfed neonates. *ABM News and Views* 1999; 5(4).

Cole MD, Peevy K. Hypoglycemia in normal neonates appropriate for gestational age. *J Perinatol* 1994; 14(2):118–120.

Committee on the Fetus and Newborn. Routine evaluation of blood pressure, hematocrit, and glucose in newborns. *Pediatrics* 1993; 92(3):474–476.

Cornblath M, Schwartz R, Aynsley-Green A, Lloyd JK. Hypoglycemia in infancy: The need for a rational definition. *Pediatrics* 1990; 85(5):834–837.

Cornblath M, Hawdon JM, Williams AF, et al. Controversies regarding definition of neonatal hypoglycemia: Suggested operational thresholds. *Pediatrics* 2000; 105:1141–1145.

Christensson K, Siles C, Moreno L, Belaustequi A, De La Fuente P, Lagercrantz H, Puyol P, Winberg J. Temperature, metabolic adaption and crying in healthy full-term newborns cared for skin-to skin or in a cot. *Acta Paediatr* 1992; 81:488–493.

Duvanel C, Fawer CL, Cotting J, Hohlfeld P, Matthiew JM. Long-term effects of neonatal hypoglycemia on brain growth and psychomotor development in small-for-gestational-age preterm infants. *J Pediatr* 1999; 134:492–498.

Holtrop BC. The frequency of hypoglycemia in full-term large and small for gestational age newborns. *Am J Perinatol* 1993; 10(2):150–154.

Hume R, NcGeechan A, Burchell A. Failure to detect preterm infants at risk of hypoglycemia before discharge. *J Pediatr* 1999; 134:499–502.

Hunter DJS, Burrows RF, Mohide PT, Whyte RK. Influence of maternal insulin-dependent diabetes mellitus on neonatal morbidity. *Can Med Assoc J* 1993; 149(1):47–52.

Moore AM, Perlman M. Symptomatic hypoglycemia in otherwise healthy, breastfed term newborns. *Pediatrics* 1999; 103:837–839.

Nylander G, Lindemann R, Helsing E, Bendvold R. Unsupplemented breastfeeding in the maternity ward. *Acta Obstet Gynecol Scand* 1991; 70:205–209.

Samson LF. Infants of diabetic mothers: Current perspectives. *J Perinat Neonat Nurs* 1992; 6(1):61–70.

Schwartz R. Neonatal hypoglycemia: Back to basics in diagnosis and treatment. *Diabetes* 1991; 40(Suppl.2):71.

World Health Organization. Hypoglycaemia of the newborn. Geneva: WHO, 1997.

# Congenital Anomalies, Neurological Involvement, and Birth Trauma

*Marsha Walker, RN, IBCLC*

## Objectives

- Discuss how congenital anomalies, neurological impairments, and birth trauma can affect early breastfeeding.
- List strategies for assisting these babies with going to the breast.

## Introduction

A number of conditions that present at birth or shortly thereafter can have a significant impact on the initiation and duration of breastfeeding. Some of these conditions are temporary while others will remain for a lifetime. Compromised babies especially benefit from the provision of breast milk and/or breastfeeding. A few babies will be unable to feed at the breast, but provision of breast milk for them can and should continue as long as possible. Some of these conditions will first be brought to the attention of a health care provider due to poor feeding, with the inability to breastfeed being a marker or symptom of the problem. Mothers of these babies can experience an enormous range of emotions. They might be frightened, frustrated, anxious, fatigued, angry, or depressed. Their emotional well-being should not be neglected in the flurry of activity surrounding the baby.

I Postmature infants—born at the onset of week 42 of gestation

  A. These infants are fully mature infants who have remained in utero beyond the time of optimal placental function.

  B. Aging of the placenta and reduced placental function impairs nutrient and oxygen transport to the fetus, placing the fetus at risk for a lower tolerance to the stresses of labor and delivery, including hypoxia.

  1. In response to hypoxia, meconium might be passed, increasing the risk for meconium aspiration.

2. Amniotic fluid might be decreased, increasing the risk for meconium aspiration, umbilical cord compression, and accidents.

C. If the placenta continues to function, the baby might become large for gestational age (LGA)—increasing the risk for shoulder dystocia and possibly resulting in a fractured clavicle.

D. Post-term infants are characterized by the following:

1. Loss of weight in utero

2. Dry, peeling skin that appears to hang due to the loss of subcutaneous fat and muscle mass

3. A wrinkled, wide-eyed appearance

4. Lack of vernix caseosa

5. Lack of glycogen stores in the liver

E. These babies might be initially hypoglycemic, requiring them to be placed at the breast early and often; mothers can be advised to use alternate massage to assure the intake of colostrum.

F. These babies might feed poorly, appear lethargic, and require considerable incentives to sustain suckling, including alternate massage, expressed colostrum incentives, skin-to-skin contact (especially as their body temperature is quite labile), and avoidance of crying episodes, which can further drop their blood glucose levels.

II Birth trauma

A. The use of forceps might result in small areas of ecchymosis on the sides of the face where the blades were placed.

B. Trauma to the facial nerves can be sustained; any muscles enervated by these nerves might temporarily show hypotonia, making latching and sucking difficult; observe for an asymmetric movement of the mouth, a drooping mouth, or a drooping eyelid.

C. Vacuum-assisted deliveries can pose an increased risk of brain damage to babies.

1. Any number of cranial hemorrhages can result from vacuum extraction.

   a. Extracranial hemorrhage (bleeding between the skin and cranial bone)

      i. Caput seccedaneum—hemorrhagic edema of the soft tissues of the scalp, usually resolving within the first week of life; usually poses no problem to breastfeeding.

      ii. Cephalhematoma—bleeding is contained within the subperiosteal space, preventing it from crossing suture lines.

      iii. Subgaleal hemorrhage can represent a significant blood loss to the infant; it presents as a fluctuant area of the scalp, sometimes increasing in size to the point of blood dissecting into the subcutaneous tissue of the back of the neck; these babies will need special help in positioning to keep pressure off the hemorrhagic area; some infants feed poorly or not at all until some of the hemorrhage has resolved; this condition presents an increased risk for high bilirubin levels as the body processes and breaks down the blood.

   b. Intracranial hemorrhage—is not visible

      i. The baby might present with common signs such as sleepiness, feeding intolerance, and decreased muscle tone.

      ii. Subdural hemorrage is the most common intracranial hemorrhage resulting from a traumatic delivery.

      iii. Some of the signs and symptoms become evident following discharge; babies who have a history of vacuum extraction that demonstrate lethargy, feeding problems, hypotonia, increased irritability, diffuse swelling of the head, and pallor need an immediate follow up.

      iv. Poor breastfeeding might be one of the first signs of this type of problem.

D. Fractured clavicle—can occur with an LGA infant or with malpresentations of the baby.

   1. The baby might display a decreased movement of the arm or distress with arm movements; the arm and shoulder will be immobilized and special positioning might be needed in order to breastfeed the baby.

   2. Some babies are not diagnosed until after discharge when certain positions are noted to cause crying in the baby; the clutch hold or placing the baby on the unaffected side at each breast might be helpful.

**III** Inborn errors of metabolism

A. Galactosemia—caused by a deficiency of the enzyme galactose-1-phosphate uridyltransferase, causing an inability in the infant to metabolize galactose.

   1. The infant can have severe and persistent jaundice, vomiting, diarrhea, electrolyte imbalance, cerebral involvement, and weight loss.

   2. These babies are weaned from the breast to a special formula.

B. Phenylketonuria (PKU)—the most common of the amino acid metabolic disorders; an autosomal, recessive, inherited disorder where the amino acid, phenylalinine, accumulates due to the absence of the enzyme that is necessary to break it down.

   1. Newborn screening for PKU is done in all 50 states in the United States and in more than 30 other countries.

   2. Babies need some phenylalinine.

   3. Infants who have PKU can continue to breastfeed when a balance is maintained between the use of a phenylalinine-free formula and breast milk.

   4. Human milk has lower levels of phenylalinine than standard commercial formulas.

5. Breastfed infants who receive a daily amount of 362ml of breast milk during the first month and 464ml of breast milk during the fourth month have lower levels of phenylalinine than infants who are fed exclusively on the low phenyalinine formula for the first six months.

6. The amount of phenylalinine-free formula and breast milk can be calculated by weight, age, blood levels, and the need for growth.

7. Another approach is to feed the baby 10–30ml of the special formula followed by breastfeeding; as long as phenylalinine levels are properly maintained, the exact calculations of breast milk and formula might not need to be made; breast milk might be more than half of the diet, giving the baby many of the advantages of breast milk.

8. Breastfeeding before diagnosis and dietary intervention has been shown to produce a higher IQ in the babies who are fed breast milk during the prediagnostic stage.

C. Cystic fibrosis (CF) is a congenital disease involving a generalized dysfunction of exocrine glands.

1. The glands produce abnormally thick and sticky secretions that block the flow of pancreatic digestive enzymes, clog hepatic ducts, and affect the movement of the cilia in the lungs.

2. Increased sodium chloride in the child's sweat is frequently the first indicator of the condition; the baby tastes salty when nuzzled.

3. Another early indicator of CF is intestinal obstruction or ileus; the meconium blocks the small intestine, resulting in abdominal distension, vomiting, and failure to pass stools (resulting in the failure to gain weight).

4. Babies who have CF produce normal amounts of gastric lipase, which combined with the milk lipase in breast milk enhances fat absorption.

5. Babies who have CF are prone to respiratory infections and benefit greatly from the disease-protective factors in breast milk.

6. Pancreatic enzymes can be given to the baby.

7. There is no need to interrupt breastfeeding.

D. Infants who have neurologic impairments often have extremely complex needs.

1. The infant's nervous system can be damaged, abnormally developed, immature, or rendered temporarily immature from insults such as asphyxia, sepsis, trauma, or drugs.

2. Infants can have an absent or depressed rooting reflex, gagging reflex, sucking reflex, or swallowing reflex.

3. Giving a bottle to a baby who is to be breastfed provides inconsistent sensory input that additionally disorganizes the nervous system.

4. A depressed or absent sucking reflex, where infants might exhibit a limited response to stimulation at the juncture of the hard and soft palate and to the tongue; these babies might have decreased muscle tone.

5. A weak sucking reflex or a poorly sustained one; the oral musculature is weakened to the point of the inability to sustain a rhythmic suck; the rhythm is interrupted by irregular pauses and sometimes a lack of the 1:1 suck-swallow cycle; adequate negative intraoral pressure is not generated, enabling the nipple to fall out of the mouth; lips do not form a complete seal; the hypotonic tongue might remain flat or bunched, not cupping around the breast.

6. Incoordinated sucking includes a mistiming of the muscle movements for the suck-swallow cycle; might see excessive movements of the mouth, head, or neck; hypersensitivity might be seen in other areas of the body; infant might have dysfunctional tongue, experience choking, and an uncoordinated swallowing.

7. Down syndrome—results from an extra chromosome at the 21 position (Trisomy 21).

   a. Common characteristics that relate to feeding include the following:

      i. A flaccid tongue that appears too large for the mouth

      ii. Generalized hypotonia, including the oral musculature

      iii. Heart defects that might require surgery

      iv. Incomplete development of the gastrointestinal (GI) tract

      v. Hyperbilirubinemia is common

      vi. Especially prone to infection

      vii. Might have a depressed sucking reflex or a weak suck, or both

   b. Babies who have Down syndrome do much better with stimulation, body contact, and communication activities—all of which are provided at the breast.

   c. Some babies have no problem sucking while others might exhibit initial sucking difficulties.

   d. Depending on the extent of the involvement, mothers might need to express colostrum and milk, place the baby skin-to-skin with short get-acquainted sessions at the breast, or place colostrum in the baby's mouth as an incentive; tube feeding devices can initially serve for supplementing at the breast and for the coordination of sucking; gentle stroking around the baby's lips and rhythmic stroking of the front half of the tongue might help prepare the baby for the breast.

   e. Positioning of the baby at the breast is important so as not to interfere with the suck-swallow rhythm through stress on the shoulder girdle; babies might benefit from being held in a nearly horizontal position across-the-lap with the hips at or near head level.

f. The Dancer hand position can benefit many of these babies because it stabilizes the jaw and supports the masseter muscles, which decreases the intra-oral space and enhances the generation of negative pressure.

g. The breast is supported by the third, fourth, and fifth fingers so that the thumb and index finger are free to form a "V" or "U"-shaped cup on which the baby's chin rests.

h. The thumb and index finger press the cheeks gently to cause them to come into contact with the breast.

i. The baby should be in a quiet alert state in order to feed.

j. The infant might need hindmilk supplementation in order to gain weight and to benefit from the use of a supplementer to deliver it.

8. Fetal distress and hypoxia (decreased levels of oxygen)

a. Infants can be compromised in utero or during delivery from low levels of oxygen due to the following:

   i. Insufficient placental reserve

   ii. Umbilical cord compression

   iii. Umbilical cord prolapse

b. Will see low Apgar scores at birth.

c. Asphyxiated infants usually cannot be fed by mouth for 48 hours.

d. If severely affected, it might be up to 96 hours before these infants can safely tolerate food in the gastrointestinal tract.

e. Colostrum is very important to this baby, because his or her GI tract might have suffered hypoxic damage; colostrum should be expressed and used as soon as the baby can tolerate feedings by mouth; mothers should frequently hand express or pump during this time.

f. Hypoxia decreases the motility of the gut and reduces the gut-stimulating hormones.

g. These infants might have a depressed suck that is not well coordinated with the swallow, and they might not do better on bottles.

h. Mothers might need to use a supplementer device, cup, or dropper to avoid nipple preference.

i. The baby might do better in a clutch hold using the Dancer hand position for jaw stability.

j. The baby might be hypertonic and should be held in a flexed position.

k. Breastfeeding interventions are similar to those for the baby who has Down syndrome.

E. Gastrointestinal tract disorders

    1. Gastroesophageal Reflux (GER)—persistent, non-projectile regurgitation (spitting-up) seen after feeds

        a. Can be mild and self-limiting, requiring no modification or interventions

        b. Can be more severe, with worsening regurgitation and weight gain or loss problems

        c. Can present as follows:

            i. Fussiness at the breast as stomach acids bathe the lower section of the esophagus

            ii. Might be more apparent in certain side-lying positions at the breast

            iv. Mothers might report increased fussing at the breast, a baby who arches off or pulls away from the breast, or a baby who cries until placed upright

            v. Descriptions of choking or coughing

            vi. Upper-respiratory infections and congestion

            vii. Feeding refusal

            viii. Micro- and macroaspiration

        d. Mothers are encouraged to keep providing breast milk, nurse the baby in an upright position (in clutch hold or straddled across her lap), nurse on one breast at each feeding to keep from over-distending the stomach, feed frequently, and keep the baby upright after feedings

        e. If the reflux is severe, the baby might undergo diagnostic tests and be placed on medication

F. Pyloric stenosis—a stricture or narrowing of the pylorus (muscular tissue controlling the outlet of the stomach)

    1. It usually occurs between the second and sixth week of life, although it can occur any time after birth.

    2. Vomiting is characteristic, intermittent at first, progressing to after every feeding, and projectile in nature.

    3. Dehydration, electrolyte imbalance, and weight loss can occur in extreme situations.

    4. If the baby does not out grow the condition or if it is severe, surgery can be performed after rehydration and correction of electrolytes.

        a. Infants can go back to the breast in six to eight hours if the duodenum is not entered; if it is, delay in breastfeeding could last several days (during which the mother should pump her milk).

        b. A breastfed baby can resume nursing earlier than a bottle-fed baby who is consuming formula due to the faster emptying time of the stomach and the lack of hard curd formation as seen with formula.

      c. Mothers should feed with one breast initially after surgery to prevent overfilling of the stomach; these limited feedings gradually expand the stomach and can be advanced as the baby tolerates it.

      d. Mothers can place the baby in an infant seat while breastfeeding to avoid positional aggravation.

G. Congenital heart defects are seen along a continuum of mild with no symptoms to severe with cyanosis, rapid breathing, shortness of breath, and lowered oxygen levels (desaturation) that requires surgical correction.

   1. Cardiac disease is not a medical indication to interrupt or cease breastfeeding.

   2. Feeding at the breast presents less work for the baby, keeps oxygen levels higher than with bottle-feeding, and keeps heart and respiratory rates stable when the baby is at the breast.

   3. A baby who has more serious heart involvement might be either unable to sustain sucking at the breast or might need to pause frequently in order to rest; if intake is inadequate, the baby will not gain weight or will exhibit weight loss.

   4. Mothers might describe these babies in any number of ways, including the following:

      a. Able to sustain sucking for only short periods of time

      b. Pulling off the breast frequently

      c. Turning blue around the lips (circumoral cyanosis)

      d. Rapid breathing; rapid heart rate

      e. Sweating while at the breast

      f. Requires very frequent feedings

   5. If surgery is planned, it is typically after the baby reaches a certain weight and/or age.

      a. Small, frequent feeds might be necessary

      b. If additional calories are needed, consider hindmilk supplementation at the breast with a supplementer device

H. Sudden Infant Death Syndrome (SIDS), also known as crib death or cot death, is the leading cause of death in infants who are older than one month in developed countries; rates vary worldwide.

   1. The etiology is unknown; it seems multi-causal.

   2. The sleeping position dramatically affects the rates. Babies placed on their backs (supine) are less prone to SIDS.

   3. The majority of deaths occur between 2 and 6 months of age with a peak at about 10 weeks of age.

   4. Breastfed infants have lower rates of SIDS than bottle-fed infants, but they can still experience the condition.

5. Breastfeeding offers dose-response protection across race and socio-economic levels; it is associated with a 50 percent reduction in risk.

6. Frederickson found that the risk of SIDS increased 19 percent for every month of not breastfeeding and 100 percent for every month of non-exclusive breastfeeding.

7. SIDS rates are higher among mothers who smoke; breastfeeding by a smoking mother reduces the rates to that equal of a bottle-fed baby.

8. The exact protective mechanism is not well understood; breastfeeding reduces minor infections such as acute upper-respiratory infections and diarrheal infections that are frequently associated with SIDS; breastfeeding and breast milk enhance the development of the central nervous system and the brain stem, which might also hold a protective effect.

9. Breastfeeding, supine sleep positioning, and co-sleeping all contribute to lower rates of SIDS and might have a synergistic effect.

# References

Berube M. Ask the expert: Gastroesophageal reflux. *JSPN* 1997; 2:43–46.

Boekel S. Gastroesophageal reflux disease (GERD) and the breastfeeding baby. Independent Study Module. Raleigh, NC: International Lactation Consultant Association, 2000.

Cannella PC, Bowser EK, Guyer LK, et al. Feeding practices and nutrition recommendations for infants with cystic fibrosis. *J Am Diet Assoc* 1993; 93:297.

Catto-Smith AG. Gastroesophageal reflux in children. *Australian Fam Phys* 1998; 27:465–473.

Cavlovich FE. Subgaleal hemorrhage in the neonate. *JOGNN* 1994; 24:397–404.

Clark BJ. After a positive Guthrie—what next? Dietary management for the child with phenylketonuria. *Eur J Clin Nutr* 1992; 46 (Suppl I): S33.

Danner SC. Breastfeeding the neurologically impaired infant. NAACOG's clinical issues in perinatal and women's health nursing: Breastfeeding 1992; 3(4):640–646.

Ernest AE, McCabe ERB, Neifert MR, et al. Guide to breast feeding the infant with PKU. Washington, D.C.: U.S. Government Printing Office, 1980.

FDA Public Health Advisory: Need for caution when using vacuum assisted delivery devices. May 21, 1998.

Frederickson DD, Sorenson JR, Biddle AK, et al. Relationship of sudden infant death syndrome to breastfeeding duration and intensity. *Am J Dis Child* 1993; 147:460.

Luder E, Kattan M, Tanzer-Torres G, et al. Current recommendations for breastfeeding in cystic fibrosis centers. *Am J Dis Child* 1990; 144:1153.

McBride MC, Danner SC. Sucking disorders in neurologically impaired infants. *Clin Perinatol* 1987; 14:109–130.

McVea KLSP, Turner PD, Peppler DK. The role of breastfeeding in sudden infant death syndrome. *J Hum Lact* 2000; 16:13–20.

Steinbach MT. Traumatic birth injury—intracranial hemorrhage. *Mother Baby J* 1999; 4:5–14.

# ORAL PATHOLOGY: CLINICAL ASSESSMENT OF THE BREASTFEEDING INFANT

*Barbara Wilson-Clay, BSEd, IBCLC*

## OBJECTIVES

- Identify abnormal infant oral anatomy and discuss its effect upon breastfeeding.
- List the oral feeding reflexes and describe their abnormal presentations.
- Discuss coordination of the suck-swallow-breathe triad in breastfeeding.
- Discuss the issue of the "fit" between the infant's oral anatomy and the mother's breast.

## Introduction

The structures and function of the mouth influence feeding behavior and later dentition, speech, and appearance. An understanding of normal appearance and function clarifies abnormal presentations.

I  Chapter overview

   A. Oral assessment of the breastfeeding infant includes the following:

      1. Observation of the infant's oral anatomy

         a. Lips

         b. Cheeks

         c. Jaws

         d. Tongue

         e. Palate

         f. Nasal passages

      2. Identification of abnormal infant oral anatomy and function

      3. Observation of infant feeding reflexes and their abnormal presentations

         a. Rooting reflex

    b. Sucking reflex

       i. An absent suck

       ii. A weak suck

       iii. An uncoordinated suck

    c. Swallowing reflex

    d. Gag reflex

    e. Cough reflex

  4. Observation of rhythmicity and effectiveness of feeding (coordination of the suck-swallow-breathe triad)

  5. Observation of the "fit" between the infant's mouth and the mother's nipple

B. Abnormal infant oral anatomy can challenge breastfeeding by altering normal oral function. Abnormal variations that the *lactation consultant* (LC) might encounter include the following:

  1. Cleft palate

  2. Cleft lip

  3. Ankyloglossia (tongue-tie)

  4. Tight labial (upper lip) frenum

  5. High arched palate/grooved or channel palate

  6. Receding chin

  7. Small nasal passages

C. Counseling the parents of an infant who breastfeeds poorly due to anatomical and/or neuromuscular issues

  1. The issue of chronic grief

  2. Protecting the milk supply

D. Case study of a breastfeeding infant who has Turner Syndrome

  1. Anatomical/neuromuscular issues

    a. Channel palate

    b. Low muscle tone/weakness of suck

    c. Coincidental tongue-tie

  2. Maternal challenges

    a. Chronic sore nipples

    b. Increased work connected with feeding

    c. Long-term pumping

  3. Delayed initiation of solids

    a. Outcome at 32 months postpartum

**II** Oral assessment of the breastfeeding infant

   A. Anatomy of the infant oral cavity

     The mouth plays a role in feeding, respiration, and speech, and the oral structures change over time with maturation and growth (Bosma, 1977). Oral structure and function can be affected by injury, congenital malformation, neurological deficits, prematurity, or illness, and these can negatively impact breastfeeding (Ogg, 1975; and Wolf and Glass, 1992).

    1. The lips (Wolf and Glass, 1992; Morris, 1977; and Ogg, 1975)

       a. Assist in drawing the nipple into the mouth.

       b. Work with the tongue to form a seal around the nipple.

       c. Help stabilize the nipple in the mouth.

       d. Flange and seal smoothly around the breast during breastfeeding.

       e. A poor lip seal can result in a loss of liquid during feeding; reflects poor motoric/muscular control of the lips.

       f. A poor lip seal is often revealed as intermittent breaks in suction with resultant smacking sounds.

       g. Low muscle tone or weakness (due to prematurity or a number of other neuromuscular issues or due to illness) can make maintaining a lip seal difficult.

       h. Assessment of lip tone includes gentle digital pressure against the lip; some resistance to this pressure should be felt.

       i. In infants who are younger than 3 months of age, drooling is uncommon and is associated with poor lip closure and weak swallowing.

       j. Jaw excursions that are too wide can also cause breaks in the lip seal.

       k. Abnormal tongue movements can break the lip seal; this problem occurs with the tongue, not with the lips.

       l. A poor lip seal impairs the amount of suction that the infant can generate; feeding efficiency is diminished and the work of feeding is increased.

       m. Tight lips (lip retraction or lip pursing) complicate latch-on and reveal instability.

       n. Sucking blisters are common but not normal.

         i. Caused by friction trauma from a retracted upper lip.

         ii. Can also be caused by a tight upper labial frenum pulling the lip under.

       o. The brief use of a firm pressure stimulus (tapping, stretching) of the lips prior to feeding might improve tone and improve the lip seal (Alper and Manno, 1996).

       p. Lip tone typically improves as the infant matures or recovers unless the underlying cause is an enduring neurological disorder or is related to a structural anomaly.

2. The cheeks (Wolf and Glass, 1992)
   a. Subcutaneous fat of the cheeks provides structural support for oral and pharyngeal function.
   b. Fat pads in the cheek are key to this stability.
   c. Poorly developed fat pads (prematurity or low birth weight) result in difficulty creating sufficient suction.
   d. Lack of cheek stability is revealed by collapsing of the cheeks during feeding.
   e. Cheek stability influences lip seal.
   f. Facial hypotonia (low tone) and weakness contribute to poor cheek stability.
   g. The use of external counter-pressure applied to the cheeks during feeding (Dancer's hand) can improve cheek stability.
3. The jaws (Palmer, 1993; and Wolf and Glass, 1992)
   a. Provide stability for the tongue, lips, and cheeks.
   b. As the jaw opens, the size of the sealed oral cavity increases, helping to create negative pressure (suction).
   c. The jaw position is normally neutral, with upper and lower gums approximating.
   d. A receding jaw can be familial, associated with chromosomal disorders, or can result from intrauterine positioning that prevents the jaw from growing forward (as in certain breech presentations).
   e. A receding jaw positions the tongue posteriorly, where it might lead to obstruction of the airway.
   f. A receding jaw can contribute to sore nipples unless the infant's head is tipped in order to bring the chin in closer to the breast.
   g. Normal jaw movements are rhythmic and graded (in other words, the excursions are neither too wide or too narrow).
   h. Abnormally wide jaw excursions can
      i. Cause breaks in the seal
      ii. Result in a loss of suction
      iii. Increase the work of feeding
      iv. Decrease infant intake
   i. Asymmetries of the jaw can be associated with the following:
      i. Asymmetrical muscle tone
      ii. Injuries
      iii. Torticollis
      iv. Abnormal jaw development

j. Jaw clenching or thrusting generally reflects hypertonia and can result in sore nipples/breasts.

k. Jaw clenching can be secondary to poor tongue function (in other words, compensatory action to hold the nipple in the mouth).

l. Neck position can affect jaw function (hyperextension and hyperflexion decrease jaw stability).

m. More appropriate postural support (hip flexion and the head in a more neutral position) can facilitate feeding.

n. Premature infants often have jaw instability due to immature muscles and low muscle tone.

   i. External jaw support (Dancer's hand) can facilitate jaw stability and control the distance of jaw excursions.

4. The tongue (Wolf and Glass, 1992; and Palmer, 1993)

a. Draws in the nipple and shapes it during feeding.

b. Helps seal the oral cavity.

c. When the tongue drops, the oral cavity enlarges—facilitating the creation of suction (negative pressure).

d. Tongue compression expresses milk out of the nipple (positive pressure).

e. The formation of a central groove provides a channel that organizes the bolus of milk for swallowing.

f. Is normally soft, thin, and flat with a rounded tip and good tone (a digital exam consists of gentle pressure on the mid-section; the tongue should press up against the finger).

g. Can extend beyond the lower lip line and lift past the mid-line of the oral cavity (a tap to the tip should elicit tongue protrusion).

h. Can lateralize (the tongue should seek the finger as it moves from side to side).

i. The normal tongue has good tone and will cup around a gloved finger and move rhythmically (formation of a central groove around the examiner's finger).

j. Abnormal presentations of the tongue

   i. Bunched or retracted tongues will not easily form a central groove.

   ii. Micrognathia (a receding jaw) can cause tongue retraction.

   iii. Abnormally high muscle tone can cause tongue retraction.

   iv. Tongue-tip elevation can make insertion of the nipple difficult.

   v. Low muscle tone can produce tongue protrusion (as in Down syndrome) and poor tongue coordination.

   vi. Tongue asymmetry can occur as a result of injury (forceps injury to the nerves innervating the tongue) or from syndromic conditions.

vii. Sometimes poor head position can negatively influence tongue position and will improve with more postural stability in the feeding positions.

viii. When the tongue moves improperly, the baby cannot suck, swallow, or breathe efficiently.

ix. Conversely, problems with free range of motion or with swallowing and breathing can make the baby compensate by using improper tongue movements.

5. The palate (Wolf and Glass, 1992)

   a. Provides stability to the structures of the mouth.

   b. Helps position the nipple in the mouth.

   c. The hard palate opposes the tongue, helping to compress the nipple.

   d. The soft palate drops when the posterior tongue rises to seal off the oral cavity during sucking (creation of suction).

   e. The soft palate lifts during swallowing to seal off the nasal cavity.

   f. The slope of the palate should be moderate and smooth.

   g. The palate should be intact.

   h. The palate should approximate the shape of the tongue.

   i. Nasal regurgitation of milk or excessive stuffiness might indicate poor soft palate seal/function that has resulted in aspiration during feeding.

   j. Prematurity and low muscle tone caused for other reasons can result in weak soft palate function.

      i. Stamina might influence soft palate function with a greater risk of aspiration as the baby becomes fatigued.

      ii. Long periods of intubation can create grooves in the palate.

      iii. Syndromic conditions (such as Turner Syndrome) can create grooved palates (Lawrence et al., 1999).

   k. Familial narrow, arched, or grooved palates can occur.

      i. Unusually shaped palates can create feeding difficulties for some infants.

6. The nasal passages (Alper and Manno, 1996; and Wolf and Glass, 1992)

   a. Should be assessed if breathing appears congested.

   b. Rarely, abnormally small nasal openings are observed.

   c. More commonly, congestion in the absence of a respiratory illness is associated with aspirated "debris" from feedings.

      i. Could be caused by a swallowing disorder.

      ii. Perhaps the infant is unable to self-pace respirations with swallows, and aspiration occurs when the infant "runs out of air."

       iii.  Reflux can cause aspiration between feedings.

       iv.  Overactive letdown can cause choking and aspiration.

B.  Infant feeding reflexes (Radtka, 1977)

    1.  The rooting reflex

       a.  Helps the baby locate the nipple.

       b.  Is present at birth; extinguishes between 2–4 months of age (although it can persist longer in breastfed infants) (Morris, 1997).

       c.  If absent or diminished, can signal poor tactile receptivity or poor neural integration.

       d.  If excessive, hypersensitivity can interfere with latching on.

    2.  The sucking reflex (Wolf and Glass, 1992)

       a.  Observed in utero as early as 15–18 weeks gestation.

       b.  Sucking with strength, rhythmicity, and stability sufficient to sustain effective feeding generally reported at 34–35 weeks gestational age.

          i.  Some infants can sustain effective feeding at these ages only for brief periods of time; fatigue abnormally shortens feeds (milk supply protection, close growth monitoring, and supplementation might be considered necessary) (Alper and Manno, 1996).

       c.  Sucking is stimulated by pressure (and perhaps chemical receptors) on the tongue and stroking of the posterior palate (the junction of the hard and soft palates).

       d.  Absent or diminished sucking might indicate the following (McBride et al., 1987):

          i.  Central nervous system (CNS) immaturity (prematurity, delayed maturation)

         ii.  CNS maldevelopment (various trisomies)

         ii.  Prenatal CNS insults (drugs in labor, asphyxia, trauma, and so on)

         iv.  Systemic congenital problems (heart disease, sepsis, and hypothyroidism)

       e.  A weak suck might indicate the following (McBride and Danner, 1987):

          i.  CNS abnormalities associated with hypotonia

         ii.  Medullary lesions

        iii.  Myasthenia gravis or botulism

         iv.  Abnormalities of the muscle; weak oral and buccal musculature

       f.  Discoordinated sucking is marked by a mistiming of normal movements or is marked by interference by hyperactive reflexes (McBride and Danner, 1987).

          i.  Can result from asphyxia

         ii.  Can result from cerebral insults in the perinatal period

       iii.  Can result from CNS maldevelopment

g. The inability to suck normally can result in impaired intake and poor growth.

h. The LC must be able to identify nutritive suck (NS) and non-nutritive suck (NNS) (Palmer, 1993; and Alper and Manno, 1996).

i. NS

  i. Organized into a series of sucking bursts and pauses.

  ii. During sucking bursts, breathing is interspersed with sucking and swallowing, so the sucking rate is slower than NNS (the ratio is one suck/second).

j. NNS

  i. Characterized by fast, shallow sucks (the ratio is two sucks/second).

  ii. Swallowing occurs infrequently.

k. The normal, term infant can sustain at least two minutes of coordinated, rhythmic nutritive sucking (Palmer, 1993).

3. The swallowing reflex (Wolf and Glass, 1992)

a. Develops early in fetal life (12–14 weeks gestation).

b. Triggered by the delivery of a bolus of fluid to the back of the tongue.

c. Also triggered by chemical receptors in the tongue.

d. Abnormalities of the tongue and palate can create problems with swallowing that lead to a risk of aspiration.

e. Swallowing dysfunction can lead to poor weight gain and aversive feeding patterns.

4. The gag reflex (Morris, 1977)

a. Protects the airway from large objects.

b. Can be hyperactive.

c. Constant activation by long nipples or invasive procedures might create feeding aversion.

5. The cough reflex (Wolf and Glass, 1992)

a. Protects against the aspiration of fluids into the airways.

b. Might be immature in premature and in some term infants.

c. The immature response to fluids in the airways might be apnea (breath holding) followed by attempts to swallow with a delayed cough.

d. Silent aspiration can occur in immature infants.

e. Coughing during feeding is generally in response to *descending* fluids (a problem while swallowing).

f. Coughing between feedings might be in response to *ascending* fluids (reflux).

C. Rhythmicity—coordination of the suck-swallow-breathe triad (Bosma, 1977; and Campbell, 1977)

1. The normal, full-term infant sucks, swallows, and breathes in a rhythmic and coordinated manner.

2. Feeding evaluation must consider all three aspects of the triad (Glass and Wolf, 1994).

3. Sucking-swallowing-breathing are functionally and anatomically interrelated (overlapping function of cranial nerves; overlapping of structures).

4. Sucking and respiratory patterns are immature in preterm infants.

5. Sucking, swallowing, and breathing patterns might be dysfunctional in ill or neurologically impaired infants; observation of feeds in compromised infants should include observation of the *entire* feed to notice evidence of fatigue, loss of rhythmicity, evidence of respiratory distress, and so on.

6. Dysrhythmic sucking and poor coordination of sucking-swallowing-breathing are not uncommon even in term infants during the first few days postpartum.

7. Indications of dysfunction can involve the following (Wolf and Glass, 1992; Wilson, 1977; and Alper and Manno, 1996):

   a. Stridor: a raspy, respiratory noise heard upon inspiration (caused by narrowing or obstruction of the airway).

   b. Wheezing: a high-pitched noise occurring during exhalation (caused by airway constriction due to inflammation or asthma or reactive airway disease caused by silent microaspiration during feeding).

   c. Apnea during feeding: periodic breath-holding while attempting to manage swallows.

   d. Sleepiness during feeding (resulting from the infant being unable to manage the work of feeding).

   e. Low feed intake.

   f. Poor growth.

8. Poor coordination of sucking-swallowing-breathing complicate feeding for the following types of infants (Palmer, 1993):

   a. Ill infants

   b. Injured infants

   c. Neurologically or congenitally impaired infants

   d. Infants who have sensory issues

   e. Premature infants

9. Poor function in any part of the triad affects the other functions.

10. Poor function of any part of the triad can negatively affect feeding behavior:

   a. Limiting intake

    b. Increasing the work of feeding

    c. Creating an aversion to feeding due to aspiration, respiratory compromise, choking, reflux, or sensory-based problems (Palmer, 1993).

11. Feeding becomes smoother and more regulated with maturation.

12. Careful attention to the feeding position can assist the compromised infant (Alper and Manno, 1996).

13. Feeding problems can be isolated and outgrown or can be red flags for enduring, persistent problems related to neurological issues (Wolf and Glass, 1992).

D. The "fit" between the infant's oral anatomy and maternal breast/nipple anatomy (Neifert, 1999; and Wilson-Clay and Hoover, 1999)

  1. The breastfeeding mother and baby form a dyad.

    a. Evaluation involves the assessment of both.

  2. The diameter, consistency, length, elasticity, and shape of the nipple might or might not be a good fit with the baby's mouth.

  3. Assessment for feeding requires observation and consideration of these issues.

  4. Nipple elasticity can be improved with various tools (breast pumps or breast shells) or by softening the engorged breast.

  5. Inverted nipples can be extended by nipple shields (Wilson-Clay, 1996).

  6. Infant growth will accommodate for long nipples.

  7. Increased infant size, strength, and stamina will accommodate meaty, non-compressible nipples.

  8. Creative positioning can accommodate for challenging nipple shapes.

  9. Certain configurations of breasts/nipples might be more or less easy for infants who have oral anomalies (refer to the next section).

E. Abnormal infant anatomy

  1. Cleft lip (Lawrence and Lawrence, 1999)

    a. Solitary clefts of the lip can pose a few breastfeeding problems.

    b. Repair is typically done in the early postpartum stage.

    c. Feeding challenges result from the following:

      i. The potential inability to form a seal with the lips

      ii. Consequent diminished suction

      iii. The risk of resultant low intake

    d. Strategies to support breastfeeding include the following:

      i. Using the mother's breast tissue to help seal the cleft (softer, more elastic breast tissue assists here better than taut or engorged breast tissue).

      ii. Using the mother's finger or thumb to "plug" the cleft while the baby nurses.

    e. Benefits of breastfeeding include the following:
        i. Strengthening of the infant's tongue and jaw muscles during sucking
        ii. Human milk contains special protections for the infant who is facing surgery (anti-inflammatory agents, growth factor, and immune protections)
    f. Post-surgical challenges include the following:
        i. A dialogue with the surgical team about the method of feeding after surgery
        ii. Some literature (for example, Weatherly-White) suggests that allowing breastfeeding prevents crying and stress on the sutures

F. Cleft palate (Curtain, 1990; Goldman, 1993; Paradise et al., 1994; Cleft Palate Foundation, 1987; Danner and Wilson-Clay, 1986; and Markowitz et al., 1979)

1. Are relatively common with an incidence of one in 60–800 births.

2. Are more common in some families and some races (for example, Native Americans, Maoris, Chinese, whites, and blacks, respectively).

3. The size and location of the cleft determine the effect on feeding.
    a. Great variability exists in severity
    b. Can be unilateral
    c. Can be bilateral
    d. Can be partial or complete (in other words, can be located in one area or can extend from the lip line to the soft palate)
    e. Can be located in the hard or soft palate
    f. Can be submucosal (identified by a notched uvula)

4. Clefts can occur as a solitary issue or can be associated with other congenital anomalies or syndromes.
    a. Clefts associated with syndromic conditions can result in feeding problems complicated by other issues associated with the syndrome (for example, heart defects that create stamina issues or airway obstruction issues in Pierre Robin Syndrome).

5. Cleft repair can be performed as early as 6 months of age or at one year or older, depending on the preferences of the surgical team.

6. Feeding challenges are considerable and include the following:
    a. The inability of the infant to form suction due to the inability to seal off the oral chamber (poor ability to create negative pressure)
    b. Difficulty holding the nipple in the mouth due to the lack of ability to create suction
    c. Difficulty pressing the nipple against the palate due to cleft (poor ability to create positive pressure)

    d. Nasal regurgitation due to fluid escaping the oral cavity and entering the nose through the cleft (Morris, 1977)

7. Consequences of cleft palate include the following:

    a. An increased incidence of infant respiratory problems

    b. An increased incidence of otitis media (due to the impaired function of Eustacian tubes resulting from the breach in normal supportive palate musculature)

    c. The potential for poor infant intake

    d. Poor growth, including failure to thrive

    e. Down-regulation of maternal milk supply if not protected

8. Feeding strategies include the following:

    a. Recognition that infants who have clefts are difficult to feed, especially in early infancy

    b. Providing growth monitoring and supplementation with human milk as needed

    c. Selection of appropriate alternate feeding methods to deliver supplement

    d. Protection of the maternal milk supply with a hospital-grade electric breast pump

    e. Consideration of palatal obturator (prosthesis that creates an artificial palate, allowing the infant to feed with an intact oral cavity)

    f. Teaching the mother to hold the breast in the infant's mouth (to compensate for the lack of ability to hold in the nipple due to weak suction)

    g. Teaching the mother to position her breast against the intact portions of the palate so that the baby can use the tongue to press against the palate to create positive milking pressure

    h. Teaching the mother to use upright feeding positions to prevent choking

    i. Using the Dancer's hand position to stabilize chin movements and to apply counter-pressure to the cheeks

    j. Demonstrating equipment such as the Haberman feeder and feeding tube devices that might assist the infant with obtaining more milk

    k. Teaching the mother to identify nutritive feeding and to distinguish it from non-nutritive sucking

    l. Reassuring the mother that as the baby strengthens and grows, his or her feeding ability will improve

    m. Providing realistic feedback on the individual infant's feeding skills: some infants with clefts never are able to breastfeed, and some breastfeed well

9. Ankyloglossia (tongue-tie) (Gorski et al, 1994; Messner et al., 2000; Fernando, 1998; Flink et al., 1994; Hazelbaker, 1999; and Wilson-Clay and Hoover, 1999):

   a. Like cleft palate, a mid-line defect (also described as a short or tight lingual frenulum).

   b. The frenulum is a thin velum formed from the mucosa of the floor of the mouth that abnormally attaches to the mid-section or tip of the underside of the tongue and restricts its movement to some degree.

   c. Can be thin and stretchy or thick and tight.

   d. When the tongue is lifted, the short, tight, or too-far forward frenulum distorts the tongue tip into a characteristic "heart" shape.

   e. Runs in families.

   f. The incidence is felt to be between 2–4 percent of infants.

   g. Can persist in some individuals into adulthood.

   h. Can create mechanical difficulties in forming certain sounds, in performing dental hygiene, and can create feeding problems for some infants.

   i. Feeding problems might involve the following:

      i. The inability to shape the tongue into a central groove (resulting in poorly managed bolus formation and swallowing problems)

      ii. The inability to maintain forward extension of the tongue over the lower gum/lip line (resulting in poor lip seal and a poor ability to hold the breast in the mouth)

      iii. The inability to use the forward position of the tongue to cushion the pressure of lower jaw closure (resulting in compensatory jaw clenching and pinched maternal nipples and the risk of mastitis)

      iv. The inability to lift the tongue past the mid-line of the oral cavity (resulting in poor creation of positive pressure used to strip the breast)

      v. Increased work of feeding because the baby is forced to rely on compensatory mechanisms in order to milk the breast (resulting in poor intake and the potential for down-regulation of the milk supply)

      vi. Risk of untimely weaning

   j. Assessment involves the following:

      i. Observation of the infant's ability to extend the tongue beyond the lower gum ridge and to sustain the forward position during feeding

      ii. Observation of the infant's ability to lift the tongue past the mid-line of the oral cavity

      iii. Observation of the infant's ability to hold and maintain the breast in the mouth

      iv. Observing for maternal comfort during normal-length feedings (absence of cracked nipples)

      v. Observation of infant intake (by test weight, growth monitoring, and diaper counts)

      vi. Evaluation by a pedodontist, pediatric ear, nose, and throat specialist, or a pediatrician who is trained to assess the condition

   j. Lactation support consists of the following:

      i. Altering the position at the breast to bring the chin closer (to shorten the distance that the tongue must reach)

      ii. Protection of the nipples by alternating pumping/feeding; topical measures to manage nipple trauma

      iii. Protection of the milk supply if endangered

      iv. Referral to an appropriate specialist

   k. Frenotomy normally involves the following:

      i. Office procedure in infants younger than 3 months of age

      ii. Can be done without general anesthesia; however, some physicians will only perform it under general anesthesia

      iii. Scant bleeding is observed

      iv. An improvement in breastfeeding is immediate in some infants

      v. Some infants need recovery time to habilitate the normal movement of the tongue (several days to several weeks)

10. Tight labial frenum (Wiessinger and Miller, 1995)

   a. Like ankyloglossia, this condition involves a slightly anomalous growth of a velum (frenum).

   b. The labial frenum attaches the upper lip to the upper gum.

   c. A tight labial frenuum lacks elasticity and might grow down to the gum ridge.

   d. Can create difficulty flanging the upper lip (causing abrasion to the breast).

   e. Can reduce the stability of the latch-on by interfering with the lip seal.

   f. Can create a cascade of problems in some dyads, resulting in sore nipples, low intake, mastitis, low milk supply, and so on.

   g. Later, this condition can influence malformations of the teeth (creating a gap between the front teeth).

   h. Some children will sever this tissue during childhood falls, or it will be corrected during orthodontia.

   i. Strategies to manage the infant who has a tight upper labial frenum presenting with breastfeeding difficulty include the following:

      i. Showing the mother how to manually flange the baby's upper lip

      ii. Referral to a pedodontist of pediatric ENT in order to ablate the frenulum surgically or with a laser procedure

11. High, arched, grooved, or channel palates (Lawrence and Lawrence, 1999; and Wilson-Clay and Hoover, 1999)

    a. The tongue helps shape and spread the palate in the developing fetus.

    b. Anomalies of the tongue or jaw can prevent the tongue from shaping and spreading the palate.

    c. Chromosomal disorders (such as Turner Syndrome) can create unusual palatal configurations.

    d. Prolonged intubation (for example, premature or ill infants) can create palatal erosion and create channels in the palate.

    e. Unusually shaped palates can create problems similar to those of clefts of the palate.

        i. The tongue has difficulty stabilizing the breast against the hard palate.

        ii. Sealing the oral chamber can become more difficult if the breast cannot fill the channel or bubble in the palate.

    f. Sore nipples might ensue if the tongue traps the face of the nipple up into the channel or bubble, where it can rub against the ridges of the palate (creating friction trauma).

    g. Later, food or other chewed objects can become trapped in the channel or bubble, and parents must check for this condition in young children (Rovet, 1995).

    h. Strategies for breastfeeding include the following:

        i. Searching for feeding positions that feel most comfortable to the mother.

        ii. Monitoring weight gain, because the infant's work of feeding is increased and there might be a tendency to fatigue before consuming sufficient calories.

        iii. Protection of the milk supply might be required until the infant grows and strengthens.

        iv. Occasionally, use of a thin silicone nipple shield helps stabilize the intra-oral space.

12. Receding chin (micrognathia, retrognathia) (Wolf and Glass, 1992; and Bull et al., 1990)

    a. Can be observed independently or associated with cleft defects.

    b. Mild jaw recession immediately after birth is common in many infants due to in utero positioning.

    c. Jaw recession can impair breastfeeding because direct opposition of the gum ridges assists compression of the milk ducts.

    d. The tongue position can altered by jaw recession.

    e. Posterior positioning of the tongue negatively impacts the creation of a seal and negative pressure (suction).

       f.  Posterior positioning of the tongue can result in sore nipples due to jaw clench as a compensatory mechanism to stabilize the breast in the mouth.

       g.  Growth will result in the lower jaw pulling forward.

       h.  Positioning that tips the chin forward, closer to the breast, assists feeding.

       i.  Protection of the nipples might be necessary (alternating pumping with feeding).

       j.  Protection of the milk supply might be necessary because the infant might fatigue early from an increased work of feeding.

   13.  Obstructed nasal passages (Bosma, 1977)

       a.  Occasionally, an infant presents with abnormally small nasal passages.

       b.  Infants are normally nose breathers but can alter to oral respirations if their nose is blocked (Wolf and Glass, 1992).

       c.  If nasal respiration is compromised, the infant might refuse to breastfeed.

       d.  Referral to an ENT for evaluation is appropriate if the infant's ability to breastfeed is impaired due to mechanical obstruction of the nares.

       e.  Referral for a swallow study is appropriate if the obstruction appears to result from aspirated debris.

**III** Counseling the parents and protecting breastfeeding

Successful feeding influences maternal satisfaction with mothering and becomes one of the ways in which a mother "measures" her ability to successfully take on the maternal role (Morris, 1977; and Minde, 1982).

A.  Failure of an infant to feed normally can contribute to a phenomenon described as "chronic grief."

B.  Poorly feeding infants require more parental effort in order to feed.

C.  Increased parental work feeding a dysfunctionally feeding infant negatively affects the family and can adversely affect bonding.

D.  Breastfeeding, while providing many benefits for the immature, ill, or injured infant, can be considered by the mother's social support system to be "too difficult" for the mother and baby.

E.  The role of the LC is to assist in developing safe, clear plans that protect the following:

   1.  The baby's intake and growth

   2.  The mother's milk supply

   3.  The potential to return to unassisted breastfeeding if possible, given the infant's condition

F.  The LC provides appropriate emotional support through counseling skills, provides information, and suggests realistic goals (Lauwers et al., 2000).

G.  The LC provides accurate information about equipment to maintain lactation:

1. Hospital-grade electric breast pumps should be provided within 6–8 hours of birth to mothers whose infants are not able to breastfeed due to prematurity, illness, neurological deficit, or oral-motor abnormality (ILCA Guidelines).

2. Pumping should imitate the normal infant's feeding frequency (for example, by day 3, 8–12 times/24 hours with a duration of nursing of about 15 minutes per breast) (American Academy of Pediatrics, 1997; and Meier et al., 1999).

3. In general, double pumping, early initiation of pumping, and frequency of pumping greater than six times/24 hours are positively associated with higher pumped milk volumes and a greater likelihood of adequate milk production over time (Hill et al., 1999).

4. Accurate human milk storage guidelines should be provided to parents and caregivers.

5. The LC evaluates the individual infant and mother in terms of the most appropriate alternate feeding method given the circumstances and the specific feeding deficits (refer to the chapter concerning alternate feeding, Chapter 33).

# References

Alper M. Dysphagia in infants and children with oral-motor deficits: Assessment and management. *Semin Speech Language* 1996; 17(4):283–305, 309.

American Academy of Pediatrics Work Group on Breastfeeding. Breastfeeding and the use of human milk. *Pediatrics* 1997; 100:1035–37.

Bosma J. Structure and function of the infant oral and pharyngeal mechanisms. In Wilson J, ed. Oral-motor function & dysfunction in children. Chapel Hill, NC: University of North Carolina at Chapel Hill, 1977, May 25–28:39, 52–53, 69.

Bull M, Givan D, et al. Improved outcome in Pierre Robin sequence: Effect of multidisciplinary evaluation and management. *Pediatrics* 1990; 86(2):294–301.

Campbell S. Oral sensorimotor physiology. In Wilson J, ed. Oral-motor function and dysfunction in children. Chapel Hill, NC: University of North Carolina at Chapel Hill, 1977, May 25–28:3.

Curtain G. The infant with cleft lip or palate: More than a surgical problem. *J Perinat Neonatal Nurs* 1990; 3(3):80–89.

Danner S, Wilson-Clay B. Breastfeeding the infant with a cleft lip/palate, *Lactation Consultant Series, Unit 10.* Wayne, NJ: Avery Publishing Group, 1986.

Fernando C. Tongue tie: From confusion to clarity. Sydney, Australia: Tandem Publications, 1998.

Flink A, Paludan A, et al. Oral findings in a group of Swedish children. *Int J Paediatr Dent* 1994; 2:67–73.

The genetics of cleft lip and palate: Information for families. Pittsburgh: Cleft Palate Foundation, 1987.

Glass R, Wolf L. Incoordination of sucking, swallowing, and breathing as an etiology for breastfeeding difficulty. *J Hum Lact* 1994; 10(3):185–189.

Goldman A. The immune system of human milk: Antimicrobial, anti-inflammatory and immunomodulating properties. *Pediatric Infect Dis J* 1993; 12:664–671.

Gorski S, Adams K, et al. Linkage analysis of X-linked cleft palate and ankyloglossia in Manitoba Mennonite and British Columbia native kindreds. *Hum Genet* 1994; 2:141–148.

Hazelbaker A. The assessment tool for lingual frenulum function. Masters Thesis, 1993.

Hill P, Aldag J, Chatterton R. Effects of pumping style on milk production in mothers of non-nursing infants. *J Hum Lact* 1999; 15(3):209–216.

Lauwers J, Shinskie D, Beck S. Counseling the nursing mother, 3rd ed. Sudbury, MA: Jones and Bartlett, 2000: 43–70.

Lawrence R, Lawrence R. Breastfeeding: A guide for the medical profession, 5th ed. St. Louis: Mosby, 1999: 489–492.

Markowitz J, Gerry R, Fleishner R. Immediate obturation of neonatal Cleft palates. *Mt Sinai J Med* 1979; 46(2):123–129.

McBride M, Danner S. Sucking disorders in neurologically impaired infants: Assessment and facilitation of breastfeeding. *Clin Perinatol* 1987; 14(1):109–130.

Meier P, Brown L, Hurst N. Breastfeeding the preterm infant, in Riordan J, Auerbach KG, eds. Breastfeeding and human lactation. Sudbury, MA: Jones and Bartlett, 1999: 449–481.

Messner A, Lalakea L, Aby J, et al. Ankyloglossia: Incidence and associated feeding difficulties. *Arch Otolaryngol Head Neck Surg* 2000; 126:36–39.

Minde K. The impact of medical complications on parental behavior in the premature nursery. In Klaus M, Robertson M, eds. Birth, interaction and attachment: Exploring the foundations for modern perinatal care. Johnson & Johnson, Pediatric Round Table, 1982: 6:98–104.

Morris S. A glossary of terms describing the feeding process. In Wilson J, ed. Oral-motor function & dysfunction in children. Chapel Hill, NC: University of North Carolina at Chapel Hill, 1977, May 25–28:160.

Morris S. Interpersonal aspects of feeding problems. In Wilson J, ed. Oral-motor function & dysfunction in children. Chapel Hill, NC: University of North Carolina at Chapel Hill, 1977, May 25–28:106–113.

Morris S. Oral-motor development: normal and abnormal. In Wilson J, ed. Oral-motor function & dysfunction in children. Chapel Hill, NC: University of North Carolina at Chapel Hill, 1977, May 25–28: 122.

Neifert M. Clinical aspects of lactation. *Clin Perinatol* 1999; 26(2):282–3.

Ogg L. Oral-pharyngeal development and evaluation. *Phys Therapy* 1975; 55(3):235–241.

Palmer MM. Assessment and treatment of sensory-versus motor-based feeding problems in very young children. *Infants and Young Children* Oct. 1993; 67–73.

Palmer MM. Identification and management of the transitional suck pattern in premature infants. *J Perinat Neonatal Nurs* 1993; 7(1):66–75.

Palmer MM. Appendix A: NOMAS—Definition of terms for jaw function. *J Perinat and Neonat Nurs* 1993;7(1):74.

Palmer MM. Appendix A: NOMAS—Definition of terms for tongue function. *J Perinat and Neonat Nurs* 1993;7(1):75.

Paradise J, Elster B, Tan L. Evidence in infants with cleft palate that breast milk protects against otitis media. *Pediatrics* 1994; 94(6):853–860.

Powers N. Slow weight Ggain and low milk supply in the breastfeeding dyad. *Clin Perinatol* 1999; 26(2):416.

Radtka S. Feeding reflexes and neutral control. In Wilson J, ed. Oral-motor function & dysfunction in children. Chapel Hill, NC: University of North Carolina at Chapel Hill, 1977, May 25–28: 96–105.

Rovet J, ed. Turner syndrome across the lifespan. Markham, Ontario: Kelin Graphics. 1995; iv.

Weatherly-White R, Kuehn D, et al. Early repair and breast-feeding for infants with cleft lip. *Plast Reconstr Surg* 1987; 79(6):879–885.

Wiessinger D, Miller M. Breastfeeding difficulties as a result of tight lingual and labial frena: A case report. *J Hum Lact* 1995; 11(4):313–316.

Wilson J. Patterns of respiration (appendix). In Wilson J, ed. Oral-motor function & dysfunction in children. Chapel Hill, NC: University of North Carolina at Chapel Hill, 1977, May 25–28: 66–68.

Wilson-Clay B. Clinical use of nipple shields. *J Hum Lact* 1996; 12(4):279–85.

Wilson-Clay B, Hoover K. The breastfeeding atlas. Austin, TX: LactNews Press, 1999: 37, 54–57, 61–62.

Wolf and Glass. Feeding and swallowing disorders in infancy. Tucson, AZ: Therapy Skill Builders, 1992.

# Slow Weight Gain/Failure to Thrive

*Elsa Regina Justo Giugliani, MD, PhD, IBCLC*

## Objectives

- Distinguish between slow weight gain and failure to thrive.
- List the main causes of failure to thrive.
- Discuss and assess parameters for an infant who has a failure to thrive.
- Develop appropriate management strategies according to the etiology of failure to thrive.

## Introduction

Inadequate weight gain in the breastfed infant is an exceptional condition that occurs mainly in infants who are younger than six months of age. In most cases, it can be reversed when the problem(s) causing it is identified and promptly corrected. True failure to thrive is potentially dangerous, requiring early recognition and action.

I Definitions

   A. Slow weight gain—when infants and children gain weight consistently, although slowly; this condition is usually familial or genetic.

   B. Failure to thrive—when infants and children fail to gain the expected weight or lose weight.

   C. Usually, their weight drops below the third percentile or is two standard deviations below the mean weight of the reference population (NCHS/WHO).

II Growth parameters

   A. Healthy newborn infants should not continue to lose weight after 10 days of life.

   B. Healthy newborn infants should regain their birth weight by three weeks of life.

     1. The median daily weight gain is 26–31g for infants in the first three months.

     2. 17–18g from 3–6 months.

     3. 12–13g from 6–9 months.

     4. 9g from 9–12 months (Desmarais and Browne, 1990).

5. The growth of breastfed children differs from that of artificially fed infants.

6. As a consequence, the current International Growth Reference (NCHS/WHO), which is based on predominantly formula-fed infants, is inadequate for the breastfed infant.

7. These infants often appear to begin faltering in weight at 3–4 months of age when compared with the reference population (Frantz, 1992).

III  Distinction between slow weight gain and failure to thrive

A. Slow weight gain

1. Alert, responsive, and a healthy appearance

2. Normal muscle tone and skin turgor

3. Dilute urine, six or more times/day

4. Frequent stools (or infrequent, but large amount)

5. Good suck

6. Eight or more breastfeeds/day, lasting 15–20 minutes

7. Good let-down reflex

8. Weight gain slow, but consistent (refer to Table 21-1)

**Table 21-1**     Weight Gain in Breastfed Infants

|          | Thriving | Concern |
|----------|----------|---------|
| Day 1–7  | Loses < 10% of birth weight | Loses greater than or equal to 10% of birth weight |
|          | Starts gaining weight again | Still losing weight |
| Day 14   | Has regained birth weight | Still under birth weight |
| Day 14–42 | Average weight gain greater than or less than 30g/d | Average weight gain < 20g/d |

Reprinted by permission: Frantz KB. The slow-gaining breastfeeding infant. NAACOG's clinical issues in perinatal and women's health nursing 1992; 3:647–655.

IV  Failure to thrive

A. Apathetic or weakly crying infant

B. Poor muscle tone and skin turgor

C. Concentrated urine, a few times/day

D. Infrequent, scanty stools

E. Fewer than eight breastfeeds/day, usually brief

F. No signs of let-down reflex

G. Poor and erratic weight gain or no weight gain

V  Conditions associated with weight-gain problems

A. Infant factors
  1. Poor intake
     a. Poor suckling
        i. Physical/structural factors
        ii. Cleft lip/palate
        iii. Short frenulum
        iv. Micrognathia
        v. Macroglossia
        vi. Choanal atresia
B. Iatrogenic conditions
  1. Maternal analgesia/anesthesia—can diminish the infant's alertness and ability to suck
  2. Bottle/pacifiers/nipple shields—can decrease suckling stimulation and cause nipple confusion (refer to Table 21-2)
C. Medical conditions
  1. Anoxia/hypoxia
  2. Prematurity
  3. Neonatal jaundice—can make infants lethargic
  4. Trisomy 21
  5. Trisomy 13-15
  6. Hypothyroidism
  7. Neuromuscular dysfunction
  8. Central nervous system impairment
  9. Abnormal suckling patterns
D. Infrequent/less feeds
  1. Mother-infant separation
  2. Pacifiers
  3. Water/juice supplementation
  4. Early solids
E. Low net milk intake
  1. Vomiting and diarrhea
  2. Malabsorption—cystic fibrosis
  3. Infection
F. High energy requirements
  1. Small for the gestational-age infant
  2. Central nervous system

**Table 21-2**  Simple Management of Breastfeeding a Newborn

| Assessment | Intervention | Rationale |
|---|---|---|
| Mother removes infant before he or she is finished or adheres to a preset time guideline | Encourage mother to let infant self-limit feedings by monitoring swallows; teach swallow sounds | Breastfed newborns take 10–60-minute feedings, mean of 31 minutes; length of feeding is equal to quantity of nutritive suckle |
| | Explain about overdressing, may need to unwrap and wake infant to finish feeding | Overheated infants decrease suckling; swaddled newborns assume sleep state |
| | Switch to second breast when swallows slow or stop and back to first breast again if infant is interested | Offering both breasts stimulates better milk volume; pauses might not mean newborn is finished; feeding refusal when switched might mean newborn is finished |
| Consistent long intervals between feedings (4 hours or more for newborn) | Feed more often, do not adhere to formula-fed 4-hour schedule | Breastfed newborns usually feed every 2–3 hours; some infants "cluster feed" after a long sleep period |
| | Discourage pacifier during first weeks | Desire to suckle is a survival mechanism but might indicate real need to feed; more suckling equals more milk volume |
| | Wake sleepy infants, feed at least 8 times every 24 hours | Drugs during labor, maternal postpartum drugs, or hyperbilirubinemia might cause infant to sleep too much |
| Trying to get infant to "sleep through the night" before 8–12 weeks | Dispel myths that parents should promote long infant sleep periods by letting infant cry or using pacifier | Newborns need to feed throughout a 24-hour period; most do not sleep for a six-hour stretch until 8–12 weeks of age |
| | Tell mother "power" feedings are at night in the first three weeks; she should rest during the day | Prolactin levels are high when mother sleeps; newborns feed best at night during the first three weeks |
| Mother offering more water than breast milk, thinking she is supposed to or because of fear of jaundice | Discontinue water for more frequent breast milk feedings | No extra water is needed because of the lower solute load of breast milk if the infant is feeding frequently |
| Mother using nipple shield | Discontinue shield | Water not proven to lower bilirubin levels faster than milk feedings; bilirubin also excreted in stool with milk feedings |
| | Use feeding tube device if infant will not breastfeed well | Shield reduces available milk by 22–66 percent |

Reprinted by permission: Frantz KB. The slow-gaining breastfeeding infant. NAACOG's clinical issues in perinatal and women's health nursing 1992; 3:647–655.

335

3. Stimulants in the milk
4. Neurologic disorders
5. Severe congenital heart disease (refer to Table 21-3)

**Table 21-3**  Underlying Pathology Associated with Slow Gain or Low Milk Supply

| Mother | Infant |
| --- | --- |
| Stress | Prematurity 36–37 weeks |
| Inverted nipples | Oral-motor dysfunction |
| Nipple shields | Neurologic problem |
| Medications | Short frenulum |
| Hormonal aberrations | Urinary tract infection |
| Pregnancy | Reflux, with or without oversupply |
| Thyroid disorder | Allergy |
| Retained placenta | Obvious or known illness |
| Hypopituitarism | |
| Breast surgery | |
| Primary glandular insufficiency | |
| Obvious or known illness | |

Reprinted by permission: Frantz KB. The slow-gaining breastfeeding infant. NAACOG's clinical issues in perinatal and women's health nursing 1992; 3:647–655.

**VI** Maternal factors

A. Inadequate milk production

1. Mismanagement—the most common cause of slow weight gain/failure to thrive
   a. Improper positioning
   b. Low frequency/duration of feedings
   c. Rigid feeding schedules
   d. Absence of night feedings
   e. "Switch nurse" technique—sometimes
   f. Use of nipple shields
   g. Engorgement
   h. Non-graspable nipples

2. Insufficient glandular development
    a. The mother experiences no or minimal breast changes during pregnancy and no postpartum breast fullness.
    b. Often, there are marked differences in the shape and size of the breasts.
3. Illness
    a. Infection
    b. Hypothyroidism
    c. Untreated diabetes
    d. Sheehan's syndrome
    e. Pituitary tumors
    f. Mental illness
    g. Retained placenta
    h. Fatigue
    i. Emotional disturbance
4. Drugs
    a. Estrogen (oral contraceptive)
    b. Antihistamine
    c. Sedatives
    d. Diuretics
    e. Large doses of vitamin B6
5. Severe diet restriction
6. Breast reduction surgery
7. Smoking
8. Pregnancy
9. Impaired milk ejection reflex
    a. Psychological inhibition
    b. Stress
    c. Pain
10. Breast surgery
11. Smoking
12. Alcohol
13. Pituitary disease
14. Abnormal milk composition
    a. Very low fat diet
    b. Strict vegan vegetarian without vitamin B12 supplementation
    c. Hypernatremia

d. Stimulants in the milk—too much caffeine (coffee, tea, cola)

15. Assessment

a. Listening attentively to the mother and helping her express her feelings is an important aspect at the assessment

**VII** History

A. Details of the breastfeeds/feedings

1. Frequency

2. Duration

3. Use of the "switch nurse" technique, or switching back and forth between breasts

4. Signs of the let-down reflex—leaking or spraying of milk; tingling or burning sensations within the breast

5. Use of nipple shields

6. Other liquids and foods

7. Use of bottles (refer to Table 21-4)

B. Infant's aspects

1. General health

2. Birth weight/adequacy for gestational age

3. Lowest weight after birth and the age at that time

4. Sleep pattern

5. Fussiness

6. Number of wet diapers—an infant is usually getting enough milk if he or she is having at least six wet diapers a day

7. Frequency/amount/color of stools

a. Usually 2–5 bowel movements/day in infants who are younger than 6 weeks of age

b. Consistent green and watery stools can be a sign of too much foremilk and not enough hindmilk

8. Use of pacifiers

C. Mother's aspects

1. General health

2. Psychological aspects

3. Presence of relatives or friends criticizing her for breastfeeding

4. The mother's level of commitment to breastfeeding

5. Dietary habits, including herbal use

6. Sleep pattern

7. Smoking

**Table 21-4** Sudden Onset of Poor Weight Gain at 3–5 Months

| Assessment | Intervention | Rationale |
|---|---|---|
| Excessive use of gratifying devices for infants (carriers, swings, fingers, pacifiers) | Offer breast when infant suckles fingers or needs comfort | Some infants love to suckle; self-gratification might interfere with feeds |
| | Feed more often if number of feedings has decreased | Infant might be too comforted by swing or carrier |
| Shorter feedings, same number | Lengthen feedings by removing fingers, objects from mouth, and putting the infant back to breast | Hindmilk with cream comes at end of feed; infant might stop before getting the heavier milk |
| | Offer cold objects to soothe mouth, then return the infant to breast | Teething can begin at 4 months |
| Highly distractable, stops before finished, will not go back to breast | Feed in quiet room with no television, radio, telephone ringing, or talking | Developmentally distracted at 4–6 months |
| | | Gets less hindmilk with shorter feeds |
| History of busy maternal schedule (holidays and so on) | Plan for longer feedings, drop unnecessary activities, ask for help with chores | Busy women will give "quick feed" because of time constraints; shortened feedings equal less hindmilk, even if they are more frequent |
| | | Infant now sleeps six hours at night and needs good day feedings |
| Early or heavy introduction of solid foods | Teach starting solids after 4–6 months | American Academy of Pediatrics/Canadian Pediatrics Society recommends starting solids 4–6 months, preferably six months |
| | Offer only after breastfeeding | Solid food might supplant a feed, decreasing feeding frequency and thus decreasing milk supply |
| Mother began taking birth control pill | Suggest progesterone-only pill | Estrogen-containing pills can lower the quantity of milk |
| Mother has sudden, severe weight loss | Make sure she is not dieting severely, over-exercising, or anorexic | Severe maternal weight loss might lower milk supply |
| Recent history of mother/infant separation with good parenting skills present | Suggest one-on-one care by nurturing person or adequately staffed, all-infant daycare setting | Infant depression caused by perceived loss of mother has been documented in some infant-care facilities |

Reprinted by permission: Frantz KB. The slow-gaining breastfeeding infant. NAACOG's clinical issues in perinatal and women's health nursing 1992; 3:647–655.

        8. Alcohol consumption

        9. Medications

**VIII** Physical assessment of the infant relative to breastfeeding

    A. Assess the hydration status.

        1. Amount of wet diapers each 24 hours

        2. Moist mucous membranes

        3. Anterior fontanelle that is not depressed

        4. Skin turgor

    B. Compare the infant's weight, length, and head circumference with previous measurements and determine the baby's pattern of weight gain.

    C. Observe anatomical abnormalities of the mouth and major neurological disturbances.

        1. Observe the ability to root and suck.

        2. Observe muscle tone and mouth, tongue, and facial movements.

**IX** Assessment of the maternal breast

    A. Breast/nipples/areolae condition

    B. Presence of scars

    C. Symmetry

    D. Signs of mastitis

**X** Observation of the feeding

    A. Typical breast fullness-to-softness changes during feeding

    B. Positioning

    C. Latch on—good grasp

    D. Infant suck

        1. How vigorous it is

        2. Coordination

        3. Rhythmic sucking-swallowing

    E. Signs of adequate let-down

        1. Milk flows from the opposite breast

        2. Milk flows when feeding is interrupted abruptly

    F. Interaction between mother and baby

    G. Duration of the feeding in each breast

**XI** Laboratory tests

    A. In specific situations, some specialized tests might be of help:

        1. Prolactin levels—to rule out inadequate glandular tissue or a primary prolactin secretion defect; intrafeeding (after 15 minutes of breastfeeding) value should be at least twice the baseline

2. Crematocrit (level of fat in the milk)—to rule out poor milk ejection reflex or poor maternal nutrition

3. Sodium, chloride, potassium, pH, blood urea, nitrogen, and hematocrit when the infant is dehydrated; when electrolyte levels are abnormal, sodium, chloride, and potassium should be measured in the mother's milk

B. Management

1. All infants who have a failure to thrive should be seen by their primary care providers.

2. If an underlying medical condition is suspected, the lactation consultant (LC) will refer the mother and/or baby for medical/surgical assessment.

3. The management of failure to thrive is based on etiology (see related chapters).

4. When the mother's milk supply is low:

   a. Be sure that the baby is correctly positioned and latched on.

   b. Suggest to the mother the following actions: increasing the frequency of breastfeeds, offering both breasts at each feeding; giving time for the baby to empty the breast; trying to switch nursing if the baby is sleepy or not sucking actively; avoiding bottles, pacifiers, and nipple shields; giving only mother's milk in the first six months; eating a well-balanced diet; drinking enough fluids; and resting.

   c. Alternate massage might increase volume and fat content per feed.

5. Supplementary feeding might be necessary, temporary or permanent; recommendations on the type and mode of these feedings depends on motivation and conditions (physical and emotional) of the mother.

6. When the mother's supply is adequate, the first choice is to supplement the child with her own fresh milk.

   a. Oxytocin as a nasal spray can be suggested to the primary care provider if the problem is the let-down reflex and simple strategies to improve it have failed.

   b. In many circumstances, when the infant has neuromuscular or central nervous system disorders, physical therapy might be necessary.

7. In some selected cases, when routine methods fail, medication (metoclopramide, domperidome) are helpful and should be discussed with the primary care provider.

8. When no obvious cause is identified, a positive attitude to breastfeeding is helpful: a positive plan for the number and length of feedings, a good diet, and rest for the mother (refer to Table 21-5).

**Table 21-5** Effect of Feeding Options on Mother and Child

| Feeding Options | Will promote goal of long-term breastfeeding? | Is infant actually breastfeeding? | What is infant energy/time expenditure? | Does infant receive human milk? | Is infant gaining weight? | Is it safe for infant? | What is effect on milk supply? | What is maternal time expenditure? |
|---|---|---|---|---|---|---|---|---|
| Continue frequent breastfeeding | Possibly | Yes | High | Yes | May be poor | Yes, if weight monitored | Decreases | High |
| Supplement after breast (bottle, cup, dropper) | No | Yes | High | If uses pumped human milk | Yes | Yes (cup = aspiration danger) | Decreases | High |
| Temporarily bottle feed pumped human milk, then resume breastfeeding | Possibly | No | Low | Yes | Yes, if enough milk pumped | Yes | Decreases | Medium |
| Bottle feed pumped human milk | No | No | Low | Yes | Yes, if enough milk pumped | Yes | Decreases if long term | Medium |

(continues)

342

**Table 21-5** Effect of Feeding Options on Mother and Child (*Continued*)

| Feeding Options | Will promote goal of long-term breast-feeding? | Is infant actually breast-feeding? | What is infant energy/ time expenditure? | Does infant receive human milk? | Is infant gaining weight? | Is it safe for infant? | What is effect on milk supply? | What is maternal time expenditure? |
|---|---|---|---|---|---|---|---|---|
| Feeding tube device with pumped human milk | Yes | Yes | Low | Yes | Yes, if enough milk pumped | Yes | Good | Medium-high |
| Feeding tube device with formula | Yes | Yes | Low | Half | Yes | Yes | Good | Medium |
| Finger feeding by tube/syringe on finger | No | No | High, if slow feeder | If uses pumped human milk | Not always | Aspiration danger | Decreases | High |
| Quit breast-feeding for bottle feeding | No | No | Low | No | Yes | Yes | Gone | Low |

Reprinted by permission: Frantz KB. The slow-gaining breastfeeding infant. NAACOG's clinical issues in perinatal and women's health nursing 1992; 3:647–655.

C. Evaluation

   1. Is the infant gaining weight within the normal limits?

   2. Is the infant correctly positioned and latched on?

   3. Have possible causes of failure to thrive been removed?

   4. Has the infant had a medical/surgical assessment?

# References

Desmarais L, Browne S. Inadequate weight gain in breastfeeding infants: Assessments and resolutions. *Lactation Consultant Series* No 8. New York: Avery Publishing Grouping Inc., 1990.

Frantz KB. The slow-gaining breastfeeding infant. NAACOG's clinical issues in perinatal and women's health nursing 1992; 3:647–655.

La Leche League International. Slow weight gain during the first years. The breastfeeding answer book. Franklin Park, IL: La Leche League International, 1991, 215–233.

Lawrence RA, Lawrence RM. Normal growth, failure to thrive, and obesity in the breastfed infant. Breastfeeding. A guide for the medical profession, 5th ed. St. Louis: Mosby, Inc., 1999, Chapter 12, 395–424.

National Research Council, Food and Nutrition Board, National Academy of Science. Recommended daily allowances, ed. 10. Washington, DC: US Government Printing Office, 1989.

Powers NG. Slow weight gain and low milk supply in the breastfeeding dyad. *Clin Perinatol* 1999; 26:399–430.

World Health Organization. Physical status: the use and interpretation of anthropometry. *Technical Report Series 854*. Geneva: World Health Organization; 1995.

# Breastfeeding Twins and Higher-Order Multiples

*Karen Kerkoff Gromada, MSN, RN, IBCLC*

## Objectives

- Discuss the ways that antenatal, intrapartum, and postnatal conditions and events often affect the initiation of breastfeeding and lactation after multiple births.

- Describe strategies for initiating and coordinating breastfeeding with multiple-birth neonates.

- Identify physiologic and psychosocial factors that often affect breastfeeding multiple-birth infants/children.

## Introduction

A number of assumptions are associated with breastfeeding twins or higher-order multiples. When providing breastfeeding/lactation care to women who have multiple-birth children, the International Board Certified Lactation Consultant (IBCLC) can assume the following:

- Multiple-birth infants/children strain maternal physical and emotional reserves, because human reproductive history indicates single-infant pregnancy and birth as the species norm; this strain on maternal reserves often extends to the breastfeeding relationship(s).

- Breastfeeding initiation and duration with multiples is more than replicating appropriate breastfeeding mechanics with two or more infants/children.

- Infant and maternal complications present at birth affect breastfeeding initiation and might have long-lasting effects on breastfeeding duration or the feeding pattern of one or more of the multiple infants.

- Coordinating the breastfeeding of two or more infants who have differing but normal suckling abilities, feeding patterns, and feeding styles might be perceived by a mother as causing breastfeeding problems as opposed to being part of the reality of having multiple infants/children.

* Older infant and toddler multiples engage in interactive behaviors between themselves during breastfeeding that might affect the maternal-child(ren) breastfeeding relationship.

I Factors associated with multiple pregnancy that might affect the initiation of breastfeeding

   A. Increased incidence of twin and higher-order multiple (HOM) births in Western cultures

      1. Twins—almost 40 percent increase between 1980–1998

         a. Dizygotic: 1980—1.9/100 live births; 1996—2.4/100 live births

         b. Monozygotic (identical): 1980—1/250 live births; 1996—1/250 live births

      2. Higher-order multiples—345% increase between 1980–1996

         a. 1980—triplets = 1/7000; quadruplets = 1/571,000; quintuplets = 1/47,000,000

         b. 1996—higher-order multiples = 1/655 live births

      3. Related factors—increase the effect on the incidence of dizygotic "twinning"

         a. Ovarian stimulation medications or ovulatory induction medications

         b. Assisted reproductive technologies (ART)—in vitro fertilization (IVF), intrauterine insemination (IUI), and gamete or zygote intrafallopian tube transfer (GIFT/ZIFT)

   B. Effect of increased incidence of multiple births on breastfeeding and lactation

      1. Increased numbers of mothers of multiples (MOMs) initiating breastfeeding

      2. The demographics of women who are using ART to achieve pregnancy are often the same mothers or the same population who are experiencing increased rates of breastfeeding initiation and duration (Gromada and Spangler, 1998; Bowers, N. personal communication, November 7, 1998)

II Risk factors of multiple pregnancy/birth (Keith and Keith, 1999)

   A. Infants—increased incidence:

      1. Preterm labor and birth (less than 37 weeks gestation; very preterm is less than 33 weeks). For example, the average length of gestation is as follows:

         a. Single infant = 39–39.5 weeks (10 percent/2 percent very preterm)

         b. Twins = 36 weeks (50-plus percent/14 percent very preterm)

         c. Triplets = 33 weeks (90-plus percent/40 plus very preterm)

         d. Quadruplets and quintuplets = 30–31 weeks

    2. Intrauturine growth restriction (IUGR)/fetal growth restriction (FGR)

        a. Decreased fetal growth curves at 27 weeks (HOM) to 30 weeks (twins)

        b. Discordant growth related to placental or cord anomalies

        c. Twin to twin transfusion syndrome (TTTS) related to vascular connections when monozygotes share a single placenta

    3. Low birth weight (LBW; less than or equal to 5lb, 8oz or 2,500g) and very, or extremely, low birth weight (V/ELBW; less than or equal to 3lb, 3oz or 1,500g)

        a. Single infant = 6 percent LBW and 1 percent V/ELBW

        b. Twins = greater than 50 percent LBW and 10 percent V/ELBW

        c. Triplets = 90 percent LBW and 30 percent V/ELBW

        d. Quadruplets or more see even higher levels of LBW and V/ELBW.

    4. Increased incidence of congenital or pregnancy-related anomalies, such as cardiac, club foot, hip dislocation, developmental delays, cerebral palsy, Down syndrome, and so on

    5. Fetal, neonatal, and infant deaths = five times higher than for single infants (NCHS, 1998)

B. Maternal

    1. Pregnancy-induced hypertension (PIH); also called preeclampsia or toxemia

        a. Symptoms often more severe in multiple pregnancy

        b. Progression to HELLP syndrome (Chapter 11) more common with multiple pregnancy

    2. Anemia

    3. Perinatal hemorrhage

        a. Antenatal or intrapartum related to placental conditions; for example, previa, abruption

        b. Postnatal related to increased implantation site(s) and increased uterine atony

    4. Surgical delivery (approximately 50 percent both twins, 12 percent second twin; greater than 90 percent HOM)

        a. Malpresentation of fetal presenting part

        b. Fetal distress (increased for second/subsequent multiple)

C. Effect on breastfeeding initiation

    1. Increased infant complications result in increase of:

        a. Immature or insult to CNS = decrease effective suck

        b. Mother-infant(s) separation related to increased need for infant neonatal intensive care unit (NICU) stays

2. Maternal complications or interventions to prolong pregnancy result in an increase of:
   a. Depletion of maternal physical and psychological/emotional reserves during the postpartum period
   b. Delayed initiation of breastfeeding or compensatory milk expression
D. Prenatal preparation (Gromada, 1999; Gromada, 1992)
   1. Infant-feeding decision—advantages and disadvantages pertinent to the breastfeeding of two or more newborns/infants
   2. Milk production adaptation for multiple infants (Mead, Chuffo, and Lawlor-Klean and Meier, 1992; Saint, Maggiore and Hartmann, 1986)
   3. Anticipatory guidance related to:
      a. Improving infant outcomes associated with a pregnancy weight gain of 45lb (20kg) for twins; 50-plus lbs (23-plus kg) for triplets (Luke and Eberlein, 1999) = improved breastfeeding initiation
      b. Initiation related to potential infant or maternal complications = maternal flexibility
      c. Short- and long-term breastfeeding goals and possible adaptations related to the reality of multiple infants

III Initiating breastfeeding (Gromada, 1999; Gromada and Spangler, 1998; and Sollid, Evans, and Garrett, 1989)
A. Healthy, full/close-to-term twins and triplets
   1. Early, frequent, "cued" breastfeeding for each
   2. Individual versus simultaneous feedings until at least one is assessed as consistent, effective breastfeeding
   3. Discharge planning
      a. Coordinating breastfeeding (see below) and other infant care
      b. Distinguishing breastfeeding issues versus "two or more infants" issues
      c. Support systems—physical, such as household help and emotional support
B. Maternal complications
   1. Direct breastfeeding
   2. Compensatory milk expression per self or caregiver (eight times or 100 minutes/24 hours)
C. Preterm or sick twins/higher-order multiples
   1. Establishing lactation for two or more newborns via milk expression—a realistic plan
      a. Initiate milk expression as soon as possible following birth for at least eight times or 100 minutes/24 hours.
      b. Increase the number of pumping sessions or the total number of minutes pumped as needed.

   c. Increased need for hospital-grade, electric pump with a double collection kit

  2. Transitioning two or more preterm or sick neonates to breastfeeding

   a. Assess and intervene based on individual infant ability

   b. Learning curve for breastfeeding—maternal patience and persistence needed as two or more preterm or sick newborns (of differing abilities) learn to breastfeed effectively

  3. Discharge planning

   a. Staggered discharge is common; one baby gets to come home/one baby is in the NICU

   b. Parental anxiety related to the growth and development of preterm or sick newborns

   c. Differing breastfeeding "learning" curves for individual infants

**IV** Maternal postpartum biopsychosocial issues affecting breastfeeding and lactation

 A. Physiologic conditions related to depleted reserves or a decreased resistance to illness

  1. Sequelae related to the stress of a multiple pregnancy; complications or interventions to prolong the pregnancy

  2. Recovery from surgical birth

  3. Profound sleep deprivation related to frequent interruptions for multiples' care/feeding

 B. Emotional; chronic feeling of being overwhelmed

  1. Incidence of postpartum depression (PPD) 2–3 times higher in mothers of multiples

  2. Unrealistic expectations for the maternal role with multiple infants

  3. Lack of support systems

 C. Mother-infant(s) attachment—different process than with a single infant

  1. Common variations (attachment terms copyright Karen Kerkhoff Gromada, 2000):

   a. Unit attachment—initial feelings of attachment are for the set of babies as a whole

   b. Flip-flop attachment—alternating focus of attention on one infant at a time

   c. Preferential attachment—a persistent, deeper attachment for one baby; harmful to all

  2. Differentiation—parental comparisons of multiples' physical and behavioral traits

**V** Maintaining breastfeeding (Gromada, 1999; Gromada and Spangler, 1998; Sollid, Evans, and Garrett, 1989)

A. Coordinating breastfeeding related to multiple infant feeding patterns

1. Individual variations related to normal variations in breastfeeding patterns (for example, the typical number of feedings per 24 hours) or breastfeeding styles (for example, the typical length of feedings)

2. Affected by zygosity (genetically based patterns) and the maternal perception of the infants as per the differentiation process

3. Individual outcome measures related to within normal limits outputs and weight gains

a. Coordinate 24-hour feeding charts by assigning a paper color per infant.

b. Outcomes might reflect individual breastfeeding ability/effectiveness of the milk transfer.

B. Feeding rotation—anything works if based on the infants' cues

1. Alternate breasts each feeding.

2. Alternate breasts every 24 hours (more often if you have an odd number of multiples); most favored.

3. Assign each multiple a specific breast.

a. Benefits—increased ability to suckle effectively or to minimize thrush consequences

b. Risks—infant refusal to feed on the opposite breast if one breast cannot be suckled for any reason

C. Individual versus simultaneous feeding

1. Affected by infants' suckling abilities and maternal choice

2. Rationale for simultaneous feeding:

a. Saves maternal time and facilitates the development of a routine

b. Theoretical increase in milk production (many mothers have had no problem with milk production when multiples are always fed individually if feedings were cue-based)

c. Effective breastfeeding of one infant might stimulate improved breastfeeding in another by triggering the milk ejection reflex (MER)

3. Most MOMs combine simultaneous with individual feedings

4. Support/"extra arms" = household pillows or a larger, deeper nursing pillow

5. Positions for simultaneous feeding (Gromada, 1999; Wilson-Clay and Hoover, 1999)

a. Double clutch/double football (variation = double perpendicular)

b. Double cradle or criss-cross cradle (variation = V-hold)

        c. Cradle-clutch combination (variation = layered/parallel)

        d. Double straddle (variation = double upright; kneeling/standing)

        e. Double prone (variation = double "alongside")

  D. Maternal comfort

    1. Because of the increased time spent breastfeeding multiple infants, many mothers create a nursing station

        a. A wide, padded chair or sofa; for example, an upholstered recliner

        b. A nearby table for snacks, beverages, portable telephone, remote controls, and so on

        c. Located in a room where the mother wishes to spend most of her time

    2. Nutrition—a natural increase in hunger and thirst

        a. Strategies for eating while breastfeeding; for example, one-handed snacks, a sports mug

        b. A suppressed/minimal appetite in a breastfeeding mother of multiples might be a symptom of postpartum depression

  E. Role of routine or "scheduling" feeds

    1. Maternal need for control

    2. Related to profound sleep deprivation/recovery from multiple pregnancy and birth

    3. Ability to anticipate infants' care/feeding needs appears to increase with higher-order multiples

    4. Strategies

        a. Discuss realistic expectations for the individual infant pattern

        b. Wake one to feed with or immediately after another; day and/or night (the risk of inadequate feeding of one or more babies/ignoring an infant's higher need for attention)

        c. Co-sleeping options to increase maternal sleep

**VI** Ongoing breastfeeding difficulties (see related chapters) (Gromada, 1999 and Auer and Gromada, 1998)

  A. Infant-related (cited as most commonly associated with early weaning by mothers of multiples)

    1. An ongoing latch-on or suckling difficulty of one might effect breastfeeding for all.

        a. Limited maternal time/effort available to work with affected multiple(s)

        b. Limited time for compensatory milk expression related to decreased milk removal by the affected infant(s)

2. Inadequate weight gain of one or more multiples
   a. Real: inadequate outputs or consistent poor gain: less than _____ oz (14–15g)/day or less than 4oz (112g)/week
   b. Perceived: genetically based, slower, but within normal limits growth/gain of one; slow, steady gain of _____ oz (14–15g)/day or 3–4oz (84-112g)/week of one

B. Maternal (cited as most commonly associated with early weaning by mothers of multiples)
   1. Milk sufficiency
      a. Real: related to sequelae of pregnancy/birth complications, underlying maternal condition, or delayed/infrequent milk emptying via direct breastfeeding or compensatory milk expression
      b. Perceived: related to confusion resulting from an increase in the total number of daily breastfeedings or confusion from variations in the infants' breastfeeding patterns
   2. Nipple or breast pain
      a. Less time to consistently intervene related to the number of infants requiring care
      b. Delayed or missed feedings combined with a decreased maternal resistance for illness might have a greater impact due to increased production; for example, a faster engorgement or the development of a plugged duct or mastitis
      c. Mastitis from milk stasis due to an abundant milk supply and erratic feeding patterns

C. Intervention—establish/maintain milk production at the expense of time with an individual infant at the breast
   1. The mother might remain more confident and more likely to continue breastfeeding when milk production is less of a concern
   2. The infant's ability at the breast often improves with time/maturity; milk production can improve or be maintained only if removed frequently

VII Full or partial breastfeeding and breast milk feeding options
   A. Descriptions
      1. Full breastfeeding—done for weeks to months with two to four multiples
      2. Partial breastfeeding—occasional "topping off" to scheduled supplementary feedings
      3. Full or partial breast milk feeding—feeding of expressed breast milk via an alternative feeding method for all/some feedings

B. Implementation of feeding options

1. Any option can be used with one/more/all multiple(s) at any time during lactation.

2. Any option can be used for short-term or long-term.

   a. MOMs have moved from breast milk feeding to partial to full breastfeeding.

   b. MOMs have moved from full to partial breastfeeding.

3. Partial breastfeeding can include the use of expressed breast milk (EBM) or artificial baby milk (ABM).

4. The rationale involved in decision-making:

   a. Affected by ongoing infant or maternal breastfeeding-related issues

   b. Psychosocial issues related to the care of two or more newborns/infants

   c. Partial breastfeeding might mean the difference between continuing to breastfeed at all versus totally weaning

D. Factors associated with partial breastfeeding:

1. Benefits (actual or perceived):

   a. Adequate infant nutrition (when intake is of concern for one or more infants)

   b. Help with some feedings

   c. Some breastfeeding/breast milk is better than no breastfeeding/breast milk related to milk properties and the maternal-infant(s) attachment

2. Risks (actual):

   a. Decreased milk production/increased difficulty improving for multiples

   b. Increased infant illnesses related to a decreased human milk intake

   c. Increased infant preference/confusion related to an alternative feeding method yet a decreased time to work in order to get one infant to the breast due to having to care for two or more infants

3. Maintaining milk production when using partial breastfeeding:

   a. Minimize use; for example, "topping off" or complementing a breastfeeding versus a supplement

   b. Supplement one or more on an as-needed basis; for example, the need for uninterrupted sleep

   c. Avoid alternating feeding methods every other feeding—full work of both methods

   d. Maintain milk removal at least 8–12 times/24 hours

VIII Breastfeeding older babies and toddler multiples

A. Supplementary vitamins or iron:

1. Based on the individual multiple's situation/outcomes

2. Iron might be needed for preterm multiples or for the "donor" of TTTS.

B. Starting solids

1. Individual multiples might demonstrate readiness at different times, especially dizygotes

2. MOMs might be encouraged to introduce solids earlier

    a. The perception that solid feedings lengthen the time between feedings

    b. Preterm multiples' GI tracts are less mature and less ready for early solids introduction

C. Weaning

1. Individual baby-led/child-led weaning:

    a. Might occur weeks, months, or years apart

    b. Early (10–12 months), abrupt baby-led weaning slightly more common

2. Mother-encouraged, baby-led weaning—imposition of some limits on breastfeeding, such as time, place, and so on; usually due to the effect of multiples' interactions while at the breast

3. Mother-led—a purposeful decrease in the number of breastfeedings by the mother; more common related feelings of being overwhelmed by the multiple infants/toddlers

    a. Gradual

    b. Abrupt—the counselor can encourage gradual weaning if listening to the mother actively

D. How multiples differ from singletons:

1. Increased nursing strikes in older infancy (etiology unknown)

2. Increased biting of the mother's breast

3. Increased interaction between the multiples during breastfeeding

    a. Playful to punching behaviors—often builds up from playful to pushing to punching

    b. Jealous breastfeeding—one requests to breastfeed only because another is breastfeeding

    c. Frenzy feeding—both or all "attack" the mother in order to breastfeed whenever she sits

IX  IBCLC role

A. Provide perspective for MOMs

B. Enhance maternal confidence

C. Encourage maternal flexibility related to adaptation to the individual infants' patterns

D. Recommend interventions that are realistic for the special situation:

1. Present the short- and long-term benefits and risks of any intervention.
2. Acknowledge the effect that multiples have on a plan of care for an individual infant.
3. Revise the plan as needed.

E. Refer MOMs to other breastfeeding MOM/breastfeeding resources.

# References

Auer C, Gromada KK. A case report of breastfeeding quadruplets: Factors perceived as affecting breastfeeding. *J Hum Lact* 1998;14(2):135–141.

Gromada KK. Mothering multiples: Breastfeeding and caring for twins or more, rev. ed. Schaumburg, IL: La Leche League International, 1999.

Gromada KK, Spangler KA. Breastfeeding twins and higher-order multiples. *JOGNN* 1998; 27(4):441–449.

Gromada KK. Breastfeeding more than one: Multiples and tandem breastfeeding. NAACOG's (AWHONN's) *Clinical Issues in Perinatal and Women's Health Nursing*, 1992; 3(4):656–666.

Keith L, Keith D. Multiple birth: Epidemiology, perinatal outcomes and long term sequelae. Chicago, IL: The Center for Study of Multiple Birth (online), 1999. Available from: www.multiplebirth.com/first.htm.

Luke B, Eberlein T. When you're expecting twins, triplets or quads: A complete resource. New York: Harperperennial Library, 1999.

Martin JA, Park MM. Trends in twin and triplet births: 1980-97. Hyattsville, MD: National Center for Health Statistics (online), 1999. Abstract from: www.cdc.gov/nchswww/releases/99facts/99sheets/multiple.htm.

Mead LJ, Chuffo R, Lawlor-Klean P, Meier PP. Breastfeeding success with quadruplets. *JOGNN* 1992; 21(3):221–227.

National Center for Health Statistics (NCHS). Update on Risk Factors for Infant Mortality. Hyattsville, MD: Author (online), 1998. Abstract from: www.cdc.gov/nchs/releases/98facts/98sheets/infmort.htm.

Saint L, Maggiore P, Hartmann PE. Yield and nutrient content of milk in eight women breast-feeding twins and triplets. *Br J Nutr* 1986; 56(1):49–58.

Sollid DT, Evans SG, Garrett A. Breastfeeding multiples. *J Perinat Neonat Nurs* 1989; 3(1):46–63.

Wilson-Clay B, Hoover K. The breastfeeding atlas. Austin, TX: LactNews Press, 1999.

# LACTATIONAL PHARMACOLOGY

*Thomas W. Hale, RPh, PhD*

## OBJECTIVES

- Describe the entry of medications into human milk.
- List the effect of postpartum timing on drug entry.
- Describe the chemistry of medications that enables or prevents their entry into human milk.
- Describe drug kinetic parameters that are important in breastfeeding mothers.
- Describe the milk/plasma ratio and its importance for evaluating drug risks in the breastfeeding mother.

## Introduction

Safely using medications in breastfeeding mothers requires a certain basic knowledge of how drugs enter breast milk, which drugs are of potential risk, and factors that might increase or decrease the infant's sensitivity to the medication. The amount of drug entering breast milk is largely determined by its maternal plasma kinetics, its lipid solubility, its molecular size, and other factors. The use of these kinetic parameters makes determining the risks of medications much less difficult, particularly with newer medications. Although there are many exceptions, a simple rule of thumb is that less than 1 percent of the maternal dose will ultimately find its way into the milk (and subsequently, to the baby). Relative infant doses of less than 10 percent are generally considered safe for the infant.

I   Determine the need for medication

    A. Is this medication really necessary, and could the mother do without the medication?

        1. Just how effective is the drug?

            a. Some antihistamines are only minimally effective and may not be necessary.

      b. If a medication is not efficacious, then its use might not be advisable.

      c. An example is the use of antihistamines for colds, and so on.

  2. Could the mother wait several months before undergoing therapy, such as for a toenail fungus or a cosmetic surgical procedure?

  3. If the drug is an herbal medication, is it really necessary?

      a. Could the mother wait to use the drug until after she has discontinued breastfeeding?

      b. Is its use really justified?

  4. Extremely high doses of vitamins could be potentially harmful and are not really necessary; thus, their risks might outweigh the benefits of their use.

**II** Maternal factors that affect drug transfer

  A. Dose of medication

    1. Is the dose of the medication greater or lesser than the normal range?

    2. How is the plasma level of the medication changed by the dose used in the mother? If a mother is using 25,000 units of vitamin A, that is significantly more risky than a 5,000-unit dose.

    3. Is the medication formulation a rapid or sustained-release product?

      a. How does this medication change the mother's plasma levels and the risk to the infant?

      b. Sustained-release drugs should be considered as if they were long half-life drugs.

    4. When is the medication dosed, and how does the dosing interval affect plasma levels and milk levels?

      a. If a mother takes a medication at night and does not breastfeed until the morning, this situation is significantly different than if she breastfeeds every two hours.

    5. Is the dose of medication absorbed orally by the mother?

      a. Thus, what are her plasma levels? Are they high or really low?

      b. Plasma levels are generally in equilibrium with the milk at all times.

      c. Higher plasma levels mean higher milk levels.

    6. Most asthma medications are used via inhalation; thus, maternal plasma levels of the medication are virtually nil and are not likely to produce milk levels at all.

**III** Entry of drugs into human milk

  A. The amount of drug excreted into milk depends on a number of factors

    1. The lipid solubility of the drug

    2. The molecular size of the drug

3. The blood level attained in the maternal circulation

4. Protein binding in the maternal circulation

5. Oral bioavailability in the infant and mother

6. The half-life in the maternal and infant's plasma compartments

B. Although this description is somewhat simplistic for a sophisticated and somewhat obscure system, these pharmacokinetic terms provide a reasonably complete system for evaluating drug penetration into milk and the degree of exposure of the infant.

**IV** Drug entry into the milk compartment

A. Drugs enter the breast milk primarily by diffusion driven by equilibrium forces between the maternal plasma compartment and the maternal milk compartment.

1. Medications enter the milk by transferring from the maternal plasma, through the capillary walls, past the alveolar epithelium, and into the milk compartment.

2. During the first four days postpartum, large gaps exist between alveolar cells.

3. These gaps might permit enhanced drug entry into human milk during the colostral period, but the absolute amount of the drug in the milk might still be quite low (refer to Figure 23-1).

4. After 4–14 days, the alveolar cells enlarge—shutting off many of the intercellular gaps—and the amount of drug entry into the milk is reduced.

5. Because the alveolar epithelium has rather tight junctions, most drugs dissolve through the bilayer membranes of the alveolar cells.

6. Dissolving through the bilayer lipid membranes is difficult for most mediations, however—particularly those that are ionic or polar.

**Figure 23-1**
Alveolar cell gaps as a function of days postpartum

(Courtesy Thomas Hale, Medications and Mother's Milk, 9th ed., 2000)

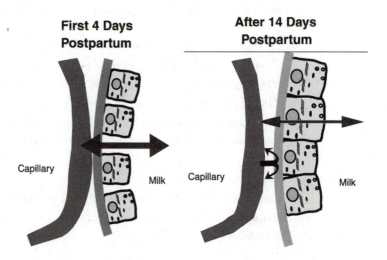

**First 4 Days Postpartum**

**After 14 Days Postpartum**

Capillary

Milk

Capillary

Milk

7. The more lipid-soluble a drug is, the greater the capability of the drug to penetrate into the milk.

8. Drugs that are active in the central nervous system (CNS) generally attain higher levels in the milk compartment simply because their chemistry is ideal for entry.

9. Drugs in the maternal plasma compartment are in complete equilibrium with the milk compartment; there might be more or less in the milk compartment, but they are still in equilibrium.

10. Several pumping systems exist, one of which is most important.

   a. For example, iodine has a rather high milk/plasma ratio and is readily pumped into the milk compartment.

   b. Therefore, high doses of iodine should be avoided.

   c. Includes vaginal Betadyne (povidone iodide) and radioactive I-131a

11. Many electrolytes, such as sodium chloride, magnesium, and so on, are tightly controlled by the alveolar cell; even high maternal levels might not produce significant changes in milk-electrolyte composition.

B. Protein binding and its effect on drug levels in milk

   1. As a general rule, most drugs are transported in blood that is bound to plasma albumin—a large molecular-weight protein that resides in the plasma.

   2. The more the drug is bound to milk, the less that is available free in the plasma compartment to enter into various other compartments, particularly the milk compartment.

   3. As the percent of drug binding increases, the level of the drug in the milk decreases.

   4. Drugs that have high protein binding can be chosen in order to attempt to reduce milk levels.

C. Lipid solubility

   1. As a general rule, the more lipid-soluble a drug, the higher the milk levels.

   2. The more polar or water-soluble a drug, the less the milk levels will be.

   3. While it is hard to determine the lipid solubility of most compounds, a good rule is that if the drug readily enters the brain compartment (CNS), then it is more likely to enter the milk.

   4. Thus, a drug that is active in the brain should be more closely scrutinized than one that is not active.

D. Half-life of the medication

   1. The elimination half-life of the medication generally describes the time interval that is required after administration of the medication until one-half of the drug is eliminated from the body.

2. It is better to choose drugs that have shorter half-lives, because the length of exposure of the infant to the medication (via milk) is generally reduced.

3. Milk levels during the day will generally be lower if the maternal peak is avoided by waiting several half-lives to breastfeed the infant.

4. Long half-life drugs might have a tendency to build up in an infant.

   a. In many instances, the half-life of the medication might be much longer in a newborn infant than in the adult.

5. Thus, prolonged exposure to long half-life medications might lead to increasing plasma levels of the medication in the infant (refer to the drug Prozac as an example).

6. In essence, long half-life medications really become a problem only if they are ingested by the mother over a long period, thus enabling the infant to build up higher and higher plasma levels.

   a. Acute use of long half-life medications is not generally a problem.

7. One cannot always avoid long half-life medications.

   a. In these instances, become aware of the clinical dose provided to the infant via milk.

   b. If this dose is still low, then accumulation is not as likely to occur in the infant.

8. A general guideline is that it takes approximately five half-lives before a drug is VIRTUALLY ELIMINATED from the system.

E. Bioavailability

1. Bioavailability of a medication is a measure of just how much medication reaches the plasma of that individual.

2. While there is not a large amount of good bioavailability data regarding infants, it is thought that it does not differ greatly from that of an adult.

3. Measured in percentage, a drug that has 50 percent bioavailability generally means that only 50 percent of the medication administered actually reaches the plasma compartment of the mother or infant.

4. Drugs that have poor bioavailability fail to reach the plasma compartment for a variety of reasons.

   a. They are sequestered in the liver and cannot exit.

   b. They are destroyed in the gut (proteins, peptides, aminoglycosides, and so on).

   c. They are simply not absorbed in the small intestine (vancomycin).

5. The drug that has the lowest bioavailability should be chosen for breastfeeding mothers because it will greatly reduce the exposure of the infant to the medication.

F. Molecular weight of the medication

1. In general, the larger the molecular weight of the medication, the less likely it is to enter into the milk compartment.

   a. While some medications might enter the milk, their levels are reduced.

2. Drugs that have molecular weights greater than 800–1,000 daltons have greater difficulty in passing the alveolar cell and entering the milk.

3. Drugs that have huge molecular weights (such as 25,000–200,000 daltons) are virtually excluded from milk in clinically relevant amounts.

4. Drugs that have huge molecular weights include heparin, insulin, interferons, and low molecular-weight heparins.

G. Milk/plasma ratio

1. Scientifically, the milk/plasma ratio is a useful tool to evaluate the relative concentration of medication in the maternal plasma compared to the maternal milk compartment.

2. High milk/plasma ratio drugs like to enter milk, while low milk/plasma ratio drugs are less attracted to the milk compartment.

   a. Unless both levels (plasma and milk) are known in the specific patient, the milk/plasma ratio might not indicate the true risk of using the medication.

3. In the case where a medication has a high milk/plasma ratio (for example, 5) and an extremely low maternal plasma level, then five times a very low level is still very low (see Bupropion).

4. Unless a great deal is known about the maternal plasma level, the milk/plasma ratio might give the clinician the wrong impression.

5. It is helpful if the health care provider knows the dose per unit of milk.

   a. This way, he or she can calculate the dose to the infant via the milk and obtain a realistic view of the clinical dose that will be transferred to the infant via milk.

V Evaluating the infant

A. Assume that the premature infant is more susceptible to maternal drugs.

1. While many medications are often used in these situations, increased attentiveness to the risks is warranted.

2. Using a medication in an 8-month-old infant is significantly less risky than with a premature infant or even a full-term newborn.

B. Be aware of the health and well-being of the infant.

1. Infants who are on apnea monitors, infants who have GI syndromes, and so on should be evaluated more closely for compatibility of medications used during lactation.

C. What medications is the infant ingesting?
   1. Drug-drug interactions might occur between medications that the mother is ingesting and medications that the infant is ingesting.
D. Sedating medications should be avoided (Valium-like drugs, barbiturates, and older antihistamines), particularly in infants who have apnea or who are susceptible to Sudden Infant Death Syndrome (SIDS); however, their use in acute, one-time situations is significantly less problematic.
E. Over-the-counter medications
   1. Over-the-counter medications are also drugs (see Figures 23-2 and 23-3).

**Figure 23-2**    Herbal products used as galactagogues

| Common Name | Evidence for Efficacy | Possible Adverse Reactions |
|---|---|---|
| Alfalfa; *Medicago sativa* | No scientific or clinical evidence for efficacy as a galactogogue | Large quantities may cause pancytopenia |
| Caraway; *Carun carvi* | No scientific or clinical evidence for efficacy as a galactogogue | None |
| Dill; *Anethum graveolens* | No scientific or clinical evidence | None |
| Fennel; *Foeniculum vulgare* | Historical use | Allergic reaction, photo dermatitis, and contact dermatitis |
| Fenugreek; *Trigonella foenum* | Historical use | None when ingested in usual quantities |
| Rosemary; *Rosmarinus officinalis* | No scientific or clinical evidence for efficacy as a galactagogue | Ingestion of large amounts of the oil can result in gastrointestinal distress, kidney damange has been reported |
| Watercress; *Nasturtium officinale* | No scientific or clinical evidence | Gastrointestinal upset |
| Chaste tree; *Vitex angus-castus* | Animal studies have found an increase in lactation and mammary enlargementt | Gastrointestinal reactions, itching, rash, headaches, and increased menstrual flow |
| Lettuce Opium; *Lactuca virosa* | No scientific or clinical evidence | |
| Milk Thistle; *Silybum marianum* | Historical use | Allergic reaction, mild laxative effects have been reported |

**Figure 23-3**   Herbal products to avoid during breastfeeding

| Common Name | Potential Uses | Reason |
| --- | --- | --- |
| Aloe vera; *Aloe ferrox*; *Aloe perryi*; *Aloe vera* | Used orally as a stimulant laxative | Contains anthranoid derivatives |
| Basil; *Ocimum Basilicum* | Delayed menstruation | The concerns of this herb are based on therapeutic use and not use as a spice. The herb contains estragole which is a procarcinogen. Long-term use is not recommended; not recommended for use during lactation. |
| Black cohosh; *Cimicifuga racemosa* | Uterine stimulant, PMS, Menopause | Safety data lacking |
| Bladderwrack; *Fucus Vesiculosus* | Thyroid deficiency | Contains iodine |
| Borage; *Borago officinalis* | Mild expectorant, diuretic | Contains pyrrolizidine alkaloids. There is no evidence for effectiveness. |
| Buckthorn berry and bark; *Rhamnus catharticus* | Stimulant laxative | Contains anthranoids, which are contraindicated in breastfeeding. Lack of toxicological information. |
| Coltsfoot; *Tussilago farfara* | Coughs, bronchila congestion | Contains pyrrolizidine alkaloids |
| Comfrey; *Symphytum officinale* | Heal stomach ulcers, purify the blood; only topical use is recommended | Contains pyrrolizidine alkaloids |
| Ginseng; *Panax ginseng*; *Panax quinquefolium* | Increased mental capacity | May cause estrogenic side effects; also can cause diminished platelet adhesiveness. Some texts recommend avoiding during breastfeeding until more information is available. |
| Goldenseal; *Hydrastis canadensis* | Travelers diarrhea, topical antiseptic | Some texts recommend avoiding during lactation. |
| Kava Kava; *Piper methysticum* | Sedation | Sedative effects possibly pass into milk |
| Licorice; *Glycyrrhiza glabra* | Flavoring | Excessive consumption can result in psuedoaldosteronism. |
| Male fern; *Dryopteris filix-mas* | Topical use only | Poisonings have occurred. Use by German E commission not recommended. |
| Podophyllum; *Podophyllum peltatum* | Topical use only | Although there are no documented adverse reactions during breastfeeding, it is systematically absorbed and toxic; use is discouraged during breastfeeding. |
| Purging buckthorn; *Rhamnus catharticus* | Stimulant laxative | Contains anthranoid derivatives |
| Rhubarb Root; *Rheum officinale*; *Rheum palmatum* | Stimulant laxative | Lack of sufficient data |
| Uva Uris; *Arctostaphylos uva-ursi* | Urinary antiseptic, diuretic | Hydroquinone primary antiseptic portion of the plant can be toxic. Lack of information on transfer into milk; German E Commission recommends against use in lactation. Other compounds work just as well and may not be absorbed. |

2. Many mothers self-medicate without consulting a health care professional.

3. Mothers should avoid medications that are labeled as extra strength, maximum strength, or long acting.

   a. Usually, the lowest dose possible is recommended and is marked or labeled as regular strength.

4. Mothers should avoid (if possible) medications that contain a variety of ingredients (refer to Figure 23-4).

---

**Figure 23-4**    Table 1. Analgesics

Acetaminophen 325 mg - Y

Acetaminophen 500 mg - N

Actron (ketoprofen) - Y

Advil (ibuprofen) - Y

Aleve (naproxen) - Y

Alka-Seltzer Effervescent Antacid and Pain Reliever (aspirin, sodium bicarbonate) - N

Anacin (aspirin, caffeine) - N

Anacin Maximum Strength (aspirin, caffeine) - N

Anacin-3 Regular Strength (acetaminophen) -Y

Anacin-3 Maximum Strength (acetaminophen) -N

Anodynos (aspirin, salicylamide, caffeine) - N

Arthritis Pain Formula (aspirin, aluminum-magnesium hydroxide) - N

Arthritis Foundation (ibuprofen) - Y

Arthritis Foundation Aspirin Free (acetaminophen) - N

Arthritis Foundation Nighttime (acetaminophen, diphenhydramine) - N

Arthritis Foundation Safety Coated Aspirin (aspirin) - N

Arhropan (choline salicylate) - N

Ascriptin Arthritis Pain (aspirin, aluminum-magnesium hydroxide, calcium carbonate) - N

Ascriptin Regular Strength (aspirin, aluminum-magnesium hydroxide, calcium carbonate) - N

Aspercin (aspirin) - N

Aspercin Extra (aspirin) - N

Aspergum (aspirin) - N

Aspermin (aspirin) - N

Aspirin 81 mg - N

Aspirin 325 mg - N

Aspirin 500 mg - N

Aspirin Free Pain Relief (acetaminophen) - Y

Azo-Diac (phenazopyridine) - Y

Azo-Standard (phenazopyridine) - Y

Backache Caplets (magnesium salicylate) - N

Back-Quell (aspirin, ephedrine sulfate, atropine sulfate) - N

Bayer Adult Low Strength (aspirin) - N

Bayer Arthritis Extra Strength (aspirin) - N

Bayer Aspirin (aspirin) - N

Bayer Aspirin Extra Strength (aspirin) - N

NOTE: Y = usually safe when breastfeeding; N = avoid when breastfeeding

Bayer Regular Strength (aspirin) - N

Bayer Plus Extra Strength (aspirin) - N

Bayer PM Aspirin Plus Sleep Aid (aspirin, diphenhydramine) - N

BC Arthritis Strength (aspirin, salicylamide, caffeine) - N

BC Powder (aspirin, salicylamide, caffeine) - N

Bromo-Seltzer (acetaminophen, sodium bicarbonate, citric acid) - N

Bufferin Analgesic Tablets (aspirin) - N

Bufferin Arthritis Strength (aspirin) - N

Bufferin Extra-Strength (aspirin) - N

Cope (aspirin, caffeine, aluminum-magnesium hydroxide) - N

Datril Extra Strength Non-Aspirin (acetaminophen) - N

Doan's Extra Strength (magnesium salicylate) - N

Doan's PM Extra Strength (magnesium salicylate, diphenhydramine) - N

Doan's Regular Strength (magnesium salicylate) - N

Dynafed EX (acetaminophen) - N

Dynafed IB (ibuprofen) - Y

Dyspel (acetaminophen, ephedrine sulfate, atropine sulfate) - N

Ecotrin Low, Regular, or Maximum Strength (aspirin) - N

Emagrin (aspirin, caffeine, salicylamide) - N

Empirin Aspirin (aspirin) - N

Empirin Free (acetaminophen, caffeine) - N

Excedrin Aspirin Free (acetaminophen, caffeine) - N

Excedrin Extra Strength (acetaminophen, aspirin, caffeine) - N

Excedrin PM (acetaminophen, diphenhydramine) - N

Feverall Adult Strength Suppository (acetaminophen) - Y

Goody's Extra Strength (acetaminophen, aspirin, caffeine) - N

Goody's Extra Strength Headache (acetaminophen, aspirin, caffeine) - N

Haltran (ibuprofen) - Y

Healthprin Brand Aspirin (aspirin) - N

Heartline (aspirin) - N

Ibuprohm (ibuprofen) - Y

Legatrin (acetaminophen, diphenhydramine) - N

Midol IB Cramp Relief Formula (ibuprofen) - Y

Midol Menstrual Maximum Strength (acetaminophen, caffeine, pyrilamine) -N

Midol Menstrual Regular Strength Multisymptom Formula (acetaminophen, pyrilamine) - N

Midol PMS Maximum Strength (acetaminophen, pamabrom, pyrilamine) - N

Midol Teen Maximum Strength (acetaminophen, pamabrom) - N

Mobigesic (magnesium salicylate, phenyltoloxamine) - N

Momentum (magnesium salicylate) - N

Motrin IB (ibuprofen) - Y

Nuprin (ibuprofen) - Y

Orudis KT (ketoprofen) - Y

P-A-C (aspirin, caffeine) - N

(continued)

**Figure 23-4**    Table 1. Analgesics (continued)

Panadol Maximum Strength (acetaminophen) - N

Percogesic (acetaminophen, phenyltoloxamine) - N

Premsyn PMS (acetaminophen, pamabrom, pyrilamine) - N

Prodium (phenazopyridine) - Y

Re-Azo (phenazopyridine) - Y

St. Joseph Adult Aspirin (aspirin) - N

Stanback AF Extra Strength Powder (acetaminophen) - N

Stanback Original Formula Powder (aspirin, salicylamide, caffeine) - N

Supac (acetaminophen, aspirin, calcium gluconate, caffeine) - N

Tapanol Extra Strength (acetaminophen) - N

Tempra (acetaminophen) - Y

Tempra Quicklet (acetaminophen) - Y

Tylenol Arthritis Extended Relief (acetaminophen) - N

Tylenol Extra Strength (acetaminophen) - N

Tylenol PM (acetaminophen, diphenhydramine) - N

Tylenol Regular Strength (acetaminophen) - Y

Ultraprin (ibuprofen) - Y

Unisom With Pain Relief Nighttime (acetaminophen, diphenhydramine) - N

Uristat (phenazopyridine) - Y

UroFemme (phenazopyridine) - Y

Valorin (acetaminophen) - Y

Valorin Extra (acetaminophen) - N

Valorin Super (acetaminophen, caffeine) - N

Valprin (ibuprofen) - Y

Vanquish (aspirin, acetaminophen, caffeine, aluminum-magnesium hydroxide) - N

XS Hangover Relief (acetaminophen, calcium citrate, magnesium trisilicate, calcium carbonate, caffeine) - N

## Table 2. Cough, Cold, Allergy Preparations

Actifed (tripolidine, pseudoephedrine) - Y*, Y**

Actifed Allergy Daytime (pseudoephedrine ) - Y**

Actifed Allergy Nighttime (pesudoephedrine, diphenhydramine) - Y**

Actifed Plus (acetaminophen, pseudoephedrine, tripolidine) - N

Actifed Sinus Daytime (acetaminophen, pseudoephedrine) - N

Actifed Sinus Nighttime (acetaminophen, pseudoephedrine, diphenhydramine) - N

Advil Cold and Sinus (ibuprofen, pseudoephedrine) - N

Alcomed 2-60 (dexbrompheniramine, pseudoephedrine) - Y*, Y**

Alka-Seltzer Plus Cold & Cough Medicine (aspirin, chlorpheniramine, phenylpropanolamine, dextromethorphan) - N

NOTE: Y = usually safe when breastfeeding; Y* = usually safe when breastfeeding, monitor infant for drowsiness; Y** = usually safe when breastfeeding, monitor for decreased milk production, mother should drink extra fluids; N = avoid when breastfeeding

Alka-Seltzer Plus Cold & Cough Medicine Liqui-Gels (aspirin, chlorpheniramine, phenylpropanolamine, dextromethorphan) - N

Alka-Seltzer Plus Cold & Flu Medicine (acetaminophen, dextromethorphan, phenylpropanolamine, chlorpheniramine) - N

Alka-Seltzer Plus Cold & Flu Medicine Liqui-Gels (acetaminophen, dextromethorphan, phenylpropanolamine, chlorpheniramine) - N

Alka-Seltzer Plus Cold Medicine (aspirin, chlorpheniramine, pseudoephedrine, acetaminophen) - N

Alka-Seltzer Plus Cold Medicine Liqui-Gels (aspirin, chlorpheniramine, pseudoephedrine, acetaminophen) - N

Alka-Seltzer Plus Cold & Sinus Medicine (aspirin, phenylpropanolamine) - N

Alka-Seltzer Plus Cold & Sinus Medicine Liqui-Gels (pseudoephedrine, acetaminophen) - N

Alka-Seltzer Plus Night-Time Cold Medicine (aspirin, phenylpropanolamine) - N

Alka-Seltzer Plus Night-Time Cold Medicine Liqui-Gels (dextromethorphan, doxylamine, pseudoephedrine, acetaminophen) - N

Allerest Headache Strength (acetaminophen, chlorpheniramine, pseudoephedrine) - N

Allerest Maximum Strength (chlorpheniramine, pseudoephedrine) - Y*, Y**

Allerest No Drowsiness (acetaminophen, pseudoephedrine) - N

Allerest Sinus Pain Formula (acetaminophen, pseudoephedrine) - N

Allerest 12 Hour (chlorpheniramine, phenylpropanolamine) - N

Bayer Select Sinus Pain Relief Formula (acetaminophen, pseudoephedrine) - N

BC Allergy Sinus Cold Powder (aspirin, phenylpropanolamine, chlorpheniramine) - N

BC Sinus Cold Powder (aspirin, phenylpropanolamine) - N

Benadryl Allergy/Congestion (diphenhydramine, pseudoephedrine) - Y*, Y**

Benadryl Allergy/Cold (diphenhydramine, pseudoephedrine, acetaminophen) - N

Benadryl Allergy Liquid or Dye-Free Liquid (diphenhydramine) - Y*

Benadryl Allergy Sinus Headache Caplets & Gelcaps (diphenhydramine, pseudoephedrine, acetaminophen) - N

Benadryl Allergy Ultratab Tablets, Ultratab Kapseals, Chewables, or Dye-Free Liqui-Gels (diphenhydramine) - Y*

Benylin Adult Formula (dextromethorphan) - Y*

Denylin Cough Syrup (diphenhydramine) - Y*

Benylin Expectorant (dextromethorphan, guaifenesin) - Y*

Benylin Multisymptom (guaifenesin, pseudoephedrine, dextromethorphan) - N

Buckley's Mixture (dextromethorphan, ammonium carbonate, camphor, balsam, glycerin, menthol, pine needle oil) - N

Cerose DM (dextromethorphan, chlorpheniramine, phenylephrine, alcohol 2.4%) - N

Cheracol-D (dextromethorphan, guaifenesin) - Y*

Cheracol Plus (phenylpropanolamine, dextromethorphan, chlorpheniramine) - N

(continued)

**Figure 23-4**   Table 2. Cough, Cold, Allergy Preparations (continued)

Cheracol Sinus (dexbrompheniramine, pseudoephedrine) - N

Chlor-Trimeton 4-Hour Allergy (chlorpheniramine) - Y*

Chlor-Trimeton 4-Hour Allergy/Decongestant (chlorpheniramine, pseudoephedrine) - Y*, Y**

Chlor-Trimeton 8- and 12-Hour Allergy (chlorpheniramine) - N

Chlor-Trimeton 12-Hour Allergy/Decongestant (chlorpheniramine, pseudoephedrine) - N

CoADVIL (ibuprofen, pseudoephedrine) - N

COMTREX Deep Chest Cold and Congestion Relief (acetaminophen, guaifenesin, phenylpropanolamine, dextromethorphan) - N

COMTREX Maximum Strength Multi-Symptom Acute Head Cold & Sinus Pressure Relief (acetaminophen, brompheniramine, pseudoephedrine) - N

COMTREX Maximum Strength Multi-Symptom Cold & Cough Relief Caplet or Tablet (acetaminophen, pseudoephedrine, chlorpheniramine, dextromethorphan) - N

COMTREX Maximum Strength Multi-Symptom Cold & Cough Relief Liquid (acetaminophen, pseudoephedrine, chlorpheniramine, dextromethorphan) - N

COMTREX Maximum Strength Multi-Symptom Cold & Cough Relief Liqui-Gels (acetaminophen, phenylpropanolamine, chlorpheniramine, dextromethorphan) - N

Contac Severe Cold & Flu (phenylpropanolamine, chlorpheniramine, acetaminophen, dextromethorphan) - N

Contac 12-Hour Caplets (phenylpropanolamine, chlorpheniramine) - N

Contac 12-Hour Capsules (phenylpropanolamine, chlorpheniramine) - N

Coricidin D Decongestant (acetaminophen, chlorpheniramine, phenylpropanolamine) - N

Coricidin HBP Cold & Flu (acetaminophen, chlorpheniramine) - N

Coricidin HBP Cough & Cold (chlorpheniramine, dextromethorphan) - N

Coricidin HBP Nighttime Cold & Cough Liquid (acetaminophen, diphenhydramine) - N

Delsym Cough Formula (dextromethorphan) - N

Dimetapp Cold & Allergy Chewable Tablets or Quick Dissolving Tablets (brompheniramine, phenylpropanolamine) - N

Dimetapp Cold & Cough Liqui-Gels (brompheniramine, phenylpropanolamine, dextromethorphan) - N

Dimetapp Cold and Fever Suspension (acetaminophen, pseudoephedrine, brompheniramine) - N

Dimetapp DM Elixir (brompheniramine, phenylpropanolamine, dextromethorphan) - N

Dimetapp Elixir (brompheniramine, phenylpropanolamine) - N

Dimetapp Extentabs (brompheniramine, phenylpropanolamine) - N

Dimetapp Tablets and Liqui-Gels (brompheniramine, phenylpropanolamine) - N

Dristan (phenylephrine, chlorpheniramine, acetaminophen) - N

Dristan Maximum Strength (pseudoephedrine, acetaminophen) - N

Drixoral Allergy/Sinus (pseudoephedrine, dexbrompheniramine, acetaminophen) - N

Drixoral Cold & Allergy (pseudoephedrine, dexbrompheniramine) - N

Drixoral Cold & Flu (acetaminophen, dexbrompheniramine, pseudoephedrine) - N

Drixoral Nasal Decongestant (pseudoephedrine) - N

Efidac-24 (pseudoephedrine) - N

Expressin 400 (guaifenesin, pseudoephedrine) - Y**

4-Way Cold Tablets (acetaminophen, phenylpropanolamine, chlorpheniramine) - N

Guaifed (guaifenesin, pseudoephedrine) - Y**

Guaitab (guaifenesin, pseudoephedrine) - Y**

Hyland's Cough Syrup With Honey (ipecac, potassium antimony tartrate) - N

Hyland's C-Plus Cold Tablets (herbs, potassuim iodide) - N

Isoclor Timesule (chlorpheniramine, phenylpropanolamine) - N

Isohist 2.0 (dexbrompheniramine) - Y*

Motrin IB Sinus Pain Reliever (ibuprofen, pseudoephedrine) - N

Nasalcrom A Tablets (chlorpheniramine) - Y*

Nasalcrom CA Caplets (pseudoephedrine, acetaminophen) - N

Novahistine (chlorpheniramine, phenylephrine) - Y*, Y**

Novahistine-DMX (dextromethorphan, guaifenesin, pseudoephedrine) - N

Oscillococcinum Pellets (herbs) - N

Pertussin DM Extra Strength (dextromethorphan) - N

Pyrroxate (chlorpheniramine, phenylpropanolamine, acetaminophen) - N

Robitussin (guaifenesin) - Y

Robitussin-CF (guaifenesin, phenylpropanolamine, dextromethorphan) - N

Robitussin-DM (guaifenesin, dextromethorphan) - Y*

Robitussin-PE (guaifenesin, pseudoephedrine) - Y**

Robitussin Cold—Cold, Cough, & Flu Liqui-Gels (acetaminophen, guaifenesin, pseudoephedrine, dextromethorphan) - N

Robitussin Cold—Night-Time Liqui-Gels (acetaminophen, pseudoephedrine, dextromethorphan) - N

Robitussin Cold—Severe Congestion Liqui-Gels (guaifenesin, pseudoephedrine) - Y**

Ryna Liquid (chlorpheniramine, pseudoephedrine) - Y*, Y**

Ryna-C Liquid (codeine) - N

Ryna-CX Liquid (codeine, pseudoephedrine, guaifenesin) - N

Scot-Tussin DM (dextromethorphan, chlorpheniramine) - N

Scot-Tussin Expectorant (guaifenesin) - Y

Scot-Tussin Sugar Free, Alcohol Free Expectorant (guaifenesin) - Y

Scot-Tussin Sugar-Free Allergy Relief Formula (diphenhydramine) - Y*

Scot-Tussin Sugar-Free DM (dextromethorphan, chlorpheniramine) - N

(continued)

**Figure 23-4**    Table 2. Cough, Cold, Allergy Preparations (continued)

Sinarest No Drowsiness (acetaminophen, pseudoephedrine) - N

Sinarest Regular and Extra Strength (acetaminophen, chlorpheniramine, phenylprropanolamine) - N

Sine-Aid Maximum Strength Sinus Medication (acetaminophen, pseudoephedrine) - N

Sine-Off No Drowsiness Formula (acetaminophen, pseudoephedrine) - N

Sine-Off Sinus Medicine (chlorpheniramine, pseudoephedrine, acetaminophen) - N

Singlet (pseudoephedrine, chlorpheniramine, acetaminophen) - N

Sinutab Non-Drying Liquid Caps (pseudoephedrine, guaifenesin) - Y**

Sinutab Sinus Allergy Medication Maximum Strength (acetaminophen, chlorpheniramine, pseudoephedrine) - N

Sudafed Cold & Allergy Tablets (chlorpheniramine, pseudoephedrine) - Y*, Y**

Sudafed Cold & Cough Liquid Caps (acetaminophen, guaifenesin, pseudoephedrine, dextromethorphan) - N

Sudafed Cold & Sinus Liquid Caps (acetaminophen, pseudoephedrine) - N

Sudafed Nasal Decongestant (pseudoephedrine) - Y**

Sudafed Non-Drying Sinus Liquid Caps (guaifenesin, pseudoephedrine) - Y**

Sudafed Severe Cold Formula (acetaminophen, pseudoephedrine, dextromethorphan) - N

Sudafed Sinus (acetaminophen, pseudoephedrine) - N

Sudafed 12-Hour Tablets (pseudoephedrine) - N

Sudafed 24-Hour Tablets (pseudoephedrine) - N

Suppressin DM (dextromethorphan, guaifenesin) - Y*

TAVIST Allergy Tablets (clemastine) - Y*

TAVIST-D Caplets or Tablets (clemastine, phenylpropanolamine) - N

TAVIST Sinus Caplets or Gelcaps (acetaminophen, pseudoephedrine) - N

Theraflu Flu and Cold Medicine (acetaminophen, pseudoephedrine, chlorpheniramine) - N

Theraflu Maximum Strength Flu, Cold and Cough Medicine (acetaminophen, dextromethorphan, pseudoephedrine, chlorpheniramine) - N

Theraflu Maximum Strength Flu and Cold Medicine (acetaminophen, pseudoephedrine, chlorpheniramine) - N

Theraflu Maximum Strength Nighttime (acetaminophen, pseudoephedrine, chlorpheniramine) - N

Theraflu Maximum Strength Non-Drowsy (acetaminophen, pseudoephedrine, dextromethorphan) - N

Triaminic AM Cough and Decongestant (pseudoephedrine, dextromethorphan) - N

Triaminic AM Decongestant (pseudoephedrine) - Y*

Triaminic Cold & Allergy Softchews (pseudoephedrine, dextromethorpham, chlorpheniramine) - Y*, Y**

Triaminic Cold & Cough Softchews (pseudoephedrine, dextromethorphan, chlorpheniramine) - N

Triaminic DM Syrup (phenylpropanolamine, dextromethorphan) - N

Triaminic Expectorant (guaifenesin, phenylpropanolamine) - N

Triaminic Night Time (pseudoephedrine, dextromethorphan, chlorpheniramine) - N

Triaminic Severe Cold & Fever (acetaminophen, pseudoephedrine, dextromethorphan, chlorpheniramine) - N

Triaminic Sore Throat (acetaminophen, dextromethorphan) - N

Triaminic Syrup (phenylpropanolamine, chlorpheniramine) - N

Triaminic Throat Pain & Cough Softchews (acetaminophen, pseudoephedrine, dextromethorphan) - N

Triaminicin Tablets (acetaminophen, phenylpropanolamine, chlorpheniramine) - N

Triaminicol Cold & Cough (phenylpropanolamine, dextromethorphan, chlorpheniramine) - N

Tylenol Allergy Sinus Maximum Strength (acetaminophen, chlorpheniramine, pseudoephedrine) - N

Tylenol Allergy Sinus NightTime Maximum Strength (acetaminophen, pseudoephedrine, diphenhydramine) - N

Tylenol Cold Medication Multi-Symptom Formula (acetaminophen, chlorpheniramine, pseudoephedrine, dextromethorphan) - N

Tylenol Cold Medication No Drowsiness Formula (acetaminophen, pseudoephedrine, dextromethorphan) - N

Tylenol Cold Multi-Symptom Severe Congestion (acetaminophen, dextromethorphan, guaifenesin, pseudoephedrine) - N

Tylenol Flu NightTime Maximum Strength Gelcap (acetaminophen, diphenhydramine, pseudoephedrine) - N

Tylenol Flu NightTime Maximum Strength Hot Medication (acetaminophen, diphenhydramine, pseudoephedrine) - N

Tylenol Flu NightTime Maximum Strength Liquid (acetaminophen, dextromethorphan, doxylamine, pseudoephedrine) - N

Tylenol Severe Allergy (acetaminophen, diphenhydramine) - N

Tylenol Sinus Maximum Strength (acetaminophen, pseudoephedrine) - N

Tylenol Sinus NightTime Maximum Strength (acetaminophen, doxylamine, pseudoephedrine) - N

Ursinus (pseudoephedrine, aspirin) - N

Vicks DayQuil LiquiCaps, Liquid (pseudoephedrine, acetaminophen, dextromethorphan) - N

Vicks DayQuil Sinus Pressure & Pain Relief (ibuprofen, pseudoephedrine) - N

Vicks 44 Cough Relief (dextromethorphan, alcohol 5%) - Y*

Vicks 44D Cough & Head Congestion Relief (dextromethorphan, pseudoephedrine, alcohol 5%) - N

Vicks 44E Cough & Chest Congestion Relief (dextromethorphan, guaifenesin, alcohol 5%) - Y*

Vicks 44M Cough, Cold & Flu Relief (dextromethorphan, pseudoephedrine, chlorpheniramine, acetaminophen, alcohol 10%) - N

Vicks NyQuil LiquiCAps (doxylamine, dextromethorphan, acetaminophen, pseudoephedrine) - N

Vicks NyQuil Liquid (doxylamine, destromethorphan, acetaminophen, pseudoephedrine, alcohol 10%) - N

*(continued)*

**Figure 23-4**    Table 3. Cough and Cold Lozenges and Sprays

Celestial Seasonings Soothers Herbal Throat Drops (menthol, pectin) - Y

Cepacol Maximum Strength Sore Throat Lozenges (menthol, cetylpyridinium, benzocaine) - Y

Cepacol Maximum Strength Sore Throat Spray (dyclonine, cetylpyridinium) - Y

Cepacol Regular Strength Sore Throat Lozenges (menthol, cetylpyridinium) - Y

Cepastat Cherry Lozenges (phenol, menthol) - N

Cepastat Extra Strength Lozenges (phenol, menthol eucalyptus oil) - N

Cepastat Lozenges (phenol) - N

Cheraol Sore Throat Spray (phenol) - N

Halls Mentho-Lyptus Drops (menthol) - Y

Halls Plus Cough Suppressant Drops (menthol, pectin) - Y

HOLD Lozenges (dextromethorphan) - Y*

Listerine Lozenges (hexylresorcinol) - N

N'ICE Lozenges (menthol) - Y

Robitussin Cough Drops (menthol, pectin, eucalyptus) - Y

Scot-Tussin Sugar-Free Cough Chasers (dextromethorphan) - Y*

Sucrets 4-Hour Cough Suppressant Lozenges (menthol, dextromethorphan) - Y*

Sucrets Maximum Strength lozenges (dyclonine) - Y

Sucrets Regular Strength (hexylresorcinol) - N

Sucrets Regular Strength Vapor (dyclonine) - Y

Vicks Chloraseptic Lozenges (benzocaine, menthol) - Y

Vicks Chloraseptic Sore Throat Spray (phenol) - N

Vicks Cough Drops (menthol) - Y

NOTE: Y = usually safe when breastfeeding; Y* = usually safe when breastfeeding, monitor infant for drowsiness; N = avoid when breastfeeding

## Table 4. Nasal Preparations

Afrin Allergy Spray (phenylephrine) - Y**

Afrin Extra Moisturizing Spray (oxymetazoline) - Y**

Afrin Moisturizing Saline Mist (sodium chloride) - Y

Afrin Original Spray, Nose Drops and Pump Mist (soxymetazoline) - Y**

Afrin Saline Mist With Eucalyptol and Menthol (Sodium chloride) - Y

Afrin Severe Congestion Spray (oxymetazoline) - Y**

Afrin Sinus Nasal Spray (oxymetazoline) - Y**

Alconefrin (phenylephrine) - Y**

AYR Saline Mist and Drops (sodium chloride) - Y

Benzedres Inhaler (propylhedrine) - N

Cheracol Spray (oxymetazoline) - Y**

Dristan Long Lasting Spray (oxymetazoline) - Y**

NOTE: Y = usually safe when breastfeeding; Y** = usually safe when breastfeeding, monitor for decresaed milk production, mother should drink extra fluids; N = avoid when breastfeeding.

Dristan Spray (phenylephrine, pheniramine) - N

Duration 12-Hour Spray (oxymetazoline) - Y**

4-Way Fast Acting Nasal Spray (phenylephrine) - Y**

4-Way Long Acting Spray (oxymetazoline) - Y**

4-Way Saline Moisturizing Mist (sodium chloride) - Y

HuMIST Saline (sodium chloride) - Y

Little Noses Saline (sodium chloride) - Y

Nasalcrom Nasal Spray (cromolyn sodium) - Y

Nasal Moist Gel (aloe vera) - Y

Nasal Moist Solution (sodium chloride) - Y

Neo-Synephrine Drops (phenylephrine) - Y**

Neo-Synephrine Extra Strength Drops (phenylephrine) - Y**

Neo-Synephrine Mild, Regular, and Extra Strength Spray (phenylephrine) - Y**

Neo-Synephrine 12-Hour Extra Moisturizing Spray (oxymetazoline) - Y**

Neo-Synephrine 12-Hour Spray (oxymetazoline) - Y**

Nose Better Natural Mist (glycerin, sodium chloride) - Y

Nostril Nasal Decongestant (phenylephrine) - Y**

NTZ Spray and Drops (oxymetazoline) - Y**

Ocean Nasal Mist (sodium chloride) - Y

Otrivin Nasal Drops and Spray (xylometazoline) - N

Pretz (glycerin) - Y

Priviner Nasal Spray and Solution (naphazoline) - N

St. Joseph Nasal Decongestant (phenylephrine) - Y**

Salinex Nasal Mist and Drops (sodium chloride) - Y

Vicks Sinex Nasal Spray and Ultra Fine Mist (phenylephrine, champhor, eucalyptol, menthol) - N

Vicks Sinex 12-Hour Nasal Spray and Ultra Fine Mist (oxymetazoline, camphor, eucalyptol, menthol) - N

Vicks Vapor Inhaler (leumetamfetamine, menthol, camphor) - N

## Table 5. Asthma Preparations

Asthmahaler (epinephrine) - x

Asthmanephrin (racepinephrine) - x

Bronkaid Caplets (ephedrine, guaifenesin, theophylline) - x

Bronkaid Mist (epinephrine) - x

Bronkoelixir (ephedrine, guaifenesin, theophylline, phenobarbital) - x

Bronkotabs (ephedrine, guaifenesin, theophylline, phenobarbital) - x

Primatene Mist (epinephrine) - x

*(continued)*

NOTE: x = consultation with a physician is highly recommended prior to use.

**Figure 23-4**    Table 6. Antacids and Digestive Aids

Alka-Mints (calcium carbonate) - Y

Alka-Seltzer (aspirin, sodium bicarbonate) - N

Alka-Seltzer Extra Strength (aspirin, sodium bicarbonate) - N

Alka-Seltzer Gas Relief (simethicone) - Y

Alka-Seltzer Gold (sodium, potassium bicarbonate) - N

Alkets/Alkets Extra Strengh (calcium carbonate) - Y

Almora (magnesium gluconate) - Y

AlternaGEL (aluminum hydroxide) - Y

Alu-Cap (aluminum hydroxide) - Y

Aludrox (aluminum-magnesium hydroxide) - Y

Alu-Tab (aluminum hydroxide) - Y

Amitone (calcium carbonate) - Y

Amphogel (aluminum hydroxide) - Y

Axid AR (nizatidine) - Y

Basaljel (aluminum carbonate) - Y

Beano (enzymes, sorbitol) - Y

BeSure (food enzymes) - Y

Chooz Antacid Gum (calcium carbonate) - Y

Citrocarbonate (sodium bicarbonate-citrate) - N

Creamalin (aluminum-magnesium hydroxide) - Y

Dairy Ease (lactase) - Y

DDS-Acidophilus (lactobacillus acidophilus) - Y

Dicarbosil (calcium carbonate)

DiGel (simethicone, calcium carbonate, magnesium hydroxide) - Y

Eno (sodium tartrate-citrate) - N

Gas-X (simethicone) - Y

Gas-X Extra Strength (simethicone) - Y

Gaviscon Extra Strength (aluminum hydroxide, magnesium carbonate) - Y

Gaviscon Regular Strength Liquid (aluminum hydroxide, magnesium carbonate) - Y

Gaviscon Regular Strength Tablets (aluminum hydroxide, magnesium trisilicate) - Y

Gaviscon-2 (aluminum hydroxide, magnesium trisilicate, sodium bicarbonate) - N

Gelusil (aluminum-magnesium hydroxide, simethicone) - Y

Kudrox (simethicone, aluminum-magnesium hydroxide) - Y

Lactaid Original, Extra Strength, and Ultra (lactase) - Y

Lactinex (lactobacillus culture) - Y

Lactrase (lactase) - Y

Maalox Anti-Gas (simethicone) - Y

Maalox Anti-Gas Extra Strength (simethicone) - Y

Maalox Heartburn Relief (aluminum hydroxide, magnesium-calcium carbonate, potassium bicarbonate) - N

Maalox Magnesia and Alumina Oral Susp. (magnesium-aluminum hydroxide) - Y

Maalox Maximum Strength (magnesium-aluminum hydroxide, simethicone) - Y

Maalox Quick Dissolve Tablets (calcium carbonate) - Y

NOTE: Y = usually safe when breastfeeding; N = avoid when breastfeeding.

Marblen (magnesium-calcium carbonate) - Y

Mylanta AR (famotidine) - Y

Mylanta Fast-Acting (aluminum-magnesium hydroxide, simethicone) - Y

Mylanta Maximum Strength (aluminum-magnesium hydroxide, simethicone) - Y

Mylanta Supreme (calcium carbonate, magnesium hydroxide) - Y

Mylanta Tablets and Gelcaps (calcium carbonate, magnesium hydroxide) - Y

Nephrox (aluminum hydroxide) - Y

Pepcid AC (famotidine) - Y

Pepto-Bismol Original (bismuth subsalicylate) - N

Pepto-Bismol Maximum Strength (bismuth subsalicylate) - N

Phazyme-125 Softgels (simethicone) - Y

Phazyme-166 Maximum Strength (simethicone) - Y

Phillips Milk of Magnesia (magnesium hydroxide) - Y

Riopan (magaldrate) - Y

Riopan Plus (magaldrate, simethicone) - Y

Riopan Plus 2 (magaldrate, simethicone) - Y

Rolaids (calcium carbonate, magnesium hydroxide) - Y

Sodium Bicarbonate (sodium bicarbonate) - N

Tagamet HB (cimetidine) - Y

Tempo (calcium carbonate, aluminum-magnesium hydroxide) - Y

Titralac (calcium carbonate) - Y

Titralac Extra Strength (calcium carbonate) - Y

Titralac Plus Antacid (calcium carbonate, simethicone) - Y

Tums E-X Antacid (calcium carbonate) - Y

Tums Regular (calcium carbonate) - Y

Tums ULTRA Antacid (calcium carbonate) - Y

Zantac 75 (ranitidine) - Y

## Table 7. Laxatives, Stool Softeners

Bisacodyl - N

Cascara Sagrada - Y

Ceo-Two Evacuant Suppository (sodium bicarbonate, potassium bitartrate) - Y

Citrucel (methylcellulose) - Y

Colace (docusate) - Y

Correctol Laxative (bisacodyl) - N

Correctol Stool Softener (docusate) - Y

Dialose (docusate) - Y

Doxidan (casanthranol, docusate) - N

Dulcolax Tablets and Suppositories (bisacodyl) - N

Effer-Syllium (psyllium) - Y

Emulsoil (caster oil) - N

Epsom Salt (magnesium sulfate) - Y

Evac-Q-Kwik (bisacodyl) - N

Ex-Lax Chocolate or Regular (sennosides) - Y

Ex-Lax Maximum (sennosides) - N

*(continued)*

NOTE: The use of products containing phenolphthalein is contraindicated. Y = usually safe when breastfeeding; N = avoid when breastfeeding.

**Figure 23-4**    Table 7. Laxatives, Stool Softeners (continued)

Fiberall (psyllium) - Y

Fibercon (calcium polycarbophil) - Y

Fiber Naturale (methylcellulose) - Y

Fleet Enema Regular (sodium biphosphate, phosphate) - Y

Fleet Laxative (bisacodyl) - N

Garfield's Tea (senna) - Y

Gentlax S (senna concentrate, docusate) - N

Gentle Nature (sennosides) - Y

Glycerin Suppositories - Y

Haley's M-O (magnesium hydroxide, mineral oil) - N

Herb-Lax (senna) - Y

Hydrocil (psyllium) - Y

Innerclean Herbal (senna, psyllium) - N

Kellogg's Tasteless Castor Oil (castor oil) - N

Kondremul (mineral oil) - N

Konsyl Fiber (polycarbophil) - Y

Konsyl Powder (psyllium) - Y

Maalox Daily Fiber (psyllium) - Y

Maltsupex (barley malt extract) - Y

Metamucil (psyllium) - Y

Milkinol (mineral oil) - N

Mitrolan (polycarbophil) - Y

Mylanta Natural Fiber Supplement (psyllium) - Y

Nature's Remedy Tablets (cascara sagrada, aloe) - N

Neoloid (castor oil) - N

Perdiem Fiber (psyllium) Y

Perdiem Overnight Relief (psyllium, senna) - N

Peri-Colace (casanthranol, docusate) - N

Phillips Gelcaps (docusate) - Y

Phillips MIlk of Magnesia (magnesium hydroxide) - Y

Phospho-Soda (sodium phosphate) - Y

Purge Concentrate (castor oil) - N

Regulace (casanthranol, docusate) - N

Regulax SS (docusate) - Y

Regutol (docusate) - Y

Senokot (sennosides) - Y

Senokot-S (sennosides, docusate) - N

SenokotXTRA (sennosides) - N

Serutan (psyllium) - Y

Surfak (docusate) - Y

Syllact (psyllium) - Y

## Table 8. Anti-Diarrheal Preparations

Dairy Ease (lactase) - Y

Diar Aid (loperamide) - Y***

Diarrid (loperamide) - Y***

Diasorb (attapulgite) - Y

Donnagel (attapulgite) - Y

Equalactin (polycarbophil) - Y

Hylant's Diarrex (arsenicum, podophyllum, phosphorus, mercurius) - N

NOTE: Y = usually safe when breastfeeding; Y*** = use of loperamide should not exceed two days; N = avoid when breastfeeding.

Imodium A-D (loperamide) - Y***

Imodium Advanced (loperamide, simethicone) - Y***

Kao-Paverin (kaolin, pectin) - Y

Paopectate (attapulgite) - Y

Kaopectate Maximum (attapulgite) - Y

Pepto-Bismol (bismuth subsalicylate) - N

Rheaban (attapulgite) - Y

## Table 9. Nausea and Vomiting, Motion Sickness Preparations

Benadryl (diphenhydramine) - Y*

Bonine (meclizine) - N

Calm-X (dimenhydrinate) - Y*

Dramamine (dimenhydrinate) - Y*

Dramamine Less Drowsy (meclizine) - N

Emetrol (phosphorated carbohydrates) - Y

Pepto-Bismol (bismuth subsalicylate) - N

Marezine (cyclizine) - N

Nauzene (diphenhydramine) - Y*

Triptone (dimenhydrinate) - Y*

NOTE: Y = usually safe when breastfeeding; Y* = usually safe when breastfeeding, monitor infant for drowsiness; N = avoid when breastfeeding

## Table 10. Hemorrhoidal Preparations

Americaine (benzocaine) - Y

Anusol HC-Ointment (hydrocortisone) - Y

Anusol Ointment (pramoxine, mineral oil, zinc oxide) - Y

Anusol Suppositories (starch) - Y

Balneol (mineral oil, lanolin oil) - Y

Calmol 4 (zinc oxide, cocoa butter) - Y

Fleet Medicated Wipes (witch hazel) - Y

Fleet Pain-Relief (pramoxine) - Y

Hemorid for Women (pramoxine, phenylephrine) - Y

Hydrosal Hemorrhoidal (benzyl alcohol, ephedrine, zinc oxide) - Y

Nupercainal (dibucaine) - Y

Nupercainal Anti-Itch Cream (hydrocortisone) - Y

Nupercainal Suppositories (cocoa butter, zinc oxide) - Y

Pazo (benzocaine, ephedrine, zinc oxide, camphor) - Y

Peterson's Ointment (phenol, camphor) - Y

Preparation H Hydrocortisone Cream (hydrocortisone) - Y

Preparation H Ointment, Suppositories, and Cream (phenylephrine, shark liver oil) - Y

Procto Foam Non-Steroid (pramoxine) - Y

Rectacaine Ointment (petrolatum, shark liver oil, mineral oil) - Y

Rectacaine Suppositories (phenylephrine) - Y

(continued)

NOTE: Y = usually safe when breastfeeding.

**Figure 23-4**    Table 10. Hemorrhoidal Preparations (continued)

Tronolane Cream (pramoxine) - Y

Tronothane Hydrochloride (pramoxine, glycerin) - Y

Tronolane Suppository (zinc oxide) - Y

Tucks Gel (witch hazel, glycerin) - Y

Tucks Pads (witch hazel) - Y

Wyanoids (cocoa butter, shark liver oil, glycerin) - Y

## Table 11. Sleep Preparations

Alka-Seltzer PM Pain Reliever & Sleep Aid Medicine (aspirin, diphenhydramine) - N

Anacin PM Aspirin Free (acetaminophen, diphenhydramine) - N

Bayer PM Extra Strength Aspirin Plus Sleep Aid (aspirin, diphenhydramine) - N

Benadryl (diphenhydramine) - Y*

Compoz (diphenhydramine) - Y*

Doan's PM Extra Strength (magnesium salicylate, diphenhydramine) - N

Dormarex and Dormarex 2 (diphenhydramine) - Y*

Dormin (diphenhydramine) - Y*

Excedrin PM (acetaminophen, diphenhydramine) - N

Goody's PM (acetaminophen, diphenhydramine) - N

Legatrim PM (diphenhydramine, acetaminophen) - N

Melatonex (melatonin) - N

Melatonin (melatonin) - N

Melatonin (pyridoxine, melatonin) - N

Melatonin Lozenge (melatonin, xylitol) - N

Melatonin PM Dual Release (calcium, vitamin B6, magnesium, niacin, melatonin, xylitol) - N

Midol PM Night Time Formula (diphenhydramine, acetaminophen) - N

Nervine Nightime Sleep Aid (diphenhydramine) - Y*

Nite Gel (doxylamine, acetaminophen, pseudoephedrine, dextromethorphan) - N

Nytol Natural (ignatia amara, aconitum radix) - N

Nytol Quickcaps and Quickgels (diphenhydramine) - Y*

Restyn 76 (diphenhydramine) - Y*

Sleep-Ettes D (diphenhydramine) - Y*

Sleep-Eze 3 (diphenhydramine) - Y*

Sleepinal (diphenhydramine) - Y*

Sleepiness (diphenhydramine) - Y*

Sleep Rite (diphenhydramine) - Y*

Snooze Fast (diphenhydramine) - Y*

Sominex Original (diphenhydramine) - Y*

Sominex Pain Relief Formula (diphenhydramine, acetaminophen) - N

Tranquil (diphenhydramine) - Y*

Tranquil Plus (diphenhydramine, acetaminophen) - N

Unisom (doxylamine) - N

Unisom Maximum Strength (diphenhydramine) - Y*

Unisom With Pain Relief (acetaminophen, diphenhydramine) - N

NOTE: Y* = usually safe when breastfeeding, monitor infant for drowsiness; N = avoid when breastfeeding.

## Table 12. Stimulants

No Doz (caffeine 200mg) - N*               Vivarin (caffeine 200mg) - N*

NOTE: N* = less than 150 mg two to three times a day has no apparent effect on breastfeeding infant. Probably better to drink a cup of coffee than to take the drug.

## Table 13. Appetite Suppressant Products

Acutrim (phenylpropanolamine) - N          Mini Thin Diet Aid (phenylpropanolamine) - N

Amfed T.D. (phenylpropanolamine) - N       Permathene (phenylpropanolamine) - N

Dexatrim (phenylpropanolamine) - N         Protrim (phenylpropanolamine) - N

Dieutrim T.D. (phenylpropanolamine, benzocaine)   Super Odrinex (phenylpropanolamine) - N
- N
                                           Thinz Back to Nature and Thinz-Span
Mini Slims (phenylpropanolamine) - N       (phenylpropanolamine) - N

NOTE: N = avoid when breastfeeding.

## Table 14. Insulin Preparations

All insulin-containing products are safe in breastfeeding; however, it is recommended that the insulin dose be reduced by 25 percent of the prepregnancy dose.

## Table 15. Artificial Sweeteners

Equal (aspartame) - Y***                   Sweet 'N Low (saccharin) - Y

NutraSweet (aspartame) - Y***

NOTE: Y = usually safe in breastfeeding; Y*** = usually safe when breastfeeding, avoid using if the mother or infant has diagnosed phenylketonuria.

---

### References for Tables

1. Wilkes D. The international perspective on the OTC market. *IMS Health Self Medication/OTC Bulletin*. December 9, 1998.

2. Findlay J, DeAngelis R, Kearney M, et al. Analgesic drugs in breast milk and plasma. *Clin Pharmacol and Ther*. 1981; 29: 625–633.

3. Anderson PO. Drug use during breast-feeding. *Clin Pharm*. 1991; 10: 594–624.

4. Rathmell JP, Viscomi CM, Ashburn MA. Management of nonobstetric pain during pregnancy and lactation. *Anesth. Analg*. 1997; 85: 1074–1087.

5. Britt R, Pasero C. Using analgesics during breastfeeding. *Am J Nursing.* 1999; 99:20.

6. American Academy of Pediatrics Committee on Drugs. The transfer of drugs and other chemicals into human milk. *Pediatrics.* 1994; 13:137–150

7. Kok TH, Taitz LS, Bennett MJ, et al. Drowsiness due to clemastine transmitted in breast milk. *Lancet.* 1982; 1:914–915.

8. Briggs G, Freeman R, Yaffe S. *Drugs in Pregnancy and Lactation: A Reference Guide to Fetal and Neonatal Risk.* 5th ed. Baltimore: Williams and Wilkins; 1998: 72–73, 217, 222, 407–408, 548, 661–662, 958–959.

9. Nice FJ. Breastfeeding and OTC medications. *Pharm Times.* 1992; 58: 114–124, 126–127.

10. Kanfer I, Dowse R, Vuma V. Pharmacokinetics of oral decongestants. *Pharmacotherapy.* 1993; 13: 116S–128S.

11. Scariati P, Grummer-Strawn L, Fein S. A longitudinal analysis of infant morbidity and the extent of breastfeeding in the United States. *Pediatrics.* 1997; 99: E5. Abstract.

12. Briggs G, Freeman R, Yaffe S. *Drugs in Pregnancy and Lactation Update.* Baltimore: Williams and Wilkins; 1998 [Update September; 1 (3)].

13. Redetzki HM. Alcohol. In: Wilson JT, ed. *Drugs in Breast Milk.* Balgowlah, Australia: ADIS Health Science Press; 1981: 46–49.

14. Hornby P, Abrahams T. Pulmonary pharmacology. *Clin Obstet and Gynecol.* 1996; 39: 17–35.

15. Meny RG, Naumburg EG, ALger LS, et al. Codeine and the breastfed neonate. *J Hum Lact.* 1993; 9: 237–240.

16. Covington T, Pau A. Oxymetazoline. *Am. Pharm.* 1985; NS25 (5): 21–26.

17. Yurchak AM, Jusko WJ. Theophylline secretion into breast milk. *Pediatrics.* 1976; 57: 518–520.

18. Stewart JJ. Gastrointestinal drugs. In: Wilson JT, ed. *Drugs in Breast Milk.* Balgowlah, Australia: ADIS Health Science Press; 1981: 65–71.

19. Hagemann T. Gastrointestinal medications and breastfeeding. *J Hum Lact.* 1998; 14:259–262.

20. Nikodem VC, Hofmeyr GJ. Secretion of the antidiarrhoeal agent loperamide oxide in breast milk. *Eur J Clin Pharmacol.* 1992; 42: 695–696.

21. Figueroa-Quintanilla D, Lindo E, Sack B, et al. A controlled trial of bismuth subsalicylate in infants with acute watery diarrheal disease. *N Eng J Med.* 1993; 328: 1653–1658.

22. Oo C, Kuhn R, Desai N, McNamara P. Active transport of cimetidine into human milk. *Clin Pharmacol Ther.* 1995: 58: 548–555.

23. Somogyi A, Gugler R. Cimetidine excreation into breast milk. *Br J Clin Pharmacol.* 1979; 7: 627–629.

24. Kearns G, McConnell R, Trang J, Lkuza R. Appearance of ranitidine in breast milk following multiple dosing. *Clin Pharm.* 1985; 4: 322–324.

25. Obermeyer B, Bergstrom R, Callaghan J, et al. Secretion of nizatidine into human breast milk after single and multiple dosing. *Clin Pharmacol Ther.* 1990; 47: 724–730.

26. Courtney T, Shaw R, Cedar E, et al. Excretion of famotidine in breast milk. *Br J Pharmacol.* 1988; 26: 639P.

27. Stoukides C. Topical medications and breastfeeding. *J Hum Lact.* 1993; 9: 185–187.

28. Committee on Drugs, American Academy of Pediatrics. The transfer of drugs and other chemicals into human breast milk. *Pediatrics.* 1983; 72: 375–383.

29. Juszczak M, Stempniak B. The effect of melatonin on suckling-induced oxytocin and prolactin release in the rat. *Brain Res Bull.* 1997; 44: 253–258.

30. Ryu J. Effect of maternal caffeine consumption on heart rate and sleep time of breast-fed infants. *Dev Pharmacol Ther.* 1985; 8: 355–363.

31. Davies H, Clark J, Dalton K, Edwards O. Insulin requirements of diabetic women who breastfeed. *Brit Med J.* 1989; 298: 1357–1358.

32. Stegink LD, Filer LJ, Baker GL. Plasma, erythrocyte, and human milk levels of free amino acids in lactating women administered aspartame or lactose. *J Nutr.* 1979; 109: 2173–2181.

33. Egan PC, Marx CM, Heyl PS, et al. Saccharin concentration in mature human milk. *Drug Intell Clin Pharm.* 1984; 18: 511. Abstract.

F.  Minimizing the effect of maternal medication on the infant

1. Avoid the use of long-acting forms of medications; the infant might have difficulty excreting it due to the requirement of detoxification by an immature infant's liver.

2. Doses can be scheduled so that the minimum amount of drug enters the milk; medications can be taken right before or right after a breastfeeding.

3. Infants should be watched for unusual or adverse signs or symptoms, such as a change in feeding patterns, level of alertness, sleeping patterns, fussiness, rash, and bowel changes.

4. Drugs can be chosen that produce the least amount in the milk.

## Radioactive Drugs

A brief interruption may be necessary to allow elimination or decay of the radioactive substance.

Follow the guidelines provided by the Nuclear Regulatory Commission provided in the reference section.

Breastfeeding should probably be discontinued following the use of radioactive I-131 due to the enhanced risk of thyroid carcinoma in the infant.

## References

American Academy of Pediatrics Committee on Drugs. The transfer of drugs and other chemicals into human milk. *Pediatrics* 1994; 13:137–150.

Briggs GG, Freeman RK, Yaffe SJ. Drugs in pregnancy and lactation, 5th ed. Baltimore, MD: Lippincott Williams and Wilkins, 1998.

Hale T. Medications and mothers' milk: A manual of lactational pharmacology, 9th ed. Amarillo, TX: Pharmasoft Publishing, 2000.

Hale T. Clinical therapy in breastfeeding mothers. Amarillo, TX: Pharmasoft Publishing, 2000.

Lawrence RA, Lawrence RM. Breastfeeding: A guide for the medical profession, 5th ed. St. Louis, MO: Mosby, Inc., 1999:351–393.

Nice FJ, Snyder JL, Kotansky BC. Breastfeeding and over-the-counter medications. *J Hum Lact* 2000; 16:319–331.

Nuclear Regulatory Commission. Activities of radiopharmaceuticals that require instructions and records when administered to patients who are breastfeeding an infant or child. *Regulatory Guide* 8.39. www.nrc.gov/NRC/RG/08/08-039.htm.

# Environmental Chemicals, Recreational Drugs of Abuse, and Drugs that Affect Milk Production

*Marsha Walker, RN, IBCLC*

## Objectives

- Discuss the issue of environmental chemicals in breast milk.
- Discuss drugs of abuse and recreational drug use in lactating women.
- Discuss drugs that affect milk production and/or suppression.

## Introduction

With rare exception, and usually on the occasion of a large environmental contamination, chemical agents have not been shown to adversely affect breastfeeding infants. Only in exceptional circumstances would the benefits derived from breastfeeding fail to outweigh the possible toxic consequences of chemical exposure through breast milk. Data relating to chemical contaminants in breast milk are often conflicting, inaccurate, or speculative—resulting in more uncertainty and less clarity. Data concerning the toxicity of chemicals in humans is often sparse and is limited to high-dose or mixed chemical exposures, often as a result of occupational exposure or accidents. The possible presence of environmental contaminants in breast milk is also used in the political arena as a justification to clean up the environment or as a weapon against breastfeeding. Because many environmental contaminants can be transported across the placenta to the fetus, it is difficult to separate the effect of prenatal exposure from that of exposure through breast milk. If the infant and the mother are exposed to the same environmental contaminants in the home (such as lead), breast milk might not be the chief route of exposure. Furthermore, exposure to environmental chemicals varies from country to country (and even in each country from region to region), making it difficult to generalize information to all populations. The *lactation consultant* (LC) will benefit from a general overview of this topic and from an understanding of the multi-factor contributors to recommendations.

I General considerations

   A. Based on the growth patterns of breastfed and formula-fed infants, a breastfeeding baby acquires more body fat during the first three months of life and theoretically would be more susceptible to lipophilic (having an affinity for fat) compound toxicity during this time period than a formula-fed infant.

   B. From 3–12 months of age, a breastfed baby becomes leaner than a formula-fed one with less body fat.

   C. If a breastfed infant is switched to formula at three months of age, there would be an increase in the risk of toxicity to lipophilic agents between 3 and 12 months because these infants possess more fat and thus potentially store more toxins.

   D. Growth or weight gain is frequently used as an index of toxicity in animals and humans and should not be the sole parameter used to establish toxicity in the first year of life, due to the differences in growth between breastfed and formula-fed babies.

   E. Lipophilic contaminants can be present in human milk, stored in mammary fat, or stored in body fat (with adverse effects related to the concentration and release from fat).

   F. The fats in breast milk arise from three sources: 30 percent from the current maternal diet, 60 percent from maternal adipose tissue stores, and 10 percent from synthesis in the mammary gland itself.

   G. Even with adequate maternal fat intake in the diet, adipose tissue stores still contribute 60 percent of the fats to the milk.

   H. Exposure to chemicals is generally over a period of years; these chemicals are mobilized during lactation and might represent a route of elimination.

   I. Women who lose a large amount of weight rapidly can contribute greater amounts of lipophilic contaminants into the breast milk.

   J. The number of children previously nursed by a mother will affect the chemical levels in her milk for her next baby.

   K. Subsequent children will consume a milk containing lower concentrations of persistent chemicals.

   L. Obese women can have up to 50 percent more body fat than women who are at or near their optimum weight. The extra fat provides a greater reservoir for chemical contaminants, diluting their presence; if the obese woman ingests greater amounts of food containing contaminants, then fat levels will equal or exceed the general population.

   M. Compounds that have a molecular weight of below 200 are likely to be found in milk, especially if they are lipophilic.

N. Many of the chemicals under consideration are ubiquitous, making it difficult to find control samples to which we can compare exposure.

O. Analytical techniques have become very sophisticated, permitting the detection of extremely low levels of chemicals that previously have been reported to be below the limit of detection.

P. Conclusions based on a single subject or a small sample size might be misleading when translating outcomes in small numbers into public health policy.

Q. Breast milk levels of contaminants are used as epidemiological markers of human exposure within a community because of the correlation between breast milk levels and levels in the fat stores.

R. Unless the circumstances are unusual, however, breastfeeding should not be abandoned on the basis of chemical presence alone; only extreme levels of contaminants in breast milk represent more of a hazard than the failure to breastfeed.

S. In most cases, the levels of pesticides in human milk are less than those in cow's milk.

II  Halogenated hydrocarbons

A. DDT (1,1-bis(p-chlorophenyl)—2,2,2-trichloroethane and its related compounds and metabolites, mirex, polychlorinated biphenyls (PCBs), heptachlor, aldrin/dieldrin, chlordane, and hexachlorobenzene (HCB)

1. Most of the early studies until 1980 showed detectable levels of DDT in nearly all women who were tested.

2. Adverse effects on infants were not shown at the levels detected.

3. Because DDT was banned in the United States in 1972, the average woman in the United States is not considered at risk for excessive levels of DDT in her milk.

4. In some developing countries, however, mothers might continue to be at risk in rural or agricultural areas.

5. The World Health Organization does not consider breast milk to be a major source of DDT.

6. DDE (dichlorodiphenyldichloroethylene) is a major metabolite of DDT and has been associated with a shortened duration of breastfeeding; this effect is thought to arise from the weak estrogen activity of DDE and related isomers possibly contributing to a reduced milk supply.

7. No adverse effects have been noted in the recipient infants.

B. Polychlorinated biphenyl (PCB) and polybrominated biphenyl (PBB)

1. Formerly used as insulation media in electrical systems, lubricants, and as paint additives, these components are now used only in closed systems in order to prevent air, soil, and water contamination.

2. These compounds can exert neurotoxic effects on the infant's developing brain.

3. Except in cases of unusually heavy exposure, there is no contraindication to breastfeeding.

4. If there is a question about environmental exposure and the safety of breastfeeding, the state health department (in the United States) can be consulted for specific advice or to measure plasma and breast milk levels.

C. Dioxins and benzofurans

1. Dioxins are a group of related compounds that are both manmade and occur naturally in low levels in the environment.

2. Dioxins are released into the air from combustion processes such as commercial or municipal waste incineration, burning fuels such as wood, coal, or oil, burning household trash, and forest fires; chlorine bleaching of pulp and paper and certain other types of chemical and manufacturing processes can create small amounts of dioxins, as does cigarette smoking.

3. One of the best known dioxins is Agent Orange.

4. The United States *Environmental Protection Agency* (EPA) will be releasing a final report on a reassessment of dioxin exposure and hazards in 2001 (*Exposure and human health reassessment of 2,3,4,8-tetrachlorodibenzo-p-dioxin (TCDD) and related compounds*); a draft of this document is available at www.epa.gov/ncea/dioxin.htm.

5. Data within this report show that it is safe to breastfeed infants in the United States relative to dioxin; the report shows that dioxin levels in the environment have decreased.

6. The findings in the EPA document include the following statements: "We believe there are overwhelming benefits of breastfeeding and encourage women to continue the practice...Findings in the draft EPA dioxin report do NOT suggest that women should stop breastfeeding. Women are encouraged to continue the practice of breastfeeding given its overall benefits to mother and child."

D. Organochlorine insecticides

1. These include aldrin, dieldrin, endrin, naphthalene derivatives, lindane, heptachlor, and chlordane; many of these have been banned in industrialized countries.

2. Lindane (used in shampoos and treatment of head lice in children) appears

in milk, but no reports of adverse effects on breastfeeding infants have been reported.

3. Heptachlor and chlordane are used for control of the cotton boll weevil; levels can be measured in milk but no adverse effects in breastfed infants have been reported.

E. Organophosphorous insecticides

1. Chlorpyrifos and malathion have both been identified in breast milk.

2. Toxicity is theoretically possible in severe exposure conditions.

F. Solvents and solvent abuse

1. Organic solvents are aromatic compounds that are present in paint, glue, resins, dyes, stain removers, polishes, paint thinner, gasoline, and aerosol propellants.

2. Benzene and butane are widespread, but most of the solvent present in frequently abused substances is toluene.

3. Heavy exposure to the dry cleaning solvent perchloroethylene has been associated with jaundice in the breastfed infant.

4. Mothers can be exposed in occupational settings (shoe repair, furniture refinishers, printing shops, and so on).

5. Inhaled volatile organic chemicals can be deposited into adipose tissue and occur in breast milk.

6. Exposure to organic solvents during pregnancy has the potential to result in toxemia and anemia in the mother.

7. Organic solvents have a high affinity for lipid-rich tissues, including the brain and central nervous system.

8. Deliberate inhalation of organic solvents is a popular form of drug abuse.

9. They are properly classified as anesthetics and typically produce a short period of stimulation before central nervous system depression.

10. When deliberately concentrated and inhaled, these highly volatile compounds are rapidly absorbed in the lungs and lead to a rapid brief "high."

11. Toluene might not be detected on routine drug screens.

12. The release of organic solvents from breast milk fat needs to be considered among solvent abusers in light of what is known about adverse effects to the fetus during pregnancy.

G. Heavy metals

   1. Little information is available concerning the effects in babies of heavy
      metal exposure through breast milk.

   2. Heavy metal exposure is related to water supplies, ingestion of cow's milk,
      intake of infant formula, consuming certain foods, and so on.

   3. Breastfed infants are exposed to lower amounts of heavy metals because
      formula is often mixed with water that can contain the heavy metal;
      boiling contaminated water concentrates the heavy metal.

   4. Lead is still present in the environment despite the lowered lead levels
      resulting from the elimination of leaded gasoline, lead solder from cans, and
      lead in paint.

   5. Lead intake still arises from lead water pipes or lead solder, leaded paint
      chips in older housing, and lead in the soil.

   6. Less lead passes into breast milk than across the placenta.

   7. Breast milk levels are one-tenth to one-fifth of maternal levels.

   8. Formula-fed infants have higher lead levels than breastfed babies.

   9. Breastfeeding is not contraindicated unless the maternal lead level exceeds
      40 micrograms/deciliter.

   10. Cadmium exposure through breast milk has not been clearly reported; the
       major route of cadmium intake is through cigarette smoke.

   11. Maternal malnutrition in cadmium-exposed, lactating women could
       increase toxicity in the breastfeeding baby.

   12. Mercury levels in breast milk are usually very low.

   13. Exposure of the general public is usually from industrial sources or from
       seafood sources; rare environmental disasters have contributed mercury to
       the general environment.

   14. Only if maternal serum levels of mercury were extremely high would the
       milk need to be tested.

   15. Any woman who has been exposed should be evaluated by her physician.

   16. Heavy metals are rarely a contraindication to breastfeeding and then only
       under extreme exposure circumstances.

H. Drugs of abuse

   1. Generally, drugs of abuse are contraindicated for breastfeeding mothers;
      however, there is not universal agreement on some of the drugs.

      a. Drugs typically contraindicated are amphetamines, cocaine, heroin, and
         phencyclidine.

b. Reports disagree about the effects of marijuana and nicotine (smoking).

c. Smoking is not a contraindication to breastfeeding.

d. Smoking can decrease milk volume and fat content as well as depress the milk ejection reflex immediately prior to breastfeeding.

e. Nicotine absorbed from milk is less than 5 percent of the average daily dose of the adult.

f. The risk of *Sudden Infant Death Syndrome* (SIDS) is significantly higher in infants who are formula-fed and whose mothers smoke; breastfeeding is protective against SIDS when mothers smoke.

I. Silicone breast implants

1. Silicon is the second most abundant element in the Earth's crust.

2. Certain foods and beverages contain significant levels of silicon (vegetables, rice, grains, and beer); silicon is also found in large amounts in simethicone preparations for infant colic, with no identifiable problems related to the silicone content; artificial nipples and pacifiers, some nipple shields, and some breast pump parts contain silicone.

3. Silicone is a synthetic compound that is a polymer of 40 percent silicon by weight; it is used in items such as prostheses, medical devices, and pharmaceutical products.

4. Silicone breast implants were widely used until their restriction in 1992 by the *Food and Drug Administration* (FDA) to be available only through clinical trials; concerns arose regarding silicone gel leakage and connective tissue disease in some women who have implants.

5. Suggestions that there was an association between the silicone implants and an esophageal disease in breastfed infants has been seriously questioned due to problematic methodology and involvement with the plaintiffs in a lawsuit against the implant maker.

6. Studies of silicon levels in the milk of mothers with and without implants show no significant differences between the two groups (Semple et al., 1998).

   a. Breast milk silicon levels of mothers who do not have silicone implants: 51.05 ng/ml

   b. Breast milk silicon levels of mothers who have silicone implants: 55.45 ngml

   c. Cow's milk silicon levels: 708.94 ng/ml (range 666.5–778.3)

   d. Mean silicon level in 26 brands of infant formula; mean 4402.5 ng/ml (range 746.0 ng/ml–13,811.0 ng/ml)

7. The biologic effects of circulating silicone remain unknown, and silicone implants do not present a contraindication to breastfeeding.

**Table 24-1**   Summary of medical contraindications to breastfeeding in the United States

| Problem | OK to Breastfeed in U.S.? | Conditions |
|---|---|---|
| **Infectious Diseases** | | |
| Acute infectious disease | Yes | Respiratory, reproductive, gastrointestinal infections |
| HIV | No | HIV-positive |
| Hepatitis | | |
|    Hepatitis A | Yes | As soon as mother receives gamma globulin |
|    Hepatitis B | Yes | After infant receives HBIG, first dose of hepatitis B vaccine should be given before hospital discharge |
|    Hepatitis C | Yes | If no co-infections (e.g., HIV) |
| Venereal warts | Yes | |
| Herpes viruses | | |
|    Cytomegalovirus | Yes | |
|    Herpes simplex | Yes | Except if lesion on breast |
|    Varicella-zoster (chicken pox) | Yes | As soon as mother becomes noninfectious |
|    Epstein-Barr | Yes | |
| Toxoplasmosis | Yes | |
| Mastitis | Yes | |
| Lyme disease treatment | Yes | As soon as mother initiates |
| HTLV-1 | No | |

| Problem | OK to Breastfeed in U.S.? | Conditions |
|---|---|---|
| **Medication/Prescription Drugs and Street Drugs** | | |
| Antimetabolites (see Table 4) | No | |
| Radiopharmaceuticals (see Table 5) | | |
| Diagnostic dose | Yes | After radioactive compound has cleared mother's plasma |
| Therapeutic dose | No | |
| Drugs of abuse (see Table 6) | No | Exceptions: cigarettes, alcohol |
| Other medications | Yes | Drug-by-drug assessment |
| **Environmental contaminants** | | |
| Herbicides | Usually | Exposure unlikely (except workers heavily exposed to dioxins) |
| Pesticides | | |
| DDT, DDE | Usually | Exposure unlikely |
| PCBs, PBBs | Usually | Levels in milk very low |
| Cyclodiene pesticides | Usually | Exposure unlikely |
| Heavy metals | | |
| Lead | Yes | Unless maternal level >40 mg/dL |
| Mercury | Yes | Unless mother symptomatic and levels measurable in breastmilk |
| Cadmium | Usually | Exposure unlikely |
| Radionuclides | Yes | Risk greater to bottlefed infants |

Note: This table provides a brief summary. Each situation must be decided individually. Contraindications are rare in the United States.

Source: Lawrence RA. 1997. A review of the medical benefits and contraindications to breastfeeding in the United States. *Maternal and Child Health Technical Information Bulletin*. Arlington, VA: National Center for Education in Maternal and Child Health.

# References

Arnold G. Solvent abuse and developmental toxicity. Chapter 23 in Kacew S, Lambert GH, eds. Environmental toxicology and pharmacology of human development. Washington, DC: Taylor and Francis, 1997.

Berlin CM, Kacew S. Environmental chemicals in human milk. Chapter 4 in Kacew S, Lambert GH, eds. Environmental toxicology and pharmacology of human development. Washington, DC: Taylor and Francis, 1997.

Jensen AA, Slorach SA, eds. Chemical contaminants in human milk. Boca Raton, FL: CRC Press, 1991.

Lawrence RA. A review of the medical benefits and contraindications to breastfeeding in the United States. *Maternal and Child Health Technical Information Bulletin*. Arlington, VA: National Center for Education in Maternal and Child Health, 1997. See Table 24-1.

Lawrence RA, Lawrence RM. Breastfeeding: a guide for the medical profession, 5th ed. St. Louis, MO: Mosby, Inc., 1999.

Levine JJ. Breast silicone implants and pediatric considerations. Chapter 7 in Kacew S, Lambert GH, eds. Environmental toxicology and pharmacology of human development. Washington, DC: Taylor and Francis, 1997.

Levine JJ, Ilowite NT. Sclerodermalike esophageal disease in children breastfed by mothers with silicone breast implants. JAMA 1999; 271:213–216.

Rogan W, Blanto P, Portier C, Stallard E. 1991. Should the presence of carcinogens in breast milk discourage breastfeeding? *Regul Toxicol Pharmacol* 1991; 13:228–240.

Rogan WJ, Ragan NB. Chemical contaminants, pharmacokinetics, and the lactating mother. *Environ Health Perspect* 1994; 102 (Suppl II):89–95.

Schreiber JS. Transport of organic chemicals to breast milk: Tetrachloroethene case study. Chapter 5 in Kacew S, Lambert GH, eds. Environmental toxicology and pharmacology of human development. Washington, DC: Taylor and Francis, 1997.

Semple JL, Lugowski SJ, Baines CJ, et al. 1998. Breast milk contamination and silicone implants: Preliminary results using silicon as a proxy measurement for silicone. *Plast Reconstr Surg* 1998; 102:528–533.

# Counseling Skills

*Judith Lauwers, BA, IBCLC*

## Objectives

- Identify three principles of adult learning that lead to the empowerment of mothers.
- State the three levels at which learning takes place, and explain their relative effectiveness.
- Explain the three components of communication and their relative impact on the message.
- List three strategies to strengthen the message received from the spoken word.
- State three elements of body language that enhance a consultant's counseling effectiveness.
- Define the four needs of a mother that are met in the counseling process, and describe strategies for meeting each of those needs.
- Distinguish between the relative roles of the consultant and the mother in guiding and leading counseling methods and the appropriate use of each method.
- Demonstrate a variety of guiding skills that will elicit information from and provide support to the mother.
- Implement effective problem solving and a follow-up within the context of consulting.

## Introduction

Effective counseling skills and communication techniques are essential tools of the lactation consultant. The use of these skills will provide mothers with the support and teaching that will help them develop confidence in their mothering and breastfeeding. The degree to which mothers are helped by support and advice from a lactation consultant is determined in large part by the lactation consultant's approach. Adult learners need to perceive themselves as having control over their outcomes. Therefore, an approach that establishes a partnership between the mother and lactation consultant will foster the mother's learning and growth. This approach also increases the likelihood of the mother complying with her lactation consultant's advice. In addition, a firm understanding of effective counseling skills and the components of communication will assist the lactation consultant with educating and supporting the mothers who are in her care.

## Content Outline

I  Principles of adult learning

    A. Approach of *learning* rather than *being taught*

    B. Develops a partnership with the mother and baby

       1. Engages the mother as an active participant in the learning process

       2. Provides choices and asks the mother to select those that will work for her

    C. Approaches counseling in a noninterfering manner

       1. Moves at the baby's pace

       2. Limits interactions to guiding unless specific intervention is needed

       3. Ensures that any intervention is focused and justified

       4. Puts the mother in control

    D. Creates an effective learning climate

       1. The consultant makes positive impressions

          a. Display of self confidence

          b. Desire to share knowledge

          c. Ability to relate to people

          d. Willingness to be flexible and to adapt

          e. Sense of humor

          f. Strong knowledge base

          g. Enthusiasm

          h. Informality

          i. Respect for the learner

          j. Frequent eye contact

          k. Positive body language

      l. Neat, clean, and stylish attire

      m. Strong voice with carefully pronounced words

  2. Encourages the learner to be an active participant

      a. Planning is done mutually by the consultant and the mother

      b. Encourages self direction, self reliance, and risk taking

      c. Facilitates the mother's development of problem-solving skills

      d. Fosters the mother taking ownership for the plan and being responsible for the outcome

      e. Encourages the mother to evaluate her own learning

E. Individualizes the consultant's approach with every dyad

  1. Recognizes uniqueness in every mother and baby

      a. Respects the mother's background and taps into it

      b. Assesses each mother's learning needs before problem solving

  2. Assesses the mother's readiness to learn

      a. Capitalizes on the "teachable moment" that will maximize her ability to learn and process information

      b. Considers the mother's physical comfort, confidence level, emotional state, and the health of the mother and baby in determining the teachable moment

  3. Keeps pace with the mother

      a. Consultant uses the mother's language style and imagery

      b. Consultant matches the mother's intensity and sense of humor

      c. Consultant tailors her actions to the mother's responses

F. Learning takes place at three levels:

  1. Lowest level: information shared verbally

      a. Does not require visual or interactive reinforcement

      b. Example: discussion of contraception or nutrition

  2. Higher level: something visual added to verbal instruction

      a. Does not require interactive reinforcement

      b. Example: use of a cloth breast to show the location of lactiferous sinuses

  3. Highest level: learner participates actively in the learning process

      a. Provides visual reinforcement to show that the mother has mastered the technique being taught

      b. Engages the mother actively in her learning

      c. Example: demonstration of the use of a breast pump with the mother giving a return demonstration

II  Components of communication

   A. Communication is the delivery and reception of a message

   B. Reception depends on a combination of three factors:

     1. 7 percent determined by the spoken word

     2. 38 percent determined by tone of voice

     3. 55 percent determined by body language

   C. The spoken word

     1. Avoid negative terminology and imagery.

       a. The conjunction "but" negates the first half of the thought.

         i. Implies that the mother is doing/saying something wrong

         ii. Undermines the mother's self-confidence

         iii. Replace "but" with "and"

         iv. Example: *"You are holding your baby in a good position, and if you turn him slightly you will find that he can get an even better latch"*

       b. The verb "should" also implies judgment.

         i. Implies that the mother is doing/saying something wrong

         ii. Undermines the mother's self-confidence

         iii. Rephrase to avoid the word "should"

         iv. Example: instead of, *"You should feed your baby whenever he wants,"* rephrase to, *"When you feed your baby whenever he wants, you will be meeting his needs"*

     2. Select words and phrases that correct any incorrect or inappropriate practices without compromising the mother's self-confidence.

     3. Avoid words that imply success or failure, adequate or inadequate.

     4. Avoid sending mixed messages; be certain that the words create the desired effect.

     5. Supplement verbal messages with demonstrations, visual aids, and written instructions in order to strengthen understanding.

   D. Voice tone

     1. The manner of speech can create a warm, friendly, humorous atmosphere.

     2. Use a moderate volume (not too loud or too low).

     3. Use a moderate rate of speech (not too fast or too slow).

     4. Use a moderate pitch, and guard against your voice becoming higher-pitched when you are angry or excited.

E. Body language

1. Based on the behavioral patterns of nonverbal communication
2. Study of the mixture of all body movements
3. Ranges from the very deliberate to the unconscious
4. Can vary culturally or cut across cultural barriers; thus, needs to be tailored to the client population
5. A smile
   a. Adds to a warm and inviting atmosphere
   b. Puts mothers at ease; elicits a smile from the mother
6. Eye contact
   a. Eyes are the most important component of body language in transmitting information
   b. Conveys the consultant's desire to communicate
   c. Establishes a warm, caring, and inviting climate
   d. Serves as a powerful tool for influencing others
   e. Try to maintain eye contact at least 85 percent of the time
   f. Failure to establish eye contact sends a negative message
7. Posture
   1. A relaxed and comfortable posture creates a warm and inviting climate
      a. Sitting or standing squarely with both feet flat on the floor
      b. Resting the arms at one's side (or, when sitting, on one's knees)
      c. Open body posture shows an openness to communicate on a meaningful level
   2. Crossing the arms or legs conveys disinterest and emotional distance
      a. Combining open posture with leaning forward further conveys interest in engaging the mother
         i. Distance
         ii. Standing or sitting too close invades another's personal space (their comfort zone)
         iii. Standing or sitting too far away conveys a message of being too busy or uninterested
      b. Establish a comfortable position—not too far away or too close—by using the mother's reactions as a guide
      c. Altitude
         i. Height in relation to another person conveys who possesses the greatest importance or control

        ii. A position equal to or below the mother puts her in control and leads to a greater self-reliance and empowerment

    d. Touch

        i. Can convey warmth, caring, and encouragement

        ii. Must come at the right moment and in the right context

        iii. Ask permission before touching the mother's breasts or her baby

  3. Reading the body language of others

    a. Be alert for nonverbal messages that the mother sends

    b. Observe and respond to her reactions and body language

    c. Watch for signs of physical discomfort

**III** The counseling process

  A. The goal of counseling is to fulfill the mother's needs for emotional support, physical comfort, understanding, and action

    1. Gives the mother the support that is needed to develop confidence

    2. Encourages the mother to express herself

    3. Educates the mother and imparts problem-solving techniques

    4. Helps the mother develop self-sufficiency and satisfaction

  B. Consultant traits are an important element in the counseling process

    1. A warm and caring attitude shows deep and genuine concern and empathy.

    2. Openness to disclosing feelings and thoughts encourages trust and openness in the mother when done appropriately.

    3. Acknowledging the mother's individuality and worth, without judgment, gives the mother the freedom to be herself.

    4. Clear, accurate communication reduces confusion and frustration.

    5. Flexibility helps the consultant respond appropriately to the mother at different stages in the counseling process.

  C. Meeting the mother's needs for emotional support

    1. Helps the mother arrive at a state where she can take in information and join in problem-solving

    2. Provides a sense of security that encourages her to verbalize her feelings and anxieties

    3. Validates her feelings, emotions, and concerns

    4. Praises her actions

     5. Listens to what the mother is *not* saying; listens to her underlying message

     6. Sends the message that the consultant genuinely cares about the mother's well-being and concerns

  D. Meeting the mother's needs for immediate physical comfort

     1. A mother who has physical discomfort might not be in a teachable moment.

     2. Offer emotional support, then help the mother relieve physical discomfort before proceeding with educating and problem-solving.

  E. Meeting the mother's needs for understanding

     1. The mother needs to understand herself and her feelings.

     2. The mother needs to clearly define and understand the problem and its cause.

     3. The mother needs to understand her options in resolving the problem.

     4. Meeting these needs will help the mother make informed choices and assume responsibility for her actions.

  F. Meeting the mother's needs for positive action

     1. The mother gains satisfaction in knowing that she is actively working on the problem.

     2. The consultant and mother mutually agree upon the action to be taken.

**IV** Methods of counseling

  A. The guiding method

     1. Helps the consultant listen attentively and empathize

     2. Helps the consultant gather necessary information and insights

     3. Encourages the mother to express her ideas and concerns openly

     4. Helps the mother hear what the consultant is saying

     5. Helps the consultant hear what the mother is *not* saying

     6. Transmits a message of acceptance and concern

     7. Begins the counseling process and is used throughout the contact

  B. The leading method

     1. Requires a more active role by the consultant in directing the conversation

     2. Helps the mother who is unable to solve a problem

     3. Helps the consultant and mother see the situation more clearly

     4. Helps define options that will lead to a plan of action

     5. Enables the consultant and mother to form a partnership

  C. The follow-up method

     1. Analyzes the effectiveness of the contact

2. Determines how and when to plan the next contact

3. Identifies what preparation is needed for the next contact

4. Determines whether the consultant's suggestions have been useful

5. Identifies the mother's need for further emotional support

6. Lets the mother know how concerned the consultant is with helping her

**V** Skills used in counseling

  A. Counseling skills in the guiding method

    1. Listening

      a. Perceiving with the ears, eyes, and imagination

      b. The consultant is silent much of the time while the mother talks

      c. Helps the consultant gain information to clarify the situation

      d. The counseling skill *attending*

        i. The consultant listens passively to indicate that the consultant is paying attention

        ii. Encourages the mother to continue talking freely

        iii. Reinforces that the mother is responsible for the discussion

        iv. Examples: eye contact, open posture, calm gestures, a silent pause, or saying "Yes" or "Mmm"

      e. The counseling skill *active listening*

        i. Also called *reflective listening*

        ii. The consultant paraphrases what she believes the mother meant

        iii. Clarifies the message so that the mother can reflect on it

        iv. Shows acceptance of the mother's viewpoint

        v. Encourages a response from the mother

    2. Facilitating

      a. Encourages the mother to give more information

      b. Helps define the situation

      c. Focuses on specific concerns

      d. Pinpoints issues and feelings on which to concentrate

      e. The counseling skill *clarifying*

        i. The consultant admits confusion about the meaning and restates what was heard

        ii. Makes a point clear

        iii. Example: "What I think I hear you saying is that your nipples hurt only when…"

      f. The counseling skill *asking open-ended questions*

       i. A question that cannot be answered by a simple "yes" or "no"

      ii. The consultant asks questions that begin with "Who, what, when, where, why, how, how much, and how often"

    iii. Example: Instead of asking, "Does your baby nurse often enough?", ask the question, "How many times does she nurse in 24 hours?"

    iv. Caution: The use of questions should be limited and balanced with other counseling skills

g. The counseling skill *interpreting*

       i. Takes active listening one step farther to empathetic listening

      ii. The consultant interprets what was said rather than merely restating it

    iii. Enables the mother to process the consultant's interpretation and to agree or disagree

    iv. Useful when the consultant has a clear impression of what was said

     v. Uses wording that describes the emotion that is being expressed

    vi. Example: "You're worried that your baby is not getting enough milk"

h. The counseling skill *focusing*

       i. The consultant pursues a topic that is helpful to explore or condenses a number of points into a summary

      ii. Selects one particular point to repeat

    iii. Useful when the mother gets into an unrelated topic

    iv. Example: "Tell me more about..."

i. The counseling skill *summarizing*

       i. The consultant makes a summary of the important points

      ii. Goes over highlights and reinforces important information

    iii. Restates the plan of action

    iv. Reassures the mother that the consultant has been tuned into her

     v. Helps the consultant know that she understood the mother

    vi Most effective when done by the mother (for example, "Let's see. In order to build your milk supply, you are going to do what?")

j. The counseling skill *influencing*

       i. Encourages the mother to continue to seek help

      ii. Instills a positive outlook in the mother

k. The counseling skill *reassuring*
   i. The consultant offers the mother perspective
   ii. Helps a mother see that her situation is normal
   iii. Assure the mother that her situation will improve
   iv. Example: "Your breasts will feel more comfortable after the fullness goes down."

l. The counseling skill *building hope*
   i. The consultant helps the mother see how her feelings relate to her situation
   ii. Encourages the mother to talk about her feelings
   iii. Helps relieve tension
   iv. Encourages the mother to take positive action
   v. Example: "I'm glad your mother could join us. Maybe if you are patient with her, she will begin to be more supportive now that she has a better understanding of breastfeeding"

m. The counseling skill *identifying strengths*
   i. The consultant helps the mother focus on her positive qualities and those of her baby
   ii. Counteracts negative factors
   iii. Encourages the mother to persevere
   iv. Encourages the mother to develop and rely on her own resources
   v. Recalls enjoyable memories
   vi. Example: "You did that really well!"

B. Counseling skills in the leading method
   1. The goal is to understand a problem and develop a plan of action
   2. Used when the mother is unable to solve a problem
   3. Provides additional resources to lead the mother toward a solution
   4. Places more responsibility for the direction of the discussion on the consultant
   5. Initiated only after enough information and insights have been obtained through guiding skills
   6. The counseling skill *informing*
      a. Consultant educates the mother
      b. Explains how something functions and the reasons behind it
      c. Corrects a misconception or mismanagement
      d. Suggests appropriate resources

    e. Needs to be done at a teachable moment

    f. Example: "When your baby suckles, that stimulates the nerve endings that in turn signal milk production. Therefore…"

7. The counseling skill *problem solving*

    a. The consultant begins helping the mother with a problem

    b. First, forms a hunch about the problem

    c. Second, looks for additional factors that will confirm the hunch

    d. Third, tests the hunch by suggesting what the problem might be

    e. When rejected, explores alternative hunches with the use of guiding skills to gain further insights and information

    f. When confirmed, develops a plan of action with the mother

        i. Limits to two or three actions for the mother in order to avoid overwhelming her

        ii. Asks the mother to summarize the plan in order to demonstrate her understanding

        iii. Sets a time limit on the actions to be taken

        iv. Follows up at the appropriate time to learn whether the plan worked or whether further suggestions are needed

B. Counseling skills in the follow-up method

1. Follow-up is an ongoing process

2. Needed after each individual contact

3. The urgency of the situation will determine how soon and how frequent follow-ups are necessary

4. The counseling skill *evaluating the session*

    a. The consultant determines whether the mother's needs were met

    b. Assesses the use of appropriate counseling skills

    c. Evaluates the information and advice given to the mother

    d. Evaluates the method of documentation

5. Enables the consultant to learn from mistakes and failures

6. The counseling skill *arranging the next contact*

    a. The consultant identifies the next contact with the mother

    b. Indicates who will initiate the contact

    c. Determines additional information or assistance that is needed

    d. Leaves the door open for the mother to contact the consultant when needed

7. The counseling skill *researching outside sources*
   a. The consultant acknowledges the mother's need for assistance
   b. Gains further input and a fresh outlook on a problem
   c. Gains support from colleagues
8. The counseling skill *renewing the counseling process*
   a. The consultant begins the counseling process anew with the follow-up contact
   b. Begins with guiding skills and progresses to leading skills and further follow-up

## References

Brammer LM. The helping relationship. New Jersey: Prentice Hall, 1973.

DeVito JA. The interpersonal communication book, 5th ed. New York: Harper & Row, 1989.

Fast J. Body language. New York: Pocket Books, 1970.

Knowles M. The modern practice of adult education/from pedagogy to androgogy. Chicago: Follett Publishing, 1980.

Lauwer J, Shinskie D. Counseling the nursing mother: A lactation consultant's guide. Sudbury, MA: Jones and Bartlett Publishers, 2000.

Northouse PG. Health communication. A handbook for health professionals. Englewood Cliffs NJ: Prentice-Hall, 1985.

# The Parenting Role

*Marsha Walker, RN, IBCLC*

## Objectives

- Describe the common emotions of new parents.
- Discuss breastfeeding in the context of a major life change.
- Recognize the signs of inadequate coping.
- Describe breastfeeding within alternative family styles.
- Discuss family planning options.

## Introduction

The nature of parenting roles and the quality of family relationships are influenced by social, cultural, and historical factors. Parents share many of the same goals across cultures but differ in how they approach meeting them. Some cultures place a strong emphasis on family and group identity, while others value individuality and independence. Child-rearing attitudes and recommendations have changed over the years, as have the roles of men and women. Mothers and fathers today are challenged with balancing multiple roles while promoting the optimal development of their children. Articles and books contain conflicting information and advice that can be confusing for both parents and children. Parents who are in nuclear families have lost the modeling and influence of the extended family in their learning and practicing for the parental role. Any number of family configurations can be found, from the traditional married man and woman with the man as the major breadwinner to blended families through divorce and remarriage. Families living in poverty face significant parenting challenges and barriers.

As hospital stays shorten, families are geographically spread out, and economic factors force women into employment after short maternity leaves, educational needs for new parents have burgeoned. The lactation consultant is in a unique position to both assist with breastfeeding and to offer valuable support to new families.

**I** Stages of parental role acquisition (Bocar and Moore, 1987):

    **A.** The anticipatory stage occurs before delivery and is the time period when parents begin learning about their new roles (reading, talking with their own parents, asking questions of other family members and parents, attending classes, and so on).

    **B.** The formal stage begins after delivery and is when parents create the "perfect parent" image or an idealized version of parenting; they are interested in mastering practical child care skills; they might lack self confidence and become easily overwhelmed and confused by conflicting information; they need concrete demonstrations and suggestions as well as acknowledgement that they are the experts on their own baby; once they develop confidence in their ability to meet the infant's basic needs, they progress to the informal stage.

    **C.** The informal stage is when parents begin interacting with their peers and other informal interactions and begin to relax the more rigid rules and directions used to acquire the caretaking behaviors.

    **D.** The person stage is when parents modify their styles and evolve their own unique parenting styles.

**II** Infant-to-parent attachment

    **A.** Attachment was viewed as a behavioral system (Bowlby, 1969).

        1. Infant attachment or signaling behaviors were described that functioned to initiate and maintain contact between the mother and infant (crying, cooing, and smiling).

        2. A secure attachment helped the infant develop a sense of security that had been described by Erikson (1950) as basic trust.

        3. The first six months of life were described as a sensitive period during which the infant's job was to develop a trusting relationship with the caregiver.

    **B.** Ainsworth (1978) has described three general patterns of infant-to-parent attachment: avoidant, ambivalent, and secure.

        1. Avoidant infants show little distress during separation, treat a stranger the same way as the mother, and avoid proximity or interaction with the mother during a reunion after separation.

        2. Ambivalent infants resist contact with a stranger and might be angry or resistant to the mother upon reunion following a separation; once contact with the mother is initiated, the infant seeks to maintain it.

        3. Securely attached infants seek proximity and contact with the mother (especially during reunions) but also explore the environment.

        4. Mothers who are sensitive and responsive to the infant's needs during the early months and who promptly met the infant's needs foster the development of secure attachment relationships.

5. Mothers who fail to respond to their infants or responded inappropriately fostered the development of avoidant or ambivalent attachments.

6. Parental sensitivity and responsiveness might be key indicators of a parent's attachment to his or her infant and can affect the infant's subsequent attachment to the parent.

7. Secure infant-to-parent attachments at age 12–18 months are related to the child's adaptive problem-solving ability at two years of age and to social competence at age three.

8. The quality of a child's early attachment relationship with the parents has long-term effects on child development.

9. Occasionally, new parents adopt the formal stage of parenting (rather than moving beyond it) by practicing one of the rigid parenting programs that prescribe scheduled feedings, limited contact, specified sleep periods, and so on in order to cause the baby to sleep through the night and exert minimal disruption to the husband-wife relationship, which might take precedence over the needs of the baby.

10. Use of some of these baby training programs can result in slow weight gain of a breastfed baby due to the limits placed on when the baby can feed, untimely weaning because the breastfed baby cannot sleep in the manner specified, and even failure to thrive.

11. These babies are at risk for attachment problems; babies who are left to "cry it out" might sleep through the night due to the abandoning of hope of being parented in the evening and might experience despair.

III  Parent-to-infant attachment

A. Many factors are related to the development of a parent's attachment to the infant; parental, situational, and infant.

B. Parents begin to form attachments to the baby in utero.

C. Early contact and bonding behaviors have been suggested as being important during the early hours following birth; Klaus and Kennel (1982) proposed a sensitive period following birth as being important in establishing attachment; while humans are capable of adaptation and growth in this area, the concept might be of special importance to those mothers who are at risk of developing maladaptive parent-child relationships.

D. Attachment behaviors of low-income or indigent women are enhanced by keeping mothers and babies together in a rooming-in environment.

E. Father-to-infant attachment is enhanced by his presence at the delivery of the baby and extended father-infant contact during the newborn period.

F. Fathers have unique ways of interacting with their infants, frequently called engrossment in the early period; the term "maternal role attainment" was first described by Rubin (1967), who described the phases of taking-in, taking hold, and letting go as characteristic of the behavior of new mothers.

G. The interactions of the parents with the baby during the early weeks is a get-acquainted process.

H. If there are discrepancies between what parents had fantasized their baby would be like and the reality of their child, parents might be delayed in their attachment progress.

I. The temperament of an infant has a great effect on parental feelings of competence and interactions.

1. Compatibility can have an effect on parenting behaviors.

2. Infants who are difficult to console or whose needs are hard to meet might have parents who feel that it is a challenge to develop quality interactions.

3. When parents perceive their efforts as successful in meeting the needs of their infants, they perceive themselves as competent and effective caregivers.

IV Emotional adjustments

A. Mood changes accompanying childbirth are usually mild and self-limiting.

B. There is disagreement in the literature as to whether postpartum psychological complications are unique to the postpartum period or are symptoms of an underlying disorder that is triggered by childbirth.

C. Possible causes have included hormonal changes, chemical imbalances, a genetic predisposition, poor ego development, low self esteem, poor interpersonal relationships, and the perception of the inability to meet others' needs.

D. As many as 50 to 80 percent of postpartum women go through a period of emotional distress beginning two to three days after delivery, partially related to hormonal readjustments as well as a feeling of overwhelming responsibility; this condition has been termed the "baby blues"; feelings of ambivalence, tearfulness, sadness, insomnia, anxiety, irritability, poor concentration, and lack of self confidence are time limited and soon pass.

E. Mothers might also feel isolated and might receive little support from friends, co-workers, or family and might remain stressed and fatigued.

F. A disappointing birth experience, poor nutrition, and a fussy baby increase these feelings of sadness.

G. A small number of women become clinically depressed starting between 2–6 weeks after delivery for several months following birth; this condition is called postpartum depression and is thought to occur in 10–20 percent of new mothers.

H. Postpartum depression is a mild to moderate depression characterized by labile emotions, mood swings, sleep disturbances, and fatigue; mothers might feel hopeless and unable to deal with even small situations; mothers might describe vague physical complaints as well as not feeling attached to her baby; mothers might describe themselves as having no control over their lives; these mothers might not refer to their babies by name.

I. Other risk factors include being a single mother, low socioeconomic level, limited education, pregnancy complications, and health complications.

J. These mothers should be encouraged to contact their physician for a referral to a professional therapist; if medications are prescribed, they must be checked for compatibility with breastfeeding.

K. Postpartum psychosis is a much more rare disorder, occurring in one to two mothers per 1,000 women.

L. This condition results in severe changes in emotions and behavior; symptoms can include hallucinations, delusions, bizarre or violent behavior, and threats of harm to herself or to her baby.

M. If severe enough, this illness might result in hospitalization, medications, and psychiatric counseling; separation might be an issue as well as medication compatibility with breastfeeding.

N. Effects on the other family members might include decreased communication, inadequate parenting, behavioral problems with other children, and marital discord.

O. The lactation consultant will be part of a team involved in the care of mothers who have postpartum affective disorders and might be called upon for help with securing a breast pump, acting as a resource for information about medications and breastfeeding, maintaining breastfeeding, or helping the mother relactate if desired.

V Sexual abuse survivors

A. As many as one in three women will be sexually assaulted in their lifetime.

B. Long-term effects of sexual abuse as a child might be manifested in at least 20 percent of survivors during adulthood.

C. Pregnancy and childbirth are often times that either remind survivors of past sexual abuse or when this feeling is recognized for the first time; triggered memories can interfere with breastfeeding.

D. Mothers might experience flashbacks, depression, anger, a loss of control, powerlessness, and a sense of confusion about relationships.

E. Mothers might or might not inform the lactation consultant about past sexual abuse.

F. Some mothers might have difficulty dealing with the intimacy of breast-feeding and prefer to pump milk and feed the expressed milk with a bottle.

G. Breastfeeding at night, in a darkened room, in a bed, or with others around might be difficult or impossible for this mother; choices of breastfeeding times and places might need to be explored in order to avoid situational flashbacks or unpleasant feelings; sometimes a mother can breastfeed if someone else handles the nighttime feedings.

H. Some women are comfortable nursing a young baby but have difficulty with an older baby who smiles and plays at the breast; the lactation consultant will need to offer information about typical older baby behavior at the breast while emphasizing the functional role of the breasts as opposed to the sexual role.

I. The lactation consultant might wish to gently encourage this mother to secure counseling from an expert in sexual abuse.

J. Attachment parenting is compatible with mothers who have experienced past sexual abuse.

**VI** Postpartum sexual adjustments

A. The birth of a baby disrupts the lives of parents, interferes with freedom and spontaneity, and requires a major commitment of time focused on the new infant.

B. The need for sexual readjustment is common to the situation of new parenthood.

C. Some women might be tired, "touched out," or so overwhelmed as not to be able to concentrate on sexual needs.

D. Some fathers might resent all the attention the baby is receiving.

E. Many physicians recommend waiting to resume sexual relations after the six-week check-up; not all couples will need to wait for that period, however.

F. Some women find that their breasts are very sensitive to touch or not sensitive at all; breasts are not off limits during lovemaking; many experienced couples simply have the mother either feed the baby or express milk beforehand to reduce leakage during lovemaking.

G. The hormones of lactation can cause a decrease in vaginal lubrication; mothers might find that a lubricant will relieve discomfort.

H. Many couples also enjoy other forms of intimacy during this time, because it presents an opportunity to explore variations in techniques or routines.

**VII** Return of fertility

A. During the immediate postpartum period and for varying lengths of time thereafter, the breastfeeding mother experiences amenorrhea or the absence of the menses.

B. The menstrual cycle absence can be followed by anovulatory cycles (absent egg release).

C. The return of menses in a breastfeeding mother is 9–30 percent in three months and 19–53 percent by six months and is dependent on factors such as exclusive breastfeeding, nighttime breastfeeding, short intervals between breastfeedings, durations of feeds, and the absence of supplemental feeds or sucking by the baby.

D. Some women do not resume their cycles until after weaning has occurred.

E. Some women experience scanty show before their true cycles resume.

F. Women can become pregnant while they are breastfeeding and have a number of family planning options.

G. Natural family planning is a group of methods that rely on fertility awareness to prevent or space pregnancies: the calendar method, basal body temperature method, cervical mucous method, symptothermal method, and lactational amenorrhea method (LAM).

1. LAM can be used under three conditions: the mother's menses has not yet returned, the baby is breastfed around the clock without other foods in the diet or a sucking displacement to pacifiers, and the baby is younger than six months.

2. If any one of these conditions is not met, then backup contraception is needed.

3. LAM offers pregnancy protection during the first six months postpartum with no side effects; the risk of pregnancy in the first six months is less than 1 percent.

H. Vaginal spermicides are 69–89 percent effective and are used after the cervix has closed; there are no side effects or contraindications while breastfeeding.

I. Barrier methods

1. The male condom and foam are very effective, with no side effects or contraindications while breastfeeding

2. The female condom (does not require fitting by a health care professional)

3. Diaphragm—must be refitted after each pregnancy

4. Cervical cap

J. Intrauterine device (IUD)—while IUDs are a very effective method, breastfeeding women are at a higher risk of expulsion of the IUD during the early nursing period because of the uterine contractions caused by suckling

K. Oral contraceptives—these contraceptives have been in use for more than 40 years; two types are on the market today: a combined estrogen/progestin pill and a progestin-only formulation

      1. Breastfeeding women usually use the progestin-only pill in the early phase of breastfeeding (the first six months).

      2. Estrogen has the risk of reducing milk quantity and can also pass into the milk.

  L. Injectable hormonal contraception (Depo-Provera)—is injected every three months

      1. The manufacturer states that in breastfeeding women, it is to be started after six weeks.

      2. Administration before leaving the hospital has been associated with interference with the establishment of lactation and subsequent milk production problems.

  M. Implanted hormonal contraception (Norplant)

**VIII** Siblings and breastfeeding

  A. Each child is different and needs time and understanding in his or her adjustment to the arrival of a new sibling.

  B. A mother can be encouraged to find at least one time each day where her total attention is devoted to the older sibling.

  C. Siblings might wish to be included during breastfeeding; mothers can read a book to the sibling or watch him or her play.

  D. He or she might wish to taste the milk, in which case hand expressing a little into a cup might satisfy his or her curiosity.

  E. Toddlers might also be tandem nursing (breastfeeding of two or more children of different ages); the new baby takes precedence over the toddler, with access to both breasts occurring before the toddler nurses.

  F. If a mother wishes to wean the older sibling (or resents the intrusion on breastfeeding), she can wean in a gradual manner by substituting activities for nursings and feeding the new baby when the older child is not around or when he or she is occupied with other things.

  G. Some mothers reserve just one time each day for the older sibling to nurse in order to provide that special time together.

  H. A child who has previously weaned might show renewed interest in breastfeeding when he or she sees the new baby at the breast; mothers need to decide how they can best accommodate the needs of both children.

**IX** Single mothers

  A. Single mothers might have sole responsibility for the baby.

  B. Women might be single by choice, through separation or divorce, or through the death of the spouse.

C. Single mothers who are divorced or in the process of divorcing might have custody issues that impact separations and breastfeeding.

D. Single mothers might live alone, with a partner or roommate, or with family members.

E. She might have the multiple responsibilities of work, school, household chores, and parenting.

F. She might have little privacy or support for what she is doing.

G. Some single mothers find that keeping the baby in their bed at night and breastfeeding through the evening and nighttime hours are beneficial to and fulfilling for both mother and baby.

H. The lactation consultant should be familiar with community resources for single mothers and should troubleshoot ways to meet the mother's and baby's needs while preserving the breastfeeding relationship.

X  The adolescent mother

A. Many adolescents elect to keep their infants and are physically and psychologically capable of breastfeeding.

B. Adolescents who have a dependent relationship with their mothers are less likely to breastfeed.

C. Adolescents respond poorly to lecturing, advice-giving, mandates, and patronizing discussions or actions; teens respond best to sincere, consistent, and honest support with a greater response to interactive learning and the right to refuse to participate if she feels threatened; they learn best in an environment that is nonjudgmental, fun, and supportive of the teen's decisions.

D. These mothers might be poorly nourished and might experience inadequate prenatal care.

E. Staff in the hospital should encourage these mothers to room-in with their baby, invite interaction between the mother and baby, and treat the mother in an adult manner, giving options and including her in the decision-making process.

F. Power struggles with the grandmother can occur; the teen's mother might be threatened by the breastfeeding especially if she did not breastfeed her daughter; some grandmothers actively oppose breastfeeding.

G. Some adolescent mothers choose to breastfeed specifically because this action gives some control over the situation.

H. Teen mothers might have difficulty seeing beyond their own needs, have unresolved issues about their bodies and sexuality, and might resent the baby and parenting because it interferes with their social life.

I. Older teens who are exposed to other breastfeeding mothers and/or prenatal breastfeeding education are most likely to breastfeed.

J. Teen mothers are concerned about modesty and the need to return to school within as little as two weeks after delivery; plans for breastfeeding around breaks and classes need to be worked out; peer counselors are a valuable addition to the support for teen mothers.

K. Teen mothers typically choose to breastfeed because it is good for the baby and because of the closeness of the relationship.

L. Other family members, especially the teen's mother, might need information about breastfeeding and can be provided with ideas for supporting it.

M. Teachers might need help to understand that breastfeeding is not being used as an excuse to miss classes.

# References

Ainsworth MDS, Blehar MC, Waters E, Wall S. Patterns of attachment—psychological study of the strange situation. Hillsdale, NJ: Lawrence Erlbaum Associates, 1978.

Bar-Yam NB, Darby L. Fathers and breastfeeding: A review of the literature. *J Hum Lact* 1997; 13:45–50.

Bocar DL, Moore K. Acquiring the parental role: A theoretical perspective. Lactation Consultant Series. Franklin Park, IL: La Leche League International, 1987.

Bowlby J. Attachment and loss: Attachment (Vol. 1). New York: Basic Books, 1969.

Erikson EH. Childhood and society. New York: W.W. Norton, 1950.

Kendall-Tackett K. Breastfeeding and the sexual abuse survivor. *J Hum Lact* 1998; 14: 125–130.

Kennedy KI, Kotelchuck M. Policy considerations for the introduction and promotion of the lactational amenorrhea method: Advantages and disadvantages of LAM. *J Hum Lact* 1998; 14(3):191–203.

Kennedy KI, Kotelchuck M, Visness CM, et al. Users' understanding of the lactational amenorrhea method and the occurrence of pregnancy. *J Hum Lact* 1998; 14:209–218.

Klaus MH, Kennell JH. Parent-infant bonding, 2nd ed. St. Louis: C.V. Mosby, 1982.

Klaus MH, Jerauld R, Kreger N, et al. Maternal attachment: Importance of the first postpartum days. *N Engl J Med* 1972; 286:460–463.

Labbok MH, Hight-Laukaran V, Peterson AE, et al. Multicentre study of the lactational amenorrhea method (LAM). 1. Efficacy, duration and implications for clinical application. *Contraception* 1997; 55:327–336.

Lauwers J, Shinskie D. Counseling the nursing mother: a lactation consultant's guide. Sudbury, MA: Jones and Bartlett Publishers, 2000.

Lawrence RA, Lawrence RM. Breastfeeding: a guide for the medical profession. St. Louis, MO: Mosby, Inc., 1999.

Leffler D. U.S. high school age girls may be receptive to breastfeeding promotion. *J Hum Lact* 2000; 16:36–40.

Nichols FH, Zwelling E. Maternal-newborn nursing: Theory and practice. Philadelphia, PA: W. B. Saunders Company, 1997.

Rubin R. Attainment of the maternal role: Part 1, Processes. *Nurs Res* 1967; 16:237–245.

Rubin R. Attainment of the maternal role. Part II, Models and referents. *Nurs Res* 1967; 16: 342–346.

Volpe EM, Bear M. Enhancing breastfeeding initiation in adolescent mothers through the breastfeeding educated and supported teen (BEST) club. *J Hum Lact* 2000; 16:196–200.

## Internet Resources for Postpartum Depression Information

Postpartum Adjustment Support Services of Canada (PASS-Can)—http://www.pass-can.volnetmmp.net/
The National Canadian Clearinghouse for education and support related to perinatal mood and anxiety disorders. We hope you find this information helpful regarding these and other services we have to offer mothers, new families, and health care professionals.

Depression after Delivery—http://www.behavenet.com/dadinc/
The corporation was formed to provide support for women with postpartum depression. It has expanded its focus to include education, information, and referral for women and families coping with mental health issues associated with childbearing, both during pregnancy and postpartum.

Pacific Postpartum Support Society—www.postpartum.org
The Pacific Post Partum Support Society is a nonprofit society dedicated to supporting the needs of distressed postpartum mothers and their families. We have been assisting women to recovery for more than twenty-seven years.

Postnatal Information for Men—http://www.pndinfo.co.uk/
This site is primarily designed for men, whose partners are suffering with Postnatal Depression, (PND). This is not to say that this is a men only site! I hope that women will find the site to be of interest also.

Online PPD Support Group—http://www.geocities.com/ppdsupportpage/
This page is devoted to mothers and families affected by Post Partum Depression. The

members of this Online PPD Support Group find information, helpful advice, and caring support through a PPD mailing list, a chatroom and a forum. Please feel free to browse our pages. We welcome you to join us.

WellMother.com, Dr. Shaila Misri's Site—http://www.wellmother.com/index.htm
WellMother.com is an online resource for women and their families designed to offer support and resources on a number of issues related to the emotional challenges specifically related to their reproductive cycle including: Pregnancy, Postpartum, Pregnancy loss, PMS, and Menopause.

Postpartum Depression Links—http://www.psycom.net/depression.central.post-partum.html
Excellent list of links to various subjects relating to PPD including breastfeeding, meds therapy, etc.

Postpartum Support International—http://www.chss.iup.edu/postpartum/
A Social Support Network, Information Center & Research Guide Concering Postpartum Mood Disorders & Depression. This site also has excellent info on research, conferences, early detection, and many resources for both new parents and professionals.

Pregnancy and Depression—http://www.angelfire.com/de2/depressionpregnancy/index.html
Professional Journal articles. Excellent information on meds during pregnancy and breastfeeding.

The British Columbia Reproductive Mental Health Program—
http://www.bcrmh.com/disorders/postpartum.htm
Emotional Disorders in the Postpartum Period. Recent research has shown that women are susceptible to psychiatric disorders during pregnancy. Most commmonly found are major depression, panic disorders, obsessive compulsive disorders, and psychosis.

The Postpartum Stress Centre—http://www.postpartumstress.com/index.html
Karen Kleinman, MSW.

Medscape Women's Health—
http://www.medscape.com/Home/Topics/WomensHealth/womenshealth.html
Do your own research on various subjects pertaining to women's health.

Parentsplace PPD Support Board—
http://boards.parentsplace.com/messages/get/pppostdepression65.html
We hope that you will find here others who understand what you are feeling and that you will find support and friendship as you work toward feeling better.

# ADOPTIVE MOTHERS AND BREASTFEEDING

*Noreen Siebenaler, MSN, RN, IBCLC*

## OBJECTIVES

- Define induced lactation.
- Define relactation.
- State three reasons why an adoptive mother might choose breastfeeding.
- Describe two factors related to the infant that influence successful adoptive breastfeeding.
- Describe two factors related to the mother that influence her ability to successfully breastfeed an adoptive infant.
- List three assistive devices that are used to initiate and increase milk production and that facilitate adequate milk transfer to adoptive infants who are breastfeeding.

## Introduction

Adoptive mothers who choose to breastfeed have many options. Adoptive mothers develop their own definition of successful breastfeeding as they progress from collecting information about breastfeeding to utilizing methods to induce lactation, to actually breastfeeding their babies when the babies arrive. Successful breastfeeding for this unique group of mothers and babies can often be achieved through exploring options, assisting the mother with choosing a method of adoptive breastfeeding, and facilitating the mother and baby through the process of adoptive breastfeeding.

    **I** Induced lactation and relactation

      A. Definitions

          1. Induced lactation—the process of initiating milk production in a woman who has never been pregnant

2. Relactation—the process of initiating or increasing milk production in a woman who has previously been pregnant. If a woman has previously lactated or breastfed, she is also considered to be relactating.

B. Important issues to discuss with the adoptive mother

1. The primary reason why the mother wants to breastfeed.

   a. The mother might expect breastfeeding to give her a feeling of "special closeness" to her baby.

   b. The mother might want to breastfeed due to the health benefits of breastfeeding for the baby.

2. How does the mother define successful breastfeeding for herself?

3. If the adoptive mother is not able to achieve a full milk supply, how will she feel?

   a. Inform the mother that patience is critical to success; it is best not to have precise expectations about when milk production will begin.

4. Does the mother have a supportive environment for breastfeeding?

5. Are her immediate family and friends supportive?

6. If her family is not supportive, will the mother have any other support system?

7. If the mother is relactating, why did she stop breastfeeding the first time?

8. If the mother is relactating, how long has it been since she last breastfed?

9. Are the mother's breastfeeding goals realistic? Provide the mother with realistic information related to milk production possibilities.

II  Pre-breastfeeding preparation options

A. Pumping

1. A bilateral, electric, hospital-grade pump is the most effective option.

   a. The mother pumps as often as the baby would breastfeed, or a minimum of six times in 24 hours.

   b. Pumping stimulates prolactin release from the pituitary.

   c. The time required for milk production to start varies from a few days to a few weeks and is difficult to predict.

   d. When the baby arrives, the mother puts the baby to her breast; further pumping for initiation or support of milk production then becomes an option.

      i. The mother might choose to breastfeed with a supplementer if milk production is minimal.

      ii. The mother might choose to partially breastfeed, combining breastfeeding with another feeding method.

B. Hormones
    1. Estrogen
        a. Can be taken orally or transdermally in order to prepare breasts for lactation
        b. Causes proliferation of the milk transporting ducts in the breast
        c. Mimics the hormonal changes of pregnancy
        d. Is usually used in combination with pumping and galactogogues
    2. Progesterone
        a. Is taken orally, by injection, or by suppository
        b. Stimulates breast development and the growth of secretory alveoli
        c. Mimics the hormonal change of pregnancy
        d. Is usually used in combination with pumping and galactogogues

C. Galactogogues
    1. Drugs or herbal preparations that cause milk secretion
        a. Metoclopromide (reglan); United States
            i. Most commonly used to increase lower esophageal sphincter tone in gastroesophageal reflux in patients who have reduced gastric tone
            ii. Commonly used in infants and children
            iii. Stimulates prolactin release from the pituitary and therefore enhances breast milk production
            iv. Side effects can include gastric cramping, diarrhea, and depression if used more than four weeks
        b. Domperidone (motillium); not FDA approved in the United States but commonly used in other countries
            i. Same uses as metoclopromide
            ii. Minimal to no risk of side effects
            iii. Can be sent to the United States through some Canadian, Mexican, and New Zealand pharmacies with a U.S. physician's prescription
        c. Herbal galactogogues are often found in local health food or grocery stores and sometimes used simultaneously
            i. Fenugreek seed (*Trigonellagraecum*)
                (1) When used in moderation is listed in the United States as (GRAS); generally regarded as safe (Hale, 2000)
                (2) Might have a hypoglycemic effect which has been noted in animal studies

        (3) Little clinical research exists on the use of Fenugreek

        (4) Safe when used in normal doses of less than 6 grams per day

   ii. Blessed thistle

        (1) No negative effects have been noted

        (2) Antibacterial and anti-inflammatory properties

   iii. Milk thistle (*Silybum marianum*)

        (1) The seeds are used in a tea with no reported side effects in infants

   iv. Mother's Milk Tea

        (1) Usually contains small amounts of Fenugreek and other herbs associated with lactation

        (2) Often used in combination with other galactogogues

        (3) Several other herbal galactogogues are often recommended (see adoptive breastfeeding Web sites)

**III** Infant factors that influence the success of adoptive breastfeeding

  A. The infant's willingness to suckle

  B. The infant's age

    1. Babies who are younger than three months old might be more willing to accept the breast (Riordan and Auerbach, 1980, 1981)

    2. The length of time since the baby has breastfed

    3. How the infant has been fed when not breastfeeding

**IV** Maternal factors that can influence an adoptive mother's ability to breastfeed successfully

  A. Maternal motivation, patience, and persistence

  B. Previous breastfeeding experience

    1. Women who have never breastfed or who have never been pregnant are somewhat less likely to establish a full milk supply (Auerbach and Avery, 1980, 1981).

  C. Condition of the mother's breasts

    1. Previous breast surgery may result in limited milk transport due to severing of the milk transporting ducts. Depending on the type of surgery, some women may be able to totally breastfeed, partially breastfeed, or choose to breastfeed with a supplementer.

    2. Flat nipples can make it difficult for some babies to latch on to the breast, maintain adequate suction, and obtain enough milk. Before the baby arrives,

assist the mother with techniques to evert nipples such as with a pump or adapted syringe.

D. Mother's ability to interact responsively with the baby

1. Does the mother have extra help at home and time off work?

2. Is the mother willing to breastfeed on demand with frequent skin-to-skin contact?

E. Support from family, friends, the community, and health professionals

**V** Adoptive breastfeeding methods (mothers' choices)

A. Supplemental nursing system (SNS)

1. Show the mother the SNS video to assist her with making a choice.

2. If the mother expresses an interest in SNS, help her put the equipment together and try it on.

B. Lact-Aid—Give the mother the Web site address so that she can see the Lact-Aid supplementer and read about how it is used

C. Breastfeeding without supplementer

D. Bottles given after breastfeeding

**VI** Psychology of adoptive breastfeeding

A. The success of adoptive breastfeeding should not be determined by the amount of milk produced.

B. The primary purpose of breastfeeding an adopted infant is to enhance the attachment process.

C. Frustration associated with not achieving expected outcomes can interfere with the attachment process.

1. Assist and encourage the mother to determine realistic priorities and expectations before she initiates the process of inducing lactation or relactation.

**VII** Counseling adoptive mothers: role of the lactation consultant

A. Facilitator

1. Encourages the mother to reach her own decisions

2. Uses a positive, realistic approach

B. Educator

1. Describes the physiology of lactation at the mother's level of understanding and as it applies to her situation

2. Provides and encourages the mother to explore resources that enable her to choose options related to adoptive breastfeeding

C. An expert practitioner providing excellent one-to-one, "hands-on" assistance with the following:

    1. Correct positioning

    2. Correct latch-on

    3. Assessment of the infant's oral anatomy and ability to breastfeed

    4. Assessment of the breasts and nipples

**VIII** Internet resources related to adoptive breastfeeding

A. La Leche League—www.lalecheleague.org

B. A Web site offering support specifically for adoptive mothers who are breastfeeding or who are interested in breastfeeding— www.fourfriends.com/abrw/

C. Bright Future Lactation Resource Center—www.bflrc.com

D. One mother's experience with adoptive breastfeeding— www.members.tripod.com/~Darillyn/

# References

Auerbach KG, Avery JL. Nursing the adopted infant: Report from a survey. Denver, CO: Resources in Human Nurturing, International, 1979.

Cheales-Siebenaler NJ. Induced lactation in an adoptive mother. *J Hum Lact* 1999; 15:41–43.

Guoth-Gumberger M. Stillen mit dem brust-ernahrungsset (Breastfeeding with the Supplemental Nutrition System). La Leche League Deutschland, Publication 68-D, Muchen, Germany, 1992.

Hormann E. Stillen eines Adoptivkindes und Relaktation (Breastfeeding an adopted child and relactation). La Leche League Germany, Publication 57–D, Munchen, Germany, 1998.

Lawrence RA, Lawrence RM. Induced lactation and relactation (including nursing the adopted baby) and cross-nursing. Breastfeeding: A Guide for the Medical Profession, 5th ed. St. Louis, MO: Mosby, Inc., 1999:633–652.

Riordan J, Auerback KG. Breastfeeding and Human Lactation. Sudbury, MA: Jones and Bartlett Publishers, 1998:553–557.

Sutherland A, Auerbach KG. *Relactation and Induced Lactation*. Lactation Consultant Series, Unit 1. Wayne, NJ: Avery Publishing Group, 1985.

World Health Organization. Relactation: Review of experience and recommendations for practice. Geneva: WHO, 1998.

# Breastfeeding and Working Women: The Role of the Lactation Consultant

*Barbara Wilson-Clay, BSEd, IBCLC*

## Objectives

- Discuss the economic value of breastfeeding.

- Identify three benefits to employers who support on-site or other types of breastfeeding support for female workers.

- Identify benefits to mothers and babies when breastfeeding is continued after the mother returns to work.

- Identify opportunities to "market" breastfeeding support in the workplace.

- Identify strategies for locating allies within communities and businesses in order to achieve mother-friendly workplaces.

- Identify legislative and policy initiatives as effective strategies for achieving social change with regard to workplace rights.

- Describe basic workplace requirements to support the lactating employee.

- Discuss issues related to the choice of breast pumps.

- Describe the safe storage of breast milk.

- Discuss issues related to handling milk in the day-care environment.

- Discuss the issue of toxic exposure or occupational hazards in the workplace in relation to breastfeeding.

## Introduction

Women have always worked, and their employment settings range from fields and factories to the corporate boardroom and the space shuttle. While separation from the infant can pose logistical problems for the nursing mother, women have developed many successful strategies to maintain their breastfeeding relationships. These techniques include maternal leave of absence for up to one year following birth, flexible scheduling, home-based employment, on-site day care, bringing the infant to the mother for feedings, hand-expressing or pumping milk in the workplace for missed feeds, and reverse-cycle feeding. The lactation consultant helps the employed mother maintain lactation in several ways. In order to do so, the lactation consultant (LC) must understand the physiology of the control of lactation so that mothers establish and maintain an adequate milk supply. The LC provides anticipatory guidance to help mothers plan a course of action and to develop strategies to support plans to return to work. The LC must be familiar with alternate methods of milk expression, including both hand expression and the use of breast pumps. He or she must be able to counsel on the issue of alternate feeding devices, milk storage, and scheduling. It is useful to provide assistance on how to communicate with a day-care provider about the handling of human milk. Finally, the LC's guidance must include discussion of any potential workplace hazards in terms of toxic exposure to the mother. On a broader plane, the LC acts as a change agent in his or her community in order to publicize the benefits of breastfeeding as a public health issue in order to influence workplace conditions to protect lactating women.

I    The economic value of breastfeeding

    A.  The social, economic, and monetary value of breastfeeding has been poorly quantified in the global market (Andrews, 1983).

        1.  Methods exist to value other unwaged activity and can be applied to breastfeeding.

            a.  Estimate the value of the product: milk.

                i.  Estimate the value of the activity/time needed to produce it.

                ii. Estimate the costs of replacing the product (including the environmental impact of all aspects of production, preparation, and disposal of human milk substitutes); Auerbach, 1984.

    B.  Under-valuing of breastfeeding results in a missed opportunity to influence policy-makers to support breastfeeding.

        1.  Awareness of the costs of *non*-breastfeeding might assist with obtaining better benefits for breastfeeding women.

        2.  Lactation consultants must be aware of and address economic issues.

            a.  Discuss this value of breastfeeding in presentations, expert testimony, and directly with clients.

    C.  Non-breastfeeding poses a health risk for infants.

        1.  Data supports decreased illness in breastfed populations (Auerbach and Guss, 1984).

D. The social cost of non-breastfeeding is related to the following:
   1. Child health costs—such costs are higher in non-breastfed populations (Auerbach, 1990; Auerbach, 1993).
   2. Child spacing—might be less significant in developed nations, but globally, breastfeeding supports longer birth intervals.
   3. The costs of growing, preparing, and delivering breast milk substitutes are an economic burden.
   4. The environmental aspects of growing, preparing, delivering, and disposing of breast milk substitute packaging impact everyone.

II General considerations
   A. 84 percent of working women return to work in six months.
   B. Breastfeeding duration is related to the number of hours worked each week (Fein and Roe, 1998):

| Hours worked per week | Not working | < 20 hours | 20–34 hours | > 35 hours |
|---|---|---|---|---|
| Average duration of breastfeeding | 25.1 weeks | 24.4 weeks | 22.5 weeks | 16.5 weeks |

   1. Breastfeeding is not a determinant of work-leave duration.
   2. Breastfeeding duration depends partly on the duration of leave.
   3. Breastfeeding intensity depends partly on work intensity.
   4. Women who have not completed high school breastfeed 17 weeks less; high school graduates nine weeks less; and women who have some college education breastfeed five weeks less than college graduates.
   5. Each one-year increase in the mother's age increases the average breastfeeding duration by .78 week.
   6. Each week of work leave increases breastfeeding duration by a half-week.

   C. Benefits to employers
   1. Less absenteeism—mothers miss less work because of a sick child (Ballard, 1983)
   2. Less staff turnover—support for mothering in the workplace helps retain female workers and saves the costs of hiring and training new employees
   3. Improved worker productivity and morale (loyalty)
   4. Lower health insurance premiums and fewer health claims
   5. Assigning value to breast milk and to breastfeeding earns women a seat at the table in terms of negotiating benefits

   D. Benefits to mothers and babies
   1. Breastfeeding promotes bonding and emphasizes the exclusivity of the mother-child relationship.

2. Breastfeeding enables the mother and child to reunite in an intimate fashion following separation.

3. Breastfeeding benefits the health and well-being of mother and child.

4. Continuing to breastfeed after returning to paid work enhances the woman's sense of meeting her maternal goals.

III Workplace breastfeeding support—the duration of exclusive breastfeeding is longer for women who receive support for breastfeeding at work (Bar-Yam, 1998).

A. Supportive work environments are assisted by:

1. Written policies (documentation of support from top management)

2. Circulation/information dissemination of policies that affect parenting/maternity benefits

3. Inclusion of information about policies in new worker orientation programs/materials

4. Ideally: on-site education pre- and postnatally about breastfeeding and working, and benefits to reimburse for pumping expenses or the creation of a company-maintained pump room with pumps provided for mothers

B. Mothers' requirements in the workplace:

1. Flexible and reasonable maternity leave

2. Flexibility of work hours (part-time, flex-time, job-sharing) is an ideal situation—even if only for a few weeks after returning to the job

3. A 15-minute break in the morning and afternoon in order to nurse the baby or express milk

4. A lunch break

   a. A private, clean area where a woman can nurse or express milk

   b. A safe place to store milk

   c. A clean water source for washing up

C. On a company-by-company basis, employers adapt their work environment and available space resources to meet the needs of breastfeeding employees (Bar-Yam, 1998).

1. Some companies design and appoint special breastfeeding rooms

   a. Connected to an occupational nurse's station

   b. Connecting off the women's restrooms

   c. Separate retro-fitting of unused office space with a sink, tables, and lockers

   d. Provision of unused space without amenities beyond privacy, electricity, and a chair

2. The company should provide the following:
   a. Space
      i. Private, comfortable room
      ii. Central location
      iii. Well lit, ventilated, and heated/air conditioned
      iv. Electrical outlets, sink, chair, and refrigerator
      v. Pump
      vi. Table
      vii. Parenting literature
      viii. Telephone
      ix. Storage space, footstool
3. Time
   a. Baby < 4 months = 3 20-minute pumping breaks
   b. Commute time between the workspace and the pumping room
   c. A hospital-grade electric pump that is capable of double pumping
4. Support
   a. Gatekeepers (a co-worker who makes sure that time, space, and support come together for nursing mothers)
   b. Lactation consultant/breastfeeding classes
   c. Human resource department/work life programs
   d. Supervisor (assures flexibility in the department for the mother to pump)
   e. Office manager
   f. Co-workers (cover phones, classroom, work station, cash register, and so on)
5. Education
   a. Lactation program
   b. Described in benefits materials
   c. Articles in company newsletter
   d. Flyers posted about program
   e. Educational offering for supervisors and co-workers
   f. Breastfeeding pamphlets, videos, and so on in resource center
6. E-mail informing pregnant women about lactation support
   a. Some companies designate resource personnel to provide a liaison to assist with a lactating worker's needs, including the following:

          i. The company or occupational health nurse (Barber-Madden et al., 1987)

          ii. The company health and fitness coordinator

          iii. The benefits coordinator

    b. Workers might designate a representative for liaison with the company.

          i. A delegate from among the workers who are currently using the pump room

          ii. A union representative

          iii. In some instances, a lactation consultant might be employed to communicate with both the employer and workers about setting up a pumping room or a corporate lactation program (Barber-Madden et al., 1986).

**IV** Creating mother-friendly work places: strategies for change

  A. Network with allies:

    1. The state department of health: is there a breastfeeding taskforce?

    2. Local branches of major corporations, most of whom have work/life programs and benefits managers

      a. If this company is supporting breastfeeding at another location, this service provides an opportunity to advocate for parity in all locations.

    3. Cities often have employers' collectives that meet regularly to discuss work- and benefits-related issues. The lactation consultant can:

      a. Offer to speak at such a meeting.

      b. Advocate the inclusion of breastfeeding/workplace benefits in benefit packages.

      c. Make a poster display of what workplace support for breastfeeding might look like.

      d. Use these meetings as networking opportunities that lead to discussions about on-site breastfeeding rooms that would fit with *their* needs/ situations.

      e. Offer to set up displays at job fairs.

      f. Offer to provide prenatal education about breastfeeding to pregnant workers in a lunch-time seminar format.

      g. Provide materials to companies (for example, lists of places to rent/buy breast pumps and local breastfeeding support services).

      h. Create a local coalition to develop a brochure to promote mother-friendly workplaces.

4. Meet with your local legislative representatives to discuss breastfeeding policy issues in your state.

   a. Public policy often drives public behavior; consider the regulation of cigarette smoking and changed attitudes about secondhand smoke exposure.

   b. Expert testimony before committees in a state legislature can help influence policy decisions.

5. Let the media in on it.

   a. Publicize every small advance as if it were a major event; companies love good press.

   b. Give awards for being family-friendly and emphasize the breastfeeding angle.

6. She might look like "just a mom," but in her workplace they call her "Boss."

   a. Helping individual women meet their breastfeeding goals sends ripples into the community.

   b. Remind powerful women of their social obligation to support breastfeeding; it might be a new idea to them.

**V** The logistics of combining working and breastfeeding (Figure 28-1)

A. Prenatal

   1. Arrange a 12-week leave or longer.

   2. Each week of work leave increases breastfeeding duration by a half-week.

   3. Returning to work within the first 12 weeks is related to the greatest decrease in breastfeeding duration.

B. Explore work intensity options/flexibility

   1. Working part time increases the number of feeds per day and the duration of breastfeeding.

   2. The median level of breastfeeding is highest among women who work 1–9 hours/week and is the lowest among those who work greater than or equal to 35 hours/week at three months (Figure 28-2).

C. Child care arrangements (close proximity to the baby increases the number of feeds/day)

D. Childbirth classes/breastfeeding classes (attending a prenatal birthing class increases breastfeeding duration by five weeks)

E. Employee benefits (leave, flexibility, lactation program, and so on)

F. Letters to the employer (if a parent misses two hours of work for the excess illness attributable to formula-feeding, more than 2,000 hours [the equivalent of one year of employment] are lost per 1,000 never-breastfed babies)(Ball and Wright, 1999)

**Figure 28-1**    Return-to-work breastfeeding assessment worksheet. (Reprinted by permission: Bar-Yam N. Workplace lactation support, part 1: A return-to-work breastfeeding assessment tool. *J Hum Lact* 1998; 14:249–254.)

|  | Yes | No | Notes |
|---|---|---|---|

*Type of Job*

1. What is the client's job?

2. Does she have her own office?

3. Does she keep her own calendar/control her own time?

4. Does the client's job involve travel out of town or out of her office?

5. Are most of her colleagues men or women?*

*Space*

Bathrooms are not acceptable breastfeeding/pumping spaces!!

1. Is there designated private breastfeeding/pumping space (Nursing Mothers' Room/NMR) in the workplace?

2. Does the space have a sink, a chair, and electrical outlets?

3. Are pumps available there?

4. Where is the space in relation to the client's workspace?

5. How long does it take to get from the workspace to the NMR?

6. Where will the client store her milk?

7. If there is no designated space, where will the mother pump?

8. Can she use the same space every day?

9. Are there electrical outlets there?

10. Where is the nearest sink?

*Time*

Pumping should not come at the expense of the mother's lunch!!

1. How old will the baby be upon return to work?

2. How often will the client be pumping/breastfeeding when she first returns to work?

3. When will the client pump?

4. What type of pump will she use? Is there a double pump?

5. How many parts on the pump must be cleaned out with each use?

6. Can breaks be taken reliably at the same time every day?

7. If there is on-site or near-site day care, can the mother go to the baby to nurse?

*Support*

1. Who at work knows that the client plans to breastfeed/pump at work?

2. Does the supervisor need to be informed or consulted?

3. If so, what are his/her feelings about the client's plan?

4. Are there other new mothers at work (at the same workplace or colleagues at other workplaces) who are nursing or planning to nurse at work?

|  | Yes | No | Notes |
|---|---|---|---|

5.  Are there mothers at work who have done so in the past?

6.  What are her partner's feelings about the mother's plan to nurse and work?

7.  Do day care providers know how to handle breast milk?

8.  How do they feel about it?

9.  Will on-site or near-site providers call the mother to nurse, if she requests it?

*Gatekeepers*

1.  If there is no lactation support program, who can help the client find time and space to pump/breastfeed?

2.  Who is responsible for signing up spare offices/conference rooms?

3.  Who keeps the calendar, answers the phone, greets visitors?

*Supervisor*

1.  Must the supervisor be consulted regarding making time and/or space available to pump/breastfeed?

2.  What is the relationship between the client and her supervisor?

3.  Has the client addressed this issue with her supervisor?

4.  If so, what was the response?

5.  If not, what are her concerns about doing so?

*Breastfeeding-Friendly Benefits*

1.  Are there any policies in the workplace regarding nursing mothers?

2.  Are there any policies regarding flexibility for new mothers returning to work?

3.  Does the client have access to any of the following programs?**

    a. earned time          e. flex-time

    b. part-time           f. compressed work week

    c. job sharing         g. telecommuting

    d. phase back         h. on-site or near-site day care

4.  If so, has the client thought about taking advantage of one or more of them?

5.  What is the procedure for doing so?

6.  If not, with whom would the client speak to try to arrange one or more of these programs?

    a. supervisor          d. Employee Relations Officer

    b. Human Resources Officer    e. Other (specify)

    c. Benefits Officer

*Note.* Space for answers is not displayed to scale.

*In some workplaces, men are more understanding and supportive than women and sometimes it is the reverse, but it is good information to have.

**See Figure 28-2 for definitions and benefits of each of these programs.

**Figure 28-2**   Descriptions of flexible work programs and their benefits for new mothers and employers. (Reprinted by permission: Bar-Yam N. Workplace lactation support, part 1: A return-to-work breastfeeding assessment tool. *J Hum Lact* 1998; 14:249–254.)

| Benefit | Definition | Advantages for New Mothers | Advantages for Employers |
|---|---|---|---|
| Earned time | Sick leave, vacation time and personal days are grouped into one set of paid days off. Workers takethese days at their own discretion. | Mothers do not have to justify time off to their supervisors. Often, earned time accrues over several years, giving new mothers substantial paid leave after birth. | Promotes loyalty because workers feel trusted and valued. Workers often willing to work extra time as need arises because their needs were met when they arose. |
| Part-time | Workers work less than 35–40 hours/week. Benefits are usually prorated to hours worked. | Gives new mothers more time at home. Often includes flexibility of which hours are worked. | Retain workers with valuable experience and training. Saves recruiting and training new workers. |
| Job sharing | Two workers each work part-time and share the responsibilities and benefits of one job. | Gives mothers more time at home while keeping the same job. | Retain workers with valuable experience and training. Saves recruiting and training new workers. |
| Phase back | Workers return from leave to full-time work load gradually over several weeks or months. | Longer return to work adjustment period for mother and baby. More time with infant, when breastfeeding is being established. | Retains workers with experience. Promotes loyalty and dedication of workers. |
| Flex-time | Workers arrange to work hours to suit their schedules, i.e., 7 a.m.–3 p.m., or 10 a.m.–6 p.m. | Can work with spouse's schedule to require less paid child care. Can arrange hours around best times of day to be with baby. Shorter commutes in less traffic. | Workplace covered for more hours/day. Workers better able to focus when schedules suit their needs. |
| Compressed work week | Workers work more hours on fewer days, i.e., 7 a.m.–7 p.m., 3 days/week. | Allows new mothers full days at home with their babies. | Workers better able to focus when schedules suit their needs. Retains workers with experience and training. |

| Benefit | Definition | Advantages for New Mothers | Advantages for Employers |
|---|---|---|---|
| Telecommuting | Workers work all or part of their jobs from home. | Can work around baby's schedule. Less commuting time. Less work clothing and travel expenses. | Retains workers with experience and training. Saves office and parking space. |
| On-site or near-site day care | Day care provided on or near site, often sponsored by the company. | Can visit baby for nursing etc. during the work day. Commuting time is with baby. | Promotes loyalty among workers. Workers better able to focus when baby is accessible. |

G. Worksite environment

H. What support exists for breastfeeding mothers?

I. Pumps (employer-supplied, rented, collection kits, and instructions)

J. Lactation consultant/breastfeeding support

K. Motivation (influences length and intensity of perseverance of breastfeeding)

L. Encourage full recovery from childbirth and the optimal establishment of lactation.

   1. Studies indicate that an early return to full employment is associated with a cessation of breastfeeding.

      a. Six to eight weeks leave might not be sufficient to provide adequate time to recover and establish lactation (Bridges et al., 1997).

   2. Additional supportive care in the hospital and during the early postpartum period contribute to breastfeeding success.

      a. The lactation consultant and visiting nurse care both contribute to successful initiation and early maintenance of breastfeeding (Broome, 1981).

      b. Working mothers are at an increased risk for mastitis; increased maternal fatigue and going too long with full breasts might be the primary factors (Christoffel et al., 1981).

         i. Anticipatory guidance can assist in the prevention of mastitis.

         ii. Increased support for the mother from other family members is critical to assist the working mother and to protect her health and energy.

   3. Immediately postpartum:

      a. Priority is an abundant milk supply (the most frequent reason for premature weaning is insufficient milk).

    b. Early resolution of problems (women who have problems wean before returning to work or do so but breastfeed for three weeks less).

    c. Resolve issues of embarrassment (women who are extremely embarrassed about breastfeeding stop breastfeeding 10 weeks earlier).

    d. Determine who is responsible for household chores.

    e. Early postpartum education should include instruction on hand-expression.

    f. Assistance and education in the selection of an effective breast pump helps mothers select appropriate equipment for their situation.

    g. A good breast pump:

        i. Imitates the negative pressure levels created by sucking infants

        ii. Excessive levels of negative pressure can damage nipple tissue (Cohen and Mrtek, 1994)

        iii. Has a flange design that is a good fit with the mother's nipple size; if the mother's nipple fits too tightly into the flange opening, constriction can irritate the nipple tissue and inhibit milk flow

        iv. Is easy to operate and does not promote repetitive stress injury (Cohen et al., 1995)

        v. Is reasonably portable

        vi. Is not noisy to operate (can contribute to concerns about privacy)

        vii. Is easy to clean; parts can be sterilized and the design does not contribute to contamination issues

        viii. Has a product warranty

        ix. Cost is an issue, but poorly designed pumps ultimately cost the consumer more and are a poor bargain if they undermine lactation

        x. Offer the option for double pumping

          (1) Double pumping saves time

          (2) Mothers prefer double pumping (Ducket, 1992)

        xi. Electric pulsatile (automatic cycling) pumps more closely imitate infant sucking and are associated with higher prolactin levels (Faught, 1994)

M. Pumping strategies: preparing to return to work

    1. The mother obtains the pump and begins to use it experimentally at 2–4 weeks postpartum.

    2. Pumping sessions might take place between feedings, or the mother might select one feed per day during which she feeds the baby from one breast and pumps from the other.

3. Pumped milk can be offered to the baby by an alternative method of the mother's choice to help accustom the baby to being fed as he or she will be fed in day care.

   a. Offering the baby a full feed is not necessary to accustom the baby to an alternate feeding method.

   b. Small volumes can serve to familiarize the baby with alternate feeding methods and might be less stressful.

   c. Feedings can be best offered by someone other than the mother.

   d. Waiting too long to introduce a bottle can cause problems with nipple confusion (Type B, bottle refusal)(Fein and Roe, 1998).

   e. Milk that is not fed to the baby can be frozen for later use or donated to a milk bank.

   f. The mother should be advised not to over-stimulate with her pump.

      i. Double pumping might be too stimulating for some mothers during this postpartum period.

      ii. Sequential pumping or pumping only the un-nursed breast might be sufficient.

      iii. Double pumping might only need to take place during separations from the baby.

      iv. Pumping sessions of 12–15 minutes are generally sufficient to obtain milk for practice feeds and to begin stashing milk in the freezer.

      v. If a mother has difficulty letting down her milk while pumping, gentle nipple manipulation, breast massage, and visualization can assist (Frederick and Auerbach, 1985).

      vi. It is not necessary to use the highest pressure settings; start on a low setting and gradually increase the pressure over the course of the pumping session as long as the pressure level remains comfortable.

      vii. The mother needs education on milk storage, thawing and warming techniques, safe milk transportation information, and on offering bottles (if applicable).

N. Ethical issues related to breast pumps

   1. The IBCLC is obligated to "remain free of conflict of interest while fulfilling the objectives and maintaining the integrity of the lactation consultant profession" and to "provide information about appropriate products in a manner that is neither false nor misleading" (Galtry, 1997).

   2. If the lactation consultant provides equipment, she must be aware of the product liability issues.

      a. This awareness includes issues related to the safety of reusing or sharing breast pumps designed and labeled by the manufacturer as "single user items" (Gielen et al., 1991).

      b. The lactation consultant is expected to remain current in terms of research regarding the safety and efficacy of equipment related to supporting lactation.

O. Milk storage guidelines for working mothers

    1. Studies indicate that human milk can be stored for various lengths of time depending on the temperature.

    2. Human milk is safely stored:

      – For four hours at 25°C (77°F)

      – For 24 hours at 15°C (59°F) in an ice-chilled cooler (Greenberg and Smith, 1991)

      – For five days in a refrigerator at 4°C (39°F)(Hamosh et al., 1996)

      – For 3–4 months in a refrigerator freezer compartment with a separate door

      – Milk can be held at −19°C (0°F) for six months in a separate deep freezer (Hills-Bonczyk, et al., 1993)

P. Counseling mothers about handling feedings in day care

    1. Mothers can handle feedings three ways:

      a. Provide exclusive breast milk feeds; requires expressing an average of three times/work shift.

      b. Provide part breast milk and part formula; might be a good choice if a mother can pump only once a day.

      c. Send formula for the baby at day-care; breastfeed when the mother and baby are together.

      d. Inform day care workers about handling human milk.

         i. Wash hands after diaper changes and before feeding.

        ii. Milk should be labeled; check the label before feeding.

       iii. Avoid warming by microwaving due to increased scalding risks and risks of changes to the milk (Katcher and Lanese, 1985).

       iv. Thaw frozen milk in the refrigerator or gently warm in hot water (do not heat milk on the stove).

        v. Leftover milk can be held over briefly in the refrigerator and fed at the next opportunity; beyond that, it should be discarded.

       vi. Gently shake the breast milk to mix the layers.

      e. Freezing can cause alteration of milk lipids; the milk might look "soapy."

f.  Freezer burn can affect milk stored in plastic bags that are not designed for freezing human milk.

g.  In descending order, the best storage media are as follows:

   i.  Glass

   ii.  Hard plastic

   iii.  Plastic bags designed to freeze/store milk

h.  Instruct caregivers that no other food is to be given without parental authorization.

i.  Use any available breast milk before using formula.

j.  Expect the baby's appetite to change from feeding to feeding.

k.  Many mothers pack bottles designated as 'meals' and some as 'drinks' or 'snacks.'

   i.  Try to avoid feeding the baby large quantities of milk in the hour before the mother arrives.

   ii.  Hold the baby for all feeds; do not prop the bottle.

   iii.  If the baby refuses the bottle, milk can be offered in a cup, spoon, by dropper, or chilled to the consistency of ice milk and spooned to the older baby (older than four months).

l.  Addressing the day care worker's concerns about the safety of handling human milk:

   i.  Milk is not currently classified by the Occupational Safety and Health Administration (OSHA) as requiring "universal precautions" while handling (Kearny and Cronenwett, 1991).

   ii.  If concerns about handling milk are expressed, mothers can 'pre-package' milk by using solid, labeled containers (no soft plastic bags that could tear and leak).

   iii.  Empty, used bottles are put in a sack for the mother to clean so that the worker never handles the milk, only the bottles.

VI  Occupational hazards and the breastfeeding woman

A.  It is undeniably true that the presence of environmental contaminants has exposed human populations to elevated levels of toxins, some of which appear in human milk. This fact might argue more for the reduction of such exposure than against breastfeeding. The long-term effects of toxic exposure via breast milk are not known. Analysis of human milk after accidental exposures to PCBs, DDE, and heptachlor have not demonstrated that the infants were harmed by breastfeeding, although level of exposure might be a mitigating factor (Kurinij et al., 1989, and Lawrence, 1994).

B. It is prudent for pregnant and lactating women to avoid optional exposure to hazardous chemicals, fumes, and materials.

C. Occupational exposures typically involve trace metals, solvents, and halogenated hydrocarbons (Lindburg, 1996).

D. Exposure to passive cigarette smoke should be avoided.

E. In general, lipid-soluble toxins are more problematic because they accumulate in fat tissue and are excreted in milk.

F. Water-based toxins are more rapidly excreted.

G. Dry cleaner solvent (inhaled as a vapor) stays in the body only a few days but might be of concern to women who work around it.

H. Artists and ceramic workers must consider lead exposure; clothing should be changed before handling the baby; hand-washing and breathing filters should be used.

I. Household herbicides, pesticides, and cleaning solvents should not be directly handled or inhaled.

J. Protective clothing, masks, goggles, and air filters are prudent strategies for lactating women who work around toxic materials.

K. Health care workers should practice universal precautions, especially given the potential for exposure to HIV and hepatitis C.

L. Accidental exposures to toxins or potential infection should be reported to the physician; milk or blood can be tested.

## Suggested Readings

Balancing Breastfeeding and Work, AusInfo, GPO Box 1920, Canberra ACT, 2601, Australia, 2000.

Breastfeeding Works for Working Women, (pamphlet) Texas Dept. of Health, 1998.

The Milk of Human Kindness: A global fact sheet on the economic value of breastfeeding, International Women Count Network and WABA, Crossroads Books, Philadelphia, PA: 2000.

Women, work and breastfeeding: Everybody benefits! The Mother-Friendly Workplace Initiative Action Folder, WABA, 10850 Penang, Malaysia: 1993.

## References

Andrews, M. A survey of the problems and strategies of working breastfeeding mothers. Midwest Nurs Res Soc Conf Proceed 1:1983.

Auerbach, K. Employed breastfeeding mothers: Problems they encounter. *Birth* 1984; 11:1.

Auerbach K, Guss E. Maternal employment and breastfeeding: A study of 567 women's experiences. *Am J Dis Child* 1984; 138:958.

Auerbach K. Assisting the employed breastfeeding mother. *J Nurse Midwifery* 1990; 35:26–34.

Auerbach KG. Maternal employment and breastfeeding. Chapter 15 in Riordan J, Auerbach KG. Breastfeeding and human lactation. Sudbury, MA: Jones and Bartlett Publishers, 1993: 401–427.

Ballard P. Breastfeeding for the working mother. *Issues Compr Pediatr Nurs* 1983; 6:249.

Bar-Yam N. Workplace lactation support, part 1: A return-to-work breastfeeding assessment tool. *J Hum Lact* 1998; 14:249–254.

Bar-Yam N. Workplace lactation support, part II: Working with the workplace. *J Hum Lact* 1998; 14:321–325.

Barber-Madden R, Cowell C, Petschek M, Glanz K. Nutrition for pregnant and lactating women: Implications for worksite health promotion. *J Nutr Educ* (supplement) 1986; 18:72–75.

Barber-Madden R, Petschek M, Pakter J. Breastfeeding and the working mother: Barriers and intervention strategies. *J Pub Health Policy* 1987; 8:531–541.

Bridges CB, Frank DI, Curtin J. Employer attitudes toward breastfeeding in the workplace. *J Hum Lact* 1997; 13:215–219.

Broome M. Breastfeeding and the working mother. *JOGNN* 1981; May/June.

Christoffel K, et al. Advice from breastfeeding mothers. (letter) *Pediatrics* 1981; 68:141.

Cohen R, Mrtek MB. The impact of two corporate lactation programs on the incidence and duration of breastfeeding by employed mothers. *Am J Health Promotion* 1994; 8:436–441.

Cohen R, Mrtek M, Mrtek RG. Comparison of maternal absenteeism and infant illness rates among breast-feeding and formula-feeding women in two corporations. *Am J Health Promotion* 1995; 10:148–153.

Ducket L. Maternal employment and breastfeeding. *NAACOG's Clini Iss Perinat Women's Health Nursing* 1992; 3:701–712.

Faught L. Lactation programs benefit the family and the corporation. *J Compensation & Benefits* 1994; September/October:44–47.

Fein SB, Roe B. The effect of work status on initiation and duration of breastfeeding. *Am J Pub Health* 1998; 88:1042–1046.

Frederick I, Auerbach KG. Maternal infant separation and breastfeeding: The return to work or school. *J Reprod Med* 1985; 30:523–526.

Galtry J. Lactation and the labor market: Breastfeeding, labor market changes, and public policy in the United States. *Health Care Women Intern* 1997; 18:467–480.

Gielen AC, Faden RR, O'Campo P, et al. Maternal employment during the early postpartum period: Effects on initiation and continuation of breastfeeding. *Pediatrics* 1991; 87:298–305.

Greenberg CS, Smith K. Anticipatory guidance for the employed breast-feeding mother. *J Pediatr Health Care* 1991; 5:204–209.

Hamosh M, et al. Breastfeeding and the working mother: Effect of time, and temperature of short-term storage on proteolysis, lipolysis, and bacterial growth in milk. *Pediatrics* 1996; 97:492–498.

Hills-Bonczyk SG, Avery MD, Savik K, et al. Women's experiences with combining breast-feeding and employment. *J Nurse Midwifery* 1993; 38:257–266.

Katcher A, Lanese, M. Breastfeeding by employed mothers: A reasonable accommodation in the workplace. *Pediatrics* 1985; 75:644.

Kearny M, Cronenwett L. Breastfeeding and employment. *J Obstet Gynecol Neonatal Nurs* 1991; 20:471–480.

Kurinij N, Shiono P, Ezrine S, Rhoades G. Does maternal employment affect breastfeeding? *Am J Pub Health* 1989; 79:1247–1250.

Lawrence R. Maternal Employment. In Lawrence R. Breastfeeding: A guide for the medical profession, 4th ed. St Louis: C.V. Mosby, 1994: 387–403.

Lindburg LD. Trends in the relationship between breastfeeding and postpartum employment in the United States. *Soc Biol* 1996; 43:191–202.

Lindburg LD. Women's decisions about breastfeeding and maternal employment. *J Marriage Fam* 1996; 58:239–251.

MacLaughlin S, Strelnick E. Breastfeeding and working outside the home. *Issues Compr Pediatr Nurs* 1984; 7:67.

Madlon-Kay D, Carr R. The effect of decreasing maternity leave on breastfeeding patterns. *Fam Med* 1988; 20:220–221.

Martinez G, Dodd D. 1981 milk feeding patterns in the United States during the first 12 months of life. *Pediatrics* 1983; 71:166.

Martinez G, Stahle D. The recent trend in milk feeding among WIC infants. *Am J Pub Health* 1982; 72:68.

Moore J, Jansa N. A survey of policies and practices in support of breastfeeding mothers in the workplace. *Birth* 1987; 14:191–195.

Morse J, Bottorff J. 1989 Intending to breastfeed and work. *JOGNN* 1989; 18:493–500.

Morse JM, Bottorff JL. Patterns of breastfeeding and work: The Canadian experience. *Can J Pub Health* 1989; 80:182–188.

Petschek M, Barber-Madden R. Promoting prenatal care and breastfeeding in the workplace. *Occup Health Nurs* 1985; 33:86–89.

Price A, Bamford N. The breastfeeding guide for the working woman. New York: Simon & Schuster, Inc., 1983.

Pryor G. Nursing mother, working mother. Boston: Harvard Common Press, 1997.

Rasch L. Working and nursing. *American Baby*, November 1984.

Reifsnider E, Myers ST. Employed mothers can breast-feed too! MCN 1985; 10:256–259.

Richardson JL. Review of international legislation establishing nursing breaks. *J Trop Pediatr Environ Child Health* 1975; 21:249–258.

Roe B, Whittington LA, Fein SB, Teisl MF. Is there competition between breastfeeding and maternal employment? *Demography* 1999; 36:157–171.

Ryan A, Martinez G. Breast-feeding and the working mother: A profile. *Pediatrics* 1989; 83:524–531.

Saloman M, et al. Breastfeeding, natural mothering and working outside the home. Chapter 27 in Stewart D and Stewart L, eds. 21st century obstetrics now. Chapel Hill: NAPSAC, Inc., 1977.

Shepard S, Yarrow R. Breastfeeding and the working mother. *J Nurs Midwifery* 1982; 27:16.

Tyler K. Got milk? Workplace lactation programs provide an inexpensive way to reduce employee absenteeism, lower health care costs and improve employee retention. *HR Magazine* 1999; 44:69–73.

Van Esterik P, Greiner T. Breastfeeding and women's work: Constraints and opportunities. *Stud Fam Plan* 1981; 12:184.

Verronen P. Breastfeeding: Reasons for giving up and transient lactational crises. *Acta Paediatr Scand* 1982; 71:447.

West C. Factors influencing the duration of breastfeeding. *J Biosocial Sci* 1980; 12:325.

# Growing and Breastfeeding

*Molly Pessl, BSN, IBCLC*

## Objectives

- Describe developmental issues that determine human breastfeeding duration.

- Contrast the belief that biological weaning is something done to a child rather than occurring spontaneously as part of human development.

- Discuss possible clinical challenges that the lactation consultant might encounter when a woman is breastfeeding a baby for more than one year.

- Discuss cultural beliefs that make long-term breastfeeding difficult.

- Recommend ways in which the lactation consultant can assist families who are breastfeeding past the cultural norm.

## Introduction

Although much of the world has implemented plans to increase the rates of breastfeeding initiation, very little energy, time, or money has been dedicated to breastfeeding issues after a mother has successfully overcome the challenges of making her initial decision to breastfeed. Most women give up breastfeeding early in the experience, but if a mother does manage to initiate and continue to breastfeed successfully, there is little in the scientific and medical literature (particularly in the western world) to guide the lactation consultant in counseling families about weaning ages in human children. Attention turns to publications from research on other primates, plus secondary references and anecdotal information from mothers who have been willing to observe and respect their child's natural progression of breastfeeding behaviors. The American Academy of Pediatrics published recommendations for exclusive breastfeeding for about six months and continued breastfeeding to one year and beyond. These guidelines have helped health care professionals look at feeding decisions from a view outside the cultural norm.

As babies breastfeed beyond the early weeks, new situations emerge through the maturation and development of the infant's physical and social domains. Breastfeeding an older baby or a toddler presents its own unique set of challenges that the lactation consultant might be called upon in order to provide advice.

I  Developmental issues suggesting long-term nursing as a biological norm (Figure 29-1)

    A.  Breastfeeding remains a very important activity for small children when the child is permitted to behave within a developmental context.

    B.  The child's immunological benefits are still enhanced by breast milk.

    C.  Babies have strong sucking needs well into the second year.

    D.  The mouth and sucking remain an area of major pleasure and comfort for children for many years.

        1.  If they hurt themselves:

            a.  Buccal stimulation releases oxytocin in the baby.

            b.  Oxytocin increases the pain threshold.

        2.  Teething.

        3.  Small children breastfeed in order to settle or to regroup.

            a.  Mothers report that nursing is often the only time that the toddler stops and relaxes.

            b.  Breastfeeding helps when a child is sick or troubled.

        4.  The mother might have returned to work; some babies begin breastfeeding more frequently at night in order to re-establish contact with the mother.

**Figure 29-1**    Natural age at weaning according to technique used

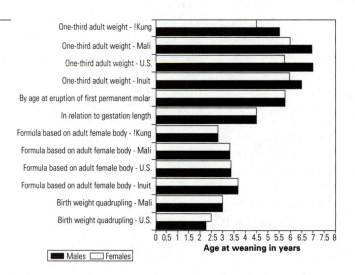

E. Dreaming and separation anxiety become prevalent in children 6–18 months of age.

1. Many children continue to have frequent night waking or begin night waking again after a period of none.

2. Some babies experience night terrors, which breastfeeding helps ameliorate.

3. Some parents institute sleep-through-the-night baby training programs during the first six months of the baby's life; in spite of these programs, some babies will begin waking at night after six months of age.

F. Young children still rely on the adult world for safety and care.

1. The mother remains the center of the child's life in the toddler years.

2. Breastfeeding requires the mother to hold and touch the child; some children nurse when they need time with their mother or to ease concerns after the mother has been away.

3. Some young children develop strong fears of activities that were previously tolerated, such as baths, new places, and strange people.

   a. Breastfeeding offers reassurance, comfort, and safety.

   b. Some mothers comment that there is no other place that the child feels safer than in their arms breastfeeding.

4. Small children are still developing the basis for total trust.

G. Breast milk remains an important nutritional component as solid food intake gradually increases to the primary source of calories in the second year of life.

II Why mothers continue to nurse after the first year:

A. Breast milk and lactation continue to offer health benefits to both mother and child.

1. Many of the outcomes of lactation are dose dependent; mothers who breastfeed into the second year or longer significantly reduce their risk for osteoporosis and breast cancer.

2. Oxytocin surges during breastfeeding promote maternal behaviors.

   a. The response to oxytocin has long-lasting effects

   b. Increased social behaviors

   c. Enhanced listening skills

   d. Tolerance to repetitious or boring tasks

      i. Mothers recognize the child's needs and are able to put the child's needs before their own.

      ii. Mothers enjoy breastfeeding.

**III** Cultural challenges of nursing an older baby or child

    A. In many breastfeeding societies, nursing an older child is normal.

    B. Cultural conflicts in non-breastfeeding (western) countries can lead to a conflict between the mother/baby needs and the cultural pressures to wean.

    C. There are a number of beliefs and attitudes that are unsubstantiated in the scientific literature that mothers are subjected to when breastfeeding an older baby or child:

        1. Continued breastfeeding creates over-dependence on the mother.

        2. Childhood dependence is bad behavior.

        3. Continued breastfeeding spoils or indulges the child.

        4. Independent behaviors need to be enforced.

        5. Continued breastfeeding is perverse, incestuous, or child abuse.

        6. There are no benefits to long-term breastfeeding.

        7. Weaning must be imposed on children, rather than having it happen developmentally.

        8. Long-term breastfeeding and nighttime breastfeeding contribute to "nursing caries."

        9. All other foods are superior to breast milk.

       10. Babies should wean by one year of age.

    D. The medical, authoritarian model of pediatric care instructs mothers by clocks and timelines, rather than by the individual child's needs.

        1. The tendency to turn parenting issues into medical issues and procedures

        2. Tendency of the culture and health care providers to judge and advise based on personal experience, personal opinions, and entrenched attitudes that are resistant to change rather than to rely on science or evidence

    E. Biologically, the human infant and child is the same throughout the world

        1. The human infant has not changed biologically since early time (Figure 29-2).

        2. Culturally imposed rules conflict with the biologic and physiologic capabilities of the child (Figure 29-3).

    F. It is difficult to be inconspicuous when breastfeeding an older baby or child.

        1. Mothers might have concerns about breastfeeding in public with a bigger, older baby.

        2. There is much "closet nursing" that occurs.

        3. Some mothers hope that the baby or child will not want to nurse when others are around.

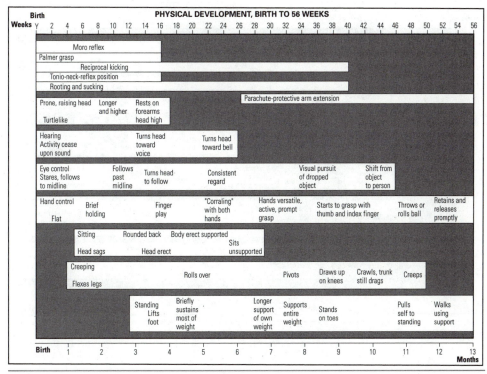

**Figure 29-2**    A child's physical development

4. The mother might resort to the bottle or inappropriate foods when she is in public.

G. Women might state that they "want their body back."

H. Issues of sexuality might surface more frequently.

1. Continued pressure from family, partner, friends, or strangers to wean.

2. Crude and hurtful questions such as, "How long are you going to do that?"

a. The lactation consultant can help mothers form a standard answer to this type of question, such as, "Until we are finished," "This is none of your business," "As long as we both continue to enjoy it," or "Until he is accepted into college."

IV Clinical breastfeeding challenges after six months and after the first year:

A. There are a few clinical problems in the last half of the first year and into the second year that are unique to these periods of time.

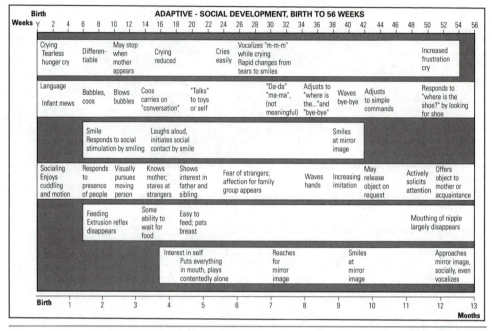

**Figure 29-3**    A child's adaptive-social development

B. Concerns such as plugged milk ducts, milk stasis, mastitis, and thrush can occur at any time throughout the breastfeeding experience.

C. Some situations that are unique to nursing the older breastfeeding baby and child include the following:

1. Return of menstruation

   a. The majority of women who exclusively or totally breastfeed for the first six months generally experience a return of the menses late in the first year or after solids are introduced around six months.

   b. Some mothers report that their baby nurses reluctantly or refuses the breast entirely right before their period or during the first day or two.

   c. Some women report a diminishing of the supply with the volume increasing in a day or two.

   d. Mothers might complain of very tender nipples and/or breasts.

   e. Mothers can hand express or pump milk and offer it in a cup if their nipples are extremely tender.

2. New pregnancy
   a. Many mothers complain of sore nipples.
   b. The majority of pregnancies while breastfeeding are preceded by menstruation.
   c. Mature milk reverts to colostral fluid at the end of the pregnancy.
   d. Some babies will wean during the next pregnancy because of diminished milk volumes or the change in the taste of the milk.

3. Nipple trauma
   a. Some older babies bite the nipple after their two upper middle teeth erupt.
   b. Some will nurse differently because of teething.
   c. Edges of teeth resting on the areola leave grooves or indentations.
   d. Mothers can gently remove the baby from the breast if he or she bites, rather than yelling at him or her or saying the word "no"; some babies cannot differentiate between "no biting" and "no breastfeeding."

4. Abrupt weaning by the baby or child is possible, as is the desire to continue nursing at special times of the day.

5. Nursing strikes
   a. Sudden onset of refusal to nurse can occur at any time during the breastfeeding experience.
   b. Some mothers feel this is a personal rejection.
   c. This situation is usually temporary and is not an indication of weaning due to insufficient milk or because the baby is finished with breastfeeding.
   d. There is no particular reason that has been identified with this behavior; it has been attributed to or associated with return of menses in the mother, unpleasant tastes in the milk, a change in odors or aromas of the mother, a cold or earache in the baby with nasal obstruction, sleep-through-the-night training programs, separations, or increased distractibility.
   e. Some interventions that might be of help include nursing in a quiet, dark location, increasing the contact between mother and baby without putting the baby to the breast, offering the breast when the baby or child is sleepy or before waking from a nap, skin-to-skin contact in a warm bath tub, offering the breast while walking with the child, and ruling out illness.
   f. Nursing strikes that last more than a day or two will often require that the mother express milk on a regular basis to prevent dwindling milk supplies.

6. Distractibility
   a. As babies get older, they can become highly distractible at the breast, smiling and laughing and coming off the breast to look around.
   b. This situation can result in a baby being more hungry at night and increased night feedings.
   c. Many of these babies need to be breastfed in a quiet and/or darkened location with no playing at the breast until the feed is finished.

V Interventions by the lactation consultant:
   A. Examine own beliefs regarding long-term nursing.
   B. Breast milk remains the optimal beverage for the baby, even after introducing solid foods.
   C. Breast milk contains the special fats that are absent in both infant formula and the low- to no-fat solid foods that are typically given to older babies.
   D. Assist the family in viewing breastfeeding within the context of the child's development (Figure 29-4).
   E. All children eventually wean from the breast.
      1. Weaning the baby does not make the challenges of parenting go away.
      2. Breastfeeding requires patience, just as all infantile behaviors do.
      3. The baby does not wish to wean at the same time the mother does.
      4. Mothers need reassurance that this situation will end someday.
      5. Continuing to nurse a toddler does not mean a mother can never say no.
      6. Help mothers deal with the value judgments offered by others about breastfeeding.
         a. What they did with their children is irrelevant to this mother/baby pair.
         b. Disgust and criticism can be met with education and firm resolve.
         c. Confusion about continued breastfeeding interfering with the ability of the child to be an independent adult.
         d. Child-led weaning might be seen as counter-culture.
         e. Most mothers would probably continue to breastfeed without too many concerns and probably enjoyment if they were not constantly questioning themselves and being questioned by others.
         f. Help the mother look closely at her own feelings and understanding of her child.
         g. Our culture values commercialism, capitalism, and independence, which are at odds with the needs and behaviors of mothers and babies.

**Figure 29-4** Infant pyschosocial and breastfeeding behaviors by age

| Age | Psychosocial Behavior | Breastfeeding Behavior |
|---|---|---|
| First day postpartum | Quiet alert state after birth, followed by long sleep. | May or may not feed following delivery. Sleepy, learning how to suckle. |
| 1 mo | Follows objects with eyes; reacts to noise by stopping behavior or crying. | Becoming efficient at suckling; feedings last approximately 17 minutes. Feedings now 8–16 times per day. |
| 2 mo | Smiles; vocalizes in response to interactions. | Easily pacified by frequent breastfeedings. |
| 3 mo | Shows increased interest in surroundings. Voluntarily grasps objects. Vocalizes when spoken to. Turns head as well as eyes in response to moving object. | Will interrupt feeding to turn to look at father or other familiar person coming into room and to smile at mother. |
| 4–5 mo | Shows interest in strange settings. Smiles at mirror image. | Continues to enjoy frequent feedings at the breast. |
| 6 mo | Laughs aloud. Shows increased awareness of caregivers vs. strangers. May become distressed if mother or caregiver leaves. | Solids offered. Fewer feedings. Feeds longer before sleep for the night. May begin waking to nurse more often at night. |
| 7–8 mo | Imitates actions and noises. Responds to "no." Enjoys peek-a-boo games. Reaches for toys that are out of reach. | Will breastfeed anytime, anywhere. Actively attempts to get to breast (i.e., will try to unbutton mother's blouse). |
| 9–10 mo | Distressed by new situations or people. Waves bye-bye. Reaches for toys that are out of reach. | Easily distracted by surroundings and interrupts feedings frequently. May hold breast with one or both hands while feeding. |
| 11–12 mo | Drops objects deliberately to be picked up by other people. Rolls ball to another person. Speaks a few words. Appears interested in picture books. Shakes head for "no." | Tries "acrobatic" breastfeeding (i.ei., assumes different positions while keeping nipple in mouth). |

*(continues)*

449

**Figure 29-4** Infant psychosocial and breastfeeding behaviors by age (*Continued*)

| Age | Psychosocial Behavior | Breastfeeding Behavior |
|---|---|---|
| 12–15 mo | Fears unfamiliar situations but will leave mother's side to explore familiar surroundings. Shows emotions (e.g, love, anger, fear). Speaks several words. Understands meaning of many words. | Uses top hand to play while feeding: forces finger into mother's mouth, plays with her hair, and pinches her other nipple. Pats mother's chest when wants to breastfeed. Hums or vocalizes while feeding. Verbalizes need to breastfeed—may use "code" word. |
| 16–20 mo | Has frequent temper tantrums. Increasingly imitates parents. Enjoys solitary play or observing others. Speaks 6–10 words. | Verbalizes delight with breastfeeding. Takes mother by the hand and leads her to favorite nursing chair. |
| 20–24 mo | Helps with simple tasks. Has fewer temper tantrums. Engages in parallel play. Combines 2 or 3 words. Speaks 15–20 words. | Stands up while nursing at times. Nursing mostly for comfort. Feeding before bedtime is usually last feeding before weaning. When asked to do so by mother, is willing to wait for feeding until later. |

# References

Bumgarner NJ. Mothering your nursing toddler. Schaumberg, IL: La Leche League International, 1994.

Huggins K. The nursing mother's guide to weaning. Boston: Harvard Common Press, 1994.

Mohrbacher N, Stock J. The breastfeeding answer book, rev ed. Schaumburg, IL: La Leche League International, 1997.

Small MF. Our babies, ourselves: How biology and culture shape the way we parent. New York: Random House, 1998.

Stuart-Macadam P, Dettwyler KA, eds. Breastfeeding: Biocultural perspectives. New York: Aldine de Gruyter, 1995.

# INTERPRETATION OF RESEARCH

*Kristen Montgomery, PhD, RNC, IBCLC*

## OBJECTIVES

- Define the research process.
- Discuss how research can be implemented into practice.
- Describe how to critique research articles.
- Describe how human subjects are protected from potential harm during research.

## Introduction

Research is the building block for scientific knowledge and helps to guide practice based on outcomes of generated knowledge. Research from a variety of disciplines is applicable to the mother-baby breastfeeding dyad, including nursing, medicine, physiology, anthropology, sociology, nutrition, psychology, chemistry, and physics. This section attempts to clarify the research process and discuss how research can be implemented into practice. Additionally, we provide information about how to appropriately critique research and protect human subjects from potential harm.

  I  Types of research
    A. There are two broad types of research: qualitative and quantitative.
       1. Qualitative research tends to focus on the words of the participant and explores issues in-depth.
       2. Quantitative research focuses on relationships among variables of interest (and statistical numbers) and attempts to discover relationships and predict behavior or certain outcomes.
    B. One type of research is not better than the other; the two types are best viewed as complementary.
    C. Additionally, qualitative and quantitative research methods can sometimes be combined via a process known as triangulation.

D. Qualitative research often serves as a building block to quantitative research in that qualitative research is often done when little previous work has been done in the particular area.

E. Additionally, qualitative research methods can be used to study problems in a more in-depth fashion or from a different angle.

F. Quantitative methods, on the other hand, can also be exploratory in nature and often evolve to more complex methods that examine relationships and predict outcomes.

II Design

A. Types of research designs
   1. Research designs are similar to a continuum that includes more basic, exploratory designs at the most simple level and randomized, controlled clinical trials at the most complex level.
   2. The most common types of research designs are summarized in Table 30-1.

**Table 30-1**    Common Research Designs (from Polit & Hungler, 1991)

| Design Name | Characteristics |
|---|---|
| **Experimental Designs** | A type of research design in which the researcher is an active participant. Includes randomization, control, and manipulation. Umbrella term for a number of types of designs. |
| Randomized Clinical Trials | An experiment involving a test of the effectiveness of a clinical treatment. |
| Solomon Four-Group Designs | An experimental design that uses a before-after design for one pair of experimental/control groups and an after-only design for a second pair. |
| Factorial Designs | An experimental design in which two or more independent variables are simultaneously manipulated; permits an analysis of the main effects of the independent variables separately, plus the interaction effects of these variables. |
| **Quasi-Experimental Designs** | A type of research design in which subjects cannot be randomly assigned to treatment conditions, although the researcher does manipulate the independent variable. |
| Non-Equivalent Control Group Designs | A type of research design that consists of a comparison group that was not developed based on random assignment. |
| Time Series Designs | A research design that involves collection of data over an extended period of time, with multiple points of data collection, both before and after the intervention. |

*(continues)*

**Table 30-1** (*Continued*)

| Design Name | Characteristics |
| --- | --- |
| **Non-experimental Designs** | Research designs in which the researcher collects data without introducing any new treatments or changes. |
| Retrospective Studies | A type of study that attempts to link a current event or condition with another event or variable that previously occurred. |
| Prospective Studies | A study that begins with the event or variable that is thought to contribute to the outcome condition and follows the individual over time to see the outcome. |
| Descriptive Correlational Studies | A type of study that aims to describe relationships between variables. |
| Univariate Descriptive Studies | A type of study that describes the behavior of one variable. |
| **Survey Research** | A type of research study that seeks to obtain information about a topic of interest by soliciting individual's opinions. |
| **Field Studies** | A type of study where data is collected in the subject's natural environment, often to describe that environment. |
| **Evaluation Research** | A type of study that investigates how well a program or project works. |
| **Needs Assessments** | A type of study where the research collects information about the needs of a particular group. |
| **Historical Research** | Research with the goal of identifying relationships and sequences of past events. |
| **Case Studies** | A type of research that investigates an individual, group, or institution at an in-depth level. |
| **Secondary Analysis** | A type of research where data are analyzed from a previous study with the goal of testing new research questions. |
| **Meta-Analysis** | A research technique for statistically analyzing multiple studies for a group effect. |

III Data collection

    A. Similar to research designs, there are many ways to collect data for the purposes of research.

    B. Data can take the form of an interview or responses to questions (a questionnaire), which can be either verbal or written, and physiological measures (such as blood pressure), body fluids (such as a breast milk sample), and others.

    C. The way data are collected depends on the type and purpose(s) of the study.

    1. For example, if the aim of the research was to understand why mothers choose to wean their infants, one would likely interview these women verbally, because "understanding" is difficult to access from a series of written questions.

    2. Additionally, if there were certain measures or concepts that the researcher was interested in measuring, the researcher might use a particular research tool to accomplish this task.

**IV** Research tools or instruments

  A. Many tools are available to measure different concepts.

    1. For example, if the researcher was interested in measuring maternal satisfaction with the breastfeeding experience, the researcher would need to locate a tool that was designed for this purpose and then administer the test to the mother.

    2. Tools are most often a series of questions (a questionnaire) that are easily answered by the participant, although occasionally tools might contain other types of measures.

    3. When a tool is used, it is important to make sure that the tool is reliable and valid for the purpose and population in which it is being used.

    4. The results of the tool are generally and statistically analyzed at the end of the study.

**V** Results

  A. Results of the study must be interpreted within the context in which the data were collected.

  B. With qualitative research, the results are generally expressed in themes or words that characterize what the participants had to say.

  C. In quantitative research, results are generally expressed in terms of relationships (or lack of relationships) that exist.

    1. Relationships are often referred to as statistically significant.

    2. In other words, the statistical analysis indicates that there is a relationship between the items (variables) of interest.

    3. When the results indicate that there is a relationship (statistical significance), it is important to assess whether this relationship is also clinically significant.

    4. For example, a new type of breast pump was designed to help mothers pump milk faster. The statistical analysis of the research project indicates that the new pump is faster than previous pumps. Therefore, the results are statistically significant. Closer examination, however, reveals that the pumping time is decreased by a mere 15 seconds. Fifteen seconds is not

likely to result in any differences in the amount of time that a mother must pump; therefore, while the statistical results are statistically significant, the implications are not clinically significant.

5. The author of the research report should address the issue of statistical versus clinical significance and discuss how the findings from their research apply to clinical practice.

VI Application to practice

A. To keep practice most current, new research needs to be incorporated.

B. New research is  incorporated into practice after several rigorous studies have found similar results.

C. How many studies and what types of studies depend on what is at risk.

1. For example, one would not want to try a new nipple in the clinical setting based on one study. We know that infants are likely to develop nipple confusion, which can interfere with the establishment of successful breastfeeding. To implement something into practice that would take the infant from the breast, we would need a large amount of well-respected research that showed there was some benefit. In other words, if there is too much at risk (the establishment of breastfeeding), we would want to make sure that we had a lot of evidence that the practice would be beneficial.

2. On the other hand, if there was not much risk involved, implementation into practice could occur much sooner, because not much is lost if the research turns out to have some faults. For example, a new infant bed is being marketed as helping babies sleep better and cry less. The hospital you work in decides to try the new beds. If the new beds are effective and the babies sleep better and cry less, then great—the goal has been achieved. If there is no difference in how much the babies cry or sleep, then nothing is lost. One can continue to use the new beds or switch back to the others (it really does not make a difference).

VII Ethical issues

A. Human rights

1. Persons involved in research have certain rights.

2. Anyone who is invited to participate in a research study must give informed consent.

3. Informed consent is the process whereby the potential participant is told everything he or she needs to know about the study to decide whether to take the risk involved with participating.

4. Risk can be minimal to quite large, so it is important that individuals adequately understand the research study.

5. Potential participants need to be aware of risks, potential benefits (often there are no potential benefits to the specific person), time involved, what

they are expected to do, any invasive procedures, and any compensation for their time or travel.

**VIII** Critique and interpretation

    A. Critique of research is an essential skill for any individual who is working in a rapidly expanding environment such as health care.

    B. The critique and interpretation of research is essential in order to maintain current knowledge.

    C. Maintaining current knowledge, however, requires that one can "judge" research to realize how, when, and where the research is appropriately used (Table 30-2).

**Table 30-2**   Common Research Terminology

| | |
|---|---|
| Bias | Any factor that might potentially influence the results of a study. |
| Clinical Significance | When the results are meaningful to practice in a clinical setting. (i.e., the results make a difference to clinical practice) |
| Control | A group of individuals that are not exposed to the experimental conditions for the purpose of having a group for comparison. |
| Dependent Variable | The variable that changes as a result of the change in the independent variable, the outcome. |
| Experiment | A research design in which the researcher is an active participant. Includes randomization, control, and manipulation. Umbrella term for a number of types of designs. |
| Informed Consent | The process of notifying potential research subjects regarding the potential risks and benefits of participating in a research study. |
| Independent Variable | The variable that is manipulated in a research study and thought to contribute to a change in the dependent variable. |
| Manipulation | The intervention or change that occurs within the study—the part that is different that the control group does not receive. |
| Qualitative Research | A broad type of research with the goal of understanding how participants behave in their natural environments. Generally more in-depth, discovering deep relationships, focusing on analysis of the "word" rather than numbers. |
| Quantitative Research | A broad type of research that focuses on identifying relationships among variables, including prediction. Results are obtained via statistical analysis. |
| Randomization | The act of assigning subjects to different groups within a research study so those subjects have an equal chance of being in any of the groups. |
| Relationship | A connection between two or more variables. |
| Statistical Significance | A mathematically-based difference between two groups. |

D. One must be able to critique the overall quality of the research and examine whether or not the research was appropriate for what the authors were trying to achieve with the research study.

1. For example, if the authors were attempting to discover some initial information on a topic, one would not expect that they would use an experimental design, because experimental designs are appropriate for testing interventions that have data to support that the intervention might be effective.

E. Essential items to consider when critiquing research include design, sample size and techniques, statistical analysis, and conceptual framework.

1. All studies begin with a hypothesis, testing the hypothesis, and then an analysis of the data to see how likely it is that the results were due to chance.

2. Statistical analysis cannot prove an experimental hypothesis to be true; it can only show how unlikely it is to be false; this is called proving the null hypothesis.

3. Good studies encompass the largest sample size that they can reasonably obtain.

4. A large sample has less of a chance for error than a small sample.

5. The statistical analysis will tell what the power of that sample size was.

6. Power indicates the ability of the study to detect a significant difference between the experimental and control groups, given a particular population.

7. Researchers want a power of 0.80 (80 percent), which means that the data have an 80 percent probability of correctly rejecting the null hypothesis.

8. Statistical significance is determined by applying a test to the data and calculating the probability of obtaining that result (Table 30-3).

9. The probability is reported as a $P$ value, with the desirable $P$ value of .05 or lower; a $P$ value of .05 (5 out of 100, or 1 in 20) or less is considered significant.

10. A $P$ value expressed as $P < .01$ says that the odds are less than one out of 100 that the difference in outcome was due to chance.

11. Significant means that the observed difference is considered a real difference and is not due to chance.

12. Another type of significance testing is applied to odds ratios and risk ratios, which compare two rates of occurrence by dividing one into the other.

13. Usually, a number is seen followed by a range as in RR (relative risk) = 0.6, confidence interval (CI) 0.4–1.3; the calculated value is 0.6 but the actual value has a 95 percent probability of falling somewhere between 0.4 and 1.3.

14. If the range includes 1.00 as it does in the previous example, then the result is not significant because a value of 1.00 means that one of the possible ratios is 1:1, meaning no difference between the two rates.

F. All research studies have strengths and limitations that must always be considered in the context of the study's goals.

G. It is important that all elements of the research project fit together and are consistent.

1. For example, is the theoretical framework consistent with the research questions that the authors address?

2. Are the research questions consistent with the purpose(s) of the study?

3. Are the statistical techniques appropriate for the type of data collected and the research design?

   a. Statistical procedures used for correlational and experimental or quasi-experimental studies are broadly classified as parametric or nonparametric.

   b. Parametric tests are generally preferred by researchers because they are more powerful; they permit the process of generalizing the findings of the study sample to the population at large.

   c. In order to use parametric procedures, the sample must be randomly selected; the dependent variable(s) must be measured at an interval level; and the variables must be normally distributed among the study groups (Table 30-4).

   d. Nonparametric statistics are used where the sample size is small, where it cannot be assumed that there is a normal distribution of variables in the sample, where parameters of the population are not known, and where the level of measurement of variables is at the lower levels of nominal or ordinal.

   e. The Chi-square test is usually used to determine whether the proportions in two groups are significantly different; large Chi-square values usually lead to low, statistically significant $P$ values.

   f. Cohen's kappa is calculated when two observers rate the same event on a scale and the researcher wants to show that the two raters are in close agreement; values at 0.7 or higher are considered good.

   g. Cronbach's alpha test is reported when the researcher is trying to give evidence of the reliability of an instrument; values can range from 0.0 to 1.0, with values closer to 1.0 having better reliability.

   h. Multivariate analysis is the concurrent analysis of three or more variables to determine whether and what are the patterns of relationships among the variables; used in complex analysis of large samples in correlational or experimental studies that have multiple dependent or independent variables.

**Table 30-3**    Appropriate Statistics for Type of Study and Level of Data

| Type of Study | Nonparametric Tests and Level of Data | Parametric Tests and Level of Data |
|---|---|---|
| **Descriptive** | | |
| One variable | Frequency, *nominal* | |
| | Percentage, *ordinal* | |
| | Mode, *nominal* | |
| | Median, *ordinal* | |
| | Mean, *interval* | |
| | Standard deviation, *interval* | |
| Two or more variables | Contingency table, *nominal* | |
| | Cross-tabulation, *nominal* | |
| | Chi-square, *nominal* | |
| **Correlational** | Spearman's rho, *ordinal* | Pearson-*r*, *ordinal* |
| | Mann-Whitney U, *ordinal* | |
| **Experimental or Quasi-experimental** | | |
| Two independent groups | Median test, *ordinal* | *t*-test (pooled), *interval**  |
| | Mann-Whitney U, *ordinal* | |
| Two dependent or paired groups | Wilcoxon signed-rank, *ordinal* | *t*-test (paired), *interval**  |
| | McNemar chi-square, *nominal* | |
| Two or more groups | Chi-square, *nominal* | ANOVA (F test), *interval**  |
| | Kruskal-Wallis, *ordinal* | |
| | Friedman test, *ordinal* | |

*Level of data of dependent variable.

**Table 30-4**   Levels of Measurement

| Type | Definition | Examples |
|------|-----------|----------|
| Nominal | Discrete categories of data that do not have any implied order. | Gender: male–female<br>Breastfed/not breastfed<br>Marital status |
| Ordinal | Assigned categories of data that can be ranked in order. Intervals between categories are not equal. | Most Likert-type scales<br>Infant Breastfeeding Assessment Scale (IBFAT) (Matthews, 1991) |
| Interval or ratio | Categories of data that are ordered and are equal distances apart. Ratio also has a known zero point. | Body temperature<br>Blood pressure<br>Weight or length<br>Duration of breastfeeding measured in specified days, weeks, months, or years |

    i. Researchers might use multiple regression, path analysis, *analysis of covariance* (ANCOVA), factor analysis, discriminant analysis, canonical correlation, and *multivariate analysis of variance* (MANOVA).

    j. All of these questions are important and need to be considered when evaluating the overall quality of the research project.

4. First, and probably most importantly, the research study needs to be evaluated in terms of its significance to the profession and clinical practice.

5. In other words, does this study make any difference?

6. It is the "So what?" question that can help one to decide.

7. If the study is not significant to either the discipline or clinical practice, it will probably not be very useful.

8. Part of determining whether the research is appropriate is evaluation of the previous research done on a given topic.

9. Does the study build on previous work or replicate previous findings?

10. Did the researchers make too large a leap in knowledge from the previous research?

11. It is important to determine the purpose of the study.

    a. The purpose should be clearly stated and easy to understand.

    b. Does the purpose flow from a literature review that identified gaps in the current literature that the study hopes to fill?

    c. Does it seem that the authors conducted a comprehensive review of the literature?

      d. If yes, then one can next progress to understanding the research questions.

      e. Again, the questions need to be concise and easy to understand.

12. Is the research design appropriate for the study purpose(s) and the research question(s)?

      a. Did the authors respect the rules regarding application of the research design?

      b. Is the sampling method appropriate for the design, and are the data being collected at an appropriate level for the types of statistical analysis that are used by the researchers?

      c. Discussions of research procedures should be clear and detailed enough so that another individual could replicate the study.

13. The analysis section should be evaluated next.

      a. Are the results presented clearly, and are implications for practice and further research identified?

      b. Does the author make a distinction between statistical and clinical significance?

      c. Does the author present the findings in the context of the original study purposes and research questions?

**IX** Summary

  A. Care to mothers and babies will be most effective after the appropriate integration of current research occurs.

  B. The integration of research keeps health care providers on the cutting edge of providing high-quality care.

  C. Careful analysis and critique of research is necessary to provide the best patient care, however.

  D. Careful analysis of research studies enables one to appropriately implement the results of the research project, providing the best care to mothers and babies (Table 30-5).

**Table 30-5**    Guidelines for Evaluating Quantitative and Qualitative Studies

| General Guidelines | Quantitative Studies | Qualitative Studies |
| --- | --- | --- |
| 1. Problem and purpose<br>Clearly stated?<br>Amenable to scientific investigation? | Provides direction for study? | Broadly stated?<br>Exploratory? |

| General Guidelines | Quantitative Studies | Qualitative Studies |
|---|---|---|
| Significant to breastfeeding knowledge? | | |
| 2. Review of literature Pertinent? Well organized? | Includes recent and classic references? Theoretical base or conceptual framework evident? | Acknowledged the existence of (or lack of) literature on the topic? |
| 3. Protection of human rights Subject's protection from harm ensured? Subjects suitably informed by written informed consent? Study reviewed by ethics board or committee? Means for ensuring privacy, confidentiality, or anonymity are explained? | | |
| 4. Method Design congruent with research question? Sampling procedure appropriate for research method? Method of data collection relevant for design? | Deductive approach used? Variables identified and defined? Sample representative of population and adequate size? Measuring tools suitable, reliable, and valid? Control of extraneous variables evident? | Inductive approach used? Key informants selected? Theoretical sampling addressed? Data collection and analysis concurrent? Process for data collection and analysis described? Data saturated? Reliability and validity explained? |
| 5. Results and discussion Analysis suitable for method and design? Results clearly presented? Interpretations clear and based on data? Research question answered? Limitations of study identified? Conclusions based on results? Implications for practice and research described? | Statistical procedures used suitable for data and sample size? Tables clear and representative of data? Successful and unanticipated results reported? | Examples of informants' accounts displayed? Rich descriptions or theory presented? Findings compared with literature? Theory logical and complete? |

# References

Breck S. Critical reading and review of research. Chapter 25 in Counseling the nursing mother, 3rd ed. Sudbury, MA: Jones and Bartlett Publishers, 2000:449–479.

Fitzpatrick JJ. Encyclopedia of nursing research. New York: Springer, 1998.

Fitzpatrick JJ. Nursing research digest. New York: Springer, 1999.

Fitzpatrick JJ, Montgomery KS. Maternal child health nursing research digest. New York: Springer, 1999.

Goer H. Obstetric myths versus research realities: A guide to the medical literature. Westport, CT: Bergin & Garvey, 1995.

Hewet RJ. Research and breastfeeding. Chapter 23 in Riordan J, Auerbach KG, eds. Breastfeeding and human lactation. Sudbury, MA: Jones and Bartlett Publishers, 1998: 747–774.

Polit and Hungler. Nursing research: Principles and methods, 4th ed. Philadelphia: J. B. Lippincott, 1991.

# A LEGAL PRIMER FOR LACTATION CONSULTANTS

*Priscilla G. Bornmann, JD*

## OBJECTIVES

- Describe the lactation consultant (LC)/client professional relationship.
- Describe legal actions most likely to be brought against lactation consultants.
- Define "informed consent" and describe how it relates to the lactation consultant.
- Discuss record retention.
- Describe how to change a medical record.
- Explain the ABCs of testifying at a deposition or at a trial.
- Detail the ten commandments for avoiding LC liability.

**I** The LC/Client Professional Relationship

A. Creation of the LC/Client Relationship

1. There is generally no duty to render care or attention unless the LC agrees to do so. If the LC "accepts" a client, however, duties are created that are contractual in nature.[1] Those duties that are created exist whether or not the LC is being paid for services.[2]

   a. The duty to render the appropriate level of care (unless authorized to withdraw)

   b. The duty to refer if unable to render appropriate care

   c. The duty not to abandon the client

2. The contract creating the client relationship can be created either by

   a. Express agreement—an actual agreement, the terms of which are stated either orally or in writing. For example: The LC agrees to counsel participants in a health plan.

   b. Implied agreement—a contract inferred in law as a matter of reason and justice from the acts or conduct of the parties or the circumstances surrounding the transaction. For example: This situation could result from a telephone conversation in which the client asks to make an appointment for a specific condition (not merely to "see" an LC).[3]

3. Occurrences that might create an LC/client relationship

   a. If periodic visits, but for different reasons: Each appointment = a new contract

   b. If ongoing visits for a *chronic* condition requiring the client to appear for follow up: Each visit = one contract

   c. Telephone conversations might create a client relationship if the lactation consultant indicates acceptance or gives comments in the nature of treatment[4]

---

[1] *MacNamara v. Emmons*, 36 Cal. App.2d. 199, 204-205, 97 P2d 503, 507 (1939).

[2] Failure to pay an account may constitute grounds for an LC to terminate a Client relationship, so long as the LC does not attempt to do so at a critical time, the LC provides notice to the Client, and the LC gives the Client an opportunity to obtain proper care elsewhere.

[3] But see, *Tsoukas v. Lapid*, 191 iLL 2D 561, 738 NE 2d 936, (Ill. 2000) in which the court held that an HMO patient's telephone calls to a physician listed in an HMO directory did not establish a physician-patient relationship between the parties.

[4] *Hamil v. Bashline*, 224 Pa Super 407, 307 A2d 57 (1973).

   d. Making an appointment
- i. This action usually constitutes an agreement to meet to determine *whether* to enter a client relationship.
- ii. In some cases, however, a client relationship is created by the act of making an appointment.

Virginia case: A blind woman and her 4-year-old guide dog went to a doctor's office. The doctor demanded that the guide dog be removed, refused to treat the woman, and did not assist her in finding other medical attention. The court noted that the appointment had been made "for the treatment of a vaginal infection" and thus created a relationship and duties—it was more than a mere appointment to see a physician.[5] Two questions would be relevant here: 1) Did the client entrust her treatment to the LC, and 2) did the LC accept the case?[6]

Practice tip: Think before turning away someone who arrives pursuant to an appointment. If the person needs immediate counseling or care, give it. If not, you can make alternate arrangements or refer that person to another competent practitioner.

   e. Examination probably creates a relationship.[7]

Practice tip: If you discover a problem beyond your competency, do not just walk away. Advise the client of your concerns; advise them of the need to obtain follow-up care; and refer them to a competent practitioner.

   f. Phone calls can create a relationship. Their content determines whether this relationship is so. To avoid creating a relationship by telephone:[8]
- i. The person receiving the call should identify himself or herself and obtain the name of the individual to whom he or she is speaking.
- ii. The person receiving the call can listen to the caller's complaints.
- iii. If an appointment is made, it should be made clear that the appointment is being made for evaluation in order to determine whether the lactation consultant can accept the new client.

---

[5] *Lyons v. Grether*, 218 Va 630, 239 SE2d 103 (1977).

[6] *Parkell v. Fitzporter*, 301 Mo 217, 256 SW 239 (1923); *Hanson v. Pock*, 57 Mont 51, 187 P 282 (1920); *Peterson v. Phelps*, 23 Minn 319, 143 NW 793 (1913).

[7] *Green v. Walker*, 910 F2d 291 (5th Cir 1990).

[8] *Hamil v. Bashline*, 224 Pa Super. 407, 307 A2d 57 (1973); But See, *Fabien v. Matzko*, 235 Pa.Super 267, 344 A2d 569 (1975) and *Childs v. Weis*, 440 SW2d 104 (Tex.Civ.App. 1969); But see, *Tsoukas v. Lapid*, 191 iLL 2D 561, 738 NE2d 936 (Ill. 2000) in which the court held that an HMO Patient's telephone calls to a physician listed in an HMO directory did not establish a physician-patient relationship between the parties.

        iv. If no appointment is made, the person receiving the call should inform the caller of her options: for example, she might go to the local emergency room, phone an appropriate physician, or phone another lactation consultant.

        v. If the LC gives comments in the nature of advice, an LC/client relationship has been created.

  4. Occurrences that usually do not create an LC/client relationship

    a. Request by a physician that the LC see a client or review the client's record (if the doctor is "relying" on the LC, however, and the LC knows, a relationship might be implied; see the client soon).

    b. The LC's hospital affiliation—generally, no relationship exists as to persons who once were in the hospital; however, this rule will not apply if the call is to a hospital "hotline." In an emergency, it would be best to see and/or refer.

B. Duration and termination of the LC/client relationship

  1. Duration—usually no duration is specified, so the law fills in by requiring the LC to continue care until either

    a. The need for LC services no longer exists

    b. The client withdraws from care

    c. The LC withdraws in a manner that does not constitute "abandonment" of the client

  2. Termination—the relationship exists until:

    a. The need for LC services no longer exists

    b. The LC and client mutually agree to discontinue the relationship

    c. The client discharges the LC either expressly or by seeking LC services from another provider

    d. The LC unilaterally withdraws from relationship by

        i. Giving the client appropriate notice of intent to withdraw

          (a) Talking by phone or in person

          (b) Sending a certified letter, return receipt requested, stating the following: 1) the status of the client; 2) the need for follow-up care; 3) the intention to withdraw by a definite, stated date (the date must give time for the client to seek alternative care); 4) stating that he or she will seek service for emergencies until the date stated; and 5) stating that the subsequent physician of the LC can obtain a copy of all records with written permission from the client.

Note: A client's failure to pay will not justify the LC's unilateral withdrawal without giving sufficient opportunity to obtain alternative care.

    ii. Referring to a competent replacement or to a specialist when a client's problem is outside the LC's competence[9]

3. Situations that might constitute abandonment

  a. The LC is called to consult (a limited contract). To avoid problems, take the following three steps:

    i. Tell the client verbally and write on the chart, "I have been called by Dr. _____ to evaluate ___."

    ii. Perform the service needed.

    iii. Tell the client verbally and write on the chart, "I am signing off this case and will no longer follow this client. I (or business name), however, will remain available if I am notified that additional consultations or assistance is required."

  b. Failure to attend the client when required under a general contract for treatment

  c. Substitution of LCs. The client is not abandoned if replacement is competent. To avoid problems:

    i. Notify the replacement of case details verbally and in writing.

    ii. If possible, give notice to the client of the intent to substitute.

    iii. Advise the new clients of the group's rotation procedure.

  d. The client's failure to keep a follow-up appointment or to follow medical advice: Under such circumstances, an LC has a duty to:

    i. Be sure that the client understands the nature of her condition

    ii. Be sure the client is informed of risks of failing to seek medical attention

    iii. Provide the client with an opportunity to visit the LC for counseling or care

Practice tip: Call the client with information in 1, 2, and 3 above. Follow up with a certified letter to the client containing the same information.

---

[9] *Brandt v. Grubin*, 131 NJ Super 182, 329 A2d 82, 89 (1974).

# Sample Telephone Log

Date: _____    Time: _____

Call From: _____

Re: _____

Complaint: _____

_____

Deposition: _____

_____

Comments:[10] _____

_____

_____

_____

---

[10] If the person taking the calls seeks advice from another, record the name of the person providing advice here. In addition, record here any follow-up instructions given (e.g., call back in 24 hours).

# Sample Letter to Confirm Discharge by Client

Dear _____ :

This will confirm the content of our _____ (date) telephone conversation in which you discharged me from providing further services to you as a lactation consultant.

In my opinion, you should continue to receive services from another lactation consultant because _____. Such services may be obtained in this area from:

(Insert List)

If you have not already done so, I suggest that you engage the services of another lactation consultant without delay. You may be assured that, with your written request, I will furnish any other medical service provider with information regarding the services you have received from me.

Sincerely,

# Sample Letter to Client Who Fails to Keep Appointments

Dear _____ :

    On _____ (date) you failed to keep your appointment at my office. It is my professional opinion that you should continue to receive the services of a lactation consultant, and I urge you not to neglect this need.

    If you wish, you may telephone my office for another appointment. However, it is possible that you might prefer to deal with another lactation consultant. If this is the case, I suggest that you make arrangements promptly. Such services may be obtained in this area from

    (Insert List)

    I am enclosing a consent form that you should fill out and return to me if you want me to release information to any other medical service provider.

    Sincerely,

# Sample Letter of Withdrawal from Client Relationship

Dear _____:

   I regret to inform you that I am withdrawing from further professional attendance upon you as a lactation consultant. I find it necessary to take such action because _____ (State a reason: For example, persistent failure to settle a bill, a pattern of not keeping appointments, refusing to follow instructions, and so on).[11]

   Because you continue to need lactation consultant services, I suggest that you immediately make arrangements with another lactation consultant to provide the attention that you should have. Lactation consultant services are available in this area from

   (Insert List)

   If you wish, I will continue to attend you for a brief period of time while you are making arrangements to retain another lactation consultant, but this period of time must not exceed seven days from the date of this letter.

   I am enclosing a consent form that you should fill out and return to me if you want me to release information another lactation consultant or other medical service provider.

   Sincerely,

---

[11] Although not required, it is wise to keep "friendly" records, thus the LC may wish to state the reason for the decision to terminate services.

## Sample Authorization to Release Lactation Consultant Records

To: LACTATION CONSULTANT'S NAME AND ADDRESS

Client: _____

Social Security Number: _____ Birth Date: _____

Address: _____

_____

This will certify that I have engaged the services of

Name: _____

Address: _____

_____.

You are hereby authorized to furnish and release to _____

_____

any and all information that he/she/it may request related to the lactation consultant services you furnished me from _____ (date) to _____ (date) without limitation, such as notes, records, opinions, and the like.

Please do not disclose this information to insurance adjusters or other persons without written authority from me. (Pursuant to confidential and privileged communications laws.) The foregoing authority shall continue in full force and effect until revoked by me in writing.

Date: _____ Signature: _____

Date: _____ Witness: _____

**II** Legal actions most likely to be brought against lactation consultants (refer to the chart on the following page)

**III** Consent, informed consent, and the lactation consultant in the United States

These comments on consent and the doctrine of informed consent, as it has been applied in the United States, are not specific to breastfeeding issues because no cases related to breastfeeding have been reported. It is hoped, however, that an overview of general principles might help LCs better understand this common law doctrine, which is gaining acceptance in a wide variety of medical settings.[12]

A. Consent principles

The distinction between *consent* and *informed consent* is legally significant. Consent occurs when the client, or one authorized on his or her behalf, agrees to a course of treatment or the performance of a medical procedure. It requires only that the client, or his or her representative, understand the nature of the proposed treatment.[13] If the LC fails to obtain consent and proceeds to touch the client, the LC might be guilty of battery (of touching the client without consent) and might be liable for an award of nominal damages to the client although no real injury results.

B. Informed consent

Even if a client's consent is given, an LC could be found liable to a client for not obtaining *informed* consent. What information is needed as the basis for informed consent? The courts have generally held that a client's informed consent is given only if the following areas have been discussed:

1. The nature of the client's problem or illness
2. The nature of the proposed therapy or treatment
3. Reasonable alternative therapies or treatments
4. The chance of success with the proposed therapy or treatment

---

[12] *Ketchup v Howard,*247 gA aPP 54, 00 FCDR 206, 2000 WL 1747538 (Ga.Ct.App., Nov. 29, 2000) [held that medical professionals, including dentists must obtain informed consent from patients by advising them about procedures' known risks and available treatment alternatives]; *Matthis v. Mastromonaco,* 733 A2d 456 (1999) [held that the informed consent doctrine applies to noninvasive procedures as well as invvasive ones].

[13] Note, however, the Client's consent, or even insistence on a certain treatment plan or procedure will not relieve a health care provider from the obligation to treat patients within the accepted standard of care.   *Metzler v. New York State Board for Professional Medical Conduct,* 610 NYS2d 334 (AD 3 Dept 1994)[homeopathic treatment].

## COMMON TYPES OF ACTION(S)

| CAUSES OF ACTION: ELEMENTS: | TORT (Physical and Emotional Safety) | | | CONTRACT (Expectation of Economic Advantage) | STATUTORY VIOLATION (Public Policy) | | |
|---|---|---|---|---|---|---|---|
| | Battery | Malpractice* | Infliction of Emotional Distress | Breach of Warranty | Unauthorized Practice of Medicine | Failure to Report Child Neglect/Abuse | Violation of Unfair and Deceptive Trade Practice Statute ** |
| Duty | To respect the rights of other persons to freedom from harmful or offense bodily contact. | To use due care on rendering LC services. | To refrain from outrageous conduct | LC promises or "guarantees" a result. | | | |
| Intent | LC intended to physically contact client. | (No proof required.) | LC knew or should have known conduct likely to cause emotional distress. | (No proof required.) | See State Statute | See State Statue | See State Statute |
| Breach | Unconsented to physical contact with one person by another. | Act/omission causing LC to fail to provide standard of care as would be provided by the "ordinary, prudent LC" under similar circumstances. | Act so outrageous (causing more than embarrassment or humiliation) that a reasonable person, normally constituted, would be unable to cope with the mental stress caused. | Result not achieved. | | | |
| Damage | Injury (to client's dignity) presumed. | Severe mental distress. | Severe mental distress. | Result less advantageous than promised. | | | |

* Failure to diagnose, initiate treatment, refer or consult, provide attention or care, or obtain informed consent

** See Quimby v. Fine, 724, P.2d 403, 406 in which a court found that physicians who unfairly or deceptively promote their skills or other medical services, or fail to disclose the risks and alternatives to the treatment performed violated the State's Statute.

5. Substantial risks that are inherent in the therapy or treatment
6. Any risks related to failing to undergo therapy or treatment[14]

Although a written consent form will be considered as evidence that the client's informed consent was obtained, it is not usually conclusive.[15] A suit for lack of informed consent is generally based on negligence.[16] The client must prove not only that the LC breached a duty to give or obtain such consent but also that this action caused injury or damage. This situation usually requires that the client prove she would have elected a different treatment or course of therapy had she been properly informed.[17]

Standard consent forms alone ordinarily do not provide sufficient information about the disclosures made to the client in order to establish that the client's consent was an adequately informed decision.[18] On the other hand, a consent form will be given effect as a defense if all the evidence supports a conclusion that the client was informed about the treatment to which he or she consented.[19]

---

[14] It is well settled that only material risks need to be disclosed. There is no duty to disclose all conceivable risks (*Gouse v. Cassell*, 532 Pa 197, 615 A2d 33 [1992]), risks that are not reasonably foreseeable (*Hondroulis v. Schumacher*, 546, So2d 466 [La 1989]), or those risks that are minimal. (*Penwick v. Christensen*, 912 SW2d 275 [Tex App Houston, 14th Dist, 1995] *writ denied* [June 28, 1996]; *rehearing of writ of error filed* [July 12, 1996]; *rehearing of writ of error overruled* [Aug 1, 1996]). However, establishing whether a particular risk is more than merely "conceivable", or "reasonably foreseeable", or greater than "minimal" is an imprecise exercise which has spawned much litigation.

[15] *Siegel v. Mt. Sinai Hospital*, 62 Ohio App 2d 12, 403 NE2d 202 (1978).

[16] The case law of the state of Pennsylvania is an exception to this rule. In Pennsylvania, if informed consent was not given, this is treated as the legal equivalent of no consent having been given, and the action is then an action for battery (not negligence). *Gouse v. Cassel*, 532 Pa 197, 615 A2d 331, 334 (1992); *Sagala v. Tavares*, 533 A2d 165,(Pa Super 1987); *Boyer v. Smith*, 345 Pa Super Ct 66, 497 A2d 646 (1985); *Salis v. United States*, 522 FSupp 989 (MD Pa 1981); *Gray v. Grunnagle*, 423 Pa 144, 233 A2d 633 (1966).

[17] *Canterbury v. Spence*, 464 F2d 772, 780 (DC Cir), *cert. denied*, 409 U.S. 1064 (1972); *St. Gemme v. Tomlin*, 118 Ill App 3d 766, 74 Ill Dec. 264, 455 NE2d 294 (1983). The 1992 Code of Medical Ethics prepared by the Council on Ethical and Judicial Affairs of the American Medical Association states that a patient's right of self-decision can be effectively exercised only if the patient possesses enough information to make an intelligent choice, that the patient should make the ultimate decision on accepting treatment, and that a physician's ethical obligation is to present the medical facts accurately to the patient and assist that patient in making choices from the therapeutic alternatives consistent with good medical practice. *Also see, Koegan v. Holy Family Hospital*, 95 Wash2d 306, 622 P2d 1246 (1980).

[18] *Pegram v. Sisco*, 406 FSupp 776 (WD Ark 1976) aff'd 547 F2d 1172 (8th Cir 1976); *LePelley v. Grefenson*, 101 Idaho 422, 614 P2d 962 (1980); *Karl J. Pizzalotto MD Ltd v. Wilson*, 437 So2d 859 (La. 1983) remd 444 So2d 143 (La App 1983); *LaCaze v. Collier*, 434 So2d 1039 (1983); *Roberson v. Menorah Medical Center*, 588 SW2d 134 (Mo App 1979); *Gray v. Grunnagle*, 423 Pa. 144, 233 A2d 633 (1966); *Cross v. Trapp*, 294 SE2d 446 (W Va 1982).

[19] See *Rogers v. Brown*, 416 So2d 624 (La App 1982). In this case the Client's consent was established on the basis of a consent form where the physician and nurse testified that risks of treatment were fully explained to the Client and the form was completed, signed, and given to the Client.

Theoretically, a client or his or her representative could waive the obligation to obtain informed consent if the client or his or her representative insisted that the client not be informed of the nature of the treatment or the accompanying risks.[20] The actual occurrence of such a waiver, however, is difficult to foresee in a breastfeeding context.

For LCs who are in a busy practice, adequate legal protection can be obtained as to courses of treatment often prescribed by writing up an information sheet and frequently updating it. The LC should ask the mother (or both parents, if they are available) to sign and date two identical forms below a typed statement, saying that she acknowledges receipt of the information. One copy of the form should remain in the LCs files, and the other should be given to the mother. When determining the information to include in such a form, consider the following recommendations:

1. Consult with other LCs to determine what risks and alternative modes they explain to their patients.

2. Consult current medical literature to determine the frequency and severity of risks and the availability of reasonable alternative modes of current treatment.

3. Supplement the above with those additional risks that are serious or life-threatening, even though infrequently encountered.

4. Add to the form additional information that you believe the average, prudent client would want to have explained to enable her to give an informed consent.

The existence of a duty to obtain informed consent is not dependent on prior legal recognition of this doctrine in the forum. The absence of any law recognizing informed consent liability at the time of the defendant's alleged breach will not preclude imposing informed consent liability if making more extensive disclosures would have been recognized as good and acceptable medical practice at the time.[21] The duty to obtain informed consent is based on the right of patients to control what will be done with their own bodies.[22, 23]

---

[20] *Putensen v. Clay Adams, Inc.*, 12 Cal App 3d 1064, 91 Cal Rptr. 319 (1970).

[21] *Halley v. Birbiglia*, 3901 Mass 540, 458 NE2d 710 (1983).

[22] *Canterbury v. Spence*, 150 App DC 263, 464 F2d 772 (DC Cir 1972) cert denied 409 US 1064 (1972); *Sard v. Hardy*, 281 Md 432, 379 A2d 1014 (1977); *Smith v. Shannon*, 100 Wash2d, 666 P2d 351 (1983).

[23] However, in many jurisdictions, this duty arises out of the fiduciary nature of the physician-patient relationship and may not apply to LC's. *Nelson v. Gaunt*, 125 Cal App 3d 623, 178 Cal Rptr 167 (1981).

Some states in the United States limit the use of the informed consent doctrine to cases involving surgical or operative medical procedures.[24] A few other states have held that their informed consent statutes do not apply to "routine medical procedures."[25] In such jurisdictions, it is doubtful that the doctrine of informed consent would be relevant to most breastfeeding situations. There is a recent case law, however, that holds that the doctrine of informed consent applies to noninvasive as well as invasive medical procedures.[26]

Currently, the *primary treating physician* has the duty to obtain the patient's informed consent for treatment but not always those personnel who merely consult with,[27] refer to,[28] or assist[29] the attending physician.[30] Depending on the jurisdiction, a hospital or clinic might be capable of escaping liability for failing to obtain the patient's informed consent before performing a procedure or conducting a course of treatment prescribed by the patient's physician.[31] In some jurisdictions, however, it is possible to impose *respondeat superior* liability on the hospital at which the patient received medical treatment without his or

---

[24] *Boyer v. Smith*, 345 Pa Super Ct 66, 497 A2d 646 (1985)[holding that the defendant had no duty to obtain a patient's informed consent to the administration of a therapeutic drug].

[25] *Novak v. Texada, Miller, Masterson & Davis* Clinic, 514 So2d 524 (La App 1987) *cert denied* 515 So2d 807 (La (1987)[administration of a flu shot held to be a "routine" medical procedure to which Louisiana's informed consent statute did not apply]; *Daniels v. State*, 532 ASo2d 218 (La App 1988)[treating a closed wrist fracture found to be a routine medical procedure to which Louisiana's informed consent statute did not apply].

[26] *Matthis v. Mastromonaco*, 733 A.2d 456 (N.J. 1999).

[27] *Halley v. Birbiglia*, 390 Mass 540, 458 NE2d 240 (1982).

[28] *Stovall v Harms*, 214 Kan 835, 522 P2d 353 (1974); *Llera v. Wisner*, 171 Mont 254, 557 P2d 805 (1976); *Johnson v. Whitehurst*, 652 SW2d 441 (Tex App 1983).

[29] *Harnish v. Children's Hospital Medical Center*, 387 Mass 152, 439 NE2d 240 (1982).

[30] *Beard v. Brunswick Hospital Center*, 632 NYS2d 805 (App Div, 2d Dept, 1995)[a physician who assisted a surgeon, but who was not the primary surgeon, found not liable]; *Foflygen v. Zemel*, 420 Pa Super 18, 615 A2d 1380 (Pa. 1993)[a physician taking a patient's medical history in conjunction with the patient's admission to the hospital for medical treatment, and a nurse assisting the treating physician during the procedure held not liable]; *Barnes v. Gorman*, 605 So2d 805 (Miss 1992)[consent obtained by an LPN may not be adequate], *but See, Perez v. Park Madison Professional Lab* (lst Dept, 1995) 212 App Div 2d 271, 630 NYS2d 37, *partial summary judgment granted, cause dismd* (NY App Div lst Dept) 1995 NY App Div LEXIS 7844 *and app dismd without op* 87 NY2d 896, 640 NYS2d 880, 663 NE2d 922; (*Sangiulo v. Leventhal*, 132 Misc2d 680, 505 NYS2d 507 (1986)[a "substitute physician" administering part of a course of treatment started by a physician for whom he was covering found not liable].

[31] *Davis v. Hoffman*, M.D., 972 F. Supp 308, 1997 WL 416261 (ED Pa, 1997) [hospital not responsible for independent contractor's failure to obtain patient's informed consent]; *Geise v. Stice*, 567 NW2d 156, 252 Neb 913, (Neb 1997)[hospital had no duty to obtain informed consent since physician was not an employee of the hospital]; *Gross v. Oklahoma Blood Institute*, 856 P2d 998 (Okla App 1990), *But See, Keel v. St. Elizabeth Medical Center*, 842 SW2d 860 (Ky 1990).

her informed consent if it can be shown that the physician who breached the duty to obtained informed consent was a hospital employee. Under certain circumstances, if the employee is the agent for a hospital, both the employee and the hospital can be held responsible.[32]

C. Who should consent?

The duty to obtain consent is owed to the patient. If the patient is a minor or has a disability, however, the patient might not be legally competent to give consent. In such cases, the LC should obtain the consent from the patient's parent or guardian. Moreover, in breastfeeding cases, who is the patient—the mother alone, or the mother and the baby? Although there is no existing case law because breastfeeding has physical ramifications for both mother and baby, it appears that both have "client" status.

D. Who can give consent for an infant?

1. The general rule in the United States is that competent adults are capable of giving valid consent. Prior to the age of majority, which usually is designated by state statute, an individual is considered incapable of consenting to medical care or treatment. Thus, is it necessary to obtain the consent of an infant's parent or guardian to consent on the infant's behalf?[33] A parent who has legal custodial rights over a child has the authority to consent to medical care and treatment for that child. So, if parents are divorced or legally separated (for example, a separation agreement has been signed), the parent who is granted legal authority for the care, custody, and control of the child has the right to consent to treatment to the exclusion of the other parent.

2. If the parent herself is a minor, the legal waters are muddied and her ability to consent to treatment for her child is less clear. Best practice would suggest that the LC receive the consent of the other parent (if that parent is not a minor) or from the minor parents (grandparents) or guardian, unless the minor parent is considered to be "emancipated" or a "mature minor."

---

[32] *Koegan v. Holy Family Hospital*, 95 Wash2d 306, 622 P2d 1246 (1980); *Shenefield v. Greenwich Hospital Ass'n*, 10 Conn App 239, 522 A2d 829 (1987)[Physician as agent for hospital.] But see the following cases holding hospitals not liable for the failures of staff physicians to obtain informed consent: *Harnish v. Children's Hospital Medical Center*, 387 Mass 152, 439 NE2d 240 (1982); *Roberson v. Menorah Medical Center*, 588 SW2d 134 (Mo App 1979); *Cross v. Trapp*, 294 SE2d 446 (W Va 1982).

[33] *People v. Messinger*, No. 9467694FH (Mich, Ingham County Cir Ct Feb. 2, 1995)[jury acquitted a father charged with involuntary manslaughter on grounds that his decision to disconnect premature infant son's respirator was the result of informed decision to withdraw life sustaining treatment in the child's "best interests"]; *Dewes v, Indian Health Service*, 504 FSupp 203 (D SD 1980).

a. Emancipation has been defined as "the relinquishment by the parent of control and authority over the minor child, conferring on him (child) the right to his earnings and terminating the parents' legal duty to support the child."[34]

b. Emancipation generally occurs when a minor lives away from his or her parents, supports himself or herself, and conducts his or her own affairs. Some states have statutes defining particular circumstances that qualify a child as emancipated.[35] Other states, to avoid encouraging runaways, require that this relationship be consensual between the child and the parent. In the absence of such a statute, the following situations have been considered to confer emancipated or "mature minor"[36] status on a minor:

   i. Military duty[37]

   ii. Marriage[38]

   iii. Living apart from the child's family independently of their support and services[39]

c. Emancipated minors are granted the same legal status as if they are already at the age of full majority. They are able to provide consent for their own medical care and might be able to consent to such care for their children as well. If the emancipated minor parent has a spouse of legal age, however, the LC is advised to obtain the consent of the spouse for the treatment of the infant whenever possible.

3. If the LC believes the parent is incompetent, another problem situation is presented even if there has been no adjudication of the parent's incompetency. Again, it is best that the LC obtain the permission of the parents' parent (grandparent) or guardian under such conditions.

---

[34] *Wallace v. Cox*, 136 Tenn 69, 188 S.W. 611, 612 (1916).

[35] e.g., see §16.1-331, *et seq.*, 3, Code of Virginia.

[36] *Belcher v. Charleston Area Medical Center*, 188 WVa 105, 422 SE2d 827 (1992).

[37] *Swenson v. Swenson*, 241 Mo App 21, 227 SW2d 103 (1950).

[38] *Bach v. Long Island Jewish Hospital*, 49 Misc2d 207, 267 NYS2d 289 (1966).

[39] *Smith v Seigly*, 72 Wash2d 16, 431 P2d 719 (1967).

# Sample Intake Form and General Consent
# for Lactation Consultant Services

| | | | | | |
|---|---|---|---|---|---|
| Baby's Last Name | First Name | Age | Date of Birth | Weeks Pregnant | Sex |

_____ lb. ____oz.     _____ lb. _____ oz.     _____ lb. _____oz.

Baby's Birth Weight    Discharge Weight   Current Weight

| | | | | |
|---|---|---|---|---|
| Mother's Last Name | First Name | Age | Date of Birth | Occupation |

| | | | | |
|---|---|---|---|---|
| Father's Last Name | First Name | Age | Date of Birth | Occupation |

**Mother's Home:**

| | | | |
|---|---|---|---|
| Street Address | City | State | Zip |

| | | |
|---|---|---|
| Telephone Number | Fax | E-mail address |

**Mother's Work:**

| | | | |
|---|---|---|---|
| Street Address | City | State | Zip |

| | | |
|---|---|---|
| Telephone Number | Fax | E-mail address |

**Father's Home:**

| | | | |
|---|---|---|---|
| Street Address | City | State | Zip |

| | | |
|---|---|---|
| Telephone Number | Fax | E-mail address |

**Father's Work:**

| | | | |
|---|---|---|---|
| Street Address | City | State | Zip |

| | | |
|---|---|---|
| Telephone Number | Fax | E-mail address |

**Attending Medical Personnel:**

_____    _____    _____
**Pediatrician** (first and last name)    Street Address    Suite #

_____    _____ _____    _____    _____
City    State    Zip    Phone    Fax

_____    _____    _____
**OB/GYN, MD, DO, CNM** (first and last name)    Street Address    Suite #

_____    _____ _____    _____
City    State    Zip    Telephone

**Referred By:**

_____
Name

_____    _____    _____    _____
Street Address    City    State    Zip

_____

Why have you requested this consultation?

I/We grant permission to NAME OF LACTATION CONSULTANT OR AGENCY to share pertinent information about this consultation with my/our family physicians and health care providers, the referring person, my/our community breastfeeding helper, and my/our insurance companies in order to further the knowledge of breastfeeding. I/We understand that all medical care is to be provided by my/our own physician(s).

Date: _____    _____
                                    Signature of Mother or Father

I give my consent to NAME OF LACTATION CONSULTANT OR AGENCY to observe me breastfeeding and/or to examine my breasts during the period of lactation assistance.

Date: _____    _____
                                    Signature of Mother

Date: _____    _____
                                    Signature of Lactation Consultant

# Sample Informed Consent Form for Lactation Consultant Care or Treatment

I acknowledge that _____ has explained to me that (I am) (I may be) (my baby is) (my baby may be) suffering from/affected by _____

and has recommended the following medical care or treatment: _____

I acknowledge that the following information has been provided to me:

Purpose of the care/treatment:

_____

_____

Alternative forms of care/treatment:

_____

_____

Risks of recommended care/treatment:

_____

_____

Risks of alternative care/treatment:

_____

_____

Risks of not undergoing care/treatment:

_____

_____

I further acknowledge that I have had full opportunity to discuss this information with _____ and hereby consent to the following lactation consultant care or treatment:

_____

_____

Date:_____    _____
                    Client or person authorized to consent for client

Date:_____    _____
                    Witness

# Sample Refusal of Lactation Consultant Care or Treatment

I have been advised by _____ that (I am) (I may be) (my baby is) (my baby may be) suffering from/affected by: _____

_____

and has recommended that (I) (my baby) undergo the following medical procedure/undergo or authorize the following treatment: _____

_____

_____

I understand that although there are no guarantees with said procedures, it is anticipated that the results of the procedure will be: _____.
I further understand that my refusing to accept the recommended course subjects (me) (my baby) to the following risks: _____

_____

I have carefully considered this matter and elect to forego the recommended treatment. In so doing, I assume all risks and release and hold harmless _____,
his or her associates, employees and agents from any and all responsibility for my care and results of my failure to follow his or her advice. I acknowledge that _____
has given me full opportunity to discuss this matter with him or her and that I understand the consequences of my act.

Date:_____     _____
                       Client or person authorized to consent for client
Date:_____     _____
                       Witness

(COMMENT: This form can also be used for patients who insist on leaving a hospital against medical advice. If a client refuses to sign the form, it should be filled in and signed by the lactation consultant with the following comment.)

The information set out above has been fully explained to _____.
The (client) (client's representative) has acknowledged that he or she understands the consequences of refusing the recommended medical procedure and yet continued to refuse said care. They have additionally refused to sign this form although capable of doing so:

Date:_____     _____
                       Lactation Consultant
Date:_____     _____
                       Witness

# Sample Authority to Admit Observers

Name of Client: _____

Place/Location:_____

    I authorize _____ and the (hospital/clinic/business name) to permit the presence of such observers as they may deem fit to admit in addition to the lactation consultants while I am undergoing lactation consultation, examination, and treatment.

Date:_____    _____
                         Client

Date:_____    _____
                         Witness

# Sample Authorization and Consent for Lactation Consultant to Take, Publish, Distribute, Sell, or Use Photographs

Client: _____     Place: _____     Date: _____

In connection with the lactation consultant services that I am receiving from my lactation consultant, _____ (name), I consent that photographs may be taken of me or parts of my body, under the following conditions:

1. The photographs may be taken only with the consent of my lactation consultant and under such conditions and at such times as may be approved by said consultant.

2. The photographs shall be taken by my lactation consultant or by a photographer approved by my lactation consultant.

3. The photographs shall be used for medical records and if in the judgment of my lactation consultant, medical research, education or science will be benefited by their use, such photographs and information relating to my case may be published and republished, either separately or in connection with each other, in professional journals or medical books, or used for any other purpose which said consultant may deem proper in the interest of medical education, knowledge, or research; provided, however, that it is specifically understood that in any such publication or use I shall not be identified by name.

4. I expressly authorize my lactation consultant to reproduce, publish, and use these photographs in any manner whatsoever, including but not limited to selling the same for profit; provided, however, that in any such publication or use I shall not be identified by name.

5. The aforementioned photographs may be modified or retouched in any way that my lactation consultant, in said consultant's discretion, may consider desirable.

Date: _____     Signed: _____
                                       Client:
                              Address: _____
                                       _____
                            Telephone: _____


Date: _____     Signed: _____
                                       Witness:
                              Address: _____
                                       _____
                            Telephone: _____

# Sample Authorization and Consent
## (Breast Milk for an Infant Who Is Placed for Open Adoption)

I, _____, the natural parent of _____, an infant male/female born on _____ at _____ hospital, being over the age of 18 years, state the following under oath, voluntarily and of my own free will:

It is my present intention to consent to the adoption of said infant, my natural child, by _____ and _____. Accordingly:

1. I give my permission for _____ to breastfeed said infant if she so desires.

2. I give my permission to _____ Hospital to administer _____'s breast milk or milk from _____ milk bank to said infant.

3. I authorize _____ and _____ to consent to any and all medical care for said infant which is deemed necessary and appropriate by a physician licensed in the state of _____. This consent includes, but is not limited to, medical and surgical intervention and elective as well as emergency care.

4. This authorization may not be changed orally, but only by a writing signed by me. In the event any portion of this authorization is found to be invalid, it is my desire that all other portions remain in full force and effect. I understand that it will be interpreted and applied under the law of the state of _____.

5. I understand that the risk of transmission of bacterial or viral agents is low. However, I agree to hold _____ Hospital harmless, in and from any and all liability, claims, or damages arising, or claimed as arising, out of or in relation to this Authorization, including but not limited to any responsibility or liability from all possible implications of any diseases or illnesses, known to mankind (such as acquired immune deficiency disease, aids-related conditions, hepatitis, tuberculosis, and CMV) and any forms of adulteration or contamination.

6. I further acknowledge that I have had full opportunity to discuss this authorization with _____.

Date: _____     _____
                                                  Natural Parent's Signature
Date: _____     _____
                                                  Witness:
Date: _____     _____
                                                  Witness:
State of _____
City/County of _____, to-wit:

On this _____ day of _____, 20___, personally appeared _____ who signed and acknowledged the foregoing authorization and consent before me, freely and voluntarily.

_____
Notary Public: 

My Comm. Exp.: _____

(COMMENT: In most jurisdictions, only one parent's signature is required. It is recommended, however, that each parent sign such a form [if both are known and available] to ensure acceptance by the hospital administration. Similarly, it is not required that the document be notarized. This notarization, however, will further ensure that the authorization will be accepted without question.)

**IV** Record retention

    A. Reasons to keep patient records (these can be medical records and/or business records)

        1. To memorialize details of the client health record for "in-house" use

        2. To make it possible to give the client her record to share with other care providers

        3. To defend professional negligence suits[40]

        4. To comply with state statutes[41]

        5. To comply with regulations of the Joint Committee on Accreditation of Hospitals (JCAH)[42]

        6. To obtain third-party payments (substantiate fees)

    B. Records that should be maintained

        1. Those relevant to the patient's welfare:

            a. Patient chart

            b. Test results

            c. Original source of documents (for example, X-rays) or reports regarding them

        2. Those that are relevant to the administrative needs of the LC or his or her employer

        3. Those relevant to the protection of the LC

            a. A record of each telephone call

            b. Long-distance telephone bills[43]

            c. Appointment calendars[44]

---

[40] In some jurisdictions, if a medical professional has failed to preserve evidence that is relevant to a patient's malpractice case, the jury or judge may infer that the missing evidence would be unfavorable to the defense. *Battochi v. Washington Hospital Center*, 581 A2d 759 (D.C. 1990); *Rodgers v. St. Mary's Hospital*, 556 NE2d 913 (Ill. 1990).

[41] If the LC works in a doctor's office, the state's medical practice act or licensing statutes may dictate the type of information to be included in the patient's record. Typically these require a written record "justifying the treatment of the patient, including but not limited to, patient histories, examination results and test results." Fla. Stat. §458.331(1)(m).

[42] To remain accredited, a hospital's records must contain: (1) identification data; (2) patient's medical history; (3) reports of relevant physical examinations; (4) diagnostic and therapeutic orders; (5) evidence of appropriate informed consent; (6) clinical observations; (7) reports of procedures and tests; and (8) conclusions at the termination of hospitalization or evaluation and treatment.

[43] Keep these in a separate file by calendar year. They can demonstrate that the LC did follow up on a Client's care, or did respond in a timely fashion to a complaint.

[44] These can corroborate dates of appoints or demonstrate that a client/patient's failure to keep an appointment.

    C. Length of time to keep

       1. Your state's statute of limitations for malpractice

       2. Comply with other state statutes (some states)[45]

       3. Tax records—at least six years

       4. Period for which Medicare or other third party payees are entitled to review files to substantiate claims for reimbursement

    D. Disposition of records (on dissolution or sale of practice or death of the provider)

       1. There might be a state statute.[46]

       2. If there is no state statute *and you do not believe you must keep records for tax purposes or any other reason set forth in section "A" above:*

          a. Maintain records for at least one year.

          b. One month following the event, publish the fact in the newspaper and state that records can be retrieved at a certain place on particular days during certain hours.

          c. As soon as possible, send a written notice to each patient regarding the change and stating that at the patient's written request within reasonable time (stated in the notice), the LC will send records to the physician of the patient's choice (or the patient can retrieve records from certain location on certain days during business hours).

          d. Ten months after the event, publish a notice for four consecutive weeks that records will be destroyed a month following the last published notice.

          e. At the end of the year, dispose of records but retain a file indefinitely that contains a list of each record (and includes notations regarding to whom you gave the records, address(es) where sent, how disposed of), copies of letters to patients/clients, copies of published notices, and so on.

  V  How to correct a medical record

"From where I sit, it seems that alteration of patient medical records is becoming a significant problem."

        —Dr. Thoms Gretter, secretary of the State Medical Board of Ohio, The State Medical Board of Ohio, Your Report 2 (Winter 1997–1998)

---

[45] E.g., Ind. Code §16-4-8-12; Nev. Rev. Stat. §629.051.

[46] E.g., Fla. Stat. §455.242.

Medical records are legal documents, and health care professionals should be careful about creating and maintaining them. In addition to being essential to patient care, these records are important to insurers for financial reasons,[47] to attorneys for medical-legal reasons,[48] and to the government for payment and regulatory reasons.

In a lawsuit, it is not unusual for the plaintiff's attorneys to engage forensic chemists, document examiners,[49] ink-dating specialists,[50] fingerprint specialists, computer specialists,[51] and even DNA specialists[52] in order to discern whether the records were "doctored." Showing that records were tampered with can prevent witnesses from committing perjury and tends to increase the case's value.

A.  The proper methodology for correcting or editing a medical record is as follows:

1.  Once detected, omissions and errors should be corrected promptly.

2.  Draw a single line through any incorrect information.

3.  Being able to read what has been edited or changed is important. The correct information should then be recorded above, below, or beside the original incorrect data and should be initialed and dated.[53]

---

[47] Intentional alteration may affect the availability of coverage, depending on the terms of the defendant's insurance policy.

[48] There are at least four legal remedies to help those abused by the alteration or spoilation of records:
1.  A jury may infer either criminal guilt or civil liability from the destruction of suppression of evidence.
2.  The process of discovery can confer protection on the parties. Federal Rule of Civil Procedure 37 and its comparable state provisions authorize courts to enter sanctions for failure to produce appropriate documentation or intentionally destroying such information.
3.  When liability is determined, in addition to awarding compensatory damages, punitive damages may be awarded on a showing of "actual malice" for the intentional alteration, falsification, or destruction of medical records.
4.  A separate tort claim for intentional spoilation of evidence is developing. By early 1999 the following states had recognized some form of a separate cause of action for the tort of spoilation: Alaska, California, Florida, Illinois, Kansas, Ohio, New Jersey.

[49] Techniques include: detecting the imprint made on the paper underneath when the original notes were written, and examining other records which may include thermal markings, such as EKG strips or fetal monitor strips. These can be examined (even if on microfilm) using scientific techniques that make legible otherwise disappearing provider notes.

[50] Ink dating may prove the entry was made at a different time that its author claims. The technique can detect an alteration made with a different pen, determine the age of the document, or determine the age of the particular insertion. Ink can be dated to within six months of use with reasonable scientific probability.

[51] With computer-generated records, "deleted" entries can often be recovered from the hard drive.

[52] For example: saliva on an envelope may link a defendant to the document.

[53] Deleting with correction fluid, erasing, blotting out, or adding information at a different time than the original note was made are not appropriate ways to correct a record. Any of these actions may be viewed as an alteration.

**VI** The ABCs of testifying at a deposition or at a trial

The following pointers are general instructions on how to act at a deposition or at a trial. You should not follow them slavishly but use them as guidelines. Everyone makes mistakes. No one bats 1000. These suggestions, however, should raise your batting average.

A. Tell the truth

1. In a lawsuit, as in all other matters, honesty is the best policy. And a lie might lose the case. Telling the truth, however, demands more than refraining from telling a deliberate falsehood. Telling the truth requires that witnesses testify accurately about what they know. Everything you say must be right, correct, and accurate.

2. To be accurate in all of your answers, you must be aware that technically you cannot possibly tell what you did yesterday, what you saw yesterday, or what you heard yesterday. Technically, you can only testify to what you remember seeing yesterday or what you remember hearing yesterday.

3. Memory is not perfect. You can talk about what you saw, what you heard, and what you did as though memory were a fact, but you are really only remembering something. That is an important distinction. Obviously, there are some things that you do remember, and you remember them clearly, and there can be no question about them. But there will probably be many things about which you might be uncertain. In those instances, you can testify only about what you remember.

B. Don't act as the advocate for any party.

Attempt to testify objectively—and only about that which you are knowledgeable. In other words, you will probably answer all kinds of questions about breastfeeding. But think twice about giving an opinion about any other topic. It will only serve to diminish your credibility. For example, in a custody case, do you really *know* what is truly best for the child? Unless you are brought in as a character witness for a friend (and not as a lactation consultant), avoid taking either parent's side.

C. Educate "your" attorney.

1. Give the attorney your resumé so that he or she has the information necessary to qualify you as an expert witness. Be prepared to explain your credentials—formal schooling, employment history, and other kinds of relevant experience. If you are an IBCLC, get a brochure from the IBLCE and make sure that the lawyer understands this credential.

2. If it is foreseeable that your testimony might be countered by that of some other health care provider, explain in detail how little formal background in

breastfeeding most professional schools include in their curriculums. If you are an IBCLC, encourage the attorney to call the IBLCE office in Virginia at (703) 560-7330 and talk with someone there about the reasons for a voluntary certification instead of a licensing procedure and the constitutional requirement for the alternative pathway. Then do the same yourself so that you can testify without hesitation.

D.  Ask "your" attorney about the mother and baby.

In many cases, you will not know the people involved. So, it is important that you ask about the background of the breastfeeding dyad. For example:

1.  Does the mother smoke (if so, be prepared to rebut any inferences to the effect that her breast milk might be harmful to the child)?

2.  Does the mother drink or do drugs?

3.  Have there been any neglect or abuse issues?

4.  You know what is relevant. The attorney might not.

E.  Supply "your" attorney with copies of the references on which you will rely.

If you know the issues that are likely to arise during the trial, assemble copies of the most authoritative articles and give them to the attorney to read. If possible, supply the attorney with a set of questions to ask.

F.  Be prepared to quote a fee.

The attorney will not be able to tell you precisely how long the proceeding will take. So be prepared to quote an hourly fee and to charge 50 percent of that hourly fee for your travel time. This charge for testifying should be about the same as what you would charge for a private consultation of the same duration.

G.  Ask "your" attorney whether you should bring some general references when you testify.

Many times, references will not be necessary. But if having a Lawrence and/or a Riordan and Auerbach with you will calm your nerves, why not bring it along? Impress upon the attorney that these are generally accepted as authoritative in case they could be used in cross-examination.

H.  Be prepared for the "hypothetical question."

Either or both attorneys might describe a scenario based on a particular set of facts and then ask you to comment on it in your "professional opinion" or to a "reasonable degree of medical certainty." Be aware that usually when this question is posed, they are asking about some issue that is very central to the case. Think about the question before answering. Then, answer with clarity. If additional facts would make a difference, say so at the outset. Unless the questions is very simple, avoid giving a bare "yes" or "no" answer.

I.  Educate the people in the courtroom or in the conference room.

Generally, you will truly be the expert on human lactation at any trial or deposition. The only time there will be someone there who knows as much as you do will be if another LC is called to testify. Try to remember how little the average person in our society knows about breastfeeding and to remember to define basic terms and to simply describe basic processes (for example, the effect of stimulation on milk supply). When possible, give a little background about the basic anthropological/social/medical theory on which your answer is built. Judges and lawyers are usually fascinated by an LC's testimony.

J.  Admit what you do not know.

The issue here is credibility. You cannot be effective if you are not prepared.

K.  Straighten out confusion.
    1.  If you should become confused about a point, straighten the matter out while the testimony is being taken. (If you are testifying at a deposition, you will have an opportunity to read the testimony over afterward and make any necessary corrections, but it is better to make your corrections at the time of the deposition.)
    2.  For example, the opposing lawyer might ask you a question that will remind you of a related question that you have already answered. The new questions might remind you that when you answered the previous one, you made a mistake.
    3.  The worst tactic you can take is to try to cover up that mistake by giving an incorrect answer. The best strategy is to correct the mistake right then. Say, "Excuse me, I just remembered back there you asked me X and I said Y. I was mistaken, I should have told you Z."

L.  Don't guess.

If you do not remember something, admit it. If you do not know something, admit it. You might be embarrassed. You might feel that you should be able to remember, but unless you really do remember, do not guess. You have nothing to gain by guessing. If you guess right, you have not won anything. If you guess wrong, you have lost. Guessing is a game you cannot win, so there is no sense playing it. You cannot answer accurately if you do not hear or understand a question. So, be sure that you hear and understand the question before you try to answer it. If you do not hear it, ask to have it repeated. If you do not understand it, ask to have it explained. It is important that you understand each question the way the lawyer intends you to understand it. It is likewise important that anyone else who hears or reads your answer understand it the same way that you mean it. Language is inexact. It is much easier to be general than to be specific. Therefore, the defense attorney's questions might have several meanings, and your answers might have several meanings. Be sure that your answers are as exact as they can be so that no one can misinterpret them.

M. Give accurate estimates.

Beware of questions involving time and dates. If you estimate, make sure that everyone understands that you are estimating.

N. Clarify multiple meanings.

You will be asked questions that have multiple meanings. You will have to answer, so if there is any doubt in your mind as to whether a question has a multiple meaning, either make sure that you understand what the questioner means or make sure that what you mean is clear.

O. Answer background questions as accurately as possible.

The lawyers will ask you for background information. They will probably ask you your address, when and where you were born, where you went to school, and what jobs you have had. You might not be able to remember all of these details, but do your best. If you do not remember, tell the questioner that you do not remember or give the best possible estimate. For example, "Well I'm not sure, but it seems to me it may have been back in 1995 or 1996, about then."

P. Beware of a question that assumes fact.

You might be asked a question that assumes a fact that is not true or assumes that you have testified to a fact when you have not. You have heard the question, "Have you stopped beating your wife yet?" You cannot answer this question "yes" or "no" without getting into trouble, because it assumes a fact that is not true.

For example, the questioner might ask, "When did you first see the baby?", and you might say, "Well, I'm not sure, on July 5th or 6th. I don't know, somewhere along in there." Later, the questioner will ask, "Well, after you first saw the baby on July 5th, what happened?" This question assumes you had testified that you first saw the baby on July 5th when in fact you testified you were not sure when you first saw the baby.

Q. Watch out for alternative questions.

Another type of question to watch out for is a question in the alternative, such as, "Well, now, is it one or is it two? Which is it?" The danger is that you might know it is not one, but you do not know whether it is two or not. Your mind might reason that if it is either one or two, and you know that it is not one, then it must be two. So you answer, "It's two" when you really do not know.

The fallacy in this type of reasoning is easy to see. "What color is this pencil? Is it red or is it blue?" You can see that it is obviously yellow. So just because questions are put to you in the alternative does not mean that the given alternatives are the only ones.

R.  Be alert to paraphrases.

The opposing attorney might paraphrase part of your testimony. He or she might say, "Well, now, let me see if I understand you correctly; if I am mistaken, you correct me," and then state what he or she understands your testimony to be. If any word is used that you do not think is correct, call it to the lawyer's attention.

Even if the paraphrase sounds perfect to you, do not give an unqualified "Yes." You might be saying "Yes" to something you really did not intend. A word might have meaning that you did not understand or appreciate. The most you can say is, "Yes, that sounds about right," or, "As far as I can tell, that's about right." Otherwise, you are putting your stamp of approval on every word used. You are letting the attorney tell your story in his or her words (some of which you might not have fully understood).

S.  Take your time.

Give the question as much thought as is required to understand it and form your answer, then give the answer. Never give a snap answer, but bear in mind that if you take a long time to answer each question, a judge or jury might think that you are making up your answers.

Do not answer while the questioner is still talking. If you are talking and the questioner is talking, you should stop. One of two things is happening

1.  You are answering before the questioner is finished the question (in which case you should stop, because you cannot listen to the question and understand it while you are answering it).

2.  The questioner is interrupting you before you have completed your answer to the first question, in which case you should also stop.

3.  When you stop because you have been interrupted, pay no attention to the question being asked, but keep in mind what you were about to reply to the first question. If you do not, chances are you will forget it. When the questioner finishes talking, say, "Pardon me, I wasn't through with my last answer." Then, give your answer and ask, "Now, what was your next question?"

T.  Answer concisely.

1.  Answer a question concisely and then wait for the next question. Say what you need to say, but do not go off on a tangent.

2.  You should not be evasive or argumentative, nor should you nit-pick about language. Do not hide anything. You are only to answer the question, but the question must be asked before you give an answer.

3. Do not invite more questions. Control this situation by the inflection of your voice. For example, the questioner might ask what shoe you put on first this morning. If you answer, "Well, I don't remember what shoe I put on first this morning," with the accent on "this," you are inviting another question.

U. Be aware of your speech and appearance.

Talk loudly enough so that everybody can hear you. Do not chew gum, and keep your hands away from your mouth so that you can speak distinctly. Speak up so that the court reporter can hear you. You must give an audible "yes" or "no" answer. The reporter cannot hear nods of the head. "Yes" or "no" sounds better than "uh-huh" or "yeah." Dress conservatively and be well-groomed.

V. Look the judge (and jurors, if any) in the eye.

Do not be afraid to look the judge and jurors in the eye while you are testifying. They are naturally sympathetic to a witness and want to hear what is said. Look at them most of the time and speak frankly and openly as you would to a friend or neighbor.

W. Don't look at your lawyer for approval.

Do not look for help when you are on the stand. You are on your own. If you look at your lawyer when a question is asked on cross-examination or look for approval after answering a question, the jury will notice and will develop a bad impression. You must appear confident about your answers.

X. Do not be defensive.

Do not argue with opposing lawyers. They have a right to question you, so do not become defensive or give evasive answers. You are not there to convince them how right you are or how wrong the other side is. You are not there to do anything except answer every question as accurately, courteously, and concisely as possible.

Y. Do not lose your temper.

You should appear to be completely disinterested. Do not lose your temper no matter how hard you are pressed.

Z. Be courteous.

One of the best ways to make a good impression is to be courteous. Be sure to address the judge as "Your Honor."

AA. Avoid joking.

1. Avoid wisecracking and joking. A lawsuit is a serious matter.
2. This advice is particularly true for depositions. Remarks that everyone present understands as a joke can haunt you after they are transcribed, because inflection made the difference. But there it is in black and white. "I could have killed her!"

BB. Do not be reluctant to admit to discussions with your attorney.

If you are asked whether you have talked to your lawyer, admit it freely. The same thing goes for when you are asked whether you are being paid. It can be particularly effective to say that "Although I am earning a fee, that will not affect the content of my answers."

CC. Beware of the "Have you told me everything?" question.

At the end, the other attorney might decide to ask you, "Have you told me everything about how this happened?" Chances are you have not, because you were not asked questions about everything. You are only required to answer what was asked, so do not "close the book" by saying, "Yes, this is all." Instead, what you can say is, "Yes, as far as I can recall, that's about all. I have tried to answer your questions. I believe I have answered them the best I know how."

DD. Relax.

If you relax and talk as you would to neighbors or to friends, you will make a more credible impression.

EE. Reread these instructions the night before you testify.

Reread these instructions the night before you testify so that you will have them firmly in your mind. They will help you.

VII Ten Commandments for avoiding LC liability

A. Become familiar with your state's laws regulating the practice of medicine.

   1. Check the Medical Practice Act—are you a "physician extender" or an "allied health professional"?

   2. Check the provisions regarding the unauthorized practice of medicine.

B. Become familiar with your hospital/clinic/office protocols. (If there are none, write your own.) Helpful references include "Standards of Practice for IBLCE Lactation Consultants" available from the International Lactation Consultant Association, 1500 Sunday Dr., Suite 102, Raleigh, NC 27607; Telephone (919) 787-4916; E-mail ilca@erols.com; and the "IBLCE Code of Ethics" available from the International Board of Lactation Consultant Examiners, 7309 Arlington Blvd., Suite 300, Falls Church, VA 22042-3215; Telephone (703) 560-7330; Fax (703) 560-7332; and E-mail iblce@erols.com.

C. Obtain malpractice insurance. You might need two policies: Your employer's "umbrella" policy plus your own personal professional negligence coverage.

D. Keep your insurance continuously in force.[54]

---

[54] Most professional liability policies are written on a "claims made" basis which means that the policy must be in force at the time the claim is presented as opposed to when the incident actually occurred. The majority of policies require that claims be reported within 30 days after the policyholder receives notice of the incident.

E. Build a positive relationship with your clients. (Common courtesy cures most claims.)

F. Do not guarantee results or create unrealistic expectations for your clients.[55]

G. Act as a consultant—do not make decisions for your clients. Instead, outline options and disclose risks.

H. Do not take certain clients (if the client gives you negative "vibrations"; if you do not have the time to handle the case; and if the case is beyond your level of competence).

I. Document what you do. Also document what you chose *not* to do and why. Create "friendly" records, because patients might see them. Organize your desk to make this activity easier.

   1. A file holder containing blanks of your most-used forms

   2. A Rolodex or file box with client information

   3. A telephone opposite your dominant hand

   4. Be compulsive—hand-write notes as you go, and do not get behind; use triplicate/carbonized forms (one copy each for the LC, doctor, hospital, or clinic [supervising or referring entity], and the client).

J. Limit your personal liability in case of a malpractice claim.

   1. Obtain legal advice.

   2. Consider holding real estate as "tenants by the entireties" with your spouse.

   3. Consider creating an entity for your practice.

   4. Investigate transferring some assets to an "inter vivos" trust.

# Appendix 31–A

## Notes on Battery

(We refer to "battery" in this chapter as possible grounds for a case against a health care provider who gives supplements or uses artificial nipples without the parents' consent.)

**Battery:**   Common-law grounds for a possible case against a health care provider who gives supplements or uses artificial nipples without the parents' consent (absent a medical emergency[56]). Although there is no case law on point, ordinary common-law battery might prove

---

[55] If the LC promised a particular result (as distinguished from a generalized statement) and the result is not as promised, a "breach of warranty" claim could be brought. *Guilmet v. Campbell*, 385 Mich 57, 188 NW2d, 601 (1971); *Depenbrok v. Kaiser Found. Health Plan*, 79 Cal App 3d 138, 144 CalRptr 724, 726 (1978).

[56] Absent emergency, patients have the right to determine not only whether surgery is to be performed on them, but who shall perform it. *Perna v. Pirozzi*, 92 NJ 446, 457, A2d 431, 439 (1983).

to be a valuable weapon in the arsenal protecting parents' desires that their infants be exclusively breastfed. Absent an emergency or other unusual medical circumstances, battery can be used as the basis for bringing a suit against health care providers who ignore the parents' directions that their infant receive breast milk only (no water and no nipples or teats).

Theoretically, two distinct interests are protected by the cause of battery. First, the interest in the physical integrity of the body—that it be free from harmful contacts—and second, the purely dignitary interest in the body that it be free from offensive contacts.

In the United States, the "perfect case" based on this theory would be one involving a routine prenatal history and a healthy, full-term baby who experienced no medical complications in which the parents notified their health care providers (pediatrician, hospital, and so on) of their wishes in writing prior to the delivery and again upon admission. A "breastfeed only" notice to this effect would also be placed on the baby's isolette.

A. Elements of the case:[57] In most jurisdictions, to prevail in a case alleging battery against a health care provider who gives a baby supplements without the parents' consent, the parents would have to prove the following elements by a preponderance of the evidence:

1. Intention:[58] That the provider intended to bring about a touching that was harmful[59] or offensive to the infant (note that a touching or other contact in a courteous or merely casual manner for a legitimate purpose[60] or one unavoidably made[61] will not usually support an allegation of battery[62]). In legal terms, a result is "intended" if the act is done for the purpose of accomplishing a certain result or with the knowledge of a substantial certainty such that a result will ensue. Usually, all that is necessary is a) that the provider engaged in volitional activity and b) that the provider intended to violate another's legally protected interest in his person. It is not necessary to show that the provider entertained

---

[57] "Elements" are the individual parts of an allegation that must be proved by a plaintiff if the plaintiff is to win the lawsuit. The plaintiff must prove each of them in order to prevail.

[58] Some courts may still extend the idea of battery to include direct but unintended injuries if they were caused by negligence. For the most part, however, battery is not regarded as including negligent injuries.

[59] See, e.g., International Lactation Consultant Association, "Summary of the Hazards of Infant Formula." Single copies may be purchased for $1.50 each by writing ILCA at 200 N. Michigan Avenue, Suite 300, Chicago, Il 60601-3821.

[60] Belcher v. United States, 511 FSupp. 476, 483 (ED Pa 1981); Gatto v. Publix Supermarket, Inc., 387 So2d 377 (Fla App. 1980).

[61] Austin v. Metropolitan Life Ins. Co., 106 Wash 371, 180 P 134, 6 ALR. 1061 (1919); Hoffman v. Eppers, 41 Wisc 251 (1876).

[62] However, in the case of a supersensitive person known to resent contact not offensive to a normal person, a deliberate touching for the purpose of offense would probably involve liability. See, e.g., Richmond v. Fiske, 160 Mass 34, 35 NE 103 (1893).

a hostile intent toward the baby or to even show the intent to cause the baby injury or embarrassment. The provider's intention to bring about an unpermitted contact is sufficient.[63]

2. Touching: That the provider actually touched the baby in an offensive or harmful way. The contact need not consist of an immediate contact between the body of the provider and the body of the person who was hurt or offended.[64] In fact, it is enough if the contact is made with anything that is sufficiently connected with the person as to have the same practical effect.[65] A baby bottle meets this standard. Moreover, there is support in the reported case law for the proposition that it is a battery to cause another to ingest a substance without his consent.[66]

3. Without consent: That the baby's parents or guardians did not consent to the touching. A touching without consent equals battery if it is not an accidental touching or a contact excused by emergency circumstances.

a. Medical Procedures/Treatments/Therapies:
In the absence of any consent, a physician is subject to liability in battery for treatments that involve touching the patient. See *Lounsbury v Capel*, 836 P.2d 188, 192 (Utah App.1992) [holding that a patient, who alleged that surgery was performed on him without his consent, stated a common law claim for battery]; the Matter of A.C., 573 A.2d 1235, 1243 (1990) [A "surgeon who performs an operation without the patient's consent may be guilty of a battery . . . or . . . (who) obtains an insufficiently informed consent . . . may be liable for negligence."]; *Tonelli v Khanna*, 238 N.J. Super 121, 569 A.2d 282, 285 (App. Div. 1990) [doctor who conducts surgery

---

[63] *Kling v. Landry*, 686 N.E.2d 33 (Ill.App.Ct. 1997). For these reasons, mistake is not a defense to battery, "inevitable accident" is. In an accident, the interest-invasion is unintended and inevitable. because the consequences alleged to be wrong are "not intended by the provider and could not have been foreseen and avoided by the exercise of reasonable care and skill." Salmond and Heuston *On The Law Of Torts* 29 (18th ed. Heuston and Chambers, 1981).

[64] It may result from the throwing of an object. *See, e.g., Singer v. Marx*, 144 CalApp 2d 637, 301 P2d 40 (1956) [Stone]; *Barbara A. v. John G.*, 145 Cal App 3d 369, 193 CalRptr 422 (1983)[impregnation that exceeded scope of plaintiff's consent to intercourse with her lawyer].

[65] *See, e.g., Crossman v. Thurlow*, 336 Mass 252, 143 NE2d 814 (1957) [battery occurred when a person deliberately drove an automobile into the rear of a vehicle in which another person was sitting]; *Garratt v. Dailey*, 46 Wash2d 197, 279 P2d 1091 (1955)[(battery committed by removing a chair on which another was about to sit]; *Reynolds v. Pierson*, 29 IndApp 273, 64 NE 484 (1902) [defendant committed battery by pushing a person on whom another was leaning].

[66] *State v. Monroe*, 121 N.C. 677, 28 SE 547, 43 LRA 861, 61 AmSt Rep. 686 (1897); *Mink v. University of Chicago*, 460 FSupp 713 (ND Ill 1978)[defendants caused pregnant women who had gone to university hospital for prenatal care to take pills of diethylstilbestrol (DES), without being told they were taking DES of that they were participating in an experiment]. *But see, Boyer v. Smith*, 345 Pa Super Ct 66, 497 A2d 646 (1985) [holding that there is no duty to obtain consent to the administration of a therapeutic drug].

without patient's consent engages in unauthorized touching and thus commits battery]; *Moser v Stallings*, 387 N.W.2d 599, 601 (Iowa 1986); *Cowman v Hornaday*, 329 N.W.2d 422, 424 (Iowa, 1983); *Perna v Pirozzi*, 92 N.J. 446, 457, A.2d 431, 438 (1983) [any nonconsensual touching is a battery]; *Lojuk v Quandt*, 706 F.2d 1456 (7th Cir. 1983) [psychiatrist's administration of electroconvulsive therapy without patient's consent, intentionally and not merely negligently, is battery and not malpractice]; but compare *Vargas v Rosal-Arcillas*, 108 Misc.2d 881, 438 N.Y.S.2d 986,987-988 (Spec. Term 1981); *Hales v Pittman*, 118 Ariz. 305, 576 P.2d 493 (1978) [if no consent to operation, then battery occurred], but see Id. n.3, referring to statutory abrogation of battery cause of action enacted after this suit arose, c.f. Ariz. Rev. Stat. Ann. §12-562(B)(1982); *Perin v Hayne*, 210 N.W.2d 609, 618 (Iowa 1973).

b. There is no need to prove injury to the baby. It is not necessary for a person who is claiming battery to have sustained any actual injury. The suit is based upon the person's right to determine what will be done with his or her own body.[67] Consequently, if a provider ignores the baby's right to physical integrity, an injury to the baby's dignity is presumed, and the baby is entitled to collect damages—even in those cases where the touching actually benefited the baby.[68] A battery claim can also arise when the parents have consented to one kind of procedure, treatment, or therapy and the provider deviates from the consent and performs a substantially different procedure or provides a substantially different treatment or therapy. In such a case, the requisite element of deliberate intent to deviate from the consent given is present.[69]

B. Damages available:

1. Nominal damages—Generally, common-law battery does not require that nonconsensual conduct be injurious; rather, proof of unauthorized invasion of

---

[67] *Schloendorff v. Society of N.Y. Hospital*, 211 N.Y. 125, 105 NE 92 (1914).

[68] *See, e.g.*, Kold E.A., Ramseyer N.: "Truman v. Thomas: Informed Refusal In Simple Diagnostic Testing." *Univ. Ca. Davis Law Rev.* 14:1105-20, 1981; *Perna v. Pirozzi*, 92 NJ 446, 457, A2d 431, 439 (1983) [Nonconsensual touching remains battery, even if performed skillfully and to the benefit of the patient].

[69] *Perin v. Hayne*, 210 NW2d 609, 618 (Iowa 1973); *Moser v. Stallings*, 387 NW2d 599, 601 (Iowa 1986); *Perin v. Hayne*, 210 NW2d 609, 617-18 (Iowa 1973); *Canterbury v. Spence*, 464 F2d 772, 782-783 (USApp DC 1972); *Berkey v. Anderson*, 1 Cal App 3d 790, 82 Cal Rptr 67 (1969) [allegation of consent to permit doctor to perform a procedure no more complicated than the electromyograms plaintiff had previously undergone, when he actual procedure was a myelogram involving a spinal puncture]; *Bang v. Charles T. Miller Hosp.*, 251 Minn 427, 88 NW2d 186 (1958) [plaintiff consented to a prostate resection when uninformed that this procedure involved tying off his sperm ducts]; *Corn v. French*, 71 Nev. 280, 289 P2d 173 (1955)[patient consented to exploratory surgery; doctor performed mastectomy]; *Bonner v. Moran*, 126 F2d 121, 122-123 (U.S. App. D.C. 1941); *Zoterell v. Repp*, 187 Mich319, 153 NW 692 (1915) [consent given for a hernia operation during which doctor also removed both ovaries].

the plaintiff's person, even if harmless, entitles him to at least nominal damages. *Lounsbury v Capel*, 836 P2d 188, 192 (Utah App. 1992) and *Perna v Pirozzi*, 92 NJ 446, 457, A2d 431, 438 (1983) [under battery theory, proof of unauthorized invasion of plaintiff's person, even if harmless, entitles him to nominal damages] explore this concept.

2. Recovery for injuries proximately caused—Under battery theory, a patient can recover for all injuries proximately caused by the mere performance of an operation to which he has not consented, whether the same is the result of negligence or not (*Perna v Pirozzi*, 92 NJ 446, 457, A2d 431, 438 [1983]).

C. Insurance coverage—Some malpractice policies might not cover battery because of an exclusion of liability for criminal acts (*Trogun v Fruchtman*, 58 Wisc2d 596, 599-600, 207 NW2d 297, 312-313 [1973]).

D. No need to prove that the provider deviated from the standard of care—A doctor has a duty to provide his or her personal services in accordance with his agreement with the patient (*Perna v Pirozzi*, 92 N. 446, 457, A2d 431, 440 [1983]). In an action against a physician predicated upon battery, the patient need not prove initially that the physician has deviated from the professional standard of care (*Perna v. Pirozzi*, 92 NJ 446, 457, A2d 431, 438 [1983]).

E. In most jurisdictions, a consented touching for which consent was induced by inadequate information is not battery but negligence (malpractice).[70]

1. The statute of limitations for negligence is often more favorable than for battery (*Canterbury v Spence*, 464 F2d 772, 793-94 [D.C. Cir. 1972]). If it is not possible for the parents to claim battery as a cause of action, however, due to the running of the statute of limitations, they might be able to allege battery as an affirmative defense entitling them to a right of set-off.[71] Alternatively, if the

---

[70] The case law of the state of Pennsylvania is an exception to this rule. In Pennsylvania, if informed consent was not given, this is treated as the legal equivalent of no consent having been given, and the action is then treated as an action for battery (not negligence). *Gouse v. Cassel*, 532 Pa 197, 615 A2d 331, 334 (1992); *Sagala v. Tavares*, 533 A2d 165 (Pa Super 1987); *Boyer v. Smith*, 345 Pa Super Ct 66, 497 A2d 646 (1985); *Salis v. United States*, 522 F Supp 989 (Md Pa 1981); *Gray v. Grunnagle*, 423 Pa 144, 233 A2d 633 (1966). Pennsylvania courts have further limited the use of the informed consent doctrine to cases involving surgical or operative medical procedures. *Boyer v. Smith*, 345 Pa Super Ct 66, 497 A2d 646 (1985) [holding that the defendant had no duty to obtain a patient's informed consent to the administration of a therapeutic drug].

[71] See, e.g., Federal Rules of Civil Procedure 13(c); 54 C.J.S. Limitation of Actions 38 and entries under West's Key Number Limitation of Actions #41 (setoff). *Basic Boats, Inc. v. United States*, 311 FSupp. 596, 14 FR Serv2d 180 (EDVa. 1970); *Stone v. White*, 301 US 532, 57 SCt 851, 81 LE 1265 (1937); and *Sullivan v. Hoover*, 6 FRD 513, 10 FRServ. 13a121, Case 1 (DDC. 1947). *Compare*, for example, D.C. Code Ann. §12-301 [granting a one year statute of limitations for bringing an action based on battery] with D.C. Code Ann. §16-3904 and *Johnson v. Fairfax Village Condo*, IV, 641 A2d 495, 508 (DCApp 1994) [permitting a defense of battery to be used as a shield (set-off and recoupment) so long as the otherwise time-barred battery claim arises out of the same transaction as the plaintiff's claim].

health care provider took affirmative action to conceal the battery, the statute of limitations might be tolled for the period of concealment.[72]

2. Parents who decide to inform their health care providers about their wishes prior to delivery should do so in writing. In many jurisdictions, the letter could be worded something like the following page:

# Appendix 31–B

A. What are the elements of an action alleging failure to obtain informed consent?

1. Duty—There must be a relationship that gives rise to the duty to disclose. In many jurisdictions, this duty is limited to the relationship between the treating physician and the patient.[73]

2. Breach—A breach of a health care provider's duty to obtain informed consent (after disclosing material facts, risks, complications, and alternatives to the proposed treatment) must be established on the facts of each case.

3. In each case, a material risk to the patient must exist. Query: Which risks associated with formula feeding are "material," and under what circumstances?

   a. There is case law to support the proposition that the disclosures should be specific to the patient's treatment.[74] Query: Does this statement mean that a physician who did not alert parents to the risk of allergy in a family that has a history of allergies apparent on the face of the medical record could be found not to have obtained their informed consent to formula feed?

   b. The Materiality Standard—In the United States, the various state courts use one of two tests for determining a material risk:

      i. The prudent patient standard (majority view)—Whether a reasonable person in the patient's position would attach significance to undisclosed

---

[72] *Mink v. University of Chicago*, 460 FSupp 713, 721 (ND Ill 1978); *Baker v. Monsanto*, 962 FS 1143, 1161, (SD Ind 1997).

[73] *Auler v. Van Natta*, 686 NE2d 172, 174-75 (Ind. Ct. App. 1997)(holding that although the physician had a duty to make "reasonable disclosures of material facts relevant to the decision the patient is required to make"a hospital had no independent legal duty to obtain the patient's informed consent, where the physician was not an agent or employee of the hospital and no other special circumstances were present. *Also see Giese v. Stice*, 252 NE 913, 567 NW2d 156, 162-63 (1997); *Krane v.Saint Anthony Hospital*, 738 P2d 75, 77 (Colo. Ct.App 1987); *Cross v. Trapp*, 170 WVa 459, 294 SE2d 446, 459 (1982). *But see, Keel v. St. Elizabeth Medical Center*, 842 SW2d 860 (Ky 1990).

[74] *Barnes v. Gorman*, 605 S02d 805 (Miss 1992).

*Parents Names*
*Parents' Address*
*Date*

*By Certified Mail, Return Receipt Requested to:*

*HOSPITAL and address*
*PEDIATRICIAN and address*
*OBSTETRICIAN and address*

*Dear _____:*

*I expect to deliver my child at _____ (name of hospital) on or about
_____ (date). I have made the decision to breastfeed. Consequently, I direct that
my newborn not be given water, formula, artificial nipples (this prohibition includes teats,
dummies, and pacifiers) or any substance other than human milk except in the case of an
unavoidable medical emergency under circumstances where consent cannot be given either by
myself or my husband, _____ (husband's full name).*

*In the event of an emergency for which supplemental feeding is necessary, donor human
milk should be used. Given this advance notice, there is virtually no reason why my newborn
should be given formula, because there is time for donor milk to be ordered.*

*IN LETTER TO OBSTETRICIAN, ADD THE FOLLOWING: Please place this
letter in my medical record.*

*IN LETTER TO PEDIATRICIAN, ADD THE FOLLOWING: Please place a copy
of this letter in a place where you will see it immediately upon my baby's birth.*

*IN LETTER TO HOSPITAL, ADD THE FOLLOWING: I am enclosing two copies
of this letter. Please place a copy of this letter in both my medical record and that of my
infant.*

*Sincerely,*

information in deciding whether to consent to treatment, considering the nature and severity of the harm and the probability of its occurrence[75]

   ii. The prudent provider standard (minority view)—What would a reasonably prudent health care provider have disclosed under the circumstances?[76] Establishing this standard at trial usually requires expert testimony unless it is obvious to lay people that a particular risk was one that should have been disclosed.

4. Proximate cause—The plaintiff in an action against a provider for failure to obtain informed consent generally will be required to show that the provider's failure to obtain the patient's informed consent was the proximate cause of any injury to the plaintiff.[77] Depending upon the jurisdiction, an objective or a subjective standard might be applied to make this determination:

   a. Subjective standard—In those courts that apply a subjective standard, the issue of proximate cause often turns exclusively on the presentation and credibility of testimony by the plaintiff that he or she would have withheld consent if he or she had been adequately informed (*Dessi v United States*, 489 F.Supp 722 [ED Va 1980]).

   b. Objective standard—Other courts have adopted an objective standard of causation because of the likelihood of a patient's bias in testifying in hindsight on this hypothetical matter. This objective test can be articulated as follows: Would a reasonable person in the plaintiff's position have consented to the treatment if the risks involved had been adequately disclosed?[78]

   Even if this objective standard is applied, however, it is usually necessary to present evidence that the patient personally would not have consented to the proposed treatment if he or she had been fully informed of the nature

---

[75] *Canterbury v. Spence*, 464 F2d 772 (DC Cir 1972); *Price v. Hurt*, 711 SW2d 84 (Tex App 1986); *Largey v. Rothman*, 110 NJ 204, 540 A2d 504 (1988); *Precourt v. Frederick*, 395 Me 689, 481 NE2d 1144 (1985); *Sagala v. Tavares*, 533 A2d 165, (Pa Super 1987); *Kennis v. Mercy Hospital Medical Center*, 491 NW2d 161 (Iowa 1992); *Wilkerson v. Mid-America Cardiology*, 908 SW2d 691 (Mo App 1995).

[76] *Geise v. Stice*, 567 NW2d 156, 252 Neb 913, (Neb 1997); Ouellette v. Mehalic, 534 A2d 1331 (Me 1988); *Royball v. Bell*, 778 P2d 108 (Wyo 1989).

[77] *Brown v. Dahl*, 41 Wash App 565, 705 P2d 781 (1985); *Jacobs v. Painter*, 530 A2d 231 (Me 1987).

[78] E.g. *Canterbury v. Spence*, 150 App DC 263, 464 F2d 772 (DC Cir 1072) *cert denied* 409 US 1064 (1972); *Guebard v. Jabaay*, 117 Ill App 3d 1, 72 Ill Dec 498, 452 NE2d 751 (1983). Under this test, the patient's testimony is relevant, but not controlling. *Hartke v. McKelway*, 228 App DC 139, 707 F2d 1544 (DC Cir 1983) *cert denied* (US) 104, SCt 425, 78 LE2d 360 (1983); *Wooley v. Henderson*, 418 A2d 1123 (Me 1980); *Roybal v. Bell*, 778 P2d 108 (Wyo 1989); *Livingston v. LaNasa*, 552 So2d 1281 (La App 1989).

and possible consequences (because failure to disclose is not actionable if full disclosure would not have precluded the plaintiff's consent).[79]

5.  Injury resulting from treatment—The plaintiff must show that the treatment performed without informed consent resulted in an injury to the patient.

    a.  In every case, the plaintiff must show that the adverse consequences that the provider failed to disclose did in fact materialize to the patient's detriment.[80]

    b.  The plaintiff might also be required to show that the injury that materialized was in fact caused by the treatment provided and was not attributable to some other cause.[81]

6.  Damages—As with any case, the plaintiff must prove the nature and value of the damages suffered.

B.  Defenses

1.  Informed consent statutes—Some states in the United States have enacted informed consent legislation. For example, a statute might describe or limit[82] the disclosures required. A statute might also limit the scope of a provider's duty to obtain informed consent by eliminating the duty to disclose the risks of treatment or by stating that a written consent conforming to statutory provisions will be presumed valid.[83]

2.  Written consent forms—Although a written consent form will be considered as evidence that the patient's informed consent was obtained, it is not usually conclusive,[84] particularly if the form is too general,[85] confusing, or ambiguous.[86]

---

[79] *Canterbury v. Spence*, 464 F2d 772, 780 (D.C. Cir), *cert. denied*, 409 US 1064 (1972); *St.Gemme v. Tomlin*, 118 Ill App 3d 766, 74 Ill Dec. 264, 455 NE2d 294 (1983); *Buzzell v. Libi*, 340 NW2d 36 (ND 1983); *Scott v. Bradford*, 606 P2d 554 (Okla 1979); *But See, Gouse v. Cassel*, 532 Pa 197, 615 A2d 331, 334 (1992).

[80] *Canterbury v. Spence*, 150 App DC 263, 464 F2d 772 (DC Cir 1972) *cert denied* 409 US 1064 (1972); *Hales v. Pittman*, 118 Ariz 305, 576 P2d 493 (1978); *Masquat v. Maguire*, 683 P2d 1105 (Okla 1981).

[81] *Cornfeldt v. Tongen*, 295 NW2d 638 (Minn 1980); *Roberson v. Menorah Medical Center*, 588 SW2d 134 (Mo App 1979); *Reiser v. Lohner*, 641 P2d 93 (Utah 1982).

[82] *See. e.g., LaCaze v. Collier*, 434 So2d 1039 (La 1983) [La Rev Stat §40:1299 requires broader disclosure of risks than that required by case law, but relieves physicians of the duty to disclose alternative treatments when written consent is obtained in compliance with statutory provisions].

[83] *See. e.g., Robinson v. Parish*, 251 Ga 496, 306 SE2d 922 (1983) [providing that under Georgia's Medical Consent Law, Ga. Doe Ann §88-2906, physicians must only inform patients of the general terms of treatment and need not disclose risks]; Meretsky v. Ellenby, 370 So2d 1222 (Fla. App. 1979) [citing the Florida Medical Consent Law, FLA STAT §768.46 (1981)].

[84] *Siegel v. Mt. Sinai Hospital*, 62 Ohio App 2d 12, 403 N. E. 2d 202 (1978); *Valcin v. Public Health*, 473 So2d 11297 (Fla App 1984) [standard consent form found insufficient to establish that patient's consent was adequately informed]; *Also See, Adams v. Richland Clinic, Inc.*, 37 Wash App 650, 681 P2d 1305 (1984).

[85] *Mederos v. Yashar*, 588 A2d 1038 (RI 1991).

[86] *Mederios v. Yashar*, 588 A2d 1038 (RI 1991).

Standard consent forms alone ordinarily do not provide sufficient information about the disclosures made to the patient to establish that the patient's consent was an adequately informed one.[87] A consent form will be given effect as a defense, however, if all of the evidence supports a conclusion that the patient was informed about the treatment to which he or she consented.[88]

a. A written consent form will also serve to establish a defense to an informed consent action if it conforms to a statute providing that consent obtained in writing and in compliance with statutory specifications will be conclusively presumed as valid. (For example, under the Georgia Medical Consent Law, Ga. Code Ann §§88-2906, physicians must only inform patient of general terms of treatment and need not disclose risks.[89])

b. Proposed practice tip: LCs who are in a busy practice can obtain a measure of legal protection with regard to courses of treatment frequently followed (for example, mastitis) by writing an information sheet as long as the same are updated on a regular basis. The LC should ask the mother (or both parents, if they are available) to sign and date two identical forms below a typed statement saying that she (or they) acknowledges receipt of the information. One copy of the form should remain in the physician's files, and the other should be given to the mother. When determining the information to include in such a form, consider the following recommendations:

    i. Consult with other care providers to determine what risks of the alternatives to breastfeeding they explain to their patients.

    ii. Consult current medical literature to determine the frequency and severity of risks and the availability of reasonable alternative modes of those alternatives.

    iii. Supplement the above with those additional risks that are serious or life-threatening, even though infrequently encountered.

    iv. Add to the form additional information that you believe the average, prudent patient would want to have explained in order to give an informed consent.

---

[87] *Pegram v. Sisco*, 406 FSupp 776 (WD Ark 1976) *aff'd* 547 F2d 1172 (8th Cir 1976); *LePelley v. Grefenson*, 101 Idaho 422, 614 P2d 962 (1980); *Karl J. Pizzalotto MD Ltd v. Wilson*, 437 So2d 859 (La. 1983) remd 444 So2d 143 (La App 1983); *LaCaze v. Collier*, 434 So2d 1039 (1983); *Roberson v. Menorah Medical Center*, 588 SW2d 134 (Mo App 1979); *Gray v. Grunnagle*, 423 Pa. 144, 233 A2d 633 (1966); *Cross v. Trapp*, 294 SE2d 446 (W. Va. 1982).

[88] *See, Rogers v. Brown*, 416 So2d 624 (La. App. 1982). In this case the patient's consent was established on the basis of a consent form where the physician and nurse testified that risks of treatment were fully explained to the patient and the form was completed, signed, and given to the patient.

[89] *Meretsky v. Ellenby*, 370 So2d 1222 (Fla App 1979); *Robinson v. Parrish*, 251 Fa496, 306 SE2d 922 (1983).

3. Negating one or more of the elements of the plaintiff's case—Nonliability in an action for failure to obtain informed consent to treatment generally can be established by negating one or more of the elements of the plaintiff's case. The defendant might be able to do so by showing that:

   a. The defendant had no duty to disclose any information about the treatment beyond that which actually was disclosed—A provider might be able to establish a lack of duty by showing that the risk was remote in the sense that it materializes only in a small percentage of the cases in which the treatment is carried out.[90] Likewise, there is no duty to disclose a risk that causes no serious adverse effects even if it does materialize.[91]

   b. The risk that materialized was not a known risk.[92]

   c. The disclosures were adequate, and there was therefore no breach of the duty to obtain informed consent.[93]

   d. The defendant's alleged nondisclosure was not a proximate cause of the plaintiff's injury.

   e. No feasible alternative available—The duty to obtain informed consent generally includes the duty to disclose the possibility of alternatives to the proposed treatment, but no such disclosures are required when no feasible alternatives are available.[94]

   f. The duty to disclose conformed to the standard of care based on the typical disclosure practices of similarly situated physicians—In jurisdictions where this standard exists, a defendant might be able to establish liability by

---

[90] *Riedinger v. Colburn*, 361 FSupp 1073 (Idaho 1973) [Idaho law; physician had no duty to disclose risk that permanent vocal cord paralysis could occur where evidence of over 600 cases in which operation had been performed without causing permanent vocal damage established remoteness of risk]. Note, however, that a physician is generally required to disclose even a small chance of death or serious disability, particularly if it would be feasible for the patient to avoid the risk by declining the treatment. *Canterbury v. Spence*, 150 App DC 263, 464 F2d 772 (DC Cir 1972) *cert denied* 409 US 1064 (1972).

[91] *Wiley v. Karam*, 421 So2d 294 (La App 1982) [dentist did not have a duty to warn patient of risk that root canal reamer would break and become lodged in tooth during root canal procedure because breakage of reamer generally has no significant consequences].

[92] *E.g., Trogun v. Fruchtman*, 58 Wis2d 569, 207 NW2d 297 (1973) [physician not negligent in failing to warm patient that drug might cause hepatitis where danger was unknown to medical community at time of treatment].

[93] *Roberts v. Wood*, 206 FSupp 579 (SD Ala 1962); *Contreras v. St. Luke's Hospital*, 78 Cal App 3d 919, 144 Cal Rptr 647 (1978); *Lindquist v. Ayerst Laboratories, Inc.*, 227 Kan 308, 607 P2d 1339 (1980).

[94] *Green v. Hussey*, 1127 Ill App 2d 174, 262 NE2d 156 (1970) [physician had no duty to disclose risk that post-mastectomy cobalt radiation therapy would create risk of fibrosis of lung where no alternative post-operative treatment was available]; *Downer v. Veilleux*, 322 A2d 82 (Me 1974) [physician did not have duty to discuss alternatives to placing patient's broken leg in traction where no feasible alternative treatment was available].

showing that the disclosures made conformed to this standard. (Refer to the discussion of the "Prudent Provider Standard" previous.)

4. Genuine emergency—There is usually no duty to make informed consent disclosures in an emergency that requires immediate action or that precludes a considered decision by a patient.[95]

5. Therapeutic privilege—The provider can withhold disclosure of a material risk when the provider reasonably foresees that the disclosure will cause the patient to become so ill or so emotionally distraught as to foreclose a rational decision.[96]

6. The patient who has waived his or her right to the particular information—Theoretically, a patient or his or her representative can waive the provider's obligation to obtain informed consent if the patient or his or her representative insisted that the patient not be informed of the nature of the treatment or of the accompanying risks.[97]

7. The duty to disclose was discharged—This situation can occur when the patient is advised of the possibility that unexpected complications might require the physician to utilize previously uncontemplated procedures, after which the patient authorizes the physician to exercise his or her discretion in determining how to proceed.[98]

8. The "undisclosed" risk was obvious.

9. The patient had independent knowledge of the information that the provider allegedly should have disclosed—Showing that the patient had independent knowledge of information that the provider failed to disclose essentially establishes that there was no duty to disclose that information[99] or that the failure to disclose was not a proximate cause of the plaintiff's injury.[100]

---

[95] e.g., *Koegan v. Holy Family Hospital*, 95 Wash2d 306, 622 P2d 1246 (1980); *Plutshack v. Univ. of Minn. Hospitals*, 316 NW2d 1 (Minn, 1982); *Mroczkowski v. Straub Clinic & Hospital, Inc.*, 732 P2d 1255 (Hawaii App 1987). *But See, Sard v. Hardy*, 281 Md 432, 379 A2d 1014 (1977) [Where the patient is capable of giving the consent to treatment and there is no immediate threat to the patient's life or health, a showing the patient was in pain will not alone be sufficient to establish an emergency]; *Cunningham v. Yanklin Clinic P.A.*, 262 NW2d 508 (SD 1978) and *Dewes v. Indian Health Service*, 504 FSupp 203 (D SD 1980) [both finding that an emergency which incapacitates the patient will not necessarily excuse a failure to obtain the consent of a person capable of acting on the person's behalf].

[96] *Roberts v. Wood*, 206 FSupp 579 (SD Ala 1962); *Nishi v. Hartwell*, 52 Hawaii 188, 473 P2d 116 (1970); *Canterbury v. Spence*, 150 App DC 263, 464 F2d 772 (DC Cir 1972) *cert denied* 409 US 1064 (1972).

[97] *Salis v. United States*, 522 F. Supp 989 (MD Pa 1981) [Pennsylvania law]; *Cobbs v. Grant*, 8 Cal3d 229, 104 Cal Rptr 505, 502 P2d 1 (1972); *Putensen v. Clay Adams, Inc.*, 12 Cal App 3d 1064, 91 Cal Rptr. 319 (1970).

[98] *Charley v. Cameron*, 215 Kan 750, 528 P2d 1205 (1974); *Carman v. Dippold*, 63 Ill App 3d 419, 20 Ill Dec 297, 379 NE2d 1365 (1978).

[99] *Canterbury v. Spence*, 150 App DC 263, 464 F2d 772 (DC Cir 1972) *cert denied* 409 US 1064 (1972).

[100] *Kinikin v. Heupel*, 305 NW2d 589 (Minn 1981).

# Appendix 31–C

## Notes on Herbal Remedies

The incredible ease with which herbal supplements can be purchased might lead some LCs to believe that it is safe to suggest that their clients use them, particularly because no prescription is necessary. Unless there is evidence to support the use of a particular supplement, however, making such a recommendation has the potential to subject an LC to liability for professional negligence.

Currently, the peer-reviewed research basis for recommending herbal remedies appears to be virtually non-existent. In addition, many (if not most) herbal supplements continue to be inadequately tested, inadequately labeled, and poorly made, causing dosages to vary greatly. For example, in the United States, the *Dietary Supplements Health and Education Act of 1994*[101] (DSHEA) has left the *Food and Drug Administration* (FDA) impotent to regulate these processes,[102] so the suppliers of these substances are free to make health claims about them for which there is little or no scientific proof indicating their effectiveness (or the absence of side effects).

# Appendix 31–D

## Tips for Organizing, Running, and Enjoying a Home Business

A. Obtain insurance.

Ask your home insurance provider about your property and liability coverage. Many home insurance policies do not automatically cover businesses that are run from the home, but you can obtain adequate coverage simply by purchasing a rider to your homeowner's policy. The cost will be nominal, provided that you do not have visitors to your home office. If you plan to see clients in your home office, however,

---

[101] Public Law 1043-417, October 25, 1994, 108 Stat. 4325.

[102] Prior to the DSHEA, the FDA asserted that it had the power to regulate supplements and sought to place the burden of proving safety and efficacy on the manufacturers and suppliers. However, the DSHEA substantially diminished federal control over these products. To its credit, despite the DSHEA, the FDA has attempted to preserve its role in preventing injury. It has advocated that nutritional statements and warnings appear on labels and it has proposed requirements that supplements meet good manufacturing practices. In addition, the FDA has used its considerable public relations powers to warn the public about the risks associated with herbal supplements and maintains a web site on the subject.

consult your insurer for advice. Whatever policy you obtain, ask about coverage for the following risks:

1. If your home burns down, will your office equipment be covered?

2. If a client is injured while visiting your home office, will you be covered if he or she sued you? Under a scenario such as this one, how can you protect yourself from the risk of losing your home?

3. If you are sued for libel, professional misconduct, or anything else related to your professional conduct as an LC, your homeowner's policy will not cover you. To protect against this kind of risk, you will need to obtain professional negligence ("malpractice") coverage.

B. Consider creating an entity.

If you expect to grow, are working with a partner, or currently have any employees, seriously consider setting up a *Limited Liability Company* (LLC). The LLC is a simple and inexpensive form of legal protection.

1. Advantages:

   a. Protection from all forms of personal liability (except for professional negligence, against which your only "hedge" is a personal malpractice policy). Types of risks that the entity can shield you from personally include slips and falls in the office, negligent hiring, employees' claims of discrimination or wrongful termination, copyright infringement, violations of noncompete agreements, and so on.

   b. Establishing an LLC or other entity adds credibility to a business card. When I ran a business from my home, people feared that I was less professional than someone who had a downtown office. Something as simple as adding "LLC" gave people the impression of a formal, more established firm.

2. To set up an LLC or other entity, you have to file a certificate (or articles of organization or incorporation) with the appropriate agency in your state. This one- or two-page form can typically be filed for $300 to $500. It is safest, though, to hire a lawyer to ensure that it is filed correctly and that it includes the appropriate indemnification provisions. You might also have publication and other costs. Discuss the following checklist with your lawyer to make sure that you have covered the most important bases:

   a. Articles of organization or incorporation (file with your state)

   b. Certificate of organization

   c. Fictitious name certificate (file with your state and/or county)

   d. Employer's ID number (file Form SS4 with the Internal Revenue Service [IRS])

   e. Operating agreement or shareholders' agreement

   f. Establish a separate bank account

   g. Keep a record of members' (or shareholders') contributions

   h. Issue to members their certificates of membership

   i. Issue to members certificates of management (if appropriate)

   j. Employees

      1. Distinguishing independent contractors from employees

      2. Engagement agreements (including confidentiality)

      3. INS I-9 forms

      4. Federal and state withholding forms

   k. Business license (Check with your town about any permits or waivers that are necessary to run a business from your home. Many insurance contracts contain clauses stating that coverage might be affected if the policyholder is not in compliance with local laws.)

   l. Registration with your state's Department of Taxation

   m. Minutes (including organization minutes) and resolutions

   n. Annual reports/registered agent

   o. Federal tax returns (Are you self-employed, or will you be an employee?)— For a one-person LLC, rules for filing income taxes are generally quite simple, and income and expenses are reported on your *personal* form 1040, Schedule C, as if there were no LLC.

   p. State tax returns

   q. Promissory note form (so you can document any loans)

   r. Office lease (even if your office is in your home)

C. Rules to work by

When well-meaning people who have home businesses run afoul of the IRS, it is almost always because of one of two reasons: 1) They cannot prove what they claim due to poor record keeping, or 2) They commingle business and personal interests. Avoid these problems by adhering to the following rules:

   1. Set up a separate checking account for the business. Pay *every* business expense through this account.

2. If you have an LLC, sign the check with the LLC's name first. (*Example*: "Widget Co., LLC, by Jane Smith, Manager")

3. When you must buy something for the business with cash or with a personal check, pay yourself back by writing a check from the company to yourself.

4. If you need to infuse personal cash into the business, write out a formal loan document between yourself and your company. When you can repay yourself, write a check from the company account to your personal account with interest.

5. If you take a home-office deduction (people who do so face an increased risk of IRS audits), apply the IRS rules properly. Pay the appropriate portion of the bills from your business account. (Example: If your office is 10 percent of your home's square footage, make 10 percent of your utility payments from your business checking account. That could be 10 percent of each payment—or just work out the amount you expect the utility bill to be for the year and pay 10 percent of the year's total from the business account toward the end of the year.)

   Also, consider the down side of claiming the home-office deduction. When the time comes to sell the home (if the home office was used for more than three out of five years before the sale), the portion of your home that you use for business purposes will not qualify for the home-sale exclusion from capital gains taxes.

6. Meet with your accountant at least once a year. Do not just hand over your documents at tax time. It might cost you $200 to $300 for each chat, but it should save you far more in the long run. This action might not be necessary after you have run a home business for a few years. But until you feel comfortable with the tax law and formalities of running a business, it is money well spent. Schedule this meeting between May and November. Accountants tend to have more free time then than during tax-crunch time.

D. Breastfeeding advocacy

As an LC, you may be asked to provide input into legislation that is meant to protect the rights of breastfeeding women. Consider sharing your thoughts about the following issues with your local legislators. The language given is offered simply to get you started:

1. Public breastfeeding

   Notwithstanding any other provision of law, a woman[103] can breastfeed her child[104] in any location, public or private, where the woman is otherwise

---

[103] Use of the word "woman" makes this applicable to adoptive as well as natural mothers.

[104] Use of the word "child" avoids the restricting term "infant."

authorized to be, regardless of whether or not the nipple of the woman's breast is covered during or incidental to the breastfeeding. Any person who violates this section shall be fined not less than $100 or imprisoned not more than 30 days or both. In addition, a private action for monetary damages and/or equitable relief can be brought in order to enforce this section by the woman who is aggrieved and/or by any person who is entitled to sue on behalf of the aggrieved child. If a violation of this section is proved in such a private action, each aggrieved party shall be entitled, in addition to any other appropriate relief, to presumed damages in an amount equal to $100 plus three times the reasonable attorneys fees and costs that party incurred.

2. Automatic excuse from jury service

A person shall be excused from jury service if the person submits written documentation verifying, to the court's satisfaction, that the person is solely responsible for the daily care of a person who has a permanent disability living in the person's household and that the performance of juror service would cause substantial risk of injury to the health of the person with a disability, or that the person is the mother of a breastfed child and is responsible for the daily care of the child. If the person is regularly employed at a location other than the person's household, however, the person shall not be excused under this section.

Refer to the chart on page 476 for more information about the material presented in this chapter.

# Bibliography

Bornmann P. Legal considerations and the lactation consultant—USA. Unit 3. The Lactation Consultant Series, Wayne, NJ: Avery Publishing Group, 1986.

Harper J, Harper G. The law of torts, 2nd ed. Boston: Little Brown and Company (as supplemented through 2000).

International Board of Lactation Consultant Examiners. IBCLC Code of Ethics. See Chapter 32, this volume.

International Lactation Consultant Association. Standards of Practice for IBCLC Lactation Consultants.

Smith LJ. Expert witness: What to emphasize. *J Hum Lact* 1991; 7(3):141.

Suhler A, Bornmann P, Scott J. The lactation consultant as expert witness. *J Hum Lact* 1991; 7(3):129–140.

Taraska J. Legal guide for physicians. New York: Mathew Bender and Co., Inc., 1990 (as supplemented through 2000).

Wold C. Managing your medical practice. New York: Mathew Bender and Co., Inc., 1989 (as supplemented through 2000).

# THE CODE OF ETHICS FOR INTERNATIONAL BOARD-CERTIFIED LACTATION CONSULTANTS: ETHICAL PRACTICE

*JoAnne Scott, MA, IBCLC*

## OBJECTIVES:

- Define the purpose of the code of ethics for International Board-Certified Lactation Consultants from the International Board of Lactation Consultant Examiners (IBLCE).
- Discuss each provision as it relates to lactation consultant (LC) practice.
- Describe how to report violations of the code of ethics.

## Introduction

The purpose of the code of ethics is to provide guidance to International Board-Certified Lactation Consultants (IBCLC) in professional practice and conduct. By virtue of seeking and using the credential, the IBCLC has accepted obligations to herself or himself, the client, colleagues, society, and the profession. According to the code of ethics, "The International Board Certified Lactation Consultant shall act in a manner that safeguards the interests of individual clients, justifies public trust in her/his competence, and enhances the reputation of the profession."

    I  The preamble to the code states that the IBCLC is "personally accountable for her/his practice" and that "in the exercise of professional accountability, the IBCLC must:"

      A.  "1. Provide professional services with objectivity and with respect for the unique needs and values of individuals."

      B.  In practice, the IBCLC will strive to remain objective; that is, to focus on the problem as presented by the client and to attempt to resolve the problem to the satisfaction of the client, regardless of whether that outcome is what the IBCLC would have chosen for himself or herself.

C. For example, a mother might choose not to breastfeed exclusively or to wean completely before the child is one year old.
   1. As long as the mother has been made aware of the advantages to herself and to her child for exclusive breastfeeding for the first six months and for continuing human milk in the child's diet until he or she reaches a minimum of one year of age, it is the mother's decision how she will breastfeed.
   2. The IBCLC will help the mother meet her own goals.
D. "2. Avoid discrimination against other individuals on the basis of race, creed, religion, gender, sexual preference, age, and national origin."
E. In practical terms, the IBCLC will provide the same skilled level of help to individuals whose circumstances or lifestyles he or she might find unsympathetic as she does to those whom he or she admires.
F. He or she will make every attempt to understand the client's goals, especially when they are expressed in an idiom, custom, or context with which the IBCLC is unfamiliar or uncomfortable.
   1. For example, when consulted by a lesbian couple who wish to induce lactation in the non-biological parent, the IBCLC—who might find a homosexual lifestyle abhorrent—will provide just as good care as he or she would to a heterosexual couple.
G. "3. Fulfill professional commitments in good faith."
H. Once a commitment has been made to help a particular client, to give a presentation, or to perform any other professional service, the IBCLC will make every effort to fulfill that commitment.
I. "4. Conduct herself/himself with honesty, integrity, and fairness."
J. The IBCLC will abide by his or her word, will make his or her best effort to serve a client once accepted, will charge a fair price for his or her services according to community standards, and will facilitate the client's best interests even if those interests do not coincide with the best interests of the IBCLC.
   1. For example, the IBCLC will schedule sufficient time to thoroughly investigate a client's problems and will refrain from "quick fixes," although he or she might be pressured by an employer to see more clients in a given period of time.
K. "5. Remain free of conflict of interest while fulfilling the objectives and maintaining the integrity of the lactation consultant profession."
L. For example, the IBCLC will not take payment from an individual or corporation that obtains its income from products or services that are not in the best interests of the public, whom it is our duty to protect.

     1. A primary example is that human milk substitutes are intended not for infants whose own mothers cannot feed them, but rather for as many infants as marketing can recruit.

M. The IBCLC who earns part of his or her livelihood from the rental or sale of breastfeeding aids and devices must remain aware of the temptation to recommend such aids when they are not needed in order to solve particular breastfeeding problems.

     1. A common example would be breast pumps, the use of which can help to preserve breastfeeding when the mother and baby must be separated (but they are not needed by every lactating mother).

     2. Another solution would be supplemental feeding devices that enable the baby to be supplemented at the breast; the use of these devices can certainly be appropriate in certain circumstances but should never substitute for careful investigation of the causes of and correction for inadequate infant weight gain.

N. "6. Maintain confidentiality."

O. Sharing case studies with colleagues is a legitimate method of learning.

P. One must be very careful, however, to disguise all details that could serve to identify the individual clients.

Q. The number of details that need to be suppressed might vary depending on the audience with whom one intends to share the case.

     1. For example, if one practices in a small community, details such as the baby's age, gender, and ethnic origin might be sufficient for the client to be identified by other health care providers in the community.

     2. Those details would not need to be altered if the presentation were done in a large metropolis or at a conference at a distant location.

     3. Even if one intends to suppress all possible identifying details, the IBCLC should always obtain permission from the client to share the case with colleagues.

     4. It is recommended that such permission be incorporated into the IBCLC's routine intake form.

R. "7. Base his or her practice on scientific details, current research and information."

S. This principle is termed "evidence-based practice."

T. The IBCLC must be careful not to base parts of his or her practice on common assumptions but rather to substantiate recommendations with published, peer-reviewed literature and scientific evidence wherever possible.

U. A corollary to this principle is that he or she must make reasonable efforts to remain current and up-to-date with published research and information.

V. Where published, substantiating, scientific, medical, or technical information does not (yet) exist but the IBCLC has clinical experience relevant to the issue at hand, he or she should inform the client.

W. "8. Take responsibility and accept accountability for personal competence in practice."

    1. Keeping up-to-date with current published information and research is a part of accountability for personal competence in practice.

    2. It is part of one's duty to clients, the public, and the profession to remain current.

    3. Taking responsibility for personal competence includes understanding research tools and terminology and developing the ability to distinguish properly designed research from faulty research.

    4. It also includes acquiring clinical skills as well as knowledge.

    5. Competence involves taking the time to study with skilled practitioners, colleagues and mentors in order to learn "hands-on" skills that cannot easily be taught by the written word.

X. "9. Recognize and exercise professional judgment within the limits of her/his qualifications. This principle includes seeking counsel and making referrals to appropriate providers."

Y. Unless the IBCLC has other health professional qualifications and is legally entitled to act within the parameters of those qualifications, he or she must keep a clear distinction in mind at all times between the "mechanical" management of breastfeeding problems and possible medical ramifications.

    1. For example, the IBCLC is within his or her scope of practice to become concerned at excessive infant weight loss or inadequate weight gain, but he or she is not qualified to recommend a specific brand of infant formula for immediate supplementation.

    2. His or her role would be to inform the appropriate primary health care provider of concerns and to help the mother maintain the breastfeeding relationship while supplementing the baby and working to increase the maternal milk supply.

    3. Another example would be when the IBCLC might suspect a fungal infection on the mother's nipples because of clinical symptoms and a predisposing history.

    4. He or she cannot make a diagnosis.

5. He or she can inform the client of what is suspected, but clinically relevant information should be forwarded to the client's primary health care provider for medical review and follow-up.

6. Where clinical concerns involve both mother and baby and each has a different primary health care provider, a copy of the report should be sent to both.

Z. Where the IBCLC encounters puzzling aspects of a case that appear to be non-medical in nature, he or she should contact colleagues for additional perspectives.

AA. Where in the judgment of the IBCLC, either member of the client pair would benefit from consultation with another allied health care provider (for example, a physical therapist or dietitian), the IBCLC should include this suggestion in the report to the primary health care provider along with names of practitioners of these specialties whom the IBCLC has found to be clinically skillful and supportive of breastfeeding.

AB. "10. Inform the public and colleagues of her/his services by using factual information. An International Board Certified Lactation Consultant will not advertise in a false or misleading manner."

AC. An IBCLC will not allow descriptions of his or her services to imply unrealistic outcomes or fees.

1. For example, not all breastfeeding problems can be solved with good information and instruction, and to imply that seeking the services of a particular practitioner will ensure success is false.

2. To advertise that fees for a standard 15- or 30-minute visit are a certain amount is misleading when it is the rare consultation that needs less than one hour, and most require even longer.

AD. "11. Provide sufficient information to enable clients to make informed decisions."

AE. It is the duty of the IBCLC to provide the client with all information that is relevant to the purpose of his or her consultation and not to select information to achieve the IBCLC's desired outcome or because of the client's perceived inability to absorb information.

1. For example, a mother might make the decision not to continue breastfeeding because the actions needed to resolve the problem might require more time and energy than she is realistically willing to give.

2. The IBCLC might have made a different personal decision under similar circumstances, but the temptation to minimize difficulties and withhold factual information in order to encourage the mother to persevere must be resisted.

3.  If barriers to communication exist between the IBCLC and the client because of significant differences in formal education, culture, or facility with language, it is the IBCLC's duty to work even harder to communicate the full range of options in a clear, simple, and unambiguous manner.

AF. "12. Provide information about appropriate products in a manner that is neither false nor misleading."

AG. The ethical advocacy of breastfeeding aids and devices for the IBCLC consists of these tools' appropriateness to solve breastfeeding problems or to make life easier for the breastfeeding mother.

AH. An IBCLC who gets no financial gain from the sale of such products is perhaps more free to advocate their use than is the IBCLC who carries them for the convenience of the client.

AI. To recommend the use of a product and then to sell or rent it to the client might be a practical necessity, but it gives the appearance of a conflict of interest.

AJ. Therefore, IBCLCs who engage in commercial promotion of these items must be especially careful not to recommend them in ambiguous situations but rather to discuss their pros and cons and to make it completely clear when a less-expensive product will serve the purpose just as well as a more expensive one would.

1.  For example, when an IBCLC recommends spoon or cup feeding to a baby who needs to be supplemented, he or she should show the parents inexpensive medicine spoons and mention cups that the parents might have at home, as well as showing relatively expensive specialized cups and soft, flexible spoons with one-way valves, and the IBCLC should allow the parents to make their own decisions about which tool they choose to use.

AK. "13. Permit use of her/his name for the purpose of certifying that lactation consultant services have been rendered, only if she/he provided those services."

1.  For example, an IBCLC who employs or supervises uncertified people who work with breastfeeding mothers and babies cannot allow clients, other health care providers, or third-party reimbursement agencies to assume that these uncertified practitioners are lactation consultants.

2.  The IBCLC must make it routinely and abundantly clear that the individuals who have provided services are not certified by the International Board of Lactation Consultant Examiners.

AL. "14. Present professional qualifications and credentials accurately, using IBCLC only when certification is current and authorized by the IBLCE, and complying with all requirements when seeking initial or continued certification from the IBLCE. The lactation consultant is subject to disciplinary action for aiding another person in representing herself/himself as an IBCLC when she/he is not."

AM. Continuing to represent oneself as an IBCLC after certification has lapsed, or permitting oneself to be described or advertised as such, is in breach of copyright and might be grounds for denying eligibility if the person should ever seek to certify again.

AN. Use of terms such as "IBCLC candidate" or "student IBCLC" are potentially misleading to the public and can also be grounds for denying eligibility should certification ever be sought.

AO. False or misleading statements on applications for initial candidacy will result in eligibility being denied or certification being revoked if discovered after the applicant has passed the exam.

AP. Such statements on an application for recertification are also grounds for decertification.

AQ. The IBCLC who allows the public to assume that he or she has other health-care credentials when he or she does not (for example nursing or midwifery) is also in breach of this tenet of the code of ethics.

AR. Knowledge that another is representing himself or herself as an IBCLC when that person is not currently certified, and not reporting it to the IBLCE, is in violation of the code.

AS. "15. Report to an appropriate person or authority when it appears that the health or safety of colleagues is at risk, as such circumstances may compromise standards of practice and care."

AT. Knowingly permitting a colleague to continue to practice as an IBCLC when that person's health or safety is at risk, and whose condition might compromise client care, endangers not only the mothers and babies whose welfare is our primary duty but also endangers the reputation of the credential.

1. For example, if a colleague is engaging in substance abuse, although that person might seem to avoid substance use when on duty, judgment might be impaired and the individual might succumb to the temptation to use when seeing clients while under unusual stress.

2. It is the duty of the IBCLC to bring such situations to the attention of appropriate authorities.

AU. "16. Refuse any gift, favor, or hospitality from patients or clients currently in her/his care which might be interpreted as seeking to exert influence to obtain preferential consideration."

1. This statement in the code is not meant to direct IBCLCs to refuse token gifts of appreciation, which are customary in many cultures.

2. It is intended to alert IBCLCs to the possibility that judgment can be influenced by significant or unusual gifts or contributions.

      a. For example, an IBCLC who owns a business or makes decisions about which products will be carried by the health-care institution in which he or she is employed is in a position to be influenced by such favors to carry certain products for sale to mothers and to exclude others.

      b. Favors might influence which products are selected to be used in connection with lactation research and what mention these products receive in published results.

      c. The IBCLC must be careful to avoid the appearance of a conflict of interest.

AV. "17. Disclose any financial or other conflicts of interest in relevant organizations providing goods or services. Ensure that professional judgment is not influenced by any commercial considerations."

    1. For example, an IBCLC who is employed by a health care facility might also engage in private practice.

    2. Referral in his or her employee capacity to the private practice, without disclosing the connection, would violate this principle of the code of ethics.

    3. An IBCLC who receives a stipend, honorarium, or grant from an organization that has commercial ties to lactation should disclose this connection when presenting or publishing, if relevant.

AW. "18. Present substantiated information and interpret controversial information without personal bias, recognizing that legitimate differences of opinion exist."

    1. The IBCLC should present substantiated, evidence-based information to clients and colleagues whenever possible.

    2. Clinical experience and new information that is not yet substantiated might have valuable bearing on the issue at hand and should be presented without personal bias and with courtesy and respect for differing opinions.

    3. In the preamble, among those who are listed to whom the IBCLC is obligated to behave in a professional manner that brings credit to the profession are "colleagues."

    4. Sometimes collegial behavior and courtesy to other members of one's profession can be problematic, especially when strong differences of opinion as to causes and the remediation of problems endure.

    5. While uncollegial behavior is seldom a factual basis for a violation of the code of ethics, the IBCLC is reminded that vituperative public arguments discredit all parties and jeopardize public trust and the profession itself.

AX. "19. Withdraw voluntarily from professional practice if the lactation consultant has engaged in any substance abuse that could affect her/his practice; has been adjudged by a court to be mentally incompetent; or has an emotional or mental disability that affects her/his practice in a manner that could harm the client."

1. Colleagues might need to help an IBCLC to realize that he or she is breaching this tenet of the code, because substance abuse, mental incompetence, or emotional or mental disability can impair the IBCLC's capacity to realize that he or she could harm clients.

2. Voluntary surrender of the credential will cause the Board of Examiners to look favorably upon resumption of its use once the disability has been ameliorated.

AY. "20. Obtain maternal consent to photograph, audiotape, or videotape a mother and/or her infant(s) for educational or professional purposes."

1. Such consent should be obtained in writing, which clearly limits the use of the material to professional purposes, and should be dated.

2. The material to which consent has been given should be described on the consent document. IBCLCs are advised to develop standard consent forms and to have the content of such forms reviewed by an attorney or legal expert.

3. The employed (as opposed to the self-employed) IBCLC is advised to obtain the consent of the employer, as well.

AZ. "21. Submit to disciplinary action under the following circumstance: If convicted of a crime under the laws of the practitioner's country which is a felony or a misdemeanor, an essential element of which is dishonesty, and which is related to the practice of lactation consulting; if disciplined by a state, province, or other local government and at least one of the grounds for the discipline is the same or substantially equivalent to these principles; if committed an act of misfeasance or malfeasance which is directly related to the practice of the profession as determined by a court of competent jurisdiction, a licensing board, or an agency of a governmental body; or if violated a *Principle* set forth in the *Code of Ethics for International Board Certified Lactation Consultants* which was in force at the time of the violation."

1. The IBCLC must inform the chairman of the Ethics and Discipline Committee of the IBLCE if he or she is convicted of a crime involving dishonesty that is related to IBCLC practice, or if the person has been disciplined by a governmental agency or court for such an action, and voluntarily surrender the credential.

2. Colleagues might need to remind an IBCLC of this duty, or to report such a conviction or disciplinary action to the chairman of the Ethics and Discipline Committee if a voluntary report is not made by the individual concerned.

3. Violations of principles of the code should also be reported by third parties if the IBCLC concerned refuses to do so.

4. Violations that took place before the relevant principles were adopted are not grounds for disciplinary action.

BA. "22. Accept the obligation to protect society and the profession by upholding the *Code of Ethics for International Board Certified Lactation Consultants* and by reporting alleged violations of the Code through the defined review process of the IBLCE."

1. It is the IBCLC's duty not only to adhere to the principles of the code of ethics himself/herself but also to bring violations on the part of other certificants to the attention of the IBLCE.

2. A careful and thorough investigation will follow and will provide the accused party with every opportunity to respond in a professional and legally defensible manner.

3. Only signed, written complaints will be considered.

4. The person against whom the complaint has been brought will receive a copy of the complaint and will be notified of the name of the complainant.

5. The IBCLC should also encourage others, members of the supervising and coordinating professions, and employers and clients who have direct knowledge of violations to report incidents that might require disciplinary action.

6. A profession that does not police itself forfeits the public's trust.
   Complaints should be sent to:
   Chairman, Ethics and Discipline Committee
   IBLCE
   7309 Arlington Blvd., Suite 300
   Falls Church, VA 22042-3215 USA

BB. "23. Require and obtain consent to share clinical concerns and information with the physician or other primary health care provider before initiating a consultation."

BC. For the IBCLC in private practice or who works in an outpatient clinic, language giving consent to share clinical concerns and information with the physician or other primary health care provider should be incorporated into routine intake forms and signed by the client before the consultation begins.

1. For employed IBCLCs, such consent is usually incorporated into admitting forms in health care facilities.

2. Entries made in patient charts, routinely reviewed by the primary health care provider, should be sufficient except in emergency situations.

3. IBCLCs who are in private practice are advised to secure a legal review of consent language and for their own safety to decline to see clients who

refuse to sign such consent or who do not wish to list a primary health care provider.

4. The IBCLC might offer assistance in securing a primary health care provider or help in any other way, but unless he or she possesses primary health care provider credentials in addition to the IBCLC credential, he or she endangers himself or herself as well as the welfare of the client by practicing without medical review.

5. These statements apply when the IBCLC is investigating a breastfeeding problem, not when she is engaged in routine informational activities such as assisting a woman with the selection of a breast pump or instructing her about how to maintain lactation when returning to paid employment.

6. The IBCLC might be the ideal person to provide such services, but they are not considered consultations.

BD. "24. IBCLCs must adhere to those provisions of the International Code of Marketing of Breast-milk Substitutes which pertain to health workers."

1. Portions of the international code that apply to health workers include the following:

   a. Do not give free samples of breast milk substitutes to parents or other relatives of a new baby.

   b. Do not promote such products in health care facilities.

   c. Do not accept gifts from manufacturers or distributors of such products, and do not accept samples for personal use.

2. Only the third item is completely under the control of the IBCLC.

3. The first two can be incorporated into policies of the health care facility where the IBCLC is employed, and he or she might be required to provide samples to parents and to promote the use of certain products.

4. The International Board of Lactation Consultant Examiners does not expect IBCLCs to risk losing their jobs to uphold the principles of either code.

5. The IBCLC is, however, expected to take every opportunity to educate co-workers, supervisors, and administrators about the detrimental effects of such practices.

# Breastfeeding Devices and Equipment

*Vergie I. Hughes, RN, MS, IBCLC*

## Objectives

- Choose the appropriate breastfeeding aids to remedy specific breastfeeding problems.
- List two advantages and two drawbacks of each specific aid.
- Describe the appropriate use of the aid.

## Introduction

When mothers experience discomfort while breastfeeding or encounter infants who have difficulty latching on to the breast or gaining weight, interventions might be necessary to correct the problem. The role of the lactation consultant is to identify potential causes of the problem and to offer intervention options in order to remedy the situation. Often, refining the mother's technique in positioning, latch-on, breastfeeding frequency and duration, and so on is the first strategy toward solving a number of problems. When additional intervention is needed, specific devices and equipment might be of help. The goal is to return the mother and baby back to direct breastfeeding as soon as possible (and if possible).

    I  Nipple shields—a device placed over the nipple and areola on which the baby sucks

      A. Types

          1. Thick rubber or latex shields

          2. Plastic or glass base with a bottle-like nipple attached

          3. Thin silicone

             a. Might cover the entire areola

             b. Might have partial coverage of the areola with the upper portion cut away to allow the infant's nose to touch the mother's skin

      B. Uses

          1. The infant is unable to latch on due to flat or inverted nipples.

          2. The baby is unable to open his or her mouth wide enough in order to achieve a deep latch.

3. The baby is unable to draw the nipple/areola into his or her mouth.

4. The mother might have an over-active let-down reflex.

5. The mother's nipples/areola might be sore, damaged, or infected.

6. The baby might have a weak, disorganized, or dysfunctional suck.

C. Advantages

1. Immediate results

2. Provides shape to a flat or inverted nipple

3. Helps stretch and improve the elasticity of a flat or inverted nipple when the baby sucks strongly over the shield

4. Reinforces a wide-open mouth position at the breast

5. Helps control the quick flow from a mother with an over-active let-down reflex for a baby who cannot handle a fast flow of fluid

6. Might reduce pain experienced by the mother

7. Helps keep the baby at the breast during remediation of the problem

8. Prolactin levels seem unaffected by the use of the thin silicone shields

D. Disadvantages

1. Thick rubber shields, bottle-like nipples, and thick latex shields have the capability to reduce milk transfer.

2. The thin silicone shields do not seem to carry this problem due to good post-feed weights in infants who are using them.

3. Inner ribbed protrusions can cause discomfort and pain.

4. Some babies will need complementary feedings to compensate until milk transfer improves.

5. Some mothers might need to pump after feedings with the shield in order to initiate and/or maintain an optimal milk supply.

6. Latex shields carry the risk of inducing a latex allergy in the mother and/or infant.

E. Techniques

1. Roll the shield back about one-third of the length of the nipple shank and apply to the breast, rolling the shield onto the nipple and areola.

2. This action places the mother's nipple deeper into the nipple shank.

3. The baby can pull the nipple even further into the shield after several minutes of vigorous sucking.

4. The shield can be removed at this time and the infant placed quickly back directly on the mother's breast before the nipple/areola loses its shape.

5. If the infant will not latch on, the mother can keep practicing latch at each feeding after the baby has sucked over the shield for a few minutes.

6. Avoid cutting pieces off the tip of the shield in an attempt to wean the baby from it; blunt uncomfortable edges might remain.

F. Shield selection (Wilson-Clay, 1999)

1. The teat height should not exceed the length of the infant's mouth from the lips to the junction of the hard and soft palates.

2. If the height of the teat is greater than this length, the probability increases that the infant's gum ridges will rest beyond where the tongue should begin to exert its peristaltic motion.

3. If this situation happens, the lactiferous sinuses might not be drawn into the teat shaft far enough for compression by the infant's tongue, reducing the milk transfer.

4. In some babies, this excessive length can trigger a gag reflex and an aversion to feeding.

5. Wilson-Clay recommends using the shortest available teat with the height under 2cm.

6. Some small shields are not wide enough at the base to accommodate larger nipples.

7. Wide bases might be too large for some babies who have small mouths.

8. Preterm infants might need to rely on a shield for longer periods of time.

9. Meier et al. (2000) describe typical problems of small preterm infants at the breast that include the failure to latch on, sucking for insufficient lengths of time, immature feeding behaviors, falling asleep as soon as he or she is positioned at the breast, and repeated slipping off the nipple (for which a small thin shield has been shown to help).

10. Shields have been demonstrated to increase the volume of milk transfer in these situations, resulting in preterm babies who breastfeed for longer periods of time at each feeding and for a greater overall duration.

11. Preterm infants might require the use of nipple shields for longer periods of time than term infants, often two to three weeks or until term-corrected age.

12. Shields have from one to five holes; milk flows best through nipple shields that have multiple holes.

13. Infant weight should be monitored frequently during nipple shield use.

14. If the shield slips despite proper fit and application, the areolar portion of the shield can be moistened or the mother can use a sticky breast cream sparingly.

II Breast shells—a two-piece plastic device consisting of a dome or cup and a concave backing contoured to fit the shape of the breast; held in place over the nipple/areola by the mother's bra.

A. Types

1. Designed to invert a flat nipple; the part in contact with the breast has a small opening that is just large enough for the nipple to protrude through.

2. The pressure on the areola was thought to break adhesions that were anchoring the nipple to the base of the areola.

3. The dome has one or more air vents to enable air to circulate around the nipple.

4. Most brands have a second type of backing with a much larger opening to place over the areola when the mother has sore nipples; the dome keeps the bra off the nipple and enables air to circulate.

5. Some brands have a cotton liner that surrounds the backing for a comfortable fit.

6. Some shells have an absorbent cotton pad that is placed in the bottom of the shell under the areola to absorb leaked milk.

B. Uses

1. To evert flat or inverted nipples either prenatally or postpartum

2. To collect leaking milk

3. To relieve engorgement

4. For sore nipple relief

C. Advantages

1. While shells are sometimes used prenatally to evert flat nipples, evidence has demonstrated that the shells actually provide little correction in the prenatal period and that many mothers dislike wearing them

2. Might provide relief from a sore nipple

3. Might encourage milk to leak and help relieve engorgement

4. Can be worn between feedings after the baby is born to help the nipple protrude prior to each breastfeed

D. Disadvantages

1. Theoretical risk of stimulating pre-term labor contractions.

2. Not effective in everting a flat or retracted nipple.

3. Might cause irritation to the nipple or areola either from contact with the skin or from moisture build-up in the shell and the resulting skin breakdown.

4. Drip milk collected in the shell should not be fed to the baby.

5. Drip milk can leak out of some shells when the mother leans over.

6. Some shells are obvious under the bra.

7. The bra might need to be a cup size larger in order to accommodate the shell.

8. Women who have fibrocystic breasts might experience discomfort from the constant pressure.

9. Shells should be removed for naps and at bedtime so that areas of the breast do not become obstructed.

E. Technique

1. Center the opening of the shell over the nipple and apply the bra to hold it in place.

2. Apply a cotton liner if appropriate.

3. Wear them for gradually longer periods of time during the day.

4. In hot weather or if moisture builds up, remove them for 20 minutes at a time, several times each day, and dry the shells well.

III Nipple everters

A. Types

1. A syringe-like device that is placed over the nipple; the plunger is gently pulled to apply suction to the nipple

2. Commercially available syringe has a soft flexible areolar cone

3. Non-commercial device can be made from a 10cc or 20cc syringe

a. The end of the barrel is cut off where the needle attaches to form a hollow tube.

b. The plunger is inserted into the cut end, leaving the smooth side to be placed over the nipple.

4. Another commercially available product is placed over the nipple prenatally and generates suction the entire time it is worn

B. Uses

1. Evert a flat or retracted nipple in the prenatal or postpartum period.

2. Form a nipple to make latch-on easier for a baby who is having difficulty grasping and holding the nipple.

C. Advantages

1. Comprises a simple, low-cost technique to aid in latch-on and nipple erection

2. Is mother-controlled to her comfort

D. Disadvantages

1. If used too vigorously or incorrectly, has the potential to cause pain or skin damage

2. The nipple might not remain everted long enough for the baby to achieve latch-on

3. Some institutions that are concerned about legal liability require the use of the commercial (FDA-approved) device, because a 10 cc or 20 cc syringe has been modified to perform a function for which it was not originally intended.

  E. Technique

    1. The mother applies the commercial or modified syringe to the nipple; she gently pulls back on the plunger to her comfort and holds the nipple everted for 30 seconds or to her comfort.

    2. She performs this action prior to each breastfeeding and can repeat between feedings if desired.

    3. The second type of device is generally used prenatally, placed over the nipple for varying lengths of time, and for varying amounts of suction.

**IV** Hydrogel dressings—three-dimensional networks of cross-linked hydrophilic polymers that are insoluble in water and that interact with aqueous solutions by swelling

  A. Hydrogel dressings are associated with the concept of moist wound healing and are used for nipples that have cracks, fissures, and deep wounds.

  B. They function to absorb excess drainage, maintain a moist wound surface that enables epidermal cells to migrate across the wound, provide thermal insulation for improved blood flow, and protect the wound from bacterial invasion or trauma.

  C. Types

    1. Are provided in gel, gauze, and sheet forms

    2. Sheet dressings are either glycerin or water based

  D. Uses

    1. Used on nipples for superficial or partial-thickness wounds in order to enhance the healing process

  E. Advantages

    1. Provides soothing relief to sore nipples

    2. Speeds wound granulation and healing

    3. Can be chilled and reused

    4. Non-adherent

    5. Oxygen permeable

    6. Maintains a clean, moist environment

    7. Comfortable and flexible

  F. Disadvantages

    1. Might macerate peri-wound skin

      2. Some brands have minimal absorption

      3. Water-based products can dry out rapidly when exposed to air

      4. Have the potential in certain situations to contribute to yeast or bacterial overgrowth

      5. Might be as effective as lanolin

      6. If the mother forgets that the gel dressing is in place and/or has cut it very small, the baby can suck it into his mouth and choke on it

  G. Technique

      1. Wash hands before handling.

      2. The dressing should be cut about one-fourth to one-half inch larger than the wound.

      3. Some dressings are manufactured specifically for nipple care and are small and round, not requiring cutting.

      4. Remove the backing to the dressing and apply the gel side to the wound.

      5. The dressing is removed before nursing, placing it on a clean surface, gel side up.

      6. The dressing can be chilled and reapplied following each feeding.

      7. The breast does not need to be washed prior to nursing.

      8. Dressings should not be applied in the presence of a known wound infection.

      9. The dressing should not be worn at night to prevent accidental ingestion by the infant if the mother fails to remove the dressing.

**V** Creams (cosmetic, non-medicated)—creams have been used to soothe and/or "treat" sore nipples for hundreds of years; most creams have a soothing effect but do not prevent or cure sore nipples

  A. Types

      1. Purified lanolin or lanolin-containing creams

      2. Combination creams that have multiple ingredients

  B. Uses

      1. Used to soothe sore nipples

      2. Some are used to create a moist wound-healing environment

  C. Advantages

      1. Can enhance granulation process in superficial and partial thickness cracks and fissures

      2. Might reduce pain and have a soothing effect

      3. Widely available

      4. Most do not need to be washed off prior to feedings

     5. Might serve to moisturize dry skin and protect it from maceration

D. Disadvantages

     1. Some products might need to be washed off before each feeding.

     2. This wiping off can remove moisture from the skin, create further damage, and slow wound healing.

     3. Some combination creams have ingredients that could provoke an allergy in the infant, such as peanut oil.

     4. Some have petroleum bases and other ingredients that could irritate nipple skin.

     5. Lanolin should have the lowest possible free alcohol content to avoid aggravating a wool allergy in susceptible mothers.

     6. Modified lanolin generally has the lowest level of free alcohol and appears to be free of pesticides.

     7. Vitamin E oil, cocoa butter, Bag Balm®, and so on are products that have never been approved for use on the nipple of a lactating mother.

**VI** Droppers—a plastic or glass tube with a squeeze bulb at one end

A. Types

     1. Some are made completely of soft plastic; some are glass with a rubber bulb; some are small, child-size.

B. Uses

     1. Provide milk incentives at the breast in order to achieve latch-on

     2. Finger-feed to take the edge off hunger before attempting latch-on

     3. Complementary feeding when breast milk intake is not sufficient

     4. Temporary aid to improve suck organization

C. Advantages

     1. Avoids the use of artificial nipples

     2. Inexpensive and widely available

     3. Easy to use and teach parents

     4. Quick way for baby to receive small amounts of milk while learning to breastfeed

D. Disadvantages

     1. Can be difficult to clean

     2. Must be continually refilled

     3. Baby does not learn to suck unless the dropper is placed in the mouth next to the adult's finger and the baby is able to accomplish a correct sucking cycle; or, milk from a dropper is gently dropped into the corner of the baby's mouth at the breast

4. Sucking on the dropper alone will not teach correct sucking patterns

5. Time-consuming

E. Technique

1. If using with a finger, place the filled dropper along the side of the finger as the baby draws the finger into his or her mouth.

2. Allow the baby to suck the milk out of the dropper.

3. If the baby is unable to perform this task, one or two drops can be placed on the baby's tongue to initiate swallowing and sucking.

4. Milk should not be squirted into the baby's mouth.

5. A dropper can be placed into the corner of the baby's mouth while latching on to the breast; one or two drops of milk can be placed on the tongue to initiate a swallow followed by a suck.

6. The infant must be alert, not sleepy, and have a functioning swallow reflex.

**VII** Spoons

A. Types

1. Teaspoon, tablespoon, plastic spoon, medicine spoon with a hollow handle, spoon-shaped device attached to a milk reservoir

B. Uses

1. Feed the baby when breastfeeding is interrupted.

2. Complementary feeding when breastfeeding is not sufficient.

3. Hand-express colostrum for a baby who is not yet established at breast; prevent hypoglycemia.

4. Prime the baby for feeding at the breast.

C. Advantages

1. Avoids the use of artificial nipples

2. Can be used as a temporary aid to effect milk intake in the baby

3. Inexpensive and easily available

4. Easy to use and clean

D. Disadvantages

1. Must be continually refilled

2. Does not teach the baby to suck at the breast

3. Fluid in the mouth is not associated with sucking

4. Does not correct improper sucking patterns

E. Technique

1. Position the baby in a semi-upright position.

2. Place the spoon just inside the infant's lips and allow the infant to obtain the milk at a rate he or she can easily swallow.

    3. Allow the infant to pace the feeding.

    4. Avoid pouring the milk into the baby's mouth.

    5. The baby should be alert with a functioning swallow reflex.

## VIII Cups

### A. Types

    1. 28cc medicine cups, plastic small drinking cups

    2. Small cups with an extended lip or edge to control the flow of milk

    3. Flexible silicone cups with a restricted outlet

    4. Paladai—a small pitcher-shaped device from India

### B. Uses

    1. Feed the infant when breastfeeding is interrupted

    2. Complementary feeding when breastfeeding is not sufficient

    3. Used with both term and preterm infants to avoid nipple preference

    4. Used when the mother is unavailable to breastfeed

### C. Advantages

    1. Avoids the use of artificial nipples

    2. Inexpensive and widely available

    3. Easy to use and to teach parents to use

    4. Reduces the incidence of bottle-feeding associated apnea and bradycardia in preterm infants

    5. Non-invasive alternative to gavage feeding; reduces the risk of esophageal perforation and oral aversion

    6. A quick way to supplement or complement breastfeeding

    7. Physiologic stability

    8. Good weight gain

    9. Use of a paladai reduces the amount of spilled milk, resulting in an increased intake in babies who are using this device

### D. Disadvantages

    1. The cup must be frequently refilled.

    2. The baby can dribble much milk, reducing intake.

    3. The baby does not learn to suck.

    4. The infant, parents, or health care providers can become dependent on the cup.

### E. Technique

    1. The baby should be in a calm, alert state (not sleepy).

    2. Position the baby in a semi-upright position, wrapped so that his or her hands do not bump the cup.

3. Fill the cup about half full.

4. Place the rim of the cup on the baby's lower lip with the cup tilted just to the point of the milk coming into contact with the upper lip.

5. Do not apply pressure to the lower lip.

6. Let the baby pace the feeding by sipping or lapping at the milk.

7. Do not pour the milk into the baby's mouth.

8. Leave the cup in the same position during the baby's pauses so that he or she needs to continually reorganize oral conformation.

9. Refill as needed.

IX  Syringes

A. Types

1. 1–50cc capacity, used with a 5 French length of tubing

2. Periodontal syringe, 10cc capacity with a curved tip

3. Regular syringes (without the needle) are usually not used because the infant might have difficulty forming a complete seal

B. Uses

1. To provide an incentive at the breast to encourage latch-on, to initiate suckling, or to aid in sustaining the suckling once started

2. To provide complementary or supplementary feeding while the infant simultaneously sucks on a caregiver's finger

C. Advantages

1. Avoids the use of artificial nipples

2. Might help improve uncoordinated mouth and tongue movements

3. Provides a source of milk flow that will work to regulate the suck

D. Disadvantages

1. More complex technique to learn and teach to parents

2. Supplies might not be widely available

3. More intrusive

4. Infant can become dependent on the method

5. Infant might demonstrate poor jaw excursion while sucking on an adult finger

a. Some periodontal syringes have a rough tip that could irritate the baby's mouth

E. Technique

1. At the breast; insert the tip of the syringe (or feeding tube) just inside the infant's lips at the corner of his or her mouth

2. Give a small bolus of milk (.25–.5cc) when the infant sucks

3. The rate might be as follows:

   a. suck:bolus:suck:bolus

   b. suck, suck, bolus: suck, suck, bolus

   c. suck, suck, suck, bolus: suck, suck, suck, bolus

4. On the finger

   a. Place the infant in a semi-upright position in the caregiver's arms or in an inclined infant seat.

   b. Parents can use a washed finger; the health care provider should wash his or her hands and use a finger cot.

   c. Use the finger that is closest in size to the circumference of the mother's nipple.

   d. Introduce the finger into the infant's mouth pad up, enabling the baby to pull the finger back to the junction of the hard and soft palate.

   e. If the infant resists, withdraw the finger slightly, pause until he or she is comfortable, and then proceed.

   f. Place the syringe or tubing next to the finger, making sure that it is positioned so that it will not poke the infant.

   g. As the infant sucks, reward correct suckling motions with a small bolus of milk.

   h. Use the rate of suck:bolus to entice a reluctant feeder, allowing the infant to gradually remove the milk from the device by himself or herself.

   i. Complete feedings in this manner should take about 15–20 minutes to avoid gastric discomfort.

   j. If this technique is being used to prime the baby for the breast, place the baby at the breast when he or she demonstrates a sucking rhythm.

   k. If the baby stops for more than 10–20 seconds, call the infant's name. Gently move or massage his or her body or stroke under the chin, or withdraw the finger slightly to stimulate the suck reflex.

   l. If the tongue lies behind the lower gum ridge, apply slight pressure to the back of the tongue to stroke it forward over the lower gum ridge.

X  Tube feeding devices—usually consist of a reservoir or container for milk, with one or two thin flexible lengths of tubing attached

   A. The container for milk can be a syringe, a bottle clipped to the shoulder area, a bottle suspended on a cord around the mother's neck, a plastic bag, or a bottle with a regular artificial nipple through which the tubing is threaded.

   B. The container might have one or two thin lengths of flexible tubing.

   C. The tubing is usually attached by tape to the mother's nipple/areola or to the feeder's finger.

D. Uses
   1. To provide complementary feeding to an infant at the breast for low milk supply, inefficient suckling, slow weight gain, adoptive nursing, relactation, preterm infant, or for neurologically affected infants
   2. The tubing can also be attached to a finger for others to feed the baby or to prime the baby for going to the breast

E. Advantages
   1. Avoids the use of artificial nipples
   2. Might help improve sucking organization and patterns
   3. Enables delivery of supplements if needed while preserving the breastfeeding

F. Disadvantages
   1. More complex technique to learn and teach
   2. Supplies might not be widely available
   3. Supplies might be expensive
   4. More intrusive
   5. Infant can become dependent on the method
   6. The infant might exhibit shallow jaw excursions while sucking on an adult finger
   7. Time-consuming to clean the equipment after each use
   8. Might be awkward at first to get both the tubing and the mother's nipple into the infant's mouth
   9. If the milk container is not positioned properly, the infant might receive milk when not suckling
   10. Some mothers might be allergic to the tape that is used to secure the tubing in place at the breast; consider paper tape or non-allergenic tapes or dressings

G. Technique
   1. Tube feeding on a finger proceeds in a similar manner as with the syringe and tubing combination.
   2. The milk reservoir can be elevated or lowered to achieve control over the milk flow speed; the milk should flow only when the baby sucks.
   3. If tube feeding at the breast, the milk container should be filled and placed so that the top of the fluid is level with the mother's nipples.
   4. The container can be elevated for small or weaker babies.
   5. If the device has a choice of tubing sizes, use the largest size for a preterm baby, a disorganized infant, or one who needs an easier flow; advance the baby to the smaller sizes as sucking improves.

6. The baby should take both the nipple/areola and the tubing into his or her mouth.

7. Tape the tubing so that it comes over the top of the nipple and its end does not extend beyond the nipple tip.

8. For some preterm infants or others who need more help, the tip of the tubing can be placed to extend beyond the tip of the nipple; however, some babies learn to suck on this device like a straw, so care should be taken in monitoring the quality of the suckling.

9. Babies need close follow-up for frequent weight checks and to be weaned off the device.

XI  Haberman feeder—a specialized feeding bottle with a valve and teat mechanism to adjust the milk flow in order to prevent overwhelming or flooding the baby with milk

A. Uses
1. Severe feeding problems, such as Down syndrome, cleft lip/palate, neurological dysfunction, disorganized sucking, a preterm infant, babies who have cardiac defects, cystic fibrosis

B. Advantages
1. Might work with an infant who is otherwise difficult to feed
2. If the baby cannot nurse at all or just needs a little help, the bottle can be squeezed to release a limited volume of milk
3. The smaller feeder has a shorter teat for smaller babies
4. Can be used as a quicker means of complementary or supplementary feedings

C. Disadvantages
1. Exposes the infant to an artificial nipple
2. Might promote a shallow latch-on when the infant goes to the breast
3. Might be difficult to obtain
4. Might be expensive

D. Technique
1. Place the nipple onto the infant's lips, allowing him or her to draw it into the mouth if capable.
2. Pull back on the nipple if the baby has a shallow gag reflex or to help him or her start sucking.
3. Rotate the nipple to adjust the rate of flow to meet the needs and capability of the baby.

**XII** Pacifiers

   A. Uses

      1. Treat delayed swallowing.

      2. In non-orally fed infants, pacifiers help maintain oral motor patterns and tactile response that will be necessary to transition to feeding at the breast.

      3. Meet high sucking needs.

      4. Act to calm a fussy baby.

   B. Advantages

      1. Enables sucking activity for an infant who might otherwise over-feed

      2. Might quiet a crying baby

      3. Non-nutritive sucking in the preterm infant might help in more rapid transition to oral feeding

   C. Disadvantages

      1. Exposes an infant to an artificial nipple

      2. Displaces sucking from the breast

      3. Might cause drowsiness in the baby and missed feedings

      4. Increased incidence of otitis media

      5. Vector for continued fungal infection

      6. Might see shorter breastfeeding duration

      7. Might see increased rates of malocclusion

      8. Increases the risk for latex allergy

      9. Pacifiers with balls on the tip enable the baby to maintain the pacifier in the mouth with a weak lick-suck motion, rather than functional sucking activity

     10. Orthodontic pacifiers might flatten the central grooving of the tongue

   D. Technique

      1. Pacifiers should be used with caution.

      2. Non-orally fed infants might benefit from sucking on a number of different-shaped pacifiers to avoid becoming accustomed to only one shape.

**XIII** Artificial nipples—no artificial nipple precisely mimics the dynamic qualities of the human breast

   A. Artificial nipples are made from silicone, rubber, or latex.

   B. Numerous sizes and shapes are available.

      1. Round, cross-section nipples tend to be straight and gradually taper to a flared base.

      2. "Orthodontic" nipples have bulb-like ends and narrow necks.

3. Some have a very wide base that is supposed to encourage the baby to keep his or her mouth open wider.

4. Artificial nipples do not elongate in the mouth as the human breast does.

5. Two types of openings occur in artificial nipples: holes and crosscuts. Hole size is one of the major determinants of flow rate.

6. Crosscut nipples do not enable milk to drip from them, but compression on them removes fluid.

7. Nipples have high, medium, and low flow rates.

C. Advantages

1. Ease and speed of feedings

2. Some artificial nipples are used in special situations to assist infants in learning sucking patterns

3. Easily obtained

D. Disadvantages

1. Flow might be faster than with breastfeeding, accustoming the baby to a quick delivery of milk.

2. Shape is different and consistency is firmer, potentially causing the infant to prefer the stronger stimulus of the artificial nipple.

3. Encourages the baby to close his or her mouth, not open wide, and even bite on the narrowed neck of some of the nipples.

4. Fast flow can contribute to apnea and bradycardia in preterm or stressed infants.

5. Orthodontic nipples cause a squash and fill type of sucking, remove the central grooving of the tongue, and enable the infant to close his or her mouth tightly around the nipple.

6. Long nipples might trigger a gag reflex in some babies.

7. Can contribute to latex allergy.

8. Weakens the strength of the suck; reduces the strength of the masseter muscle.

9. Muscles involved in breastfeeding are either immobilized, overactive, or malpositioned during bottle-feeding, which can contribute to abnormal dental and facial development in the child.

10. Bottle-feeding has been positively correlated with finger sucking, which can deform the palate.

11. Can contribute to malocclusion.

E. Technique

1. If artificial nipples are used, choose those that have a long shank, wide base, and slow flow of milk.

2. Tickle the infant's lips with the nipple and allow him or her to draw the nipple into the mouth himself or herself.

3. Observe for signs of a milk flow that is too fast or too slow.

4. Switch sides halfway through the feeding.

**Table 33-1**    Selecting and Using Breastfeeding Devices and Equipment

Selecting the proper solution to lactation management problems is a complex blend of

(1) the lactation consultant's experience

(2) the infant's capabilities and limitations

(3) the mother's anatomy and physiology

(4) the mother's ability to cope with the situation

This is a general guideline for using breastfeeding aids in various clinical situations. It is only a guide. The lactation consultant must consider all factors before recommending a plan of care. More than one problem may be present.

Often the plan of care moves from the first choice solution, if unsuccessful, to the second choice solution and if it is unsuccessful, to the next choice. This may take a matter of minutes, days, or weeks. As the situation improves, the plan may move from the last choice to the next higher choice and so on, until resolution.

During treatment phase of care, move from left to right as the situation warrants; more than one intervention may be used at a time . During the recovery phase of care, move the right to the left as the situation improves.

| Problem | First choice solution | Second choice solution | Third choice solution | Fourth choice solution |
|---|---|---|---|---|
| Difficult latch-on | Correct positioning and latch-on | Curved tip syringe with milk used at the breast to entice baby to latch-on | Nipple shield to assist with latch-on. May also use curved tip syringe to assist with latch-on | Add FTD system to increase the milk flow |
| Breast refusal | Skin-to-skin time with mother | Correct positioning and latch-on | Nipple shield to assist with latch-on | Bottle—Long shank with wide base |
| Sore, damaged nipples (abraded skin) | Correct positioning and latch-on | Lanolin preparation and breast shells | Temporarily use breast pump until nipples heal | Nipple shield to relieve mother's pain—short term use |

| Problem | First choice solution | Second choice solution | Third choice solution | Fourth choice solution |
|---|---|---|---|---|
| Sore, damaged nipples (broken skin) | Correct positioning and latch-on | Hydrogel dressing | Temporarily use breast pump until nipples heal | Nipple shield to relieve mother's pain—short term use |
| Flat or inverted nipples | Breast shells during last 2–3 weeks of pregnancy and first weeks of breastfeeding | Breast shells and/ or nipple everter used near time of delivery and the first weeks of breastfeeding | Nipple shield; Breast pump to pull nipples out and increase elasticity | |
| Shallow latch-on Tight mouth | Correct positioning and latch-on | Nipple shield to encourage wider open mouth | Bottle—Long shank wide base nipple. Place bottle so wide part of nipple is at infant's gum line to encourage a wider mouth while suckling | Eyedropper or spoon or cup feeding |
| Over-active let down; Baby chokes at breast | Hand compression blocking some milk ducts during let-down, then release. Supine positioning ("Australian Hold") | Nipple shield temporarily until baby can handle flow | Institute measures to reduce milk supply if over-active let-down is due to over-supply | |
| Low maternal milk supply | FTD at breast to increase infant intake and maternal breast stimulation. Correct positioning and latch-on | Pumping with hospital grade breast pump | Herbal supplements | |

*(continued)*

**Table 33-1**    Selecting and Using Breastfeeding Devices and Equipment (continued)

| Problem | First choice solution | Second choice solution | Third choice solution | Fourth choice solution |
|---|---|---|---|---|
| Infant displays incorrect tongue position and/or movement | Suck training and put baby to breast; Correct positioning and latch-on | Suck training with finger feeding and curved tip syringe or finger feeder device | Suck training with finger feeding with FTD | |
| Infant requires supplementation due to hospital policies or medical condition | Supplement at breast with curved tip syringe or FTD | Supplement with cup | Supplement with bottle with long shank, wide base nipple. | Supplement with eye dropper or spoon |
| Adoptive nursing | FTD at the breast; Use breast pump regularly | Supplement with bottle with long shank, wide base nipple until milk supply increases | | |
| Neurologically impaired baby, preemie baby, low muscle tone | Correct positioning and latch-on. Use Dancer hand position | FTD at the breast; Use breast pump regularly | Use Haberman bottle | |
| Cleft lip and/or palate babies | Correct positioning and latch-on. Use nipple skin to fill in defect | Use Haberman bottle; Obtain palatal obturator if used in institution | | |
| Baby with high sucking needs, fussy baby | Allow to feed at the breast until satiated | Use pacifier after feeding to settle baby | | |

FT—Feeding tube device: Commercially made device commonly called a Supplementary Nurser System or Lact-aid, or made from bottle of milk and a 5 Fr feeding tube.

# References

Aarts C, Hornell A, Kylberg E, et al. Breastfeeding patterns in relation to thumb sucking and pacifier use. *Pediatrics* 1999; 104:e50; http://www.pediatrics.org/cgi/content/full/104/4/e50.

Alexander JM, et al. Randomized controlled trial of breast shells and Hoffman's exercises for inverted and non-protractile nipples. *Br Med J* 1992; 304(6833):1030–1032.

Armstrong H. Feeding low birthweight babies: Advances in Kenya. *J Hum Lact* 1987; 3:34–37.

Arsenault G. Using a disposable syringe to treat inverted nipples. *Can Fam Phys* 1997; 43:1517–1518.

Auerbach KG. The effect of nipple shields on maternal milk volume. *J Obstet Gynecol Neonatal Nurs* 1990; 19:419–427.

Barros FC, et al. Use of pacifiers is associated with decreased breastfeeding duration. *Pediatrics* 1995; 95:497–499.

Biancuzzo M. Creating and implementing a protocol for cup feeding. *Mother Baby J* 1997; 2:27–33.

Biancuzzo M. Breastfeeding the newborn: Clinical strategies for nurses. St. Louis, MO: Mosby, Inc., 1999.

Billet J. Aids to breastfeeding: A look at some of the products. *Prof Care Mother Child* 1994; 4:19–20.

Bodley V, et al. Long-term nipple shield use—a positive perspective. *J Hum Lact* 1996; 12:1–4.

Brent N, Rudy SJ, Redd B, et al. Sore nipples in breast-feeding women: A clinical trial of wound dressings vs conventional care. *Arch Pediatr Adolesc Med* 1998 November; 152(11):1077–1082.

Brigham M. Mother's reports of the outcome of nipple shield use. *J Hum Lact* 1996; 12: 91–97.

Bull P, Barger J. Fingerfeeding with the SNS. Rental Roundup 1987; Summer.

Cable B, Stewart M, Davis J. Nipple wound care: A new approach to an old problem. *Hum Lact* 1997; 13(4):313–318.

Cable B, Davis J. Hydrogel dressings not to be used on infected tissue. *J Hum Lact* 1998; 14:205.

Clum D, et al. Use of a silicone nipple shield with premature infants. *J Hum Lact* 1996; 12:87–90.

Coates MM. Bottle-feeding like a breastfeeder: An option to consider. *J Hum Lact* 1990; 6:10–11.

Coates MM. Learning at the conference. *J Hum Lact* 1991; 7:174.

Cronenwett L, et al. Single daily bottle use in the early weeks postpartum and breastfeeding outcomes. *Pediatrics* 1992; 90:760–766.

Cockburn F, et al. Breastfeeding, dummy use, and adult intelligence. *Lancet* 1996; June 22 347:1765–1766.

Darzi MA, Chowdri NA, Bhat AN. Breast feeding or spoon feeding after cleft lip repair: A prospective, randomised study. *Br J Plast Surg* 1996; 49(1):24–26.

Davis HV, et al. Effects of cup, bottle, and breastfeeding on oral activities of newborn infants. *Pediatrics* 1948; 2:549–558.

Drane D. The effect of use of dummies and teats on orofacial development. *Breastfeeding Rev* 1996; 4:59–64.

Drosten F. Pacifiers in the NICU: A lactation consultant's view. *Neonatal Network* 1997; 16:47, 50.

Edgehouse L, Radzyminski SG. A device for supplementing breastfeeding. *MCN* 1990; 15:34–35.

Frantz K. Breastfeeding product guide 1994. Sunland, CA: Geddes Productions, 1993.

Fredeen RC. Cup feeding of newborn infants. *Pediatrics* 1948; 2:544–548.

Glover J, Sandilands M. Supplementation of breastfeeding infants and weight loss in hospital. *J Hum Lact* 1990; 6:163–166.

Gupta A, et al. Cup feeding: An alternative to bottle feeding in a neonatal intensive care unit. *J Trop Pediatr* 1999; 45:108–110.

Hagen RL. Lanolin for sore nipples. *Arch Pediatr Adolesc Med* 1999; 153:658.

Harlan G. Feeding device follow-up. *MCN* 1990; 15:326.

Henrison MA. Policy for supplementary/complementary feedings for breastfed newborn infants. *J Hum Lact* 1990; 6:1–14.

Hewat RJ, et al. A comparison of the effectiveness of two methods of nipple care. *Birth* 1987; 14:41–45.

Hill PD, et al. Does early supplementation affect long-term breastfeeding? *Clin Pediatr* 1997; 36:345–350.

Howard CR, de Blieck EA, ten Hoopen CB, et al. Physiologic stability of newborns during cup- and bottle-feeding. *Pediatrics* 1999; 104:1204–1207.

Howard CR, Howard FM, Lanphear B, et al. The effects of early pacifier use on breastfeeding duration. *Pediatrics* 1999; 103:e33 http://www.pediatrics.org/cgi/content/full/103/3/e33.

Huml S. Sore nipples: A new look at an old problem through the eyes of a dermatologist. *Pract Midwife* 1999; 2:28–31.

Hunter HH. Nipple shields. A tool that needs handling with care. *Pract Midwife* 1999; 2:48–52.

Inoue N, Sakashita R, Kamegai T. Reduction in masseter muscle activity in bottle-fed babies. *Early Hum Dev* 1995; 42:185–193.

Jackson JM, Mourino AP. Pacifier use and otitis media in infants twelve months of age or younger. *Pediatr Dent* 1999; 21:256–261.

Johnson SM. Further caution re: nipple shields. *J Hum Lact* 1997; 13:101.

Jones B. Choosing a supplementation method. J Hum Lact 1998; 14:245–246.

Kesaree N, Banapurmath CR, Banapurmath S, Shamanur K. Treatment of inverted nipples using a disposable syringe. *J Hum Lact* 1993; 9:27–29.

Kuehl J. Cup-feeding the newborn: What you should know. *J Perinatal Neonatal Nurs* 1997; 11:56–60.

Lang S, Lawrence CJ, Orme RL. Cup feeding: An alternative method of infant feeding. *Arch Dis Child* 1994; 71:365–369.

Lang S. Cup-feeding: An alternative method. *Midwives Chron Nurs Notes* 1994; 107:171–176.

Lang S. Breastfeeding special care babies. London: Bailliere Tindall, 1997.

Lennon I, Lewis B. Effect of early complementary feeds on lactation failure. *Breastfeeding Rev* 1987; 11:25–26.

MAIN Trial Collaborative Group. Preparing for breastfeeding: Treatment of inverted and non-protractile nipples in pregnancy. *Midwifery* 1994; 10:200–214.

Malhotra N, Vishwimbaran I, Sundaram KR, Narayanan I. A controlled trial of alternative methods of oral feeding in neonates. *Early Hum Dev* 1999; 54:29–38.

Marriott M. Nipple shields used successfully. *J Hum Lact* 1997; 13:12.

Matthew OP. Science of bottle feeding. *J Pediatr* 1991; 114:511–519.

Matthew OP. Nipple units for newborn infants: A functional comparison. *Pediatrics* 1988; 81:688–691.

McGeorge DD. The "Niplette": An instrument for the non-surgical correction of inverted nipples. *Br J Plast Surg* 1994; 47:46–49.

Meier PP, Brown LP, Hurst NM, et al. Nipple shields for preterm infants: Effect on milk transfer and duration of breastfeeding. *J Hum Lact* 2000; 16:106–114.

Morse J. The hazards of lanolin. *MCN* 1989; 14:204.

Morse J. Lanolin recommended to breastfeeding mothers to prevent nipple discomfort and pain. *Birth* 1989; 16:35.

Musoke RN. Breastfeeding promotion: Feeding the low birth weight infant. *Intl J Obstet Gynecol Suppl* 31 1990; 57–68.

Neifert M, Lawrence R, Seacat J. Nipple confusion: Toward a formal definition. *J Pediatr* 1995; 126:S125–S129.

Neimela M, Uhari M, Mottonen M. A pacifier increases the risk of recurrent acute otitis media in children in day care centers. *Pediatrics* 1995; 96:884–888.

Newman J, Pitman T. Dr. Jack Newman's guide to breastfeeding. Toronto: Harper Collins, 2000.

Newman J. Caution regarding nipple shields. *J Hum Lact* 1997; 13:12–13.

Newman J. Breastfeeding problems associated with the early introduction of bottles and pacifiers. *J Hum Lact* 1990; 6:59–63.

Nicholson WL. The use of nipple shields by breastfeeding women. *J Aust Coll Midwives* 1993; 6:18–24.

Noble R, Bovey A. Therapeutic teat use for babies who breastfeed poorly. *Breastfeeding Rev* 1999; 5:37–42.

North K, Fleming P, Golding J, et al. Pacifier use and morbidity in the first six months of life. *Pediatrics* 1999; 103:e34 http://www.pediatrics.org/cgi/content/full/103/3/e34.

Nowak AJ, Smith WL, Erenberg A. Imaging evaluation of artificial nipples during bottle feeding. *Arch Pediatr Adolesc Med* 1994; 148:40–42.

Nowak AJ, Smith WL, Erenberg A. Imaging evaluation of breastfeeding and bottle feeding systems. *J Pediatr* 1995; 126:S130–S134.

Palmer B. The influence of breastfeeding on the development of the oral cavity: A commentary. *J Hum Lact* 1998; 14:93–98.

Pugh LC, et al. A comparison of topical agents to relieve nipple pain and enhance breastfeeding. *Birth* 1996; 23:88–93.

Righard L. Are breastfeeding problems related to incorrect breastfeeding technique and the use of pacifiers and bottles? *Birth* 1998; 25:40–44.

Righard L, Alade MO. Breastfeeding and the use of pacifiers. *Birth* 1997; 24:116–120.

Rowe L, Cumming F, King R, Mackey C. A comparison of two methods of breastfeeding management. *Aust Fam Physician* 1992 March; 21(3):286–294.

Savage-King F. Helping mothers to breastfeed. Nairobi, Kenya: African Medical and Research Foundation, 1992.

Schubiger G, et al. UNICEF/WHO baby friendly hospital initiative: Does the use of bottles and pacifiers in the neonatal nursery prevent successful breastfeeding. *Eur J Pediatr* 1997; 156:874–877.

Sealy CN. Rethinking the use of nipple shields. *J Hum Lact* 1996; 12:29–30.

Stine MJ. Breastfeeding the premature infant: A protocol without bottles. *J Hum Lact* 1990; 6:167–170.

Thorley V. Cup feeding: Problems created by incorrect use. *J Hum Lact* 1997; 13:54–55.

Turgeon-O'Brien H, et al. Nutritive and non-nutritive sucking habits: A review. *ASDC J Dent Child* 1996; 63:321–327.

Venuta A, Bertolani P, Pepe P, et al. Do pacifiers cause latex allergy? *Allergy* 1999; 54:1007.

Victora CG, Behague DP, Barros FC, et al. Pacifier use and short breastfeeding duration: Cause, consequence, or coincidence? *Pediatrics* 1997; 99:445–453.

Walker M, Auerbach KG. Breast pumps and other technologies. Chapter 13 in Riordan J, Auerbach KG, eds. Breastfeeding and human lactation. 2nd ed. Sudbury, MA: Jones and Bartlett Publishers, 1998:393–443.

Wight NE. Cup-feeding. ABM news and views. *Acad Breastfeed Med* 1998; 4:1–5.

Wilson-Clay B, Hoover K. The breastfeeding atlas. Austin, TX: LactNews Press, 1999.

Wilson-Clay B. Clinical use of silicone nipple shields. *J Hum Lact* 1996; 12:655–658.

Wilson-Clay B. Nipple shields: Just another tool. *J Hum Lact* 1997; 13:194.

Wolf LS, Glass RP. Feeding and swallowing disorders in infancy. Tucson, AZ: Therapy Skill Builders, 1992.

Woodworth M, et al. Transitioning to the breast at six weeks: Use of a nipple shield. *J Hum Lact* 1996; 12:305–307.

Woolridge MW, Baum JD, Drewett RF. Effect of a traditional and of a new nipple shield on sucking patterns and milk flow. *Early Hum Dev* 1980; 4:57–64.

Wright A, et al. Changing hospital practices to increase the duration of breastfeeding. *Pediatrics* 1996; 97:669–675.

Ziemer M, et al. Evaluation of a dressing to reduce nipple pain and improve nipple skin condition in breastfeeding women. *Nurs Res* 1995; 44:347–351.

# DONOR HUMAN MILK BANKING

*Mary Rose Tully, MPH, IBCLC*

Donor human milk banking is the process of providing human milk to a recipient other than the donor's own infant. This process involves recruiting and screening donors, storing, treating, and screening donated milk, and distributing the milk based on the physician's orders. This process should not be confused with storage and handling of the mother's own milk for her own child in any setting, however.

There are many uses for donor milk, including supplementing a mother's own supply until she has sufficient milk for her child(ren)'s needs.

I  Preterm infants who are fed human milk, including banked donor milk, have improved outcomes related to the nutritional qualities, ease of digestibility, and immunological components of human milk.

   A. There is a lower risk of developing necrotizing enterocolitis (NEC), a devastating bowel disease that is frequently fatal.

   B. A large study in the United Kingdom found that infants who were fed at least some human milk (donor or the mother's own, all by gavage) in the first month of life had higher IQs at 7.5–8 years of age, even when controlling for psychosocial influences.

   C. A U.S. study at a large neonatal unit showed that using fortified human milk (the mother's own) was related to decreased infections and a more rapid achievement of full feeds with no untoward effects related to slower weight gain because the feedings were better tolerated.

   D. Donor milk has also been used effectively for treatment of a variety of conditions or to provide appropriate nutrition in full-term infants and older children, including chronic renal failure, metabolic disorders, IgA deficiency, and allergy. Many cases of feeding intolerance and allergy have been treated with donor milk but are not reported in the literature, including infants who have failed to thrive on anything but human milk. Donor milk is typically a treatment of last resort in these cases, primarily because of the expense.

E. There are also some adult conditions that respond to human milk, including hemorrhagic conjunctivitis, IgA deficiency in liver transplant recipients, and gastrointestinal problems, such as severe reflux. Human milk also contains a unique protein that induces apoptosis (programmed cell death) in certain cancer cells. Isolating this protein for clinical use is now being studied at the University of Lund.

F. Some families will request donor milk for an adopted baby or for a baby whose mother cannot lactate, simply because of the advantages of human milk feeding for all infants. Again, cost becomes a factor if there are no medical reasons for needing the donor milk.

G. Generally, donor milk is acceptable to the families of the recipient babies, but many need to understand how the donors are screened and how the milk is processed and tested.

H. Milk donors are always anonymous, except in special circumstances. Few milk banks are set up to perform directed donations. Among Muslims, however, it is important that the recipient mother and donor mother meet, because the Koran decrees that all babies who receive milk from the same mother are siblings and the two women's children cannot marry when they are older.

I. Donor milk banking is found in most parts of the world and is typically associated with a neonatal intensive care unit (NICU). The use of donor milk is more common in some countries than in others. For example:

1. In South America, there are milk banks in several countries, including Brazil, where there are 154 active donor milk banks and where donor milk is the feeding of choice for all infants who do not have their mother's own milk meeting their needs.

2. In the United States and Canada, donor milk is the feeding of choice when the mother's own is not available in a few NICUs, but it is typically the therapy of last resort. The United States currently has five milk banks with two more hospitals considering opening banks. Canada has one active milk bank.

3. Many European countries have donor milk banks. In the United Kingdom and Scandinavian countries, donor milk banking and the use of donor milk is common but is not universal. In the former East Germany, donor milk banking is more common than in the former West Germany, and in France there are 19 donor milk banks that serve the entire country. The largest of French milk bank is free-standing and lyophilizes (freeze dries) milk before shipping to the many hospitals in the surrounding region. Italy has 18 donor milk banks associated with NICUs primarily in the northern part of the country.

4. India is beginning to develop milk banking guidelines and establish milk banks.

5. China has donor milk banks in many hospitals.

6. Kuwait has one donor milk bank.

J. Typically, donors are not paid for their donations; however, in some countries donors are sufficiently compensated at the end of the their donation to cover the cost of electric pump rental.

1. The Human Milk Banking Association of North America (HMBANA) guidelines, which are used in the United States and Canada, prohibit compensation to donors, as do the Brazilian government guidelines. The French government discourages payment to donors but does allow it.

2. A few European banks compensate donors nominally (usually the compensation is sufficient to cover pump rental), and some milk banks loan breast pumps to donors during the period of donation.

3. Most donors have altruistic motives of helping others and sharing with babies who are not as healthy as their own. Donating milk can also be an important and therapeutic part of the grieving process for mothers whose babies have died.

K. In Europe and North America, donors typically use electric breast pumps; however, in many countries milk is hand expressed, and a few milk banks still accept "drip milk."

L. Donor milk banks usually operate in a hospital within the NICU, the food service department, or the blood or tissue banking department; however, some milk banks are free-standing and regulated by the government just as blood banks are.

1. Milk banks are staffed by a milk bank director/coordinator who oversees day-to-day operations and supervises donor recruiting and screening as well as milk processing and dispensing, and a medical director might or might not do a physical exam on each donor and her infant but always supervises medical decisions.

a. The milk bank director/coordinator might be an IBCLC lactation consultant, a nurse, a physician, or a trained milk bank coordinator.

b. Frequently, a trained technician does the milk processing.

c. The medical director is often, but not always, a neonatologist and is responsible for clinical decisions and oversight of the milk banking operations.

d. In Brazil, there is a 40-hour training course required for milk bank personnel.

    e. Most donor milk banks are also sources of breastfeeding support and counseling. In many countries, they are a part of implementation of the Baby Friendly Hospital Initiative.

    2. A few countries, including Poland, Brazil, France, and India have national milk banking regulations through the ministry of health. Many others are regulated through professional organizations or general tissue banking guidelines, however.

M. Milk donors and the donor milk are carefully screened, just as other donor tissues are. Although serum screening of donors is expensive, milk banks in developed nations do serum screening for communicable diseases such as TB, HIV, HTLV, Hepatitis B and C, and syphilis. Because cost is prohibitive and the donor milk is so vital, however, the banks in some developing countries rely on heat treatment to kill viruses and other pathogens and use verbal/written screening to eliminate high-risk donors.

    1. The cost of serum screening is born by the milk bank or the national health system, not by the donor.

    2. In some situations, physicians on the milk bank staff perform a physical on each mother and her infant. Other milk banks require a form completed by the donor's physician and her infant's physician.

N. Donor milk is stored frozen at about –20°C until it is heat processed, then it is refrozen until it is distributed. Although freezing preserves most of the nutritional, immunologic, hormonal, and other unique properties of the milk, it does not destroy many pathogens. Careful heat treatment with Holder pasteurization (62.5°C timed for 30 minutes after the center container reaches that temperature) preserves as many of the properties of the milk as possible.

O. In Germany, some milk is dispensed raw after donor screening. HMBANA guidelines also enable dispensing of milk raw in rare circumstances; however, since 1988 no bank has reported a request for raw milk in the United States or Canada.

    1. Either a commercial human milk pasteurizer or a standard laboratory shaking water bath is used. The shaking water bath is considerably less expensive but more time intensive because the milk containers must be physically moved to a vat containing an ice slurry for quick chilling after heat treatment. In Brazil, the central standards bank has developed a chart for processing time based on container volume, which minimizes even further the damage to the milk components.

P. Milk banks use a wide variety of containers for processing and storing milk. Some decisions have been based on scientific investigation, and some have been based on convenience.

Q. Most milk banks will accept initial donations in whatever container the donor has been using but will then provide containers for the donor's future donations.

1. Many banks use glass because it is a good heat conductor, preserves the components of the milk well, and can often be reused.

2. The commercial human milk pasteurizers have been designed to process milk in food-grade plastic bottles sold expressly for the purpose.

# References

Al-Naqeeb NA, et al. The introduction of breast milk donation in a Muslim country. *J Hum Lact* 2000; 16(4):346–350.

Anderson A, Arnold LDW. Use of donor breastmilk in the nutrition management of chronic renal failure: Three case histories. *J Hum Lact* 1993; 9(4):263–264.

Arnold LDW. A brief look at drip milk and its relation to donor human milk banking. *J Hum Lact* 1997; 13(4):323–324.

Arnold LDW. Donor milk banking in China: The ultimate step in becoming baby friendly. *J Hum Lact* 1996; 12(4):319–321.

Arnold LDW. Donor milk banking in Scandanavia. *J Hum Lact* 1999; 15(1):55–59.

Arnold LDW. The lactariums of France: Part 1. The lactarium Docteur Raymond Fourcade in Marmande. *J Hum Lact* 1994; 10(2):125–126.

Arnold, LDW. Recommendations for collection, storage, and handling of a mother's milk for her own infant in the hospital setting. Raleigh, NC: Human Milk Banking Association of North America, 1996.

Arnold LDW. Use of donor milk in the treatment of metabolic disorders: Glycolytic pathway defects. *J Hum Lact* 1995; 11(1):51–53.

Arnold LDW, Courden M. The lactariums of France, Part 2: How association milk banks operate. *J Hum Lact* 1994; 10(3):195–196.

Baum JD. Donor breast milk. *Acta Paediatr Scand Suppl*, 1982. 299:51–57.

de Almeida JA. Personal communication, 2000.

De Nisi G. Personal communication, 2001.

Deolankar RP. Personal communication, 1999.

Gutiérrez D, de Almeida JA. Human milk banks in Brazil. *J Hum Lact* 1998; 14(4):333–335.

Hakansson A, et al. Apoptosis induced by a human milk protein. *Proc Natl Acad Sci USA* 1995; 92(17):8064–8068.

Lucas A, et al. Breast milk and subsequent intelligence quotient in children born preterm. *Lancet* 1992; 339:261–64.

Lucas A, Morley R. Breast milk and neonatal necrotising enterocolitis. *Lancet* 1990; 336:1519–23.

Merhav HJ, et al. Treatment of IgA deficiency in liver transplant recipients with human breast milk. *Transpl Int* 1995; 8(4):327–329.

Morbidity and Mortality Weekly Report. Acute hemorrhagic conjunctiveitis—American Samoa. *MMWR* 1982; 30(54):1–132.

Munshi N. Personal communication, 2000.

Penc B. Organization and activity of a human milk bank in Poland. *J Hum Lact* 1996; 12(3):243–246.

Royal College of Paediatrics and Child Health and UK Associaton of Milk Banking. Guidelines for the establishment and operation of human milk banks in UK, 2nd ed. London: Royal College of Paediatrics and Child Health, 1999.

Schanler RJ, Shulman RJ, Lau C. Feeding strategies for premature infants: Beneficial outcomes of feeding fortified human milk versus preterm formula [comment]. *Pediatrics* 1999; 103(6):1150–1157.

Springer S. Human milk banking in Germany. *J Hum Lact* 1997; 13(1):65–68.

Tully DB, Jones F, Tully MR. Donor milk: What's in it and what's not. *J Hum Lact* 2001 (in press).

Tully MR. Banked human milk in treatment of IgA deficiency and allergy symptoms. *J Hum Lact* 1990; 6(2):75–76.

Tully MR. Cost of establishing and operating a donor human milk bank. *J Hum Lact* 2000; 16(1):57–59.

Tully MR. Donating human milk as part of the grieving process. *J Hum Lact* 1999; 15(2):149–151.

Tully MR, ed. Guidelines for the establishment and operation of a donor human milk bank, 2000 ed. HMBANA, 2000.

Tully MR. Human milk banking in Sweden and Denmark. *J Hum Lact* 1991; 7(3):145–146.

Weaver G. Every drop counts: News from the United Kingdom Association for Milk Banking. *J Hum Lact* 1999; 15(3):251–253.

Wiggins PK, Arnold LDW. Clinical case history: Donor milk use for severe gastroesophageal reflux in an adult. *J Hum Lact* 1998; 14(2):157–159.

# SKILLS AND TECHNOLOGY
*Marie Davis, RN, IBCLC*

## OBJECTIVES

- Describe the criteria for comfortable maternal positioning.
- List three types of breast support.
- Demonstrate four infant positions for breastfeeding.
- Demonstrate three special positions for breastfeeding difficulties.
- List three objective findings that contribute to poor maternal and infant positioning for breastfeeding.
- Describe the components of proper latch-on.
- List the signs of milk transfer.
- Describe three criteria for assessing sufficient milk intake.
- List three signs of swallowing.

## Introduction

Proper maternal and infant positioning forms the cornerstone of the breastfeeding experience. Comfortable, pain-free, and effective breastfeeding can be achieved through exploring what works best for each mother/baby pair. Numerous options and variations exist for standard positioning. Mothers do not need to know all of these positions, and their positioning preference should be respected.

    I Maternal and Infant Positioning

      A. Assessment

        1. History

          a. Previous breastfeeding experience

            i. Has the mother breastfed previous children? If so, for how long?

            ii. Did she have sore nipples or other problems?

        iii. When and reason for weaning

        iv. Previous breastfeeding education (classes, reading, videos, and so on)

   b. Cultural influences

        i. Assess the mother's concerns regarding modesty.

        ii. What are her feelings about breastfeeding in front of other people and in public places?

        iii. Who functions as her support system?

2. Intrapartum

   a. Did she have a vaginal birth?

        i. Episiotomy pain will influence the mother's comfort and position.

        ii. What type (if any) labor medications did she receive? Some might cause sedation or poor responsiveness in the infant.

        iii. Is she taking pain medication? Pain medication 20 minutes prior to feedings might increase her comfort level. Large amounts might sedate her and her baby.

   b. Did she have a cesarean delivery?

        i. Type and location of incision.

        ii. Pain might limit her early positions.

        iii. What type of medications did she have during labor and for subsequent pain control?

        iv. Is she on any other medications?

   c. Are there any complications from childbirth?

        i. Extension of episiotomy

        ii. Bladder, cervical, uterine, rectal, or perineal problems

        iii. Fever

        iv. Level and location of pain

           (1) Perineum

           (2) Back

           (3) Legs, arms, neck, shoulders

           (4) Wrist (carpal tunnel syndrome)

   d. What are her limitations?

        i. Physical

        ii. Psychological/social

           (1) Feelings of inadequacy

           (2) Lack of self confidence

           (3) Sensitivity to comments and criticism

(4) Fatigue

(5) Overwhelmed

   iii. Medical

   iv. Environmental

(1) Where will she breastfeed at home?

(2) Who else is in the household?

**II** Breasts and nipples

  A. Size and shape of breasts

    1. Large, pendulous breasts might require that a rolled up towel or receiving blanket be placed under them for support

    2. The direction that the nipple points will influence where the baby's mouth is placed

    3. Anomalies (tubular, asymmetric)

  B. Condition of the nipples and areola

    1. Everted, flat, retracted

    2. Edematous areola from IV fluids can flatten a normal nipple as it is enveloped by swollen areolar tissue

    3. Nipple anomalies, supernumerary nipples

**III** Behavioral state of the baby

  A. Deep sleep

    1. Limp extremities, no body movement

    2. Placid face

    3. Quiet breathing

    4. Cannot be easily aroused

  B. Light or active sleep

    1. Resistance in extremities when moved

    2. Mouthing or suckling motions

    3. Facial grimaces

    4. More easily awakened, more likely to remain awake if disturbed

    5. If left undisturbed, will easily fall back asleep

  C. Drowsy

    1. Eyes open and close intermittently

    2. Might make sounds (murmur or whisper)

    3. Might yawn and stretch

  D. Quiet alert

    1. Looks around; interacts with environment

2. Body still and watchful

3. Breathing even and regular

4. Excellent time for breastfeeding

E. Active alert

   1. Moves extremities

   2. Wide eyed, irregular breathing

   3. More sensitive to discomfort (wet diaper or excessive stimulation)

F. Crying

   1. Agitated, disorganized

   2. Needs comforting

   3. Poor state to attempt breastfeeding

**IV** Planning and implementation

A. Position of mother

   1. Structure the environment for privacy.

      a. Assess the mother's comfort with visitors and family.

      b. If indicated, ask them to leave and return after the feeding.

      c. Turn off the television, radio, and telephone. Have an answering machine or family member handle phone calls.

   2. Ensure the mother's comfort.

      a. Pain medication prior to feedings if necessary.

      b. The mother can empty her bladder if needed and wash her hands.

      c. Washing the nipples and areolae is unnecessary.

      d. Ensure a comfortable room temperature, quiet environment, and a cushion for episiotomy if needed.

   3. Ensure physical support.

      a. If the mother is seated on a straight-backed chair:

         i. Knees should be slightly higher than the hips.

         ii. Provide a footstool to raise the mother's knees so that the baby faces her body and prevents back strain.

         iii. Pillows can be placed behind her back for comfort and support.

         iv. A firm pillow (or commercial nursing pillow) can be placed in the mother's lap to raise the baby to the level of the breasts if necessary.

         v. The mother should not lean back or forward over the baby.

      b. If the mother is seated in a bed:

         i. Raise the head of the bed to a 90-degree angle or to the comfort of the mother.

        ii. Use pillows behind her back if necessary.

       iii. Place a pillow under her knees and/or under her arms if needed.

       iv. A pillow can be placed on her lap to raise the baby to the level of the breast if needed or to protect a cesarean incision.

  c. If the mother is lying down:

        i. Mothers might experience less fatigue if breastfeeding while lying down.

        ii. Some mothers express concern over the number of pillows needed to nurse in a side-lying position (suffocation hazard or too cumbersome for them to arrange by themselves).

       iii. Mothers can be assisted onto their side if necessary, with the baby placed facing toward the breast to be used for the feeding.

       iv. A pillow can be placed between her legs lengthwise to level the hips and to relieve lower back pain.

        v. A pillow can also be placed behind her back if needed.

       vi. A rolled baby blanket or towel can be used if needed behind the infant to prevent him or her from rolling onto his or her back.

      vii. The mother can cradle the infant with her lower arm or place the arm behind her head.

  d. If the mother is flat on her back:

        i. Not an optimum position for breastfeeding.

        ii. The weight of the infant against her breast might be painful.

       iii. The infant's face might become buried in the breast.

       iv. Might be needed if the mother has complications from an epidural or spinal.

        v. Might help the infant cope with a fast milk flow (see Australian hold).

B. Position of the infant

  1. Positioning points

    a. The infant should be well supported so that the baby is flexed and the limbs are tucked into the body.

    b. The infant should face the mother's body with the ear, shoulder, and hip in a straight line.

    c. Calling it "tummy to tummy" positioning is misleading and might cause the mother to hold the baby's body too low.

    d. The baby's body should be level.

    e. The baby's lower end should not drift into the mother's lap.

    f. In the cradle hold, the mother's elbow should be at a 90-degree angle.

**Figure 35-1**    Cradle position

    g. Avoid twisting the infant's neck.

    h. Avoid pressure against the back of the infant's head (occipital area), because this action will cause the baby to arch away from the breast.

2. Madonna or cradle hold (Figure 35-1):

    a. Most commonly used position.

    b. Feels the most natural to the mother.

    c. Offers the least amount of control over the infant's head.

    d. The baby lies across the mother's forearm on the side that the mother will be using for the feeding.

    e. The baby's head is either in the bend of the mother's elbow or midway down her forearm, whichever results in the best positioning.

    f. The mother holds the baby's buttocks with her hand.

    g. The mother's arm should be level.

    h. The mother avoids dropping the baby's bottom toward her lap.

    i. If the baby is not level, this situation might put downward pressure on the breast.

    j. Might alter the latch, pulling the breast out of the baby's mouth.

    k. The baby's lower arm can be placed around the mother's back or tucked down along next to his or her body.

    l. The baby's legs should be wrapped around the mother's waist.

**Figure 35-2**     Football hold

3. Clutch or football hold (Figure 35-2):
   a. The football hold is often preferred when a new mother is having difficulty with latch-on.
   b. Gives the mother better control of the infant's head.
   c. Improves the mother's view of the baby's mouth.
   d. Improves the mother's view of her nipple and areola.
   e. Place two pillows beside the mother if needed.
   f. Place the infant on the pillows with the baby's hips flexed bottom-up against the back of the chair/couch/bed, the feet aiming towards the ceiling.
   g. The feet should not touch the back of the chair.
   h. Pressure on the feet can trigger arching and the stepping reflex.
   i. The baby's arms can be placed across his or her chest or around the breast.
   j. Slide the arm under the infant's back with the hand at the base of the baby's head.
4. Elevated clutch hold:
   a. Use the same positioning as for the clutch hold.
   b. Place the baby in a sitting position next to the mother.

**Figure 35-3**    Cross-cradle hold

5. Cross-cradle hold (Figure 35-3):
    a. Principles are the same as for the cradle hold.
    b. The baby lies across the forearm of the opposite arm from the breast being used for the feeding (the left arm for the right breast).
    c. The baby's head is held just below the ears at the nape of the neck.
    d. The breast is supported with the hand on the same side as the breast to be used for the feeding.
    e. Also used for preterm infants
6. Sidelying (Figure 35-4):
    a. Position the mother in the sidelying position.
    b. The baby is placed on the bed turned toward the breast.
    c. The mother can use her arm to hold the infant in position.
    d. The breast is held by the mother's upper hand.
7. Australian or posture feeding:
    a. The baby is placed on his or her abdomen across the mother's chest with the mother lying back.
    b. The mother might need to support the forehead of the baby with the heel of her hand to prevent the baby's head from falling forward.
    c. Used for mothers who have a forceful milk ejection reflex that is overwhelming the baby.
    d. Also used for babies who bite or retract their tongue; helps the jaw and tongue move down and forward.
    e. Care must be taken that the breasts are adequately drained when using this position.
  See Table 35-1 for a summary of the various advantages and disadvantages of the basic positions.

**Figure 35-4**    Lying down
position

**Table 35-1**    Advantages and Limitations of Basic Positions

| Position | Advantages | Limitations | Pertinent Points |
|---|---|---|---|
| Cradle hold | • Women are most likely to have seen this position used<br>• Works best for most situations | • Difficult to achieve good sitting position in hospital bed; use chair if possible<br>• Requires sitting; cesarean incision or hemorrhoids may make sitting a less desirable position | • Be sure that infant is chest-to-chest rather than chest-to-ceiling<br><br>• Infant should be at the level of the nipple |
| Side-lying | • Helpful after cesarean birth<br>• Great for nighttime feedings | • Difficult to visualize latch | • Be sure that infant is chest-to-chest rather than chest-to-ceiling<br>• Use folded receiving blanket behind infant to maintain chest-to-chest position<br>• Mother's body should be at a slight angle to the mattress, leaning backward just a bit against a pillow |
| Football | • Helpful after cesarean birth<br>• Helpful for women with especially large breasts<br>• Provides better visualization of latch-on process | • Often difficult to do sitting up in hospital bed | • Be sure that infant is chest-to-chest rather than chest-to-ceiling |

C. Latch-on:
1. A good latch-on will prevent many breastfeeding problems.
2. Essential to the prevention of sore nipples.
3. Essential to adequate milk intake.
4. Things to avoid during latch-on:
   a. Avoid moving the breast out of its resting position.
   b. Avoid taking the breast to the baby.
   c. Avoid twisting of the mother's or infant's body.
   d. Avoid pushing down on the baby's chin to force the mouth open.
   e. Avoid pushing the baby's head into the breast.
   f. Avoid flexing the baby's neck (chin to chest).
   g. Avoid extending the baby's neck.
   h. Avoid allowing the arms and legs to flail.

D. Breast support
1. Key points:
   a. Fingers need to be far enough back to allow full access to the mother's areola.
   b. The weight of the breast should be supported with the mother's hand.
   c. Large-breasted women may benefit from a rolled wash cloth or towel placed under the breast to elevate it and to prevent the baby from pulling down on the nipple.
   d. Small-breasted women might not need to support the breast but will need to place the heel of the hand against the chest so that the infant's access is not obstructed.
   e. The mother cannot easily see her finger position on the breast.
   f. Most women grasp the breast with the thumb well up on the breast but the fingers too close to the areola on the underside of the breast.
   g. Suggest that the mother practice holding her breast in front of a mirror.
   h. C-hold (thumb on top of the breast with all four fingers below) is preferred.
      i. Gentle compression of the breast tissue between the thumb and fingers, making the areola more oblong than round
      ii. Push slightly back into the chest wall to cause the nipple to protrude.
      iii. Gentle pressure applied with the thumb so the nipple points slightly upward

iv. The baby is then brought to the breast, mouth open wide, lower lip catching the bottom of the areola and then brought up onto the top of the areola.

v. Sometimes helps to tell the mother to envision trying to eat a sandwich larger than her mouth and go through the steps she would make to take the first bite

i. The scissors hold (breast grasped between the index and middle fingers) might work better for some mothers as long as the fingers are well away from the areola.

j. The dancer hold (breast grasped from below with the thumb and index fingers and the baby's face resting in the fleshy part between the thumb and index finger) might be needed for preterm infants or for infants who have poor jaw support.

E. Bringing the baby to the breast:

1. Brush the lower lip lightly with the nipple.

   a. The mother should do this by gently moving her breast up and down.

   b. Caution the mother to keep her fingers away from the baby's mouth.

   c. Some babies might respond better when the upper lip is stimulated.

2. The baby will open his or her mouth slightly at first, then gape.

   a. Mouth open wide, tongue to the floor of the mouth (Figure 35-5).

   b. A crying baby might open the mouth wide but the tongue will be at the roof of the mouth.

**Figure 35-5**
Latch-on.

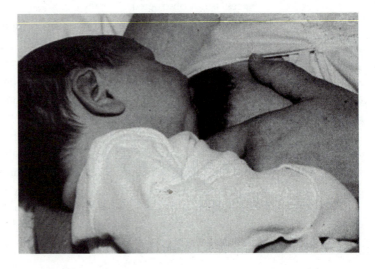

    c. Cues given to the baby, such as the mother saying "open" and opening her own mouth wide might assist with latch-on.

    d. With the mouth open wide, the mother should quickly pull the baby into the breast.

3. Avoid the rapid arm movement (RAM) technique, because this action often startles the baby and is counter-productive.

4. A baby should never be pushed or shoved into the breast.

5. The baby's chin should touch the breast first, with both the chin and the tip of the nose touching the breast.

6. The baby's mouth should be brought up and over the areola with the baby leading with his or her chin.

    a. Opinions differ as to the position of the baby on the areola.

    b. Some say centered.

    c. Some say asymmetrical, with the lower jaw covering more of the areola than the upper jaw.

    d. The most important things are maternal comfort and good milk transfer.

17. Concerns over the infant's nose:

    a. Many mothers naturally push into the breast to keep it away from the baby's nose.

    b. This action will alter the latch-on, pulling the breast out of the baby's mouth.

    c. Might be a cause for sore nipples and/or plugged ducts.

    d. If the mother cannot see the baby's nose, she should alter the position of the baby's body or her hand.

    e. Raising the infant's bottom half so that it is more level with the head might clear the nose, or wrapping the baby's legs around the mother's waist might also work.

    f. Lifting up slightly on the breast might clear the nose.

8. Mouth position:

    a. The baby's mouth should be wide open.

    b. The angle at the corner of the mouth should be 150 degrees or better.

    c. The baby will not have a dimple in the cheek (indicates that the tongue is drawn behind the lower gum and that the baby is sucking as if from a straw).

    d. Both lips should be flared outward.

    e. The nipple and approximately one-fourth to one-half inch of the areola should be in the mouth; it is unnecessary or impossible for the baby to draw in an entire areola into his or her mouth.

    f. The breast is not placed into the baby's mouth; it is the baby who draws the breast into its mouth.

9. Signs of swallowing:

    a. Puff of air from the nose

    b. "Ca" sound from the throat

    c. Deeper jaw excursion preceding each swallow

    d. Vibration on the occipital region of the head

    e. Can hear the swallow with a stethoscope placed on the baby's throat

    f. Top of the areola moves inward toward baby's mouth

F. Breastfeeding assessment tools:

1. There are a number of tools used to assess and document various aspects of breastfeeding; validity and reliability of some tools have been studied showing advantages and disadvantages of each.

2. Systematic Assessment of the Infant at Breast (SAIB) (Shrago and Bocar, 1990) (Table 35-2)

**Table 35-2**    Evaluating the Effectiveness of Latch-On and Suck

**Proper Alignment:**

- Helps keep nipple and areola in infant's mouth
- Reduces traction on mother's nipples
- Facilitates swallowing

| Proper Alignment | Improper Alignment | Nursing Interventions |
| --- | --- | --- |
| Infant is flexed and relaxed | Muscular rigidity | Comfort and calm the infant<br>Try a football hold to get flexion |
| Head and body are at breast level | Head and body sagging; baby "reaching" for the breast | Provide pillows to facilitate baby's head and body at breast level |
| Head squarely facing breast | Head turned:<br>• Laterally<br>• Hyperextended<br>• Hyperflexed | Help mother to adjust her hold on infant<br>Do not force baby's head against the nipple. Instead, help mother to move arm to align infant |
| Infant's body aligned from shoulder to iliac crest | • Trunk facing the ceiling instead of skin-to-skin with mother<br>• This results in poor compression of the sinuses and obstructed swallowing | Hold "tummy-to-tummy" |

**Areolar Grasp:**

Peristaltic motions of tongue result in effective areolar compression, i.e., compression of the lactiferous sinuses.

| Proper Areolar Grasp | Improper Areolar Grasp | Nursing Interventions |
|---|---|---|
| Infant's mouth opens widely to cover lactiferous sinuses | Pursed lips indicate that mouth is not open wide enough | Tickle lips with nipple or finger Move mother's arm quickly toward breast when baby finally opens wide (see text) |
| Lips flanged outward | Lips pursed: lip(s) curled under | As above |
| Complete seal formed around areola; strong vacuum | Incomplete seal; baby can be easily pulled away from nipple | Hook your finger (or have mother hook her finger) under infant's chin |
| Approximately 1.5 inches of areolar tissue is centered in infant's mouth | Only nipple is in mouth, or nipple is not centered | Break suction and reposition |
| Tongue is troughed and extends over lower alveolar ridge | Tongue partially inside mouth Nurse has "biting" sensation if she inserts her finger in infant's mouth Results in sore nipples and diminished milk supply Likely to happen if infant does not open wide | Break suction and reposition |

*Note:* Data in left column expanded from Shrago L, Bocar D. The infant's contribution to breastfeeding. *J Obstetr Gynecol Neonatal Nurs* 1990; 19(3): 209–215. Table from Biancuzzo M. *Breastfeeding the Healthy Newborn* 1994: 31–32. Copyright 1994 by March of Dimes Birth Defects Foundation. Reprinted by permission.

**Areolar Compression:**

Removes milk from breast

| Proper Areolar Compression | Improper Areolar Compression | Nursing Interventions |
|---|---|---|
| Mandible moves in a rhythmic motion | Mandible moves in tiny motions up and down; appears more like "chewing" instead of gliding | Break suction and reposition |

*(continued)*

**Table 35-2**    Evaluating the Effectiveness of Latch-On and Suck (*continued*)

| Proper Areolar Compression | Improper Areolar Compression | Nursing Interventions |
|---|---|---|
| If indicated, a digital suck assessment reveals a wave-like motion of the tongue from the anterior mouth toward the oropharynx; tongue is cupped or "troughed" | Incorrect tongue motions include:<br>• Side-to-side movement<br>• Deviation of the tongue to one side<br>• Peristaltic movement from the posterior region to the anterior region of the tongue<br>• Frank tongue thrusting (actively pushing the finger out of the mouth with the tongue)<br>• Diminished negative pressure<br>• Absence of seal around lips<br>• Tongue not troughed | Digital suck assessment is not routinely performed<br>Break suction and reposition<br>Suck training has been advocated but has not been proven effective in well-controlled, scientific studies<br>Sucking is a reflex, and deviations in reflexes should be followed up with a complete neurologic assessment |
| Cheeks full and rounded when sucking | Cheeks dimple when sucking | Break suction and reposition |

**Audible Swallowing:**

(Most reliable indicator of milk intake)

| Proper | Improper | Nursing Interventions |
|---|---|---|
| Audible swallowing present | Lack of audible swallowing | Reevaluate alignment, areolar grasp, areolar compression |
| Quiet sound of swallowing is heard | No swallowing is heard | Break suction; take baby off breast and try again. Be sure to get baby to open wide, which frequently solves the problem |
| May be preceded by several sucking motions, especially in first few days | Even after many rapid sucks, infant does not display rhythmic sucking motion and swallowing is not heard | Reevaluate latch-on<br>Evaluate milk supply<br>Evaluate milk ejection reflex |

| Proper | Improper | Nursing Interventions |
|---|---|---|
| May increase in frequency and consistency after milk ejection reflex occurs | No change in observable pattern after milk ejection occurs; flutter-sucking more common | Reevaluate latch-on Evaluate milk supply Evaluate milk ejection reflex |

**Table 35-3    Infant Breastfeeding Assessment Tool**

| Score | 3 | 2 | 1 | 0 |
|---|---|---|---|---|
| **Readiness to feed** | Baby starts to feed readily without effort (alert) | Needs mild stimulation to start feeding | Needs more stimulation to rouse and start feeding | Cannot be roused |
| **Rooting** | Roots effectively immediately | Needs some coaxing, prompting, or encouragement to root | Roots poorly, even with coaxing | Did not try to root |
| **Fixing ("latch-on")** | Starts to feed immediately | Takes 3–10 minutes to start | Takes over 10 minutes to start | Did not feed |
| **Sucking pattern** | Sucks well on one or both breasts | Sucks on and off, but needs encouragement | Weak suck, suck on and off for short periods | Did not suck |
| **Maximum possible** | 12 | 8 | 4 | 0 |

Data derived from Matthews MK. Developing an instrument to assess infant breastfeeding behavior in the early neonatal period. *Midwifery* 1988; 4(4): 154–165. Table adaptation reprinted from Biancuzzo M. *Breastfeeding the Healthy Newborn: A Nursing Perspective.* White Plains, NY: March of Dimes Birth Defect Foundation; 1994.

    a. Assesses the mechanics of positioning, latch-on, and swallowing

    b. Is easy to use

    c. Validity and reliability have not been thoroughly studied.

  3. Infant Breastfeeding Assessment Tool (IBFAT) (Matthews, 1988) (Table 35-3)

    a. Looks at the readiness to feed

    b. Lacks a measurable criteria for swallowing or milk transfer

**Table 35-4**   The Latch Scoring System

| | 0 | 1 | 2 |
|---|---|---|---|
| Latch | • Too sleepy or reluctant<br>• No latch achieved | • Repeated attempts<br>• Hold nipple in mouth<br>• Stimulate to suck | • Grasps breast<br>• Tongue down<br>• Lips flanged<br>• Rhythmic sucking |
| Audible swallowing | • None | • A few with stimulation | • Spontaneous and intermittent, 24 hours old<br>• Spontaneous and frequent >24 hours old |
| Type of nipple | • Inverted | • Flat | • Everted (after stimulation) |
| Comfort (breast/nipple) | • Engorged<br>• Cracked, bleeding, large blisters, or bruises | • Filling<br>• Reddened/small blisters or bruises<br>• Mild/moderate discomfort | • Soft<br>• Tender |
| Hold (positioning) | • Full assist (staff holds infant at breast) | • Minimal assist (i.e., elevate head of bed; place pillows for support)<br>• Teach one side; mother does other<br>• Staff holds and then mother takes over | • No assist from staff<br>• Mother able to position/hold infant |

From Jensen D, Wallace S, Kelsay P. LATCH: a breastfeeding charting system and documentation tool. *J Obstet Gnecol Neonatal Nurs* 1994; 23: 29.

4. LATCH (Jensen, Wallace, and Kelsay, 1994) (Table 35-4)
   a. Evaluates the amount of help a mother needs to physically breastfeed
   b. Does not clearly evaluate the latch-on component
5. Mother-Baby Assessment (MBA) (Mulford, 1992) (Table 35-5)
   a. Has a strong evaluation component of the mother's developing skills in both recognizing when it is time to feed the baby and how to feed the baby

**Table 35-5**    Using the MBA Scoring System

| Steps | Points | What to Look For/Criteria |
| --- | --- | --- |
| 1. Signaling | 1 | Mother watches and listens for baby's cues. She may hold, stroke, rock, talk to baby. She stimulates baby if he is sleepy, calms baby if he is fussy. |
| | 1 | Baby gives readiness cues: stirring, alertness, rooting, sucking, hand-to-mouth, vocal cues, cry. |
| 2. Positioning | 1 | Mother holds baby in good alignment within latch-on range of nipple. Baby's body is slightly flexed, entire ventral surface facing mother's body. Baby's head and shoulders are supported. |
| | 1 | Baby roots well at breast, opens mouth wide, tongue cupped and covering lower gum. |
| 3. Fixing | 1 | Mother holds her breast to assist baby as needed, brings baby in close when his mouth is wide open. She may express drops of milk. |
| | 1 | Baby latches on, takes all of nipple and about 2 cm (1 in) of areola into mouth, then suckles, demonstrating a recurrent burst-pause sucking pattern. |
| 4. Milk transfer | 1 | Mother reports feeling any of the following: thirst, uterine cramps, increased lochia, breast ache or tingling, relaxation, sleepiness. Milk leaks from opposite breast. |
| | 1 | Baby swallows audibly; milk is observed in baby's mouth, baby may spit up milk when burping. Rapid "call-up sucking" rate (two sucks/second) changes to "nutritive sucking" rate of about one suck/second. |
| 5. Ending | 1 | Mother's breasts are comfortable; she lets baby suckle until he is finished. After nursing, her breasts feel softer; she has no lumps, engorgement, or nipple soreness. |
| | 1 | Baby releases breast spontaneously, appears satiated. Baby does not root when stimulated. Baby's face, arms, and hands are relaxed; baby may fall asleep. |
| | 10 | |

This is an assessment method for rating the progress of a mother and baby who are *learning* to breastfeed.

For every step, each person—both mother and baby—should receive a "+" before either one can be scored on the following step. If the observer does not observe any of the designated indicators, score "0" for that person on that step.

If help is needed at any step for either the mother or the baby, check "Help" for that step. This notation will not change the total score for mother and baby.

From Mulford C. That mother-baby assessment (MBA): and "Apgar score" for breastfeeding. *J Hum Lact* 1992; 8:82.

6. Potential Early Breast Feeding Problem Tool (PEBPT) (Kerney, Cronenwett, and Barrett, 1990)
    a. Developed to determine which breastfeeding problems are rated highest among breastfeeding mothers
    b. 23 questions, four-point Likert scale
    c. The higher the score, the more breastfeeding problems occurred
7. Maternal Breast Feeding Evaluation Scale (Leff, Jeffries, and Gagne, 1994)
    a. Consists of three subscales: maternal enjoyment/role attainment, infant satisfactions/growth, and lifestyle/maternal body image
    b. Designed to measure positive and negative aspects of breastfeeding that mothers have identified as important in defining successful lactation

Table 35-6 compares the various breastfeeding assessment tools.

**Table 35-6**   Comparison of Breastfeeding Assessment Tools

| Characteristic | IBFAT | MBA | LATCH | SAIB |
|---|---|---|---|---|
| Focus on | Infant | Infant and mother | Infant and mother | Infant and mother |
| Scored by | Mother or nurse | Nurse | Mother or nurse | Nurse |
| Time frame | Progressive; beginning to ending | Progressive; beginning to ending | Static | Any point in the feeding |
| Analysis of sequential scores | Use mean of scores | Use best of scores | Expect increase in scores | Does not apply; this is a yes-no tool |
| Measures | Signaling Rooting Suckling | Readiness Position Latch-on; milk transfer Outcome | Latch-on Audible swallowing Nipple comfort Assistance needed with positioning | Alignment Areolar grasp Areolar compression Audible swallowing |

Modified from Riordan JM, Koehn M. Reliability and validity testing of three breastfeeding assessment tools. *J Obstet Neonatal Nurs* 1997; 26:183.

G. The LC systematically evaluates the mother's and infant's positioning throughout the feeding. The LC:
    1. Avoids positioning and latching the baby for the mother; rather, this process is facilitated so that the mother learns to do this action herself

2. Avoids pushing on the back of the baby's head, compressing the mother's areola, or inserting the areola into the baby's mouth

3. Notes how the nipple appears immediately after feeding

   a. The nipple comes out of the infant's mouth round and of equal color with the areola.

   b. The nipple shows no evidence of trauma.

   c. Notes abnormal nipple shape, blisters, and/or blanching.

   d. Following a feeding, the baby should be calm, satiated, and relaxed.

   e. Note irritability and/or fussiness.

   f. The mother reports the absence of shoulder, neck, or back pain.

   g. The mother appears relaxed.

   h. The mother verbalizes confidence in positioning herself and her infant.

   i. The LC corrects positioning and latch-on techniques only as needed.

   j. The LC observes a return demonstration of skills learned by mother.

   k. The LC documents the consultation.

   l. Complete lactation consultation chart.

   m. Written instructions given to mother for ongoing self-care.

   n. The LC arranges for follow-up care.

   o. In-person follow-up within a reasonable amount of time.

   p. Telephone follow-up if appropriate.

   q. The LC consults with another health care provder if needed.

   r. Immediate contact of the medical provider where warranted.

   s. Provides a consultation report to the health care provider.

Table 35-7 provides information regarding various positions not gone into detail earlier in this chapter.

**Table 35-7**    Specialty Positions

| Type Position | Baby's Position | Mother's Position | Indications for Use |
|---|---|---|---|
| Horizontal Prone | Baby lies horizontally across mother's chest, his or her body perpendicular to hers | Mother lies on her back with her head slightly elevated | Baby having problems coping with fast milk flow, baby having trouble extending tongue, baby having trouble staying on the breast, mother with a persistent plugged duct |

*(continues)*

**Table 35-7**    Specialty Positions (continued)

| Type Position | Baby's Position | Mother's Position | Indications for Use |
|---|---|---|---|
| Vertical Prone | Baby lies parallel to mother, feet resting on the same-side leg as the breast he or she is latched onto | Mother lies on her back with her head slightly elevated | Baby having problems coping with fast milk flow, baby having trouble extending tongue, baby having trouble staying on the breast, mother with a persistent plugged duct |
| Lateral Prone | Baby lies parallel to mother but slightly off to the side; most of weight is on side of his or her body nearest mother's arm and he or she is cradled by her arm | Mother lies on her back with her head slightly elevated | The mother of twins can use this position with a baby at each arm. Baby having problems coping with fast milk flow, baby having trouble extending tongue, baby having trouble staying on the breast, mother with a persistent plugged duct |
| Over-the-Shoulder Prone | Baby lies on a pillow, approaches breast over mother's shoulder | Mother lies on her back with her head slightly elevated | Works best with older baby who has some head control Baby having problems coping with fast milk flow, baby having trouble extending tongue, baby having trouble staying on the breast, mother with a persistent plugged duct |
| Upside Down Side Lying | Baby lies on his or her side upside down in relation to her, feet point toward mother's head | Mother lies on her side | Mother with sore nipples, baby with poor suck, mother with persistent plugged ducts |
| Hands and Knees | Baby lies flat on back elevated by pillows to breast height | Mother raises herself on her hands and knees above baby | Mother of twins, persistent plugged ducts |

| Type Position | Baby's Position | Mother's Position | Indications for Use |
|---|---|---|---|
| Straddle Position | Baby sits in mother's lap, faces mother with legs straddling mother's abdomen | Mother is sitting with baby in lap, facing her and straddling legs around mother's abdomen | Baby having problems coping with fast milk flow, baby with a cleft palate |
| Straddle Position | | Mother uses pillow to bring small baby to breast level and tips head back as baby latches to position better | |
| Combination Cradle and Clutch Hold | One baby in cradle hold, other baby in clutch hold with head on sibling's abdomen | Mother is sitting upright with pillows under mother's elbows and babies | Breastfeeding two babies simultaneously |
| Criss Cross | Two babies' bodies in cradle hold, criss-crossed in mother's lap | Mother is sitting upright with pillows under mother's elbows and babies | Breastfeeding two babies simultaneously |
| Parallel | Babies' bodies extend in same directions, one baby in cradle hold, head in crook of mother's arm and body across mother's lap, other baby's body extends in same direction as sibling off mother's lap, with head supported by mother's hand and arm | Mother is sitting upright with pillows under mother's elbows and on her lap | Breastfeeding two babies simultaneously |
| Double Clutch Hold | Both babies in clutch hold, lying on firm pillows at mother's sides | Mother is sitting upright with feet propped on footstool, chair, books, low horizontal structure such as table, base of hospital tray table | Breastfeeding two babies simultaneously |

*(continued)*

**Table 35-7**    Specialty Positions (continued)

| Type Position | Baby's Position | Mother's Position | Indications for Use |
|---|---|---|---|
| Babies at Side | Babies lie at mother's sides, partly on their sides facing each other with feet in mother's lap | Mother is sitting upright | Breastfeeding two babies simultaneously |
| V-Position | Babies' heads are at mother's breasts, forming V with knees touching in her lap | Mother is lying nearly flat on back with two pillows under head and upper body | Breastfeeding two babies simultaneously, safe and comfortable for night position |
| Slide-Over | Baby begins nursing on preferred breast and mother slides baby over to less preferred breast without changing baby's body position | Mother nurses first on preferred breast; after milk-ejection reflex, mother slides baby over to less preferred breast without changing baby's orientation to mother's body and finishes feeding at less preferred breast | Persuading baby who is refusing one breast to nurse on the less preferred breast |
| Cross-Cradle, Modified Clutch, or Transitional Hold | Baby is supported in mother's lap on a pillow or cushion in horizontal or semi-upright position, baby's mouth at level of nipple or slightly lower, baby's body on his or her side facing her extends along length of mother's forearm, baby's neck and head supported by mother's hand | Mother holds baby using the arm opposite the breast to be used for feeding, right arm when nursing left breast, mother's hand opposite the breast to be used for feeding supports baby's neck and head, baby's body extends along length of forearm, uses same-side hand to support breast | Babies having difficulty latching on, low-birth-weight babies, babies with low muscle tone, babies with weak rooting reflex, babies with weak suck |

Source: Compiled from information in Nohrbacher N, Stock J (1997). *The Breastfeeding Answer Book*. Schaumburg IL: La Leche League International, pp. 50–52, 321–323. Art by Donna Wilson used with permission.

# References

Adams D, Hewell SD. Maternal and professional assessment of breastfeeding. *J Hum Lact* 1997; 13:279–283.

Biancuzzo M. Breastfeeding the newborn: Clinical strategies for nurses. St. Louis, MO: Mosby, Inc., 1999.

Jenks MA. Latch assessment in the hospital nursery. *J Hum Lact* 1991; 7:19–20.

Jensen D, Wallace S, Kelsay P. LATCH: A breastfeeding charting system and documentation tool. *J Obstetr Gynecol Neonatal Nurs* 1994; 23:27–32.

Kearney M, Cronenwett L, Barrett J. Breastfeeding problems in the first week postpartum. *Nurs Res* 1990; 39:90–95.

Leff E, Jeffries S, Gagne M. The development of the maternal breastfeeding evaluation scale. *J Hum Lact* 1994; 10:105–111.

Matthews MK. Developing an instrument to assess infant breastfeeding behavior in the early neonatal period. *Midwifery* 1988; 4:154–165.

Minchin M. Positioning for breastfeeding. *Birth* 1989; 16:67–73.

Mulford C. The Mother-Baby Assessment (MBA): An "Apgar score" for breastfeeding. *J Hum Lact* 1992; 8:79–82.

Renfrew M, Fisher C, Arms S. Bestfeeding: Getting breastfeeding right for you. Revised ed. Berkeley, CA: Celestial Arts, 2000.

Riordan JM, Koehn M. Reliability and validity testing of three breastfeeding assessment tools. *J Obstetr Gynecol Neonatal Nurs* 1997; 26:181–187.

Riordan J. Predicting breastfeeding problems. *AWHONN Lifelines* 1998; December: 31–33.

Riordan J, Bibb D, Miller M, Rawlins T. Predicting breastfeeding duration using the LATCH breastfeeding assessment tool. *J Hum Lact* 2001; 17:20–23.

Schlomer JA, Kemmerer J, Twiss JJ. Evaluating the association of two breastfeeding assessment tools with breastfeeding problems and breastfeeding satisfaction. *J Hum Lact* 1999; 15:35–39.

Shrago L, Bocar D. The infant's contribution to breastfeeding. *J Obstetr Gynecol Neonatal Nurs* 1990; 19:209–215.

Walker M. Management of selected early breastfeeding problems seen in clinical practice. *Birth* 1989; 16(3):148–158.

Walker M. Functional assessment of infant feeding patterns. *Birth* 1989; 16(3):140–147.

Walker M. Do labor medications affect breastfeeding? *J Hum Lact* 1997; 13(2):131–137.

# EXPRESSING/PUMPING BREAST MILK

*Ruth E. Worgan, RN, CM, C&FH, IBCLC*

## OBJECTIVES

- Describe indications for hand and mechanical expressing.
- Discuss the various types of pumps available.
- Describe the techniques of hand expressing
- Describe the action of the various pumps on the market.
- List the advantages and disadvantages of the different types of expressing techniques.
- Discuss selected guidelines for expressing milk.

## Introduction

Many women at some time during their breastfeeding experience might wish to express their breast milk. Whether to initiate or to preserve breastfeeding, the removal of a mother's milk from her breasts either by hand or with a breast pump is a learning experience. Women will benefit from clear instructions and guidelines to express milk in an efficient manner and of an optimal quantity to meet their individual needs.

I   Mothers might wish to express milk for a number of reasons

   A. To increase the milk supply

   B. To initiate lactation in the absence of the baby

   C. To have milk available when she wishes to go out

   D. To provide the baby with breast milk if she is at work or at school

   E. To supply breast milk for a baby who is ill or hospitalized due to prematurity

   F. To relieve or prevent milk engorgement

   G. To remove milk and stimulate the milk supply if the baby is not feeding efficiently

H. To maintain or increase milk production if the mother is traveling, hospitalized, taking medications that are not recommended during breastfeeding, or if milk production has decreased due to infrequent feedings or a slow start in the hospital

I. To contribute to a milk bank

II Hand-expressing breast milk

A. The ability to hand-express breast milk is a learned skill. It is the most common form of expressing throughout the world as no equipment or electricity is required

B. Hand-expressing is performed for a number of reasons

1. To soften the areola

2. This hand-expression enables overfull milk pools to be drained a little to make it easier for baby to latch on

3. To remove milk from an overfull breast if the mother is away for a feeding

4. To collect milk and stimulate milk production if the baby does not feed vigorously

5. To initiate lactation when the infant cannot be put to breast

   a. To save milk for future feedings

   b. To elicit the milk ejection reflex prior to breastfeeding or pumping

C. Helpful hints to facilitate successful expression

1. Some mothers find it easier to learn this technique in the morning when the breasts tend to be fuller.

2. Mothers can express milk right after the baby feeds or between feedings; there is always milk in the breasts.

3. If milk is expressed between feedings, the baby might want to feed a little more frequently until milk production adjusts.

4. Some mothers learn and practice hand expression while the baby is nursing.

   a. The milk in the other breast will have started to flow and might be dripping out.

5. The first few times that a mother tries, hand expressing might seem awkward.

D. Technique

1. The mother should wash her hands well before beginning.

2. Milk can be expressed into any type of container—a bottle, cup, glass, jar, bowl, and so on.

3. It helps if the container has a wide opening.

4. Sterilize the container by boiling it, soaking it in sterilizing solution, microwaving it, or running it through the dishwasher before using it for milk collection.

5. Avoid touching the inner surface of the container to keep it as clean as possible.

6. To elicit the milk ejection reflex, mothers can:

   a. Take a hot shower.

   b. Apply a warm, damp wash cloth to the breasts.

   c. Find a comfortable location and turn on music.

   d. Think of the baby or look at his or her picture.

   e. Massage the breasts.

7. Hand expression should be gentle so as not to damage the breast tissue or skin.

8. For preterm or ill babies, or for babies who are unable to latch to the breast, the mother can hand express droplets of colostrum that are drawn up with a syringe as they appear on the nipple.

   a. Mothers will start by massaging the breast.

      i. This action encourages the milk to move down from the milk-making glands deep in the breast to the milk pools behind the areola.

      ii. The breasts can be massaged in different ways, with the mother deciding which method works best for her.

         (1) Hold the breast with one or both hands (depending on the size of the breast) so that the thumbs are on top of the breast and the fingers are beneath it. Gently compress the breast between the fingers and thumbs, rotating the fingers and thumbs around the breast.

         (2) Or, using the fingertips to massage in small circles all around the breast and under it as well also works.

         (3) This circular motion can cover some of the harder-to-reach areas on the underside of the breast and under the arms.

         (4) This type of massage can also be used while expressing to encourage more milk to flow down to the nipple.

         (5) The mother can place the container under the breast and grasp the areola by putting the thumb on the top margin and her index finger on the bottom margin.

         (6) She will press back toward her chest and then squeeze her thumb and index finger together about 3 centimeters behind the nipple.

         (7) She will do this a few times and then rotate her thumb and index finger about a half inch to the left or right and compress again.

(8)  She will continue to rotate her finger position around the areola so that all lactiferous sinuses are expressed and all sections of the breast are drained.

(9)  She can establish a rhythm of using her other hand to massage, then compress, and so on.

iii.  Another method that some mothers find helpful is to hold the breast so that the thumb is on the top margin of the areola and the other four fingers are cupping the breast from underneath, with the little finger touching the rib.

(1)  To express milk, she will start a wave-like motion from her little finger, pushing gently into the breast followed by the fourth finger, then the third, then the index finger while the thumb compresses from above.

(2)  She can perform this action a few times and rotate the hand position so that all areas of the breast are reached.

(3)  When she is finished on the first breast, she will continue on the second one.

(4)  To obtain more milk, she can return to the first breast again, alternating back and forth to take advantage of the several milk ejection reflexes.

(5)  Many women find this type of milk expression very easy to do and become quickly efficient at removing several ounces of milk at a time from the breasts.

(6)  Other mothers might find this process tiring or too slow.

   (a)  They might also need to express milk more quickly than they can by hand, due to short work breaks or while the baby is napping.

(7)  Some mothers who have physical impediments, such as carpal tunnel syndrome or arthritis, might find this method difficult and painful, or impossible to use. Other expression techniques are available for these women.

(8)  For some mothers, a breast pump is a good option.

**III**  Breast pumps

A.  The choice of a pump depends on the availability and how it will be used.

B.  The pump should be efficient, comfortable, easy to find, affordable, easy to clean, and easy to use.

C.  The two issues most frequently mentioned by mothers when they are choosing or using a pump are the amount of milk that can be pumped and the time that it takes to pump it.

D. Pumps do not suck, pull, or pump milk out of a breast.

E. Pumps create a vacuum that forms a pressure gradient, encouraging milk in the breasts under high pressure (from the let-down reflex) to flow to an area of low pressure in the pump.

F. The pump is different from the specialized sucking method used by babies at the breast.

G. A well full-term baby is much more efficient than a pump at withdrawing milk, so a mother can spend 10–20 minutes pumping milk but not remove as much as an efficiently nursing baby would.

H. There are manual/hand pumps, battery-operated pumps, and electric pumps.

1. Manual or hand pumps

   a. Hand pumps are small, inexpensive, and easily found in maternity catalogs, baby stores, drug stores, large toy stores, department stores, discount stores, hospitals, clinics, groups providing postpartum and breastfeeding support, and hospital supply stores.

   b. They are used for occasional milk expression.

   c. The limitations of this class of pumps will pose less of a problem if the mother has an abundant milk supply and a vigorously nursing baby, and is using the pump only a few times a week.

   d. There is a large variety of hand pumps available.

   e. Bicycle Horn-Type Hand Pumps

      i. Mothers should avoid those that use a rubber bulb to create a vacuum by squeezing and releasing it.

      ii. The ones shaped like bicycle horns are usually inefficient, provide a poor fit between the breast and the pump, can cause nipple pain and damage, and can contaminate the milk if it flows back into the bulb.

      iii. They have a very small area that collects the milk, so the pump has to be emptied frequently.

      iv. These pumps are inexpensive and can still be found in many countries.

2. Cylinder pumps are a category of pumps made up of two cylinders, one inside the other.

   a. A vacuum is generated when the outer one is pulled while the inner remains over the areola.

   b. The inner cylinder with the flange (the part of the pump placed on the breast) has a gasket at the other end to help form a seal with the edge of the outer cylinder.

   c. These work better than the rubber bulb pumps, are easier to clean and use, and are not very expensive.

    d. Most come with small plastic or silicone inserts that are placed into the flange to improve the fit between the breast and the pump.

    e. They require less frequent emptying than the rubber bulb pumps, usually after about 2–3 ounces have been collected in the outer cylinder.

    f. Some cylinder pumps use standard baby bottles to collect milk.

       i. This eliminates the need to transfer milk to another container while pumping.

    g. Several brands of these pumps can be adapted for use on the large electric pumps.

    h. A few of these types of pumps have an adjustable vacuum and/or a mechanism that automatically interrupts the vacuum at the end of the outward pull on the cylinder.

       i. These are desirable safety features, because some of these types of pumps are capable of generating very high vacuum levels on the nipple and areola.

       ii. Too high of a vacuum can be generated if the mother pulls the outer cylinder out so far that it becomes painful.

       iii. This situation can also cause the outer cylinder to come completely off the inner one, spilling all the collected milk.

    i. Some mothers find improved milk collection by pulling and holding while others get more milk by using shorter, more frequent pulls.

    j. Be aware that as the cylinder fills with milk, the mother will need to shorten the pull because of the higher negative pressure.

    k. Another group of manual pumps are the ones that generate a vacuum when the mother squeezes and releases a handle.

       i. These pumps are lightweight, inexpensive, easy to use, can be quite efficient, and are easily cleaned.

       ii. They can cause the wrist and arm to tire quickly with repeated use.

       iii. Their operation will be difficult if the mother has hand or arm problems, such as carpal tunnel syndrome, arthritis, and so on.

       iv. Several of these have soft silicone inserts that can be placed in the flange for a better fit between the breast and the pump.

I. Using a hand pump

    1. Mothers should be advised to read and follow the directions that come with the pump.

       a. These instructions tell how it is designed to be used and how to clean it.

    2. Mothers should have all equipment ready before they begin.

    3. She should wash her hands before each pumping session.

4. The pump should be sterilized before the first use, after which washing in the dishwasher or with hot soapy water is usually sufficient to keep it clean.

   a. All parts that come in contact with the milk should be washed in hot, soapy water, rinsed, and air-dried after each use.

5. Milk should be expressed in a private, comfortable place.

6. If the mother's arm gets tired, she can prop the pump on a pillow, table, or wide chair arm while she pumps.

7. She can get something to drink, like juice or water, unplug the phone or let the answering machine take care of calls, and create a private, uninterrupted time.

8. If she is pumping at work, she should avoid using a bathroom stall.

   a. This area is a germ-ridden place where no one's food should be prepared.

9. If the pump has inserts, she should select the one that gives the best fit.

   a. All of the nipple and at least some of the areola should be covered by the flange depending on the size of the areola.

   b. The flange should not extend way beyond the areola, nor should the areola extend way beyond the flange.

   c. The correct fit of the flange enables part of the areola and all of the nipple to slip easily and comfortably into it.

   d. Some women find that if they moisten the flange with warm water, it prevents the flange from moving when they are manipulating the pump.

   e. The flange should be centered over the nipple and areola.

      i. Some pumps have different-sized flanges to accommodate larger nipples and breasts; the mother should be fit with a flange that accommodates the anatomical configuration of her breast.

J. Using a cylinder pump

1. The mother should gently pull the outer cylinder away from her body several times until the milk begins to spray out.

2. She should pull on the cylinder just enough to create a constant suction and stream of milk.

3. When the flow slows or stops, she will push and pull on the cylinder again to restart the milk flow.

4. She can massage her breast while she pumps to help the milk flow.

5. When she can no longer see milk flowing while she massages the breast, she can push the outer cylinder toward her breast and insert her finger into the side of the flange to remove the pump from her breast.

6. She can massage the breast again and apply the pump to the same breast or massage the other side and repeat the process.

7. If she is using a pump with a pressure setting, she should start on low and gradually increase the vacuum to where she is comfortable and removing the maximum amount of milk.

8. Many women express both breasts twice following breast massage.

9. If she is using a squeeze-handle pump, she will need to practice a little to find the most efficient rhythm of squeezing the handle, holding it, and releasing it.

10. Tips to assist in successful expression:

   a. There are two things that can make pumping easier and faster, and often increase the amount of milk expressed.

      i. Encourage the milk to let down or flow before she starts pumping.

         (1) This action decreases the amount of time the pump's pressure is applied to the breast and creates a way to make the milk flow more easily.

         (2) She can facilitate this by thinking about her baby, hand expressing, massaging the breast, applying warm compresses to the breast, looking at a picture of the baby, or by using slow, deep breathing.

         (3) Mothers can also express when the milk lets down between feedings or first thing in the morning when the breasts are fullest.

      ii. The other technique that helps the milk flow faster is to massage and compress the breast while the pump is applying vacuum pressure.

         (1) She can gently compress the breast on the outward stroke of a cylinder pump, massage the breast as the outer cylinder is pushed toward the breast, and squeeze again on the outward pull.

         (2) With a squeeze handle pump, she would compress the breast as she squeezes the pump handle and massage the breast when she releases the handle.

         (3) The let-down reflex can become conditioned with some mothers finding that if they pump in the same place at the same time, their body comes to associate these cues with milk flow.

K. Battery-operated pumps

   1. Battery-operated pumps are small, portable, hand-held pumps that use a small motor to generate a vacuum.

   2. They usually require two AA 1.5 volt batteries or size C batteries.

   3. Some of these pumps can work well for a mother who has a good milk supply and a quick, strong let-down reflex.

4. They use batteries very quickly, however, and might not provide enough stimulation for a mother who needs to increase her milk supply or for long-term pumping.

5. These pumps generally have a dial or a way to select the level of vacuum that the pump will generate.

6. Except for a couple of brands of these pumps, the vacuum needs to be released manually for the pause part of the cycle, otherwise a continuous vacuum is created causing nipple damage.

7. When a baby swallows at the breast, he or she interrupts the suction placed on the areola.

8. Suction on a non-automated pump cannot just be turned on and left to run.

   a. If using a pump that does not automatically interrupt the suction, ensure that the mother presses the release button every few seconds to mimic a baby's suck-pause cycle.

9. Alkaline batteries are recommended to get the highest number of cycles (suction and release) per minute.

10. As the batteries wear down, the pump takes longer and longer to generate suction after it is interrupted.

    a. This process can hurt the nipple if left on too long.

11. Rechargeable batteries usually need to be charged daily and might not produce as many cycles and as strong a vacuum as alkaline batteries.

12. Most of these pumps have models that accept an A/C adapter so that they can be plugged into wall electricity.

    a. This allows the pump to generate as many cycles as the motor is capable of doing.

13. Battery pumps require only one hand to operate and are popular with mothers who pump several times each week.

14. Some mothers use two battery pumps to pump both breasts at the same time if they are on a tight schedule.

15. If the mother is using a battery pump that does not automatically interrupt the suction, she must make sure to press the suction release button every few seconds to her comfort.

    a. She should set these pumps to the lowest suction level and increase it gradually as needed.

    b. Massaging and compressing the breast as she pushes the suction release button will increase the pressure inside the breast as the suction in the pump builds again.

L. Electric pumps

1. There are small, medium, and large electric breast pumps.

2. The smaller pumps are usually semi-automatic.

   a. In other words, the mother can set the level of suction but must interrupt it every couple of seconds by uncovering and covering a small hole with her thumb or index finger.

3. A few models are automatic and have collection kits that enable mothers to pump both breasts at the same time.

   a. Mothers who work part time or who pump numerous times each week might find these a good choice if they have a well-established milk supply.

4. The medium-sized electric pumps are somewhat more expensive and represent a committed investment in breastfeeding.

   a. Mothers who are employed full time might find these a good choice because they have car adapters and carrying cases with ice packs, and are small and lightweight

   b. They usually have the capability to pump both breasts at the same time.

   c. They can also be run on batteries.

5. The large electric pumps are preferred for mothers who require long-term expressing for ill babies, preterm babies, babies who have special problems where the mother must initiate and maintain her milk supply until the baby can be put to the breast, and sometimes by mothers who are in school or who are employed full time.

   a. These pumps are usually very expensive and are generally rented from depots in the community.

      i. Hospitals usually make these available to mothers while their baby or they are hospitalized, and some employers have these on site for use by their breastfeeding employees.

      ii. In a long-term pumping situation, it is actually less expensive to rent the pump on a long-term basis than it is to buy formula for the feedings that the mother would miss.

   b. The large electric pumps are also used by mothers who have a low milk supply that they wish to increase.

      i. All have the option to pump both breasts at the same time.

      ii. Decreases the time it takes for each pumping session to about 10 minutes and better maintains milk production when mothers and babies are separated

      iii. These pumps cycle in a way that is closer to what a baby does.

        iv. They can be rented from a hospital, a hospital supply house, a pharmacy, a breastfeeding support group, a lactation consultant, a breastfeeding counselor, and a clinic.

            (1) All of the companies have lists of where to find their rental depots in the community.

            (2) Many insurance carriers reimburse mothers for electric breast pump rental if their baby is hospitalized.

            (3) A prescription for breast milk from the baby's physician might be required to secure the rental and to extend it for use after the baby is discharged.

M. Tips to assist successful expression:

  1. Clean all the pieces before first using them.

  2. Assemble the collection kit according to the directions that come with the pump.

  3. Set the pump on the lowest suction setting, increasing it only if needed.

  4. Start the milk flowing first, put the flanges on the breasts, and massage the breasts while pumping.

  5. If using the double collection kit, hold the flanges with the forearm to free the other hand for breast massage.

  6. This process might be easier if the collection bottles are placed on a table while pumping.

  7. Some women secure the flanges to their bra to free one or both hands.

  8. Frequency of breast expression: depends upon the reason for expressing.

    a. For occasional expressing, pump during, after, or between feedings, whichever gives the best results.

    b. Express as many times as required to obtain the amount of milk needed to use or store.

    c. Many mothers tend to express more milk first thing in the morning.

    d. For employed mothers, expressing may be needed on a regular basis for at least the number of breastfeeds that are missed.

    e. To prevent a gradual decline in the milk supply if returning to work within 6–8 weeks, she should express enough milk during her maternity leave to increase her production by about 50 percent.

    f. This milk can be frozen for later use.

    g. To increase a low milk supply, she can express after each feeding to increase stimulation to the breast.

    h. For preterm or ill babies, the mother should begin expressing milk within two hours of the birth and 8–12 times each 24 hours thereafter;

she should not delay expressing, and can use a large rented electric pump with a double collection kit.

   i. For engorgement, she can pump a little before she nurses in order to soften the breasts and pump after she nurses if she still feels full or uncomfortable.

9. Duration of expression

   a. Duration of expression depends on the reason for expressing, the type of expressing, the equipment used for expressing, and the time of day.

      i. If pumping one breast at a time: pump for about 10–15 minutes with an electric pump and 10–20 minutes with a manual or battery pump.

      ii. Some mothers switch from the first breast to the second and back again a couple of times until there is little to no milk flowing when the breast is massaged.

      iii. If pumping both breasts at the same time with an electric pump: pump for about 10 minutes or until the flow decreases.

10. Cleaning the expressing equipment:

   a. After expressing milk, rinse all parts with cold water that have come into contact with the milk.

   b. Wash the parts in hot soapy water, rinse well, and air dry.

   c. Some pump parts can be put on the top rack of a dishwasher.

   d. In some countries, health departments recommend to sterilize the equipment by boiling, microwaving, or using cold water sterilizing solutions.

   e. Check the directions that came with the pump.

   f. Some mothers boil pump parts, especially if they are expressing milk for a preterm or ill baby.

      i. To avoid melting the pump in the saucepan, either set a timer or add a couple of marbles to the water; if the mother hears them rattling around, the water level is getting too low.

      ii. Be careful with the rubber gasket on cylinder pumps and other gaskets on hand-held or electric pumps.

         (1) Boiling these or running them through the dishwasher might cause the rubber to shrink or harden.

         (2) Such gaskets will no longer be able to maintain a seal to provide suction.

         (3) The gasket must be removed for cleaning because it can harbor bacteria if left on the inner cylinder or in a bottle.

         (4) Some pumps come with extra gaskets, or more can be ordered from the manufacturer.

**IV** Common expressing/pumping problems:

   A. Sore nipples

      1. Some mothers find that their nipples become sore from pumping.

         a. This condition usually gets better with time, but there are a few things that can be done to prevent or ease the situation.

            i. She can massage her breast and start the milk flowing before using the pump.

            ii. Continue massaging the breast while she pumps in order to speed things up.

            iii. Check that the flange fits properly and is not chafing the areola or putting pressure on the junction of the nipple and areola.

            iv. Pump for shorter periods of time but more frequently until the nipples feel better.

            v. Apply breast milk to the nipples after each pumping session and allow to air dry.

            vi. Avoid creams, lotions, ointment, and so on because they usually do not function to heal sore nipples.

            vii. Check the pressure settings on pumps that have these.

               (1) Put it on the lowest setting.

            viii. If she is using a cylinder pump, she should not pull out as far on the outer cylinder.

            ix. If she is using a battery pump or a semi-automatic electric pump, interrupt the vacuum more frequently.

            x. Avoid having the nipples sit in wet nursing pads between pumping sessions.

            xi. Try a different-size flange.

            xii. Use or discontinue using the inserts in the flange to see whether either of these actions results in a better fit.

            xiii. Change to a different manufacturer's collection kit with a big electric pump, or change pumps to find one that gives a better fit.

            xiv. Try hand-expressing milk until the nipples feel better.

   B. Fluctuation or decrease in milk supply

      1. Many women experience fluctuations in their milk supply if expressing over a long period of time.

         a. This may cause the mother distress and she may question her ability to continue providing milk for her baby.

            i. Some anxiety may be relieved by discussing this with the mother prior to it happening and having a plan of action if and when it does.

2. If the mother knows that she will be pumping for an extended period of time, for example, with a preterm baby or early return to work, one way to avoid this gradual decline in milk production is to intentionally over-produce milk during the first couple of weeks after the baby is born.

   a. She then continues expressing as much milk as possible, even if it is way more than her baby needs at that time.

   b. This situation sets milk production at a very high rate right from the start, and a gradual fall in amount will not be a problem.

3. The following is a list of questions to ask the mother to help discover where the problem might lie and what might help increase the milk supply:

   a. Are you eating a well-balanced diet, or have you recently begun a weight-reduction program?

   b. If you have tried to lose weight quickly, is it more than a half-pound per week?

   c. Have you returned to work or increased your commitments outside the house?

   d. Have you changed your pumping routine or decreased the number of times per day that you pump?

   e. Have you been ill or under a lot of stress?

   f. Are you taking medications or herbal preparations that could affect the milk supply?

   g. Are you getting enough rest?

   h. Have you recently had a lot of company, houseguests, or functions to attend?

   i. Is it a busy holiday period?

   j. If your baby is hospitalized, has his or her condition changed?

4. Troubleshoot and correct any of the above situations.

5. For long-term pumping, she can try some of the following tips:

   a. Talk to a friend or another mother who has experienced this type of pumping situation.

   b. If the baby is hospitalized, she can bring home a blanket or other object from her baby's crib or isolette.

   c. If possible, express at the hospital next to the baby's isolette.

   d. If the baby's condition permits, she can hold him while she pumps or hold his or her hand.

   e. Skin-to-skin holding of the baby can increase milk production, especially if the baby can nuzzle the breast while he or she is there.

   f. Use a relaxation audio tape to help her relax before and during each pumping session.

g. Medications such as metoclopramide (Reglan) or domperidone (Motilium) can sometimes be used to boost a milk supply.

h. Many mothers have found several acupuncture sessions quite helpful in increasing milk production.

V  Storing breast milk

A. Breast milk can be stored in plastic bottles, plastic nurser bags, breast milk storage bags, glass bottles, glass containers, or ice cube trays.

B. All containers should be clean and have covers.

C. Mothers should always leave extra room in the container if she is freezing milk, because it expands when frozen.

D. Label the containers with the date and time she expressed the milk, using the oldest first.

E. If she is taking milk to her hospitalized baby or day care provider, she should make sure the baby's name is on the label.

F. Milk from each pumping session can be put in the same container in the refrigerator and frozen at the end of the day.

G. If pumping for a preterm baby, it is better to keep the milk from each pumping session in a separate container to avoid contamination when it is handled, opened, and closed repeatedly.

H. Special care nurseries usually give mothers the container in which they want the milk stored.

I. Cooled milk can also be added to containers of previously frozen milk.

J. Some mothers express milk directly into nurser bags attached to an electric pump or into very small bottles for use with preterm infants.

K. Freeze milk in small amounts of 2–4 oz to avoid waste and to thaw quickly.

L. If storing milk in a plastic or glass bottle, cap it tightly with the cap and disc and do not store it with the nipple unit in place.

M. If storing milk in plastic nurser bags, use a twist tie to seal the top, double bag the milk (because these bags puncture easily), and place the bag in a paper cup inside an air-tight container.

N. Do not use nurser bags for storing milk for preterm babies.

O. Avoid touching the inside of any of these containers.

VI  Milk storage times

A. Room temperature (77°F–27°C)—four hours for a healthy, full-term infant (not for a preterm or ill infant)

B. Cooler with blue ice (59°F)—24 hours. Employed mothers frequently use small coolers with frozen ice packs to keep milk chilled at work and during their commute

C. Refrigerator (35°F)—3–5 days. If milk will be stored longer than this period, freeze it. Keep it in the back of the refrigerator, not on the door

D. Freezer compartment inside a refrigerator—two weeks

E. Self-defrosting freezer compartment that is separate from the refrigerator (0°F) (on top, on the bottom, side by side)—several weeks to several months. Milk should be kept in the back of the freezer, not on the door, and off of the bottom where it becomes warm during the defrost cycle

F. Deep freezer with no defrost cycle (0°F)—6–12 months

G. Previously frozen breast milk in the refrigerator—24–48 hours

H. Most mothers want to know how much breast milk their baby will take so that they do not defrost too much and waste it or so the day care provider, sitter, or father has enough for feedings. The following is a rough guide for average feeding amounts:

1. 2–3 oz (60–80ml) for a baby up to two weeks

2. 3–5 oz (80–150ml) for a baby up to two months

3. 4–6 oz (150–180ml) for a baby 2–4 months

4. 5–8 oz (180–200ml) for a baby 4–6 months

5. She can keep a few 1–2 oz (30–60ml) containers of milk for snacks or if the baby needs more than expected at a particular feeding

VII To use stored breast milk

A. Breast milk should be served at body temperature (36–37°C). This assists in reactivating the antibodies in breast milk.

B. To warm refrigerated milk, stand the container in a bowl or pan of warm water or hold the container under warm running water.

1. Shake it gently several times, because the milk separates into layers when it is stored.

2. The mother will notice skim-looking milk on the bottom, richer-looking milk in the middle, and a layer of cream on the top.

a. This appearance is normal and is exactly how human milk should look.

b. Stored milk might also have different-colored layers depending on what the mother has eaten.

C. To thaw frozen milk, keep it in its container and thaw it in a bowl of warm water.

1. It can also be thawed under warm running water or overnight in the refrigerator.

2. Do not thaw or warm breast milk on the stove or in a microwave oven.

a. Microwaving breast milk can destroy some of the disease-protective factors in the milk and risks burning the mouth and throat of the baby due to the uneven heating by microwave ovens.

        b. Mothers should leave instructions with anyone taking care of the baby that the milk is not to be microwaved.

    3. Babies do not need anything warmer than room temperature.

    4. If the baby does not take all the milk in the bottle, it can be placed in the refrigerator for a couple of hours and given to the baby when he or she is hungry.

        a. After that, discard the milk.

  D. Glass or plastic bottles for collecting and storing milk should be washed in hot soapy water, scrubbed with a bottle brush, rinsed thoroughly, and air-dried.

    1. Mothers can also wash them in a dishwasher according to the manufacturer's directions.

  E. Breast milk that has been frozen for several weeks or months or that has been stored in a self-defrosting freezer might have a stale or soapy odor or taste.

    1. This is generally attributed to lipase breaking down some of the milk fat during storage.

    2. It has no effect on the safety or nutrition of the milk.

  F. Refrigerated milk can be transported in an insulated box, chest, or cooler bag by using blue ice.

  G. Frozen milk should be put in an insulated box, cooler bag, or chest with no ice.

    1. The ice is actually warmer than the frozen milk and can partially defrost the milk.

    2. Frozen milk that is transported over long distances is packed in dry ice.

**VIII** Pump considerations for helping mothers choose the pump that is best suited for their needs.

  A. Vacuum amounts

    1. < 150 mmHg might result in little milk output.

    2. > 200 mmHg might result in pain and damage to the nipples.

        a. Manual or automatic cycling

        b. Time needed to generate the vacuum

        c. Pressure curve

        d. Cycling frequency

        e. Quality of fit between the flange and the breast

        f. Flange dimensions and characteristics

        g. Compression stimuli

        h. Teat deformation

        i. Milk yield

        j. Summary of expression parameters

## Negative Pressure Ranges

| Baby | Hand Expression | Hand Pump | Battery Pump | Electric Pump |
|---|---|---|---|---|
| 50–241mmHg | None | 0–400mmHg | 50–305mmHg | 10–500mmHg |
| 50–155mmHg average | | | | |
| Basal resting pressure to keep nipple in mouth 70–200mmHg | | | | |

## Positive Pressure Ranges

| Baby | Breast and Milk Ejection Reflex | Hand Expression | Hand Pump | Battery Pump | Electric Pump |
|---|---|---|---|---|---|
| Tongue 0.73–3.6mmHg | 28mmHg when breast is full | Theoretically could exert >760mmHg, which is atmospheric pressure | None to minimal | None to minimal | Without compression stimulus, none to minimal |
| Jaw 200–300g | 10-20mmHg with milk ejection reflex | | | | With compression stimulus |

## Hormonal Response Ranges

| | Baby | Hand Expression | Hand Pump | Battery Pump | Electric Pump |
|---|---|---|---|---|---|
| Prolactin | 55–550ng/ml | 67ng/ml | 67ng/ml | 59.7ng/ml | 46–405ng/ml |
| Basal levels up to 200ng/ml first 10 days 10–90 days 60–110ng/ml | | 28–42 days postpartum | 28–42 days postpartum | 28–42 days postpartum | Single pumping 92.1 ± 29.2ng/ml Double pumping |

|  | Baby | Hand Expression | Hand Pump | Battery Pump | Electric Pump |
|---|---|---|---|---|---|
| 90–180 days 50ng/ml 180 days to 1 year 30-40ng/ml |  |  |  |  | 136 ± 31.6ng/ml |
| Oxytocin | 5–15 units/ml |  |  |  |  |
|  | 100mU released during 10 minutes |  |  |  |  |

**Mechanics**

|  | Baby | Hand Expression | Hand Pump | Battery Pump | Electric Pump |
|---|---|---|---|---|---|
| Cycles per minute | 36–126 | variable | Variable | 5–60 | 2–84 |
| Duration of vacuum | 0.7 seconds | none | Variable | 1–50 seconds | 1–3 seconds |
| Duration of rest | 0.7 seconds intersuck interval | Variable | Variable |  |  |
| Volume of milk per suck | 0.14ml/suck at the beginning of a feeding |  |  |  |  |
|  | 0.01ml/suck at end of feeding |  |  |  |  |

© Marsha Walker, RN, IBCLC 2000

B. Flanges
   1. There are many different flange types and sizes. It is important to facilitate successful expressing to consider the availability in your community of the different pump types and what is best suited for the size and shape of the nipple and breast.
   2. Flange Types
      a. Hard plastic
      b. Flexible silicone

c. Glass

d. Solid casing with a collapsible liner

e. Inserts

f. Irregularities

g. Different-size flanges and shanks (for better fit to anatomical configuration of the breast)

h. Dimensions of the higher rated manual pumps

   i. Diameter of flange = 60–69mm

   ii. Depth of flare = 25–30mm

   iii. Inner opening (shank) = 21–26mm

   iv. Range of shank or inner opening diameter in pumps currently on the market: $1/_2$"–$1^1/_2$" (12.69mm–38mm)

i. Simultaneous (SIM) and sequential (SEQ) pumping comparisons

| | |
|---|---|
| Neifert and Seacat 1985<br>n=10<br>2–7 months<br>postpartum<br>SEQ=20 minutes<br>SIM=10 minutes<br>Term infants | Milk yield similar, volume obtained in $1/_2$ the time with SIM with lower vacuum levels; increased prolactin rise with SIM |
| Auerbach 1990<br>n=25<br>5–35 weeks<br>postpartum<br>term infants | SIM=highest milk yields in 7–12 minutes; higher milk volume<br>SEQ=10-15 minutes to reach maximum milk yield |
| Groh-Wargo et al., 1995<br>n=32<br>preterm infants<br>pumped 3–5<br>times/day | SIM=16 minutes per session; 7.6 +3 hours per week<br>SEQ=24 minutes per session; 11.1 ± 3.1 hours per week<br>Average 28 pumping sessions per week=400ml/day of milk<br>did not see increased prolactin |
| Hill et al., 1996<br>n=9<br>preterm<br>pumped × 5 | SEQ 5 × 5 × 5 × 5, 20 minutes total; milk volumes decreased after 25 days;<br>proportion of prolactin at day 42 was 52 percent of level at day 21; milk yield |

during hospital stay
pumped × 8 at
home through day 42

ranges 158.4g day 3–505.8g day 20
SIM milk volumes continued to rise over
entire study time; prolactin at day 42 was 85%
of level at day 21; milk volume ranges 41.4g
day 3 to 741g on day 41

Hill et al., 1999
n=39
preterm infants
pumped × 8/24h

SIM 10 minutes; milk weights higher each week
of the study in SIM;
pumping frequency=31 ± 11.93 times per week
to 45 ± 10.88 times
SEQ 5 × 5 × 5 × 5 for 20 minutes; pumping
frequency=28 ± 8.9 times per week to 41 ±
9.05 times per week
Hours from birth to initiation of pumping:
SEQ 9.7 hours to 101 hours (4.2 days)
SIM 28.28 hours to 84.3 hours (3.5 days)
Milk weights inversely correlated to number of
hours from birth to initiation of pumping
Milk weights positively correlated with weekly
frequency of pumping and Kangaroo Care

# References

Arnold LDW. Recommendations for collection, storage and handling of a mother's milk for her own infant in the hospital setting, 3rd ed. Denver, CO: Human Milk Banking Association of North America, 1999.

Asquith MT, Harod J. Reduction of bacterial contamination in banked human milk. *J Pediatr* 1979; 95:993–994.

Asquith MT, Pedrotti PW, Harrod JR, et al. The bacterial content of breast milk after the early initiation of expression using a standard technique. *J Pediatr Gastroenterol Nutr* 1984; 3:104–107.

Asquith MT, Sharp R, Stevenson DK. Decreased bacterial contamination of human milk expressed with an electric breast pump. *J California Perinatal Assoc* 1985; 4:45–47.

Auerbach KG. Sequential and simultaneous breast pumping: A comparison. *Int J Nurs Stud* 1990; 27:257–265.

Auerbach KG, Walker M. When the mother of a premature infant uses a breast pump: What every NICU nurse needs to know. *Neonatal Network* 1994; 13:23–29.

Biancuzzo M. Selecting pumps for breastfeeding mothers. *JOGNN* 1999; 28:417–426.

Blenkharn JI. Infection risks from electrically operated breast pumps. *J Hosp Infect* 1989; 13:27–31.

Boutte CA, Garza C, Fraley JK, et al. Comparison of hand and electric-operated breast pumps. *Human Nutr:Applied Nutr* 1985; 39A:426–430.

Bowles BC, Stutte PC, Hensley JH. New benefits from an old technique: Alternate massage in breastfeeding. *Genesis* 1987-1988; 9:5–9, 17.

Breier BH, Milsom SR, Blum WF, et al. Insulin-like growth factors and their binding proteins in plasma and milk after growth hormone-stimulated galactopoiesis in normally lactating women. *Acta Endocrinologica* 1993; 129:427–435.

Budd SC, Erdman SH, Long DM, et al. Improved lactation with metoclopramide: A case report. *Clin Pediatr* 1993; January:53–57.

Chetwynd AG, Diggle PJ, Drewett RF, et al. A mixture model for sucking patterns of breast-fed infants. *Statistics in Med* 1998; 17:395–405.

Clavey S. The use of acupuncture for the treatment of insufficient lactation (Que Ru). *Am J Acupuncture* 1996; 24:35–46.

Costa KM. A comparison of colony counts of breast milk using two methods of breast cleansing. *JOGNN* 1989; May/June:231–236.

Daly SE, Kent JC, Huynh DQ, et al. The determination of short-term breast volume changes and the rate of synthesis of human milk using computerized breast measurement. *Exp Physiol* 1992; 77:79–87.

Daly SEJ, et al. The short-term synthesis and infant regulated removal of milk in lactating women. *Exp Phys* 1993; 78:209–220.

Daly SE, Hartmann PE. Infant demand and milk supply. Part I. Infant demand and milk production in lactating women. *J Hum Lact* 1995; 11:21–25.

Daly SEJ, Hartmann PE. Infant demand and milk supply. Part 2: The short-term control of milk synthesis in lactating women. *J Hum Lact* 1995; 11:27–37.

DeCarvalho M, Anderson D, Giangreco A, et al. Frequency of milk expression and milk production by mothers of non-nursing premature neonates. *Am J Dis Child* 1985; 139:483–485.

De Sanctis V, Vitali U, Atti G, et al. Comparison of prolactin response to suckling and breast pump aspiration in lactating mothers. *La Ricerca Clin Lab* 1981; 11:81–85.

Donowitz LG, Marsik FJ, Fisher KA, et al. Contaminated breast milk: A source of Klebsiella bacteremia in a newborn intensive care unit. *Rev Infect Dis* 1981; 3:716–720.

Drewett RF, Woolridge MW. Sucking patterns of human babies on the breast. *Early Hum Dev* 1979; 3/4:315–320.

Egnell E. The mechanics of different methods of emptying the female breast. *J Swed Med Assoc* 1956; 40:1–8.

Ehrenkranz R, Ackerman B. Metoclopramide effect on faltering milk production by mothers of premature infants. *Pediatrics* 1986; 78:614–619.

El-Mohandes AE, Schatz V, Keiser JF, et al. Bacterial contaminants of collected and frozen human milk used in an intensive care nursery. *Am J Infect Control* 1993; 21:226–230.

El-Mohandes AE, Keiser JF, Johnson LA, et al. Aerobes isolated in fecal microflora of infants in the intensive care nursery: relationship to human milk use and systemic sepsis. *Am J Infect Control* 1993; 21:231–234.

Ehrenkranz R, Ackerman B. Metoclopramide effect on faltering milk production by mothers of premature infants. *Pediatrics* 1986; 78:614–619.

Feher S, et al. Increased breastmilk production for premature infants with a relaxation/imagery audiotape. *Pediatrics* 1989; 83:57–60.

Frantz K. Breastfeeding product guide 1994. Sunland, CA: Geddes Productions, 1993.

Frantz K. Breastfeeding product guide supplement. Sunland, CA: Geddes Productions, 1999.

Grams M. Breastfeeding source book. Sheridan, WY: Achievement Press, 1988, 100–142.

Green D, Moye L, Schreiner RL, et al. The relative efficacy of four methods of human milk expression. *Early Hum Dev* 1982; 6:153–159.

Gransden WR, Webster M, French GL, et al. An outbreak of Serratia marcescens transmitted by contaminated breast pumps in a special care baby unit. *J Hosp Infect* 1986; 7:149–154.

Groh-Wargo S, Toth A, Mahoney K, et al. The utility of a bilateral breast pumping system for mothers of premature infants. *Neonatal Network* 1995; 14:31–35.

Gunn AJ, Gunn TR, Rabone DL, et al. Growth hormone increases breast milk volumes in mothers of preterm infants. *Pediatrics* 1996; 98:279–282.

Gunther M. Sore nipples: Causes and prevention. *Lancet* 1945; November 10:590–593.

Hill PD, Brown LP, Harker TL. Initiation and frequency of breast expression in breastfeeding mothers of LBW and VLBW infants. *Nurs Res* 1995; 44:352–355.

Hill PD, Aldag JC, Chatterton RT. The effect of sequential and simultaneous breast pumping on milk volume and prolactin levels: A pilot study. *J Hum Lact* 1996; 12:193–199.

Hill PD, Aldag JC, Chatterton RT. Effects of pumping style on milk production in mothers of non-nursing preterm infants. *J Hum Lact* 1999; 15:209–216.

Hill PD, Aldag JC, Chatterton Jr RT. Breastfeeding experience and milk weight in lactating mothers pumping for preterm infants. *Birth* 1999; 26:233–238.

Hill PD, Aldag JC, Chatterton RT. Initiation and frequency of pumping and milk production in mothers of non-nursing preterm infants. *J Hum Lact* 2001; 17:9–13.

Hopkinson JM, Schanler RJ, Garza C. Milk production by mothers of premature infants. *Pediatrics* 1988; 81:815–820.

Hurst NM, Valentine CJ, Renfro L, et al. Skin-to-skin holding in the neonatal intensive care unit influences maternal milk volume. *J Perinatol* 1997; 17:213–217.

Johnson CA. An evaluation of breast pumps currently available on the American market. *Clin Pediatr* 1983; 22:40–45.

Meier P, Wilks S. The bacteria in expressed mothers' milk. *MCN* 1987; 12:420–423.

Milsom SR, Breier BH, Gallaher BW, et al. Growth hormone stimulates galactopoiesis in healthy lactating women. *Acta Endocrinologica* 1992; 127:337–343.

Moloney AC, Quoraishi AH, Parry P, et al. A bacteriological examination of breast pumps. *J Hosp Infect* 1987; 9:169–174.

Morse JM, Bottorff JL. The emotional experience of breast expression. *J Nurse Midwifery* 1988; 33:165–170.

National Health and Medical Research Council. Infant feeding guidelines for health workers. Canberra: Australian Government Printing Service, 1995.

Neifert MR, Seacat JM. Milk yield and prolactin rise with simultaneous breast pumping. Ambulatory Pediatric Association Annual Meeting, Washington, DC, May 7–10, 1985.

Nwankwo MU, Offor E, Okolo AA, et al. Bacterial growth in expressed breast milk. *Ann Trop Paediatr* 1988; 8:92–95.

Paul VK, Singh M, Deorari AK, et al. Manual and pump methods of expression of breast milk. *Indian J Pediatr* 1996; 63:87–92.

Pittard WB, Geddes K, Brown S, et al. Bacterial contamination of human milk: Container type and method of expression. *Am J Perinatol* 1991; 8:25–27.

Prieto CR, Cardenas H, Salvatierra AM, et al. Sucking pressure and its relationship to milk transfer during breastfeeding in humans. *J Reproduction Fertility* 1996; 108:69–74.

Ruis H, Rolland R, Doesburg W, et al. Oxytocin enhances onset of lactation among mothers delivering prematurely. *Br Med J* 1981; 283:340–342.

Saint L, Maggiore P, Hartmann PE. Yield and nutrient content of milk in eight women breastfeeding twins and one woman breastfeeding triplets. *Br J Nutr* 1986; 56:49–58.

Stutte PC, Bowles BC, Morman GY. The effects of breast massage on volume and fat content of human milk. *Genesis* 1988; 10:22–25.

Thompson N, Pickler RH, Munro C, et al. Contamination in expressed breast milk following breast cleansing. *J Hum Lact* 1997; 13:127–130.

Tyson JE, Edwards WH, Rosenfeld AM, et al. Collection methods and contamination of bank milk. *Arch Dis Child* 1982; 57:396–398.

Walker M. How to evaluate breast pumps. *MCN Am J Matern Child Nurs* 1987; 12:270–276.

Walker M, Auerbach KG. Breast pumps and other technologies. Chapter 13 in Riordan J, Auerbach KG. Breastfeeding and human lactation, 2nd ed. Sudbury, MA: Jones and Bartlett Publishers, 1998:393–448.

Weber F, Woolridge MW, Baum JD. An ultrasonographic study of the organization of sucking and swallowing by newborn infants. *Dev Med Child Neurol* 1986; 28:19–24.

Wennergren M, Wiqvist N, Wennergren G. Manual breast pumps promote successful breastfeeding. *Acta Obstet Gynecol Scand* 1985; 64:673–675.

Whittlestone WG. The physiologic breastmilker. *NZ Fam Phys* 1978; 5.

Wilks S, Meier P. Helping mothers express milk suitable for preterm and high-risk infant feeding. *MCN* 1988; 13:121–123.

Williams J, Auerbach K, Jacobi A. Lateral epicondylitis (tennis elbow) in breastfeeding mothers. *Clin Pediatr* 1989; 28:42–43.

Woolridge MW. The anatomy of infant sucking. *Midwifery* 1986; 2:164–171.

Zinaman MJ. Breastpumps: Ensuring mothers' success. *Contemporary Ob/Gyn (Technol)* 1988; 55–62.

Zinaman MJ, Hughes V, Queenan JT, et al. Acute prolactin and oxytocin responses and milk yield to infant suckling and artificial methods of expression in lactating women. *Pediatrics* 1992; 89:437–440.

Zoppou C, Barry SI, Mercer GN. Dynamics of human milk extraction: A comparative study of breast feeding and breast pumping. *Bull Math Biol* 1997; 59:953–973.

Zoppou C, Barry SI, Mercer GN. Comparing breastfeeding and breast pumps using a computer model. *J Hum Lact* 1997; 13:195–202.

# International Statements and Documents to Promote, Protect, and Support Breastfeeding

*By Karin Cadwell, PhD, RN, IBCLC*

## Objectives

- Discuss international statements and documents that are used as tools to protect, promote, and support breastfeeding.

## Introduction

Alarmed over the unnecessary deaths related to the industry-created bottle-feeding culture, two agencies of the *United Nations* (UN), the *World Health Organization* (WHO), and the *United Nations Children's Fund* (UNICEF) held an international meeting in 1979 concerning infant and young child feeding. The ultimate result was the creation of the International Code of Marketing of Breast Milk Substitutes and subsequent resolutions that have been approved in the World Health Assembly. This document and others strive to replace the commercial barriers to breastfeeding with protection for a health-related behavior that is in danger of extinction.

   I   The International Code of Marketing of Breast Milk Substitutes and subsequent relevant resolutions

   A. Doubts and pressures about "not enough milk" have been cleverly communicated to mothers by manufacturers of breast milk substitutes, feeding bottles, and teats.

   B. WHO and UNICEF drafted the Code of Marketing of Breastmilk Substitutes, which was adopted by the World Health Assembly in May 1981.

   C. An international recommendation, the code is put into effect at the national level.

D. By 1997, only 17 countries had turned all of the code into law. More than 60 countries have taken significant action to implement some or all of the code.

E. The *International Baby Food Action Network* (IBFAN) set up the *International Code Documentation Centre* (ICDC) with the task of keeping track of code compliance both by governments and by companies.

F. Further resolutions have clarified and strengthened the code, including a statement that member states "ensure that there are no donations of free or subsidized supplies of breast milk substitutes and other products" covered by the code. This resolution forbids health care facilities to accept free or lost cost supplies.

G. The 1996 World Health Assembly Resolution urged member states to "ensure that complementary foods are not marketed for or used in ways that undermine exclusive and sustained breastfeeding."

II The scope of the code applies to the marketing and practices related to:

A. Breast milk substitutes, including infant formula; other milk products, foods, and beverages, including bottle-fed complementary foods, when marketed or otherwise represented to be suitable, with or without modification, for use as a partial or total replacement of breast milk

B. Feeding bottles and teats

C. The quality, availability, and information concerning the use of products mentioned in A and B

III Definitions of terms used in the code

A. "Breast milk substitute" means any food being marketed or otherwise represented as a partial or total replacement for breast milk, whether or not suitable for that purpose.

B. "Infant formula" means a breast milk substitute formulated industrially in accordance with applicable Codex Alimentarius standards, to satisfy the normal nutritional requirements of infants up to between four and six months of age, and adapted to their physiological characteristics. Infant formula can also be prepared at home, in which case it is described as "home-prepared."

C. Complementary food means any food, whether manufactured or locally prepared, that is suitable as a complement to breast milk or to infant formula, when either becomes insufficient to satisfy the nutritional requirements of the infant. Such food is also commonly called "weaning food" or "breast milk supplement."

IV Relevant parts of World Health Assembly resolutions

A. WHA 39.28 "Any food or drink given before complementary feeding is nutritionally required may interfere with the initiation or maintenance of breastfeeding and therefore should neither be promoted nor encouraged for use by infants during this period; The practice being introduced in some countries of providing infants with specially formulated milks (so-called follow-up milks) is not necessary."

B. WHA 47.5 Member States are urged to "foster appropriate complementary feeding from the age of about six months."

C. WHA 49.15 Member States are urged to "ensure that complementary foods are not marketed for or used in ways that undermine exclusive and sustained breastfeeding."

V Promotion to the public and the health care system of products covered by the code:

A. There should be no advertising or other form of promotion (such as free samples or gifts of articles or utensils) to the general public of products within the scope of the code.

B. There should be no promotion to health workers as a means of indirect promotion to the public.

VI The code also charges governments with the responsibility to "ensure that objective and consistent information is provided on infant and young child feeding."

A. Covered are the planning, provision, design, and dissemination of information or their control.

B. There is a gray area between information and promotion which may be easily crossed by manufacturers and cast doubt on a woman's ability to breastfeed.

VII Labeling is also covered under the code.

A. Labels should offer information about the appropriate use of the product in a way that does not discourage breastfeeding.

B. The label should be clear and understandable, using appropriate language, with no pictures of infants.

C. Some countries also require the age recommended for introduction of particular infant foods, certain health claims (such as the use of the word "hypoallergenic").

VIII The Baby-Friendly Hospital Initiative

A. The Baby-Friendly Hospital Initiative (BFHI) was designed to rid hospitals of their dependence on breast milk substitutes and to encourage maternity services to be supportive of breastfeeding.

B. Launched in June 1991 at a meeting of the International Pediatric Association in Ankara, Turkey, by WHO and UNICEF.

C. The global initiative is aimed at promoting the adoption of the *Ten Steps to Successful Breastfeeding* in hospitals worldwide.

D.  The BFHI is designed to remove hospital barriers to breastfeeding by creating a supportive environment with trained and knowledgeable health workers.

**IX**  The ten steps to successful breastfeeding

A.  Have a written breast-feeding policy that is routinely communicated to all health care staff.

B.  Train all health care staff in skills necessary to implement this policy.

C.  Inform all pregnant women about the benefits and management of breastfeeding.

D.  Help mothers initiate breast-feeding within a half-hour (one hour in the United States) of birth.

E.  Show mothers how to breastfeed and how to maintain lactation even if they should be separated from their infants.

F.  Give newborn infants no food or drink other than breast milk unless *medically* indicated.

G.  Practice rooming-in: enable mothers and infants to remain together 24 hours a day.

H.  Encourage breastfeeding on demand.

I.  Give no artificial teats or pacifiers (also called dummies or soothers) to breastfeeding infants.

J.  Foster the establishment of breastfeeding support groups and refer mothers to them upon discharge from the hospital or clinic.

K.  The FAO/WHO International Conference on Nutrition.

**X**  The FAO/WHO International Conference on Nutrition was held in Rome, Italy in December 1992, and signatories adopted the World Declaration on Nutrition and the Plan of Action for Nutrition.

A.  Article 19 of the World Declaration on Nutrition pledged "to reduce substantially within this decade social and other impediments to optimal breastfeeding."

B.  The plan of action endorsed breastfeeding under sections on preventing and managing infectious diseases and preventing and controlling specific micronutrient deficiencies. The action also called for the promotion of breastfeeding by governments by providing maximum support for women to breastfeed.

**XI**  Innocenti Declaration

A.  The Innocenti Declaration was adopted at a meeting sponsored jointly by UNICEF, WHO, USAID, and the *Swedish International Development Authority* (SIDA) in Florence, Italy in August 1990.

   B.  The Innocenti Declaration calls for concrete actions for governments to take by 1995.

   C.  Attainment of Innocenti goals requires, in many countries, the reinforcement of a "breastfeeding culture" and the vigorous defense against incursions of a "bottle-feeding culture."

**XII** Operational targets——All national governments by the year 1995 should have:

   A.  Appointed a national breastfeeding coordinator of appropriate authority and established a multisector national breastfeeding committee composed of representatives from relevant governmental departments, nongovernmental organizations, and health professional associations

   B.  Ensured that every facility providing maternity services fully practices all 10 of the *Ten Steps to Successful Breastfeeding* set out in the joint WHO/UNICEF statement "Protecting, promoting and supporting breastfeeding: the special role of maternity services"

   C.  Taken action to give effect to the principles and aim of all articles of the International Code of Marketing of Breast-Milk Substitutes and subsequent relevant World Health Assembly resolutions in their entirety

   D.  Enacted imaginative legislation protecting the breastfeeding rights of working women and established means for its enforcement

**XIII** All international organizations are called upon to:

   A.  Draw up action strategies for protecting, promoting, and supporting breastfeeding, including global monitoring of the evaluation of their strategies

   B.  Support national situation analyses and surveys and the development of national goals and targets for action

   C.  Encourage and support national authorities in planning, implementing, monitoring, and evaluating their breastfeeding policies

**XIV** The Innocenti Declaration was adopted by the World Summit for Children in September 1990 and by the 45th World Health Assembly in May 1992 in Resolution WHA 45.34.

   A.  United States Surgeon General's workshop on breastfeeding and human lactation

   B.  First time (1984) a U.S. national leader called attention to breastfeeding and human lactation

   C.  First national meeting in the United States focused exclusively on supporting breastfeeding

   D.  Three publications resulted from the workshop: *The Report of the Surgeon General's Workshop on Breastfeeding and Human Lactation* (1984), *The Followup*

*Report: Surgeon General's Workshop on Breastfeeding and Human Lactation* (1985)
and *Second Followup Report: the Surgeon General's Workshop on Breastfeeding and
Human Lactation* (1991).

**XV** Recommendations of the work groups:

A. A national breastfeeding promotion initiative directed to all those who
   influence the breastfeeding decisions and opportunities of women involved
   in school, job training, professional education, and employment is needed.

B. Public education and promotional efforts should be undertaken through the
   education system and the media. Such efforts should recognize the diversity of
   the audience; should target various economic, cultural and think groups; and
   should be coordinated with professional education.

C. It is imperative for all health professionals to receive adequate didactic and
   clinical training in lactation and breastfeeding and to develop skills in patient
   education and the management of breastfeeding.

D. The health-care system needs to be better informed and more clearly supportive
   of lactation and breastfeeding.

E. The successful initiation and continuation of breastfeeding will require a broad
   spectrum of support services involving families, peers, care providers, employers,
   and community agencies and organizations.

F. An intensified national research effort, including a broad range of research
   studies, is needed to provide data on the benefits and contraindications of
   breastfeeding among women in the United States. Research is also needed to
   evaluate strategies/interventions and to determine progress in achieving goals
   related to the promotion of breastfeeding.

**XVI** IBFAN—The International Baby Food Action Network

A. IBFAN was generated at the WHO/UNICEF Meeting on Infant and Young
   Child Feeding, which took place in Geneva, Switzerland in October 1979.

B. By the end of the meeting, representatives from six of the NGO's attending
   decided to form the IBFAN.

C. One of IBFAN's objectives was to monitor the marketing practices of the
   industry around the world and to share and publicize the information gathered.

D. The group also stated that "there should be an international code of marketing
   of infant formula and other products used as breast milk substitutes."

E. IBFAN has also set up the *International Code Documentation Centre* (ICDC)
   with the task of keeping track of code compliance both by governments and by
   companies.

F. WHO Global Data Bank on Breastfeeding.

G. The WHO Global Data Bank on Breastfeeding is maintained in the Nutrition Unit of the World Health Organization (WHO) in Geneva.

H. Information from national and regional surveys and studies are pooled that deal specifically with breastfeeding prevalence and duration.

I. Reports are prepared on breastfeeding trends in countries for which data are available.

J. Every effort is made to achieve worldwide coverage.

K. Pontificiae Academiae Scientiarum Documenta 28.

L. The Pontifical Academy of Sciences and the Royal Society held a Working Group on: Breastfeeding: Science and Society on May 11–13, 1995, at the Vatican.

M. Part of an overall study on population and resources.

N. Pope Pius XII had urged Catholic mothers to nourish their children themselves (1941).

O. Pope John Paul II emphasized that "mothers need time, information and support in order to breastfeed . . . no one can substitute for the mother in this natural activity."

# References

Division of Child Health and Development. Evidence for the ten steps to successful breastfeeding. Geneva: World Health Organization, 1998.

Nutrition Unit, Division of Food and Nutrition. The international code of marketing of breast-milk substitutes: A common review and evaluation framework. Geneva: World Health Organization, 1997.

Pontificia Academia Scientiarum. Working group on: Breastfeeding: Science and society. Citta Del Vaticano: Pontificia Academia Scientiarum, 1996.

Sokol EJ. The code handbook: A guide to implementing the international code of marketing of breastmilk substitutes. Penang, Malaysia: International Code Documentation Centre, 1997.

U.S. Department of Health and Human Services. Report of the surgeon general's workshop on breastfeeding and human lactation. Washington, D.C. DHHS Publication No. HRS-D-MC 84–2, 1984.

World Health Organization and Wellstart International. Promoting breast-feeding in health facilities: A short course for administrators and policy-makers. Geneva: World Health Organization, 1996.

# Resources

Armstrong HC, Sokol E. The international code of marketing of breastmilk substitutes: What it means for mothers and babies world-wide. International Lactation Consultant Association, 1994.

Baby Friendly Hospital Initiative: Learning to be baby friendly (video).

Barriers and solutions to the global ten steps to successful breastfeeding: A summary of in-depth interviews with hospitals participating in the WHO/UNICEF BFHI interim program in the US.

Best of the best: A selection of materials from hospitals with certificates of intent to the UNICEF/WHO BFHI.

Breaking the rules: Stretching the rules 1998 A worldwide report on violations of the WHO/UNICEF International Code of Marketing of Breastmilk Substitutes.

Chetley A, Allain A. Protecting infant health: A health worker's guide to the International Code of Marketing of Breastmilk Substitutes, 9th ed. IBFAN, 1998.

Complying with the code? A manufacturers' and distributors' guide to the code. Penang, Malaysia: IBFAN, 1998.

Hospital self appraisal tool: Promoting breastfeeding in health facilities: A short course for administrators and policy-makers.

Innocenti declaration on the protection, promotion, and support of breastfeeding in the 1990s global initiative. WHO/UNICEF sponsored meeting, Florence, Italy, 1990.

International Baby Food Action Network (IBFAN) Penang, Malaysia.

International Code of Marketing of Breast Milk Substitutes. World Health Organization, Geneva, Switzerland, 1981.

Protecting breastfeeding: Making the code work. World Breastfeeding Week Action Folder, 1994: WHO Code Action Kit.

Protecting, promoting, and supporting breastfeeding; The special role of maternity services. Geneva: WHO/UNICEF, 1989.

Sokol EJ. The code handbook: A guide to implementing the International Code of Marketing of Breastmilk Substitutes. International Code Documentation Center/IBFAN, Penang, 1997.

The International Code of Marketing of Breastmilk Substitutes: A common review and evaluation framework.

United Nations Conventions: Convention on the Elimination of All Forms of Discrimination Against Women; Convention on the Rights of the Child; International Labor Organization Convention on Maternity Protection; International Convention on Economic, Social, and Cultural Rights; World Breastfeeding Week

WBW Action Folder
La Leche League, International
1400 N. Meacham Rd.
Schaumburg, IL 60173
(847) 519-7730

WBW Action Kit
INFACT Canada

WBW Action Pack
International Lactation Consultant Association (ILCA)
1500 Sunday Dr., Suite 102
Raleigh, NC 27607
(919) 787-5181

WHO and Wellstart International, Geneva, 1996.

WHO Publications Center: Evidence for the Ten Steps to Successful Breastfeeding (1998).

World Alliance for Breastfeeding Action (WABA)
PO Box 1200
10850 Penang, Malaysia
60.4.6584816
Fax 60.4.6572655

World Health Organization, Marketing & Dissemination; CH-1211 (27), Geneva, Switzerland.

# United States Breastfeeding Improvement Documents

American Academy of Pediatrics, Work group on breastfeeding: Breastfeeding and the use of human milk. *Pediatrics* 1997; 100:1035–1039.

Breastfeeding in the United States: A national agenda and strategic plan.
United States Breastfeeding Committee, 2000.
US Breastfeeding Committee.

Call to action: Better nutrition for mothers, children, and families (1991).
National Center for Education in Maternal & Child Health, Washington, DC.

Followup report: The surgeon general's workshop on breastfeeding and human lactation. HRS-D-MC 85-2, 1985

HHH Blueprint for Action on Breastfeeding.
US Department of Health and Human Services
Office on Women's Health
Washington, DC, 2000

Healthy people 2010.
DHHS, Public Health Service: National Health Promotion and Disease Prevention Objectives (2000). Washington, DC.

Lawrence RA. A review of the medical benefits and contraindications to breastfeeding in the United States. Maternal and Child Health Technical Information Bulletin. Arlington, VA: National Center for Education in Maternal and Child Health, 1997.

Nutrition action themes for the United States: A report in response to the international conference on nutrition.
Center for Nutrition & Policy Promotion.
USDA
1120 20th St, NW, Suite 200-North Lobby
Washington, DC 20036

Rep. Carolyn Maloney
Breastfeeding legislation in Congress
www.house.gov/maloney

Report of the surgeon general's workshop on breastfeeding and human lactation. HRS-D-MC84-2, 1984.

Richter J. Engineering of consent: Uncovering corporate PR. Dorset, UK: The Corner House, March, 1998.

Salisbury L, Blackwell AG. Petition to Alleviate Domestic Infant Formula Misuse and Provide Informed Infant Feeding Choice. Public Advocates, Inc., 1535 Mission St., San Francisco, CA 94103, 1981.

Second followup report: The surgeon general's workshop on breastfeeding and human lactation. Spisak S, Gross SS: National Center for Education in Maternal & Child Health, Washington, DC, 1991.

Sethi SP. Multinational corporations and the impact of public advocacy on corporate strategy: Nestle and the infant formula controversy. Norwell, MA: Kluwer Academic Publishers, 1994.

Shuber S. The international code of marketing of breast-milk substitutes: An international measure to protect and promote breastfeeding. Cambridge, MA: Kluwer Law International, 1998.

Slusser W, Lange L, Thomas S. Report of the national breastfeeding policy conference. UCLA Center for Healthier Children, Families and Communities. Washington, DC, November 12-13, 1998.

State breastfeeding legislation
http://www.lalecheleague.org/LawMain.html

Waggett GG, Waggett RR. Breast is best: Legislation supporting breastfeeding is an absolute bare necessity—a model approach.

# EDUCATION AND CHANGE

*By Karin Cadwell, PhD, RN, IBCLC*

OBJECTIVES

- List resources for professional education and change in lactation.

## Introduction

Almost all national and international statements regarding lactation call for changes to improve education for health care providers and lactation management based on evidence. Changing current practice is a slow process that needs a well thought-out plan. This chapter looks at resources to help make changes.

I A Blueprint for Policy Makers to Promote, Protect, and Support Breastfeeding, published by UNICEF in 1999

   A. Establish national breastfeeding committees.

   B. Promote the Baby-Friendly Hospital Initiative.

   C. Implement and enforce the code.

   D. Establish maternity protection.

   E. Train medical personnel and health workers.

   F. Support exclusive and sustained breastfeeding throughout the community.

   G. Provide resources for support groups.

   H. Promote breastfeeding campaigns.

   I. Integrate breastfeeding messages into child health activities.

   J. Improve women's social and economic status.

II The Evidence-Based Practice Paradigm is an emerging model for objective examination of the validity of policy and is an underpinning of change.

   A. The paradigm offers tools to address the tension between folklore and medicine by authority and between observed experience and authority.

B. Evidence-based practice might level the field by providing a forum for interdisciplinary discussion.

C. A hierarchy of evidence has been accepted in medical research literature as proposed by Guyatt and colleagues.

1. Systematic reviews and meta-analyses

2. Randomized controlled trials

3. Cohort studies

4. Case-controlled studies

5. Cross-sectional surveys

6. Case reports

D. Planning for change

1. Form a multidisciplinary practice committee.

2. Develop a philosophy of care.

3. Gather information.

a. What is the basis for current practice?

b. Standards and guidelines from professional organizations.

c. Review standards from regulatory agencies.

d. Hospital policies and procedures.

e. Search the published literature.

f. Grade the literature by using the following framework:

   i. Evaluate your current practices into rituals (for example, "We have always done it this way") and rationales (based on scientific principles, standards of care, and evidence).

   ii. Standing orders for healthy newborns

   iii. Standing orders for common complications or problems

4. Evaluate current protocols.

a. Risks/benefits

b. Informed decision-making of parents

5. Develop best practices for the breastfeeding family.

a. Can be in the form of clinical pathways or routine order sets

6. Evaluate current practice.

a. No published standards or guidelines for care, but enough literature support (cup feeding for preterm infants)

b. No published standards or guidelines for care and limited data (cabbage leaves for engorgement)

c. Published standards and guidelines for care and literature support (unrestricted breastfeeding times and frequency)

       7. Benefits of evidence-based care

         a. Care practices that are defensible during budget cuts and restrictions

         b. Multidisciplinary collaboration

         c. Assurance of patient safety

         d. Reduction of liability claims

         e. Prevents cost-containment (based on financial targets) decisions that affect patient care and replaces with cost consciousness (allocation of services based on risk/benefits and long-term patient outcomes)

    E. Evidence-based examinations of breastfeeding policies and practices have been published.

       1. The International Lactation Consultant Association (ILCA) published *Evidence-Based Guidelines for Breastfeeding Management during the First Fourteen Days* in 1999.

       2. The World Health Organization, Division of Child Health and Development, published *Evidence for the Ten Steps to Successful Breastfeeding* in 1998.

       3. The Healthy Children Project published *Toward Evidence-Based Breastfeeding Practice* in 1999.

**III** Naylor and colleagues have suggested three levels of objectives for lactation management education:

    A. Level I: Awareness

       1. Target group: medical students (pre-service education).

       2. Example objective: Discuss, in general terms, findings from the basic and social sciences of lactation.

       3. Describe the general benefits of breastfeeding for the infant.

    B. Level II: Generalist

       1. Target group: pediatricians, obstetric-gynecology physicians and residents, family medicine residents, and advanced practice nurses.

       2. Example objective: *Apply the findings from the basic and social sciences to breastfeeding and lactation issues.*

       3. Describe the unique properties of human milk for human infants.

       4. Describe the advantages of preterm milk for the preterm infant.

    C. Level III: Specialist

       1. Target group: advanced/independent study, fellowships.

       2. Example objective: *Critique the findings from the basic and social sciences and evaluate their applicability to clinical management issues.*

       3. Discuss in detail the components of human milk and their functions.

4. Describe in detail the suitability of preterm human milk for the preterm infant.

**IV** Education specific to the field of breastfeeding and human lactation has been considered by WHO and UNICEF and described as follows:

A. Promoting Breastfeeding in Health Facilities: A Short Course for Administrators and Policy Makers

1. Goal: To sensitize administrators and directors of health facilities to the importance of breastfeeding and the Baby-Friendly Hospital Initiative
2. Target Group: Health facility directors and administrators
3. Length: 10–12-hour course

B. Breastfeeding Management and Promotion: An 18-hour course for maternity staff

1. Goal: To change maternity care to be breastfeeding-friendly
2. Target Group: All staff of a maternity facility
3. Length: 18-hour course plus 3 hours of clinical practice

C. Breastfeeding Counseling: A Training Course

1. Goal: To develop clinical and counseling skills in breastfeeding
2. Target Group: Key health workers in all parts of the health system
3. Length: 40-hour course plus eight hours of clinical practice

D. Training Guide in Lactation Management

1. Goal: To prepare a cadre who can become trainers or Baby-Friendly Hospital Initiative assessors
2. Target Group: Trainers, policy makers, doctors, and senior community workers
3. Length: 80 hour course plus 6 hours of clinical practice

**V** Components of professional knowledge as set forth by Schein include the following:

A. An underlying discipline or basic science component upon which the practice rests or from which it is developed

B. An applied science or "engineering" component from which many of the day-to-day diagnostic procedures and problem solutions are derived

C. A skills and attitudinal component that concerns the actual performance of services to the client using the underlying basic and applied knowledge

# References

AWHONN: Achieving consistent quality care. Washington, DC: Association of Women's Health, Obstetric and Neonatal Nurses, 1998.

Breastfeeding Support Consultants. Creating change . . . in the face of resistance. Chalfont, PA: 1995.

Cadwell K. Using the quality improvement process to affect breastfeeding protocols in United States hospitals. *J Hum Lact* 1997; 13:5–9.

Cadwell AL, Turner-Maffei C. Toward evidence-based breastfeeding practice. Sandwich, MA: Health Education Associates, Inc., 1999.

Canadian Task Force on the Periodic Health Examination. The periodic health examination. *Can Med Assoc J* 1979; 121:1193–1254.

DeGeorges KM. Evidence! Show me the evidence! Untangling the web of evidence-based health care. *AWHONN Lifelines* 1999; 3:47–48.

Dickerson K, Manheimer E. The Cochrane collaboration: Evaluation of health care and services using systematic reviews of the results of randomized controlled trials. *Clini Obstet Gynecol* 1998; 41:315–331.

Dolan MS. Interpretation of the literature. *Clinil Obstetr Gynecolo* 1998; 41:307–314.

Enkin M, Keirse MJNC, Renfrew M, Neilson J. A guide to effective care in pregnancy and childbirth, 2nd ed. Oxford: Oxford University Press, 1995.

Family and Reproductive Health, Division of Child Health and Development. Evidence for the ten steps to successful breastfeeding. Geneva: World Health Organization, 1998.

Heinig MJ. Evidence-based practice: Art versus science? *J Hum Lact* 1999; 15:183–184.

Greenhalgh T. How to read a paper: The basics of evidence based medicine. London: BMJ Publishing Group.

Guyatt GH, et al. User's guides to the medical literature. IX. A method for grading health care recommendations. *JAMA* 1995; 274:1800–1804.

International Lactation Consultant Association. Evidence-based guidelines for breastfeeding management during the first fourteen days. Raleigh, NC: April 1999.

Leff EW, Schriefer J, Hagan JF, DeMarco PA. Improving breastfeeding support: A community health improvement project. *J Qual Improv* 1995; 21:521–529.

McKibbon KA. Evidence-based practice. *Bull Med Library Assoc* 1998; 86:396–401.

Naylor AJ, et al. Lactation management education for physicians. *Semin Perinatol* 1994; 18:525.

Schein E. *Professional education*. New York: McGraw Books, 1973:43.

Sikorsk J, Renfrew MJ. Support for breastfeeding mothers. *Birth* 1999; 26:131.

Simpson KR, Knox GE. Strategies for developing an evidence-based approach to perinatal care. MCN 1999; 24:122–131.

Sinclair JC, et al. Introduction to neonatal systematic reviews. *Pediatrics* 1997; 100:892–895.

UNICEF. Breastfeeding: Foundation for a healthy future. New York: UNICEF, 1999.

US Preventive Services Task Force. Guide to clinical preventive services, 2nd ed. Washington DC: US Department of Health and Human Services, 1996.

World Health Organization and Wellstart International. Promoting breast-feeding in health facilities: A short course for administrators and policy-makers. WHO/NUTR/96.3. Geneva: WHO, 1996.

## Internet Resources

HealthWeb: Evidence Based Health Care: http://www.uic.edu/depts/lib/health/hw/ebhc

Cochrane Collaboration: http://www.update-software.com/cochrane.htm

In Canada: http://hiru.mcmaster.ca/cochrane

University of Alberta: http://www.med.ualberta.ca/ebm/ebm.htm

National Guideline Clearinghouse: http://www.guidelines.gov

Cumulative Index to Nursing & Allied Health Literature (CINAHL): http://www.cinahl.com

Medline  National Library of Medicine: http://www.nlm.nih.gov

HealthSTAR: http://www.nlm.nih.gov

# Caring for Vulnerable Populations

*By Cynthia Turner-Maffei, MA, IBCLC*

## Objectives

- Describe cultural competency vis-à-vis breastfeeding.
- Identify two strategies that have been successful in promoting breastfeeding in vulnerable populations.
- Demonstrate awareness of the rationale for special concerns regarding breastfeeding and vulnerable populations.

## Introduction

Lactation consultants strive to promote, support, and protect breastfeeding among all families. The benefits of breastfeeding are particularly advantageous for families who are in vulnerable situations. Special emphasis must be placed on meeting the needs of those who are less able to access breastfeeding help because of financial, language, and cultural barriers. Lactation consultants should endeavor to develop culturally competency in order to address these barriers.

    I  Issues of vulnerable populations regarding breastfeeding

      A.  Low-income families

          1.  In some nations, low-income mothers breastfeed at the highest rates; in other nations, the reverse is true.

          2.  Perceived value of breastfeeding versus formula

              a.  Formula is beyond the economic reach of low-income women in many developing nations.

              b.  Often, formula has a greater perceived value than breast milk. The ability to purchase formula is a status symbol in some communities.

              c.  Gifts of formula from hospitals, health care providers, and government programs have been associated with declines in breastfeeding initiation, exclusivity, and duration.

3. In some nations, low wage earners do not receive the degree of workplace accommodation of nursing or milk expression breaks that is attained by higher wage-earning cohorts.

4. Accessibility of breastfeeding help

   a. Low-income populations often have limited access to health care services, including breastfeeding help.

   b. Where lactation care is available largely on a fee-for-service basis, breastfeeding help might be beyond the financial means of many families.

5. Minority families

   a. Traditions, beliefs, and values surrounding breastfeeding vary widely among the world's cultures.

   b. Statements of authority figures can be received positively or negatively by members of minority cultures.

      i. Some cultures value authority figures; others seek authority within.

      ii. Rejecting medical advice might be perceived as an act of autonomy by some. Authority-based breastfeeding promotion programs have the potential to be counterproductive if not carefully designed.

6. The racial and ethnic prejudices prevalent within the majority culture can influence the choices of individuals of minority cultures.

   a. The publicity surrounding the tragic starvation death of a breastfed African-American infant and the subsequent legal action against his mother is a case in point for the "dangerous" image of breastfeeding. While this mother was indicted and found guilty in the death of her infant, several white, middle-class mothers who experienced similar tragic losses have been heralded as cautionary martyrs, rather than criminals.

   b. Mothers who belong to minority cultures might thus conclude that breastfeeding is a dangerous activity.

7. Access to health care services, including breastfeeding care, might be limited within minority communities due to financial, language, geographic, and cultural barriers.

B. Immigrant families

   1. Families migrating from lesser-developed to developed nations often assume very different breastfeeding patterns in their new nation. Dramatically, 98 percent of a group of Chinese emigrants breastfed their last baby born in China; only 2 percent of the sample chose to breastfeed the first child born in the United Kingdom.

   2. Researchers have theorized that these changes in breastfeeding patterns might reflect women's assimilation of the infant feeding norms of their new

nation. In many developed countries, breastfeeding is relatively invisible, practiced largely in private homes, while bottle-feeding is the visible cultural norm.

3. Other factors that might influence breastfeeding include:

   a. Availability of formula

   b. Presence or absence of support provided by larger family networks

   c. Ease of integrating breastfeeding with employment outside the home

4. Refugee families

   a. The trauma and brutality experienced by many refugees can have a long-lasting, unspoken effect on all aspects of daily life, including infant feeding.

   b. The visible presence of formula donations in refugee camps might be a deterrent to continued breastfeeding.

C. Cultural competency

1. Cultural competency describes "the interpersonal skills and attitudes that enable individuals to increase their understanding and appreciation of the rich and fluid nature of culture and of differences and similarities within, among, and between cultures and individuals . . . [Cultural competency] is a process that . . . providers must learn to adapt to each new individual encounter."

2. The first step toward developing cultural competency is for each provider to undertake self-assessment. Care is enhanced when each care provider identifies and endeavors to remain conscious of his or her own cultural values and biases.

3. Care providers and their clients might have divergent beliefs about issues such as the etiology of problems, appropriate care plans, and so on.

   a. Exploring the client's viewpoint is key in arriving at mutually acceptable care plans.

   b. Cultural beliefs and practices such as colostrum taboos have an impact on breastfeeding. The practice of feeding an infant other foods (including formula) during the first days of life might lead health care workers to assume incorrectly that women have chosen not to breastfeed.

      i. The identity of the most influential person in a woman's feeding decision varies among cultures. Some identified individuals are health care providers, maternal grandmothers, partners, relatives, and friends.

      ii. Several sources have identified general medical beliefs and values of different cultures. Such information can provide a framework for initial exploration with clients.

        iii. While it is possible to generalize about the experience of many groups of people, it is impossible to predict the meaning of an experience for any individual. Truly culturally competent care makes no assumptions about the experience, practices, or viewpoints of others.

        iv. New educational media and strategies should be designed, tested, and evaluated based on input from members of the target community.

D. Strategies for individual encounters

    1. Establish an environment of trust and respect.

       a. Ask respectful, open questions.

       b. Practice sensitivity to differing customs regarding eye contact, body language, touching, and so on.

E. Seek to understand the unique perspective of each woman.

    1. Invite each woman to express her knowledge and concerns.

       a. A series of questions designed for this purpose (Kleinman) can be helpful in elaborating a woman's understanding and cultural knowledge of the situation.

       b. Without such knowledge, the care provider might unwittingly provide information that violates a client's belief structure.

    3. Offer understanding and carefully targeted educational messages.

    4. Invite the client's feedback regarding suggested action plans.

       a. One author suggests, "If I tell you something and your mother has told you something different, please let me know and we'll see how we can work together."

       b. For example, the goal of treatment of the postpartum woman in the "hot-cold" medical systems practiced by many of the world's cultures is to keep the woman warm, eating, drinking, and surrounding herself with substances classified as "hot." How might this woman perceive her lactation consultant's suggestion to apply ice to her engorged breasts?

F. Include partners and family members in encounters as much as possible.

    1. Develop careful follow-up plans.

       a. Integrate breastfeeding follow-up with other services (pediatric follow-up) to the extent possible.

       b. Identify whether the woman is expected to contact the consultant or vice-versa.

       c. Many clients move frequently and do not have regular access to a telephone. Establish back-up communication plans.

    G. Know that women who have familial or financial problems might require special attention and extra counseling sessions so that they can be helped to identify how to achieve and sustain exclusive breastfeeding.

        1. Develop and invite her to participate in a peer counseling program:

            a. Peer counseling programs have been identified among the most effective strategies for breastfeeding promotion and preservation.

            b. "[P]eers are more persuasive spokespersons than health professionals or celebrities because they offset the lack of role models and doubts many women have about the ability of low-income women to lactate successfully."

            c. Women who have had successful breastfeeding experiences and who are members of the target community are recruited and trained to counsel and support pregnant and parenting mothers.

            d. Peer counseling programs are often low-cost methods of providing breastfeeding help.

II. Improving support for vulnerable populations in the health care system.

    A. Integrate breastfeeding support into comprehensive medical care.

        1. Several researchers have shown that providing continuous lactation care within the framework of comprehensive prenatal, postpartum and pediatric care is most effective in increasing incidence, duration, and exclusivity of breastfeeding.

        2. Encourage breastfeeding training for all health providers.

        3. Increase awareness of community breastfeeding support systems and services among health care providers.

    B. Develop cultural competency programs within health care systems and among health care providers.

        1. Identify individuals within the target community who are willing to serve as "cultural brokers," providing cultural interpretation when needed for lactation consultants and other members of the health care team.

        2. Encourage cultural assessment to identify the major values, health beliefs, and practices of target populations.

        3. Encourage systems and providers to study the impact of health care practices (for example, distribution of formula samples) on breastfeeding outcomes.

        4. Explore barriers to breastfeeding through interviews with community members and use this information to design new programs and strategies.

    C. Offer education regarding the identification of breastfeeding as the safest infant feeding method for refugee populations.

## Summary

Through self-assessment, respectful counseling, and developed skill, lactation consultants can help families have satisfying breastfeeding experiences. Just as breastfeeding is an empowering and satisfying experience for many women and their families, working with families who are in vulnerable situations provides many opportunities for professional growth and fulfillment for lactation consultants.

## References

Ad Hoc Group on Infant Feeding in Emergencies. Infant feeding in emergencies: Policy, strategy & practice. Dublin, Ireland: Emergency Nutrition Network, 1999.

Armotrading DC, Probart CK, Jackson RT. Impact of WIC utilization rate on breast-feeding among international students at a large university. *J Am Diet Assoc* 1992; 92(3):352–353.

Balcazar H, Trier CM, Cobas JA. What predicts breastfeeding intention in Mexican-American and Non-Hispanic white women? Evidence from a national survey. *Birth* 1995; 22(2):74–80.

Bernstein N. 1999. Trial begins for mother in breast-fed infant's starvation death. *New York Times*, April 28, 1999.

Brent NB, Redd B, Dworetz A, et al. Breastfeeding in a low-income population. *Arch Pediatr Adolesc Med* 1995; 149:798–803.

Bryant CA. 1982. Impact of kin, friend and neighbor networks on infant feeding practices. *Soc Sci Med* 1982; 17:57–65.

Bryant CA, Coreil J, D'Angelo S, et al. A new strategy for promoting breastfeeding among economically disadvantaged women and adolescents. *NAACOG's Clin Iss Perinat Women's Health Iss: Breastfeeding* 1992; 3(4):723–730.

Carter P. Feminism, breasts and breast-feeding. New York: St. Martin's Press, 1995.

Chesapeake Institute. National agenda for achieving better results for children and youth with serious emotional disturbance, 1994. URL: http://cecp.air.org/resources/ntlagend.html. Accessed 01/27/00.

Fadiman A. The spirit catches you and you fall down: A Hmong child, her American doctors, and the collision of two cultures. New York: Noonday Press, 1997.

Freed GL, Jones TM, Schanler RJ. Prenatal determination of demographic and attitudinal factors regarding feeding practice in an indigent population. *Am J Perinatol* 1992; 9(5/6):420–424.

Gabriel A, Gabriel KR, Lawrence RA. 1986. Cultural values and biomedical knowledge: Choices in infant feeding. *Soc Sci Med* 23(5):501–509.

Gross SM, Caulfield LE, Bentley ME, et al. Counseling and motivational videotapes increase duration of breast-feeding in African-American WIC participants who initiate breast-feeding. *J Am Diet Assoc* 1998; 98:43–148.

Gunnlaugsson G, Einarsdottir J. Colostrum and ideas about bad milk: A case study from Guinea-Bissau. *Soc Sci Med* 1993; 326(3):283–288.

Haider R. Reasons for failure of breast-feeding counselling: Mothers' perspective in Bangladesh. *Bull of WHO* 1997; 75(3):191–196.

Jones D. Effect of a lactation nurse on the success of breast-feeding: A randomized controlled trial. *J Epidemiol Comm Health* 1986; 40(1):45–49.

Kistin N, Benton D, Rao S, Sullivan M. Breastfeeding rates among black urban low-income women: Effect of prenatal education. *Pediatrics* 1990; 86(5):741–746.

Kleinman A. Patients and healers in the context of culture. Berkeley, CA: University of California Press, 1980.

Long DG, Funk-Archuleta MA, Geiger CJ, et al. *J Hum Lact* 1995; 11(4):279–284.

Lutter CK, Perez-Escamilla R, Segall A, et al. The effectiveness of a hospital-based program to promote exclusive breast-feeding among low-income women in Brazil. *Am J Public Health* 1997; 87:659–663.

Narayanan I, Dutta AK, Philips E, Ansari Z. Attitudes, practices, and socio-cultural factors related to breastfeeding: Pointers for intervention programmes. In Atkinson SA, et al., eds. Breastfeeding, nutrition, infection and infant growth in developed and emerging countries. St. John's, Canada: ARTS Biomedical Publishers and Distributors, 1990.

Romero-Gwynn E. Breast-feeding patterns among Indochinese immigrants in Northern California. *Am J Dis Child* 1989; 243:804–808.

Romero-Gwynn E, Carias L. Breast-feeding intentions and practices among Hispanic mothers in Southern California. *Pediatrics* 1989; 84:626–632.

Sciacca JP, Phipps BL, Dube DA, Ratliff MI. Influences on breast-feeding by lower-income women: An incentive-based, partner-supported educational program. *J Am Diet Assoc* 1995; 95:323–328.

Taylor MM. Transcultural Aspects of Breastfeeding—USA. Lactation Consultant Series, Unit 2. Wayne, NJ: Avery Publishing Group, 1985.

Tripp-Reimer T, Brink PJ, Saunders JM. Cultural assessment: Content and process. *Nurs Outlook* 1984; 32(2):78–82.

UNICEF. 1999. In emergencies, breastfeeding is safest method. *BFHI News*. Sept/Oct 1999: 1.

Waxler-Morrison N, Anderson J, Richardson E. Cross-cultural caring: A handbook for health professionals. Vancouver, BC: University of British Columbia, 1990.

Wiemann CM, DuBois JC, Berenson AB. Racial/ethnic differences in the decision to breastfeed among adolescent mothers. *Pediatrics* 1998; 101(6):e11.

Winikoff B, Castle MA, Laukaran VH, eds. Feeding infants in four societies: Causes and consequences of mothers' choices. New York: Greenwood Press, 1988.

Young SA, Kaufman M. Promoting breastfeeding at a migrant health center. *Am J Public Health* 1988; 78(5):523–525.

# Appendix A

# ILCA

## Preface

This text is the second edition of Standards of Practice for IBCLC Lactation Consultants, published by the *International Lactation Consultant Association* (ILCA). ILCA recognizes the certification conferred by the *International Board of Lactation Consultant Examiners* (IBLCE) as the professional credential for lactation consultants.

All individuals representing themselves as IBCLC lactation consultants should adhere to these standards of practice and to the code of ethics for International Board-Certified Lactation Consultants in any and all interactions with clients, clients' families, and other health care professionals.

## Introduction

Quality practice and service constitute the core of a profession's responsibility to the public. Standards of practice have been defined as stated measures or levels of quality that serve as models for the conduct and evaluation of practice. Standards promote consistency by encouraging a common, systematic approach. They also are sufficiently specific in content in order to meet the demands of daily practice.

These standards are presented as a recommended framework for the development of policies and protocols, educational programs, and quality-improvement efforts. They are intended for use in diverse settings, institutions, and cultural contexts.

## Standard 1. Clinical Practice

The clinical practice of the IBCLC lactation consultant focuses on providing lactation care and clinical management. This goal is best accomplished within the framework of systematic problem solving in collaboration with other members of the health care team and the client. IBCLC lactation consultants are responsible for decisions and actions that are undertaken as a part of their professional role, including the following:

- Assessment, planning, intervention, and evaluation of care in a variety of situations
- Prevention of problems
- Complete, accurate, and timely documentation of care
- Communication and collaboration with other health care professionals

  1.1  Assessment

1.1.1  Obtain and document an appropriate history of the breastfeeding mother and child.

1.1.2  Systematically collect objective and subjective information.

1.1.3  Discuss with the mother and document as appropriate all assessment information.

  1.2  Plan

1.2.1  Analyze assessment information to identify concerns and/or problems.

1.2.2  Develop a plan of care based on identified concerns or problems.

1.2.3  Arrange for follow-up evaluation.

  1.3  Implementation

1.3.1  Implement the plan of care in a manner that is appropriate to the situation and acceptable to the mother.

1.3.2  Exercise principles of safety and universal precautions.

1.3.3  Demonstrate procedures, techniques, equipment, and devices.

1.3.4  Provide appropriate instruction.

1.3.5  Provide a written report to the primary health care provider as appropriate, including the following:
- Assessment information
- Suggested interventions
- Instructions provided

1.3.6  Facilitate referral to other health professionals, community services, and support groups as needed.

  1.4  Evaluation

1.4.1  Evaluate outcomes of planned interventions.

1.4.2  Modify the plan based on the evaluation of outcomes.

1.4.3  Document and communicate to the primary health care provider(s) as appropriate:
- Evaluation of outcomes
- Modifications to the plan
- Follow-up

## Standard 2. Breastfeeding Education and Counseling

Breastfeeding education and counseling are integral parts of the care provided by the lactation consultant.

2.1  Provide education to parents and families in order to encourage informed decision making about infant and child feeding.

2.2  Provide anticipatory teaching in order to:
- Promote ideal breastfeeding practices.
- Minimize the potential for breastfeeding problems or complications.

2.4  Provide emotional support for continued breastfeeding in difficult or complicated circumstances.

2.5  Share current, evidence-based information and clinical skills with other health care providers.

## Standard 3. Professional Responsibilities

The IBCLC lactation consultant has a responsibility to maintain professional conduct and to practice in an ethical manner and is accountable for professional actions and legal responsibilities.

3.1  Adhere to these Standards of Practice and the IBLCE Code of Ethics.

3.2  Practice within the scope of the International Code of Marketing of Breast-Milk Substitutes and subsequent relevant resolutions and maintaining an awareness of conflict of interest when/if profiting from the rental or sale of breastfeeding equipment.

3.3  Act as an advocate for breastfeeding women, infants, and children.

3.4  Assist the mother in maintaining an intact breastfeeding relationship with her child.

3.5  Use breastfeeding equipment and devices appropriately by:
- Refraining from unnecessary or excessive use.
- Discussing the risks and benefits of recommended use.
- Evaluating safety and effectiveness.
- Assuring cleanliness and good operating condition.

3.6  Maintain and expand knowledge and skills for lactation consultant practice by participating in continuing education.

3.7  Undertake periodic and systematic appraisal for evaluation of one's clinical practice.

3.8  Support and promote well-designed research in human lactation and breastfeeding and base clinical practice, whenever possible, on such research.

## Standard 4. Legal Considerations

IBCLC lactation consultants are obligated to practice within the laws of the geopolitical region and setting in which they work. They must practice with consideration for clients' rights of privacy and with respect for matters of a confidential nature.

4.1  Work within the policies and procedures of the institution where employed, or if self-employed, have identifiable policies and procedures to follow.

4.2  Clearly state applicable fees prior to providing care.

4.3  Obtain informed consent from all clients prior to:
   • Assessing or intervening
   • Reporting relevant information to the primary health care provider or other health care professional(s)
   • Taking photographs for any purpose
   • Seeking publication of information associated with the consultation

4.4  Protect client confidentiality at all times.

4.5  Maintain records according to legal practices within the work setting.

## Glossary

Client—the party for whom professional services are rendered; the breastfeeding woman employing the services of the lactation consultant

Lactation consultant—a health care professional who is an IBCLC

Primary health care provider—a health professional such as a physician, nurse practitioner, or midwife who manages, directs, and coordinates the health care of a client

Universal precautions—a method of infection control involving the use of personal protective equipment (for example, gloves, a gown, or goggles) for the handling of blood and selected body fluids

# The Code of Ethics for International Board-Certified Lactation Consultants

## Preamble

It is in the best interests of the profession of lactation consultants and the public it serves that there be a Code of Ethics to provide guidance to lactation consultants in their professional practice and conduct. These ethical principles guide the profession and outline commitments and obligations of the lactation consultant to self, client, colleague, society, and the profession.

The purpose of the *International Board of Lactation Consultant Examiners* (IBLCE) is to assist in the protection of the health, safety, and welfare of the public by establishing and enforcing qualifications of certification and for issuing voluntary credentials to individuals who have attained those qualifications. The IBLCE has adopted this code to apply to all individuals who hold the credential of *International Board-Certified Lactation Consultant* (IBCLC).

## Principles of Ethical Practice

The International Board-Certified Lactation Consultant shall act in a manner that safeguards the interests of individual clients, justifies public trust in his or her competence, and enhances the reputation of the profession.

The International Board-Certified Lactation Consultant is personally accountable for his or her practice and, in the exercise of professional accountability, must:

1. Provide professional services with objectivity and with respect for the unique needs and values of individuals.

2. Avoid discrimination against other individuals on the basis of race, creed, religion, gender, sexual orientation, age, and national origin.

3. Fulfill professional commitments in good faith.

4. Conduct himself or herself with honesty, integrity, and fairness.

5. Remain free of conflict of interest while fulfilling the objectives and maintaining the integrity of the lactation consultant profession.

6. Maintain confidentiality.

7. Base his or her practice on scientific principles, current research, and information.

8. Take responsibility and accept accountability for personal competence in practice.

9. Recognize and exercise professional judgment within the limits of his or her qualifications. This principle includes seeking counsel and making referrals to appropriate providers.

10. Inform the public and colleagues of his or her services by using factual information. An International Board-Certified Lactation Consultant will not advertise in a false or misleading manner.

11. Provide sufficient information to enable clients to make informed decisions.

12. Provide information about appropriate products in a manner that is neither false nor misleading.

13. Permit the use of his or her name for the purpose of certifying that lactation consultant services have been rendered only if he or she provided those services.

14. Present professional qualifications and credentials accurately, using IBCLC only when the certification is current and authorized by the IBLCE, and complying with all requirements when seeking initial or continued certification from the IBLCE. The lactation consultant is subject to disciplinary action for aiding another person in violating any IBLCE requirements or aiding another person in representing himself or herself as an IBCLC when he or she is not.

15. Report to an appropriate person or authority when it appears that the health or safety of colleagues is at risk, as such circumstances might compromise standards of practice and care.

16. Refuse any gift, favor, or hospitality from patients or clients who are currently in his or her care that might be interpreted as seeking to exert influence to obtain preferential consideration.

17. Disclose any financial or other conflicts of interest in relevant organizations providing goods or services. Ensure that professional judgment is not influenced by any commercial considerations.

18. Present substantiated information and interpret controversial information without personal bias, recognizing that legitimate differences of opinion exist.

19. Withdraw voluntarily from professional practice if the lactation consultant has engaged in any substance abuse that could affect his or her practice; has been judged by a court to be mentally incompetent; or has an emotional or mental disability that affects his or her practice in a manner that could harm the client.

20. Obtain maternal consent to photograph, audio tape, or videotape a mother and/or her infant(s) for educational or professional purposes.

21. Submit to disciplinary action under the following circumstance: If convicted of a crime under the laws of the practitioner's country which is a felony or a misdemeanor, an essential element of which is dishonesty, and which is related to the practice of lactation consulting; if disciplined by a state, province, or other local government and at least one of the grounds for the discipline is the same or substantially equivalent to these principles; if committed an act of misfeasance or malfeasance which is directly related to the practice of the profession as determined by a court of competent jurisdiction, a licensing board, or an agency of a governmental body; or if violated a principle set forth in the Code of Ethics for International Board Certified Lactation Consultants that was in force at the time of the violation.

22. Accept the obligation to protect society and the profession by upholding the Code of Ethics for International Board Certified Lactation Consultants and by reporting alleged violations of the code through the defined review process of the IBLCE.

23. Require and obtain consent to share clinical concerns and information with the physician or other primary health care provider before initiating a consultation.

24. Adhere to those provisions of the International Code of Marketing of Breast-Milk Substitutes that pertain to health workers.

## To Lodge a Complaint

IBCLCs shall act in a manner that justifies public trust in their competence, enhances the reputation of the profession, and safeguards the interests of individual clients.

To protect the credential and to assure responsible practice by its certificants, the IBLCE depends on IBCLCs, members of the coordinating and supervising health professions, employers and the public to report incidents that might require action by the IBLCE Discipline Committee.

Only signed, written complaints will be considered. Anonymous complaints will be discarded. The IBLCE will become involved only in matters that can be factually determined and will provide the accused party with every opportunity to respond in a professional and legally defensible manner.

Complaints that appear to fit the scope of the Discipline Committee's responsibilities should be sent to the following address:

Chair of the Discipline Committee
IBLCE
7309 Arlington Blvd., Suite 300
Falls Church, VA 22042-3215 USA

# Summary of the International Code of Marketing of Breast Milk Substitutes and Subsequent World Health Assembly Resolutions

## Summary

"Inappropriate feeding practices lead to infant malnutrition, morbidity, and mortality in all countries, and improper practices in the marketing of breast milk substitutes and related products can contribute to these major public health problems." *Code Preamble*

The international code was adopted by the World Health Assembly on May 21, 1981. The code is intended to be adopted as a minimum requirement by all governments and aims to protect infant health by preventing the inappropriate marketing of breast-milk substitutes.

## Scope

The code covers the marketing of all breast milk substitutes (Article 2), and these include the following:

- Infant formula (including so-called "hypo-allergenic" formula, preterm milks, and other "special" baby milks)
- Follow-up milks
- Complementary foods such as cereals, teas and juices, water, and other baby foods that are marketed for use before the baby is six months old
- The code also covers feeding bottles and teats.

## The Provision of Clear Information

Informational and educational materials dealing with the feeding of infants that is intended to reach health professionals, pregnant women, and mothers of infants and young children should include clear information about all of the following points:

- The benefits and superiority of breastfeeding
- Maternal nutrition and the preparation for and maintenance of breastfeeding

639

- The negative effect on breastfeeding of introducing partial bottle feeding
- The difficulty of reversing the decision not to breastfeed
- Where needed, the proper use of infant formula

When such materials contain information about the use of infant formula, they should include the following points:

- The social and financial implications of its use

- The health hazards of inappropriate foods or feeding methods

- The health hazards of unnecessary or improper use of infant formula and other breast-milk substitutes

- Such materials should not use pictures or text that might idealize the use of breast-milk substitutes (Articles 4.2, 7.2).

## No Promotion to the Public

There should be no advertising or other form of promotion to the general public of products that are within the scope of the code. There should be no point-of-sale advertising, giving of samples, or giving any other promotional device in order to induce sales directly to the consumer at the retail level, such as special displays, discount coupons, premiums, special sales, loss-leaders, and tie-in sales. Marketing personnel should not seek direct or indirect contact with pregnant women or with mothers of infants and young children (Article 5).

## No Gifts to Mothers or Health Workers

Manufacturers and distributors should not distribute to pregnant women or mothers of infants and young children any gifts of articles or utensils that might promote the use of breast-milk substitutes or bottle feeding. No financial or material inducements to promote products within the scope of the code should be offered to health-care workers or members of their families. Financial support for professionals who are working in infant and young-child health professions should not create conflicts of interest (Articles 5.4 and 7.3, WHA 49.15 [1996]).

## No Promotion to Health-Care Facilities

Facilities of health-care systems should not be used to promote infant formula or other products within the scope of the code, nor should they be used for the display of products, placards, or posters concerning such products, or for the distribution of material bearing the brand name of products covered by the code (Articles 6.2, 6.3, and 4.3).

## No Promotion to Health Workers

Information provided to health professionals by manufacturers and distributors regarding products covered by the code should be restricted to scientific and factual matters and should not imply or create a belief that bottle feeding is equivalent or superior to breastfeeding. Samples of products covered by the code, or equipment or utensils for their preparation or use, should not be provided to health-care workers except where necessary for the professional evaluation or research at the institutional level (Articles 7.2 and 7.4).

## No Free Samples or Supplies

Neither manufacturers nor health-care workers should give pregnant women or mothers of infants and young children samples of products covered by the code. Free or low-cost supplies of breast-milk substitutes should not be given to any part of the health-care system (which includes maternity wards, hospitals, nurseries, and child care institutions). Donated supplies in support of emergency-relief operations should only be given for infants who have to be fed on breast-milk substitutes and should continue for as long as the infants who are concerned need them. Supplies should not be used as a sales inducement (Articles 5.2 and 7.4). Note: Articles 6.6 and 6.7 of the code have been superseded by WHA. *Resolutions 39.28 (1986), WHA 45.34 (1992), and WHA 47.5 (1994)*

## No Promotion of Complementary Foods Before They Are Needed

It is important for infants to receive appropriate complementary foods at about six months of age. Every effort should be made to use locally available foods. Any food or drink given before complementary feeding is nutritionally required might interfere with the initiation or maintenance of breastfeeding and therefore should not be promoted for use by infants during this period. Complementary foods should not be marketed in ways that undermine exclusive and sustained breastfeeding. *(Code Preamble; WHA Resolution 39.28 [1986], WHA 45.34 [1992], WHA 47.5 [1994], and WHA 49.15 [1996])*

## Adequate Labels: Clear Information, No Promotion, and No Baby Pictures

Labels should provide the necessary information about the appropriate use of the product and should not discourage breastfeeding. Infant formula manufacturers should ensure that each container has a clear, conspicuous, and easily readable message in an appropriate language that includes all of the following points:

- The words "Important Notice" or their equivalent
- A statement about the superiority of breastfeeding

- A statement that the product should only be used on the advice of a health-care worker as to the need for its use and the proper method of use

- Instructions for appropriate preparation and a warning of the health hazards of inappropriate preparation

Neither the container nor the label should have pictures of infants or other pictures or text that might idealize the use of infant formula. The terms "humanized," "maternalized," or similar terms should not be used (Articles 9.1 and 9.2).

## Companies Must Comply with the International Code

Monitoring the application of the international code and subsequent resolutions should be carried out in a transparent, independent manner, free from commercial influence (WHA 49.15 [1996]).

Independently of any other measures taken for implementation of the code, manufacturers and distributors of products covered by the code should regard themselves as responsible for monitoring their marketing practices according to the principles and aim of the code.

Manufacturers should take steps to ensure that their conduct at every level conforms to all provisions above (Article 11.3).

# INDEX

Note: **boldface** numbers indicate illustrations; italic *t* indicates a table.